C0-BXA-705

LABOR IN POWER

LABOR IN POWER

The Labor Party and Governments in Queensland 1915-57

Edited by
D.J. Murphy, R.B. Joyce and
Colin A. Hughes

University of Queensland Press 

Typeset by Press Etching Pty. Ltd., Brisbane

Printed and bound by Silex Enterprise & Printing Co., Hong Kong

Distributed in the United Kingdom, Europe, the Middle East, Africa, and the Caribbean by Prentice-Hall International, International Book Distributors Ltd, 66 Wood Lane End, Hemel Hempstead, Herts., England

National Library of Australia
Cataloguing-in-Publication data

Labor in power.

Index
ISBN 0 7022 1428 0

1. Australian Labor Party. 2. Queensland — Politics and government — 1915-1957. I. Murphy, Denis, J., joint ed. II. Joyce, Roger Bilbrough, joint ed. III. Hughes, Colin Anfield, joint ed.

320.9'94'3

Contents

Illustrations

Tables

Chapter 9

Figures

Contributors

B.J. Costar, Lecturer in Political Studies, Caulfield Institute of Technology

Barry Cotterell, Postgraduate student in Public Administration, University of Queensland

Margaret Cribb, Senior Lecturer in Political Science, University of Queensland

Raymond Evans, Lecturer in History, University of Queensland

S.K. Fox, Honours graduate in Political Science, University of Queensland

Joy Guyatt, Undergraduate Librarian of the University of Queensland

Colin A. Hughes, Professorial Fellow in Political Science, Australian National University

P.K. Jordan, Honours graduate in Social Work, University of Queensland

R.B. Joyce, Professor of History, La Trobe University

K.H. Kennedy, Lecturer in History, James Cook University of North Queensland

J.R. Laverty, Director of External Studies of the University of Queensland

J.R. Lawry, Dean of Education, Gippsland Institute of Advanced Education

Ian Moles, Associate Professor of History, James Cook University of North Queensland

D.J. Murphy, Reader in History, University of Queensland

Diana Shogren, Honours graduate in Government, University of Queensland

M.G. Sullivan, Lecturer in Education, Monash University

E.I. Sykes, Emeritus Professor of Law, University of Melbourne

Kenneth Wiltshire, Senior Lecturer in Public Administration, University of Queensland.

Foreword

I should like to commend this book and its authors for the timely, useful and factual guide it will be to those interested in politics, and that should include everyone. The authors have spent much time in research, and their interpretations of events and conclusions reached carry my endorsement.

Prior to my entry into parliament in 1935 I had a great admiration (which the passage of time has not diminished) for E.G. Theodore and W. McCormack, former Labor premiers. W. Forgan Smith who succeeded to the premiership in 1932 was of a different mould. In every respect he was a canny Scot. He had a comparatively easy time, as he dominated the Parliament, the cabinet, the caucus, and the Queensland Central Executive (QCE) of the Australian Labor Party (ALP). Even the newspapers were kinder to him than to other Labor leaders. It was said, and I think fairly, that he often supported mediocre candidates so that his own abilities shone more brightly. He exercised a strict control, enforcing cabinet unanimity in all matters, including the filling of cabinet vacancies. This regimented bloc vote with that of people like the Speaker, chairman of committees, secretary and whip, ensured that a candidate enjoying his blessing was assured of fifteen or sixteen votes. He also insisted, and was able to insist, unlike later Labor leaders, that members absent from party meetings entrust their proxies to him. He had a close and warm relationship with C.G. Fallon, secretary of the Australian Workers Union, and president of the QCE of the ALP. Once important or contentious matters were resolved to their mutual satisfaction, such decisions were seldom if ever challenged successfully. He believed in the gradual implementation of Labor's policy. Whilst occasionally regaling his audience with philosophical homilies, he was a pragmatist of the first order. Although arrogant, conceited and susceptible to flattery, he was a great leader and premier.

Frank Cooper was a most courteous man and because of his quiet manner and personal qualities was able to avoid much of the wrangling which occurs in political parties.

E.M. Hanlon first made his mark as minister for health. His development of hospital and associated services enhanced his reputation as an innovator and administrator. Although involved in major strikes involving meat, railway and electricity undertakings, which caused much dislocation of industry and personal bitterness, he enjoyed a good rapport with the unions and their leaders. He was essentially a man of common sense, a quality more uncommon than it should be. In cabinet he was a sound reasoner although occasionally one wondered whether his reasoning abilities were over influenced by his prejudice of enemies, or his loyalties to friends.

The last of the Labor premiers in Queensland was V.C. Gair. He was a good organizer until the concluding stages of his term of office. Because of my close official association with him up until Labor's disintegration and defeat in 1957 and my deep involvement in that situation I think it more appropriate for others to make an evaluation of his service to the Labor party.

I think Labor, without abandoning its altruistic aims and objectives, must to restore its credibility become more responsible, disciplined and pragmatic. The role of the crusader is less relevant today than forty years ago. The complexities of modern society and our involvement with the world at large place a heavy burden on modern political parties.

Labor policies have been an instrument for good in Queensland and Australia. Its resurgence to a position of power and authority will gain impetus and speed if we learn some of the lessons which must emerge from the publication of this excellent work.

John E. Duggan

Acknowledgements

The editors wish to acknowledge assistance received from the Queensland State Library, the John Oxley Library, the University of Queensland Library, the Fryer Library, the Mitchell Library, the National Library, the Queensland State Archives, the Australian National University Archives, Sir John Egerton and Fred Whitby at the Trades and Labor Council, Kath Gallogly, Bart Lourigan, Tom Burns and the staff at the QCE office, those unions that made their records available; Peggy Burke, Noeline Hall, Mary Kooyman, Mavis Little, Merryn McKenzie, Sue Elsom, Lyn Abnett, who typed or retyped much of the manuscript, and finally those trade union officials and ALP members who gave various authors interviews.

Introduction

In 1970, when the editors of this book published *Prelude to Power: The Rise of the Labour Party in Queensland 1885-1915*, they promised in "succeeding volumes . . . to trace how the labour movement used its power, within the limits set by its perennial problems". This volume, covering the years from 1915 to 1957, is the first fulfilment of that promise.

Labor in Power covers a period of forty-three years during which the Labor party was almost continuously in office. The only break was the crisis of the Depression (1929-32) when, in common with the experience of every other Australian government except Tasmania's, a significant proportion of the electors temporarily switched political allegiance.

A clear theme of this volume is to suggest explanations for the repeated successes of the Labor party in Queensland. The political party had existed for less than thirty years when T.J. Ryan became premier in 1915. Although his success in Queensland followed Labor victories in federal, New South Wales, South Australian and Western Australian elections, those other Labor governments did not last. It can profitably be asked how such a young party was repeatedly able to defeat its older opponents and why a majority of voters remained satisfied with its achievements and its use of its powers for almost forty years.

These questions gain an added piquancy from the perspective of the period after 1957. In 1979, after twenty years of Labor party debate, should its leaders look back enviously to these years of victories: or did the electors or the party change after the events — culminating in the split in the party in 1957 — which end this volume? Clearly, complete answers will require a third volume, for which the obvious title would be *Labor out of Power*, which again would need to be centred on the interplay between the organization and structure of the party, its goals and the calibre of the Labor officials, politicians and candidates.

This volume is arranged in three sections. The first, in two chapters, gives a necessary background. The changing internal workings of the party are analyzed. The second section, in fifteen chapters, concentrates on the programmes of the party while in government. These are arranged, as far as compartmentalization is possible, under political, economic and social headings. They cover both intention and fulfilment and lead on to the third section with its eight chapters. These concentrate on crises which reveal the perennial problems of the party and which culminated in the split and electoral defeat. The final chapter on this 1957 split provides the first detailed analysis of the Labor split in Queensland, especially of the rival personalities, which so far have been lacking.

The whole book represents the views of eighteen individual authors who have studied various aspects of the Labor party's history and achievements. The editors have imposed an overall pattern on these varied views; but have endeavoured to leave each chapter as a unit in itself, even if this has meant that some events are covered more than once. The editors have insisted neither on complete unity of interpretation nor on uncritical assessment of Labor's use of power.

Indeed one recurrent theme of interpretation reflects a suspicion that this enjoyment of power may have altered the party's aims, and that the views of many of the politicians and trade union leaders shifted markedly away from radicalism, let alone socialism, between 1915 and 1957. In the first ten years, many radical measures were introduced: the Legislative Council was abolished; experimental state enterprises were established; adult franchise was provided for local government elections. Other radical measures were proposed, for example, the initiative and referendum and Ryan's attempt to extend the vote to those aged eighteen Theodore sought the appointment of Australian-born governors, and opposed imperial titles.

More importantly for the Queensland worker, during the whole period of the Labor governments, his wages reached a level "above the national . . . and about equal to or above the average . . . of the other states". His hopes for an "industrial utopia" were encouraged by legislation limiting his hours of work (to forty-eight, then to forty-four and finally to forty), providing him with insurance payments during short-term unemployment, and protecting him and his family through compulsory workers compensation, Some of these measures were to be copied by other states. The Queensland farmer also welcomed Labor insofar as it was involved "far more deeply in trying to alleviate the problems of rural instability than had been attempted elsewhere in Australia". This involvement proved successful, particularly in the sugar industry, but also in other farming industries, by the provision of marketing boards and stabilization schemes for primary products. Electorally, Labor "undercut the Country party's support".

Increasingly as oligarchy took over in the administration of the party, there was a stress on conformism, and a suspicion of rebels and militants. *Prelude to Power* suggested that Michels' emphasis on organization implying oligarchy may be relevant: *Labor in Power* reinforces this view. By 1957 the party was not as distinctive as it had seemed likely to be, nor as revolutionary as had been feared by most conservatives.

Labor won elections through the consistent support of the majority of Queensland voters. A coalition of electoral support was established by Ryan in 1915 and maintained through to Gair in 1957. This included workers in cities and towns; sugar farmers; small farmers and selectors; small businessmen; public servants and Catholics. This coalition was maintained because the voters were satisfied by the moderate reformism of the successive Labor leaders. Thus for the small sugar growers the legacy of the Labor governments "was a stable and prosperous sugar industry" and for other primary producers it was the system of marketing boards and stabilization schemes which were to be copied elsewhere in Australia at both the national and state levels. These

The Australian Workers' Union float passes the General Post Office in Queen Street, Brisbane, during the Labour Day Procession in 1920. (Reprinted from *The Worker* 10 May 1920 with the permission of Australian Workers Union; Photograph by courtesy of the John Oxley achievements went beyond a "ringing fundamentalist agrarian rhetoric", to measurable benefits for all Queenslanders.

In the introduction to *Prelude to Power*, the editors confessed that they were "very much aware of the gaps in . . . [that] work". Gaps are easily discernible in this volume too, especially as the seven years between the two publications have not produced as much new research as had been anticipated. The availability of the records of the QCE was one of the inspirations for attempting *Prelude to Power* and they have again been used extensively for this volume, though they have been closed for the period of the split. Patrick Weller's editorship of the caucus minutes (the records of the meetings of the federal parliamentary Labor party) has shown how much can be obtained from official Labor records, and these minutes have been used by some of the contributors to this volume. But their very publication suggests how much more could be uncovered, especially from the records of unions and from private papers. Definitive histories of many unions are still needed, notably in Queensland, of the Australian Workers Union where, it is hoped, wise counsels will prevail in making the records, like those of the federal caucus, more widely accessible than at present. Although S.K. Fox, in this book, analyses the emergence of the Protestant Labour party, much more needs to be written on the influence of religion in the Labor party. The party in Queensland desired to keep church and state apart, but allegations of disproportionate Catholic influence persisted. *Prelude to Power* included a section on biographies of the men who made the party, but space in this volume has allowed only glimpses of the leaders, their chief lieutenants and a few other personalities. The gap was partly filled by the publication, in 1978, of *Queensland Political Portraits*, which includes most of the Labor premiers.

Likewise, the history of Labor cannot be written in isolation from the history of capital, nor indeed let it be stressed, from the history of Queensland or its other political parties. These have yet to be written. For general political history of the period, there remain only C.A. Bernays, *Queensland, Our Seventh Political*

Decade and Clem Lack, *Three Decades of Queensland Political History*.

For the labor movement in Queensland any modern student is indebted to the writings of Jim Larcombe. He was a Labor member of the Queensland parliament almost continuously from 1912 to 1956 who published nine studies of his party between 1925 and 1944. These remain invaluable contemporary sources.

At this pioneering stage, any book such as this must have deficiencies, both in relation to its wider context and in particular areas of detail. Yet the book goes further than straight political history. For instance, Evans on the Aborigines and Lawry on education suggest relationships between this largely political study and the social effects of the policies being adopted, even if there is insufficient knowledge from research for useful overall pronouncements on social structure in Queensland, whether on class or other lines. In other ways, *Labor in Power* makes original contributions, providing as it does detailed analyses of the working of a state government, correlating elements often ignored in other Australian studies, combining the social aspects with economic sections on agricultural, fiscal, manufacturing and mining policies.

Perhaps the most significant are the chapters on industrial and agricultural policy since Queensland Labor emerges as a pioneer in labor legislation which was subsequently followed by other states and the Commonwealth Arbitration Court, and in marketing legislation and co-operatives.

There are few references to women, although deductions about the nature of those controlling the party can be made from the fact that only one of that sex was ever accepted as a Labor candidate. Nor has John Wren appeared sufficiently in research to support allegations common at the time and since of his influence.

Positively, this book reveals much about the Labor party in Queensland: its main emphasis is from above, from the inside of the power structure, stressing the effect of organization and the prolongation of power on individuals. The structure is, however, always related to the mass of Labor party members and to all electors, the majority of whom continued to vote Labor.

Queensland never became a workers' paradise, but the state seemed better than the rest of Australia for most of its inhabitants. Having accepted the challenge of Labor to the power of the previously dominant, conservative establishment, most Queenslanders were content to accept Labor's moderate reformism and were, at the very least, rewarded by forty years of stable and predictable government.

R.B. Joyce

SECTION A

PARTY

1 Organization, Structure and Finance*

D.J. Murphy

In May 1915, the Labor party won its first Legislative Assembly election. It was to lose office in May 1929 but was returned in June 1932 and retained control of the Queensland parliament until the split of 1957. Its structure and organization were crucial to its success electorally and also as a reform party.

It is possible to see a correlation between the general efficiency of the central executive, the flow-on of this to the electorate organizations and the support the party was able to obtain at elections. Put in negative terms, when the efficiency of the party's secretary and central executive was low, this was reflected in election results. The lowest votes that the Labor party obtained in Queensland between 1915 and 1956 were at those times when the party organization was at its weakest.

The distinctive feature of the Labor party in 1915 was its extra-parliamentary organization.[1] It was not a party formed around one prominent political leader nor around any group of leading politicians. It was a party which had trade unions directly affiliated with it and a large rank and file. It had a central executive, a full-time secretary — Lewis McDonald, appointed in 1910 — and held a policy-making and rule-making conference every three years. This body, called the Labor-in-Politics Convention, was composed of delegates elected by the branch members and affiliated unionists in each of the state electorates. The convention was the supreme body of the Queensland Labor party and its decisions were binding on, and accepted by, all members of the party. In between conventions, the administration was in the hands of the Central Political Executive (CPE) which consisted of eleven members elected by the convention,

* For membership of the Queensland Central Executive, 1916-60, see Apendixes B and C, pp. 536-48.

two each from the state and federal Parliamentary Labor Parties (PLP) and five from the Australian Workers Union (AWU), the largest and best organized union in the state.

In June 1913, the CPE had moved its office from the cramped quarters in the Trades Hall in Turbot Street to the more spacious three-storied *Worker* newspaper building in Elizabeth Street, which the AWU had acquired when it absorbed the defunct Australian Labour Federation. By 1915, a comprehensive set of rules had been codified. Among the most important of these, and the ones that gave the most continuing problems, related to finance and the plebiscite system of selecting parliamentary candidates. Workers Political Organisations (WPO), the title of the local branches, and unions registered with the CPE, paid an annual registration fee of one pound and threepence per member capitation fee. This gave them the right to vote in plebiscites to select Labor candidates and convention delegates. Apart from a break between 1905 and 1909, the leader of the PLP had also been president of the CPE. In 1916, however, Billy Demaine, a printer and newspaper proprietor from Maryborough, defeated T.J. Ryan, the parliamentary leader, by one vote and Ryan became the last PLP leader to hold the presidency of the party.

Between the election of the first Labor government of Ryan in 1915 and the fall of the Labor government of V.C. Gair in 1957, the history of the Labor party falls into three periods. The first closes with the exclusion of three ARU delegates from the central executive in 1926 and the onset of the Depression; the second stretches to the close of World War II and the emergence of the "Movement" and the Industrial Groups; while the third ends with the expulsion of Gair and the loss of office, after almost forty years of continuous Labor rule.

The biggest single changes were made to the party's organization at the 1916 Convention. Thereafter, the convention would consist of state electorate delegates together with delegates elected by and from the affiliated unions. The CPE would also have delegates representing the affiliated unions, while the representation of the state and federal PLPs was reduced to one each. In 1916, the election of eleven delegates from the convention to

Billy Demaine defeated the parliamentary leader, T.J. Ryan, by one vote for presidency of the CPE. (Photograph by courtesy of the John Oxley Library.)

the CPE was retained and became the means of allowing the leader of the PLP, the CPE secretary and organizer and certain other persons to be elected to the central executive. An earlier rule prevented politicians from constituting more than half the membership of the CPE; this became outdated once unions were given direct representation on the CPE. At conventions after 1916, only small changes were made in the rules governing the general organization. Changes were made in plebiscite rules to try to cover loopholes, capitation fees were raised and the ceiling on union delegations to the convention and to the central executive was raised to take account of the growth of the AWU beyond its 1916 figure. However the organization of the party in 1957 was basically that laid down in 1916. The one major change, and a most important one, was the addition by the central executive itself of an executive committee, or "inner executive" as it was more generally known in the party, which was to become the dominant power in the party and almost a law unto itself.

The Development of Central Authority

The party that had emerged by 1915 had been marked by its optimism, its strong localism in regard to the exercise of power and by its unity. With Ryan as its parliamentary leader, it could maintain these ideals. The most serious complaint about the party's organization and operation followed the defeat in May 1917 of the government's referendum to abolish the Legislative Council. As a consequence, John Mullan, a former member of the Legislative Assembly, who had been defeated as a senator in the 1917 elections, was appointed as an organizer. He resigned this position on his re-election to state parliament in March 1918.

Two centres of power, the CPE and the PLP, were to emerge during the war and post-war period. However it was the PLP that held the initiative within the party. It alone could implement party policy and the leader of the PLP, by virtue of his being premier, could and did demand that his views and those of his cabinet and caucus prevail, or at least not be easily set aside. The presence of these two powerful bodies was a source of potential friction. However, there was also a good leaven of commonsense and political nous, qualities that had to be developed by participants in politics.

The Labor party was different from other political parties. From its inception in 1890, it had required a signed pledge from Labor candidates to support any political reform demanded by the party. In 1901, a new clause, requiring candidates to go through with the contest if selected, was added. The pledge had been further expanded by 1905 to bind candidates to vote in parliament as a majority of caucus decided. It was not envisaged that a political reform demanded by the party at a convention might be rejected or at least not supported by a majority of the PLP. The Labor party was an immense coalition of radicals and reformers, and of clerical and manual workers, farmers, small businessmen and some professionals. It was a party which continued to draw reformers to it. It was a party strongly committed to democratic state government and to a democratic organization within itself. However, not all Labor politicians, party officials and trade union leaders maintained both the theory and practice of democratic control. The exercise of power, particularly for any period of time, has a tendency to produce a drift to oligarchy and autocracy in most human beings. The solidarity, so needed if Labor and the unions were to hold together against the concerted attacks of the more powerful forces of capitalism and conservatism, could so easily be forced into conformism.

Between 1915 and 1957, the question to arise on a number of occasions was whether members of the party or politicians could be directed as to how they should vote or act in political matters. As a general principle, it was accepted that the parliamentary party, when in government, would legislate according to the platform laid down by the conventions. The timing and the specific wording of the legislation were left largely to the good sense of the PLP. It was held by convention, on several occasions, that Labor-in-Politics delegates could not be instructed by their unions or branches how they should vote on particular items. The question also arose regarding Queensland delegates to the interstate (federal) conference. In May 1918, a specific motion empowering the CPE to instruct federal conference delegates was defeated. The central executive, meeting prior to the 1921 Federal Conference, decided that a general discussion on agenda items could be held for the information of delegates, but no instructions could be issued.[2]

This was a clear extension of the power of the central executive to make rules, but its powers were never to be adequately or precisely defined. From 1918 onwards, the rules of the party became a combination of those initiated by the central executive (and usually confirmed at subsequent conventions) and those made by convention itself. An illustration of this lack of clarity concerning power in the party can be noted regarding the name of the party. The official title "Queensland Labour Party" was adopted at the 1905 Convention. At the 1918 Convention, held in January and February, a motion to change the name to the "Queensland Branch of the Australian Labour Party" was defeated. However at the CPE meeting in November that year, the title "Australian Labor Party, Queensland Branch" was adopted and the Central Political Executive became the Queensland Central Executive (QCE) of the Australian Labor party.[3] This had been a recommendation of the Federal Conference held in June that year, but Queensland did not then, or subsequently, show any particular eagerness to accept federal decisions on the internal running of its organization. The new title was approved at the 1920 Convention and the Workers Political Organizations were renamed branches of the Australian Labor Party.

It was not that there was any conscious desire on the part of the CPE or the QCE in the early 1920s to centralize power or to erode the authority of the conventions. However, as the party became larger and was confronted with the practical problems of being in government, the very structure and nature of the convention left it with little real power, though it retained immense potential power if this was skilfully organized (as it was in 1905 and 1956 before the two great splits in the Queensland party).

Cabinet ministers and "inner executive" members were aware of its potential power and its authority and came to conventions prepared to argue against any too great extensions of the platform and the rules. Nevertheless convention still passed rule and platform changes and the history of the conventions after 1918 contains many examples of the QCE and the PLP quietly neglecting to implement those platform changes which they considered to be impractical, too difficult or too sensitive to implement. What was required here was a tacit agreement between cabinet and the executive committee that the matter would be quietly deferred unless some group with power in the party made an issue of it.

The convention was characterized by its emphasis on rank and file control. It elected its own chairman, vice-chairman and secretary; it decided its own standing orders; it decided who could be admitted in to the convention hall; it appointed its own credentials, press, agenda and appeals committees and could overrule the decisions of any of these if it chose; it elected its own returning officer and scrutineers for any ballots. Its weakness was that it met only once every three years for one five-day period. Its agenda was usually so long that it would have taken three weeks to debate it properly. Furthermore, it met just prior to the state election and there was a general unwillingness to push contentious items too hard for fear of "rocking the boat" and affecting the government's chances at the election. It relied on the agenda committee's decisions as to what items there was time to debate and when these would be debated. Time was necessarily taken up with official speeches, central executive reports, lengthy ballots and appeals. If there were contentious items brought forward for debate (and few conventions did not have a long list of such items) then the time left for the remainder of the agenda became smaller. A practice developed of referring items, not debated, to the QCE which dealt with them rather imperfectly or left them to the "inner executive" to handle. At the 1926 Convention, 178 items were referred back to the QCE and in 1928, 172 items were dealt with in this manner. Attempts by delegates to have the convention sit every night or vote on each item not debated were unsuccessful. After 1923, when the convention ruled that the QCE itself could also submit items, these naturally found themselves high on the agenda committee's list.

Finance continued as a pressing problem limiting the organizational work of Lewis McDonald and his organizer Joseph Silver Collings, who had been appointed in July 1919. Registration and capitation fees maintained the office and paid the salaries of the two full-time officials and two female office staff. McDonald and Collings were paid the same salary, that of a member of the Legislative Assembly and Collings received an extra allowance when he went on organizing trips. There was no finance for broadening and increasing the membership, for political education, and little for fighting election campaigns. Local campaigns were financed by rank and file members through raffles with the AWU providing donations for selected candidates. To compensate for this lack of finance and the consequent weakness in the organization in many electorates, Theodore, after he became premier, tried to persuade the AWU to appoint political

Finance was a problem for the QCE. Secretary, Lewis McDonald (left), and organizer, Joe Collings (right), were full-time officials, paid out of the fees from registration and capitation. (Photographs by courtesy of the John Oxley Library and the Commonwealth Handbook.)

organizers, but W.J. Riordan, the AWU president, rejected this as not being possible. Nevertheless, the AWU, in fact, assumed tacit responsibility for conducting Labor party affairs in areas away from the major population centres.

Conscious of its poor financial base, the QCE turned to the convention for ways and means of finding additional finances. The 1920 Convention increased capitation fees for branches from threepence to sixpence, but rejected increases to one shilling for both unions and branches. Union capitation fees remained at threepence per member. It decided that the broader problems of finance "be referred back to the QCE for fullest consideration". A request by the QCE for a further increase in capitation fees at the 1923 Convention was similarly "passed back to the QCE for consideration". For election campaigns, the party was forced to rely on private donations, usually made to the premier, and on donations from the affiliated unions where the AWU donations dwarfed those of other unions. The QCE and the Labor evening newspaper, the *Daily Standard*, took a six months' lease on the Lyceum Theatre in George Street to see if a chain of Labor picture theatres would be feasible. The venture does not seem to have been successful. However, a series of fairs and carnivals kept the party solvent and enabled it to finance its election campaigns. Between December 1923 and August 1924, £5777 was raised by this method.[4] When capitation fees were raised from sixpence to a shilling for branch members and from threepence to sixpence for unionists at the 1926 Convention, the fairs dropped off. At the same time, McDonald's efficiency as a secretary was beginning to wane and the party consequently found itself in a poor financial position when the Depression came.

Meetings of the QCE during the war had been frequent, but not regular. They were called by McDonald and Demaine when needed. The QCE was still reasonably small with only twenty-one members in 1918. However, there were 230 branches and fifty-two affiliated unions, which meant a great deal of correspondence had to be read and numerous minor disputes settled at QCE meetings. Consequently, at the end of 1918, Theodore proposed that an executive committee of three be appointed "to examine and deal with correspondence, preliminary investigation of all matters brought before the central executive and to report thereon to the full Executive meetings".[5] The executive committee was to meet fortnightly and the QCE monthly. Demaine, McDonald and Riordan constituted the first executive committee. In March 1920, W.J. Dunstan, the AWU state secretary, replaced Riordan, and Robert Carroll, secretary of the Amalgamated Society of Engineers, who had been arrested twelve months before for flying the red flag, was added, giving representation to the Trades Hall affiliated unions. In Demaine's absence, Dunstan and, after 1925, Riordan,[6] became in effect chaiman of the "inner executive" and more powerful than either Demaine or McDonald.

Robert Carroll was appointed to the executive committee of the QCE, twelve months after he was arrested for flying the red flag.

Although Demaine was president of the QCE for twenty-two years, he was elected chairman of the convention in 1923 only. Either George Pollock, chairman of committees and later Speaker in the Legislative Assembly, or the AWU state secretary, chaired the conventions. Demaine was not really a strong or commanding convention chairman, though he performed well and with impartiality in the smaller QCE meetings. His continued presidency was a measure of his general respect in the labor movement. In the early 1920s, no members of the parliamentary party showed any desire to be elected to the executive committee.

The intention of the QCE to meet monthly faltered in 1923. After the convention in March that year — a particularly hectic convention that had followed a year of public wrangling involving the government, the QCE, the TLC and some of the more militant unions[7]— QCE meetings were held less frequently. Two months often elapsed between meetings during which time the party was administered by the executive committee. Meetings of the full QCE were called during 1925 to draw up the platform for the first Greater Brisbane City Council elections, to endorse state and federal candidates, to elect Federal Conference delegates and to deal with the forty-four-hour week issue, the restoration of the five shillings taken off the basic wage in 1922, relationships with the Communist party and the pledge specifically repudiating the Communist party. By the end of 1925, most internal problems had been settled and only four meetings of the QCE were held in 1926 and five during 1927.

Between 1918 and 1926, the executive committee had been composed of non-parliamentary members. With the power that the executive committee was acquiring to influence QCE decisions, particularly in relation to how the PLP should act, the parliamentary party moved to gain direct representation on the executive committee. In the election of officers that followed the 1926 Convention, the "inner executive" was expanded to eight — the three officers, plus five executive members. The executive committee would at times have only seven members when the QCE secretary was a voting member (McDonald did not have a vote). Collings, as organizer, also attended all executive committee meetings. William Forgan Smith, Maurice Hynes and David Gledson, members of the PLP, were elected with Carroll and J.C. Lamont, the southern district secretary of the AWU. Smith was then deputy premier, Hynes was vice-president of the AWU and Gledson, minister for labour and industry, had been a small unions' delegate on the QCE since 1916.

Increasingly, after 1926, the executive committee acted on its own initiative, confident that its actions would not be challenged at later QCE meetings. There now appeared more frequently in the QCE minutes directions that matters on the QCE agenda not finalized or which were likely to be sensitive were to be "left to the Executive Committee" or "referred to the Executive Committee".

The Communist Party

The QCE made rules and asserted its right to be obeyed by delegates and party members. Delegates to its meetings were not permitted to report to their unions or to anyone else what happened at QCE meetings. To bring recalcitrant militants into line, the QCE issued a manifesto entitled *Solidarity or Disruption*, in March 1919, which set out how far criticism of the party could be taken by radicals inside the party. In August 1919, the QCE added two new rules to those regarding plebiscites, prohibiting any branch or union from specifically endorsing any candidate in a plebiscite and prohibiting party members from canvassing, circulating literature or "using undue influence on behalf of any candidate, with or without the knowledge of the candidate" on the penalty of expulsion. It was the QCE which laid down that simple majority voting would be used in Senate plebiscites and optional preferential voting in other plebiscites. It was the QCE that ruled that facsimile ballot papers for plebiscites could be printed in the *Worker* and later in the *Advocate*, the Australian Railways Union (ARU) journal, for use by unionists far away from voting centres. It was the QCE that ruled that a person could belong only to the branch covering the geographical area in which he lived. The convention ratified these only after they had already been in operation.

The most dramatic assertion of QCE authority came in early 1925 following the Federal Conference resolutions excluding Communists from membership of the Labor party. The Communist party in the early 1920s was a new, untried organization, uncertain of its local political role, its membership or its immediate future and contained many former members of the Industrial Workers of the World (IWW). It was considerably less a challenge to parliamentary democracy in Australia than the many virulent anti-communist groups that had emerged after the war. In November 1922, a deputation from the Trades and Labor Council and from the Communist party had met with the QCE "to give effect to the resolution of the Council of Action [which was to carry out the decisions of the 1921 All-Australian Trade Union Congress] having for its object the closer union of all working class organisations and their affiliation with the ALP". The report of this meeting, in the QCE minutes, merits repeating in full.

> The ALP in Queensland would welcome the affiliation of all Industrial Unions not affiliated and it was agreed that the TLC should urge all Unions affiliated with the Council which were not affiliated with the ALP to carry resolutions to affiliate with the ALP.
>
> The principal difficulty was the question of affiliation of such bodies as the Communist Party. The ALP rules at present debar from membership any person who is a member or a known supporter of any other political party.
>
> However a friendly and free discussion took place and it was finally agreed that the representative of the Communist Party [J.B. Miles, the state secretary] should report back to his organisation the result of the deputation and endeavour to get his Party to formulate a concrete proposal which would pave the way for the Communist Party linking up with the ALP.
>
> During the discussion, Mr. Miles stated that his Party was not a revolutionary party, but desired to bring about a state of Communism by constitutional means. It was understood that any linking up of the Communist Party with the ALP would first

> necessitate an amendment of ALP rules, and if necessary, the matter could be considered at the State Convention in next March.[8]

There was no agenda item regarding the Communist party submitted by the QCE to the 1923 Convention. In fact, the Labor party was moving away from, not closer to, association with the communists.

For some members of the ALP, particularly Theodore who had long been an opponent of the anti-political Industrial Workers of the World and who had substantially drafted the *Solidarity or Disruption* manifesto, there was a hardening of attitudes towards communists, syndicalists, militants who were disruptive and those theorists who wanted the Labor party changed from a working man's party committed to reform through constitutional means, to a revolutionary socialist party. Theodore saw communists and their sympathizers as saboteurs who were "white anting" the trade union movement and the Labor party. On the other hand, George Rymer and Tim Moroney, the president and secretary of the ARU, the two men at whom much of Theodore's ire was directed, were never to join the Communist party, but regarded the communists as merely another militant working class group committed to the downfall of capitalism.

At the Federal Conference in 1924, two resolutions had been passed regarding the Communist party. They were: (i) "Neither the Communist Party nor a Branch thereof may be or become affiliated with the Australian Labor Party"; (ii) "No member of the Communist Party may be, or become a member of the Australian Labor Party". When the QCE met in February 1925 to consider these resolutions, Carroll and George Lawson of the Carters and Drivers Union sought to refer "the exclusion and refusal of admission of Communists" to the following convention. This was rejected by thirteen votes to eleven. The two Federal Conference resolutions were then adopted by the QCE by eighteen votes to six.[9] The problems arose when the QCE then decided that each member of the Labor party should sign a pledge declaring that he was not a member of the Communist party. This was an extension of the QCE's practice of making rules which should really have been the province of the convention.

The Pledge

While there had been a pledge for candidates since 1890, it was not until 1924 that the QCE decided that a pledge was required for all party members. The question of such a pledge had emerged from the acrimonious disputes which had arisen between the government and several unions in 1920. As the postwar recession settled on Queensland, the government looked for ways of economizing. Men on temporary work in government employment were dismissed. The Railway Department suffered the largest cuts. With a fall of over 10 per cent in the cost of living throughout 1921, the Arbitration Court reduced the basic wage and later the government sought, successfully, to have public servants' wages reduced by five shillings per week. It also passed a bill cutting the salaries of politicians, judges and senior public servants, not covered by awards. Resolutions were passed by the QCE and the TLC seeking the restoration of the five shillings and deputations were sent to Theodore. All had no success. The government would not move, but it indicated that it would compensate the loss in wages by introducing a child endowment scheme related to earnings.[10]

A debate at the 1923 Convention to force the government to restore the five shillings to the basic wage was lost by thirty-seven votes to thirty-five. Later in the convention, there was a motion, initiated by the ARU, to give the QCE the power to interpret any plank in the platform and instruct the parliamentary party accordingly. Theodore strongly opposed the motion in terms that were to be paraphrased and repeated thirty-three years later.

> The previous speakers had looked at things in an entirely wrong perspective. If the motion was carried, instead of responsible Government, they would have Government by organisations outside. In New South Wales where similar provisions as proposed existed, what had happened — schisms and chaos . . . .

> No Parliamentary Party or Minister could accept responsibility if he had any backbone in him at all. He would be a mere puppet and would jump as the strings were twirled. While the Labor member stuck to his pledges, and the Cabinet carried out those pledges, they should have confidence in them. If they had not that faith, Parliamentary action was all a myth. No one could say that in seven and a half years in office they had not tried to interpret the Labor platform and carry it out.[11]

Forgan Smith warned of the possible consequences of passing such a motion, but the convention delegates were in no mood to heed such warnings. They reflected the widely held belief in the Labor party that politicians should not be able to do as they pleased, but should accept the will of the party and carry out its decisions. An amendment by Riordan to insert a new rule in the construction giving the QCE power: "To interpret the planks of the platform, or any resolutions, or decisions of Convention which may at any time be in dispute and to expel from membership of the Party any member who refuses to abide by such interpretations or such decisions" was carried by fifty-five votes to eleven.[12]

After the 1923 election, when the QCE settled down to consider the resolutions from the convention, the railway union delegates took up the question of the forty-four-hour week which the convention had written into the platform. On their initiative, the QCE passed a resolution instructing the PLP to amend the Arbitration Act, to provide for the forty-four-hour week and to make this the first business of the following session. The government, however, was not prepared to legislate immediately for the reduced working week. In the environment created by disagreements over matters of great principle and concern, enormous pressures developed inside the Labor party for branch members and QCE delegates to take sides and for a strict observance of the rules. Ill-defined ideological divisions were often formed about particular personalities. Solidarity and conformity became intermixed and it was often unclear which was which.

In May 1924, it was decided that all members of the party, not merely candidates, should be required to sign a pledge.

To the few letters seeking clarification of the wording,

McDonald replied that new members could not be admitted to the party unless they signed the pledge. The position of existing

AUSTRALIAN LABOR PARTY (State of Queensland)

....Branch

MEMBER'S PLEDGE

I..

hereby pledge myself to the principles of the Australian Labor Party's Federal, State, and Local Government Platforms, and to do everything in my power to further the objects of the Australian Labor Party as set forth in the Constitution and General Rules.

Signed..

Witnessed..

Date.. Worker Typ., Brisbane

All members of the party were required to sign this pledge in May 1924.

members was not made clear. However, in 1925, when McDonald informed branches of the additional sentence in the pledge regarding the Communist party "I hereby declare that I am not a member of a Communist Organization or Party or of any political party having objects and methods in any way opposed to the Australian Labor Party" — he left no doubt whether new and existing branch members were required to sign the new pledge. He wrote to all branches:

> I am directed by the QCE to communicate with all ALP Branches and inform them that any person who refuses to sign the new form of pledge drawn up by the QCE declaring that such person is not a member of the Communist Party, is not eligible to become or remain a member of an ALP branch and any Branch which declines to accept the Federal Conference decision as conveyed by the QCE shall forfeit all rights and claims to recognition as a Branch of the ALP.[13]

Lists were kept of branch responses and a final warning in October contained the threat of automatic expulsion of branches which had not sent affirmative replies by November. Apart from a few branch members, who held out on the grounds that only the convention, not the QCE, had the authority to make such a rule, the opposition collapsed and the pledges were signed as members collected their tickets at the beginning of 1926.

Before a person could become a Labor candidate, he was now required to sign a pledge which bound him:

- not to oppose the Labor nominee in the event of losing plebiscite or other selection
- to go through with the contest if selected
- to support offical Labor policy
- to vote in parliament as a majority of caucus decided
- to accept the interpretation of the QCE regarding any disputed policy question
- to abide by the constitution and rules of the ALP
- not to become a member of a Communist (and later Fascist) organization or any other body having aims in conflict with the ALP

The anti-communist pledge issue reached a climax with the exclusion of the four ARU delegates, Rymer, Moroney, E. Foley and V. Hartley, from the 1926 convention on the grounds that they had not signed the pledge unconditionally. They had signed under protest on the grounds that the QCE did not have the authority to institute such a rule.[14] (See Chapter 18). However there were deeper issues in this exclusion than the matter of how the pledge was to be signed. The animosity towards Moroney, Rymer and Foley, which had been building up since their criticism of the government before 1920, was carried over to the QCE after the convention when the QCE would not accept these three as ARU delegates, even though they had now signed unconditional pledges. The QCE would continue to accept the ARU's affiliation, but demanded three different delegates.[15] In the imbroglio, the ARU's affiliation lapsed and subsequent requests by that union to reaffiliate were either held up with the demand for the payment of back levies of £132 15s. or simply received and left standing.

Prior to the 1926 Convention, the government had responded to QCE and union pressure and to a majority vote by the PLP, to amend the Arbitration Act to provide the forty-four-hour week (in 1924) and had restored the five shillings to the basic wage (after the 1925 strike).[16] Thereafter it became the goal of men like Forgan Smith, Riordan, McDonald, Collings and even Carroll to ensure, through a tight control by the executive committee over party affairs, that there would be no similar disputes that could endanger the Labor government. Expelling Moroney, Rymer and Foley and tacitly expelling the ARU, the most militant and syndicalist union, were symptoms of the end of the radical period for Labor in Queensland. The goals were now to retain what had been achieved and to press for more moderate reforms.

In the ideological environment of Queensland in the late 1920s, guaranteeing conformity in the labor movement was no easy task. An organization called the "Minority Labour Movement" was formed at the beginning of 1926 "to clean the Labour Movement of the reactionary element which at present controls". It did not last long, but was succeeded by an attempt at the TLC to form a political "Industrial Section" under the control of the TLC and independent of the ALP.[17] This also failed, but such were the fissures between the moderate and militant unions that several unions — the shop assistants, the clerks and many small unions — left the TLC, but retained their ALP affiliation. The AWU declined to take part in the 1927 Labor Day procession (which was subsequently abandoned for that year) and withdrew from the TLC in 1928 expressing a willingness to reaffiliate only when the TLC changed to a card system of voting.[18] This would have given the AWU a commanding influence in council decisions. It did however reaffiliate in 1929 and maintained this affiliation until 1939. In Maryborough, the QCE president himself felt the consequences of the divisions in the labor movement when an Independent Labor party team contested the municipal elections; it split the Labor vote and reduced the previous ALP majority of five aldermen to a minority of five.

The schisms within the labor movement came to a further head in the South Johnstone strike[19] (see Chapter 19). The animosity between the AWU and the ARU and between the other railway unions and the ARU worsened; the premier, McCormack, in particular, and the government in general, were condemned by even moderate unions for their repressive handling of the strike. In contrast with the QCE's positive role on behalf of the unions in the basic wage and forty-four-hour disputes, it took a non-partisan position on the strike and Carroll's own union, the Amalgamated Engineering Union, passed a vote of no-confidence in it. The 1927 Trade Union Congress confirmed the lowering of confidence of even many of the moderate unions in a Labor party so dominated by the PLP and QCE. It issued a leaflet over the signatures of George Lawson, its president and R.J. Mulvey, its secretary, both moderate union men, denying the right of the QCE to be considered the voice of the labor movement.[20] At the 1928 Labor-in-Politics Convention, debates on reports of ministerial shareholding in the Mungana shares, the South Johnstone strike, the power exercised by the QCE, the right of politicians to attend conventions or to sit on the QCE, a levy of 2½ per cent on politicians' salaries and a call for annual conventions, all reflected the frustrations of a large body, though not a majority of rank and file delegates.

Branch Organization

Despite all this, there was a recognition among the affiliated unions of the significant achievements of Labor governments for farmers and workers and, when the Labor party lost the state election in May 1929, the Trade Union Congress that met in October voted, by a large majority, to reaffirm its faith in the political Labor movement and urged unions to affiliate with the QCE and unionists to join their local ALP branches.

The debates and conflicts outlined here took place in the upper echelons of the party, largely among politicians and trade union leaders. Rank and file members, who made up the base of the party, passed resolutions at their branch and union meetings supporting or opposing the various issues at stake and tried to "have a talk" with their member of parliament, with Collings on his organizing tours, or with union officials who were on the QCE. In 1918 there were 230 branches with 4025 members and fifty-two affiliated unions with 51,158 members.[21] It was not necessary for a member of an affiliated union to be a member of an ALP branch in order to vote in a plebiscite, attend the convention as a delegate or be a representative on the QCE. Indeed the branch membership figures understated the size of the rank and file, since local branches of affiliated unions often regarded themselves as being responsible for political as well as industrial labor questions. Affiliated unionists often regarded their union membership as being the equivalent of ALP branch membership. In 1928, there were 237 branches with 4270 members and sixty-two affiliated unions with 97,776 members. The proportion of union members throughout the state who were affiliated with the Labor party dropped, between 1918 and 1928, from 66 per cent to 61 per cent.

Branches did not exist in all state electorates. There were often no branches in hard core Country party areas in south-eastern Queensland and in the solid Labor areas of the west and the north. Here the AWU organized election campaigns and acted as the ALP organization, a situation that Collings regarded as being quite unsatisfactory. In Brisbane, a Metropolitan District Council existed until 1924. It had been formed in the 1890s to organize election campaigns in the metropolitan area and, after 1901, co-ordinated federal election campaigns in the capital city. In those electorates where there was more than one branch, an Electorate Executive Committee (EEC) had been formed and consisted of an equal number of delegates from each branch. Branches and EECs were largely autonomous and maintained significant power in their own areas. New members could be admitted only through their local branch which also had the power of expulsion for breaches of the rules. A Labor member of parliament was responsible to his own local EEC and branches. These watched his actions carefully, and it was common during the 1920s for sitting members to be opposed at pre-selection plebiscites by one or more branch members or by unions. Sitting members tended not to favour large branches.

Despite its fourteen years of continuous government in Queensland, the Labor party there did not throw its weight fully into federal election campaigns after 1919 or into the federal politics of the party. It resisted the suggestion that there should be uniform constitutions among the state branches and, on more than one occasion, McDonald found himself searching back in the minutes to find how federal conference delegates had been previously chosen and agenda items submitted. In 1916 and 1918, the federal conference delegates had been elected by the convention, but at the latter convention it was decided that federal conference delegates should be chosen by exhaustive ballot of QCE members. The QCE also chose the federal executive delegates. Although Federal Divisional Executives (FDE) were established in federal electorates in 1924, on the same basis as the EECs, i.e., equal branch representation, federal candidates were difficult to attract during the 1920s and EECs continued to hold local power and to organize federal campaigns. In 1914, at the federal election after the double dissolution, Labor won seven of the ten Queensland House of Representatives' seats and all six Senate seats. However it won only two House of Representatives seats in 1922, one in 1925, two in 1928 and three in 1929. After 1914, it did not win a Senate seat until 1931 when in the swing against the Moore government, it won all three. Federal election campaigns were starved for funds at both the central and local level, where the concentration was on holding office in the state parliament.

Branch members paid two shillings and sixpence a year in fees and spent a considerable time raising money for election campaigns and to pay for their delegates to attend the convention. Where there was no local branch or where branches could not afford to send a delegate, the QCE appointed one, usually a politician or trade union official. Branch meetings were held monthly. Here the problems of the party were debated, letters were written to the QCE, interviews arranged with members of parliament and visiting cabinet ministers over employment, local projects, marketing laws, awards, labour conditions and so on. Cabinet ministers and local members kept close touch with rank and file attitudes and thinking, which meant that they seldom went too far or too fast in the reforms they proposed. There were a number of Labor newspapers which acted as a source of two way communication within the party. Brisbane had its *Daily Standard*, owned by a company of almost wholly union shareholders which in the 1920s were increasingly dependent on the AWU for grants and loans to keep the paper going. There were also, in Brisbane, the *Patriot*, a weekly, and the *Worker*, regarded by many as the official ALP paper, though wholly owned by the AWU. Along the coast, the Gympie *Truth*, the Maryborough *Alert*, the Rockhampton *Critic* and the Townsville *Clarion* appeared weekly. The Rockhampton *Daily Record*, which T.J. Ryan had owned, continued to be regarded as a Labor paper as were many other local papers which had once been classed as Labor, but were now regarded as being sympathetic, rather than being specifically in the Labor camp. Many of the pro-Labor papers that had been started before the war had gone out of business during the war through the increased cost of paper or struggled on only to cease publication during the post-war recession.

The ALP was a workers' social club as well as being a political organization. Branches acquired halls for meetings and for letting out; dances were held regularly; there were annual picnics and excursions by boat or train; Labour Day or Eight-Hour Day was celebrated with marches, sports days for the children and dinners in the Labor halls or at the Trades Halls; children's Christmas parties were held for members' and supporters' children; bursaries and prizes were presented at school "breaking up" days and receptions arranged for visiting cabinet ministers. Above all, and despite disagreements within the party, branch members exhibited a pride in what they saw their party having achieved in so short a time after its foundation and in so short a time in government. Socialism was a term they liked to debate, but it was the practical reforms that had benefited workers and farmers that made them spirited defenders of their party in newspaper

Alec MacDonald, Ned Hanlon, Harry Harvey and Mick Healey, marching in the 1946 Labour Day Parade. (Photograph by courtesy of the Trades and Labour Council.)

columns, in pubs and over smokos. ALP members were stronger Australian nationalists than were their political opponents. Though they did not subscribe to republicanism, they objected to the appointment of British governors and through the 1920s sought the appointment of Australian-born governors. When the 1923 Convention adopted Theodore's motion on imperial titles: "No further granting to Queenslanders of Imperial honours, more especially those which confer titles upon the recipients be part of their Fighting Platform", it reflected a deep-seated mistrust of such titles and of the services for which they were rewards.[22] The Queensland ALP has never rescinded this resolution.

Decline of QCE Efficiency

The loss of the 1929 election was to have important consequences for the Labor party. The first was the resignation of McCormack as leader of the PLP and his replacement by Forgan Smith. Though Forgan Smith had not been a union official he had had four years' experience in dealing with unions in the Public Works portfolio and had been highly regarded by them.[23] He held a tight rein over the parliamentary party and over the QCE. This was to be strengthened by his close association with Clarrie Fallon, then the north Queensland district secretary of the AWU, who became Queensland state secretary of the AWU in 1933. A second consequence was to be a further hardening of attitudes towards trade union militants who were wrongly blamed for the 1929 defeat. To ensure that they did not frustrate the party's chance of regaining and retaining office, the militants were to be squeezed out of any influential roles in the party. In 1934, the QCE drafted new rules for expulsions from and re-admissions to the party. Previously this had been left to individual branches. The memories of the loss of office in 1929, exemplified in the excessive eagerness of the Moore government to repeal most of Labor's reforms, made the tight centralization of Forgan Smith and Fallon easier to accept, at least until memories dimmed in the late 1930s. Moreover electoral success gave Forgan Smith a place

Clarrie Fallon's close association with Forgan Smith helped strengthen the tight rein over the parliamentary party and the QCE during the Depression.

of prestige in Labor ranks and the stability of his government together with the return of the state to more normal conditions were welcomed by an electorate shocked by the Depression.

Among the first to feel the adverse effects of the Depression and to fear the threats of the Moore government were the trade unions (see Chapter 20). Labor required a united front to meet this challenge. In October 1929, the TLC suggested a unity conference of all recognized industrial unions and ALP branches. The "inner executive" was prepared to go as far as a meeting between themselves and the TLC executive, but by mid-1930, it had backed away from the broader conference sought by the TLC, "as the Platform and Constitution of the ALP is sufficient to provide for representation of all who are in sympathy with the aims and objectives of the ALP".[24] The problem was that, as the Depression worsened, it seemed to those of a more ideological bent that "the present system was breaking down" (a much over-used sentence in the early 1930s). In their public speeches, they were seeking, not the unity that Labor needed to regain office, but a polarization of capital and Labor forces which would meet on some final battlefield. Such an ideological environment had neither place nor meaning in the practical world of the ALP where jobs and job security had first place. No unity conference was held and the QCE and PLP together sought their own means of returning to office.

The loss of office and the problems raised for the ALP by the Depression made more clear the decline in Lewis McDonald's efficiency. He had been twenty years in the position and had been unsuccessful in several attempts to enter politics. He now complained of poor health and it is evident from the QCE records of the 1920s that minutes, lists of delegates, correspondence, and financial reports were not as thoroughly maintained as they had been in his first ten years. Collings, in fact, had been carrying much of the organizational load that belonged to McDonald. With Labor in office and the initiative lying with the parliamentary party, the QCE secretary's role had been overshadowed by that of the premier and senior cabinet ministers. However with Labor in opposition, the organization of the party fell back to a greater extent on the permanent officials. In July 1931, Riordan criticized the office efficiency at an Executive Committee meeting. It was the QCE office, he said, to which the organizations had a right to look for a lead, "yet it appeared . . . that but little was done in that connection and very little initiative displayed".[25] The disarray of party finances was a major source of complaint.

In February 1931, McDonald had prepared a report on the financial situation of the QCE. This showed that during 1930 income had been £2490 and expenditure £3079. He estimated that capitation fees from branches and unions for 1931 would be down 40 per cent to around £1300. A "Back to Power" campaign, initiated early in 1930 had been deferred as the problems of the Scullin government, the economic and social effects of the Depression, the shock of the Mungana Royal Commission and the lack of initiatives in the central office, took

W.J. Riordan resigned all his Labor party offices, in 1933, to take a position on the Industrial Court Bench. (Photograph by courtesy of Queensland Newspapers Ltd.)

Syd Bryan, former president of the TLC, became vice-president of the QCE in 1938. (Photograph by courtesy of Queensland Newspapers Ltd.)

their toll. In May 1931, McDonald issued a lustreless circular letter to branches and unions appealing for funds, but it produced nothing. Following Riordan's criticisms, Collings was asked to prepare a report on the party's finances. This showed the ALP, in August 1931, having only £411 in the bank with state and federal elections looming within twelve months.

Forgan Smith opened a direct appeal for funds with a donation of £10. Though Collings was elected to the Senate in December 1931, he remained the party's organizer and was the force in the central office behind the "Back to Power" campaign which increased in intensity in 1932 after the good Labor vote in the federal elections and in the face of moves by Moore to extend the life of the parliament and to revive the Legislative Council. The AWU had more to gain from a Labor government than most unions and donated over £1000 to the campaign funds.[26] Whatever else Forgan Smith received in private donations enabled the party to fight a successful campaign and a financial report in May 1933 showed the party having £244 in credit with all debts paid. Now that Labor again held office the QCE could apply successfully to the attorney-general for permission to hold new fairs and carnivals.

At the QCE meeting on 15 March 1933, Riordan resigned all his offices in the Labor party to take a position on the Industrial Court bench. Fallon, who had not previously been a member of the executive committee, defeated Syd Bryan, by fifteen votes to seven for the vice-presidency. Bryan was then TLC president and secretary of the Electrical Trades Union (ETU), the Miscellaneous Workers Union, the Theatrical Employees Union and the Jewellers, Watchmakers and Allied Trades Union.[27] After 1933, nothing was done by the "inner executive" or by the QCE, or by the PLP unless Forgan Smith and Fallon agreed to it.

Both Forgan Smith and Fallon demanded efficiency from those who served them. McDonald's conduct of the office now came under tougher scrutiny. Following two meetings of the executive committee, for which Demaine came down from Maryborough, he was called back to explain discrepancies in the auditor's report. These were accepted as being due to his negligence, not dishonesty, but he was lucky to hold his position as secretary. Collings favoured dividing McDonald's position between a secretary who administered the office and an organizing secretary who co-ordinated the running of the party. This change was discussed, deferred and ultimately forgotten, but McDonald's salary was reduced from £11 10 s. a week to £9 a week,[28] and he was given the number three position on the unsuccessful Senate ticket in 1934.[29] In October 1935, Carroll was appointed as an organizer by the executive committee.

As McDonald's health improved and he paid closer attention to the efficiency of the office, his place in the party was restored. He was re-elected as a federal conference delegate in 1936 after having been defeated in a similar ballot in 1933 (the only Federal Conference he missed in twenty-four years). His salary was restored in May 1935, however he died in September 1936 and in February 1937, Carroll became secretary. A proposal to establish a scholarship to commemorate McDonald, similar to those for T.J. Ryan and Frank McDonnell was discussed, but lapsed. Carroll completed a revision of the party's rules and sought the appointment of a new organizer. Finances did not allow for this and it fell to the Labor members of parliament and the AWU to provide the organizers outside the metropolitan area. A further break with the past came in December 1938 when Demaine stood down from the presidency of the QCE and Fallon was elected as his successor. Bryan who had lost the TLC presidency in 1937, but who was still secretary of the ETU and the Jewellers and Watchmakers Union, became vice-president.

An Imperious "Inner Executive"

The Depression period accentuated the power of the executive committee. Though it was resolved, in July 1929, to hold QCE meetings quarterly, such meetings continued to be held irregularly and none at all was held between March 1933 and June 1934, a break of fifteen months. The executive committee, by contrast, met fortnightly or at least monthly with Collings continuing to attend, often as acting secretary, even after his election to the Senate. It was the executive committee that made the decision on Queensland's attitude to the Premiers' Plan; the executive committee decided that Langites had to be brought to heel and expelled, if necessary, but that Douglas Credit supporters were harmless enough and could be tolerated provided they did not nominate candidates against the ALP. It was the executive committee that proscribed the Friends of the Soviet Union, the Anti-War Campaign Organisation, the Unemployed Workers Movement and other communist or suspected communist fronts. The executive committee decided that the *Worker* could print facsimile ballot papers for the plebiscites at the 1932 state election.

A close watch was kept by the executive committee on the

unions and on all non-Labor political organizations. On its recommendation, a Clerks Union delegate was excluded from the QCE for his association with the Nationalist party in the 1932 elections. His rejection followed the Moroney-Rymer-Foley precedent of 1926 and the rejection of Jack Roche of the Storemen and Packers Union in 1927 and Andy Brown of the Waterside Workers Federation in 1929. Both had been associated with suspected communist meetings. The closeness of the scrutiny of all communist or left wing organizations and meetings is amply demonstrated in the case of Roche's application for re-admission to the ALP in 1933. Forgan Smith, as premier, had maintained the same police watch on meetings of the unemployed as the Moore government had initiated. When Roche's application came before the executive committee (branch secretaries referred "doubtful" applications to the QCE), it was decided to hold this over for six months. The minute read: "The Secretary reported having, in company with Mr. J. Reid [a Storeman and Packers Union official elected to the executive committee in 1937], inspected the reports of the Chief Secretary's Department which disclosed that Mr. Roche had, the day after his application for re-admission to the Party, attended a meeting organised by the Communist Party."[30]

At times, the "inner executive" became quite imperious in its dealings with party members. F.W. Brazier, the secretary of the Camp Hill branch, was summoned before the executive committee, following a reply he wrote to a QCE circular instructing branches not to associate with certain organizations. Forgan Smith framed the resolution of recantation: "The letter from the Camp Hill Branch is offensive and couched in terms which are indicative of defiance of the Executive's authority and we instruct the Branch to withdraw the letter".[31] Reports of executive committee meetings were not given to the QCE nor did the QCE members have any notion of what correspondence had been received and how it had been dealt with. Rank and file branch members remained largely ignorant of the composition and workings of the executive committee. An enquiry by the Bulimba branch regarding the personnel of the "inner executive" received the cold reply that "there is no Inner Executive of the QCE, but there is an Executive Committee as provided under Rule 30(k)".[32]

The executive committee members took their positions seriously. They fought elections seriously and allowed the political leaders to do this with some professionalism. While they were anxious to retain their own positions of power in the party they received no financial rewards or other "perks" for their work. They saw their role as maintaining a broadly based political party which could retain government and thereby protect workers and small farmers in their jobs, in marketing produce and in the prices of necessary commodities. They were determined that Labor should govern in Queensland because of the observable benefits that Labor governments had brought to farmers and workers. To achieve this goal, they were equally determined to keep radicals, militants and other non-conformists away from any sharing of administrative power.

Rank and file branch members, and also union leaders who were outside the small group who exercised power, often saw the executive committee in a different light. Their notions of democratic control of the Labor party did not extend to the "democratic centralism" which seemed to be exercised by the "inner executive". Indeed, a large amount of their time was spent in the frustrating exercise of trying to lessen the oligarchic power of the "inner". These were the radicals, the rebels and the non-conformists of the party who ran the constant risk of being "chopped off", "cut down" or "thrown out".

Bringing a rebel or non-conformist to heel by calling him in for a "talk" was a common practice. One person who found himself called in on more than one occasion was Frank Waters, a postal employee, who was elected to the Legislative Assembly in 1932. Waters had made a reputation at the TLC in the previous six years as a coming leader in the labour movement. At the 1932 Convention, he was one of a group of delegates who sought to break the tight hold of the executive committee over the Labor party, to commit the ALP to a more radical platform and to make its internal administration more receptive to rank and file

Calling a rebel or non-conformist in for a "talk" was common practice. Frank Waters, a coming leader in the Labour movement, found himself called in on more than one occasion.

initiatives. Waters sought the establishment of a socialization committee by the QCE to popularize the party's socialist objective; he sought night meetings of the QCE to enable delegates who were neither politicians nor full-time union officials to attend; he sought annual conventions and the limitation of the right to vote in plebiscites to those who had attended three ALP branch or union meetings in the twelve months prior to the plebiscite; he sought to lessen the power of the AWU by giving smaller unions greater representation at the convention. In 1932, he was defeated on all of these, but others would continue to seek similar reforms in the following forty years.

Solving the continuing problems that arose through the plebiscite system of selecting candidates remained a major question for QCE officers and rank and file members alike. These problems included: branch members who never attended branch meetings, but whose tickets were paid for, and often held, by the local member of parliament; too eager canvassing of voters by candidates and their supporters; unionists who borrowed their mates' union tickets and voted "early and often" and some not too scrupulous union officials who provided union tickets for those who would support particular candidates. Later, the large number of facsimile ballot papers, clipped from the *Worker* in electorates where the AWU organizer backed a particular candidate, would be added to the list. These infringements caused rancour within branches and headaches for the QCE officials. Demaine led the debate in 1932 and advocated disbanding the plebiscite system and having candidates selected by the QCE. There was no great faith in the QCE selecting candidates more impartially and this alternative found little support. In the end, more rules were added to try to close loopholes since the plebiscite system, with all its shortcomings, continued to hold strong rank and file support particularly among those away from Brisbane.

The 1932 addition to the rules provided that, under threat of suspension or expulsion, ALP members were prohibited from issuing circulars or printed material or from providing vehicles to take voters to the booth. A move to abolish optional preferential voting in plebiscites was lost as was an attempt to make voting compulsory for branch members. A candidate for a plebiscite was now required to have three, instead of two, years membership of an ALP branch or affiliated union (Fallon wanted five). The QCE was given power to refuse endorsement to any candidate who was shown to be "lacking in the necessary character, loyalty and ability to be a satisfactory representative of Labor in any elected capacity". The convention re-admitted Jim Kane who had refused to sign the anti-communist pledge in 1926. It approved the establishment of separate women's branches though there was opposition from those who thought that women should continue to be members of ordinary ALP branches. Most women in fact did. A later attempt to obtain direct QCE representation for women was rejected by the QCE.

While the 1930s was a turbulent decade in many parts of the world, filled with great debates about economic systems, capitalism, socialism and communism, about wars, the emergence of fascism, nazism and collective security, such debates were dampened in the Queensland ALP for whom it was a decade of stability and even conformism.

Fallon's first report as AWU secretary, in May 1933, indicated his views of the goals of Labor in politics. These were lower unemployment, a high basic wage with a high purchasing power, a reasonable working week (forty-four hours) and prosperous industries in the state.[33] The Forgan Smith governments quickly reintroduced the reforms enacted prior to 1929 and, according to Fallon's criteria, Queensland employees fared better than those in other states. Both Forgan Smith and Fallon were anxious not to disturb the balance between the ideal and the reality of Labor in politics. Consequently delegates at conventions wishing to disband the arbitration system or have a forty-hour week introduced immediately or have the government legislate for the restoration of the basic wage to its 1921 level of £4 5s. (the Queensland basic wage had dropped to £3 14s. in 1931 and returned to £4 1s. in 1938) were confronted by Forgan Smith and Fallon quoting comparisons with other states, harking back to Moore and warning of what might happen if, in forcing the PLP to move too quickly ahead, the convention brought about a loss of government.

Primary industries had always been more important in Queensland than secondary industries, and the lands, and agriculture and stock portfolios were carefully allocated along with health and home affairs, and labour. The broad coalition of blue collar workers and white collar workers, farmers, small businessmen and reformers that Ryan and Theodore had carefully built was just as carefully preserved by Forgan Smith. This concept of balance was reflected also within the party in the composition of the "inner executive", where rural, urban and provincial city interests were represented along with the cabinet, the AWU and Trades Hall unions. An oligarchy ruled the Labor party, but it was an oligarchy that was able to tap rank and file and union views on what was wanted from a Labor government. While Forgan Smith ordered, he did not crash ahead alone, but consulted those closest to him in the parliamentary party and the unions. A good example concerned the toll on a new bridge (the Story Bridge) to be built over the Brisbane River at Kangaroo Point. After the cabinet and caucus had discussed the project and recommended the financing through a toll, Forgan Smith took the question to the executive committee which ruled that the toll was not "a violation of any plank or principle of the ALP".[34]

If Forgan Smith and Fallon were seen by their supporters in the party as benevolent despots, they were anything but benevolent when the question of the Communist party was involved. Both were rigidly opposed to any dealings or association with the Communist party or any of its front organizations. Members of the ALP who were known to associate with communists or to attend or sponsor meetings where communists had even the slightest influence were sought out, cautioned and disciplined. The clear line between indigenous radical and socialist thought, which had a long history in the Labor party and the trade unions, and communist ideology was rarely sought. Fallon constantly warned of communists in the industries covered by the AWU and they were prohibited from holding any AWU offices. The "inner executive" proscribed organizations even suspected of having communist influence. A letter from the Communist party in 1937 seeking affiliation with the ALP was not acknowledged. When Jack Beasley, the minister for supply in Curtin's government and a former president of the New South Wales Labor Council, was scheduled to address the Queensland Trades and Labor Council in July 1943, he was ordered away by the executive committee who objected to any ALP association with the TLC while there was strong communist influence there.

Strangely, while the ALP was moving into a more rigid anti-communist position, it came under a Protestant sectarian attack of being dominated by Catholics. Sectarianism had been rampant during the conscription campaigns of World War I, but had abated somewhat during the 1920s. In the mid-1930s, it emerged strongly and found an outlet in the Protestant Labour party which contested twenty-three seats at the 1938 election, receiving 8.75 per cent of the vote and winning one seat, that of Frank Waters in Kelvin Grove. ALP branches found themselves receiving applications for membership from persons who, previously, had not been regarded as Labor supporters and branch secretaries received letters and bundles of leaflets with strong sectarian bias, to be read at ALP meetings. The executive committee struggled with the new threat and Carroll issued a manifesto. "Labor's Policy Towards Religious or Other Bodies", and a further warning against "Subversive Activities of Anti-A.L.P. Individuals and Bodies". Forgan Smith had a table prepared on public service recruitment, since his accession to the premiership, which showed that Catholics and non-Catholics had been employed in about the same proportions as they constituted the Queensland population.[35] The "Catholic dominated" charge was to die down, but emerged in a different form in the years prior to 1957.

Despite the great increase in QCE power and the even greater increase in executive committee power, the convention remained, for the rank and file delegates, the one open forum in which the oligarchic power in the party could be challenged. However the 1935 Convention indicated how strongly Forgan Smith and Fallon were in control (and how far ahead of their opponents they were on tactics) in debates on the abolition of the arbitration system, the establishment of socialization committees, broader representation on the QCE and the introduction of the forty-hour week. Even when Bryan led the opposition, the numbers were with Forgan Smith and Fallon. In between ten ballots to elect the eleven representatives to the QCE, the delegates attempted to debate a miscellany of items on plebiscites, which changed nothing there. The debates were long and drawn out and 577 items out of 700 were sent back to the QCE.

The same pattern followed at the 1938 Convention. By now, the conventions had lost their coherence. The debates centred on a few major issues of importance to particular unions, ballots were held for almost every committee and 350 items were referred on to the QCE. It was at the 1938 Convention that an attempt was made to find a solution to the whole plebiscite problem. Forgan Smith obtained from the convention an instruction to the QCE to consider the method of selecting candidates and have firm recommendations for the following convention. Three years before, after a particularly large number of plebiscite disputes concerned with the 1935 election, the full QCE had instructed McDonald to procure from the other states details of their methods of selecting candidates. McDonald died soon after and the problems posed by communists and sectarians, codifying the rule changes from several conventions, and the greater effort put into the 1937 federal election, kept Carroll too busy to prepare a report from McDonald's correspondence.

When the 1938 Convention instruction on plebiscites was considered by the executive committee in July 1939, it was referred to Forgan Smith for action, not to Carroll who was in any case too sick to devote himself to such a complex problem. On the other hand, Forgan Smith, himself, was far too busy to devote his attention to it and the questions were deferred and deferred again until, prior to the 1941 Convention, it was decided that no further action would be taken. There was no report on the plebiscite system to the 1941 Convention which reaffirmed its faith in plebiscites, despite amendments for QCE selection of candidates and for plebiscites only in non-Labor held seats (Forgan Smith's proposal). That a convention instruction had not been carried out was not new. The 1926 Convention, for example, had decided that Labor policy was the abolition of the optional preferential system of voting in state elections. It was obeyed, and contingent voting abolished — in 1942.

Changes with the Past

The 1930s saw the end of the chain of Labor newspapers that had been optimistically established by early Labor stalwarts to serve as the educators of Labor party members, unionists and voters. The Maryborough *Alert*, the Rockhampton *Critic* and the Gympie *Truth* had carried on through the Depression despite financial losses, but radio, paper costs, higher wages and loss of advertizing caused them finally to close. The Townsville *Clarion* struggled on with some financial support from the AWU. The *Worker* maintained publication, but at a financial loss. The *Daily Standard* had represented so many hopes, but despite the efforts of Carroll, chairman of its board, and the AWU which had become its chief financial supporter, it was forced to close in 1936. It is difficult to estimate just how much the unions put into keeping the *Daily Standard* afloat in the 1920s and 1930s. Most unions took whatever additional shares they could manage, but they were characterized by their own constant shortage of funds. Consequently, it was to the AWU that the *Daily Standard* board had principally turned. When it was finally closed down the AWU paid its remaining bills and its assets passed to the AWU, its principal creditor.

Though considerably greater effort had been exerted at the 1931 federal elections, the ALP in Queensland soon reverted to its former concentration on state politics. The concentration of unions on state politics was understandable. More than 80 per cent of employees in Queensland were covered by state awards determined by an Arbitration Court whose membership and terms of reference were laid down by the Queensland government. In 1938, the state basic wage remained higher than that of any other state; the average male rate of wages was the highest in Australia; hours of work per week were the lowest and the percentage of unionists registered as unemployed was the lowest.[36] Nevertheless, federal politics did, necessarily, intrude into the state party. The executive committee decided that the Queensland ALP opposed Australian involvement in any war resulting from the Italian-Abyssinian dispute. There was disagreement between executive committee and the Federal PLP on the attitude to the 1937 referendum on marketing and Queensland members of the federal caucus were forced to follow the QCE direction and vote for the referendum.[37] When uniform taxation was to be introduced in 1942, the QCE, on Forgan Smith's initiative, protested against the infringement of the state's sovereignty and sent Bryan and Fallon to Canberra to put their objections to the federal government. The TLC supported Curtin and Chifley.[38]

Queensland opposed the establishment of a federal secretariat in 1935 and rejected any change in the federal structure of the party. Again in 1944, Queensland had "no suggestions to make" regarding the federal executive or a federal secretariat. John Curtin's leadership and Fallon's acceptance of the federal presidency in 1938 redressed the federal-state balance somewhat. An extra effort was put into the 1937 federal elections. Queensland provided £1350 out of £4000 spent on a propaganda and publicity campaign which preceded the election. A special levy of two pence per member was placed on unions and branches to help raise this and the QCE contributed £500. The QCE spent around £3000 on this campaign. In 1938, it spent in excess of £6000 on the state campaign of which Forgan Smith contributed £2000 and the AWU £1500.

These two campaigns together with four subsequent state and one federal by-election and the 1940 federal election left the party in debt to £2000. Carnivals had been resumed in late 1939 but the party remained in debt. When Carroll died in February 1940, to save money, Bryan was appointed only as acting secretary, retaining his position as secretary of the ETU until 1944. (He remained a part-time commissioner with the State Electricity Commission until June 1948 and remained secretary of the small Jewellers and Watch Makers Union until 1955). Capitation fees for unions were increased also to one shilling at the 1941 Convention. Forgan Smith and Fallon were the principal advocates for the increase with Fallon citing £15,000 collected in disputed wages by the AWU through laws initiated by Labor governments as ample reason for the increases. To him the higher fees were a cheap price to pay for maintaining the financial solvency of the QCE office and the Labor party. Other unions thought differently and sixteen of them withdrew their affiliation because of the increase and nine others had their affiliations cancelled when they failed to pay the new capitation fees.

One of the reasons that unions left the ALP, on the pretext of objecting to the increased capitation fees, was their opposition to the authoritarian actions of the QCE and particularly those of Forgan Smith and Fallon. A motion expressing dissatisfaction with the leadership of the ALP and its dealings with the trade unions was the first item debated at the 1941 Convention. It had no chance of success, but it was symptomatic of the gulf that was emerging between a number of unions and branches, not yet organized into any coherent unit, and the AWU-PLP coalition that controlled a permanent majority on the QCE and at conventions. So long as this AWU-PLP coalition held, the party forged by Forgan Smith and Fallon would survive and probably remain electorally successful.

World War II

The effects of Hitler's attack on the Soviet Union on 22 June 1941 were felt throughout the ALP in Queensland. There was an admiration for the Russian armies who, alone, seemed to be physically fighting nazism until the British offensive began in the western desert on 18 November. Blankets, medical aid and supplies were collected for despatch to the Russians. But to the QCE, communists were communists even if they were on your side in the war and the federal executive ruling that the Australian Russian Association was a communist organization was obeyed by the QCE with great vigour. Two Labor members of parliament, George Taylor and George Marriott, who had been regarded as troublemakers in the 1930s, were expelled for their association with the Australian Russian Association's Medical Aid for Russia Committee (see Chapter 22). Frank Waters, who had been refused endorsement by the QCE for his former seat of Kelvin Grove in 1941, became joint secretary of a Combined ALP Protest Committee seeking the reinstatement of Marriott and Taylor and thereby lost his ALP membership. A ballot for continued affiliation of the Australian Federated Union of Locomotive Enginemen (AFULE) with the ALP was taken among its members with the increased capitation fees, the Taylor and Marriott expulsion and the dictatorial methods of Fallon being given as the reasons for the ballot. Affiliation was maintained by only 653 votes to 647.[39] Fallon ruled that ALP members and politicians were prohibited from addressing any meeting of the Australian Russian Association and in 1942, Tom Aikens' North Queensland Labor Party was born out of those who refused to buckle under to this rule. In September 1942, telegrams were sent to Curtin and the Queensland federal Labor politicians by the executive committee protesting against the removal of the Australian government's ban on the open existence of the Communist party.[40]

Although branch membership had grown in the 1930s, there had been a reduction in the number of branches. In the metropolitan area, where possible, the QCE had attempted to combine local branches into one branch in each electorate. Disciplinary action against branches supporting Lang and "Aid to Russia" or failure of branches to pay their dues further reduced the number of branches. In 1941, there were 210 branches with a membership of 10,654, a drop from the 1938 figure of 11,139. Due to service enlistments, this fell to 5728 members in 177 branches by 1944. Union affiliation remained steady at 59 unions with 92,810 and 129,559 members in 1938 and 1941 respectively. By 1944, this had dropped to 37 unions with 106,884 members. From about 54 per cent of unionists being affiliated with the Queensland ALP in 1938, the figure had risen to 67 per cent in 1941 and dropped back to 55 per cent in 1944.

The 1944 Convention was significant as being the first that tried to come to grips with the size and breadth of its agenda. To arrange items for debate, sixteen separate committees of five delegates and a cabinet minister were formed, at the instigation of the new premier, Frank Cooper. Even so, over three hundred items were still not considered and were referred on to the QCE. The convention upheld the early ruling that delegates could not be directed by their branches or unions on how to vote. It requested the QCE to appoint an organizer; it abolished contingent voting in plebiscites; it established a Labor youth organization and amended the pledge to read: ". . . I am not a member of a Communist or Fascist Organisation or Party . . .". It deferred a motion to establish a Labor daily newspaper, but asked the QCE to continue to try to obtain a licence for a radio station. The convention debated the government's amending the Arbitration Act to provide a forty-hour week. There was ministerial opposition to the timing, but the minister for labour, Vince Gair, satisfied a majority with an amendment linking the forty-hour week with post-war full employment and having the government legislate for the shorter week "as soon as [is] practicable".

In 1944, there was a feeling of satisfaction within the Queensland branch of the Labor party. Farmers and workers had benefited from some of the most advanced legislation passed by a state government in any part of Australia. Ned Hanlon, as minister for health and home affairs, for a decade, had provided a significant range of health and welfare services. Curtin's government had successfully fought the war and introduced more economic and social reforms in its two and a half years of office than any previous commonwealth government. Queensland had spent £8400 on the 1943 federal election campaign and returned six out of the ten members of the House of Representatives and all three senators. There had been many resolutions from the TLC, unions and branches, prior to the convention, calling for Labor unity to face the post-war problems. A unity resolution, which extended a tacit amnesty to those expelled for "Aid to Russia" activities was passed unanimously by the convention. However there was the other side to the quest for unity. A report by Hanlon in 1943 recommending the restoration of membership rights to Tom Aikens' Hermit Park branch at Townsville, in effect the North Queensland Labor Party, was rejected by the QCE. A motion to establish a unity committee from the PLP, AWU and the TLC affiliated unions was carried at the convention by only forty-three votes to forty-two and its application by the QCE was continually deferred. In February 1945, when the ARU sought reaffiliation, it was informed that this could be effected only when the disputed £132 15s. in capitation fees of 1926 were paid. Frank Waters' application to rejoin the party was merely acknowledged and he was to wait until 1956 before he regained his ALP ticket.

Internal Struggles

The post-war period was to be one of conflict within the trade unions and the Labor party as the traditional ALP forces struggled with those of the Communist party and the Catholic Social Studies Movement, better known simply as "The Movement", for the loyalty of trade unionists and control of the whole labor movement. The party outwardly was to remain stable, but this stability was also a reflection of the complacency that long years in office had produced. In April 1946, Cooper was "promoted upstairs" to the lieutenant-governor's position and Hanlon became premier. He then joined Fallon in dominating the political Labor movement.

Fallon was a tough, shrewd and skilful political leader, perhaps the most able president the Labor party has had. He maintained a balance on the ALP executive committee by having the vice-president from a Trades Hall union, and having another AWU member, the premier and deputy premier, two Trades Hall union officials together with one other union official of a "right wing" disposition, constitute the "inner executive". However the presence of communists in many unions made it difficult and in places impossible to maintain a broadly unified trade union movement associated with the ALP. There was moreover a loss of much common ground for informal meetings and discussions between several unions and the Labor government. A further consequence of the presence of many communists was that, in the unsettled industrial conditions of the post-war period when the aspirations of so many working men and their families were not being fulfilled, it was easy to see the major strikes as being communist inspired, organized, maintained and manipulated.

The two longest and most bitter strikes in Queensland after the war were those in the meat industry in 1946 and in the railways in 1948. Both had justifiable industrial reasons; neither was inspired nor manipulated by the Communist party. However the Communist party certainly made its presence felt and tried to keep the strikes going as long as possible and to portray the Labor government and the Industrial Court in the worst possible light. In both strikes, a state of emergency was declared. In 1946 the government fined railwaymen, for refusing to handle bacon products declared "black". During the 1948 dispute (see Chapter 19) the government blocked union opportunities to state publicly the case of the striking workers and passed anti-picketing legislation that brought criticism from a wide range of unions including the AWU.

What held the unions to the Labor party, apart from their traditional loyalty, was their respect for the Chifley government which was implementing Labor policy despite the most highly organized and best financed opposition that any federal Labor government, until then, had experienced. Further, despite the government's heavy handling of the 1946 and 1948 strikes, there was a genuine affection for Hanlon which differed from the respect which had been shown to Forgan Smith. Hanlon's welfare reforms in the 1930s combined with his negotiation of the free hospital scheme which the Curtin and Chifley governments had provided, and his provision of sick leave for Queensland workers in 1946, placed him in a class with Ryan and Theodore as a Labor leader. He was a personal friend of many of the Trades Hall union officials and attended the AWU annual conference. In 1947, he had also legislated directly for the forty-hour week. Moreover, he carried with him that badge of honour in union circles as a man who had been dismissed from his job for his part in a major strike. In Hanlon's case, this had been the general strike of 1912.

Throughout the 1946 and 1948 disputes, the QCE remained a neutral agent. Correspondence from unions seeking QCE action or asking for special QCE meetings to put pressure on the government were referred to the PLP or simply not acted upon. Syd Bryan, the QCE secretary, was no longer the Labor activist he had been. He wanted to keep internal disputes to a minimum, with no "rocking the boat". In 1947 he was displaying greater interest in the new radio station 4KQ, and reflected a complacency about Labor's retaining office indefinitely, which others also in the ALP were coming to exhibit.

All was not well within the ALP. Despite the existence of six Labor governments throughout Australia at the beginning of 1947, the Queensland ALP was not reflecting any of the nation-wide support for Labor. Its contribution to the bank nationalization campaign was token at best. Branch membership at the end of 1946 was still only 6479 compared with 5728 in the middle of the war, three years previously. Affiliated union membership had dropped from 106,884 to 104,058 in the same period. It was not that the cost of party membership was too high. It remained at two shillings and sixpence for adult males and one shilling and sixpence for females and juniors. Capitation fees were still only one shilling for both unions and branches. The party's financial position reflected its internal lack of organizational energy. After the 1947 state election, Bryan had been forced to seek a £5000 overdraft from the Commonwealth Bank.

The Labor-in-Politics Convention that met in Townsville in February 1947 reflected the mood of the rank and file that the Labor party had to be revived in spirit and organization. It was simply not matching the Country party, the Queensland Peoples party (which had recently become the Queensland division of the Liberal party) or the Communist party in its grass roots organization. Each of these parties had full-time organizers in the field, while the ALP had no organizer, only Bryan, whose position as secretary was not completely full-time. Bryan was singled out by the convention delegates as being at least partly to blame for the malaise. He was not re-elected as one of the eleven convention delegates to the QCE (the first time this had happened to the QCE secretary) and after the loss of Labor votes at the 1947 election, he finished last in the QCE ballot for the six delegates to the Federal Conference.

After a lengthy debate on the re-establishment of the sub-committees used in 1944, the convention got down to its first major item — the appointment of an organizer. The problem, as those close to the executive committee appreciated, was financial.

At one shilling a head capitation fees, the 6479 branch members did not even pay Bryan's salary, let alone the cost of the office staff or any organizing work. The 104,068 affiliated unionists' capitation fees of one shilling per head provided only half the cost of the 1946 federal election campaign and much less than half the cost of the state campaign in 1947. While everyone wanted an extra organizer, the reception among many of the unions to the increased capitation fees in 1941 was a warning of what could happen. Bryan himself did not seek any increase in fees in 1947. He required £35,000 in capital to finance 4KQ and did not seem to want to divert needed union investments away from the radio station. Both union and branch delegates at the convention declined to get down to the hard facts of financing the organizer's position, and were more anxious to write into the platform, planks on the forty-hour week, the assessment of the basic wage, workers compensation and consultation with unions before any new industrial legislation was introduced. When an organizer was appointed after the 1947 election, he was Ted Walsh, the deputy premier, who lost his seat in 1947. His salary was paid by the AWU.

A forty-hour week based on five days' work each of eight hours had long been a goal of the labor movement. In 1947, there was an application by federal unions before the Commonwealth Conciliation and Arbitration Court for a forty-hour week. The Queensland government was supporting that application. However this would not cover employees under Queensland state awards and unions, at the convention, wanted an amendment to the Queensland Industrial Conciliation and Arbitration Act providing, specifically, for a forty-hour week in Queensland. Hanlon was not opposed to this and recognized the role of previous Queensland Labor governments in giving the national lead in industrial reforms. However, he also wanted the forty-hour week to become universal in Australia so that Queensland industries would not be placed at any disadvantage. His amendment to the motion of Artie Cole, of the Railway Maintenance Union, calling for an amendment to the Queensland Act was carried. It read:

> As the Government of Queensland has consistently supported the establishment of a national 40 Hour Week before the Federal Arbitration Court, Convention urges the Queensland Government to amend its Arbitration Act to establish a standard 40 Hour Week for the State of Queensland in the event of the Federal Court failing to do so.
> Convention believes that a standard 40 Hour Week in industry need not reduce the output of consumer goods, and calls upon all workers to honour their obligations to the citizens of this State by maintaining production at the highest possible level.

The first paragraph was ambiguous as the Commonwealth Court could not make a judgment for those under state awards. However a specific question at the end of the debate: "Will Mr Hanlon give an undertaking that reference to a 40 hour week will be embodied in the policy speech?" received an unequivocal answer from Hanlon. "It will be. We cannot hide that from the public".[41]

Hanlon carried through his promise to the convention and, after the 1947 election legislated directly for the forty-hour week for Queensland workers under state awards. The loss of Walsh's seat at the 1947 election brought Vince Gair, then minister for labour and industry into the post of deputy premier. Walsh, however, maintained his position, with Hanlon, on the executive committee.

In the light of events that were to take place ten years later, 1947 was to be an important year in Queensland Labor history. Industrial groups had been organized in Victoria and New South Wales in 1946 with the official endorsement of the ALP conferences there. They were introduced into Queensland after the 1947 Convention had passed a resolution giving the QCE authority to establish the Groups. Joe Bukowski, southern district secretary of the AWU, Tom Rasey, an alderman in the Brisbane City Council and formerly an official of the Transport Workers Union, and Ted Walsh, were appointed by the QCE as the ALP Industrial Group executive committee.

The Industrial Groups

Fallon died in January 1950 and was to be greatly missed by his union and by the Labor party. Harry Boland succeeded Fallon as AWU secretary and as president of the QCE. Boland had come through a tough political school; he had commonsense and was loyal to both his union and to the ALP. Unfortunately he had little of Fallon's political skill. This was to be missed in 1956.

Two other changes occurred, in 1952, that were to have significant repercussions in the emerging battle for ascendancy in the ALP. Hanlon died in January 1952 and was succeeded by Vince Gair, who despite his period as minister for labour, did not have the same rapport with the unions as had Hanlon. He had been a member of the Railway Salaried Officers' Union before his election to parliament and had rejected the membership of the AWU which was offered to ALP politicians.[42] In July 1952, Syd Bryan retired as QCE secretary and was replaced by Jack

Jack Schmella, a capable administrator, became federal secretary of ALP in 1954. (Photograph by courtesy of Queensland Newspapers Ltd.)

Schmella, an industrial officer with the AWU. On Fallon's death, in 1950, Schmella had tried to stand for election as the state secretary of the AWU. He was soon recognized as a capable administrator and became the protege of Pat Kennelly, the ALP federal secretary. Kennelly, a Catholic and public enemy number one of the "Movement" in Victoria, resigned as federal secretary in July 1954 and Schmella took his place.

By 1950, the Industrial Groups were becoming a major, but not the only, organizational issue of contention and importance. Because of the redistribution of electoral boundaries in 1949 and complaints about the quality of some of the Labor candidates put up in state elections, the QCE sent a three-man committee throughout the state to recruit and recommend candidates. On the basis of their report, the QCE disbanded plebiscites and selected the candidates for the 1950 election itself. However, while the convention endorsed the QCE's decision, for this election only, it reaffirmed its faith in the plebiscite system and reversed five of the QCE selections (including its rejection of "Johnno" Mann, then chairman of committees in the Legislative Assembly). Abolishing plebiscites or restricting the eligibility of plebiscite voters appeared on the agendas of the 1953 and 1956 Conventions and were again rejected.

Labor's socialism had always been a practical matter concerned with reforms to favour workers, farmers and the "small man" generally (see Chapter 6). There had been little of the theory that marked European debates on socialism. However under the post-war sway of a new wave of anti-socialist ideologies, many of them influenced by the Catholic Social Studies Movement, there was a demand for Labor either to repudiate its traditional socialism or to define it more clearly. It was Hanlon who chose to do the latter at the 1950 Convention when Paul Hilton, a state member of parliament and an intense supporter of the Industrial Groups and the Catholic Social Studies movement, asked the convention to re-define the socialist objective, rather than simply affirm it in the traditional debate for opening a convention. Hanlon told the delegates that Labor should not "duck around" corners on the issue. "Socialization of industry", he said, "meant coming eventually to a state of society in which industry would be for the service of humanity instead of for the exploitation of humanity". "Labor", he continued, "rejects private property as being the prime motive of human activity, but does not aim at the destruction of private property. Labor demands that all shall have an equal right to own property".[43] With some additions this was accepted by the convention as the interpretation of Labor's socialism in Queensland.

Each convention found itself debating, again, the establishment of a daily or weekly Labor newspaper, but the practical problem of finding the capital together with the memories that some retained of the last years of the *Daily Standard* made this a theoretical debate. As a substitute, an ALP bulletin (later *Labor News*) was published monthly and sold to the branches and unions. An ALP debating union had been formed after the war and a Labor club at the University of Queensland. In 1947, a radio broadcast licence was obtained and 4KQ went on the air. After Schmella became secretary, an ALP youth movement was formed. The 1953 Convention debated whether the membership fee for this organization should be five shillings or ten shillings a year. Ironically, the membership fee for ALP branches was still two shillings and sixpence and the QCE was hesitant about having it raised to five shillings. Despite a 1947 Convention decision to establish a Labor college, it was not until the 1956 Convention that Schmella could outline a definite programme and recommend the establishment of a Labor College Council.

Schmella was an energetic secretary but, after Walsh's re-election to parliament in 1950, he had no organizer to assist him. Frank Forde, the former prime minister, who had been a member of the state parliament from 1917 to 1922, was taken on as an organizer in 1953 but was elected to state parliament in a by-election in March 1955. Schmella's job as secretary was made more difficult by the reassertion of the QCE against the "inner executive" as more unions affiliated and used QCE meetings to demand action by the government on industrial questions. Between 1950 and 1953 there were forty-eight executive committee meetings but only fifteen meetings of the full QCE.

However in the following three years, there were forty-six meetings of the "inner executive", and thirty-four meetings of the QCE. Schmella was confronted by a chronic shortage of finance. Unions wanted a more effective QCE, but as in 1941 resisted strenuously attempts to raise capitation fees to provide for this. It was unfortunate that a QCE decision in 1953 to increase capitation fees from one shilling to two shillings was made at the same time as state parliamentarians received a salary increase. The reaction does not need describing. A compromise of sixpence increase was agreed upon in 1954 and in 1956, a new organizer, Jim Keeffe was appointed. Keeffe was a returned serviceman who had completed his trade training as a cooper. In 1956 he was working as a clerk in the office of the Plumbers Union. The resistance of unions to paying increased dues was a manifestation of their feeling that they were not receiving the same legislative and administrative support as they had over past years and to which they felt they were due as affiliates of the ALP.

In the early 1940s these attitudes had resulted in a loss of union and branch membership. There was to be no repetition of this in the early 1950s. Through the internal battle for power after 1950, the various groups and factions inside the ALP sought to increase their size and therefore their voting potential. At the beginning of 1950, there were 216 branches with a total membership of 7066. By the 1953 and 1956 Conventions these had increased to 266 branches with 8088 members and 298 branches with 8822 members respectively. The pattern was repeated among the unions. Four new unions affiliated and one other re-affiliated between 1950 and 1953; in the following three years, three new unions affiliated, six others re-affiliated and seven unions increased the membership for which they paid capitation fees to the point where they were entitled to a full delegate or an additional delegate on the QCE. Affiliated union membership increased from 149,742 in 1950 to 177,262 in 1953 and to 211,112 in 1956. The party was then at its largest for almost twenty years and its affiliated unionists represented 69 per cent of all union members in the state.

While the ALP grew in size in these years and had outstanding electoral success in the 1953 and 1956 state elections, following the 1953 Convention and, after the expulsion of Gair in 1957, a number of changes occurred that marked the end of an era in Queensland labour history. These are dealt with in Chapter 24 but may be briefly listed here. The Trades Hall affiliated unions emerged as a force within the ALP; the AWU-PLP coalition which had begun around 1913 was broken up; the AWU was isolated and declined dramatically as the principal force inside the party; the power and influence of the Industrial Groups was destroyed and Queensland was drawn firmly into national Labor politics.

These were hectic days for the participants whether they operated at the QCE or PLP or branch level of the ALP. Secret meetings abounded; "the numbers" were organized for ALP branch and union meetings; special meetings for selected people were held at the Trades Hall on the Sunday morning before the QCE meeting (held on a Monday morning); meeting places of opposing factions were watched; unflattering roneoed sheets were distributed by both sides and tension built as the plebiscites for the 1956 Labor-in-Politics Convention approached.

It was to be at this convention that a major trial of strength would be held. In the midst of this plotting and scheming before the 1956 Convention came the dramatic revelations by the federal Labor leader, Dr. H.V. Evatt, of the existence of a secret outside body called "The Movement" which had endeavoured to gain control of the ALP. These were followed by the split in the Labor party in Victoria and the consequent defeat of the Labor government there. Then came the walkout by five of the six Queensland delegates at the 1955 Federal Conference at Hobart and the withdrawal of ALP endorsement from the Industrial Groups. Schmella, as QCE secretary and federal secretary, was at the centre of the turmoil.

The power struggle in the Labor party revolved about four issues: the person of Gair, the oligarchic power of the "inner executive", the composition of the "inner executive" and the industrial question of three weeks' leave for Queensland workers. The last of these was the catalyst on which the coalition of forces was built to tackle the first three issues. It was at the Labor-in-Politics Convention at Mackay in March 1956 that the authority of the premier over the Labor party was broken. Theodore had survived a similar challenge in 1923 on the basic wage issue, but in 1956 the convention passed a resolution to have the promise of three weeks' leave incorporated into the policy speech for the forthcoming election and to write in an assurance that this would be implemented in the first session of the new parliament. Debates were held on establishing a daily Labor newspaper, appointing an organizer, making branch meetings more atractive and developing women's branches. Gair with 126 votes easily headed the ballot for the eleven QCE delegates elected by the convention. However, four QCE delegates, Mick Brosnan, Artie Cole, Cyril Muhldorff and Ted Walsh, all aligned with the Industrial Groups, were defeated. Jack Egerton, the principal organizer of the Trades Hall affiliated unions, finished in eleventh place with seventy-eight votes. The change in those who now exercised power in the party was further emphasized at the QCE meetings after the convention when a new executive committee was elected. Gair remained a member, but his Industrial Group colleagues were swept aside (see Appendix B at the end of this book).

The Split

Despite the convention decision on the granting of three weeks' leave and indications that Gair had given to union and other delegations that he would legislate for three weeks' leave, he refused to do so. Instead he built a coalition against himself and provided for his own downfall. On 24 April 1957, the QCE met and after a five-hour debate, expelled Gair from the Labor party. Gair was by no means solely responsible for the split in the ALP that occurred in April 1957 (see Chapter 25). Given different parliamentary, union and QCE leaders from those exercising power in 1957, such a crisis could and would have been avoided.

Dramatic consequences followed the split. The ARU which

had been out of the party for thirty years was re-admitted, but the Federated Clerks, the Ironworkers and the State Service Unions all disaffiliated. In December 1958, the president of the QCE, R.J. Bukowski, who had succeeded Boland as secretary of the AWU in July 1956, was suspended from the presidency of the party. In February 1959, the AWU disaffiliated from the Labor party which lost yearly capitation fees of £6000 as a result.[44] The Labor party vacated its offices in Dunstan House, the AWU building, where it had been since 1913. Its radio station 4KQ had to be found new premises also. Clem Jones, the lord mayoral candidate for Brisbane, negotiated the purchase of a building on the corner of Edward and Elizabeth Streets, which became known as "Labor House". By the close of 1959, affiliated union membership was down to 138,334; branch membership figures were not revealed.

What of those ALP branch members who ran the party out in the electorates, who conducted innumerable small raffles to pay election bills and who constituted the party's "grass roots" organization? It was not to be until the 1968 Labor-in-Politics convention that they were to obtain direct representation on the QCE when three delegates were elected on a state-wide poll. The truth was that the members of the QCE, and more especially the members of the "inner executive", lived in a different political world from the rank and file branch members.

Some ALP branch members rejected the QCE's expulsion of Gair and left the party of which many had been loyal members for many years. Others remained solidly with the party and rejoiced that the old regime had been defeated. They believed that the new QCE would be characterized by openness, free speech and an end to the control of the party by a small clique. Some of these ALP members welcomed the expulsion of Gair as a cleansing of the party and as a "return to Socialism". For most rank and file branch members and affiliated unionists, however, it would seem that the expulsion of Gair, the split in the Labor party and the loss of government had left them stunned as they would not again be stunned until 11 November 1975. Experience had warned them that the new regime, when it settled in after the civil war was over, might not in fact have been any better than the old. It was their basic commitment to the high ideals for which the Labor party stood and their faith that the party would continue to produce figures like Ryan, Theodore, Forgan Smith, Hanlon, Curtin, Chifley and others, which held a majority of branch members to the Labor party in 1957.

With the changes in the party organization at the 1916 Convention, the Labor party became tied to the fortunes of the trade unions. So long as these were led by capable and politically intelligent men who understood the nature of Queensland politics and who recognized that the party operated on a much broader stage than the trade unions, the ALP could continue its primary role as the party of reform and a party that could win elections. Equally, the nature of the Labor party organization placed a responsibility on Labor members of parliament to acquire an understanding of the trade unions and to appreciate their view of the ALP as a party representing the interests of the wage earner. The Labor politician had to have this awareness as well as his own appreciation of the much broader stage on which the ALP performed. Both of these sets of conditions had been present for most of the forty years between 1915 and 1957. They were absent in the last years of the Labor government when they were required most.

NOTES

1. For the evolution of the Labor party in Queensland before 1915, see D.J. Murphy, "The Changing Structure of the Party", in *Prelude to Power, The Rise of the Labour Party in Queensland, 1885-1915*, eds. D.J. Murphy, R.B. Joyce and Colin A. Hughes (Brisbane: Jacaranda Press, 1970) and D.J. Murphy, ed., *Labor in Politics, The State Labor Parties in Australia, 1880-1920* (St Lucia: University of Queensland Press, 1975), chap. 3.
2. Queensland Central Executive (QCE) minutes, Labor House, Brisbane, 30 September 1921.
3. The two spellings "Labour" and "Labor" continued to be used until about 1920. The 1918 Convention report is of a "Labor" party, while a printed document issued by the QCE in March 1919 came from a "Labour" party.

4. QCE minutes, 30 September 1921.
5. Ibid., 12 December 1918.
6. In 1925 Dunstan was appointed to the Board of Trade and Arbitration and Riordan became AWU secretary.
7. See M.B. Cribb, "Some Manifestations of Ideological Conflict within the Labor Movement in Queensland, 1924-1929" (B.A. thesis, University of Queensland, 1964); and K.H. Kennedy, "The Public Life of William McCormack: 1907-1932" (Ph.D. thesis, James Cook University, 1973).
8. QCE minutes, 24 November 1922.
9. QCE minutes, 20 February 1925.
10. For more details on this, see chapters on Theodore and McCormack in D.J. Murphy and R.B. Joyce, eds., *Queensland Political Portraits* (St Lucia: University of Queensland Press, 1978).
11. *Official Record of the Eleventh Labor-in-Politics Convention* (Brisbane, 1923), pp. 50-51.
12. Ibid.
13. L. McDonald, circular to branches and unions, 11 August 1925, QCE files.
14. See Cribb, "Some Manifestations"; Kennedy, "The Public Life".
15. QCE minutes, 27 November, 21 December 1925, 29 January, 17 September 1926.
16. See chaps. on Theodore and McCormack in Murphy and Joyce, eds., *Queensland Political Portraits*; J. Larcombe, *Notes on the Political History of the Labour Movement in Queensland* (Brisbane: Worker Newspaper, 1934); A.A. Morrison, "Militant Labour in Queensland", *JRAHS* (November 1952); Cribb, "Some Manifestations"; Kennedy, "The Public Life".
17. Brisbane Trades and Labor Council (TLC) minutes, Trades Hall, Brisbane, 6 September-12 November 1926; QCE minutes, 17 September 1926.
18. TLC minutes, 17 September 1926, 30 November 1927, 23 January, 30 May, 8 August, 7 September 1928.
19. See also K.H. Kennedy, "The South Johnstone Strike and Railway Lockout, 1927", *Labour History* 31 (November 1976).
20. *Official Report*, Trade Union Congress (1927).
21. Branch membership and affiliated union figures are taken from the official reports of the Labor-in-Politics Conventions.
22. *Official Record of the Eleventh Labor-in-Politics Convention* (Brisbane, 1923), p. 19.
23. TLC minutes, 11 March 1925. For a short biography of Forgan Smith see Murphy and Joyce, eds., *Queensland Political Portraits*, chap. 14.
24. QCE, Executive Committee minutes, 13 May 1930.
25. Ibid., 20 July 1931.
26. QCE records make it difficult to list exactly the size of individual union donations.

27. The union offices held by Syd Bryan were supplied to the author by Mrs Elizabeth Bryan and Mr Archie Dawson.
28. QCE, Executive Committee minutes, 12 April, 4 May, 11 May 1933.
29. The ticket was R.J. Carroll, F.P. Byrne and L. McDonald.
30. QCE, Executive Committee minutes, 12 October 1933.
31. Ibid., 31 October 1933.
32. Ibid., 26 November 1935.
33. *Worker*, 29 May 1933.
34. QCE, Executive Committee minutes, 14 September 1933.
35. Ibid., 14 December 1938.
36. *Labour Report*, no. 29 (1938).
37. QCE minutes 15, 23 October 1936; Executive Committee minutes 12, 22 October 1936.
38. Executive Committee minutes, 1, 12 May, 8 July 1942; QCE minutes, 14, 26 May 1942.
39. Australian Federated Union of Locomotive Enginemen (AFULE), Divisional Council Minutes, 24 November 1941, E212/1, Australian National University Archives.
40. QCE, Executive Committee minutes, 30 September 1942.
41. For this debate see *Official Record of the Nineteenth Labor-in-Politics Convention* (Brisbane, 1947), pp. 29-35.
42. Interview with Mr Gair, Dublin, January 1975.
43. *Official Record of the Twentieth Labor-in-Politics Convention* (Brisbane, 1950), pp. 53-56.
44. *Official Record of the Twenty-Third Labor-in-Politics Convention* (Brisbane, 1960), p. 185.

2 Labor in the Electorates

Colin A. Hughes

The defeat of the Denham government on 22 May 1915* brought to an end almost seven years of conservative government. After the collapse of the arrangement between the moderate faction led by Kidston and the Labor party in 1908, the coalition of Kidstonites and Philpites set Queensland firmly on the way to a two-party system once more. At the 1909 election the Ministerialist team with about half the vote collected forty-one of the seventy-two seats; Labor with about 36 per cent of the vote held twenty-seven and the so-called "Independent Opposition", the left-overs from the formation of the coalition, was reduced to four seats and 10 per cent of the vote. By 1912 the process of polarization was complete: the Ministerialists, now called Liberals, with slightly more than 51 per cent of the vote, secured forty-six seats. The Labor party with less than 47 per cent of the vote gained twenty-five, whilst the half-dozen candidates standing outside the two parties could muster only 1.74 per cent of the vote and win only one solitary, and remote, seat. The Electoral Districts Act 1910 had replaced the previous system of eleven two-member districts and fifty single-member districts, varying greatly in enrolment and with boundaries drawn by the government of the day, with seventy-two single-member districts, with a permitted variation at the time of distribution of no more than 20 per cent above or below the state average enrolment (or quota) and boundaries drawn by these officials appointed by the governor-in-council. As a consequence, at the 1912 election Queensland constituencies were more equal in their numbers of electors than those of Victoria, South Australia and Western Australia, and comparable to those of New South Wales and Tasmania.

* For details of Labor vote, 1915-57, see Apendix A, pp. 526-35.

Although the election was something of an electoral triumph for the Liberals' new leader, Digby Denham, he was subsequently threatened by internal dissension and the onsurge of the Labor party under Ryan. At the beginning of 1915, Denham barely retained the leadership, and his government's earlier substitution of postal voting for absent voting, which was supposed to advantage the more literate and thus anti-Labor voters, and introduction of compulsory voting, which was supposed to drive the apathetic and possibly antipathetic non-Labor voters to the polls, failed to tune up the electoral system sufficiently.

The swing to Labor of more than 5 per cent destroyed Denham's government and moved the premier and five of his ministers from the Legislative Assembly. Labor went from twenty-four seats to forty-five; the Liberal party fell from forty-seven to twenty-one while a further five seats in the south-east of the state were captured by Farmers' Union candidates. Labor's old reliance on the north and west, which had been reinforced at the 1912 election by gains in working class areas of Brisbane, now extended through all regions of the state. The party's grip on old strongholds was consolidated: of twenty-three seats in the north and west only three remained outside the Labor camp; in six the Labor candidate was unupposed and in another seven the Labor candidate polled more than two-thirds of the votes. This was the heartland from which the labor movement had sprung in 1893 and onto which the Labour party had fallen back in its bad years. Newer territory in Brisbane was almost as profitable: the party held all but one of the eleven truly urban constituencies and three of the six suburban, i.e., suburban fringe electorates. Labor consolidated its hold on the central district around Rockhampton where it collected the remaining seats to establish a monopoly. In the remaining districts of Queensland, however, the party was still confined to the provincial cities — Ipswich, Gympie, Maryborough and Bundaberg — while on the Darling Downs it failed to win a single seat. Now it was the anti-Labor forces which fell back on their corresponding heartland — the rural electorates of south-eastern Queensland. These accounted for twenty of their twenty-six seats.*

*For all endorsed Labor candidates, 1915-57, see Appendix E pp. 551-68.

The 1918 election was conducted on the same boundaries but under Labor's first electoral act, which reduced the period of residence in an electorate to one month, so as to gain the benefit of Labor support among migratory workers. That change and the impressive activities of the Ryan government raised the Labor vote by about 1½ per cent and Labor parliamentary representation by three members. The rural wing of the anti-Labor front, which in 1915 had become sufficiently irritated with their colleagues to run a handful of Farmers' candidates and in 1918 had at least indicated a separate endorsement of a similar number, now opened a new challenge to the two-party system. In 1918 the Farmers' Union quit the National Political Council around which anti-Labor groups had previously rallied, and the following year joined with the graziers and canegrowers to form the Primary Producers' Union which had a brief run on the political stage. In July 1920, half the Nationalist parliamentarians broke away to form the Country party, and were backed at the ensuing election by the Primary Producers' Union. For the following fifteen years the anti-Labor camp remained uncertain whether it wished to maintain two parties in the field, or merely one — or perhaps even three as the brief, separate existence of the Northern Country party (1918-21) suggested. In 1923, a group of Country party MLAs broke away to re-unite with the Nationalists as the United party; in 1925 the United party and the Country party rump combined as the Country Progressive party, whereupon some United party members hived off and revived the Nationalist party, only to be reabsorbed again in what thereafter was called the Country and Progressive National party. This merger lasted from the end of 1925 to 1935 when a separate Country party organization was reformed, or 1936 when the CPNP split into Country party and United Australia party. The devious ins and outs of the changes are the history of today's non-Labor parties, the National (formerly Country) party and the Liberal party, rather than the ALP, but the obvious instability of the opposition no doubt helped Labor stay in office through the 1920s and left a tradition of bitterness and rivalry between the two groups, whether separate or in temporary unity, which helped Labor then and in later decades.

Through the 1920s the electoral pattern of 1915 prevailed, with slight fluctuations in the level of Labor dominance. In 1920, the Theodore government, beset by the difficulties of the post-war economy, suffered a 6 per cent swing in votes and dropped ten seats. The Country party with 17.2 per cent of the vote and eighteen seats, the Nationalists with 26.7 per cent of the vote and thirteen seats (an inbalance between votes and seats that reappears regularly in non-Labor electoral results and has kept the rural wing the dominant partner ever since 1920), and the Northern Country party with 7.5 per cent of the vote and three seats, came close to turning the government out. Theodore responded with a redistribution that transferred three seats from the Darling Downs (two) and Wide Bay (one) to the Brisbane area, whilst the re-drawing of boundaries nominally shifted one seat from the north-west zones to the northern. Enrolments, which had started to spread out, were brought back closer to state average once more. It should be added that the "zones" employed in Appendix A at the end of this book are arbitrary and devised for ease of identification; in several cases, near Cairns and Rockhampton for example, somewhat arbitrary instances of assignment to a zone rest on an estimate of the character of the majority of electors within a constituency. At the 1923 election, an increase of less than 0.5 per cent in the vote meant another five seats for Labor, and a comfortable majority in the House was restored. In 1926 the vote again crept up by a whisker, but with no corresponding gain in seats.

However, by the May 1929 election, the internal dissensions of the labor movement cut into the support the Labor politicians had come to expect. At the statewide level the party's vote dropped by almost 8 per cent, and sixteen seats fell with it. A cursory examination of table 2 shows that the losses, both of votes and of seats, spread unevenly over the map. Even in Brisbane, where one might suppose personal followings of members to be smallest, there were wide variations in the flight from Labor — if it occurred at all. Losses were worse around Rockhampton in the central zone where four seats (Fitzroy, Keppel, Rockhampton and Port Curtis) changed hands and the swing from Labor in votes exceeded 15 per cent in three cases and came close to it in a fourth. In Brisbane, another five seats went Country-National — Bulimba, won by the first woman to sit in the Legislative Assembly, Miss Irene Longman, Kelvin Grove, Maree, Merthyr and South Brisbane. Four seats were lost in or adjacent to provincial cities — Gympie, Ipswich, Rosewood and Toowoomba, whilst north and west of Cairns a further three were lost — Cook, Eacham, and the final sign of how times had changed, Theodore's old constituency of Chillagoe. After fourteen years in office the Labor party was back to where it had been before the great victory of 1915, at least in terms of its parliamentary representation. The one minor distinction in comparison with the 1909 election, twenty years earlier when the party had also returned only twenty-seven members, was that whereas then there had been only two members elected in Brisbane, now there were five. But in 1909 there had been nineteen members from the north and west, and now there were still eighteen, two-thirds of the parliamentary party.

The state's voters were in for a rude awakening. The shock of the Depression and the Moore government's failure to cope with an intensifying crisis drove them hastily back to Labor's arms. This time the swing exceeded 8 per cent, but Moore had sought to improve his circumstances by having a redistribution under a new Electoral Districts Act which gave some weighting to rural areas, and reduced the size of the Legislative Assembly from seventy-two to sixty-two members. (The formula imposed on the commissioners by the act was that no constituency containing a city or part of a city could be below the state average in enrolment, or less than 7000 — the state average in 1932 being 8400.) Only the Darling Downs and northern zones retained their previous number of seats; each of the others lost one seat, and the three western zones (which are collapsed into one in 1932 and subsequent years, see Appendix A at the end of the book) dropped from fourteen seats to eight, a punishment for declining population and consistency in voting Labor. Thus the huge swing back to the Labor party, now led by Forgan Smith, was temporarily contained. The Country-National contingent dropped from forty-two to twenty-eight, but the Labor membership went up only from twenty-seven to thirty-three, so that Labor's majority was relatively small. The answer was yet another redistribution under Moore's legislation which, as between zones, was minor in that Brisbane gained one seat and the central zone lost one, but as between electorates entailed substantial changes. At the ensuing election in 1935, Labor votes rose to an all-time high, 53.43 per cent; with Labor holding six uncontested seats and its opponents only two, the notional two-party preferred vote would have been higher. Labor's parliamentary dominance was equally overwhelming: forty-six seats to the Country-National's sixteen of which only three were in Brisbane (Hamilton, Oxley and Toowong), the furthest north was Keppel and the furthest west Dalby.

The 1938 election was complicated by the re-division of the CPNP into Country and UAP teams, and the temporary intervention of the Protestant Labour party which cut sharply into the Labor vote but had a minimal impact on Labor's parliamentary representation. The Protestant Labour party won one seat in Brisbane, and delivered another to the UAP so that the latter party was blessed with a total of four. In the rest of the state the Labor party won one seat from the Country party and lost a nearby one to them. The Protestant Labour party polled 8.75 per cent of the total vote, contesting twenty-three of the fifty-nine seats in which there was a contest; given the intervention of Social Credit (Douglas) candidates in substantial numbers in both 1935 and 1938 it is difficult to be certain what proportion of the Protestant Labour vote came from the Labor total, but overall the Labor vote dropped by just over 6 per cent. By 1941 the Protestant Labour party had almost vanished and the Labor vote surged up again to 51.4 per cent. Nevertheless, the party dropped three seats in Brisbane — Maree, Sandgate and Windsor, and lost Bundaberg to "Bombshell" Barnes standing as an Independent Labor candidate. When his brother won Cairns from the Labor party at a by-election the following year, the government removed the right to cast "contingent" votes, i.e., optional preferential votes, which electors had enjoyed since 1892. Thereafter Queensland alone among the states employed first-past-the-post voting.

Between the 1941 and 1944 elections there was a certain amount of re-organization with the parties. The Country party and UAP negotiated a new union as the Country-National party; this led first to a split within the Country party, and then to the birth of the Queensland People's party amid the ashes of the UAP. In 1941-42 the Labor party expelled two parliamentarians and a number of branches for various leftwing offences. At the 1944 election, the Labor vote dropped noticeably, and only thirty-seven Labor members were returned to the Legislative Assembly, a loss of six from 1941; however the number of "Independent Labor" members had risen from one to four and a communist member, Fred Paterson, had entered the House, so Labor's losses were not entirely anti-Labor gains. Labor now had 44.7 per cent of the total vote. The Country party with 17.6 per cent held twelve seats, the QPP with 24.7 per cent seven. In 1947 the Labor party slipped back a further notch, dropping 1 per cent of the vote and two seats. Its thirty-five seats still ensured a comfortable majority over the twenty-three (fourteen plus nine) of the Country party and QPP combined, but it was a suspect margin for the opposition parties between them had 46.4 per cent of the vote compared to Labor's 43.6. Suitable adjustments can be made to these figures in the light of the 4 per cent of the vote secured by the fourteen "Frank Barnes Labor" candidates, the 1.8 per cent of four other Independent Labor candidates, and the 1.3 per cent of the five Communists, not to mention the 3 per cent of the sixteen Independents, to challenge the assertion that a majority of electors were deprived of their right to choose the government they wanted; the fact remains that with the vote divided about equally between Labor and anti-Labor, Labor secured a clear majority of seats.

At this point the Labor government resorted to the distribution machinery again. Previously Queensland had avoided the system of electoral "zones" introduced in Western Australia in 1922, Victoria in 1926, New South Wales in 1927, and South

Australia in 1929. It had also maintained the principle of "one vote, one value" more effectively than any of these states, apart from New South Wales. Now, the Hanlon government started Queensland on an electoral rake's progress which in terms of complexity, if not in measures of gross inequality, equalled the lamentable records of the other states. The Electoral Districts Act, 1949, divided the state into four electoral zones, and enlarged the Legislative Assembly to a record seventy-five seats. The western and northern zones, i.e., those which were traditionally solid for the Labor party, with ten and thirteen seats respectively, had conspicuously lower quotas than the south-eastern, dominated by the Country party, and the metropolitan where Labor held a majority of seats but Liberal strength was concentrated. At the 1950 election the Country and Liberal parties combined had 49.16 per cent of the vote but won only thirty-three seats; if allowance is made for the three uncontested electorates, all solid Country party, and the "independent" pro-Country party candidate who won Burdekin, it is indisputable that the anti-Labor share of the vote exceeded 50 per cent, yet fell far short of a majority of seats. This was the high point of the anti-Labor vote in Queensland after 1929, and it was never reached again until 1974. At the 1953 election there was a substantial swing of more than 6 per cent to Labor which gained eight seats — three in Brisbane (Kedron, Norman and Sandgate), three in grazing, mining and sugar areas where Labor had traditionally done well (Roma, Cook and Mulgrave respectively), and two in farming areas where Labor could win seats only at the top of its electoral appeal — Condamine and Somerset. In 1956, the vote slipped back 2 per cent and one marginal seat was lost, but the party's position appeared unassailable.

Labor's steady string of successes in all parts of the state except the rural south-east masked something of a shift in influence at the top of the parliamentary party, representation in cabinet. When the party returned to power under Forgan Smith in 1932, seven of ten ministers sat for northern and western seats. By the time that Forgan Smith retired and Cooper became premier, only four of ten ministers represented northern and western

Frank Cooper was the first Labor premier to hold a seat in south-eastern Queensland. (Photograph by courtesy of the John Oxley Library.)

electorates. Cooper was the first Labor premier to hold a seat outside the party heartland (Bremer at Ipswich), and he was followed by two premiers from Brisbane — Hanlon (Ithaca) and Gair (South Brisbane). Slowly the party had begun to adapt to changes in Queensland demographic and economic balance of power.

The split in 1957 produced an even more drastic reversal of electoral fortunes than the troubles of 1929 had done, and the party's losses were correspondingly heavier. The year before the united Labor party had won forty-nine seats: now the Australian Labor party held only twenty and the Queensland Labor party eleven. The other eighteen Labor seats had been collected by the opposition coalition, eight going to the Country party and ten to the Liberals. Once again the weighting given rural electorates enabled the Country party (twenty-four seats on 20 per cent of the vote) to secure the advantage over the Liberal party (eighteen seats on 23.2 per cent of the vote) and obtain majorities in both the joint party room and in cabinet — and thus control over the three subsequent redistributions which retained rural weighting, although in somewhat different forms from that which Labor had applied in 1948. The last time the Labor party had held so few seats in the Legislative Assembly had been after the 1907 election, exactly fifty years earlier, when after a comparable defection of a leader the party had split but without losing so many of its senior members. But unlike previous disasters in 1907-8 and 1929, this time the heartland in the north and west failed to hold: only five seats in the north and two in the west stayed true to Labor. Another five (three in the west, two in the north) were held by sitting members who had gone with Gair and the Queensland Labor party, but the break with the party's foundations was complete. At the 1960 election, which followed a redistribution which sharply reduced the number of outback seats whilst enlarging the Assembly slightly to seventy-eight, although the Labor party collected another five seats to raise its total to twenty-five, the contribution of the west (three) and the north (four) was still minor. The party's electoral strength now rested on Brisbane and the provincial cities, and this ensured that a different sort of party would exist in the 1960s and 1970s.

In 1915 there had been 335,000 electors on the roll; by 1957 the total had risen to 792,000, more than double. This growth had taken place without any significant extension of the franchise, merely as a result of population growth. Ryan's Elections Act 1915 had restored the franchise to wife-beaters, drunkards, rogues and vagabonds, and inmates of charitable institutions, other than hospitals who lost it in 1905, but maintained the disqualification of "aboriginal natives" of Australia, Asia, Africa, and the islands of the Pacific. It also permitted the election of women to the Legislative Assembly; women had been enfranchised in 1905. The Moore government extended the franchise to natives of British India and naturalized Syrians, but disfranchised Torres Strait islanders and Aboriginal half-castes subject to the control of the Protector of Aborigines. Such changes had a minimal impact on the size of the electorate, but over the period 1915-57 the balance of electoral power within the state had shifted somewhat: in 1915, Brisbane contained seventeen of the seventy-two seats;

in 1957, twenty-four of seventy-five. In 1915, the north and west accounted for twenty-three seats; in 1957, still twenty-three though the numerical edge had shifted from the interior west to the coastal north. However, what in 1915 had been a proper recognition of the distribution of population, of the difficulty of communication, and of the economic strengths of the state, by 1957 was obviously the product of electoral rigging. The manipulated zones of 1948 were clearly intended to keep the Labor party permanently in office, and at that a particular sort of Labor party, still dominated by the AWU and the rightwing parliamentarians the AWU had supported over the years. The split of 1957 ended that sort of Labor party, but it also delivered the key to power via the machinery of redistribution and electoral weighting to Labor's opponents, whilst freezing the balance within the anti-Labor coalition in favour of the rural partner. Thus subsequent redistributions have given advantage to rural areas where Labor's support had been weakest. Where in the past Labor redistributions had designed wedges of provincial cities to dominate adjacent bits of countryside and maximize the Labor seats, now boundaries were drawn tightly around the provincial cities to lock up their Labor majorities as tightly as possible. The detailed history of boundary-drawing at the state level remains to be written, but it is likely to be the story of unashamed pursuit of party advantage. What has been provided in this chapter is a broader account of the ebb and flow of the electoral tide which for forty years, with one exception, brought a Labor majority at each election.

SECTION B

POLICIES

3 The Machinery of Government

Barry A. Cotterell

The Labor party in government chose the leader and deputy leader and members of cabinet by exhaustive ballot of the caucus where each successful candidate was required to obtain 50 per cent plus one vote of the total vote. According to Morrison "selection was affected by the need to secure some balance among the electoral zones, by the strength of cliques within the party, and by any major internal conflicts". However, others have doubted the importance of zonal considerations and suggested that other internal Labor factors were as important.[1] The premier was then responsible for the allocation of the portfolios.

To assist the ministers to carry out the administration of tasks allocated to them, Queensland, like the other Australian states adopted an idiosyncratic mixture of ministerial departments and statutory corporations. While Labor established statutory corporations, it was wary of giving them a high degree of autonomy and, for example, the State Government Insurance Office, was established as a sub-department within the public service and in the main within the Treasury Department.

Examination of government agencies over a period of forty-two years would be an impossible task unless a classification system of some sort could be devised to illustrate as simply as possible, for comparative purposes, the vast number of changes that took place over the period.

The classification system adopted is based on the character of ministerial control and the relationship to the Public Service Act.[2] In looking at ministerial control the agencies' relationship to the "Permanent Head" has been a significant characteristic and has been used in designing the classification.

The classification system adopted is as follows:

1. Ministerial Public Service Department, i.e.,
   - subject to the minister
   - employees subject to the Public Service Act
   - responsible to a permanent head (as defined in the Regulations since 1951).

1a. Ministerial Public Service sub-Department, i.e.,
   - subject to the minister
   - employees subject to the Public Service Act
   - responsible to the permanent head of the department (as defined in the Regulations since 1951).

2. Ministerial Non-Public Service Department, i.e.,
   - subject to the minister
   - employees not subject to the Public Service Act
   - responsible to the board or commissioner appointed under the relevant Act.

3. Non-Ministerial Public Service Department, i.e.,
   - not subject to the minister except for matters dealing with the Public Service Act
   - employees subject to the Public Service Act
   - responsible to the permanent head (as defined in the Regulations since 1951).

4. Ministerial other, e.g., the Auditor-General's Department.

Departmental corporations and public corporations, two classifications suggested by Wettenhall,[3] have been eliminated because in Queensland they were either Ministerial Public Service departments or sub-departments or Ministerial Non-Public Service Departments, despite their "corporate" status in legislation. The method used in Queensland has normally been to "incorporate" the permanent head, as for example, happened in the Department of Main Roads and the Lands Department.

Administrative agencies moved in and out of these five categories over the period under investigation.

In 1915, there were nine Ministerial Public Service Departments and the Railway Department, the sole Ministerial Non-Public Service Department. The Ministerial Public Service Departments were as follows:—

(1) Chief Secretary's Department; (2) Home Secretary's Department; (3) Department of Public Works; (4) Department of Justice; (5) Treasury Department; (6) Department of Public Lands; (7) Department of Agriculture and Stock; (8) Department of Public Instruction; (9) Department of Mines.

The Labor party elected eight ministers and two honorary ministers, who were in effect ministers without portfolios, to administer these ten departments. One honorary minister was appointed to assist Ryan as assistant minister for justice and the other was appointed to assist Bowman, the home secretary, whose health was failing. In order to exercise overall control of cabinet and to pay particular attention to the legislation that he regarded as important, Ryan had the assistant minister for justice supervise the day-to-day running of the Justice Department and the secretary for public lands assumed control of many of the functions of the Chief Secretary's Department.[4]

In 1915 the government introduced the Workers' Compensation Bill which established a state insurance office to provide workers' compensation without the expense of court proceedings. The following year the passing of the Insurance Act enabled the government to conduct any class of insurance that it chose to introduce. This act later provided for the establishment of a State Government Insurance Office (SGIO) to be managed and controlled by the insurance commissioner appointed under the Workers' Compensation Act of 1916 and the State Accident Insurance Office also established under that act was to be renamed the Workers' Compensation Department of the SGIO.[5] There were two reasons for the creation of the SGIO. Firstly, it was to give immediate benefits to the public by reducing premiums by at least 15 per cent below the uniform tariff adopted by the mainly overseas-owned insurance companies. Secondly, it was to retain investment funds within the state for developmental work. The SGIO was established as a Ministerial Public Service sub-Department of the Attorney-General's Department, but in 1923 it was transferred to the Treasury Department where it has remained ever since.

In 1915, the government also introduced the Public Curator

Bill in order to reduce the costs of administration of the estates of deceased persons, the preparation of wills, and the conveyancing of documents on the purchase, transfer of mortgage of land, houses and other property. The Public Curator also was to handle the legal affairs of persons who were unable to manage their own affairs, such as those who were mentally ill or long term prisoners. On its establishment it took over functions of the Offices of Curator of Intestate Estates, Curator in Insanity, Official Trustee in Insolvency and Principal Receiver in Insolvency. The Public Curator was constituted a corporation by the act and was to be appointed by the governor-in-council. It was established as a Ministerial Public Service sub-Department of the Department of Justice which it has remained to this day.

The third administrative innovation in this period was the establishment in 1918 of the position of commissioner for trade together with the State Trade Office, a Ministerial Non-Public Service Department. The establishment of a State Trade Office was initially suggested by the auditor-general in 1916 but the Commissioner for Trade Bill of 1916 was defeated by the Legislative Council. After the 1918 election the government introduced the State Enterprises Bill which grouped under one control the state stations, butchers shops, sawmills, iron and steel works, canneries, batteries, hotels, and fisheries. By this means, only one statutory corporation, the corporation of the commissioner for trade, was responsible for all of the state enterprises. The State Trade Office was established as a Ministerial Non-Public Service Department headed by the commissioner.

The introduction and growth of industrial unionism in the state public service had been encouraged by the Labor government. In 1916, with the passing of the Industrial Arbitration Act, industrial associations of employees became eligible for registration as industrial unions under that act. Six associations covering public servants registered: the Queensland Government Professional Officers' Association, the Public Service General Officers' Association (subsequently the Queensland State Service Union), the Queensland Teachers Union, and the Prison Employees' Union. Industrial agreements determining rates of pay and conditions of employment were negotiated between the government and the Teachers Union, the Police Union and the Asylum Employees Union as from 1 July 1917, and between the government and the Prison Employees Union as from 1 July 1918. The rest of the public service had to wait because, as the Public Service Board said:

> On account of the ramifications of the Public Service with its nine large departmental staffs of administrative, technical, judicial, commercial, instructional, inspectorial and clerical officers stationed throughout the State, the occasion called for a thorough and complete classification of the Public Service.[6]

On 7 February 1918, a Classification Committee, consisting of the under-secretaries to the Treasury, Public Instruction, and Home Secretary's Departments, and the commissioner of the Queensland Government Savings Bank produced a classification scheme for the general public service. Their classification was not acceptable to the Queensland Government Professional Officers' Association and after much negotiation between the government and the association, the matter became the subject of an award determined by the president of the Court of Industrial Arbitration on 24 April 1918. The award was for twelve months from that date.

Because of the severe criticism of the scheme devised by the Classification Committee, on 19 September 1918 the government appointed the under-secretary for Public Instruction, John Douglas Story, as a royal commissioner to inquire into the classification system. Despite the very specific terms of reference, the consequences of the appointment of J.D. Story and the reaction of his subsequent report were, to use Premier E.G. Theodore's words, "to make a very drastic change, and a desirable one, I think, in connection with the system of controlling the public service".[7]

Theodore had taken over as premier on 22 October 1919. At this date there were eight ministers in charge of ten portfolios with the premier holding two as chief secretary and treasurer, and Fihelly as minister for Justice and secretary for Railways.[8] In addition, another member of the Legislative Assembly was appointed as a member of the executive council and became minister without portfolio and acted as assistant minister.

The government was impressed with the breadth and insight of Story's report and such was the reception of the report that in late 1919 it proposed to vest the control of the public service in a single public service commissioner — J.D. Story, in whom were vested practically all the powers previously held by the Public Service Board composed of ministers. Later in the year, the Government introduced a bill to amend the Public Service Act and the premier said of the bill: "It provides for the appointment of a Public Service Commissioner, who will have vested in him practically all the powers which are now vested in the Public Service Board. . . ."[9]

From his wide-ranging investigations, Story had reported not only upon the subject matter of his commission but also on other aspects of public administration. In his report he said, "My visits to the various offices have impressed upon me the urgent necessity for the regular and thorough inspection of the work of the various departments, sub-departments and district offices",[10] and later "I am certain that the Public Service suffers through the lack of systematic and searching inspection of the work of its officers".[11] He went on to recommend regular inspections and suggested the duties to be carried out by the inspectors. As public service commissioner he was able to start implementing the recommendations of his report and to follow up on other matters that he had drawn to the attention to the chief secretary in a separate communication.

In his first Annual Report, the commissioner referred to the necessity for a comprehensive amendment of the Public Service Act which he found "defective in many respects". The government accepted the commissioner's recommendations; on 22 September 1922, Theodore introduced the Public Service Bill which amended the classification system by creating five divisions in place of the previous two, the professional division and the ordinary division. The new divisions arose from the various industrial awards which had been made with the relevant associations and the amendment of the act reflected acceptance of the existing classification scheme that had resulted. The new Public Service Act also substantially increased the commissioner's powers to include recommendations to the governor-in-council with respect of the grouping or regrouping of sub-departments or branches, the co-ordination of the work of the various departments, the control, reorganization or readjustment of any departments and generally the more efficient administration and control of the public service.[12]

World War I had ended in 1918 and the government was anxious to proceed with implementing its agricultural and industrial policies. However, by 1920 loan funds had become difficult to obtain and the London loan market was particularly opposed to the Queensland government's land tax proposals. To add to its difficulties, the government was faced with finding revenues for loan servicing and repayments from earlier governments. Loan funds were necessary for developing land for settlement, main roads, forestry and irrigation which were all connected with its agriculture policy.

Labor's agriculture policy affected the growth of departments in Queensland in two ways. One arm of the government's agricultural policy involved the establishing of a system of policy advising and industry control through a three-tier structure outside the ministerial department, Agriculture and Stock. The director of the Queensland Producers Association was the highest paid public servant when appointed in 1922 and it was his responsibility to establish this structure (see Chapter 8). The scheme involved the improvement of distribution and marketing of primary produce. By 1926, the director of marketing, as he was then called, had established the Council of Agriculture and Commodity Boards under the Primary Producers' Organization and Marketing Act. The council's functions were to co-operate with the Department of Agriculture and Stock, the local producers' associations and other bodies concerned with agriculture. This structure proved successful in alleviating some of the problems of rural instability. It also had distinct political benefits for Labor, in that farmers no longer had the same need for country or farmers' parties to press their needs.

The second arm of the government's agricultural policy involved land settlement and the provision of the necessary services in order to encourage closer settlement. In this regard several important changes took place in the period. The first departmental change involving land settlement policy occurred in 1919 when the secretary for Agriculture, W.N. Gillies, introduced legislation which created an important new Ministerial Non-Public Service Department, the Main Roads Board. Gillies said it was " . . . the first time that any Government in this State has recognised the obligation of the central Government so far as road construction is concerned".[13]

The 1918 Convention had inserted a plank in the Labor platform which proposed that control and maintenance of main roads be handled at the state level and following upon this convention three ministers were appointed to investigate and recommend the best system of main road construction for Queensland. The board established under the act was based on that established by the equivalent Victorian act with the significant difference that one of the three members had to be an expert road engineer. This requirement resulted in the appointment of J.R. Kemp as chairman of the board. In 1925, the Main Roads Board was abolished and Kemp was appointed the single commissioner in charge of the Main Roads Commission. This charge which is still in effect today, and which was to be constantly cited as a successful example of the single commission system of administration, was not made on any administrative principle regarding the benefits of a commissioner over a board. It occurred because Kemp had applied for the better paid position of chairman of the New South Wales Main Roads Board. The secretary for Public Lands, W.McCormack, obtained cabinet approval to appoint him commissioner of Main Roads and give him complete control of main roads in Queensland with a salary commensurate with the position, in order to retain his services.

In 1922, in order to provide the administrative machinery for the proper control of schemes such as the Dawson Valley Irrigation Scheme, which were part of the government's land settlement programme, the government established the position of commissioner for Irrigation. The sub-department of Water Supply was transferred from the Treasury to become a new Ministerial Public Service Department responsible to the minister for public lands.

The next year following the Prickly-pear Royal Commission's report, the government established the Prickly-pear Land Commission which assumed administrative and judicial functions in areas affected by prickly-pear in order to eradicate the pest and subsequently develop the land for settlement. The legislation provided for the appointment of a commission of three persons, a chairman and two members, to sit both as a commission and as a Land Court, with jurisdiction over areas designated as prickly-pear areas. A feature of the commission was that, as a judicial body, it was answerable directly to the parliament and not to the minister. On its administrative side it controlled its own operations, subject to the approval or disapproval of the governor-in-council. The minister argued that these powers retained over the commission's administrative functions were necessary to maintain responsible government.

That same year the sub-department of Forestry, also within the Department of Public Lands, attracted the attention of the government. Because the government considered that forestry operations would be better managed by an organization outside the public service, the position of director of Forests was abolished and a Provisional Forestry Board was constituted to be responsible to the minister for the proper management and control of State Forests and National Parks.

Because of its dependence upon a rural economy, Queensland was severely affected by the economic downturn stemming from the drought that had started in 1926. This had concentrated attention on certain shortcomings of the land administration. In 1927, the report of a committee of inquiry called the Land Settlement Advisory Board referred to the secretary for Public Lands having responsibility for the Department of Public Lands, the Main Roads Commission, the Irrigation Commission, the Prickly-pear Land Commission and the Forestry Board and said: "Apart from the fact that the Minister for Lands exercises control over these five Departments, each is independent of the other, and there is no system in force for co-ordinating their work. Any co-ordination that is achieved depends on the character, temperament, and capacity of the respective departmental heads".[14]

The recommendations of the advisory board were implemented by the Lands Acts Amendment Act of 1927. The legislation replaced the under-secretary of the Department of Public Lands with a Land Administration Board. Its duties were to advise the minister as to land administration matters generally, to carry out investigations as directed, and generally, subject to the minister, to administer the lands of the state. In effect, the Prickly-pear Land Commission became the model for the Land Administration Board and two members of the commission, with the under-secretary of the department, became the Land Administration Board.

The Labor government's other main area of concern was industrial policy, and embodied in this was the provision of employment at fair and reasonable wages and in safe conditions. The 1919 Story Royal Commission into the Public Service Classification system and the subsequent appointment of Story as public service commissioner were part of the government's approach to industrial policy, but many other changes were made as well. In 1926, the government increased the number of ministers from nine to ten and created a Department of Labour and Industry. The functions transferred to it had previously been within the Department of Public Works. It was made responsible for the supervision and control of the sub-department of Labour; the Industrial Registrar's Office (Board of Trade and Arbitration); the State Trade Office; Electricity Workers Board and the majority of state enterprises established under the State Enterprises Act of 1918. This move gave prominence to the priorities of the government with regard to industrial matters.

Another change that occurred in this period was the long delayed amalgamation of the Department of Harbours and Rivers, the Marine Department and the Office of the Marine Board into the Department of Harbours and Marine. While these agencies were called "Departments" they had been in fact Ministerial Public Service sub-Departments of the Department of Treasury. The government had not placed a high priority on reforming harbour and port administration which in the main was in the hands of Harbour Boards in which local government had taken part. Ryan and Theodore initially proposed to bring all ports under state control but when this was stopped by the Legislative Council it was not proceeded with. Labor liberalized the franchise agreements for the election of Harbour Boards but apart from this showed little interest. The amalgamation occurred in January 1929 after the retirement of the portmaster of Brisbane, who was also chairman of the Marine Board.

The McCormack Labor government lost office on 11 May 1929 but Labor was fortunate to be free of the reins of government during the worst years of the economic crisis. Unemployment had been mounting in Queensland since the start of the drought in 1926 and was to remain the major problem for the Queensland government until the start of World War II in 1939.

Upon assuming government, the Moore Country Progressive National government made very few changes to the portfolios that existed under Labor. The premier relinquished the portfolio of treasurer to a former treasurer, W.H. Barnes, and those of secretary for Public Instruction and secretary for Public Works were held jointly. During 1930-31, the registrar-general's office was transferred from the Justice Department to the Department of Labour and Industry in a transfer designed to amalgamate all statistical services under that department. The establishment of the Bureau of Economics and Statistics was in fulfilment of an election promise, but the one specific reason given for the bureau's establishment was later to result in Labor amending its powers. The secretary for Labour and Industry, H.E. Sizer, said with regard to the tightly organized system of wage regulation that had been established under Labor, "Obviously if we are going to regulate industry by Tribunals such as we have established, then those Tribunals must have reliable information in order to enable them to come to proper decisions".[15] The Moore government became electorally unpopular because of its interference with these wage fixing tribunals when it used the tribunals and the Bureau of Economics and Statistics to reduce wages in the community. It did not however abolish the wage fixing system.

The CPN government was ideologically opposed to state enterprise and it set about selling them off to private enterprise. It repealed the legislation, abolished the position of commissioner for Trade and the State Trade Office and appointed the under-secretary of the Department of Labour and Industry as a corporation to liquidate the business side of the enterprises.

The Moore government also amended the Lands Acts in 1931 to establish the Lands Administration Board on a permanent basis and also constituted it as the Irrigation and Water Supply Commission. Under the amendment the Irrigation and Water Supply Commission was to be co-ordinated with and administered as a sub-department of the Department of Public Lands.

On 9 December 1931, the government introduced the State Transport Co-ordination Bill which provided for the appointment of an advisory board, composed of experts, to inquire into all forms of transport. The bill did not establish a new department at this stage, and the board was purely a co-ordinating instrument. However, it did occasion a change in the title of the portfolio of secretary for railways to that of minister for transport and to allow for better co-ordination the minister was given responsibility for the Main Roads Commission from Public Lands.

Labor was returned to power on 11 June 1932, committed to purging what it considered to be the harmful effects of the Moore CPN government from the statute books. It was also committed to a policy of job-creating, public works and to a continuation of its agricultural policy, involving state development through closer settlement. Dominated as it still was by the AWU, its basic beliefs had not altered. Labor was still committed to a moderate social and industrial reform through the parliamentary process but "gradualism" was to be more in evidence than in previous governments. Radical change was opposed within the party on the basis that it could lead to loss of office and the return of another conservative government, which would undo the gains made under Labor.

The new government was led by W. Forgan Smith who assumed the portfolio of chief secretary and treasurer. Separate secretaries for public instruction and for public works were appointed once more and several changes also occurred within portfolios. Five major departmental changes occurred in this period, all of them involving co-ordination of functions. The Labor party had opposed the election eve action taken by the Moore CPN government without legislative approval, to abolish the Provisional Forestry Board and to establish a forestry board with members appointed for five years. This was one contributing reason for Labor's legislative amendments in 1932. The other was the 1931 report of the Royal Commission on the Development of North Queensland (Land Settlement and Forestry) which had pointed out that Queensland's land policy and forestry policy were diametrically opposed and that the tendency for forestry to break away and establish itself as a separate administrative agency incurred additional costs. Labor introduced a Prickly-pear Land and Forestry Administration Bill which continued the co-ordinating process for land administration by providing that the Land Administration Board would become the Prickly-pear Land Commission and the Forestry Board and that the commission and the forestry board would be administered as sub-departments of the Department of Public Lands. The abolition of the forestry board also achieved a political objective of abolishing positions filled by appointees of the Moore government.

The second departmental change resulted from the Labor election promise to abolish the Bureau of Economics and Statistics. This policy was the result of union opposition to the bureau's role of advising the Industrial Court and the latter's policy of reducing wages, but it also reflected Labor's opinion of all the Moore government's actions as regressive and requiring repeal. However, while Labor abolished the Bureau of Economics and Statistics, in its place it established a Bureau of Industry as a Ministerial Public Service sub-department of the Treasury Department to carry out almost the same functions plus some new ones. The bureau was placed under the control of the premier, and its operations involved the problems of unemployment, consideration and recommendation of proposals for the development of the state and its industries, and co-ordination of government policy in these areas. In 1933, the bureau was also established as a construction authority to enable it to construct the Kangaroo Point Bridge, later named the Story Bridge after J.D. Story. It was also to be responsible at a later stage for construction of the Somerset Dam, the Petrie Bight wharves and several of the early buildings at the University of Queensland. Unfortunately its construction function meant that its attempts at co-ordination and public works planning had to be abandoned after early 1934.

The third change in this period involved the establishment, in 1934, of the position of director-general for Health and Medical Services and in 1935 the re-organization of the functions of the Home Secretary's department which was consequently renamed the Department of Health and Home Affairs. The home affairs part of the department remained responsible for local government, police, prison and welfare functions. The major aim of these changes was once again the better co-ordination and delivery of services.

The fourth change followed the recommendations of the Royal Commission on Electricity in 1936 for the establishment of a State Electricity Commission. The State Electricity Commission Bill was introduced on 3 November 1937, based upon the royal commission. The premier said upon introducing it: "The Bill now makes a step forward in Labor's policy of organised planning in the internal economy of the State. The Labor Party and Labor Governments hold it to be vital in the public interest that the development of electricity supply should be a planned development." This legislation became the basis for co-ordination and amalgamation of the electricity supply industry, under the control of the State Electricity Commission and the Department of Electricity Supply, a Ministerial Non-Public Service Department. Up to this time the electricity industry was in the hands of private enterprise and local electricity authorities.

The fifth change resulted from several factors. At the 1938

election, Forgan Smith announced that the government's policy of providing full-time employment would continue with a view to abolishing relief work entirely. Intermittent relief work had become politically unpopular and after the election the premier indicated that a thorough investigation into the scheme would be made by the government and its officers. On 8 August 1938, the government announced that unemployment relief work would be abandoned and state projects would be undertaken on planned lines. Planning was also essential because funds available from Loan Council sources for public works were scarce and had to be deployed for maximum benefit. The change that occurred pioneered, in Australia at least, the principles adopted at the 1937 International Labour Conference at Geneva, and reflected Labor's union affiliations. These principles emphasized the importance of public works planning in reducing fluctuations in economic conditions. The State Development and Public Works Organization Bill of 1938 established the position of co-ordinator general of Public Works to be given the duty of determining priorities for public works in Queensland carried out by both state and local government bodies. J.R. Kemp, the main roads commissioner, was appointed as the first co-ordinator general and he held both posts until 1949. It is perhaps ironic that a change planned to co-ordinate all those activities with a view to securing the maximum employment of labour and the utmost efficiency in carrying out the work involved received its first test under war-time conditions when it was required to achieve the utmost efficiency by carrying out the maximum amount of work with the minimum amount of labour. The system of co-ordination not only proved up to the task but was used as a model by the commonwealth and several of the states. In 1940, the co-ordinator general was also given power to act as a construction authority, in part because of his responsibilities on behalf of the commonwealth government.

Changes in government administration after 1941 were affected by the constraints of wartime administration, shortages of manpower, materials and finance. Priority, of necessity, had to be given to policies and programmes that furthered the success of the war effort. Very few major changes to the existing administration were required during this period despite the fact that state departments and officers not only carried out their own duties efficiently but also acted as agents for the commonwealth government to ensure maximum co-ordination and benefit for the war effort.

Two changes that did occur involved local government. The first involved the transfer in 1942 of the administration of local government law from the secretary for health and home affairs to the secretary for public works. The secretary for health and home affairs at this time was deputy premier but more importantly was responsible for civil defence and it was to relieve him of some of his duties that this move occurred. At the same time administration of the Water Authorities Act was transferred from the sub-Department of Irrigation and Water Supply to the new Ministerial Public Service sub-Department of Local Government, under the secretary for public works.

The second change aimed at introducing a uniform policy of land valuation for rating purposes. The Legislative Council had rejected this reform in 1917 and Labor did not resurrect it until 1943 when it was again withdrawn owing to opposition objections and a pending state election. In 1944 the Valuation of Land Act was passed establishing the position of valuer-general as the single valuing authority in Queensland.

Subsequently the government was concerned with post-war reconstruction and development, a field which embodied the party's concern with the use of public works to create employment. After the 1944 election, the government also promoted public works involving the provision of economic infrastructure as part of its policy to encourage private enterprise to invest in Queensland.

The next round of departmental changes arose partly out of federal government funding initiative but mainly out of the recognition by the state and commonwealth government of the post-war need for housing. However, the State Housing Bill introduced on 14 November 1945 was not a new initiative with regard to the functions involved but rather a consolidation of existing arrangements under one new authority, the Queensland Housing Commission. The act dissolved the State Advances Corporation, a Ministerial Public Service sub-Department established in 1920, when the Queensland Savings Bank was merged with the Commonwealth Savings Bank. The Queensland Housing Commission took over all of the activities of the corporation, together with its assets and liabilities. Three facts in the Queensland Housing Commission's establishment should be mentioned because of their subsequent adoption as guidelines for other commissions. Firstly, the commissioner was appointed by the governor-in-council, making him responsible to the government of the day. Secondly, his tenure was established by the appointment being for a maximum term of seven years with eligibility for re-appointment. Thirdly, the commission was established as a Public Service Department.

In December 1946, the State Transport Commission of three was also replaced with a single commissioner and a permanent organization in the form of a Ministerial Non-Public Service Department was established.

That same month, following the report of the Queensland Secondary Industries Development Committee and an election promise by the opposition to create a ministry for secondary industries, the government established a Secondary Industries Division within the Department of Labour and Industry to encourage and promote secondary industry in Queensland. At the same time the government created a new Bureau of Industry to take the place of both the existing Bureau of Industry and the State Employment Council. This eliminated a duplication and waste of effort which had become evident in administration. The Irrigation and Water Supply Commission was also separated from the Land Administration Board in December 1946 and a commissioner appointed to administer it as a Ministerial Public Service Department.

After the 1947 election the process of administrative rationalization continued. The State Electricity Commission Acts Amendment Bill introduced on 12 March 1948 reconstituted the State Electricity Commission as a single commissioner although still outside of the Public Service Act. In 1949, Labor amended the Officials in Parliament Act to increase the size of the ministry to eleven. This was to be the last increase under Labor because as the premier, V.C. Gair, said in 1956, ". . . one hesitates to [increase the ministry] in times like the present. I do not want to add to the cost of government if I can afford it. My Ministers and I are prepared to do our job to the best of our ability. We are not afraid of work.[16]

On 28 November 1950, the Public Service Acts Amendment Bill was introduced to bring under the Public Service Acts all permanent salaried officers in the employ of the commissioner for Main Roads, the State Electricity commissioner and the commissioner for Transport. This development honoured a promise the government had made to the State Public Service Union and also made easier the transfer of officers within the public service. Under the act the Department of Main Roads, the Department of the State Electricity Commission and the Department of the Transport Commission were established as Ministerial Public Service Departments.

In 1954, the government introduced the State Development and Public Works Organization Acts Amendment Bill to give permanent operation to the original Act. It also made the co-ordinator general and his deputy responsible to the government of the day as opposed to the parliament which had been the case under the original legislation. This was to be the last departmental change made prior to Labor losing office in August 1956.

At the end of Labor's period of office, eleven ministers controlled seventeen Ministerial Public Service Departments and one Ministerial Non-Public Service Department, the Railway Department. In the main, Departments were single function oriented while the principal co-ordinating departments, with the exception of the Treasury, were controlled by the premier. One change that the Liberal-Country party government introduced immediately in 1957 was the establishment of a Cabinet Secretariat. Under Labor governments, cabinet submissions had not been circulated before meetings and no minutes were kept. Individual ministers were responsible for noting cabinet decisions on the relevant files and this sometimes led to difficulties in determining exactly what had been decided.

However, the basic administrative structure developed under the Labor government has not been altered dramatically by its National Liberal party successors. Sub-departments have been upgraded to departments and much "bureau-shuffling" occurred in the following twenty years but none of the functions adopted under Labor or the departments established to administer them have been abolished.

Perhaps the most basic legacy of Labor administration was the close involvement of ministers and cabinet itself with the detail of administration. This grew out of Labor's desires to maintain political control through ministerial responsibility. By 1957 there was a fairly uniform system of administration with all salaried staff except railways employees and the police force under the Public Service Act and several Ministerial Public Service Departments carrying out functions which in other states were administered by statutory corporations. The process had been incremental and evolutionary as might have been expected, but by 1957 it appeared reasonably consistent in its internal logic and efforts to achieve co-ordination. It is therefore not surprising that the incoming Country-Liberal party government found little need to alter the basic structure.

NOTES

1. A.A. Morrison. "The Government of Queensland", in *The Government of the Australian States*, ed. S.R. Davis (Melbourne: Longmans, 1960), p. 309.
2. R.L. Wettenhall, "State Departmentalism — Some General Questions", *APSA News* 8, no. 3 (September 1963) :17.
3. Ibid.
4. D.J. Murphy, *T.J. Ryan: A Political Biography* (St Lucia: University of Queensland Press, 1975), p. 120.
5. Insurance Act of 1916, Clause 6 (1) to (3).
6. Report of the Public Service Board (1917-18), p. 2.
7. *QPD* 134 (22 January 1920): 2448.
8. It is interesting to note that this was the first mention of the term

"Premier" in the ministerial title but that it did not involve extra responsibilities as the chief secretary was in fact the premier. The first mention of Premier's Department in the Estimates occurred in 1917. (See *QVP* I (1917) : 312) The first official mention of "Premier" was on 26 April 1919. (See *Queensland Government Gazette* CXIII, 137, 26 April 1919, p. 1180). From 1919 to 1963, when the title "Chief Secretary" was abandoned, the office of Chief Secretary remained combined with the office of Premier.

9. *QPD* 134 (22 January 1920): 2448.
10. The Report of the Royal Commission on Classification of Officers of the Public Service (1919), p. XLII, para 31.
11. Ibid., p. XLIII.
12. The Civil Service Act of 1922, Clause 14.
13. *QPD* 133 (4 November 1919): 1810.
14. *The Report of the Land Settlement Advisory Board* (Government Printer 1927), p. 12.
15. QPD 155 (20 August 1930): 511.
16. *QPD* 215 (18 October 1956): 957.

4 Abolition of the Legislative Council

D.J. Murphy

Political theory in the Australian colonies in the nineteenth century had called for two houses of parliament. The lower house, the Legislative Assembly or House of Assembly, was elected on a broadening franchise that ultimately provided manhood, i.e. male, suffrage more or less, while the upper house, the Legislative Council, was either nominated by the governor or elected on a high property qualification for its electors and an even higher one for its members. The Legislative Council was to be the bulwark against democracy, then still regarded by the possessors of wealth and property as something of a dirty word.

As enthusiasm for parliamentary democracy grew in the later part of the century, it was inevitable that there would be clashes between the more representative lower house and the less representative, unusually unrepresentative, upper house. How to deal with deadlocks between the two chambers, to preserve the right of the lower house of final responsibility for money bills, and for ultimate responsibility for other pieces of legislation, were continuing problems in Queensland's constitutional history. The four principal reforming premiers all clashed with the Legislative Council. Griffith was forced to appeal to the Privy Council. Kidston reduced the Council's power to reject legislation indefinitely, but did not really affect the obstructive power available to it. Ryan established that the Council could be abolished constitutionally, but failed at a referendum to secure its abolition. Theodore provided the satisfactory solution, making Queensland the only Australian state to be governed by a single chamber.

Members of the Queensland Legislative Assembly were not paid a salary until 1889. Members of the Legislative Council were never to be paid a salary or even an attendance allowance, though they did receive free railway passes. An obvious consequence was that only those persons of wealth who could afford to be in Brisbane for several months of the year, or had law practices or businesses in Brisbane, were nominated to the Council. Before 1890 there had not been much contrast in the social backgrounds of the members of the two houses, but from the election of sixteen Labor members to the Assembly in 1893, social and economic differences between the two houses grew. By the time Ryan's government was elected in 1915, there was a social chasm between the elected majority in the lower house and the nominated majority in the upper house.

The first members of the Council had been appointed by the governor of New South Wales for a five-year term. Subsequent members were appointed by the governor of Queensland for life. Although official doctrine was that appointments should be made on the advice of the governor's ministers, though he might choose not to appoint all nominated, in practice new appointments were made so as to give the government of the day a reasonable opportunity to have its legislation passed through the upper house. Not until 1903, when Kidston engineered the Labor-Liberal coalition, which broke the thirteen years of unbroken rule by the Conservative "Continuous Ministry", were the first Labor members appointed to the Council. These were Albert Hinchcliffe, manager of the *Worker* newspaper, Charles McGhie, co-owner of the Maryborough *Alert*, a weekly Labor paper, Peter Murphy, an hotel owner and businessman, and later Frank McDonnell, formerly Labor MLA for Fortitude Valley who was to establish a successful departmental store in George Street. When Ryan became the first Labor premier with a majority in the lower house, he was confronted by a Legislative Council of thirty-nine members, some of whom had been appointed as long ago as 1879 and only four of whom supported his government.

Of the various issues that produced confrontation between the two chambers, none was as important as finance. Under the Queensland Constitution, all money bills had to originate in the Legislative Assembly, but there was no provision regarding the right or otherwise of the Legislative Council to amend such bills. Throughout the nineteenth and early twentieth centuries, ministries had argued for the right of the Assembly to determine questions relating to finance. On occasions the Assembly was forced, by the realities of politics, to accept Council amendments to money bills, but it did not concede the right of the Council to this power and it was more usual for the Assembly to refuse to continue debate on money bills amended by the Council than to concede the Council's power to amend. In 1885 there had been a significant trial of strength when the Council rejected a bill for payment of MLAs' expenses. The dispute was ultimately referred to the Privy Council[1] which held that the Legislative Council did not have co-ordinate power with the Legislative Assembly, and the Assembly alone had authority over money bills, but Griffith's opponents in the Council claimed that he had unfairly included in the papers sent to the governor for transmission to London a letter which attempted to influence the Privy Council and refused to be bound by its findings.

The presence of a nominated Legislative Council packed with opponents of reform stung the democratic instincts of the emergent Labor party. When the general council of the Australian Labor Federation met in Brisbane in August 1890 to draw up the platform and rules for a political labour party, the first plank in the "People's Parliamentary Platform" read: "Universal White Adult Suffrage for all parliamentary and local elections; no plural voting; no nominee or property qualification chamber". This plank was refined through the 1890s: "Universal White Adult Suffrage" was replaced in 1893 by "one man, one vote", and in 1901 by the more exact intention of "one adult, one vote". The phrase "no nominee or property qualification" was changed to "Abolition of the Nominee Chamber" in 1893 and "Abolition of the Legislative Council" in 1901. Throughout, electoral reform remained the first plank in both the fighting and general platform.[2] As the Labor parties in all colonies were to find out when they came into government, it was one thing to place abolition of the Legislative Council at the top of the list of reforms to be achieved, but another matter to carry it out.

Kidston's coalition had given Queensland the Adult Suffrage Act of 1905 which abolished plural voting whereby an elector was entitled to vote in each constituency in which he held the requisite property qualification, and enfranchised women. Although he broke away from the Labor party in 1907, he continued to press his reform programme. When the Council drastically amended his bill to establish Wages Boards, Kidston sought sufficient appointments to the Legislative Council to ensure its passage. The governor, Lord Chelmsford, rejected his request, whereupon Kidston resigned and the governor — in an extraordinary use of his vague prerogative powers — appointed Robert Philp, the leader of the opposition. Philp did not and could not comand a majority in the Assembly, but he secured supply and then the parliament was dissolved and a new election held only eight months after Kidston had been returned as premier. Kidston won the election and forced through a chastened Legislative Council two pieces of legislation designed to limit the Council's power to frustrate the government of the day. The Constitution Act Amendment Act deleted the clause requiring a two-thirds majority in each chamber for amendment of the Constitution, and the Parliamentary Bills Referendum Act provided that a bill twice rejected by the Council would become law if approved by a majority of electors at a referendum. Kidston's last service to electoral reform was his 1910 Electoral Districts Act which effectively provided "one vote, one value" for Queensland elections.

At the 1915 election, Labor's fighting platform had as its first plank: "Abolition of the Legislative Council and the office of State Governor and the institution of the Initiative and Referendum". Ryan made no mention of this plank in his policy speech. He gave no indication ever of favouring the abolition of the position of governor, though he supported the appointment of Australian rather than British governors. In his early days as premier, he took a cautious and conciliatory approach towards the Council for he appreciated that the Council existed, its powers were real and could not be aside merely because Labor had won an Assembly election. But in caucus many Labor parliamentarians wished to govern without reference to the Council, and it took two caucus meetings before Ryan could persuade his colleagues to allow a minister to be appointed to the Council to look after government business there.

One of the Ryan government's first important pieces of legislation was a new Elections Act. Voting rights were extended to British subjects who had been resident in Australia for six months, in Queensland for three months and in their particular electorate for one month. Provision was made for joint commonwealth-state rolls and electoral machinery — which have never been effected. Women were given the right to stand for election to the Assembly, and it was laid down that elections should be held on one day, a Saturday, not stretched over several weeks as previously.

Despite Ryan's conciliatory approach, the non-Labor majority in the Council soon showed that it was determined not to recognize the changes that had occurred as a result of the recent election. In the first six months, bills to allow the government to take over and operate meatworks for the duration of the war, to provide adult suffrage in local government elections, to establish a new and comprehensive system of conciliation and arbitration and to open up land for small farmers on a perpetual lease system, were all rejected. The Workers Compensation Bill was first emasculated, then on its second appearance before the Council, the vital sections passed when the insurance company directors neglected to read and understand all the clauses. Bills rejected a second time could be put to a referendum, but with these examples of deliberate obstruction of bills promised in Ryan's policy speech, caucus was unanimous that the Council should be abolished. The question was how it could be done with certainty. A minority wanted to swamp the Council with government nominees who would then vote for its abolition, a majority preferred to have it abolished by a clear vote of the people through the Parliamentary Bills Referendum Act.[3]

On 17 November 1915, Ryan opened the second reading debate on the Constitution Act Amendment Bill to abolish the Legislative Council. His careful speech had two goals: to show that the Council could be constitutionally abolished and to argue the specific grounds for its abolition.[4] The first was, at this stage, more important. The crux of his case was that under the Order-in-Council of 6 June 1859, the legislature of Queensland had full power and authority "to make laws, altering or repealing all or any of the provisions" of the order in the same way as any other laws of the state could be altered or repealed. On this rested the validity of Kidston's Constitution Act Amendment Act on which, in turn, depended the validity of the Parliamentary Bills Referendum Act.

The debate that followed the normal week's adjournment was predictable. The Liberal opposition in the Assembly argued against the validity of Ryan's case and defended the Council's role in rejecting important government legislation. The principal case for retention of the Council was set out in an amendment moved in the Council by A.J. Thynne, MLC, a leading Brisbane solicitor and a minister in earlier conservative governments. Thynne gave twenty-two constitutional, political and general reasons for the retention of the Council and retention in its present form.[5] His amendment was carried twenty-six to three, with eleven members absent from the vote including two Labor supporters. Their number had been augmented by the appointment of William Hamilton, the former shearer jailed for his part in the 1891 strike and now minister for mines and government leader in the Council.

Ryan had to leave for England in March 1916, and the future of the Council was left standing. On his return in August it was made clear in the governor's speech to open the new session that the government was determined to push ahead with the referendum to abolish the Council. In September the bill passed the Assembly again, and was amended by the Council in December and not returned to the lower house. It was therefore declared "lost" and thus coming under the Parliamentary Bills Referendum Act. Complementary to the bill to abolish the Council was the Popular Initiative and Referendum Bill.[6] The initiative and the referendum had been significant parts of the Labor parties' commitment to electoral reform and a greater involvement of the people in the democratic processes of government. Under the bill, 10 per cent of the electors could requisition legislation (provided that it involved no additional expenditure) which would then have to be put to a referendum and, if passed, would become law. Liberals opposed the bill on the grounds that such power could not safely be entrusted to the people at large, whilst in the upper house it was seen as a means by which unions, the Labor party or other groups could organize a referendum for the abolition of the Council itself. An impasse was reached on this bill between the two houses.

The turmoil caused by the first conscription referendum in October 1916 prevented further action being taken on the future of the Council. The vote in Queensland — 158,051 against, 144,200 for conscription — gave hope to both sides of the abolition dispute, supporters of abolition that a similar majority could be secured, upholders of the Council that the reversal of fortunes which had already destroyed five Labor governments around Australia might also carry off the Ryan government in Queensland. In December 1916, the Council again challenged the Ryan government by amending the Income Tax Bill despite a ruling from the non-Labor chairman of committees that the Council did not have power to amend money bills. There was no option but to meet the challenge and assert the prerogative of the lower house. In order to save money, cabinet decided to hold the referendum on the same day as the federal elections, 5 May 1917, together with a second referendum on the reduction of liquor outlets as required under the Liquor Act. The Central Political Executive objected to this decision and declined to take any part in the abolition campaign, arguing that one major political question should be taken at a time. Ryan persuaded the members to change their minds,[7] but this left only six weeks in which to organize a campaign which would compete for time and finance with the crucial federal election in which Billy Hughes now led the anti-Labor forces. Ryan made few political mistakes, but insisting on holding the Council referendum on the same day as the federal election was probably his greatest mistake.

Amid these essentially political problems, a legal challenge emerged when three MLCs sought to test the validity of the referendum by seeking an injunction against the government from the Supreme Court.[8] The application was set down for hearing for 24 April, twelve days before the poll. The campaigning for and against abolition continued, but the litigation added an element of uncertainty. Ryan appeared for the government, together with the former Liberal attorney-general, James Blair, who had drafted the original legislation for Kidston. On Saturday, 28 April, the Full Court decided that holding of the referendum was without legal authority and issued the injunction sought. Blair asked for and was granted leave to appeal to the High Court. In Sydney, Ryan's preliminary application was heard on the Tuesday before the poll, then referred to the full High Court the following day. On the Friday morning, the day before the poll, the High Court decided that the referendum could be held with the points of law being decided later. When the case resumed in Brisbane in August, the High Court overturned the Queensland Supreme Court's decision and unanimously decided that the Constitution Act Amendment Act and the Parliamentary Bills Referendum Act were valid, and that the Queensland parliament had the power to abolish the upper house, by referendum if it so desired. Appeal to the Privy Council was refused as the referendum had by then been held.

After receiving Ryan's telegram with the High Court's decision on the Friday, Theodore tried desperately to have advertisements placed in the Saturday morning's newspapers informing the electors that the referendum would still be held and that it was legal and valid. Confusion reigned on the Saturday, whilst at the polling booths no one seemed to be quite certain just what the status of the referendum was. Moreover, the question was put in such a way that many booth workers later reported that voters had been unsure of how to cast their vote. To vote *against* the Council, an elector had to vote *for* the bill. A vote against the bill, and thus in favour of the Council, was cast by marking the lower square — and in the second referendum the well advertised and well conducted campaign against reducing the number of liquor outlets in south-east Queensland had asked voters to place their

"X" in the bottom square. That campaign won handsomely 43,460 to 23,999.

When the Council referendum votes were counted, 179,105 had voted for retention of the Council and 116,196 for abolition. The later sinking of the *Mongolia*, carrying soldiers' votes in the referendum, provided a convenient technical excuse for declaring the referendum invalid, but whatever excuses Labor members might have made, the size of the vote for the Council indicated that a substantial majority of Queenslanders were not yet prepared to countenance its abolition.

In his two years as premier, Ryan had gained the confidence and respect of the governor, Sir Hamilton Goold-Adams. When the premier sought the appointment of thirteen Labor members to the Council following the defeat of the referendum and the Council's continued rejection of government bills, Goold-Adams agreed, seeing this as a reasonable request to give the government sufficient numbers to provide a quorum in the absence of large numbers of non-government members, a not infrequent occurrence, rather than as an attempt to swamp the Council.[9] Whilst at least a third of caucus were opposed to Labor appointments being made, cabinet was able to command sufficient support to get the appointments approved. Nominees had to be financial members of the Labor party and had to fulfil all the conditions required for the normal selection of Labor candidates by plebiscite. They had to sign an additional clause to the pledge, promising to support abolition of the Council and to support the Labor party in all divisions. Endorsement was to be first by the PLP and then by the CPE.

The thirteen new members selected were: W.R. Crampton, manager of the Labor newspaper, the *Daily Standard*, and formerly director of labour; H.C. Jones, a returned soldier with service at Gallipoli and a founder of the Plumbers' Union; H. Llewellyn, a Gympie bookseller; G. Page-Hanify, president of the Good Templars; I. Perel, proprietor of the weekly newspaper, the *Patriot*; W.J. Riordan, president of the AWU; R. Bedford, journalist and shareholder in several large mines; F. Courtice, a sugar-farmer from Bundaberg; E.B. Purnell, secretary of the

Waterside Workers Federation at Rockhampton, T. Nevitt, formerly a MLA and now a quarantine officer at Townsville, and W. Demaine, R. Sumner, and L. McDonald, president, vice-president, and secretary of the CPE respectively. The new appointments brought a shower of complaints and protests from newspapers and non-Labor MLCs.

The ferocity of the second conscription campaign in Queensland in November-December 1917 and the second rejection of conscription by Queensland voters increased the animosity of non-Labor MLCs towards Ryan and the Labor government, and it was clear that whether or not Ryan mentioned the Council in his policy speech at the 1918 election, the Council's future would inevitably be an election issue. Recognizing that abolition of the Council was not an issue to win votes among non-committed electors, Ryan included it along with the matters a Labor government would deal with if re-elected but did not press the point in the campaign. By contrast, leading figures in the Nationalists' campaign deliberately made the future of the Council a central election issue. The parliamentary leader, E.H. Macartney, in an apparent concession to changes in feeling towards the Council, promised to change it from a nominated to an elected chamber, but with a restrictive property franchise. Large newspaper advertisements exhorted electors to "Keep the Council, Keep Your Homes, Keep Your Savings Banks Deposits" by voting National.[10]

Ryan won the election with a two to one majority in seats, but whilst he was in Perth at the Federal Conference of the Labor party, the Council once more rejected Theodore's Income Tax Bill and a Land Tax Bill. On his return to Queensland, Ryan conferred with Goold-Adams who agreed that the Council's action was wrong, but argued that he had no power to override it and declined to appoint new members to ensure passage of the bills. They were passed again by the Legislative Assembly and when they went back to the Council, Ryan let it be known that the government would consider taking the Council to a referendum if these bills were rejected again. It was not clear from his remarks whether the referendum would concern abolition of the Council or merely seek to pass the two money bills, but as the crisis mounted in intensity some MLCs began to reflect on Ryan's sweeping electoral victory only six months previously and the possibility that abolition could be carried. A free conference on the Income Tax Bill failed to reach agreement, but then the Council backed down on both bills. It is possible that Goold-Adams let it be known privately that he might reconsider his refusal of new appointments, but this is not known.

Ryan and the government had secured a major victory, but without any real solution to the problem the Council presented to any elected government bent on reform. Ryan again unsuccessfully sought further appointments from Goold-Adams, and then caucus voted twenty-two to twelve for a second referendum on abolition, but with the bill containing the novel suggestion that an all-parties committee of the Assembly should scrutinize all bills to ensure that they were in order before being sent to the governor, thereby meeting the need for a house of review. This time the issue was much simpler than it had been in 1915. There was no longer any question as to the legality of abolishing the upper house. The central question now was the unnecessary obstruction by the Council of a large number of vital and significant government bills. Bereft of any arguments against the legality of the measure, the Nationalist opposition argued that the Council as the "bulwark of the true interests in Queensland" was better constituted to study the questions which came before it than the Assembly as the Council's members were not responsible to the votes of constituents.[11]

The Legislative Council rejected the Constitution Act Amendment Bill and deferred pending a free conference an accompanying Appropriation Bill which provided £12,000 with which to conduct the referendum and £13,000 to pay a campaign allowance of £200 to each of the sixty-five non-ministers in the Assembly. At the free conference, a confident Ryan was unwilling to concede anything and threatened a general election at which public servants would hold the Council responsible for their salaries not being paid. Council representatives in the free conference recommended passing the

Appropriation Bill, but the QCE in December 1918 established a special Legislative Council Abolition Committee with a separate abolition fund and it appeared that Queensland was set for a second popular challenge to the upper house.

Theodore, acting premier whilst Ryan was in England, appearing before the Privy Council, formally opened the abolition campaign in Ipswich in May 1919, but because of the post-war influenza epidemic, all campaigning was brought to a halt. In August he reintroduced the abolition bill in the Legislative Assembly in accordance with the requirements of the Parliamentary Bills Referendum Act. However, the death of two non-Labor MLCs and the appointment of three Labor members to the Council — T.L. Jones, a provisions merchant, director of Foggitt, Jones and Co and long standing friend of H.E. Boote and who had beaten Liberal Premier Digby Denham at the 1915 election, G. Lawson, secretary of the Carters' Union, and A. Skirving, secretary of the Hairdressers' Union and former president of the Brisbane Industrial Council — suggested the possibility of obtaining a majority in the Council by appointments and perhaps using this majority for abolition without having to face the problems of a second referendum. After August 1919, the government's determination to proceed with the referendum lessened through a number of factors. Ryan left state politics to enter the federal parliament; Theodore and McCormack became the driving forces in caucus; the Labor vote in Queensland declined at the federal election in December and lost the state seat of Maranoa which had been held for twelve years; and finally, at the end of 1919, Goold-Adams left Queensland on his six months' retirement leave. While a new governor was being appointed, a lieutenant-governor with full powers was normally appointed by cabinet. The government had made no recommendations regarding a successor to Goold-Adams; indeed it had made it clear that he was regarded as the last imported governor and appointment of an Australian to the position would be sought. William Lennon, then the Speaker of the Legislative Assembly, a former banker and minister in Ryan's government, was sworn in as lieutenant-governor on 3 February.

The Colonial Office had accepted his appointment only after a strong recommendation of Goold-Adams that Lennon was a suitable choice.

The non-Labor majority in the Legislative Council had learned nothing in their previous four years' experience of the Labor government. On 11 February, despite a warning of swamping from the *Daily Standard*, the Council amended four clauses of the Income Tax Act Amendment Bill, rejected outright the Land Act Amendment Bill, and amended the Profiteering Prevention Bill. This was to be the Council's last defeat of the government. Cabinet recommended that Lennon appoint fourteen new members to the Council to give Labor thirty-five members in a Council total of sixty-four. The central executive endorsed sixty-three candidates, and on 19 February, Lennon appointed the fourteen chosen by the PLP. They were: R.J. Carroll, secretary of the Amalgamated Society of Engineers; W.P. Colborne, secretary of the Printing Industry Employees Association; J.S. Collings, party organizer; J.F. Donovan, a publican; T.J. Donovan, manager of the *Worker*; W.J. Dunstan, secretary of the AWU; W.F. Finlayson, MHR for Brisbane 1910-19; J.S. Hanlon, editor of the *Worker*, E.J. Hanson, secretary of the Plumbers' Union; C. Kilpatrick, a miners' union official and mines inspector; H.G. McPhail, MLA for Windsor 1915-18; R.J. Mulvey, secretary of the Brisbane Industrial Council; J.G. Smith, a Queen Street pieman, G.H. Thompson, a compositor and overseer on the *Daily Standard*. A majority to pass an abolition bill could therefore be quickly assembled, although the *Daily Standard* affirmed that Labor, bowing to the electors' earlier verdict, was endeavouring to mend rather than end it.[12] Theodore himself attempted to end speculation regarding the new appointees:

> The additional members have been appointed to prevent the Government measures from being unceremoniously flung out of the Council. The Government will not take advantage of its new strength in the Council to abolish that Chamber. At any rate until it gets a fresh mandate from the people. That could be either by

Fourteen new members were appointed to the Legislative Council, to give Labor the majority to pass vetoed bills. (Reprinted from *The Worker* 26 February 1920 with the permission of Australian Workers Union; Photograph by courtesy of the John Oxley Library.)

> making the abolition the principal issue at an election or by way of another referendum.[13]

He added that there would continue to be no payments or salaries for MLCs, thereby avoiding putting any temptation in the way of Labor appointees to become too comfortable in their new surroundings and to "rat" if they were ever called upon to exercise an abolition vote.

With the new Council majority the Profiteering Prevention Bill was passed, along with a Fair Rents Act, the amendments to the Land Acts and the new Income Tax. However, some members of caucus were having second thoughts about other electoral bills, and there were no plans for reintroducing the Initiative and Referendum Bill and Ryan's bill to give eighteen-year-olds the vote, which had also been previously rejected by the Council, and shelved. At the tenth Labor-in-Politics Convention in Townsville in June 1920, while Theodore was still in London, abolition of the Council was debated. Lewis McDonald, the QCE secretary, had reported that the literature and the abolition committee were fully prepared for the abolition campaign when it resumed. However, the question that was raised centred on why the government had not proceeded immediately with abolition as soon as the Council majority had been obtained. Was there a lack of resolve inside the Labor government? Harry Bruce, an AWU official from north Queensland, expressed the feeling of many delegates when he said: "Now they had a majority they seemed afraid to do it. Once they were very hot on the scent, now they seemed to be stone cold".[14]

John Mullan, a new recruit to cabinet, explained to the convention that immediate abolition had not been feasible and put to the delegates the two problems that the government had faced in February 1920, when it looked squarely at abolishing the Council by a vote of both houses. The first had been the necessity of obtaining royal assent, i.e., agreement by the British government, to a bill which amended the Queensland Constitution. The second was the possible electoral consequences of abolishing the Council without some further referral to the electors. The convention rejected the call for immediate abolition and passed a motion submitted by the QCE calling on the government to make abolition an issue at the next election and, when returned to power, to pass an abolition bill through the two houses of parliament.[15] The next state election had not been due until March 1921, but was brought forward to October. In his policy speech, Theodore promised that the Council would be abolished, the initiative and referendum would be introduced and adult franchise provided for local government elections. The Nationalist and Country parties joined in making retention of the Council a central election issue.

Labor won the election, but Ryan's majority of twenty-four in 1918 was reduced to four. Adult franchise was introduced for local government elections, but the initiative and referendum were dropped. If Theodore had intended to abolish the Council, it would seem that the months immediately after the election would have been most suitable. He chose not to act, and the surviving minutes of the separate caucus of Labor MLCs gave no indication that the question of formal abolition was raised in the parliamentary session after the election.

The Labor appointees to the Council were later to be called the "suicide squad". They were certainly to prove themselves unpaid heroes. Their party required that they attend all Council sessions, without pay or allowances. Whilst they were allowed to attend normal PLP caucus meetings and speak, they might not vote at such meetings, a restriction which rankled with many of them. Earlier, in May 1918, the Labor MLCs decided to ask the general PLP meeting to take steps to abolish the Council or to allow expenses to its members, but the PLP refused to consider the payment of special allowances. Aside from their abhorrence of paying allowances to support their most vigorous opponents, the non-Labor majority in the upper house, cabinet members were aware of the problems in having such a bill passed through both houses. The dual problems of caucus voting rights and allowances for Council sittings were raised again at the end of 1919. Voting rights were again rejected, but as a large number of Labor appointees had now served two unpaid years in the upper house, cabinet members were more sympathetic to their problems. How-

The theme of this float in the Labour Day procession of 1923 was the Nationalist and Country Parties' promise to restore the Legislative Council.

ever, as the second abolition campaign was expected to be held soon, the matter was left in abeyance. When the idea of another referendum was informally dropped at the beginning of 1920, cabinet agreed to an allowance of £2 2s. per sitting day but only to the Council's caucus secretary and whip. Throughout 1920 and 1921 the Labor Councillors carried on their duties as the majority party in the upper house, electing their own deputy leader, their representatives on PLP committees, and their own chairman of committees. They did not see their roles as mere ciphers who voted when and as required, but sought copies of bills before they were introduced into the Council so that they could prepare themselves to speak on the merits. Still they were unpaid labourers and in the last recorded minute of their separate caucus meeting, on 28 September 1921, they appointed their chairman and secretary as a deputation to interview the premier again about means of defraying the attendance expenses of members of the Council.

When Sir Matthew Nathan opened the Queensland parliament for its new session in August 1921, he made no reference to the Legislative Council apart from listing its abolition among the bills to be introduced. The government's small majority had been further eroded by the defection of J.C. Peterson to the Country party. By contrast to the tense position in the Legislative Assembly, the Council had become quiet. Government bills passed easily; few non-government members bothered to attend and the problem was to form and hold quorums under the standing order that required an absolute majority of members to be present. Theodore was non-committal when asked about his intentions, and it was rather the Country party section of the opposition which seemed to display more interest in abolition. Seeing themselves as the next government when Labor was inevitably defeated at the following election, Country party members did not look forward to a Labor-dominated upper house obstructing repeal of important Labor legislation of the previous six years nor to the problem of convincing the new governor that he should nominate more non-Labor members to the Council which would take its size up to around seventy. During the

Address-in-Reply debate early in September, W.J. Vowles, leader of the Country party and opposition, taunted Theodore about his unwillingness to proceed with abolition, and when the Council estimates came before the Assembly, Vowles moved their reduction by a formal £1. The Country party, it developed, would prefer an elected upper house chosen on a restricted franchise — like Victoria's — and saw abolition as a first step to its introduction. The Council estimates passed, but Theodore set the Justice Department to investigating whether the royal assent would be granted to such a measure.

A 1916 despatch from Walter Long, then colonial secretary to Goold-Adams, that the alteration of the Queensland constitution by the abolition of the Council was "*prima facie* . . . one entirely for local decision"; the Privy Council decision in the McCawley case which laid down that the Queensland legislature was master of its own constitutional fate; and Theodore's own discussion with Colonial Office authorities in London in 1920 all indicated the likely absence of British government restraints.[16]

Theodore, who was to attend the Premiers' Conference in November, had decided that the parliamentary session would end on Friday, 21 October, after the Supply Bill and certain other pieces of legislation had been passed. At what was expected to be the last caucus meeting for the year on 12 October, there was no mention of any bill to abolish the Legislative Council and the matter seemed to have been dropped for another session. However by Friday, 14 October, Theodore had been advised that there should be no problem with royal assent to an abolition bill and judged it a good time to have done with the Council quickly. With parliament adjourned and Christmas approaching, the matter could well be expected to have been forgotten by the New Year and there would be a further eighteen months before the next election. Caucus was told that the abolition bill would be reintroduced on the following Monday — without any complementary Initiative and Referendum Bill which retained some support at the party's grass roots, but left Theodore and McCormack quite unenthusiastic.

Theodore's opponents were already divided. The Country

party wanted the Council abolished and replaced, the Nationalists wanted it retained, appreciating the difficulty of reconstituting any Legislative Council once the present body disappeared. They favoured making the existing Council elective, returning three members from each federal division, with adult franchise. Both opposition proposals were put forward as amendments to Theodore's initial motion to introduce his bill; the Country party's failed forty to twenty-one, the Nationalists' forty-one to fifteen, as in each case the other opposition party crossed the floor to vote with the government. The passage of the first reading of the Bill, fifty-two to fourteen, indicated that Labor's swamping of the Council had rendered it useless in the eyes of its own supporters and removed much of the earlier resolve to retain the Council as a nominated body.

Theodore's second reading speech was masterful. His principal argument was for a unicameral legislature and against the need for an upper house of any kind. One that duplicated the composition of the Legislative Assembly would be superfluous; one that obstructed a properly elected Assembly with a clear mandate from the people would be completely against parliamentary democracy: "What we want in a democratic community is a system which will give a ready, free and direct expression of the will of the people. That can only be got by having frequent appeals to the people, the appeals not less frequent than once in three years at most."[17] The Country party indicated that it would not support any memorial that the royal assent be withheld, and Theodore indicated that he was confident that assent would be given. A Nationalist amendment to put the question to a referendum once more failed thirty-five to thirty-four. The second reading was carried thirty-nine to thirty, and the second clause that specifically abolished the Council, by fifty-one to fifteen. The clause providing the revisory committee of members of the Legislative Assembly was deleted when Theodore expressed his own lack of commitment to it. The third reading was carried forty-six to seventeen. Clearly, in a chamber where the government had a majority of only two, these votes indicated that there was no longer a large or determined minority supporting retention of the Council.

In the upper house itself a lack-lustre debate was varied only by the stand of one Labor member, Gerald Page-Hanify, a long-time advocate of the initiative and referendum, who objected to the government's "unseemly haste" in bringing down the abolition bill and the absence of the Initiative and Referendum Bill. Only thirty-nine members of Council attended the debate where the second reading was carried twenty-eight to ten. At 8.37 p.m. on Thursday, 27 October 1921, the Legislative Council of Queensland adjourned for the last time. Under the 1907 Australian States Constitution Act, the Constitution Act Amendment Act was reserved for royal assent. Non-Labor MLCs presented a memorial to the governor, and the Constitution Defence Committee which had been formed in 1917, with Robert Philp as its chairman, sent a petition. Nathan sought the premier's advice on each, and sent all documents forward to London with the single comment: "Generally, I am unable to say that there is evidence of any strong or widespread feeling in the country against this assent being given". The secretary of state for the Colonies agreed with Theodore's advice that the matter was one for Queensland concern only and recommended that the King assent.[18] The Act was proclaimed on 23 March 1922, and the most important single constitutional reform in Queensland history had been accomplished. The Legislative Council was abolished.

Had the anti-Labor parties won the 1923 election, a new Legislative Council might have been introduced. An increase in the Labor vote and divisions among and within the anti-Labor parties gave Theodore an easy win. The restoration of the Council remained in the election platforms of the anti-Labor parties throughout the 1920s, but when A.E. Moore became Country party premier in 1929, the problems of governing in the Depression and indecision about how to tackle the upper house question prevented any decision being taken. His only action was to remove railway passes and authority to use the parliamentary library from MLCs appointed during the Ryan and Theodore governments. The Labor party prepared a campaign committee against any resurrection of the Council, but the victory of William Forgan Smith in 1932 removed the threat. In 1934,

Forgan Smith secured a further Constitution Act Amendment Act which provided that the Legislative Council could not be re-introduced without the electors' approval at a referendum, and since then there have been no serious suggestions to restore the Council. Railway passes and library privileges were restored to the unpaid heroes of the suicide squad whose part in the abolition of the Council had broken the dominance of wealth and property over the Queensland parliament.

NOTES

1. For the debate and related correspondence, see *QPD* XLVII, (10 November 1885): 236-55; *QPD* XLVII, (17 November 1885): 157-63, 1575-78; and C.A. Bernays, *Queensland Politics During Sixty Years, 1859-1919* (Brisbane: Government Printer, 1919), pp. 248-54.
2. See Appendix A in *Prelude to Power, The Rise of the Labour Party in Queensland, 1885-1915*, eds., D.J. Murphy, R.B. Joyce and Colin A. Hughes (Brisbane: Jacaranda Press, 1970).
3. Parliamentary Labor Party, minutes (21 October 1915).
4. *QPD* CXXII (17 November 1915): 2163-71.
5. Ibid. (8 December 1915): 2747-49.
6. *QPD*, CXXIII (1 September 1916): 278-82.
7. Central Political Executive minutes (12, 15, 28 March 1917).
8. *Taylor and Others* v *Attorney General of Queensland and Others*, 1917, StRQ 208, 23 CLR 457. Lengthy reports of the arguments appeared in the *Brisbane Courier* and *Daily Standard*.
9. Goold-Adams to secretary of state for colonies, Governor's Outward Despatches and Telegrams VIII (12 October 1917), GOV/57, QSA.
10. *Brisbane Courier*, 12, 13, 15 March 1918.
11. *QPD* CXXXI (26 September 1918): 2640.
12. *Daily Standard*, 18 February 1920.
13. Ibid., 19 February 1920.
14. *Official Record of the Tenth Labor-in-Politics Convention* (Brisbane, 1920), p. 62.
15. Ibid., p. 63.
16. Long to Goold-Adams (18 December 1916), GOV/A84, QSA; *McCawley* v *The King and Others*, 28 CLR 106; interview with Sir William Webb.
17. *QPD* CXXXVIII (24 October 1921): 1729-44.
18. For these documents see *QPP* I (1922) :21-66.

5 Greater Brisbane and Local Government

J.R. Laverty

Despite the obvious connection between living conditions and the amenities and services provided by local governing bodies, the Labor party's interest did not begin to focus on local government until about 1910. Concern with state and national politics and concentration on policies designed to improve working conditions and raise living standards diverted attention from matters of purely local concern. Moreover, the plural, ratepayer franchise for local elections did not offer the party much hope of success on that level of government, so it is understandable that Labor should seek office first in national and state parliaments where electoral laws could be changed in its favour. Such interest as was shown in local government during the early years was, for the most part, confined to the franchise. Other local government questions were left for Labor organizations on the spot to determine.[1]

However, interest in local government began to grow. The 1910 Convention adopted a series of proposals as the basis for a local government platform, the 1913 Convention instructed the Central Political Executive (CPE) to draw up a municipal platform modelled on the 1910 proposals, and the 1916 Convention appointed a committee whose report was accepted as the party's platform for the 1917 municipal elections and subsequently inserted into the Rules and Constitution.[2] The 1910 proposals had been concerned with the payment of aldermen and councillors, the rating of unimproved land values only, the execution of municipal works by day labour, good working conditions for municipal employees, municipal ownership of local facilities and utilities, and improvement of local amenities and services. Although a motion calling for a municipal convention to formulate a "Labor Municipal programme" was narrowly defeated, the 1923 Convention approved a local government section of the state platform which followed the ideas of 1910:

1. Adult franchise for local elections.
2. No disfranchisement for arrears of rates.
3. Election of mayors and chairmen of shires by direct vote of electors.
4. Allowance of members for lost time in serving on local government bodies.
5. No alienation of public land by local authorities.
6. Legislation to unify the metropolitan area into a Greater Brisbane under the jurisdiction of a single municipal council.
7. Municipal ownership of tramways, wharves, electric lights, abattoirs and other public utilities.[3]

Resolutions were passed providing for the use of state rolls in local government elections and for compulsory voting in all municipal and water and sewerage board elections. Thus the main principles of Labor's local government platform were established by 1923 after which planks added were largely concerned with the implementation of principles already laid down.

Labor influence on Queensland governments prior to 1915 had already shaped local government. The coalition led by Morgan and Kidston had set up a public fish market in 1915 under the control of the Metropolitan Fish Marketing Board, consisting of members elected by the local authorities in the area. Responsibility for Brisbane's water and sewerage undertaking was transferred in 1909, by the Kidston government, to the Metropolitan Water and Sewerage Board elected by ratepayers exercising a single vote; in 1915 the board was authorized to open, to acquire and operate coal mines to meet its own requirements. Although gas supply was not municipalized, standards of heating, power, purity and pressure were prescribed in 1916, and gas examiners appointed to police them, while the price of gas was placed under control of a gas referee. The conservative Denham government's

Tramway Act 1913 had provided for the compulsory purchase of the entire undertaking in 1920, but once in opposition the anti-Labor majority in the Legislative Council blocked action until the Council had been swamped. The Brisbane Tramway Trust Act 1922 created a trust which acquired and operated the tramways until they were transferred to the Greater Brisbane Council. The desirability of bringing electricity supply under public control was also recognized, even though its full potential in the provision of lighting and power had not been clearly demonstrated and franchise conditions were not propitious for public acquisition. The Local Authorities Acts Amendment Act 1917 empowered local authorities to establish electric light systems in their areas without having to purchase those of existing companies, and the Labor government refused to grant the City Electric Light Company franchises to extend supply to suburban areas. Eventually the local authorities were persuaded to establish the Metropolitan Electricity Board in 1922 to purchase power in bulk from the City Electric Light Company, and distribute it in metropolitan areas outside the cities of Brisbane and South Brisbane. During the 1923 Convention the appointment of a board to organize electrical undertakings throughout the state was made plank 9 of the platform.

As already suggested, the drive of the Parliamentary Labor Party (PLP) for municipal reform focused on municipal elections, especially on the objectives of one-adult-one-vote, direct election of mayors and chairmen, and triennial elections, reforms resisted by the conservative majority in the Legislative Council until it was swamped in 1920. However, there were broader interests as well. Welfare objectives were sought by authorization of the remission of rates payable by disabled soldiers, widows, invalids and other needy citizens. Legislation and regulations fixed minimum levels of competency for clerks and engineers, whilst wages and working conditions for other local authority employees were increasingly determined through the industrial tribunals. Some quite enlightened town planning provisions were enacted in

1923 and, as part of the government's public health policy, attention was given to abuses associated with unduly high house densities, overcrowding and erection of houses on low-lying, unhealthy allotments in 1922. Labor politicians appear to have been particularly concerned about the prevalence of venereal disease, and soon after coming to power the Ryan government amended the Health Acts to deal more effectively with the problem. The system under which the public hospitals operated was changed in 1923. Previously, public hospitals had been supported by subscriptions and government grants, and were operated by boards representing subscribers and the state government. However, local authorities were responsible under the Health Acts for the treatment of infectious diseases and often paid public hospitals on a *per diem* basis to provide such treatment. The Hospitals Acts Amendment Act 1923 constituted the Brisbane and South Coast Hospitals Board to assume responsibility for providing a public hospital service for an area stretching from Brisbane to the New South Wales border. Local authorities were required to elect three representatives to the board and pay 40 per cent of any difference between expenditure and revenue.

In his Barcaldine speech, T.J. Ryan had pledged that the party would "undertake to cope with the problem of bad roads", but the problem was not tackled at once. Concern over road conditions led the 1918 Convention to resolve that "the State take over construction and maintenance of all main roads, stock routes and reserves in the State".[4] After a wide-ranging investigation of the practices followed in other states and countries, the Main Roads Act 1920 was passed providing for the co-operative development of a main roads system by local authorities and the state government under the general direction of a Main Roads Board of expert engineers.

Labor's interest in a Greater Brisbane came only after the idea had been about for some time.[5] Greater cities became an election issue in 1915 with both parties advocating reform. Ryan committed the Labor party in his Barcaldine speech: "In order the more thoroughly to permit of the control of public utilities, a scheme will be considered (subject to the approval of the places concerned) for the amalgamation of the municipal and town councils in Brisbane, Toowoomba, Rockhampton, Townsville and other cities."[6] In the event, the Ryan government "greaterized" the cities of Ipswich, Charters Towers, Maryborough, Toowoomba, Bundaberg, Townsville and Rockhampton by administrative action with scant reference to the councils and residents of the local authorities concerned. Orders-in-Council were issued under the Local Authorities Acts after giving three months' notice of the action it was proposed to take. However, it was necessary to enact special legislation before the Greater City of Brisbane could be created. Obvious advantages — economy and efficiency, the wider use of experts, increased borrowing potential, greater public interest and involvement in city government and the attraction of aldermen of first rate ability — made overt opposition to the creation of a Greater Brisbane difficult. But critics attacked the size of its area, the alleged lack of community of interest due to the mixing of urban and rural areas, the opportunities inherent in the scheme for the high value central city to be exploited in the interests of suburban development, the coercive nature of the legislation, and the small number of aldermen proposed to perform the work envisaged.[7]

The area defined by the City of Brisbane Act 1924 was 375 square miles, incorporating two cities, six towns, ten shires and portions of two other shires. In the government's view there was definite community of interest throughout the area, which centred on the city. In any case, the Greater Brisbane Council could only take over the undertakings of *ad hoc* authorities and joint local authorities — water supply and sewerage, electricity distribution, tramways, ferries, boundary bridges and the Victoria Bridge — if the defined area were adopted. Moreover, the larger area was essential to effective public health administration, to the proper supervision of milk and meat suppliers, and to the development of a satisfactory storm water drainage system, and was vital to effective town planning. There would be a council of twenty aldermen elected every three years under adult franchise for single electoral wards corresponding to the state electoral districts, and a mayor elected under the same franchise by the city as a whole. The council was granted both "general" and "express" powers which were subject only to the approval of the governor-in-council and the veto of parliament, but could not be repugnant to the provisions of other statutes. Thus the new council would have the greatest freedom to govern the city consonant with the sovereignty, and needs, of the state.

Labor's drive to rationalize and reform local government continued after 1925. A Royal Commission on Local Authority Boundaries was set up in 1927 which advocated larger authorities to meet changing circumstances, such as the development of motor transport. It recommended that two cities and fifteen towns be abolished and amalgamated with the adjoining shires and that the number of shires should be reduced from 124 to seventy-four, and proposed reforms in administrative arrangements.[8] Strong opposition from local government and conservative politicians, the onset of the Depression, and the election of the unsympathetic Moore government prevented dispassionate consideration of these recommendations for several years, and even after Labor returned to power in 1932 the primacy of measures to promote economic recovery and to reduce unemployment diverted attention from local government matters. It was not until 1948 that the Labor government implemented a limited number of the boundary changes recommended by the royal commission: twelve local authorities in the south coast region were merged into four, and two similar adjustments were made to boundaries in the West Moreton and Darling Downs regions.[9]

The government moved more expeditiously on some of the other recommendations of the royal commission. Financial divisions within local authorities were abolished in 1932, although divisons could be established for electoral purposes. During the consolidation of local government legislation in 1935, the opportunity was taken to grant all local authorities broad powers similar to those of the City of Brisbane. Uniform valuations were secured under the Valuation of Land Act 1944 which set up the Valuer-General's Department to undertake land valuations on a state-wide basis. In the 1930s and 1940s electoral matters had a somewhat convoluted history. In 1929, the Moore government replaced the adult franchise with an occupier franchise and plural voting where property was held in more than one ward or division, and popular election of mayor or chairman by an exhaustive ballot of fellow aldermen or councillors. When Labor was returned to power in 1932, adult franchise and direct election were restored. Direct election was unsuccessfully challenged at the Labor-in-Politics Conventions in 1947 and 1953 by party members involved in the Brisbane City Council on the grounds that the costs of standing made it difficult to find suitable candidates and gave too much kudos to the candidate, but the advantages of the method in rural local authorities ensured its retention.[10]

Commissions also reported on water supply and flood control, public hospitals, electricity, and transport. The state government intruded into the sphere of municipal government by undertaking the construction of the Stanley River Dam for water supply and flood control and the Story Bridge. The royal commission which inquired into the public hospital system in 1930 produced a comprehensive report on the operation and financing of the state's hospital system, and financial relief for local authorities came only in 1943 when their contributions were reduced and in 1944 when the commonwealth government began to subsidize hospitals.

Electricity supply proved a difficult problem for while party policy was clear enough — public ownership and control by commissioners — electric light companies had supply franchises which could only be terminated by costly resumptions.Rather than pay a huge price to the City Electric Light Company, the Brisbane City Council had established its own powerhouse and distribution system. It soon became evident that some electric light companies were using their monopolistic position to earn high dividends and to make unreasonably large appropriations to reserve funds instead of passing on the benefits of reduced production costs to consumers. After enacting legislation to remove the grossest forms of exploitation in 1933-34, in 1937 the government acted on the recommendations of a royal commission to establish the State Electricity Commission which subsequently negotiated an agreement with the City Electricity Light Company to develop an integrated electricity supply system for South Eastern Queensland outside the City of Brisbane which was supplied by the Brisbane City Council. The commission's co-ordinating activities were extended to the remainder of Queensland in 1938, and in 1945 it was given wider powers to co-ordinate, control and plan the development of a statewide electricity supply system. The scheme was to be based on regional electricity authorities consisting of the local authorities in the area, and one representative of the commission. The State Electricity Commission was placed under the control of a single commissioner in 1947.

The numerous pieces of legislation dealing with main roads, heavy vehicles and transport co-ordination indicate the desire of Labor governments to promote closer settlement and economic development through the construction of a state-wide network of main roads to supplement railway transport, an objective which often required the raising of funds in urban areas for expenditure on country roads. Over the years the financial contributions of local authorities to main and developmental road construction and maintenance were reduced as revenue from motor transport rose and the commonwealth government increasingly subsidized road construction from fuel excises. Co-ordination of transport was of particular concern, primarily because of an over-riding desire to protect the state railways against competition from private enterprise road transport. At first this was achieved through a judicious programme of main road construction and the taxation of road transport, but after 1931 a more effective system of licensing was developed. The consolidating Transport Act 1938 implemented a number of the recommendations of the Royal Commission on Transport, including creation of a State Transport Commission to co-ordinate transport and ensure adequate provision for the public. However, when the Queensland Harbours Trust was created in 1952, it was not given power to co-ordinate port services as the royal commission had recommended but only to control and develop ports not administered by local Harbour Boards. Thus the local authorities retained a good deal of control over ports through their representatives on the Harbour Boards, although the Port of Brisbane continued under the jurisdiction of a government department.

Although traffic control was obviously a local function, experience had shown before the turn of the century that local authorities were ill-fitted to exercise it and that police were more effective in controlling traffic in urban areas. The responsibility for the regulation of traffic was therefore vested in the hands of local authorities elsewhere. For a time Labor governments flirted with the idea of transferring traffic control in Brisbane to the city council,[11] but eventually the conflicting responsibilities and jurisdictions created by legislation dealing with local government, traffic, police, main roads and transport led to the enactment of consolidating traffic legislation in 1949 which ensured uniform regulations, penalties and administration. Traffic control was taken out of the hands of local authorities and other bodies and vested in the police commissioner.

Public health was, as we have seen, always a matter of deep concern to the Labor party. When Labor came to power the main features of the system were already established with local government responsible for public health under the stringent control of the commissioner of public health.Some of the new areas of health care accepted by Labor governments became the responsibility of the state Health Department, but for many others the traditional sharing of activities with local authorities continued. However, in the case of meat and milk supply, especially in Brisbane, local responsibility was transferred to statutory authorities. The Moore government set up the Queensland Meat Industry Board to establish and operate an abattoir in Brisbane. Its success led the Labor government in 1949 to extend its jurisdiction to the whole state, but the rights of local authorities outside Brisbane to establish local abattoirs were preserved. In 1938 a milk board was established to regulate and stabilize milk supply in the metropolitan area in the interests of both producers and consumers, and its success induced the government to extend its operation to the whole state in 1952. Perhaps the most remarkable aspect of these incursions of the central government into local affairs is the failure to ensure adequate representation of either consumers or local authorities on the statutory authorities.

Labor governments relied heavily on local authorities in their schemes to reduce unemployment. The Brisbane City Council, for example, provided work for over nine thousand four hundred men under the scheme in force during 1953. Despite some wasteful expenditure, the contribution of local authorities to the government's programme of unemployment relief was quite substantial. Moreover, by 1938 many former relief workers, especially in Brisbane, had been given full-time employment at award rates and conditions on sewerage and other works subsidized by the state government. Although at the 1938 Convention some delegates objected to this as Labor policy on the grounds that it shifted responsibility for the unemployed from the state government to local authorities, the State Development and Public Works Organisation Act, 1938, empowered the government, on the advice of the coordinator-general, to compel local authorities to carry out works in the interests of increased, stable employment and general state development. Instead of the wider and more independent powers promised local government by the secretary for health and home affairs in 1936, there was a prospect that local authorities might become agents of central government in the implementation of its plans for national development; fortunately the legislative powers were seldom exercised.

In spite of its local government reforms the Labor party had little success in local authority elections. During its early years, isolated members of the party were elected aldermen or councillors for areas with predominantly working class residents, but the plural, ratepayer franchise militated against any concerted attempt to win control of local authorities. Nevertheless, procedures for selecting Labor candidates were evolved and organizations established to conduct local government election campaigns, especially within the metropolitan area. These initiatives were rewarded in Water and Sewerage Board elections, largely because of the adult franchise, but few Labor men secured the support needed to win seats on the councils of local authorities. The belief that the extension of the adult franchise to local government elections would enable the party to win control of many local authorities was badly shaken by the results of the elections for metropolitan local authorities in 1921. Between 1915 and 1957 the Labor party's success in local government elections was less than inspiring.

In the first place, relatively few Labor candidates were ever endorsed, sometimes only a few dozen, never more than a hundred when there were close to one thousand local government councillors to be elected. Labor teams could win control of councils at Ipswich, Maryborough, Rockhampton, Mackay, Townsville and Cairns, cities which invariably returned Labor MLAs, and occasionally carried shires in sugar and grazing areas. But given the very limited financial resources of local government, tied as they were to politically-sensitive rating levels, and the conservatism of the electorate on local issues, the impact of Labor councils when they existed was normally confined to the bread-and-butter issues of day labour and wage rates for council public works. The enthusiasm for municipal socialism displayed for a time in Townsville was an exception, and on the rare occasion when a local authority undertook some novel responsibility it was in pragmatic response to a local need that could not otherwise be met. Quite possibly the multiplicity of elections in which party workers gave priority to winning power in Brisbane and Canberra helped keep Labor out of local government, except for Brisbane and some of the provincial cities, but even when the party was entrenched in office at both state and federal levels in the 1940s there was no demand for a systematic move into the third tier of government. Certainly there was never a Queensland tradition of a Labor style in local government comparable to the Tammany machines of inner Sydney and Melbourne.

Because of the size and responsibilities of the Brisbane City Council, the Queensland Central Executive (QCE) was more directly involved in organizing elections and determining policy. It had general responsibility for the endorsement of local authority candidates and the hearing of appeals on these matters, but after Greater Brisbane was created the QCE was largely responsible for developing the platform for the first city elections and subsequently "election manifestos" drawn up by sitting aldermen and the Lord Mayoral candidate had to have its approval. The QCE also arbitrated in disputes between ALP aldermen. Caucus control of municipal Labor parties and membership of progress associations proved to be troublesome problems. Municipal parties were expected to form "properly constituted caucuses", but the QCE concluded that members could only be bound by majority decisions on questions covered by the party's platform; although it believed that loyalty to caucus decisions was preferable, members were given the right to appeal against them.[12] It was not until 1957 that a definitive policy was laid down by the QCE covering membership of local progress associations: it was a matter of individual choice provided the association's constitution was not opposed to Labor platform and policy and provided the association did not endorse candidates who opposed Labor candidates.[13]

The Labor party entered the first Greater Brisbane elections with a good deal of enthusiasm, and more than sixty candidates nominated for the twenty aldermanic seats. A Greater Brisbane conference of branches and affiliated unions drew up policy proposals from which the QCE drafted a Greater Brisbane municipal platform. The manifesto placed considerable stress on the employment of union labour and the observance of union working conditions, and provided for the representation of employees on all bodies controlled by the council and for the setting up of an appeal board for all employees.[14] There were a great many similarities between the election policies of Labor and those of its United party opponents. The main differences were the stress Labor placed on conditions of employment, its concern to establish safeguards against excessive profits by contractors, and its proposed experiments in "municipal socialism" for all "communal" undertakings, including omnibus services, and municipal ownership and control of bread, meat, and milk supply, laundries, baths and washhouses, public abattoirs, and a crematorium. Even though Labor condemned the United party as the creature of big business and argued that as the initiator of Greater Brisbane it deserved to be given the opportunity of establishing the new authority in the city, it was soundly defeated. W.A. Jolly won the mayoralty and his supporters won fourteen of the twenty wards.

The Jolly administration's vigorous and imaginative programme of city development did nothing to alienate electoral support and Labor aldermen had few opportunities to make political capital out of its mistakes. The electorate's decision in 1928 was unequivocal. Jolly won a personal majority in seventeen wards and his supporters carried twelve wards, whilst two had not secured re-endorsement were returned as Independents; Labor could only retain its six seats.

Labor had been more successful in elections for the Metropolitan Water Supply and Sewerage Board, winning majorities on each occasion, but the party's record there was not good. There had been repeated conflicts between the board and its expert engineers and embarrassing examples of patronage in employment, unnecessary concessions to unions were alleged, and there was an obvious tendency to court electoral popularity at the expense of efficiency and economy. Eventually the government took the easy way out by transferring the undertaking to the Brisbane City Council, thereby relieving itself of any further embarrassment.

Following the McCormack government's defeat in 1929, the Moore government moved quickly to change radically the system of municipal government in Brisbane. There had been widespread dissatisfaction with the operation of the city council for some time, not least on the part of Lord Mayor Jolly himself, and various forms of "cabinet" or "city manager" government had been proposed.[15] The Moore government's solution was to restore a plural, ratepayer suffrage, provide for the election of the Lord Mayor by his fellow aldermen, and require the creation of a responsible, executive committee, or inner cabinet, to control the administration. In the ensuing controversy the two-party system was destroyed through the fragmentation of the non-Labor bloc into the Nationalist, Civic Reform League and Progress parties. It is not surprising, therefore, that no party secured a majority at the 1931 municipal election, or that a compromise executive was elected which soon came into conflict with the remainder of the council over its unpopular economic and retrenchment policies. The lord mayor, J.W. Greene, found great difficulty in grappling with the serious financial problems of the council which was saved from bankruptcy only by the timely intervention of the state government. Eventually the municipal budget was balanced, but only at the cost of severe retrenchments and economies which emasculated city developmental programmes. Government unemployment relief funds provided the council with finance or some "improvement" works, but the state government began to look elsewhere, to the Bureau of Industry and private industry, for the construction of major projects such as the Stanley River Dam, the Story Bridge and the Indooroopilly Bridge.

The new system of city administration had been operating for only a year when the Moore government was swept from power. The amendments to Labor's Greater Brisbane scheme were quickly reversed, although the council itself was left with the option of retaining the executive or returning to the committee system. In the 1934 municipal elections, the voters vented their disapproval of Depression-induced policies on Greene and his non-Labor supporters, now united as the Nationalist Citizens' party. Labor's mayoral candidate, A.J. Jones, promised a vigorous programme of public works to absorb unemployed at award rates, of sewerage development and the improvement of civic amenities neglected by Greene — all this to be accomplished without any increase in rates. Labor won fourteen seats and Jones became lord mayor.

The committee system was restored and refined. A programme of development in sewerage, water supply, transport, electricity and health was undertaken, largely financed by loans. Work on the preparation of a town plan revived, and the system of arterial roads developed during Jolly's administration was extended and many suburban streets were upgraded, but the emphasis of development was on sewerage works. In 1937, Jones was returned with a relatively small majority, and Labor won twelve of the twenty seats, but its promise to reduce the general rate, to lower electricity tariffs and passenger fares and to undertake a municipal housing scheme were, to say the least, injudicious.

Unfortunately, the Jones administration chose to finance its "work and wages, progress and prosperity" programme through loan expenditure, government subsidies and the profits of the tramways and electricity undertakings, rather than through increased rates. It became increasingly clear that it was resorting to improper accounting methods and was guilty of patronage. The Labor government became concerned at the inefficiency, extravagance and malpractices of the Labor council, and worried that its own public image would be tarnished by the ineptitude and corruption of its counterpart. In 1936, amending legislation had laid down the method of budgeting the council was to employ and provided for the annual auditing of city accounts by the auditor-general. In an effort to control the exercise of patronage, Jones himself issued a minute confining the engagement of staff to departmental heads and the town clerk, while the Labor party took the rather drastic step of refusing to re-endorse half of the sitting aldermen, including the chairmen of five committees, for the 1936 elections. After abortive attempts to reform the administration, the mayor eventually sought government assistance to re-organize the council's activities in 1937. The report, prepared by John McCracken and E.H. George after a searching inquiry, was an indictment of the Jones administration. It revealed a lack of co-ordination between departments, serious understaffing, inadequate supervision and planning, neglect of some important responsibilities, inefficiency, wastage of resources and some patronage.[16]

Meanwhile, the 1937 auditor-general's report was highly critical of the way in which the profits of the trading undertakings were being used to avoid rate increases instead of being held in reserve to meet the future costs of replacements, and of accounting methods which permitted a true deficit of £66,000 to be converted into a surplus of £120,000 by not charging depreciation and renewals against the city fund. The poor financial and administrative management and improper accounting practices of the Jones administration eventually exacted their toll. When the state government withdrew both the subsidies on municipal works and relief labour in 1938, the council was forced not only to curtial its sewerage programme, but also to raise the rate by one penny in the pound. The outbreak of war in 1939 adversely affected the loan market, thereby causing the council acute financial embarrassment. The council, in an election year, was forced to re-frame its budget, under the supervision of the auditor-general, to provide for a 40 per cent increase in the rate and to have it validated by special legislation.

Not surprisingly, Jones and his team were soundly defeated in the 1940 elections by the Citizens' Municipal Organisation (CMO), led by J.B. Chandler. Labor lost the mayoralty and the number of Labor aldermen was reduced from eleven to seven. The state government had already taken steps to completely reorganize the city administration. It chose R.H. Robinson, assistant under-secretary of health and home affairs, to undertake this task through secondment to the council. Robinson's re-organization sought to achieve the separation of policy formulation from the administrative functions of the council by reducing the number of committees from seven to four; creating an executive committee consisting of the mayor and the chairmen of these four committees; setting up the Registration and Administrative Boards; elevating the town clerk to the position of town clerk and city administrator, that is co-ordinating officer of the council; instituting specific departments with defined duties under the control of a permanent head; laying down codes for the recruitment, promotion and discipline of municipal officers and defining their powers and duties. Each of the departments was reorganized and the relations between them regulated. The Metropolitan Works Board, consisting of a chairman and selected city and state engineers, was established to "manage and control" the city works programme and to encourage closer co-operation at the executive level between the two spheres of government. Budget procedures to be followed by the council were clearly set out. Finally the council was required to publish annual reports and statistics to keep the public informed of its activities.[17]

Thoroughly discredited, not only by its own ineptitude, maladministration and corruption, but also by the sweeping reforms of the city administrative system the Labor government saw fit to implement, the Labor municipal party was to spend a long frustrating period in the political wilderness. It was unable to dislodge the well-disciplined, forward-looking CMO administration dominated by the charismatic J.B. Chandler. For its first two terms that administration was affected by wartime difficulties. Developmental projects had to be wound down and the council concentrated on maintaining existing services in the face of a rapidly growing community. Eventually Chandler's poor record with sewerage and water supply, together with his persistence with plans to beautify the river banks, undermined his popularity so that Labor, led by Frank Roberts, was able to win the 1952 election by carrying seventeen of the twenty-four wards.

In the event, the Roberts administration proved unable to fulfil its promise of an ample water supply, to completely sewer Brisbane and avoid high rates. The credit squeeze of the early 1950s had radically altered the financial situation so that, while inflation was brought under control and shortages of manpower and materials eased, there was a dearth of loan funds. The heavy demand for electricity forced the council to devote the greater part of its resources to the construction of the Tennyson power house. Roberts was forced to raise, rather than reduce, the rates and found, as Chandler had done in the preceding period of high inflation, that the financial resources of the council were totally inadequate for the diverse responsibilities it was expected to carry out.

These problems in themselves were sufficient to reduce electoral support for the Municipal Labor party, but its dispute with the QCE over aldermanic salaries destroyed its prospects completely. The evidence suggests that Labor aldermen were made the scapegoats in an acrimonious dispute between the QCE and the PLP over substantial increases in salaries and allowances the latter had "voted themselves" despite strong opposition from the QCE and party branches and affiliated unions. When the QCE directed the Municipal Labor party to rescind the resolution approving increased salaries for aldermen, Roberts resigned from the party. The vice-mayor, Alderman C.J. Bennett, was subsequently elected leader of the Municipal Labor party. Roberts had obviously frustrated attempts to expel him from the party by resigning, but the QCE took steps to ensure that he could not rejoin without its approval. Although he had the support of a number of metropolitan branches and would have made a strong candidate, the "inner executive" of the QCE refused to let him rejoin, whereupon he decided to stand as an Independent mayoral candidate destroying any chance Labor might have had of winning the 1955 elections.

Indeed, the party had considerable difficulty in finding a suitable candidate before it settled on M.G. Lyons. The choice was unfortunate in that he was a prominent member of the Industrial Group movement and therefore unable to command the support of a growing number of party members. He complained bitterly at the 1956 Convention of the lack of support, especially from some "prominent industrial unionists", and the treasurer, E.H. Walsh, told delegates that opposition to Lyons' candidature had led disgruntled members of party branches to leave his name off the how-to-vote cards of some endorsed candidates. The CMO candidate, T.R. Groom, defeated his two "Labor" opponents easily, and the CMO won fourteen of the twenty-four wards. Roberts attracted more votes than the official Labor candidate, Lyons.

Although concern with broader state and national issues delayed the formulation of the Labor party's policy on local government, the main planks of that policy had been spelt out by

1923. The emphasis was placed on making local government more responsive and more effective. The adult, one-man-one-vote franchise made it more responsible to the people and combined with triennial elections provided Labor with the opportunity to contest local government elections in a systematic way. The election of the mayor or chairman by the electors voting as a single electorate strengthened the trend towards policies which benefited the whole local authority area, and reduced opportunities for the pursuit of parochialism and self-interest in the provision of works and services. Queensland had a long strong-chairman tradition in local government, and under Labor his executive position was legally recognized. Election at large greatly enhanced his authority, which was an important development, especially in rural areas where the geographical dispersion of councillors made the exercise of executive authority essential to the effective operation of local government.

The Labor government's most spectacular reform of the local government structure was undoubtedly the creation of Greater Brisbane. It succeeded where other state governments failed, probably because there was general agreement that an enlargement of the city was essential, and because the opponents of its scheme were of another political persuasion. Labor drew a major part of its support from non-metropolitan electorates and did not, therefore, have to consider the electoral consequences of its actions closely. The population of the metropolitan area had not reached a size which would make the enlarged city council appear as a competitor of the state government. Moreover, a greater city seemed the logical method of achieving the party objective of municipal ownership of public utilities and Labor, with some justification, expected to win control of the new council. In the final analysis Labor was a reforming government and Greater Brisbane was clearly part of the innovative programme it had progressively implemented.

However, the ideal of self-reliant, effective local authorities proved difficult, if not impossible, to achieve. Labor governments were unable, or unwilling, to provide the revenues which would make them self-reliant. More importantly, as the needs of the community became more extensive and complex, it was found that local authorities could not effectively provide the more sophisticated facilities and services on a state-wide basis. Attempts were made, sometimes successfully, to integrate local authorities into the wider administrative systems as they developed, but in many cases the ideal of local government was sacrificed to efficiency and uniformity. Even the statutory authorities themselves became more authoritarian as boards and commissions were replaced by sole commissioners. In any case, the Labor party's initiative and innovative drive were exhausted by the end of the 1930s and in the post-World War II period the dead hand of bureaucracy lay heavy on government.

NOTES

1. *Official Record of the Fifth Labor-in-Politics Convention* (Rockhampton, 1907), p. 63.
2. *Sixth Convention* (Townsville, 1910), p. 16; *Seventh Convention* (Brisbane, 1913), p. 16; *Eighth Convention* (Rockhampton, 1916), pp. 6-7.
3. *Eleventh Convention* (Emu Park, 1923), p. 64.
4. *Ninth Convention* (Brisbane, 1918), p. 37.
5. See *Brisbane Courier*, 1 August 1900; 22 September 1900; 2 February 1901.
6. *Worker*, 29 March 1915.
7. See G. Greenwood, and J. Laverty, *Brisbane, 1859-1959: A History of Local Government* (Brisbane: Brisbane City Council, 1959), chap. 10.
8. Report of the Royal Commission on Local Authorities Boundaries, 1928, *QPP* II (1928) :1209-38.
9. For detail see K. Window, "Local Government Reform: A Case Study of the Restructuring of Local Authorities in South-East Queensland" (M.Pub.Ad. thesis, University of Queensland, 1976).
10. *Nineteenth Convention* (Townsville, 1947), pp. 42-45; *Twenty-First Convention* (Rockhampton, 1953), pp. 131-35.
11. See *QPD* CLI (5 September 1928): 60-61.
12. QCE General Meeting minutes, 23 March 1923 to 16 October 1925, pp. 234, 236-38; ibid., Executive Committee minutes, 22 March 1934 to 24 October 1934, pp. 110-12, 114, held at ALP offices, Brisbane.
13. QCE Executive and General Meeting minutes, 28 March 1957 to 30 July 1958, pp. 217, 227, 249, held at ALP offices, Brisbane.

14. QCE General Committe minutes, 16 January 1925, pp. 276-80, held at ALP offices, Brisbane.
15. Greenwood and Laverty, *Brisbane, 1859-1959*, pp. 489-91.
16. *Queensland Government Gazette* CXLIX (1937) :1400.
17. Brisbane City Council minutes, 1939-40, held at Brisbane City Hall.

6 State Enterprises

D.J. Murphy

During the nineteenth century, the Australian colonies had experimented with a wider variety of state business undertakings and initiatives than would have been possible in Britain, Canada or the United States. This "colonial socialism" had an acceptance among both liberal and conservative factions in colonial politics and was to carry over to the parties of the twentieth century.[1] The advent of the Labor parties and their quick movement to becoming the alternative governments heightened the possibility of a greater range of state business undertakings and initiatives that would go beyond the "colonial socialism" of the nineteenth century.

When the Labor government was elected in Queensland in May 1915, there had already been Labor governments in New South Wales, Western Australia and the commonwealth which had begun to introduce a range of state business enterprises.[2] Not that Labor in Queensland required these examples to pursue its own course. Since the first unofficial Labor-in-Politics Convention in 1892, there had developed in the platform an extensive programme for state business undertakings. Not only was the Labor party itself enthusiastic about what state enterprises would achieve, but its parliamentary leader, T.J. Ryan, was also convinced that much useful reform could be achieved by the state's undertaking certain business enterprises itself, in competition with private enterprise.[3]

Nationalization of industries was not favoured by Ryan or his Labor colleagues. The Labor party was more concerned with establishing enterprises that would compete with private enterprises and thus force the latter's prices down. If some private

Parliamentary leader, T.J. Ryan, was convinced that useful reform could be achieved by the state undertaking business enterprises. (Photograph by courtesy of the John Oxley Library.)

enterprises were thereby forced out of business, there would be no tears shed over this. Only in areas of public service such as railways, where Labor members were aware of the corruption that private railroads had brought to the United States, did the Labor party see the state having an exclusive role. One other area of exclusive state operation that Ryan and Theodore favoured was that of workers' compensation insurance which both sought as a compulsory state monopoly.

Labor fought the 1915 election campaign on the issues of high prices, price rings and monopolies.[4] In his policy speech, Ryan promised "vigorous action in regard to state and municipal enterprises" and argued that "by a further extension of public ownership and the establishment of state enterprises, the community will be saved from a great deal of exploitation at the hands of private capitalists". His list of proposed state business enterprises included batteries, coal mines, iron and steel works, steamships, sawmills, agricultural machinery works, freezing works, granaries, sugar mills and refineries, produce agencies and markets and abattoirs. Local councils were given power to acquire and control all public utilities, under which he listed gas, power, street car services, fish markets, bakeries and meat depots.

It was all heady stuff and with Labor's winning the election so handsomely, the *Worker*, then the most important Labor newspaper in Queensland, featured Ryan in its front page cartoon, leading the state to the hallowed land of "Socialism". It advised the new government to "establish State trading with as little delay as is commensurate with natural expediency and free ourselves from the heavy taxation levied by private enterprise". It went further and commissioned a series of special articles on state enterprises outlining the problems to be faced, economically and administratively, but urging the government to begin the programme as soon as possible.

The governor's speech opening the new parliament indicated that the commitment to state enterprises remained strong. "The want of effective machinery to protect the community from persons who continue unduly to inflate prices and to amass large fortunes out of necessary commodities", said the governor, "makes it incumbent on my advisers to seek your authority for measures to regulate trade and cope with trusts and combines and for a further extension of public ownership and the establishment of State enterprises". To the opposition leader's criticism of having a legislative programme "filled with contentious matter which would invite political strife" when only the war and the Empire should be considered, Ryan made it clear the the containment of prices was central to the whole government programme. "Private enterprise", he said, "more so in time of war than even in peace should be encroached upon in the interests of the whole people".

Between 1915 and 1925, the Ryan and Theodore governments bought or instituted a state insurance office, a public curator, state butcher shops, cattle stations, sawmills, coalmines, arsenic mines, gem mines, a hotel, a fishery and trawler, a cannery, cold stores, a produce agency, batteries, a treatment work, plant nurseries, and a state lottery — the Golden Casket. They chartered a small number of ships for the coastal service, took over the railway refreshment rooms, bought the Chillagoe railways, mines and smelters and built a state sugar mill at Tully. The Ryan government's bill to establish a state iron and steel works was rejected by the Legislative Council, but Theodore took the first steps to begin such an enterprise. Successive Labor governments, between 1915 and 1957, fostered state planned agricultural settlements on leasehold land and provided for dams and power to go with these; with assistance from the Curtin and Chifley governments, they established a system of free state-operated hospitals and maintained the free hospital system after 1953 even when this meant receiving lower commonwealth assistance than the other states and having to provide a greater share of running costs out of normal state revenues. They provided the only state unemployment insurance scheme to operate in Australia before the Depression. They built homes under the day labour scheme through the Housing Commission and established new farms at Peak Downs after World War II to provide food for Britain. The State Savings Bank, established by earlier non-Labor governments, was transferred to the Commonwealth Bank by Theodore on very favourable terms that guaranteed the Queensland government access, at low interest rates, to 70 per cent of the increased annual deposits. These Labor governments established co-operatives for primary producers and marketing boards for agricultural products plus irrigation and power schemes to open up new land for small farmers. Had not World War I, conscription, war induced financial restraints and problems with the non-Labor dominated Legislative Council distracted so much of the time and energy of the Ryan government, there would also have been established a comprehensive free legal service to complement the Public Curator and also a state shipping line.

Why were the Ryan government and the early Theodore governments so intent on the principle of state enterprises? The explanation provided in the 136-page booklet, published before the 1918 election, and entitled *Socialism at Work. The Results of the Working of the Various State Enterprises Established by the Queensland Ryan Government*, is worth recalling. Far from these enterprises being the foundation of a state governed on socialist principles and methods or which intended to nationalize all private industry, the first chapter explained:

> The object has not been to secure monopoly or to squeeze out of business legitimate private traders, but to protect the public by competing with the latter on fair and efficient lines. Present indications point to competition from the State proving a more efficient method of keeping down prices and ensuring good services than any amount of direct regulation could do.

Accepting that there was a strong element of political rhetoric in this, one can yet discern that state enterprises were seen as a basic means of regulating prices. At the same time, one should also note that in regard to sugar, the most important agricultural crop in Queensland, the government found that passing the Sugar Acquisition Act and the Regulation of Sugar Cane Prices Board Act removed the near monopoly control which the Colonial Sugar Refinery exercised over the industry through its ownership of mills and the only refinery and also removed the necessity for the establishment of a competing state refinery. The explanation here also omits the more complicated set of beliefs which were behind the individual enterprises. The late nineteenth and early twentieth centuries were periods of attack on trusts, combines and price rings by many governments having no associations, trade unions or Labor parties. While Labor parties applauded and applied similar laws to those of the anti-trust governments, they saw state enterprises as an additional and perhaps better means of combating monopolies and price rings. Their economic theories may have been oversimplified and based on an incomplete knowledge of commerce and business, but there were sufficient examples of price fixing by trusts in Europe and the United States and sufficient examples of successful government enterprises to give support to their theories.

The advocates of state enterprises saw their value in more than just containing or lowering prices. They argued that such enterprises would produce higher quality goods and services because the profit motive would not be supreme, in fact, many advocates saw no great virtue in state enterprises making large profits. State enterprises were seen as a means of reducing the costs of government and thereby reducing the general level of taxation. The sawmills were seen as a means of reducing the cost of timber used in workers' dwellings by removing middlemen; the coal mines were to reduce the cost of coal to the Railway Department; while taking over the railway refreshment rooms from private operators would reduce the costs of meals to travellers, provide a small profit for the Railway Department itself and provide something better than cold tea and stale sandwiches to long suffering train travellers. The state hotel at Babinda, in the middle of a sizeable sugar district, was built to provide good lodgings and food at reasonable prices, but it was also to remove the need for sly grog merchants along the road, whose formulae for concocting alcoholic brews had resulted in grave sickness and even death among sugar workers. Legislation and more thorough licensing and inspection of hotels, however, removed the need for expanding the state hotel business. There had been an additional reason for state hotels. Labor was the party that attracted reformers and liquor reform was one of the great campaigns throughout Australia, Europe, North America and the British Empire until the 1920s. In 1915, Labor, in Queensland, was a prohibitionist party seeking in its platform "State Manufacture, Importation and Sale of Intoxicating Liquor with the ultimate view of Total Prohibition, subject to Local or State option". The Babinda Hotel was also to serve as the first step towards a state monopoly in the manufacture and sale of liquor, since in this way total prohibition could most easily be effected, or so it was argued.

Among other reasons for establishing state enterprises were the goals of assisting mining and agricultural development and thereby providing greater employment opportunities. The concept here was to assist the small entrepreneur, whether he was a farmer or a miner, and enable him to stand on his own against merchants, bankers, shippers and big companies. The cannery, the cold stores, the produce agency, the batteries and treatment works and the Chillagoe smelters all served this goal. Building a state sugar mill at Tully enabled new sugar lands to be opened up there for men wanting to move into sugar farming and, by planning to turn this over to the farmers themselves as a co-operative, fulfilled the broad Labor goals of maintaining the "small man's" independence.

The Theodore governments borrowed heavily overseas to provide the infrastructure for a state, based on large numbers of small farmers. Labor governments, which were accused by their opponents of wanting to destroy private enterprise, saw no contradiction in using the power of the state to establish business enterprises, provide bounties and subsidies and make substantial reductions in railway freight rates to assist private farmers and miners. Indeed, they prided themselves on the assistance they gave to these "small men" to enable them to survive against their "natural enemies", the banks, merchants, combines and big companies. By combining the state enterprises and other state initiatives with a series of acts that provided for guaranteed prices through marketing boards and co-operatives, and by having an enlightened Arbitration Court taking account of living costs and productivity, together with acts that protected the health and safety of workers, the Labor governments hoped to ensure good returns for farmers, in particular, and reasonable wages and working conditions for their employees.

Of all the enterprises, the State Insurance Office exhibited the greatest planning. As a barrister appearing for unions, Ryan had experienced the gross faults of the old Workers Compensation Act. In 1907, before he was elected to parliament, he advocated scrapping the legalistic system of workers compensation, which made nearly as much money for lawyers as for injured workers, and replacing this with a system of state insurance, paid for by industry, and providing compensation with automatic payments for injuries sustained either at work or going to and from work. In addition he wanted compensatory payment for the loss of limbs or the loss of the use of any part of the body. There was to be complete accord in this with Theodore, the experienced union official. By 1915, other State Insurance Offices had been established in Victoria and in some of the states of the United States. When Ryan became premier and attorney-general, he found that the Crown Solicitor, Thomas McCawley, was also conversant with overseas experiments in workers compensation and was soon able to draft the bill that was to make workers' compensation not only compulsory, but also a state monopoly. Despite efforts by the anti-Labor majority in the Legislative Council to emasculate the bill, these opponents outsmarted themselves, passed inconsequential amendments and, in their own inspired confusion, left the compulsory state monopoly provisions untouched.[5]

The State Insurance Office, after surviving a Privy Council challenge, became one of the immediate successes for the government. It was conducted efficiently; it charged lower rates for workers compensation insurance than had the private companies before 1916; it made higher payments for injuries and was, in all ways, a successful social institution removing the major problem of loss of earnings through injuries, which, along with unemployment, was the greatest fear that workmen and their families experienced. Following its early success, the State Insurance Office was broadened to cover all insurance, but at rates that competed heavily with private insurance offices. By 1918, it was offering house insurance at 33$^{1}/_{3}$ per cent below the rates of the private companies and offering fire and other insurance at 20 per cent below. In 1918, it was empowered to transact business outside Queensland and establish agencies outside the state.

The state butcher shops were established and administered in their first years by Charles Ross, the imperial meat officer, who also acted as supervisor of the butchery. There were ninety shops established in all, though some were closed down soon after establishment when sites were found to be too unprofitable. Ross had originally been appointed by the Denham government to supervise the export of Queensland meat to Britain during the war. He had been the chairman of the Queensland Meat Export Company for fiteen years and was certainly no die-hard Labor supporter. However, he found in Ryan and John Hunter, the minister for lands who administered the butchery, two men whose concern was to provide cheap meat to as many people in

Queensland and other states as was possible, to deal fairly with the meat companies and to maintain as their first priority the provision of regular supplies of cheap meat for the allied troops. For reasons that had nothing to do with ideology, Ross was convinced that the financial success and community value of the state butcher shops were such that their operation should be vigorously expanded. At the end of 1917, he drew up a scheme which would have provided meat through the state stations and the state butchery to 75 per cent of people living in Queensland, i.e., to all people within five miles of a railway line. The political problems raised by the war and the concurrent problems of finance prevented the scheme being taken further. In 1919, Ross retired as the imperial meat officer. The state butcher shops continued to expand in their operation for political as well as economic reasons, but there was developing among the Labor parliamentarians a feeling that state business enterprises, at the small business level, might not be the best means of protecting the worker and his family. When the overcoming of the non-Labor majority in the Legislative Council allowed the Profiteering Prevention Act to be passed in 1920, it seemed that prices could be regulated with less political hostility and less drain on the government's capital funds than by establishing a number of small competing government businesses. After the defeat of the 1948 referendum to give the commonwealth control of prices, the Hanlon government passed a new Profiteering Prevention Act for Queensland.

For the other enterprises, apart from the fishery and the Chillagoe venture, their establishment and operation had to be done by administrative, not legislative action, because of the opposition of the non-Labor majority in the Legislative Council to the whole concept of state enterprises. If one omits the stations, the butchery and the Chillagoe mines and smelters, the state enterprise operations were a comparatively small part of government even though they generated much political heat. They were spread among several departments until 1918 and were to suffer, generally, from a combination of inexperienced and sometimes poor management and the bad economic conditions of the 1920s.

On the question of the profitability of the state enterprises there was to be a vast chasm between the Labor supporters of the undertakings and their Nationalist (Liberal) and Country party opponents. The latter coalition was appalled that so much money had been lost on the state business undertakings and refused to accept that gains of cheaper meat for hundreds of thousands of people, employment and assistance to small farmers and workers to keep them in production, could offset these losses. After 1919, when the general economic conditions of the state worsened and the state enterprises were in debt to the Treasury, this absence of profits in some of the undertakings was of growing concern to Theodore and later McCormack, and placed them, as the principal treasurers, in difficult positions. While both could repeat in public the stock arguments about the thousands of Queenslanders who had benefited from the enterprises, as the cabinet ministers responsible for the finances of the state throughout most of the 1920s, a most difficult decade for any treasurer, both men could appreciate the validity of what some of the less extreme opposition members said. After the 1926 election, McCormack made it clear, in delivering his budget speech, that he would not continue to support uneconomic enterprises or uneconomic railway lines. "The Government intend to cut the loss in respect of those activities which do not give a reasonable prospect of success and will shut down, or dispose of, any enterprise which continues to be worked at a loss",[6] he said. This attitude did not affect the general theory that the state government had a responsibility to borrow funds for development works to increase agricultural and mining production, the main areas of industry in Queensland.

The enterprises varied in their commercial successes. The State Insurance Office was the most profitable. The butchery sold over £5 million of meat in its fourteen years of operation at an overall profit to the Treasury of £185,000 but when interest and other charges were added in, it lost about £6000. It worked on a margin of one-fifth of a penny a pound profit across the counter. The hotel made a profit each year; the fishery lost money and its trawler had be sold; the sawmills lost money in several years through bad accounting, but made profits in other years; a similar pattern emerged regarding the coalmines and it is difficult to ascertain with any certainty whether the lower prices charged to the railway for state coal matched the losses by the mines. The cannery lost money by keeping farmers in production longer than a private cannery would have been able. It gave them hope that once the economic corner was turned their problems would be at an end. The government turned down an offer from Sir Henry Jones to buy the cannery as a going concern before the 1926 election. The cold stores similarly lost money by assisting farmers with what were really concealed subsidies. It was eventually leased by the Moore government and recouped its losses. The produce agency made a small working profit each year but when interest and other charges were added it lost £20,000 over eleven years. It made some valuable contributions to the state's agriculture through distribution of seed at low cost and the sale of some produce, but its role was eclipsed by the later co-operatives and marketing boards.

Two enterprises sustained the major losses and gave the overall state enterprise programme whatever reputation it achieved for economic failure. These were the state stations and the Chillagoe mines and smelters, which, together, by 1929 had accumulated losses of £2 million. Both were the results of unsuitable purchases made on what seemed reasonable commercial grounds; both were the victims of the economic problems that confronted similar private enterprises and caused similar financial losses in the 1920s and both suffered from inadequate management in industries that required the most competent managers.

State stations had been bought during the war after private meat export companies had tried to exclude the state butchery from supplies and for meat intended for the allied troops. During the war, no meat from state stations was supplied to the state butchery which drew on private supplies acquired by the government under the Meat Supplies for Imperial Uses Act. Meat from the state stations was sold interstate and to Britain. The war years provided a regular market at negotiated prices for all the state beef produced. These were to be the profitable years. However, the expansion in the number of stations, which involved heavy capital expenditure, left the government in a bad position in the

1920s when it was confronted by a combination of a fall in meat export prices and a fall in the quantity of meat exported from Queensland. Serious drought in the middle of the decade compounded the problems. In addition, some of the stations had been bought on a book muster and not on a bang tail muster. Local station managers had not always been the keenest and cattle duffers seemed to regard the state stations as good sources of free cattle. By the mid-1920s, the government was selling the state stations off to private buyers and had the Moore government not sold the remainder, it seems likely that, by the 1930s, all the state stations would have passed back into private hands. They had lost over £1.5 million and there were other means of regulating the price of meat and lessening price rings among the meat companies.

There were great hopes attached to all the enterprises, but it was the mines and smelters at Chillagoe that gave the greatest promise of fulfilling all the hopes. It was to be an enterprise that would be profitable to the Treasury; it would provide employment in a high unemployment area; it would keep small, independent miners in production; and it would assist in the development and population growth in north Queensland. However, none of the enterprises was to have such a run of bad fortune associated with its other problems.

The Chillagoe field had bankrupted two private companies before 1914, yet there remained a firm belief that there was payable ore there in large quantities. Ryan had negotiated with the debenture holders in London in 1916 for the sale of the mines, smelters and railways at half the price asked by the company of the previous Liberal government in 1914. Ryan intended to use the mines to produce copper for the munitions needed by the British government. The price quoted to him in London by that government was £100 a ton for the duration of the war. In wanting the state to buy and operate the mines, smelters and the private railway, Ryan argued that even if the price of copper dropped after the war, or if there was not sufficient ore remaining for economic mining after the war, then the government would still have achieved two worthwhile goals: provision of munitions for the allies and employment for those men in north Queensland who had lost their jobs in the mining industry as a result of the war. Both would have been achieved at a profit to the state. However the Legislative Council referred the bill to select committees, rejected it as being unsound commercially, but finally agreed that it was a worthwhile venture and passed the bill in October 1918, three weeks before the end of the war.

The end of the war was not to see the end of the Chillagoe venture. In the 1918 debate, it is worth noting the speeches of two men — Theodore the treasurer and one who knew the north Queensland mining fields well, and William Stephens, an affluent Brisbane businessman, opponent of state enterprises and chairman of the Legislative Council select committee which had investigated the mines and smelters in 1918. Both reflected the belief that the state would gain from the purchase and operation of the Chillagoe concern. Theodore told the Legislative Assembly: "I think there is no doubt about the mineral resurces in the district, the extent and proportion of the ore bodies and the grade of ore . . .the smelters . . . are up to date plant, kept in efficient order and condition and requiring no great expenditure . . . to bring them to an efficient condition for smelting". The problem for the Chillagoe Company, he said, which had ceased operations in April 1914, had been the low price of copper, then £65 a ton, and the absence of cheap supplies of good coal for the smelters. Copper in 1918 was bringing £110 a ton and the railway line to Mount Mulligan, where there were plentiful supplies of good coal, had been completed. Theodore explained: "If they [the Chillagoe Company] had only been able to continue for a few months, until Mount Mulligan had been opened up, and the metal market firmed a little, they would have been in an excellent position". The only problem that Theodore envisaged was that the price of copper might fall, but "authorities in America hold out the opinion that the market is bound to be sustained, because the demand for copper is bound to be sustained and increased. Copper will never be less than £100 a ton".[7]

Despite continued doubts from some mining people and others in the Chillagoe area, Stephens' endorsement removed most parliamentary doubts about the viability of the purchase. He told the Legislative Council: "There is ample evidence that there is plenty of ore in the district only waiting for the smelter. We think that the smelter would pay. It is a certainty and not a guess that you would be able to get this ore".[8] The auditor-general was to reinforce these opinions in his 1920 report: "I am of the opinion that, provided metals maintain reasonable prices and that the undertaking receives fair treatment, the Chillagoe proposition has every indication of proving a success".

The optimism regarding Chillagoe and other state mining ventures was high, possibly an indication of the influence of the large number of Labor politicians representing mining electorates. The Irvinebank treatment works, not far from Chillagoe, was acquired by the government after it had been idle for some years; the state battery at Bamford was treating independent miners' tin; a battery was purchased to assist gold miners around Charters Towers and preparations were well in hand for the state iron and steel works, though this was not to go beyond the planning stage. However, when the Mount Morgan gold mines threatened to close down in the face of rising wage claims and falling profits, the government preferred to subsidize railway haulage rates to keep the mines going and the men employed, rather than to consider taking it over as a state concern.

Soon after its purchase, Chillagoe was to revert to its earlier troubled history and did not fulfil the optimistic projections. The metals were not there in sufficient quantities to keep the smelters fully operative and when two additional mines were bought at nearby Mungana, the Lady Jane and the Girofla, again on reliable reports of payable ores being present, these also proved disappointing and were closed down in 1926. By then the price of copper had fallen to below £80 a ton, which Theodore said would be the minimum at which a profit could be returned. There was now a debt to the Treasury of £1.3 million even after £280,000 had been written off in 1924. The mining industry generally was suffering depression and private mines at Cloncurry were given a 75 per cent freight rebate. The minister for mines, Alf Jones, told parliament in 1926 that there had been only intermittent smelting at Chillagoe for the previous three years and that the smelters could not pay because of their obsolete method of recovering metals. To cut further losses, McCormack closed the smelters, but in response to local pressures had to re-open them. The losses at Chillagoe, and rumours of cabinet ministers being involved in deals regarding the mines, set off demands by the opposition parties for a royal commission into the whole Chillagoe affair which was to culminate in the Mungana Royal Commission of 1930.

Governments wishing to establish business undertakings now have the advantage of the considerable research and study that has been done on the administration of statutory corporations and public enterprises. There was no such body of knowledge available in 1915. Government departments were not geared to administer business undertakings that were politically sensitive and involved in large tradings. The State Insurance Office could be set up as a statutory corporation, with some ministerial responsibility, but away from the sensitivities of job provision, consumer prices and losses of Treasury investments. Such was not the case with other enterprises. Only with the butchery, in the period of Ross and Hunter, were similar administrative successes recorded. Quite early, Ryan and Hunter were concerned tht there should be proper legislative backing and proper administrative control of the enterprises. Because of Legislative Council opposition, they had tried, through the Sugar Acquisition Act and the thrice defeated Meatworks Bill, to obtain general legislative authority for existing and future enterprises. The auditor-general, in his 1916 report, recommended legislation to place all the enterprises under one department. The government tried to satisfy this request in the Commissioner for Trade Bill in 1916 which the Legislative Council defeated. It was only after the 1918 election that the government could pass the State Enterprises Act which validated all existing enterprises and gave legal approval for the establishment of further enterprises provided that administrative and other conditions were met.

It was this legislation that allowed for the establishment of a Department of Trade under a commissioner who reported to parliament each year. In addition, of course, there was the annual report of the auditor-general on all the enterprises. When these were losing money and becoming something of a political liability in the 1920s, the government conveniently tabled the auditor-general's report on the last days of the parliamentary session so that there could be little opportunity for informed opposition criticism. However not all the enterprises were included in the state trading department. The coal mines, the insurance office, the Chillagoe smelters and mines and the sugar mill at Tully were all under other departments.

The placing of most of the enterprises under a commissioner for trade did not establish a series of statutory corporations. A problem for the state enterprises, throughout the 1920s, was the question of how much political control or political influence was to be allowed. In practical terms, it was difficult for any politician to resist approaching a minister to request a butcher shop (or an additional shop) in his electorate or to find a job in a state enterprise for an unemployed constituent. Equally, it was difficult for a Labor minister, in a decade of relatively high employment, to recommend the closure of a state butcher shop that was providing cheap meat or to close a mine or smelter or treatment works that was keeping men in jobs or to close a railway line that was providing jobs and also freight subsidies to farmers, even when there were good economic reasons for this. Interviews with the late Frank Bulcock, a Labor member of parliament from 1919 and a minister after 1932 and with other surviving contemporaries of the state enterprise period, suggest that political influence was certainly exerted, particularly to find jobs. With most of the archival records of the state enterprises destroyed in the early years of World War II, and the politicians concerned, now dead, it is impossible to ascertain, with any precision, the extent of this influence. However, it is evident from the state butchery records of 1915-19, which have survived, that both Ross and Hunter, strenuously and successfully, resisted some moderate amount of interference. From the electors' viewpoint, it seemed that cheap meat, cheaper workers' dwellings, jobs in the railways and in the mines, were more important than reports of annual financial losses by the auditor-general or by the Nationalist and Country party politicians. Even the Moore government thought it politically inexpedient to close down the Chillagoe smelters.

State enterprises were business undertakings conducted by the government. To their opponents they represented the dreaded word "socialism"; to those on the left of the Labor party, they were not examples of socialism, but of state capitalism. To the Labor governments of Queensland which instituted them they fitted easily into neither of these ideological camps, but had much more pragmatic goals. This point needs to be emphasized despite the title, *Socialism at Work*, that was given to the series of essays about them in 1918. This title was an attempt to remove some of the red bogey fear of the term socialism and convince Queenslanders that it was a good, not a bad term. It was also to convince left wing members in the labor movement that re-electing the Labor government in 1918 was more important than being caught up in exotic ideological theories, then at a high point, concerning the immediate fall of capitalism.

They were business undertakings to assist workers as consumers and producers; they were not in any sense concerned with exploring theories of worker control of industry. Nor is there any evidence that workers employed there or the unions involved saw them in such terms. Employers in the state butchery, initially, received five shillings a week above award wages, but none of the Labor premiers, treasurers or ministers in charge of the enterprises saw them as pace-setters for private industry. When Ryan was in London in 1919, he was asked by the British government to give evidence before the commission investigating the nationalization of the coal mines. Three aspects of Ryan's evidence are relevant here. He rejected the idea of state employees necessarily receiving higher wages than those in private enterprise as being opposed to the ideal of arbitrational tribunals fixing wages. He saw the role of state enterprises as reducing the price of goods and services by demanding less profit and, by competing with private enterprises, forcing these to lower their charges. While he argued that it was both useful and necessary to have consultative committees of both workers and managers, he firmly rejected the idea of handing control of an industry over to those employed there.

For most of the state enterprises, their life came to an end with the defeat of the McCormack government in 1929. The Country-National government of A.E. Moore quickly moved to sell off most of the enterprises. Those that survived were in the mining industry but these were finally closed for economic reasons during World War II, by V.C. Gair, then minister for mines. The Hamilton cold stores survived only through the personal intervention of Hubert Sizer, the minister for labour and industry. The re-election of a Labor government under William Forgan Smith in 1932 revealed a changed attitude towards state business undertakings but not a diminution in the faith that the state could and should enter directly into the economic life of the state. The Fish Board had taken over the conduct of fish marketing from the old state fishery. A Central Coal Board was established in 1933 to regulate the production, price and sale of coal in southern Queensland. Post-depression Labor governments made no attempt to enter into the range of business undertakings that had characterised the Ryan and Theodore governments. Instead they channelled their faith into a more sophisticated system of price regulation and a comprehensive state hospital system, a greater range of welfare agencies, electricity generation and reticulation, and house building through the State Housing Commission. The Golden Casket, established during World War I to provide funds for the Queensland War Council, became a source of funds for hospitals and welfare in 1920. It contributed £18 million to hospitals by 1958 and had also provided funds for dental clinics, the university medical school and work for the unemployed.

Any overall estimation of the worth of the state enterprises involves political, economic, administrative and social judgments. Which of these takes priority is not a question easily answered. From the Queensland experience, it seems clear, however, that the state can successfully undertake business ventures when these are involved in large corporate industries such as banking, insurance, transportation, communication, power generation, hospitals, and in the provision of services. At the level of the small businessman whether he be a farmer, shopkeeper or independent tradesman, the state's best role seems to be guarding his right to make profits and to continue to exist in business against the pressures of monopolies, price rings and big companies. The state also has a role to protect employees and consumers, whether these are dealing with large or small concerns. These were the broad lessons that ministers like Forgan Smith had learned from their direct involvement in the administration of the State Trade Department.

Comparisons between the successes of private and public enterprises were not always based on valid grounds. The government did not have the luxury of withdrawing from a field when it became apparent that profits were not to be made immediately or in such a degree after a reasonable time that initial losses would soon be wiped out. Practical political considerations compounded with a special social and economic ideal made the establishment and administration of state business enterprises a complicated exercise.[9]

NOTES

1. See N.G. Butlin, "Colonial Socialism in Australia 1860-1900", in *The State and Economic Growth*, ed. H.G Aitken (New York: Society for Scientific Research, 1959); W.P. Reeves, *State Experiments in Australia and New Zealand* (London: Grant Richards, 1902).
2. R.S. Parker, "Public Enterprise in New South Wales", *AJPH* IV, no. 2 (November 1958); J.R. Robertson, "The Foundations of State Socialism in Western Australia", *HSANZ* 10, no. 39 (November 1962).
3. D.J. Murphy, "The Establishment of State Enterprises in Queensland, 1915-1918", in *Labor History*, no. 14 (May 1968).
4. See D.J. Murphy, *T.J. Ryan: A Political Biography* (St Lucia: University of Queensland Press, 1975), chaps. 4, 5, 6, for discussion of the election and the new government.
5. Ibid., pp. 123-27, 146-48.
6. *QPD* CXLVII (25 August 1926) :326.
7. Ibid., CXXIX (18 June 1918) :311-15.
8. Ibid., CXXI (23 October 1918) :3402.
9. For a contemporary assessment by a leading Australian economist, see J.B. Brigden, "State Enterprises in Australia", *International Labour Review* 16 (1927).

7 Public Finance

Kenneth Wiltshire

In 1915, state governments in Australia possessed considerable autonomy and hence responsibility in matters of public finance. The vast bulk of all taxes, including income taxes, were collected by state governments, although during World War I the commonwealth government entered the fields of income tax and land tax; the states also raised and controlled their own loan requirements. Since the removal of the Braddon Clause in 1909, the states had received a fixed per capita payment of £1 5s. from the commonwealth in lieu of the previous refund of customs revenue. It was the era of the balanced budget when the performance of governments was judged according to the magnitude of surplus or deficit. A direct consequence of according such attention to formal budget results was that incredible ingenuity was applied to juggling government accounts to produce a favourable result when necessary. The concept of Trust Funds helped substantially, and money would pop in and out of these caches depending on how healthy the Consolidated Revenue and Loan Funds were at the time. Such practices, together with the fact that not all state government financial affairs came within the scope of the budget, made any assessment of true fiscal performance extremely difficult, with no independent body, state or commonwealth, to unscramble the kaleidoscopic patterns of income, expenditure, and borrowings.

Queensland resembled the other states in all these features and more. For 1914-15 the recorded sources of revenue were: commonwealth 11.5 per cent; state taxation 13.8 per cent; land revenue 13.4 per cent; mining receipts 0.4 per cent; railways 52.7 per cent; and other 8.2 per cent. This had been the pattern since 1910. Railways dominated government activity in Queensland, as was also evident from expenditure figures where railways accounted for 33.5 per cent, the other major item being interest on the public debt at 27.4 per cent, swollen by the inclusion of railway debt charges. The high debt charge was testimony to the heavy borrowing in which Queensland had engaged to expand rail lines to all points of the compass to aid land settlement. In the period since Federation, Queensland had incurred heavier expenditure on railways than any other state, and by 1914-15 loan expenditure on railways was two-thirds of the total, other major items being loans to local authorities, the establishment of state government sugar mills, and the construction of government buildings. In loan raising Queensland, like the other states, had experienced difficulties with wartime restrictions on the availability of funds, but had still fared reasonably well, and in 1914-15 the actual charge of debt on annual budget revenue (i.e., net of receipts from loans works and services) had fallen to 3.72 per cent, the lowest figure for many years.

Relations between the Queensland and commonwealth governments had fluctuated considerably. Like the other states, Queensland had little to gain from fixed per capita payments when steady inflation eroded their worth, and it had been the only state to get back less than three-quarters of customs and excise revenue under the previous system.[1] However, the state savings bank was thriving and Queenslanders were encouraged to support it to prevent competition from the commonwealth. The state bank had 25 per cent of all savings bank business when all states signed an agreement in 1914 to transfer "ordinary" banking business provided they could retain all savings bank business. Although Queensland did not participate fully in this arrangement,[2] the Commonwealth Savings Bank agreement was subsequently to prove of immense benefit to the state because of the ready access it gave to loan money from ever-increasing depositors' balances at interest rates invariably lower than anywhere else. So Queensland was able, in 1914, to describe its relationship with the commonwealth as "most satisfactory".

Labor came to power in 1915 with well-developed fiscal policies. The party had been ambivalent on commonwealth-state relationships, wishing to defend the state's rights but reluctant to do so vocally when the party was in office at the national level. However, it was clear what action was going to be taken in state finances. Theodore had already displayed considerable acumen in financial debates and had formulated a comprehensive scheme for increasing revenue by a policy of graduated taxation which would also redistribute income by reducing the tax burden on low paid trade unionists and placing it squarely on the private trusts and combines which he believed were harmful to the community.[3] In the five months prior to the presentation of its first budget, Labor had made some minor financial adjustments. Retrospective salary increases had been paid to low-ranking public servants, and a new practice adopted in respect of certain former loan expenditure — wooden school buildings and some of the depreciation charges on loan conversion — which was properly transferred to being a charge on revenue. These book adjustments had the effect of increasing expenditure, but this was offset by large increases which had occurred in revenue, and a small surplus ensued for the year's operations. However, the year ahead posed problems for a party voted to power on a platform of increased welfare expenditure. To live within the constraints of a balanced budget the government would have to increase revenue or cut back expenditure in other fields, a course which was anathema to Labor because it would be construed as retarding development and making vital government services adequate.

The justification for the significant changes which appeared in the budget was along very different lines:

> As the government holds the view that all expenditure for services and administration, interest on the public debt, payments to sinking fund, and non-productive works should be met as far as possible out of revenue in the year when it is incurred, and that it would be unwise to pass on a deficit obligation to add to the burden of future years, it is therefore proposed to meet the shortage (a) by adjusting and increasing the income tax (b) by imposing a land tax.[4]

Thus budgetary principles were employed to justify radical

changes in taxation. There would be an increased tax on all, with a £15 exemption for each child up to sixteen years of age. Company tax was increased and made progressive, there was a higher rate of tax on companies controlling public utilities and monopoly companies, a land tax was introduced on all freehold land with an unimproved value exceeding £300 and a higher rate of tax would apply to underdeveloped freehold land. It was anticipated that all these measures would increase revenue by £375,000, converting an estimated deficit into a surplus of £4500. Expenditure would include large increases in railway spending to promote closer settlement and education. A state sawmill would be established with its own forest, and state coal mines because the government was the largest consumer of coal. Plans were announced for state monopoly control of the marketing and distribution of fish and expansion of local government activity suggested. It had not been possible to submit a loan programme because in London, the traditional source of funds, the British government had raised a huge war loan. All states were in the same position and had agreed in principle that a single borrower, the commonwealth, acting on behalf of all Australian governments would be more efficient and, no doubt, more effective. However, the terms of the arrangement had caused disagreement and not been finalized. Nevertheless, Theodore felt that the required amount would be raised.

In November 1915, the second reading of the Land Tax Bill brought to light more of the philosophy behind Labor's fiscal policies. A land tax would charge those best able to contribute to the state's development, and it possessed the added advantage of: "destroying, or tending towards destruction of private monopolies on land . . . . It also enables the government to impose a tax on the truest economic basis, upon the unearned increment of land values."[5] The aim of the measure was, according to Theodore, to ensure that all land in the state would be employed economically.

The land tax was but a foretaste of things to come when the Income Tax Amendment Bill was introduced. Anyone who might find income tax a hardship was exempt, viz., with an income below £300. The new tax would operate on a sliding scale and hit companies particularly severely: in place of the fixed scale of 5 per cent (a shilling in the pound) of all distributed profits, that would apply only to the first 60 per cent of distributed profits and a sliding scale would operate on the remaining 40 per cent. Both bills met extreme opposition in the Legislative Council which since the introduction of a state income tax by Philp in 1902 had been anxious to assert its claim to powers with respect to taxation. The Council attempted to limit the period of operation of the two bills to two years, but both parties in the Legislative Assembly agreed that this was a gross infringement of the lower house's rights. At a free conference, Theodore convinced the Council that it should withdraw its amendments but he was forced to make some minor concessions before the bills were passed. Thereafter, each year the Council attempted to frustrate Labor's changes in fiscal practices with inevitable free conferences and concessions following. Frustration over fiscal questions was one of the major influences on Labor's efforts to get rid of the upper house.

Theodore's next budget, after a full year in office, gives a better guide to Labor's priorities. There had been a severe drought in Queensland and war stringencies still existed, but the demand for the state's products was buoyant. Despite concessions to those affected by seasonal conditions and higher wages and overtime paid to government employees, a budget surplus had appeared. Whilst economies had been affected in some areas, it was a change in book-keeping practice which had the greatest impact. This involved the refusal to incorporate departmental disbursements where vouchers had not been received by 30 June, which were included as part of expenditure for July of the following financial year, thereby averting a £100,000 deficit. The action drew sparks from the auditor-general, but was sound financial practice if implemented consistently — as it was.

By this time the states had agreed to allow the commonwealth to do their loan raising, and Queensland fared satisfactorily. Once again the bulk of loan money went on the railways which had been badly hit by the drought when the government gave concessions as high as 75 per cent for the movement of fodder to starving stock. Policy was not to concentrate spending on lines which would open land for settlement after the war. The period of this budget also saw the introduction of a number of state enterprises financed in a variety of ways, including loan, trust, and revenue funds, with every hope for their success but little consideration of the way in which any losses sustained might be accommodated.

To remedy the forecast deficit two proposals were advanced.[6] First, the incidence of income tax would be further adjusted by providing two additional resting places in the progressive scale for incomes earned by personal exertion and income derived from property, and an additional resting place in the progressive scale of incomes of absentees — as well as the application of a higher rate of tax to the incomes affected by these new resting places. Second, a "super tax" would be imposed equal to a 20 per cent increase in the tax payable on all taxable incomes from £200 upwards but with the proviso that all gross incomes below £400 would be exempt. The super tax would cease to operate after the year in which peace was declared. The Legislative Council rejected both measures, and such a deadlock arose that the large deficit which loomed could be met only by the issue of short-date Treasury Bills. The years which followed, up to the demise of the Council, saw a recurring pattern whereby measures rejected one year would be reintroduced in the next budget along with further tax changes invariably aimed at property owners or those on higher incomes, only to be rejected again in the upper house. It was a crazy spectacle, and played havoc with the goal of achieving budget surpluses — indeed it produced some very large deficits. The government was determined not to reduce public spending and persisted with a number of award payments to government employees which were very costly but a fundamental part of Labor policy. The net effect of its tactics was to lay the blame for economic crisis with the Council and force it to consent to some revenue-increasing measures. After 1918, revenue became more buoyant, and by the early 1920s Theodore could claim that Queensland had the highest purchasing power and the lowest cost of living of any state, but it had also acquired a reputation of having the highest taxes, a stigma that plagued the state for years to come.

Entry into the 1920s saw a shortage of funds to undertake public works. Joint arrangements for loan raising by the states had broken down. Strong demands by the unions for extension of public works were rejected because the government was short of money. Efforts were made again to redistribute the tax burden and improve revenue by revising tax scales. The commonwealth's scheme was adopted so that the minimum rate commenced at the first pound of taxable income and the rate increased arithmetically in definite ratio with each additional pound of taxable income until the maximum rate was reached.[7] Loopholes by which businessmen could claim income really derived from property as income from personal exertion taxed at a lower rate were closed, companies were hit by measures aimed to remove many of their concessions and exemptions and to make their taxation rates steeper and more progressive, and numerous exemptions relating to trust estates and partnerships were removed or modified. Generous deductions for dependants were introduced, but their benefits confined to income earners in the lower to middle bracket. Pastoral rents were increased sharply and amendments to the Land Act promised which would remove unfair advantages which large pastoralists enjoyed in the fixing of rents. Railway freight rates were reviewed, but found to be comparatively low; only suburban fares were raised. These were drastic measures with two objectives — to further improve the lot of the low income earner and transfer the tax burden away from him, and to improve the revenue position at a time when money was very short.

The real problem was the shortage of loan money, and in March 1920 Theodore left for London to arrange a loan. The simultaneous arrival of a delegation of three "prominent men", Sir Robert Philp, Sir Alfred Cowley and J.A. Walsh, sent to protest the misdeeds of the Labor government to the secretary of state for the Colonies, created considerable uncertainty among investors on the London market. Theodore promised to amend some of the government's stern financial measures in such items as pastoral rents, industrial legislation, insurance, and succession duties, in order to raise the required amount of loan money.[8] The only reward from Theodore's trip was a temporary loan from the Bank of England, and after the 1920 elections Theodore gave notice of a Loan Bill to raise a loan locally by compulsion if necessary by which everyone with an annual income greater than £1000 might be compelled to subscribe to the £2 million loan at an interest rate to be determined by the government. In the event the money was raised without recourse to compulsion, but at a very high rate of interest, the subscription coming mainly from a large number of small investors. The next major innovation in loan financing occurred in 1922 when two loans, totalling $US22 million were raised in the United States, a major achievement in view of the scarcity of loan funds from other sources. But such excitement was dampened to some extent by the problem of repaying loans which matured about this time, for former governments had made no provision for sinking funds. By 1924, loan money was more freely available locally, and also from London, after another visit by Theodore when he had again offered to make some concessions to overseas investors, including stabilizing pastoral rents for holdings reassessed under his 1920 legislation.

Queensland had been reasonably happy with commonwealth efforts at loan raising on its behalf during the war, but reacted adversely to the commonwealth remaining in the field of income and other taxes after the war. Co-operation with the commonwealth in financial matters became more apparent about the mid-1920s. Queensland was pleased with the loose arrangement whereby the commonwealth acted as a central borrowing authority, and also with the agreement of October 1924, whereby a single authority was constituted to assess and collect commonwealth and state taxes and use one income tax return to meet the dual requirements. But the state added its voice to the howls of protest when in 1925 the commonwealth proposed discontinuing per capita payments under the Surplus Revenue Agreement, and vacating the field of personal income tax and leaving it to the states whilst making some transition grants to ease the changeover.

At this stage the railways and the state enterprises were causing

Theodore, on behalf of Queensland, refuses to back down from the threats of the London money market in September 1920. (Reprinted from *The Worker* 20 September 1920 with the permission of Australian Workers Union; Photograph by courtesy of the John Oxley Library.)

some financial concern. McCormack radically changed policy by arguing that too much had been spent in the past on new construction instead of concentrating on improving lines already opened.[9] Capital in the state enterprises was written down, and losses written off, with scarcely a voice raised at the re-allocative effects such measures would produce, viz., taxpayers subsidizing the users of the services the particular undertakings provided. Larger deficits in Consolidated Revenue accounting were held over as an overdraft and carried forward to be written off as circumstances permitted.

A series of special publications by James Larcombe, secretary for railways, 1920-29, cast some further light on Labor policies. One, dealing with financial administration, made it very clear that Labor's taxation policy was based squarely on the concept of "ability to pay". "The money must be secured from those who have it and from those who enjoy the protection and services of the State". Larcombe was quite prepared to admit that the proportion of the population paying income tax in Queensland — only 3 per cent in 1926-27 — was much lower than in any other state. This, he remarked, instead of being a source of complaint, ought to be a source of compliment. According to Larcombe, if the Tories had their way more people would pay taxes and this would mean increasing the tax on lower incomes and lowering it on higher incomes. "Such a policy violates the soundest canon of taxation; it increases the burden on the businessman, the primary producer and the industrial worker, and relieves the representatives of the wealthy concerns and foreign companies". Figures were then produced to demonstrate that low income earners in Queensland paid lower taxes than was the case in any other state, and considerable mileage was sought from the taxation relief which had been given to primary producers and taxpayers with dependent children.[10]

By the time Labor lost office in 1929, a number of features of Queensland's fiscal pattern were evident. Taxation was very high and exceeded levels in any other state. Revenue came from the following sources: commonwealth 6.8 per cent, state taxation 29.8 per cent; land revenue 8.2 per cent; mining receipts 0.3 per

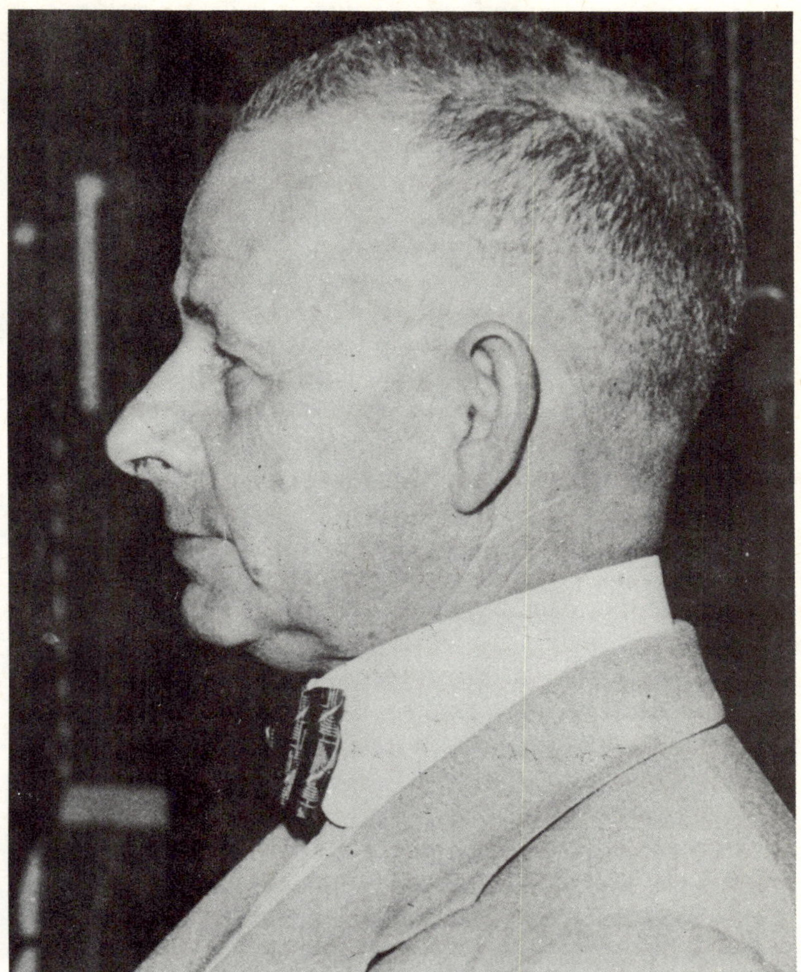

James Larcombe, in a series of articles, made it clear that Labor's taxation policy was based on the concept of "ability to pay". (Photograph by courtesy of Queensland Newspapers Ltd.)

cent; railays 44.1 per cent; other 10.8 per cent. Thus state taxation had become a much larger component of government revenue in the years of Labor government. The big charges on expenditure were still railways, interest on the public debt, education, health, and law and order. Railways still took 39 per cent of loan money, followed by workers' dwellings 18 per cent, loans and subsidies to local authorities (including water conservation grants) 13 per cent, the Agricultural Bank 8 per cent, and main roads (excluding federal subsidy) 6 per cent. Interest on the public debt had doubled whilst Labor was in office, and now represented 16 per cent of revenue; in 1929 over half the public debt was still redeemable in London, just one-third in Australia.

Thus, during their first period of office Labor had taxed, spent, and borrowed heavily in an effort to develop the state and provide full employment. Expenditure had been spread thinly across the whole state. The tax burden had shifted to a large extent from the shoulders of lower income earners to the high income earners, including companies and property owners residing outside the state. The state enterprises had not been successful in financial terms, and there was little proof that they had been successful in their other major objective — keeping down prices and providing stiff competition for the private sector. Queensland had been guilty of the shortcomings which Maclaurin attributes to all the states in this period:

- failing to spend borrowed money on self-liquidating, i.e., revenue-producing works, so that in the Depression the projects on which the money was spent could not pay their way;
- minimal provision of sinking funds to repay loans when they would fall due;
- manipulation of state accounts to minimize the deficits which were a constant feature;
- failure to provide for depreciation on railways and other assets which were subject to deterioration.[11]

In order to appreciate Labor fiscal policies after the return to office in 1932, it is necessary to note some of the developments under the Moore government. Most state enterprises were closed down. Queensland cut back on loan expenditure, and resorted to some borrowing in its own name. Belief in the ideal of the balanced budget was strongly reaffirmed. Although Moore had come to power promising tax relief, the exigencies of the Depression had forced higher taxes which hit higher income earners hardest. An effort was made to redirect expenditure towards reproductive projects, and borrowing large sums by the issue of Treasury Bills, resorted to by other states, was avoided. Relief work was financed by a special tax which rose from 1.25 per cent (1 August 1930) to 2.5 per cent on all incomes in excess of £104 (1 October 1931) to 3.75 per cent on incomes of £208-£499 and 5 per cent above £499 (1 August 1932). The other valuable mechanism used during the Depression was the Unemployed Workers' Insurance Act, introduced by Labor in 1923, which had required contributions to a fund by practically all workers. During the Depression the fund had huge demands made upon it and it became indebted to the Treasury but subsequently recovered its financial stability. Other important, and politcally unpopular, moves adopted by the Moore government included reduction in the basic wages and cuts in the salaries and wages of public servants and railway workers.

In 1932, Labor was back in office and its leader, Forgan Smith, quickly displayed his financial predilections. Labor had not been a party to the Premiers' Plan — which had split the party in other states — and so would not abide by it. Forgan Smith accepted the wisdom of each government reducing its deficit, but he was far from an unquestioning advocate of the balanced budget: "Unbalanced government budgets would, after all, be of minor importance compared with social upheavals, and although I am at all times an advocate for sound methods of dealing with government finance I cannot ignore the fact that sound government is impossible while excessive unemployment exists."[12] In Queensland the Bureau of Industry would figure prominently in rehabilitation by preparing a plan of works and schemes to use all funds to maximum benefit; public works spending was to be encouraged, not discouraged, on a premise that Forgan Smith expounded throughout the 1930s that spending on public works was part of national planning.

In the first Labor budget for three years, consolidated expenditure was pruned as much as possible but this alone could not effect the required reduction in the deficit. The only alternative was to increase revenue, and so a super land tax was reintroduced, income tax was increased as were railway fares and freights, and there was some use of trust funds. The reduction in loan money was reflected in Queensland in railway spending which was cut back to a negligible sum compared with its former dominance. The big items of loan expenditure now were for unemployment relief in general, loans and subsidies to local authorities, buildings, the Agricultural Bank, and workers dwellings. In 1932-33 interest on the public debt was 17.1 per cent of budget revenue; it had risen as high as 18.4 in the height of the Depression.

The creation of the Commonwealth Grants Commission was relatively unheralded in Queensland because the state was not to be a claimant. However, the commission provided, for the first time, an independent comparison of interstate fiscal performance which always proved revealing and was, at times, embarrassing. The commission would frequently reveal that Queensland had a lower taxable capacity than most other states, but its incidence of taxation was higher than any other state's. Indeed it showed that in 1915-16, the first year of Labor in office, actual taxation collections per head had risen to be the highest of any state, and this situation had continued throughout nearly all of Labor's first period of office.[13] Consolidated revenue expenditure per capita under Labor placed Queensland at the top of the list, apart from Western Australia with a dispersed population, and occasionally South Australia. Public debt per capita in Queensland had been high throughout the period, though not quite as high as in Western Australia and South Australia. Despite the fact that Labor had always placed heavy emphasis on public works expenditure, loan fund spending in Queensland 1915-29 did not increase any faster than in any other state. However, some interesting patterns were revealed in state expenditure on social services. By 1932, Queensland was spending about the average of all states on education, with a slightly heavier outlay on technical education; well below average in the total area of health (public health above average, care of sick and mentally afflicted average, and relief of aged and indigent and infirm and child welfare well below average); and a little below average on law, order and public safety despite a higher outlay than any other state on the police force.

The period up to World War II was not marked by any radical changes in fiscal policy. There were some recurring themes: the deficits left by the Moore government which were blamed for all the ills of the Depression; persistent advocacy of public works expenditure with employment rather than development the overriding consideration; commonwealth-state financial relations where Queensland had a number of grievances. Forgan Smith was frequently criticized for continuing the two unemployment measures, the insurance and special taxation schemes, after they were no longer necessary, and for drawing on trust fund balances when expedient to avoid criticism for deficits in consolidated revenue accounts.

The 1938 budget produced some changes in fiscal practices which appeared radical because of the relative absence of change, apart from easing the unemployment relief tax, since 1932. F.A. Cooper, who had recently become treasurer, called for a rethinking of financial support for the railways with fares and charges increased to be consonant with the cost of services provided. Local authority capital expenditure would be aided by a state contribution to interest and redemption costs instead of loan expenditure and subsidies, reducing the state's cash outlay but committing it to support of local government over a long period instead of on an annual basis. The greatest shift in Labor thinking concerned full employment measures. The previous intermittent relief work scheme, financed largely from the special tax, would be replaced; the amount of tax would be lowered and redirected to works to provide full-time employment. Motor vehicle registration fees, which had not been altered since 1927, would be assessed on a power-weight unit which would increase revenue to be paid into a Main Roads trust fund to be available for additional employment on road construction and maintenance. Machinery would be established to co-ordinate all phases of development projects designed to stimulate employment. Cooper conceived a dual role for loan expenditure: (a) the development of the state through works of permanent value which it would not be fair to charge in their entirety to the present generation of taxpayers, and (b) to provide useful employment at times when large numbers of men had been left idle as a result of the workings of private enterprise.

The 1939 budget produced the first surplus since 1927-28, and sparked off renewed criticism of the high levels of taxation which, although they had not altered substantially since the Depression, still remained the highest of any state, a constant source of political embarrassment which would remain until the introduction of uniform taxation during World War II Dissatisfaction was also expressed continuously with the way that the Moore government's deficits were carried forward each year instead of being written off, a practice which not only eased pressure on current funds but also rubbed salt into the opposition's wounds each year. A start to writing off these debts was not made until 1943.

Under wartime co-ordination of loan expenditure, Queensland received some compensation because defence spending in Queensland was proportionately much lower than in other states. However, Queensland's indebtedness was worse than that of other states because it had a higher proportion overseas and had not been receiving as favourable conversion arrangements.[14] That situation was substantially rectified in 1941 when the Australian Loan Council, at Queensland's insistence, pressed British authorities for a favourable conversion of Queensland debts.

The financial event of the war years was the Uniform Taxation scheme whereby the commonwealth took over all income taxes and levied them on a uniform basis throughout the nation. Forgan Smith had been unhappy about the introduction of the scheme and Queensland had joined with other states in presenting a High Court challenge to its constitutional validity. Despite all its supposed evils, uniform taxation was in many ways a blessing for the Labor governments. In practical terms it provided in the first year a repayment of £5,821,000 to Queensland, based on the average collections from the income tax and income (state development) tax for the two financial years 1939-40 and 1940-41, allowance being made for the savings in administration. The politically unpalatable task of taxing incomes was removed, and at a stroke the differences in taxation levels between the states were destroyed and so an end put to persistent complaints about Queensland being the most heavily taxed state. (In the overall burden of income tax, in 1940-41 Queensland was collecting £6 3s. per head of population, New South Wales £6, Western Australia £5 7s., South Australia £4 5s., Victoria £3 10s., and Tasmania £2 8s. The rates of tax in Queensland were considerably higher on upper income groups than in other states, and the figures understate the relative severity of Queensland's income tax because they do not allow for the state's relatively lower taxable capacity). Uniform taxation also served to simplify the revenue picture by identifying a discernible transfer of finance vertically from commonwealth to state, and thus also facilitated inter-state comparisons of the benevolence of the commonwealth. The switch in sources of revenue can be seen from the following figures: commonwealth (contribution to interest on the public debt) 3.7 per cent; commonwealth (state grants) 19.9 per cent; state taxation 6.4 per cent; land revenue 5.2 per cent; mining receipts 0.2 per cent; railways 57.8 per cent; other 6.8 per cent. Clearly Queensland was now more dependent on commonwealth sources with some 24 per cent of revenue now coming from Canberra compared with only about 5 per cent previously.

Queensland's public finances benefited in a number of ways from the war period. The most noticeable was a very large boost to railway revenues brought about mainly by the carriage of troops up the eastern coast. Other rail freight increased as well because of wartime activity to such an extent that generous concessions could be given in general rates and fares. In 1943, Cooper was able to announce that a sum of £1,250,000 had been set aside for railway maintenance when the labour became available. Savings bank deposits grew, and under the old arrangement the state benefited through its entitlement to the use of Commonwealth Bank deposits. Defence works expenditure escalated in the later years of the war, and again Queensland derived some advantage though not to so large an extent as those states which had more sophisticated manufacturing sectors.

The improvement in the state's financial position is best seen in a move made in 1943, under the Post-war Reconstruction and

Development Trust Fund Act, whereby machinery was provided to create reserves for deferred maintenance and post-war development schemes. The 1943 budget speech revealed that £4 million had been charged to Consolidated Revenue and paid to the credit of this Trust Fund. The practice was to be followed for a number of years thereby building up phenomenal reserves out of buoyant wartime revenue. It incurred criticism from the opposition which objected to keeping funds in watertight compartments and not reducing state taxes and levies when such large balances existed.

At the 1944 state elections, Cooper promised relief in income and company taxation when taxing rights reverted to the state, reflecting the prevailing opinion that uniform taxation would soon terminate, but by 1946 it had became an established element in Australian fiscal policy and even an offer by Prime Minister Menzies in 1951 to return income tax powers to the states did not produce a reversion to former practices. This development took much of the life out of state public finance, for although the distribution of funds still remained basically a state prerogative, the raising of revenue was now largely in the hands of the national government. The post-war period in Queensland was marked by a gradual worsening of commonwealth-state relations, although the 1946 agreement was to provide substantial assistance since the distribution formula for the first time included a "betterment factor" recognizing sparsity of population and the proportion of school children in the population of each state. (Perhaps the latter addition was not too surprising in the light of Colin Clark's leading role in the construction of the formula.[15]) Hanlon resisted all attempts to tamper with this formula in later years because of the benefits it brought to Queensland, and also because of unhappy memories of the difficulties always encountered in attempting to tax people who earned income in Queensland but did not live there.

The election of a non-Labor national government in 1949 changed the flavour of Queensland's financial debates. Although Labor premiers had chafed under the bit of the Uniform Taxation Agreement and other controls, they had been reluctant to cause too much embarrassment to a national government of their own persuasion. However, the 1949 election was the signal for every fiscal problem in Queensland to be blamed upon Canberra. Delivering his first budget speech in 1950, Premier Gair criticized the formula for distributing money to the states because it made no allowance for rapidly changing conditions, although he did say that he was basically happy with it. He complained that the commonwealth could charge the whole of its capital works programme to revenue whereas the states had to borrow, and the commonwealth retained most of currently buoyant revenues whilst giving the states an inadequate increase in grants to offset increasing expenditure. As a consequence he was budgeting for a deficit in excess of £750,000.

In the hot debate over commonwealth-state financial relations which occurred in the early 1950s, Queensland public opinion, which at first had favoured regaining state taxing powers, gradually came to a realization of the disadvantages of such a move. After the dust had settled, Queensland, like the other states, came to accept the permanent loss of taxing power. But while Labor remained in power, abuse was hurled across the southern border, mainly about the commonwealth's refusal to provide funds for a number of large-scale works projects which the state had undertaken, such as the Burdekin, Tully and Tinaroo water schemes, which totalled more than £100 million. There were several possible explanations for this refusal: the national government favoured states with non-Labor governments — as Labor spokesmen alleged; the documentation provided by Queensland was inadequate — as anti-Labor spokesmen claimed; or that the commonwealth was reluctant to recommend grants to a state government sitting on a large pile of reserves gained fortuitously. (The Grants Commission complained frequently of Queensland's failure to use its large trust balances, and even in the early 1950s the government was still tucking millions away into the Post-war Reconstruction and Development Fund.) It is of course possible that all these factors operated against Queensland's receiving loan money or special grants in this period for such projects.

An even more serious allegation by the Queensland government was that the state was receiving a declining share of taxation reimbursement money. Queensland's situation was compared with that of other states to show that they received a greater amount of commonwealth money per capita than went to Queensland, and the premier often threatened to make Queensland a claimant state, though there seems to be little doubt that the state's reserves would have thwarted this manoeuvre. As was lamented so frequently, the "wisdom" of accumulating large reserves in the war years was being negated by the commonwealth's attitude. Whatever the causes, Labor found it difficult to make ends meet during the 1950s, particularly in the light of the heavy commitment to hospitals made by the Hanlon government just after the war with the support of the federal Chifley government, altered by the Menzies government which insisted that a charge would have to be imposed on hospital patients if commonwealth contributions were to continue.

By 1957, Queensland was receiving a relatively low amount of commonwealth money per capita from all sources, loan, trust, or tax reimbursement. The consequence was that spending on public works had to be funded increasingly from reserves, and those reserves began to be depleted. Even so, by this time Queensland was receiving one third of its budget revenue from commonwealth sources compared with one quarter at the end of the war, a level of dependence which was hard to deny or replace. Although rail freights and fares had been raised a few times and other state taxes and charges were increased sporadically, there was little the state could do to improve its position. In Labor's last budget, delivered by E.J. Walsh in 1956, Queensland recorded a deficit of £1.75 million — all states had a deficit — and an envious eye was cast on the large surplus in the commonwealth's budget that year. It was pointed out that the states as a whole were being duped by the national government which retained most of the taxation money, but in the end state estimates had to be pruned and state departments told to employ the strictest economies. Serious reduction in expenditure had never been acceptable to Labor in Queensland in the 1950s; instead every attempt was made to increase capital and current expenditure in each ensuing year, and then look for the funds afterwards.

NOTES

1. A situation brought about by "bookkeeping clauses of the constitution which prevented distribution on a per capita basis", and affected by the pattern of the flow of imports to Australia; see *Treasurer's Financial Statement 1911-12*, p. 6.
2. Because of an agreement in Queensland with bankers which covered the period to 1921, Queensland did not participate immediately in this scheme. Instead, the state deposited £250,000 (to increase to £500,000 in three years) in the Commonwealth Bank, pending full participation.
3. D. Greenwood, "Edward Granville Theodore, Political Tactician and Financial Administrator" (B.A. thesis, University of Queensland, 1958), pp. 47ff.
4. *Treasurer's Financial Statement 1915*, p. 18.
5. *QPD* CXXII (23 November 1915) :2297.
6. *Treasurer's Financial Statement 1916*, p. 22.
7. *Treasurer's Financial Statement 1920*, p. 21.
8. See P.J. Bray, "E.G. Theodore and the Queensland Labor Movement 1909-1925" (B.A. thesis, University of Queensland, 1951), pp. 110ff.
9. *Treasurer's Financial Statement 1926*, p. 10.
10. J. Larcombe, *Labour Government and Financial Administration*, (Brisbane: Queensland Government Printer, 1927[?]).
11. W.R. Maclaurin, *Economic planning in Australia 1929-1936* (London: King & Son, 1937), pp. 21-37. A number of these shortcomings were revealed in the first budget speech delivered by Barnes for the Country Progressive Nationalist government.
12. *Treasurer's Financial Statement 1932*, p. 17.
13. See tables in *Grants Commission Report 1938*, Appendix No. 32, pp. 166-67.
14. *Treasurer's Financial Statement 1940*, p. 16.
15. See R.F. Cranston, "Some Aspects of Australian Federalism 1945-59" (B.A. thesis, University of Queensland, 1969), pp. 81-83.

8 Agriculture: 1915-29

Diana Shogren

Between T.J. Ryan's accession to power in 1915 and the defeat of the McCormack government in May 1929, Queensland Labor governments provided the legislative backing for an extraordinarily comprehensive programme of agrarian reform, encompassing not only improved distribution and marketing schemes, but the establishment of an institutional basis for policy-advising and industry control by delegation to the farmers themselves. In so doing, the state government involved itself far more deeply in trying to alleviate the problems of rural instability than had been attempted elsewhere in Australia, and at the same time consolidated its support in the countryside by broadening its base to include not only the rural workers of the AWU, but also a good number of the sugar growers and small farmers.

Until the end of World War I, state governments had confined their agricultural concerns mainly to the administration of regulatory measures for the control of plant and animal pests, such as Victoria's Milk Supervision Act of 1905, under which stock inspections were carried out. In Queensland, control measures were sometimes the subject of specific legislation such as the Diseases in Cattle Act of 1862, and sometimes included in clauses to the various Land Acts, such as the inducements to control prickly pear and erect rabbit-proof fencing in the Land Act Amendment Act of 1905. Agricultural research was supported by state governments: in Victoria, under Swinburne, departmental extension activities to disseminate the results of the scientific staff's work were developed from 1904 to 1908 into a quite extensive programme of agricultural education to university level;[1] and in Queensland, although the administrative arrangements did not include Agriculture and Stock as a separate portfolio of full cabinet rank until 1911, a separate Department of Agriculture had been established in 1893, and research had been fostered in State Nurseries in the 1880s and 1890s; and in response to representations from the sugar industry, the Bureau of Sugar Experiment Stations had been set up under the Sugar Experiment Stations Act of 1900.[2]

No attempts were made by pre-war Queensland governments to organize the farmers themselves or to interfere with their right to market their produce as they wished, although commonwealth controls and the Colonial Sugar Refining Company monopoly and the dependence on millers to produce a marketable commodity limited the real choice for the cane growers, and distribution problems militated against any real choice for producers of most other commodities. State governments did, however, provide assistance for the establishment of the necessary manufacturing infrastructure. As early as 1893, the McIlwraith government had passed the Sugar Works Guarantee Act, under which growers offered their land on mortgage as security for advances made for building mills and tramways, and, following an investigation into the affairs of some of the mills thus established, in 1904 the government established a Bureau of Central Sugar Mills under the treasurer to control or take part in the management of those mills that were in arrears in their obligations.[3]

B.D. Graham has pointed out that the populist character of the country party movements in Australia has tended to be overlooked.[4] Certainly, by the turn of the century in Queensland, small farmers on the Darling Downs and in the south-east dairying districts had developed vocal representative organizations intent upon influencing the political process which they felt had neglected their needs. The expansion of the sugar industry away from the plantation system towards a small yeomanry supplying central mills reinforced this movement. There is evidence that there was strong awareness among Darling Downs settlers of North American developments, and in the history of the development of farmer political movements in Queensland, the agonizing over one fundamental question — whether an agrarian party should place more stress on realizing its supporters' demands at the expense of alliance or fusion with an existing party, or maintain its independence — allowed a "breathing space" which the Ryan government was able to exploit to its advantage in the case of the sugar industry. This was the first step toward the eventual reorganization of Queensland agriculture.

As early as 1891, the first steps toward united political action by farmers had been taken with the formation, on the Darling Downs, of the Queensland Farmers' Alliance.[5] In 1895, a number of parliamentary representatives of country electorates formed a Farmers' Union to watch over agricultural interests generally. Various splinter groups formed, disbanded, and re-formed, and eventually, in 1909, a Farmers' Parliamentary Union based on south-east electorates but with E.B. Swayne, member for Mirani, as secretary, was established and continued in existence until 1915. With the support of this party-within-a-party, whose purpose was described by Swayne as the discussion of draft legislation and proposals for amendments,[6] the Co-operative Agricultural Production Act of 1914, which provided for advances to be made by the state toward the establishment of factories to process primary products such as cheese, butter and jam, and the Co-operative Sugar Works Act of 1914, enabling co-operative groups of cane growers to obtain state aid to help them acquire existing sugar mills, were passed.

At the 1912 general election, Labor had polled well in the metropolitan area, increasing the number of seats held there from two to six, and polling better than 40 per cent in another seven. On the other hand, Labor had not performed so well in the west, where its representation dropped from sixteen to thirteen. Neither had it secured the farmers' votes in the wheat and dairying areas, winning only one seat in the whole of the south-east, Darling Downs and Wide Bay areas combined. Of the sugar areas, Labor held Bundaberg and Herbert, won Cairns and the new seat of Eacham which was represented by a cane farmer, William Gillies, but made no headway in the Mackay district.[7] It was obvious that a greater proportion of the farmers' votes would have to be secured if Labor were to win the 1915 election. The agricultural issue that helped tip the balance in Labor's favour was a matter involving sugar.

From 1912 onward, cane growers had become increasingly dissatisfied with the Liberal government of Digby Denham, first, because of its procrastination over the establishment of three new mills whose erection had been recommended by a royal commission in 1911, and later because of its failure to enact legislation to regulate cane prices. Denham had refused to support a private bill to that end sponsored by one of its own members, Colonel Rankin, who was also a member of the Farmers' Parliamentary Union, and a cane grower himself. The growers were caught in a cost-price squeeze between the miller, on whom they were wholly reliant for the transformation of their cane into a marketable commodity, and the farm workers, whose conditions had been materially improved under an award made by Judge MacNaughton in 1914. T.J. Ryan was provided with a convenient opportunity to marry two previously separate aims: to secure the farmers' votes and at the same time to further the interests of the rural workers already committed to Labor's cause. It was probably true that the cane grower, beholden as he was to the miller, could not be held directly accountable for the level of wages he paid his workers to quite the same degree as the grazier or wheatgrower might be. While this point was not openly conceded, it was implied in the adoption of the concept of a "natural alliance" between farmer and worker as an ideological lynchpin of Labor's agricultural policies. Labor's policy if it were to be elected in 1915 included the establishment of cane boards, "whose function will be to fairly and impartially adjust sugar cane prices between mills and growers.[8]

Labor romped home at the 1915 election, with 52 per cent of the vote to the Liberals' 21 per cent. The party's strength, as always, was in the west and in the metropolitan area; however, Charters Towers, Cook, Bowen, Mackay and Townsville also swung to Labor, as did Gympie, Maryborough and Musgrave. With the exception of Mirani, held by Swayne, all of the northern sugar electorates were now held by Labor.[9]

The implementation of Labor's policy to control cane prices

was complicated by the wartime situation. Overseas prices for sugar rose during 1914 and 1915 owing to the restriction of beet sugar production in Europe, and difficulties in transport to Europe from tropical cane-growing countries. For years, the Australian industry had been heavily protected and growers had received a bounty incentive to prevent the employment of coloured labour. Following the federal royal commission in 1912, the excise and bounty system was abolished and replaced by a straightforward prohibition of coloured labour under the Sugar Cultivation Act of 1913. This exacerbated the growers' problems, for despite the fact that the Denham government had also passed a companion Sugar Growers' Act making provision for prompt payment of 2s.2d. per ton to suppliers of cane, which represented the difference between the old excise and bounty previously retained by the commonwealth government, its failure also to enact cane prices legislation meant that some millers simply altered their price for cane to accommodate the 2s.2d., and the growers gained not at all. Costs had increased as a result of the MacNaughton Award, and the growers' situation was made more acute when price-fixing boards in New South Wales and Victoria, where most sugar was consumed, reduced the wholesale price of refined sugar from £22 to £21 per ton. At the same time it was feared that the main refining companies would denude the local market to take advantage of inflated overseas prices, and indeed severe shortages set in.

The solution negotiated between the Fisher government and Ryan was announced on 29 June. The commonwealth government imposed an embargo on imports and exports of sugar, and took responsibility for purchasing from abroad sufficient quantities to make up any shortfall in production for domestic requirements. At the same time, it fixed the price paid to the mills for raw sugar. The Queensland government undertook to acquire by proclamation the whole of the domestic crop at an average price of £18 per ton raw and sell it to the commonwealth at cost, the latter agreeing to pass on the refined product at the lowest possible retail price. On 6 July the commonwealth attorney-general, W.M. Hughes, and the general manager of CSR, E.W. Knox, signed an agreement on refining of sugar under the new arrangements.[10]

There was some question as to the legality of the proclamation, and the Ryan government immediately introduced the Sugar Acquisition Bill to ratify it. The bill actually went much further, however, for it contained provision for extending the power of acquisition to other commodities. With the co-operation of the opposition, many of whom were as delighted as the growers at Ryan's success in stabilizing the industry, the bill quickly passed through both houses, but fears were expressed that the extended provisions might well in future be used to socialize other industries when the conditions were inappropriate.[11]

In August 1915, the long-awaited Regulation of Sugar Cane Prices Bill was introduced. It provided for a Central Sugar Cane Prices Board, consisting of a district court judge as chairman, one growers' and one millers' representative, an accountant and a chemist; and local boards each consisting of a growers' and a millers' representative, and a chairman appointed by the governor-in-council (usually a stipendiary magistrate or clerk of petty sessions). The central board was to hear appeals and determine prices for those districts without a local board. Local boards were to be constituted in those districts where twenty or more growers signified their desire for such a board to be established to determine local cane prices. The legislation provided for the appointment of check chemists and weighers at every mill. In fixing a base price for cane, deductions might be allowed in respect of burnt, frosted or diseased cane, or trashy cane, or varieties of cane the growing of which had been disapproved by the local board with the sanction of the central board. This was considered perfectly justifiable "seeing that the State Government of Queensland have been expending a considerable sum of money for some time past in the establishment of experimental stations . . . and sending their experts to different districts to advise as to the best kind of cane which ought to be grown in that district".[12] The foundation was thus laid for the complex network of regulations administered by the Central Sugar Cane Prices Board during the subsequent sixty years.

These initiatives in respect of the sugar industry were not remarkable for their establishment of a pool system in a field where previously an open market had existed. Pools had, after all, been operated voluntarily by groups of primary producers for years. Where the innovation lay was in the institution of compulsory market regulation by statutory bodies in which the producers were required to play an active part. After the war this principle was applied to other areas of production, and a pattern of agricultural marketing reform began to emerge from the existing laissez-faire chaos.

The commodities scene in pre-war Queensland was notable for a complete lack of organized marketing and distribution on a scale sufficient to prevent the operation at cross-purposes of one co-operative with another, or of co-operatives with independent growers.[13] This was particularly true of highly-perishable produce such as fruit, and the many attempts to organize co-operatives failed because these organizations had no powers of compulsion. Even a very small proportion of the commodity concerned, sold independently of the co-operative's operations, was capable of affecting the whole market and depressing the market price to a degree. Except where it had monopolistic control of an essential marketing facility such as storage or transport, or the produce was in chronic short supply, the co-operative tended, unless it defeated its own objective by price-cutting, to be left with goods on its hands, while the independent seller reaped the benefit of market stability to the cost of which he had not contributed.[14]

Wartime conditions did, however, show the man on the land what it was like to have the state regulate sale of produce and prices, and altered the focus of rural politics from the tariff, or land laws, to the new marketing arrangements. The extended powers of the federal government under the War Precautions Acts had aroused controversy, engaged the interest of farmers across Australia, and persuaded many of them of the possibilities of achieving more stable conditions through self-regulation. When the wartime wheat pools were first established in 1915, farmers organized themselves to meet the challenge of a completely new apparatus of regulation and price control. They set out to reform the pools' administration and later sought admittance of their own representatives to the boards of management, and still later requested that the system be continued after the war and permanent marketing agencies be established. In rising to the challenge, "the farmers asked their pressure groups to undertake a wider range of tasks and, above all, to work more seriously towards the objective of creating independent country parties in Parliament".[15] Gradually, the agrarian psychological climate was altering, at least among commodities producers, who, while resenting the restrictions, acknowledged the advantages of the pools.

Wheat acreages in Queensland fluctuated considerably between 1914 and 1918. In 1914, the area under crop was 127,015 acres, in 1915, 93,703 acres. In 1916, a peak of 227,778 acres was attained, but this decreased rapidly to 127,815 in 1917 and 21,637 in 1918.[16] The government attributed much of the blame for the fall-off in production to the operations of the Federal Wheat Pool which was administered by an Australian Wheat Board, consisting of the prime minister and a minister from each of Victoria, New South Wales, South Australia and Western Australia, and from which Queensland had been excluded on the ground that it did not produce enough for its own state consumption. This would not have precipitated a serious crisis were it not for the fact that the southern states controlled the pool to their own advantage, imposing a high price per bushel without entering into any negotiations with the Queensland government. In March 1920, the Queensland government corresponded with the commonwealth on supplies of wheat for the forthcoming year, and the federal government demanded a price of 7s. 8d. per bushel. Queensland objected to this on the grounds that it had not demanded world parity price for sugar on the domestic market, but was forced to accept the offer or suffer a severe shortage. Discussions were held with growers, and the Queensland cabinet, with Theodore now premier, decided to legislate to put the industry on a sound footing and assist its development to the point where it was self-supporting. This decision was supported by the opposition, whose leader had led a deputation to Theodore and

Gillies, secretary for agriculture and stock, urging the formation of a compulsory pool. A conference of farmers' representatives at Toowoomba on 22 October 1920 supported the notion, and the Wheat Pool Act was passed by the end of the year. Under the act, the State Wheat Board was established. It was chaired by a government official and consisted of five representatives of the growers, and a financial expert appointed by the associated banks. The board was empowered to classify, market and finance the pooling scheme, control all grain sheds and nullify any unfair contracts that had been entered into.[17] This was the forerunner of all the other commodity boards established from 1922 onward under the Queensland plan.

No official announcement of the government's plans to place the marketing of all Queensland primary produce on a sounder footing was made before February 1922. During the second reading debate on the Wheat Pool Bill, however, Gillies had foreshadowed a wider scheme and emphasized the importance of ensuring good prices for butter, sugar, cheese, maize, fruit or "anything the civilised man requires to keep him alive".[18] The Labor party was aware that a strong rural policy was essential to its survival, for the landslide victory of 1918, Ryan's last state election, when Labor won forty-eight of the seventy-two seats, had been undermined in 1920 when it lost ten seats — two to the Northern Country party, four to the Country party which had formed under the leadership of Vowles as a breakaway from the National party, and four to the Nationalists.[19] Many country voters had been alienated by Theodore's determination to amend the Land Act in order to abolish concessions granted by the Denham government in time of depression — increases in land rent had been limited and its retrospective payment allowed. The act was finally amended when the government stacked the Legislative Council, which had rejected labor's amendment on five previous occasions.[20]

The Wheat Pool Act of 1920 was followed in 1921 by a Cheese Pool Act along similar lines, and a Banana Industry Preservation Act, which was introduced to protect the industry against domination by Chinese labour. The Cheese Pool Act was the outcome of representations from both the producers and the cheese manufacturers. After the act was passed, a referendum of producers was held to determine whether or not it should be brought into force, with the result that of those who voted, 91 per cent were in favour of the establishment of the cheese pool. An election was then held for five members to constitute a cheese board, which took over cheese marketing for the state. The bill for the cheese pool was not prepared until there was an assurance that the suppliers and manufacturers were in agreement with the proposal.[21] A similar procedure, the establishment of a consensus among relevant producers before taking legislative action, was subsequently followed in the establishment, as part of the Queensland plan, of the Council of Agriculture.

Labor's new agricultural policy was unveiled at Laidley, where Theodore delivered an interim policy speech on 21 February 1922.[22] The scheme outlined was an optimistic one. It was intended to encourage an increase in rural population by improving the living conditions of farmers, and that could only be achieved by making the rural life more remunerative. To this end, it was proposed to remove the middleman from the rural marketing scene by employing co-operatives and pools, to open up land for settlement, establish advisory boards for the various sections of agricultural industry, and improve main roads and agricultural education.

Theodore argued that effective agricultural reform would not be realized until a great deal of preliminary organization had been undertaken in the farming communities, and proposed that the new plan be designed along the lines of the American Farm Bureau to the extent that it be based upon a grassroots organization of farmers who would be assisted to solve the problems of production and marketing, and become the driving force towards co-operative effort. Farmers had already successfully handled the marketing of a record wheat crop: they should now proceed, through a Council of Agriculture working in close co-operation with the Department of Agriculture, to develop and administer policies covering the whole range of state agriculture and most aspects of rural life, from fruit marketing to extension services to help control pests and diseases, and including the provision of advice on rural education.

To direct the Council of Agriculture and establish its supporting structure of local associations and district councils, which three tiers were to form the Queensland Producers' Association, and to oversee the preparation of the enabling legislation, the government imported from Western Australia a canny Scot by the name of Lewis Macgregor, who had managed the Westralian Farmers' Co-operative and had also advised the federal government on both commodities and repatriation matters during the war. On taking up duty in 1922 at the age of 36, the new director of the Queensland Producers' Association was the highest-paid public servant in Queensland, on a salary of £1500.[23] He quickly set about implementing the Queensland plan, and by the end of the year the Primary Producers' Organisation Act and the Primary Products Pools Act were on the statute books.

The Primary Producers' Organisation Act of 1922 provided for the formation of local producers' associations of not fewer than fifteen members, which elected district councils of agriculture, which in turn elected representatives to the Council of Agriculture. The Council of Agriculture included not fewer than five representatives of the government, and was chaired by the secretary for agriculture and stock. While the legislation was under preparation a provisional council representative of the dairying, sugar, fruit growing, wheat growing and general agricultural industries was established to get the local organization underway and prepare for the first election under the act. By the end of 1922, 707 local associations had been formed, with a registered membership of 18,361 producers. Four hundred producers nominated for election to the nineteen district councils. Each was invited to nominate a representative to the Council of Agriculture, and the provisional Council retired on 22 March 1923. District agents were appointed to prepare submissions for the various sectional interests represented in each district, and act as secretary to the district council, and district organizer.[24]

The Primary Products Pool Act gave the governor-in-council power to proclaim "any grain, cereal, fruit, vegetable, or any other product of the soil in Queensland, or any dairy produce or any article of commerce prepared other than by any process of manufacture from the produce of agricultural or other rural occupations in Queensland" a commodity for the purpose of the act, and provided for the establishment of pools so long as a majority of producers of the commodity in question agreed. Pools were administered by marketing boards representative of producers. It was not necessary for such boards to have state-wide coverage: in 1923, a state-wide poll failed to gain the 75 per cent majority needed for the establishment of a Queensland maize pool, but in the same year it was possible to establish the Atherton Tableland Maize Pool.[25] The important thing was that producers were consulted before pools were established, and they were represented on those bodies that administered them. The cost of administering the Queensland Producers' Association was initially underwritten by the government, and sustained after the first year by levies which were paid into the Queensland Producers' Association Fund.

For much of its first year of operation, the Council of Agriculture was concerned with developing legislation to encourage the co-operative movement, and investigating systems of rural credit. The passing, in 1923, of the Primary Producers' Co-operative Association Act made possible the formation of co-operative companies to deal with primary products, and the Agricultural Bank Act of 1923 provided, *inter alia*, for advances to co-operative companies and associations connected with primary production. Within a few months of the co-operative Association Act being passed, all of the co-operative associations in the fruit industry, and most of these engaged in cheese manufacturing, had embraced its provisions. Meanwhile, Macgregor addressed himself to the problems of the fruit industry, following extensive consultation of fruit growers, and in 1923 the Fruit Marketing Organization Act established the Committee of Direction of Fruit Marketing (COD) with wide-ranging powers to control the transport and disposal of all fruit grown in Queensland. The fruit industry was organized under the act on a base of local associations which elected sectional group committees, and these in turn elected representatives to the COD. An amending act in 1925 extended the powers of the COD by broadening the definition in the act of "marketing" to include "everything involved in the preparation and packing of fruit for sale, and the offering thereof for sale and selling thereof, and in the transmission of fruit from the producer to the consumer",[26] and providing for the issuing of directions by the committee in order to exercise compulsory powers of control over any fruit crop or portion of any crop. Such directions could be challenged by growers within thirty days of a notice of intention having been issued, and a poll held. It is a matter of record that very few such directions have been challenged: growers' sentiment has been sounded out before notice of intention has been issued.[27]

In 1923 alone, fourteen acts bearing directly on the interests of the state's primary producers were passed by the parliament, and, by proclamation under the Sugar Acquisition Act of 1915, the sugar board was established.[28] In 1926, the Primary Producers' Organisation and Marketing Act consolidated the previous Primary Products Pools Acts and Primary Producers' Organization Acts, and made a number of important changes to the existing legislation. In response to continued complaints that organization of the Queensland Producers' Association on a regional basis rather than along commodity lines was ineffective, it was proposed to reorganize on a commodity basis. Commodity boards, established either with, or without a marketing function, were to be elected by growers, and the Council of Agriculture composed of representatives of the boards. There were to be no government nominees on the council, although the director of marketing (Macgregor's altered title) would be *ex officio* a member of each board and act as liaison officer between the boards, council and government. The commodity boards would finance their own expenses, the council's activities, and an insurance fund, through levies. The council's functions were: to co-operate with the Department of Agriculture, the local producers' associations and other bodies in—

1. Developing the rural industries.
2. Advising upon matters to the interest of primary producers.

3. Advising the minister upon matters he may refer to the council.
4. Advising upon matters brought before the council by associations or boards.

The act also related the sugar industry to the overall organization by providing for the establishment of the Queensland Cane Growers' Council (QCGC), which was to be supported by mill suppliers' committees at each mill, and district cane growers' executives to deal with sugar industry business in each district.[29] The QCGC effectively replaced the United Cane Growers' Association.

Between 1920 and 1929, upwards of forty pieces of legislation dealing with primary industry were added to the statute book. Macgregor has recorded that,

> . . . controlled marketing . . . was applied to such products as sugar, wheat, Indian corn (maize), barley, cotton, butter, cheese, ground nuts, tobacco, arrowroot, eggs, fruit, broom millet and honey, some over the whole of Queensland, some regional. Not one of the government guarantees we gave was ever defaulted. All were liquidated . . . I did not favour socialization of means of production, distribution and exchange, as advocated by socialists. Therefore, from the inception I encouraged these control boards to continue to utilise the pre-existing private distributing enterprises as far as possible, and if necessary, under conditions which the control boards could prescribe. Uniformly they followed my advice.[30]

Notwithstanding his disclaimer, Macgregor presided with W.N. Gillies and W. Forgan Smith as successive secretaries for agriculture and stock over the systematic development of a remarkable, statutory infrastructure for commodities marketing and policy advising. In so doing, the government had, as A.A. Morrison has pointed out, undercut the Country party's support: with sectional organizations formed to channel the farmers' wishes to government and help administer their own affairs, party organizations tended to be superfluous to the producers' needs.[31]

Although Labor lost office in 1929, it had built a solid electoral base among large sections of Queensland farmers. It had done this for two reasons: the size of the rural vote in Queensland with capacity for unseating governments and the fulfilment of an ideal of workers and farmers being "natural allies."

NOTES

1. F.H. Sugden and F.W. Eggleston, *George Swinburne: a Biography* (Sydney: Angus & Robertson, 1931), pp. 197-222.
2. These details of the early history of the Agriculture portfolio are based upon A.A. Morrison, "The Government of Queensland"; Chapter IV in *The Government of the Australian States*, ed. S.R. Davis (Melbourne: Longmans, 1960), p. 316; Colin A. Hughes and B.D. Graham, *A Handbook of Australian Government and Politics, 1890-1964* (Canberra: Australian National University Press, 1968), p. 176; and Queensland. Bureau of Sugar Experiment Stations, *Fifty Years of Scientific Progress* (Brisbane: Government Printer, 1950), p. 5.
3. For an account of the Queensland sugar industry to 1928 see Harry T. Easterby, *The Queensland Sugar Industry: An Historical Review* (Brisbane: Government Printer, n.d.).
4. B.D. Graham, *The Formation of the Australian Country Parties* (Canberra: Australian National University Press, 1966), pp. 1-30; see also D.B. Waterson, *Squatter, Selector and Storekeeper: a History of the Darling Downs, 1859-93* (Sydney: Sydney University Press, 1968), p. 110 and chap. 13, "Voting Behaviour and Group Politics on the Downs".
5. For details of the organization of farmers' parliamentary representatives, see Z. Abidin, "The Origins and Development of the Queensland Country Party, 1909-1932" (M.A. thesis, University of Queensland, 1958); and Charles Arrowsmith Bernays, *Queensland Politics During Sixty Years (1859-1919)* (Brisbane: Government Printer, 1919), p. 147.
6. Campaign speech during 1912 election, *Daily Mercury*, 8 April 1912.
7. Colin A. Hughes, "Labor in the Electorates", chap. 5 in *Prelude to Power, The Rise of the Labour Party in Queensland, 1885-1915*, eds., D.J. Murphy, R.B. Joyce and Colin A. Hughes (Brisbane: Jacaranda Press, 1970), p. 82. D.J. Murphy has pointed out that Labor's wins in Bundaberg, Cairns and Herbert owed much to the sizable town populations of waterside workers, carriers and labourers; see *T.J. Ryan: A Political Biography* (St Lucia: University of Queensland Press, 1975), p. 70.
8. T.J. Ryan's Election Speech at Barcaldine, 1915, as reprinted in Murphy, Joyce and Hughes, *Prelude to Power*, p. 294.
9. Based on Hughes, "Labor in the Electorates", pp. 82-87.
10. "Sugar Supply: Memorandum of Arrangement between the Government of the Commonwealth and the Colonial Sugar Refining Company about

the Sugar Supply of Australia", *CPP* V (1914-15-16-17): 1065-68.

11. *QPD* CXX (1915) :190, 225. Murphy has pointed out that these fears were justified, for the Labor party had been corresponding with the Scaddan Labor government in Western Australia and discovered that Scaddan had used administrative, not legislative, action to establish state business enterprises, thus avoiding rejection of legislation by the Legislative Council; see *T.J. Ryan: A Political Biography* (St Lucia: University of Queensland Press, 1975), pp. 119-120.
12. William Lennon, Secretary for Agriculture, during Second Reading Speech; *QPD* CXX (1915-16) :418.
13. For an account of these problems as they existed in the fruit industry, see Diana Shogren, "The Creation of the Committee of Direction of Fruit Marketing", *Queensland Heritage 2, no. 5 (1971) :31-38.*
14. For a discussion of pools and their operation, see H.S. Hunter, "Co-operative Marketing in Queensland", *Queensland Agricultural Journal* 63 (1946) :240.
15. Graham, *The Formation of the Australian Country Party*, p. 96.
16. Department of Agriculture, *Report*, 1918-19, p. 106.
17. Second Reading Speech, *QPD* CXXXVI (1920) :138-40.
18. Ibid., p. 128.
19. Hughes and Graham, *A Handbook of Australian Government and Politics*, pp. 517-18.
20. Ulrich Ellis, *A History of the Australian Country Party* (Melbourne: Melbourne University Press, 1963), pp. 56-57.
21. Department of Agriculture, *Report*, 1921-22; *QPP* II (1923) :4.
22. *Brisbane Courier*, 22 February 1922.
23. Macgregor eventually settled in the United States. His memoirs contain many anecdotes about Queensland and federal politicians during the 1920s; see Lewis R. Macgregor, *British Imperialism: Memories and Reflections* (Millbrook, N.Y.: Dymer Communications Inc., 1968), chaps. 20-23.
24. Council of Agriculture, *Report*, 1922-23; *QPP* II (1923) :157-83.
25. Ibid., pp. 173-74. The required majority was reduced to two-thirds by the Primary Products Pools Act Amendment Act 1925.
26. *QPD* CXLVI (1925) :1345.
27. Shogren, "The Creation of the Committee", p. 38.
28. *QGG* CXXI, No. 5, 4 July 1923.
29. *QPD* CXLVIII (1926), 1058-62, 1404.
30. Macgregor, *British Imperialism*, p. 286.
31. Morrison, "Government of Queensland", pp. 297-98.

9 Agriculture: 1932-57

D.J. Murphy

Agriculture, land usage, sugar, dairying and the pastoral industries were among the most important areas of Labor's legislative and administrative actions between 1932 and 1957. It was to be the sugar industry that continued to represent the most notable Labor achievement in agriculture. In the 1930s, its production doubled, it emerged as an export industry of significance and by 1957 it was almost equalling meat as the second most valuable export of Queensland. More importantly it enabled a number of cities and towns along the coast to prosper. In the dairying industry the quality of the produce and the efficiency in production and marketing increased. The producers attained a measure of prosperity and butter, cheese and pigmeat became significant export commodities. In the 1930s, particularly, other primary producers in the maize, cotton, banana, tobacco and peanut industries were saved from having to walk off their properties and their industries were placed on a stable footing for production and marketing. Wheat was not to be a really major Queensland crop until after World War II, when its expansion was guaranteed by the stabilization programmes of the Chifley and Hanlon Labor governments. Forestry did not develop as a major industry until after the war. (See tables 1 and 2).

The fourteenth Labor-in-Politics Convention met in Brisbane in January 1932, five months before the state election. A sizable proportion of Labor's voting strength since 1915 had come from farming electorates and it might have been expected that the convention would have devoted some time to policies designed to win back support there. However, such was the over-riding importance of unemployment and working conditions among workers generally and among affiliated unionists specifically, that it was not until the last day of the convention that two items on agriculture were raised. The convention was not concerned to alter the agricultural and rural policies introduced in the 1920s; but it was concerned about restoring employment in rural areas and working conditions affected by the Moore government's industrial legislation. This pattern of little or no discussion of agricultural policies continued at subsequent conventions. Labor's agricultural programmes were initiated by the parliamentary party, not by the conventions.

Two Labor cabinet ministers stand out as being the architects of Queensland's agricultural programmes in the 1930s. These were William Forgan Smith and Frank Bulcock. While Bulcock was to raise the proficiency of the Agriculture and Stock Department in aiding primary industry, both he and Forgan Smith were

Labor premier, William Forgan Smith, son of a gardener, was successful in organizing the Queensland scheme of commodity boards and orderly marketing in the 1920s. (Photograph by courtesy of the John Oxley Library.)

to draw on the advice of the economist J.B. Brigden, who became director of the Bureau of Industry in 1932 and held that position until 1938. Forgan Smith, premier after 1932, was himself the son of a gardener and had been successful in organizing the Queensland scheme of commodity boards and orderly marketing in the 1920s as secretary for agriculture and stock.[1] While he appreciated the reality of Queensland politics, that any party wishing to govern had to hold the support of a considerable proportion of farmers and rural workers, he believed implicitly in the advantages of an agricultural as against an industrial society. He saw agriculture as being a "natural" state for man:

> I take the view that, no matter how much secondary industry may be established in Queensland, this State will continue for all time to be largely a primary producing state. It is desirable that this should be so. Primary production is the natural occupation of mankind. No one would desire for this state the industrialised type of civilisation, which exists in many countries today.[2]

While South Australia sought to avoid the worst effects of any future recessions by transforming itself from an agricultural to a predominantly manufacturing state, Queensland turned its back on increased manufactures and sought, instead, to increase the quality and area of its agricultural base. There was, however, more than fundamentalist agrarian sentiment in this. Queensland's manufacturing industries had been affected by the removal of interstate customs barriers at federation, but agriculture and the pastoral industry had proved to be areas where Queensland could compete with the southern states. It was only after World War II when manufacturing was officially encouraged that manufacturing industries became even half the gross value of primary industries in Queensland.[3]

Orderly marketing by primary producers' co-operatives was the key to Forgan Smith's agricultural Queensland. In the debate on the Bureau of Industry Bill, he told the parliament:

> We agree that there should be orderly marketing, and also that produce should be held and the markets controlled. Abolish gluts at one period as far as you can and do away with artificial

Table 1. Principal Agricultural Production 5-year average

Year	Raw Sugar 1000 tons	Maize 1000 bushels	Wheat 1000 bushels	Sorghum 1000 bushels	Cotton 1000 pounds	Peanuts 1000 pounds	Tobacco 1000 pounds	Potatoes tons	Bananas 1000 bunches	Pine-apples 1000 dozens	Butter 1000 pounds	Cheese 1000 pounds	Area under crop acres
1921-26	346	3,773	1,980	-	10,678	-	-	-	2,180	925	57,755	11,641	928,760
1926-31	486	4,688	3,204	-	10,692	-	-	-	2,978	914	75,050	12,761	1,048,695
1931-36	591	3,359	3,497	-	17,388	5,612	1,445	19,544	2,095	1,234	115,586	11,866	1,281,357
1936-41	787	3,459	5,366	-	14,863	14,258	2,241	20,325	1,593	1,586	125,226	12,220	1,664,017
1941-46	615	3,803	5,667	-	9,958	22,133	1,587	30,101	1,429	1,835	102,553	23,704	1,761,998
1946-51	754	3,060	9,254	2,920[1]	1,745	27,641	1,972	26,963	1,423	2,121	100,873	19,931	1,910,448
1951-56	1,059	2,784	13,374	3,794	3,715	23,956	4,029	33,778	1,115	2,920	96,118	16,301	2,398,535
1956-61	1,263	3,638	10,867	5,308	7,198	44,088	8,229	52,749	1,214	3,935	83,270	17,123	2,774,685

Source: *Queensland Year Books* 1. 1949-50-51 only.

Table 2. Gross Value of Production Average 5 years (£ 1000)

Year	Agriculture	Dairying Poultry Bees	Pastoral	Mining	Forestry Fishing	Total Primary	Manufacturing (Net)
1916-21	7,204	5,268	17,167	3,585	2,032	35,258	9,514
1921-26	11,466	6,856	19,166	2,023	2,849	42,362	15,055
1926-31	13,204	7,309	15,440	1,671	2,386	40,011	15,698
1931-36	12,017	6,889	12,748	2,047	2,100	35,802	13,781
1936-41	16,111	10,401	18,481	3,478	3,193	51,666	19,541
1941-46	22,271	14,326	23,583	3,871	3,356	67,409	29,051
1946-51	34,859	20,740	63,424	6,820	5,640	131,285	53,715
1951-56	69,201	34,874	95,179	19,690	10,314	229,259	109,586
1956-61	91,166	36,248	112,356	34,098	11,756	285,626	154,168

Source: *Queensland Year Book*, no. 25, 1964

> scarcity. That is the whole basis of orderly marketing . . . under a system of orderly marketing such as this Government believes in, the control of the marketing will be in the interests of the producers in the industry and in the interests of the general public.[4]

To underpin his orderly marketing and the development of the agricultural and rural industries of the state, Forgan Smith disbanded Moore's Bureau of Economics and Statistics and established in its place the Bureau of Industry. The bureau was concerned with the investigation of projects that would be economically viable, of value to the state's development and that would provide long-term employment. One of its three subcommittees was the Rural Development Committee which was to be most concerned with land usage and agriculture. *Economic News*, a four-page monthly news sheet, established by Brigden, provided short articles and statistics of value, principally to Queensland's primary producers.

Frank Bulcock was only 25 when he succeeded T.J. Ryan as the member for Barcoo in 1919. Although he was then working as an organizer with the AWU in western Queensland, he was in fact a trained agricultural and veterinary scientist with diplomas in both these areas from the Sydney Technical College and further training at the Wagga Agricultural College. By 1932, when he was appointed secretary for agriculture and stock, Bulcock was able to combine his experience as a politician with exceptional knowledge of primary industry, to become one of the foremost primary industry ministers in Queensland history. He was to remain secretary for agriculture and stock for ten years. During that time he developed a very close relationship with primary producers and their organizations. When there were requests from farmers for new legislation or amendments to existing legislation, Bulcock used his own personal contacts as well as setting his department to work to determine how widespread the movement for change was. On several occasions, he indicated that he would like to go further and faster in introducing reforms, but was holding back until he had convinced a majority of producers in the particular industry of the wisdom of his proposals and had their support. Because of this close association with primary pro-

As a trained agricultural and veterinary scientist, Frank Bulcock was able to combine this knowledge with his experience as a politician, to become one of the foremost primary industry ministers in Queensland's history. (Photograph by courtesy of Queensland Newspapers Ltd.)

ducers, and their marketing boards, and through his own continued study of overseas and interstate developments in primary production and marketing, Bulcock was far in advance of the Country party members of the opposition when it came to new legislation. In regard to the sugar industry, he and Forgan Smith operated a *de facto* sharing of responsibilities.

During Bulcock's ten years as minister, the level of expertise and advice to farmers by the Department of Agriculture and Stock was constantly raised. He saw his role as being not only an administrator and initiator of new legislation, but also as something of an overseeing agricultural teacher. He hammered constantly at the themes of quality and the use of science to aid dairymen, fruit growers, tobacco farmers, sugar growers and other producers. When, for example, the tobacco industry in north Queensland suffered a setback in 1932, through the commonwealth's lifting the embargo on the quantity of tobacco to be imported, Bulcock not only pressed for the reinstatement of the embargo, but recruited a suitable graduate in agricultural science and sent him to north Queensland to assist in the improvement of the quality of the tobacco leaf. In December 1933, Bulcock introduced a Tobacco Industry Protection Bill under which the Department of Agriculture and Stock established pure seed districts where pure tobacco seed supplies could be propagated and provided at subsidized prices for the growers. "Since tobacco is very susceptible to various diseases", he told the parliament, "it becomes the obvious duty of the State to safeguard the interests of the individual [grower] and endeavour to put the tobacco industry on a safe foundation."[5]

As with Forgan Smith, Bulcock saw agriculture under-pinning the whole social and economic development of Queensland and, through maintaining a productive, prosperous, rural population, providing ultimately for the defence of northern Australia.[6] To achieve this, agricultural education would have to be expanded and agriculture developed on efficient and economic lines. "As an agricultural State," he said, "Queensland's destiny lies along the road of agriculture. We cannot afford to take the less efficient when the more efficient is offering; so we must steadfastly set our faces in the direction of agricultural education."[7] A Chair of Agricultural Science had been established at the University of Queensland while Forgan Smith had been secretary for agriculture and stock and this was complemented by a Chair in Veterinary Science in 1936. Farm training schools were established at St Lucia, Riverview, near Brisbane and in north Queensland.

By 1932, there were already several Acts of Parliament, introduced by Labor and earlier non-Labor governments which protected or assisted primary industries. These related to farmers' co-operatives, marketing boards, land, the dairying and sugar industries, Agricultural Bank and financial assistance to farmers, and diseases in plants and animals. Between 1932 and 1942, these were amended, consolidated and updated and new acts were passed aimed at improving the quality of animals raised and crops grown, maintaining rural producers and population, maintaining processing factories such as sawmills or butter factories as economically viable units, and increasing the export of certain primary products.

Queensland Labor governments in the 1920s had pioneered the "compulsory co-operative" marketing boards which were later adopted by New South Wales and the other states.[8] In 1932, there were twenty-one of these pools in Queensland, each formed on a majority vote of the growers in the particular industry and each controlled by the growers there. They were not merely marketing boards, but through their representation on the Council of Agriculture, they were a major channel of communications between farmers and the government. One of Bulcock's first actions as minister was to extend their mandate beyond the marketing of produce to the expansion of the industry, if this was feasible, through seeking new markets and having power over the conditions of the growth of the product. On the other hand, the board could, with the support of the government, limit the production of a crop. This occurred in the banana industry.[9] The marketing of fruit and the control of its quality were vested in the Committee of Direction of Fruit Marketing whose continuation the growers and the Country party opposition endorsed in 1934.[10]

Bulcock was not in favour of bounties or subsidies to uneconomic producers, although he argued that this was better than allowing agricultural industry to collapse. In fact primary industry was subsidized through low railway freight rates and the charges made for irrigation water supplies. In addition, throughout the 1930s, cash advances were made to cotton growers in the Dawson Valley and maize growers on the Atherton Tableland to allow them to harvest their crops and maintain their farms. Nor did Bulcock favour subsidizing export crops which he said was "simply giving cheap food overseas, paid for partly by the Australian taxpayer".[11] However, this was being somewhat ingenuous. Throughout the 1930s, economists like Brigden, L.F. Giblin and D.B. Copland made it clear that the "home price" scheme for commodities such as dairy products and sugar, which Bulcock supported, was really another way of providing a subsidy to sustain local producers against cheaper imported produce.[12] There were other methods used to get around the question of direct subsidies to growers and at the same time seek an improvement in quality. Grading by the marketing boards was successfully used in the case of pig meat, butter and cheese.

The peanut industry in the 1930s afforded a good illustration of how the commodity boards plus direct government intervention were used to preserve and protect a primary industry which could otherwise not compete openly with imported produce.[13] Peanut growers in the Kingaroy district had successfully approached the Queensland government in 1924 to form a peanut board. The Queensland government in 1928 guaranteed Commonwealth Bank loans to build silos for the co-operative. An embargo on imported peanuts was introduced by the Scullin government in 1930, but was lifted in 1933 when the growers were not able to supply the local market. The industry was further weakened when a group of growers insisted on marketing their peanuts outside the board and, in 1934, the High Court in the "Peanut Case" ruled that the compulsory marketing provision of the Primary Producers' Organization and Marketing Acts were invalid under section 92 of the Commonwealth Constitution.[14] The problems caused by this decision, the later Privy Council decision in the James case and the loss of the 1937 referendum on marketing,[15] made joint commonwealth-state co-operation necessary in addition to any specific assistance the Queensland government could provide to the peanut industry. In 1939, the Peanut Board was again given control over the industry through the use of commonwealth health powers and the passing of the Peanut Industry Protection and Preservation Act by the Queensland government. Under this act, a first pool was created to absorb the expected Australian market for Queensland peanuts for which a stable price would be paid, while the surplus would go into a second pool for peanut oil. Bulcock told the parliament: "The result will be that although it is not sought to impose any restriction on the production of nuts, everybody who is engaged in the industry will get a fair share of the Australian edible nut trade."[16] Both Bulcock and the government were complimented by James Edwards, the Country party member for Nanango which then included Kingaroy, for their work on behalf of the peanut farmers.[17] Perhaps the reaction of peanut growers is best summed up in the conclusion of John Laverty in his paper on the peanut industry where he says: "There can be little doubt that the industry would have died in infancy had it not been sustained by a system of co-operative marketing under the tutelage of the Queensland Government."[18]

The two primary industries where the government was most involved were dairying and sugar. When Bulcock took over the agriculture and stock portfolio in 1932, he found the organization of the dairying industry a mess. There were different bookkeeping methods employed by adjacent butter factories so that a farmer could not readily compare the price of cream paid by each; further he found that factories were paying secret commissions to induce farmers to by-pass nearby factories and send their cream great distances to other factories. In October 1932, a royal commission listed more than a dozen substantial secret commissions paid for a variety of favours in regard to the dairying industry including one of £1500 to Harry Walker, the secretary for agriculture and stock, in the Moore government.[19] For the remainder of the decade, Bulcock set about placing the dairying industry on an efficient basis in terms of the quality of its herds, milk, cream, butter and cheese and the management of butter and cheese factories. His goal was a profitable export industry which could establish a sound footing on the large but highly competitive United Kingdom market. He was to achieve some success here and butter became Queensland's second most profitable export between 1936 and 1941 (see table 3).

An amendment to the Dairy Produce Act prohibited freight commissions on cream and instituted common bookkeeping procedures at butter and cheese factories. In the Dairy Cattle Improvement Act of 1933, an initial £10,000 was set aside for herd testing with no cost to the farmers. At that stage Queensland had the second lowest level of butter fat per cow of any Australian state, which Bulcock said "was not caused solely by climate conditions". He tried also to introduce a scheme of licensing bulls

Table 3. Queensland Rural Exports
(5 year average, value in £1000)

Year	Wool	Butter	Meat	Sugar	Total Overseas Exports
1921-26	12,944	2,063	2,582	1,106[1]	18,976
1926-31	8,340	2,820	2,422	1,770	17,937
1931-36	7,558	3,413	2,385	2,643	18,010
1936-41	9,173	5,251	4,830	4,567	27,239
1941-46	10,110	3,289	2,652	1,783	20,635
1946-51	48,331	8,240	10,569	9,329	89,913
1951-56	57,337	7,548	25,093	22,805	142,544
1956-61	63,063	5,293	32,570	31,175	172,379

Source: *Queensland Year Book*, no. 25, 1964

1. 1923-26 only

to provide better herds, but was to be unsuccessful here. In the same year, the Pig Industry Act set up machinery for tracing and eradicating disease in pork and for the grading of pork products. To assist in raising the quality of export pork to capture more of the United Kingdom market, a subsidy-refund scheme was devised to induce farmers to purchase better breeding stock. Arising out of the 1932 royal commission report, the Dairy Produce Act was amended to provide that no new butter or cheese factories could be erected without government consent and that employees of dairy companies could not hold any confidential agencies for separators, fertilizers or seeds.

After his first three years as minister, Bulcock was still distressed by the substantial lack of improvement in the quality of dairy herds and in the butter and cheese for export. He was having difficulty in convincing many dairy farmers of the importance of quality if they were to compete on the United Kingdom markets. He introduced further amendments to the various acts. Cream carriers were licensed; cream could not be diverted from one factory to another without twenty-eight days notice of intent; differential payments were introduced for different qualities of cream and the herd testing stepped up. A drought in the dairying districts in 1937 did not improve matters, but by 1938, he was able to report that the quality of butter had risen and that if the trend continued the prospects for butter exports seemed good. This proved to be the case in the ten years after the war. In 1938, the government turned to legislating for the quality of milk sold in Brisbane.

Overall Bulcock had some success in improving the quality of dairy products and raising the standard of living of the dairy farmers. While the number of dairy cows in the state increased from 775,301 in 1932 to 1,080,430 in 1940 and the number of persons permanently engaged in the industry rose from 33,500 in 1932 to 36,000 in 1940, the yield in gallons of milk per cow in Queensland in 1938 was still only 237, compared with the overall Australian yield of 360 gallons and New Zealand's 509 gallons. On the other hand, while cheese production rose from 103 million pounds in 1932 to 142 million pounds in 1939, milk production rose from 233 million gallons to 325 million gallons and, in the same period, the total value of dairy products increased from £5.4 million to £10.5 million.[20]

Sugar had a special place in the Queensland economy and also in the decentralization of population along the coast from the New South Wales border to Mossman, north of Cairns. Nambour, Maryborough, Bundaberg, Proserpine, Mackay Ingham, Innisfail and Cairns all owed their existence wholly or partly to sugar. It fulfilled the goal of nineteenth and twentieth century liberals and social democrats for a large number of small, prosperous farmers and was the one industry that could satisfy the Australian desire to fill the empty spaces in the north. The defence argument remained strong in any discussion of the sugar industry. From 1934, the Central Sugar Cane Prices Board ruled that only British subjects (natural born and naturalized) could acquire cane assignments. The 1939 royal commission into the industry stated that: "It is thought that only persons who can be called upon to defend the country in the event of war should be allowed to hold land in the exposed coastal districts which contain the sugar areas."[21] Sugar also assumed a special place with Labor governments which gained substantial votes in the sugar areas and, in turn, had done more to provide the growers with a fair and reasonable return than any other previous governments. The Industrial Arbitration Act and the Workers Accommodation Act had reduced friction between growers and sugar workers and, apart from the dispute in 1927, had provided a stable industry.

After 1924, the industry developed as an exporter as well as a supplier of the local Australian market. By 1929, more than a third of the raw sugar produced was exported. From 140,000 tons of raw sugar being produced in 1915, Queensland was producing 520,000 tons in 1929 of which about 200,000 tons was being exported. In 1929, peaks were applied to all mills to try to regulate the amount of sugar grown and marketed. The fixed price of Queensland sugar during the Depression meant that the sugar industry did not suffer as did other primary and secondary industries and this cushioned the effects of the Depression on areas of Queensland.[22]

The sugar industry remained one of the most closely regulated and most efficient industries. The legislation affecting the sugar indusry that was passed during the 1930s amended the existing acts and provided for changes sought largely by the industry itself. Through the work of the Sugar Experiment Stations, cane per acre increased from 17.32 tons in 1929 to 21.21 tons in 1939 with a consequent increase in sugar per acre from 2.41 tons in 1929 to 3.09 tons in 1939. The industry's problems, so far as the state government could solve these in the 1930s, related to the reduction of ½d. per pound in the home price for sugar in 1932, the increasing tonnage of sugar being produced and the need to export the surplus. In 1939, over 920,000 tons of sugar were produced and almost 60 per cent of this was exported. The export price of sugar had remained around £8 a ton until 1939 when it rose to £10 7s. 6d. a ton compared with around £24 a ton for home market sugar. During the years 1915 to 1957 the export price exceeded the home price only from 1947 to 1951,[23] leaving sugar a highly protected industry whose continued support rested on the grounds of population decentralization, provision of employment and a continued belief in the worthiness of permanent and concentrated settlement in north Australia.

Forgan Smith had no success in persuading the commonwealth government to increase the home price of sugar. His perseverance in the other two problem areas brought him greater success. In 1934 and 1936, he went to London to argue for the continuance of British preferential rates on Queensland sugar. While Britain agreed, in 1936, to maintain existing preferences for a further eighteen months, not the five years sought, Forgan Smith was aware of the limitation on the increase in sugar exports and the consequent need to limit the production of sugar in Queensland. His basic philosophy had always been for the industry to regulate itself and for the government to legislate according to the desires of the industry. However the mill peaks applied in 1929 had not been observed and Queensland was in danger of over-production of sugar that it could not sell either on the home market or on the world market. In 1937, Forgan Smith again went to London to take part in a British attempt to produce an international sugar agreement. Although the conference broke down, Forgan Smith was able to secure an annual Australian quota of 400,000 tons with Britain plus a share of any increase in the market.

He had been unsuccessful in having the industry regulate its own level of production and, early in 1939, the government appointed a five-member royal commission, under Mr. Justice W.F. Webb, then chairman of the Central Sugar Cane Prices Board, to report on sugar peaks. The royal commission reported that: "unless production is checked the industry will be in a position within two years of producing sugar for which there is no market." It recommended that the maximum safe production of sugar for Queensland should be about 737,000 tons per year, a figure greatly exceeded in 1939. (New South Wales was to have a recommended limit of 40,000 tons.)[24]

In October 1939, Forgan Smith introduced amendments to the Regulation of Sugar Cane Prices Act to give effect to the royal commission recommendations. Farm peaks were established as well as mill peaks, but there could not be any reduction in the acreage planted for farmers having assignments below 200 tons. The Central Sugar Cane Prices Board was given more supervisory power over the industry. No longer was the chairman of the Central Board required to be a Supreme Court judge, but could be

William Forgan Smith depicted at the height of his power in 1940. (Photograph by courtesy of the John Oxley Library.)

"a man well versed in the sugar industry".[25] Despite speculation, Forgan Smith did not immediately move to that position which was more highly paid than the premiership.

By the end of the 1930s, the Queensland government was turning its attention towards commonwealth schemes of marketing and price stabilization. This had been partly the result of the James case in the Privy Council, which indicated that the commonwealth had less marketing power under Section 92 than had been thought and which also endangered intrastate marketing powers. Such price and stabilization legislation involved the state and commonwealth governments in passing complementary legislation. Through the 1938 Wheat Stabilisation Act, Queensland wheat growers were protected from cheaper southern wheat flooding onto the Queensland market . Although Queensland was not a producer of dried fruits, Bulcock argued that Queensland complementary legislation was necessary to prevent "any illicit trade" under Section 92. Consequently in November 1939, the Fruit and Vegetable Act was amended regarding the price to be paid in Queensland for dried fruits.

Queensland was given the responsibility for drafting the bill, which all states would then pass, to limit the manufacture and distribution of margarine from imported products. Table margarine was to be sold in cubes, not in the shape of butter, and licences were to be issued for the manufacture and sale of margarine with quotas based on 1938 production. Bulcock was not prepared to discriminate against one set of primary producers, the oil seed producers, in favour of another set of primary producers, the dairy farmers, through a total ban on margarine.

> There cannot be any possible objection to the desire of people to buy vegetable margarine from our own production provided that they know they are buying margarine. I should be disinclined to place a cotton producer at a disadvantage in the production of cotton-seed oil in favour of a dairy producer who, no doubt would desire to see the complete elimination of all margarine from the market of Australia.[26]

In 1942, three changes occurred that marked the end of a fruitful decade in Queensland agricultural history during which the value of the state's agricultural production had been increased by over 50 per cent. Only New South Wales exceeded this.[27] Forgan Smith retired as premier in 1942 but continued his role as a guardian of the sugar industry by becoming chairman of the Central Sugar Cane Prices Board. In that same year, the prime minister, John Curtin, called on Bulcock to become director of agriculture in charge of food production for the war effort. It was perhaps fitting that in his last major speech on agriculture to the Queensland parliament, Bulcock concluded on tones that reflected the strong agrarian fundamentalism that had underpinned so much of Labor legislation. "No section of our community", said Bulcock, "is worthy of greater admiration by virtue of its efforts than the rural producers in Queensland."[28] In 1942, the commonwealth became the main initiator in agricultural policy and Queensland agriculture became a part of the wider war production.[29]

Tom Williams of Port Curtis succeeded Bulcock as minister for agriculture and stock. He did not have the same grasp of the portfolio as Bulcock and when Ned Hanlon replaced Frank Cooper as premier in 1946, Williams was moved to public instruction and Harold Collins, the member for the north Queensland electorate of Cook, became the new minister. Collins was to be a competent administrator, but was not the initiator that Bulcock had been, and was to hold the agriculture and stock portfolio until Labor lost office in 1957. Williams' principal piece of legislation had been to amend the Fruit Marketing Organisation Act in November 1945 to establish a vegetable group within the COD and extend the power of that body to bring about a better distribution of fruit and vegetables throughout the state. This had emerged from the report of a 1944 royal commission into fruit and vegetables. In November 1943, Cooper as premier and treasurer had liberalized the loans available under the Rural Development Co-ordination of Advances Act by increasing the maximum loan from £1800 to £5000 and increasing the maximum term of repayment from twenty-five years to thirty years. Lending for the purchase of specific items of agricultural equipment was also increased.

With the end of the war there was a return to the long-standing Queensland goals of agricultural development and land settlement. Despite the warnings from the Rural Reconstruction Commission regarding new ventures in agriculture at a time of uncertain markets and uncertain levels of farm income, Queensland plunged into new developmental projects which related to agricultural expansion. This had two goals: increasing exports and increasing agricultural production to the level of Queensland's rural population. Rural exports boomed in the post-war years due largely to the demand for wool and negotiated agreements for butter, meat and sugar (see table 3). Queensland remained closely tied to the British market. While agricultural production increased in value and in volume in certain areas (see table 1), it was not possible to stem the movement of population away from rural areas (see table 4). All that can be said was that Queensland did better than Australia as a whole at maintaining its rural working population.

Soldier settlement schemes again were proposed for ex-servicemen, but with a great deal more caution and planning than had been possible after World War I. Hanlon, an ex-serviceman from World War I, was aware of the problems caused and the hopes that were dashed by the partial failures of the soldier settlement schemes of the 1920s. A royal commission was established in February 1946, to consider ways of providing cane assignments in the sugar industry for ex-servicemen. It made a guarded recommendation for the priority sale of existing farms to ex-servicemen rather than opening new sugar areas.[30] The government accepted this viewpoint.

In 1947, Hanlon was able to have the halfpenny per pound for sugar, lost in the depression years, restored and two further increases, each of one halfpenny a pound, were negotiated with the commonwealth government in 1949. In that year also, Hanlon led the Australian sugar delegation to London where he secured an export quota of 600,000 tons, an increase of 200,000 tons on the 1937 agreement. The increased export quota allowed for expansion of sugar assignments with 3 per cent of the total production being reserved for ex-servicemen. New and increased

Table 4. Proportion of the Working Population in Rural Industries

Year	Queensland	Australia
1901	30.6	25.5
1911	28.6	23.0
1921	29.6	21.9
1933	29.3	20.9
1947	23.2	14.5
1954	20.6	13.3
1961	17.3	10.8

Source: *Commonwealth of Australia Year Books*

assignments were also given to ex-servicemen in those mill areas where average mill peaks were not being reached.

In the immediate post-war years, dairying and wheat were still covered by price stabilization schemes instituted by the commonwealth government. After 1942, the dairy industry enjoyed a commonwealth subsidy on butter and cheese to make up the difference between the cost of production to the farmer (i.e., his actual costs, plus interest charges plus a profit margin) and the return he received from the factory. In 1951, when the commonwealth Liberal-Country government refused to renew the dairy stabilization programme, Queensland farmers had already received over £11 million in subsidies. For the four previous years, butter production had exceeded 100 million pounds of which two-thirds, on average, had been sold overseas.

The refusal of the commonwealth government to renew the dairy stabilization programme coincided with a year of devastating drought when producers threatened to withhold supplies unless prices were increased. Collins' solution was to advise an increase in production, but to protect Queensland consumers, he amended the Primary Producers Organisation and Marketing Act to force the butter board to acquire sufficient butter from the producers to satisfy Queensland consumption. The amended act was then extended to all marketing boards and not repealed until 1955. Production rose again in 1952 and until 1957, on average, half the Queensland butter was exported. However, with the removal of commonwealth assistance in

1952, the return per pound to the farmers did not keep pace with rising costs and in fact declined both relatively and absolutely.

Under the Wheat Stabilisation Act of 1946, passed by both the Queensland and commonwealth governments, the Queensland wheat industry was to be allowed to expand to a million acres at a guaranteed price per bushel. The peak acreage harvested had been 442,000 acres in 1938-39 and even by 1960 one million acres had not been reached. Nevertheless, in 1947-48, more than 10 million bushels were produced, this being the first time ever that Queensland had reached such a level of production and was double the normal pre-war amount. The Queensland Wheat Board now became the agent for the Australian Wheat Board and the act was renewed when its time limit ran out.

Where Forgan Smith and Bulcock had been most concerned with preserving and protecting the primary producers who had been through the Depression, and with increasing the quality of Queensland's primary produce with an eye to the export market, Hanlon's goal was population growth and defence through small-scale agriculture. The state's primary function as he saw it was to provide the infrastructure of subsidized water, power and transport and the maintenance of the orderly marketing system. Hanlon was the first Labor premier to come from Brisbane. Yet his early years as the son of an unsuccessful selector who was forced to return to the city to find work seems to have left its mark. Like Forgan Smith, Ryan, Theodore and other political Labor leaders of his generation, Hanlon easily dropped into the ringing fundamentalist agrarian rhetoric. Unfortunately he lacked Forgan Smith's experience as minister for agriculture and stock and Bulcock's combination of theoretical and practical knowledge of agriculture and agricultural economic efficiency.

Understandably, having just survived a war in which the Japanese — those evil demons who had haunted Australia since the Russo-Japanese war — came so close to Australia and to Queensland, Hanlon saw the development of large-scale small farming as the continuation of the Labor policy of protecting Australia through "development" and "filling the empty spaces". He spelled out this theme clearly in the debate on the Tully Hydro-Electric Project Bill:

> To the best of our ability, we must try to convince the Commonwealth people that their only safety lies in developing and populating not only North Queensland, but the whole of North Austraia. The developing and peopling of that part of the country is essential to the safety of the people of Sydney and Melbourne, only a fool would think otherwise.[31]

Yet Queensland was not prepared to develop a large post-war migration programme to augment "filling the empty spaces". Its migrant intake between 1946 and 1951 was the lowest of any state at 4.06 per 1000 of population compared with Victoria 9.66, South Australia 9.9, New South Wales 10.28, Western Australia 15.72 and Tasmania 17.39.[32] Migrants were to be encouraged only after the new farms were established so that they would not compete with Australians for jobs and would not congregate in the capital city.

The Burdekin Dam, for which Hanlon obtained some imprecise verbal commitment by Chifley for commonwealth financial assistance, along with the Tully Hydro-Electric Project, the Mareeba-Dimbulah irrigation scheme and a weir on the McIntyre River were the tangible manifestation of the government's faith in its programme of increased agricultural settlement. Gair, treasurer at the time the Burdekin scheme was announced, argued that there would be five thousand irrigated farms in the area producing crops to the value of £5 million.[33] In his *Campaign Manual* for the 1956 election, when he was premier, he estimated that the population in the Mareeba-Dimbulah area would increase from four thousand five hundred to sixteen thousand, with production being of an annual value of £6 million.[34]

Behind Hanlon and Gair was Colin Clark who shared their views on agrarian settlement. After 1946, Clark was not only director of the bureau of industry, but also under-secretary for labour and industry (Gair's department), government statistician and financial adviser to the treasury. In the 1930s, Clark had argued for growth in secondary and tertiary industries, but after the war became a propagandist for agricultural and pastoral settlers.[35] It was noticeable that under Clark, the *Economic News* changed its emphasis from providing economic news of value to primary producers, as it had done under Brigden, to one of publicizing Clark's religious-economic views. Articles on marriage, population, fertility and birth rates with their relation to land settlement now took up issues of *Economic News*.[36] When Clark gave evidence before the 1950 royal commission on pastoral land settlement, he reprinted this in *Economic News*.[37] His case was for two hundred and fifty thousand people being settled in the agricultural and pastoral areas of the state. Aside from his conversion to agrarianism, Clark struck a note of urgency in his argument: "Sooner or later Australia must expect to face a military challenge from Asia, quite probably within twenty years." The way to resist that challenge in Clark's view was a repetition of the "fill the empty spaces" thesis. These new settlements would be centred on small towns of fifteen hundred persons, with a priest or pastor being among the first of the citizens provided for. As William Jackson noted in his thesis, "The Government and Economic Growth in Queensland, 1946-1951": "there is a striking similarity between Clark's views and those put forward by [B.A. Santamaria's] Catholic Social Studies Movement after world war II."[38] Paul Hilton, who was to be elected to the cabinet after the 1950 election (defeating Ted Walsh) attempted to have the 1950 Labor-in-Politics Convention commit the ALP to Clark's land and agricultural policies.

Others advising the government were not so convinced of the soundness of Clark's proposition. The 1947 annual report of the Department of Lands warned against the notion that there were large areas of land suitable for closer settlement. "The true position is" said the report "that most of the usable land is under occupation and in order to secure closer land settlement, existing tenants must be dispossessed of either part or whole of their holdings."[39] The government established the royal commission, referred to earlier, whose report supported permanent residential family properties against company or absentee owners in the west, but in no sense echoed Clark's notion of ten thousand settlers in the pastoral industry.[40]

Surprisingly, while schemes like those at the Burdekin and at Mareeba-Dimbulah, with their emphasis on closer settlement, seemed to fulfil the goals advocated by Clark, he was to become a bitter critic of these irrigation schemes after he left the Queensland government. In his book, *Australian Hopes and Fears* (published in 1958), he wrote:

> New depths in political chicane and in bogus economics were reached by the State politicians in Queensland in respect of the Burdekin Project . . . There is a case for flood mitigation works; but no case whatever for combining these with a grandiose project for irrigation . . . Every time the estimate is revised it comes out a great deal higher. The final figures look like a project costing over £100,000,000 to create a few hundred farms, generate some electric power and mitigate the floods.

Other economists besides Clark shared his later scepticism about the economic costs and values of the Burdekin project and other heavily subsidized schemes of irrigation.[41]

The post-war Labor governments took a different view from the economists. They argued that the social and defence value of increased numbers of small farmers, of the maintenance of a large rural population and decentralization of the state's industries far outweighed any economic arguments. Moreover, the system of marketing boards, stable home prices and liberal assistance through the Agricultural Bank, guaranteed that Queensland's farmers would not be forced into peasant-like survival agriculture. Although the Labor-in-Politics Convention in the 1940s and 1950s continued to exhibit a greater interest in the conditions of the worker than in agriculture, there was no challenge to the fundamental agrarian ideology that the government and the largest affiliated union, the AWU, shared.

In only one instance did the Labor government step outside the long-standing commitment to the small farmer as the basis of its agricultural programme. That was in the Peak Downs scheme where five hundred thousand acres of former grazing property and £2.5 million capital were combined to produce food for post-war Britain[42] (see Chapter 10). It was a major attempt at corporation as against family farming and was motivated by a genuine desire to help the British people over what seemed to be a desperate shortage of food. There was no collectivist theory of farming behind it. The project was begun in 1948 and wound up in 1953 showing a large financial loss though there was some gain in the sale of sixty mixed grazing and agricultural farms each around five thousand acres. The Peak Downs scheme departed from the pattern of agricultural development laid down by successive Labor premiers after Ryan. It ran counter to Theodore's 1922 proposal for agricultural development and lacked Bulcock's perception of how economically efficient farming could be carried on. While both Forgan Smith and Bulcock would certainly have been moved by the British government's need for food, it is more likely that they would have attacked the question through existing or new individual farmers, not through a government corporation actively involved in state farming.

With the death of Hanlon in 1952, the dreams of unlimited agricultural settlement and development subsided. Progress was now seen more in conserving what had been achieved than in venturing into brave new worlds. Soil conservation, extension of the sizes of farming leases, a steady development of weirs and irrigation projects, increases in sugar production, consolidation of farmers in the tobacco industry and a further strengthening of the marketing board system: these were agricultural policies pursued by Gair and Collins. Confident of the inability of the opposition to defeat the government in the parliament or at an election, Collins spent more time in the Legislative Assembly joining in the debates than ever Bulcock had. Here, he recited the virtues of primary producers, the superiority of the agrarian life and the achievements of the Queensland and recent commonwealth Labor governments in agriculture, much as a monk recited his office. In September 1955, he told the parliament during the Address in Reply debate:

> The prosperity of Australia is wrapped up with the prosperity of its primary industry . . . . It is plain that Australia has and still does ride on the back of the primary producer. For that reason, the primary producer is entitled at least to receive the full value of the cost of production for his products in order to retain the solvency of this country.[43]

Ryan and Theodore had won office for Labor in 1915 by building a coalition of urban workers, rural workers and farmers. These they saw as being "natural allies" against the city bankers, merchants and middlemen. It was Theodore as premier and Forgan Smith as minister for agriculture and stock who had provided the farmers' "Bill of Rights" through the Primary Producers Organisation Act, the Council of Agriculture and the co-operative marketing boards. It was fortunate for Labor electorally in the 1930s and for Queensland farmers that there were two such competent ministers as Forgan Smith and Bulcock supervising the government's role in agriculture as the state recovered from the Depression. Forgan Smith and Bulcock together cemented the coalition that Ryan and Theodore had developed between the Labor party and large sections of the rural and non-metropolitan population. While later Labor premiers and cabinet ministers might not have equalled the capabilities of Forgan Smith and Bulcock, they were no less sympathetic to the farmers and no less prepared to use government power in the interests of farmers than they were to use this power on behalf of workers.

The system of marketing boards, which other states later adopted, and the stabilization schemes which were also to be adopted on a national level remain the Labor governments' legacies to the Queensland primary producers. Their other legacy was a stable and prosperous sugar industry where the successive Labor governments raised the economic security of the small growers beyond the dreams of Griffith and the nineteenth century proponents of the sugar industry producing the "nation of yeoman farmers" or the "small man's paradise".

NOTES

1. On Forgan Smith, see Brian Carroll's chapter, "William Forgan Smith, Dictator or Democrat" in *Queensland Political Portraits 1859-1952*, eds. D.J. Murphy and R.B. Joyce (St Lucia: University of Queensland Press, 1978); and Michael J. Thompson, "The Political Career of William Forgan Smith — As It Influenced Economic and Political Development in Queensland" (B.Econ. thesis, University of Queensland, 1965).

2. *QPD* CLXI (23 November 1932) :1731.
3. Two very useful theses that look both at the importance attached to primary industries and the retardation of manufacturing industries in the 1930s and 1940s are M.A. Jones, "The Government and Economic Growth in Queensland 1946-56", (B.A. thesis, University of Queensland, 1968).
   Growth in Queensland 1946-1956", (B.A. honours thesis, University of Queensland, 1968).
4. *QPD* CLXI (23 November 1932) :1732.
5. Ibid. CLXIII (6 December 1933) :1972.
6. Ibid. CLXI (20 October 1932) :1071.
7. Ibid.
8. For assessments of these marketing boards see H.S. Hunter, "Co-operative Marketing in Queensland", *Queensland Agricultural Journal*, new series, no. 63 (October 1946); D.R. Lewis, "A General Review of Primary Producers' Co-operatives in Queensland", *Queensland Agricultural Journal*, new series, no. 83 (June 1957); J.N. Lewis, "Organized Marketing of Agricultural Productivity in Australia", *Australian Journal of Agricultural Economics* 5, no. 1 (September 1961); D.B. Copland and C.V. James, *Australian Marketing Problems, A Book of Documents 1932-1937* (Sydney: Angus & Robertson, 1938).
9. See Frank Bulcock's remarks in "Economic Balance", in *Australian Marketing Problems*, Copland and James, p. 232.
10. See B. Flewell-Smith, "The Queensland Fruit Trade", *Historical Society of Queensland Journal* 5 (1955); and comments of Frank Nicklin in the debate on the Fruit Marketing Organization Act Amendment Bill, *QPD* CLXV 9 (October 1934) :544.
11. *QPD* CLXXII (24 August 1938) :86.
12. See introduction and chap. 1, Copland and James, *Australian Marketing Problems*; Lewis, "Organized Marketing"; and J.B. Brigden, "The Home Price Principle", *Economic News* 4, no. 6 (June 1935); A.J. Little, "Some Aspects of Government Policy Affecting the Rural Sector of the Australian Economy with Special Reference to the Period 1939/45-1953, *Economic Record* 38, no. 83 (September 1962).
13. This section relies heavily on J.R. Laverty, "Organized Marketing and the Development of the Peanut Industry", *Historical Society of Queensland Journal* 5 (1953); and the debate on the Peanut Industry Protection and Preservation Bill, *QPD* CLXXV 9 (16 November 1939) :1467-69, 1679-80.
14. *Peanut Board* v *Rockhampton Harbour Board* 48, CLR 266.
15. For brief discussions on these see G. Sawer, *Australian Federal Politics and Law, 1929-1949* (Melbourne: Melbourne University Press, 1963), pp. 82-83, 94-95.

16. *QPD* CLXXVI (9 November 1939) :1468.
17. Ibid., p. 1469.
18. Laverty, "Organized Marketing", p. 839.
19. "Report of the Royal Commission Appointed to Inquire into and Report upon Alleged Payments of Secret Commissions etc. in the Dairying Industry", *QPP* 2 (1932).
20. Jones, "The Government and Economic Growth", pp. 49-59.
21. "Report of the Royal Commission on Sugar Peaks and Cognate Matters", *QPP* 2 (1939) :9.
22. B.J. Costar, "The Great Depression. Was Queensland Different?", *Labour History* 26 (May 1974); D.J. Stalley, "The Sugar Industry", in *The Economics of Australian Industry*, ed. Alex Hunter (Melbourne: Melbourne University Press, 1963).
23. Stalley, "The Sugar Industry", p. 375.
24. "Report of the Royal Commission Appointed to Inquire into and Report upon Alleged Payments of Secret Commissions etc. in the Dairying Industry", pp. 14-15.
25. *QPD* CLXXV 17 (24 October 1939) :921, 1076-81.
26. Ibid. CLXXV (7 November 1939) :1404.
27. Commonwealth Grants Commission, *Report* 1940, cited in Jones, "The Government and Economic Growth", p. 34.
28. *QPD* CLXXIX (17 September 1942) :233.
29. See J.G. Crawford et al, *Wartime Agriculture in Australia and New Zealand* (Stanford: Stanford University Press, 1954).
30. "Report of the Royal Commission on Soldier Settlement on Sugar Lands", *QPP* 2 (1946).
31. *QPD* CXVIII (18 October 1950) :729.
32. Jackson, "The Government and Economic Growth", p. 107.
33. *QPD* CXCVII (22 November 1949) :1739.
34. *Australian Labor Party Campaign Manual State Elections* (Brisbane: Australian Labor Party, 1956), p. 26.
35. This change in Clark's views is outlined in Jones, "The Government and Economic Growth", pp. 142-53 and Jackson, "The Government and Economic Growth", pp. 75-80. See also Colin Clark, *The Conditions of Economic Progress* (London: Macmillan, 1940); and Colin Clark, *Australian Economic Progress Against a World Background* (Joseph Fisher Lecture, Adelaide, 1938).
36. *Economic News* 14, no. 9 (1945); 15, no. 7 (1946); 16, nos. 8-9, 10-12 (1947); 17, no. 1 (1948); 18, nos. 7-9 (1949); 19, nos. 2, 7-8 (1950); 20, nos. 1, 10 (1951).
37. Ibid., 19, nos. 7-8 (July-August 1950).
38. Jackson, "The Government and Economic Growth", p. 41.
39. Ibid., p. 42.

40. "Report of the Royal Commission on Pastoral Land Settlement", *QPP* 2 (1951-52).
41. For example, B.R. Davidson, *The Northern Myth* (Melbourne: Melbourne University Press, 1965).
42. The Peak Downs scheme is well covered in H.W. Herbert, "The 'Peak Downs' Scheme", *Australian Quarterly* 25, no. 4 (December 1953); and Penelope Rogers, "The 'Failure' of the Peak Downs Scheme", *AJPH* XI no. 1 (April 1964).
43. *QPD* CCXII (13 September 1955) :296-97.

10 Land and Settlement

Colin A. Hughes

Immediately upon separation from New South Wales, the new Queensland parliament had addressed itself to legislation dealing with Crown land. In 1860, three acts were passed, two dealing with pastoral leases and the third with general settlement. For the next quarter century, the problem of land tenures exercised the community for, on the one hand, there was widespread commitment to more intensive settlement and, on the other, the dominant pastoralists sought stability of tenure to protect such improvements as they had made on raw grazing land. In the 1870s the process of subdivision of the large holdings began; between the passage of the Land Act 1868 and the Land Act 1884 some 6,300,000 acres of Crown land were alienated, but only 120,000 acres were brought under crop, while extensive dummying frustrated much of the intent for closer settlement.

The Griffith government's Land Act 1884 was at once a consolidating measure to tidy up the clutter of almost annual tinkering with land law, and a revolutionary step forward. Administration of public lands was removed from the secretary for public lands, a portfolio dating back to 1862, and given to a tribunal, the Land Board, of two members, subject only to a limited right of appeal to the Supreme Court. Pastoral lessees were dealt with firmly: their pre-emptive rights were withdrawn in the settled districts and the scheduled areas of unsettled districts which, together, amounted to about one-half the area of the colony. Thereafter, when a pastoral lease fell in, the leasehold would be divided into two parts, one to be returned to the lessee on a new lease, the other to be made available for settlement. In the settled districts new leases would run for only ten years, in the unsettled districts for fifteen (extended to twenty-one in 1886 with the proviso that after fifteen years any part of the run except the head station might be resumed without compensation).

Settlement would be promoted through the selection of both agricultural farm and grazing farm selections. The grazing farm selector, who it was expected would gradually replace the big pastoralist, might select up to 20,000 acres for an initial period of two years followed by a lease of thirty years, his rent fixed by the Land Board first for ten years, then at five-year intervals. The agricultural farm selector might select up to 960 acres, and after the initial period secure a lease of fifty years with the right after ten years to convert to freehold at a price proclaimed by the board. Both grazing and agricultural selectors were required to reside continuously on their selections, but their leases might be sold or transferred. Soon after, the Land Act 1886 turned the selection of agricultural lands into conditional purchase, provided a scheme for village settlement that never proved attractive, and in a concession that came home to roost with the Ryan government fixed the maximum increase permitted on the five-yearly review of pastoral rents at 50 per cent of the previous rental..

The broad policy embodied in the 1884 Act sought to avoid the general alienation of public lands to corporate and individual speculators, which it was feared could mean that land would have to be repurchased for public needs when development of railways and roads at public expense had made closer settlement possible. To that end, the principle of leasehold would be used to maintain a steady supply of land in the hands of the Crown so as to meet demands for land, at least until the entire colony was settled for agricultural purposes. There would be a three-stage progression: first, pastoral leases for a fixed term but without restriction as to area which would be attractive to big capitalists; second, when the big pastoralists were no longer required, the land would be broken up into grazing selections for extensive use, until the land was needed for agricultural settlement; finally, when required, there would be further subdivision into farming units at which stage freehold would be granted. The advance of the agricultural frontier would sustain a steady flow of immigrants, and as each worker left the labour market to become a farmer a new worker would replace him. This policy dominated successive Queensland governments, so that as late as 1950 a royal commission would affirm: "The soundest land policy is that which will create the greatest number of permanently resident families, consistent with a reasonable way of life, and only closer settlement can offer this. In short, the welfare of the inland is to be measured by the number of families it can be brought to support."[1]

Improved conditions from the mid-1880s ensured a steady demand for selection. The Co-operative Communities Land Settlement Act 1893, in part a response to Labor ideas but partly also a development of the earlier idea of village settlement, showed the limited appeal of any alternative to individual selection; the dubious merit of sites selected for the purpose helped defeat co-operation.[2] Selectors' reluctance to go far from transport and markets directed attention to areas of good agricultural land previously alienated but held by graziers; the Agricultural Lands Purchase Act 1894, authorized the government to buy back such land, by compulsion if necessary. Its application was mainly to the Darling Downs where, by mid-1898, 140,000 acres had been purchased and turned over to agricultural occupation; in all by 1915, 664,000 acres had been acquired for £1.7 million and 570,000 acres allotted in 2600 farms.[3] There were minor refinements of the 1884 system; the Crown Lands Act 1897 turned the Land Board into the Land Court with an additional member; the Crown Lands Act 1894 created the grazing homestead (a lease with a five years' residence requirement) with a maximum area of 2560 acres, and the Prickly-pear Selections Act 1901 introduced a new tenure for settlers who would have to clear the pest from infested land. There were frequent amendments to give relief to lessees and selectors — extensions of time in which to meet obligations, easing of rent requirements, reduction of initial payments, easing of qualifications for selectors. In 1897, the 1884 act was replaced by a new consolidating act, and in 1910 there was yet another consolidating act which provided the framework within which Labor governments from Ryan to Gair operated.[4]

In the years immediately preceding Labor's electoral victory in 1915, closer settlement had proceeded steadily. Each year between two thousand and three thousand applications for conditional purchase of agricultural lands were accepted, involving one to two million acres; about two-thirds of the applications were for agricultural farms, most of the remainder for prickly-pear selections which were substantially larger in area. The proportions of Queensland's total area (429,120,000 acres) which had been alienated or was in the process of alienation had crept up from 3.70 per cent (3.10 per cent alienated, 0.60 per cent in process) in 1900 to 6.26 per cent (3.79 per cent alienated, 2.47 per cent in process) in 1914, but it was still a tiny part of the state and generally confined to the coast and south-east with isolated patches of freehold elsewhere. The process of closer settlement for grazing showed comparable success: each year there were one hundred and fifty to two hundred and fifty grazing farm applications accepted involving one and a half to three and a half million acres, and two hundred and fifty to three hundred and fifty grazing homestead applications accepted involving two and a half to four million acres. However, rather more than half the total area of the state remained subject to pastoral leases; despite the low rental per square mile such leases contributed significantly to state revenues. Overall, Queensland was still predominantly pastoral, with almost half Australia's cattle and almost a quarter of the country's sheep, but less than 5 per cent of the area under crop and accounting for barely 1-2 per cent of wheat production.

Labor's policy in general accepted the 1884 system, and the desirability of closer settlement on which it was based. Herbert Hardacre, the party's leading spokesman on land matters in opposition, concluded his principal speech on the 1910 act with verse to commemorate the US Homestead Act of 1861 which ended:

The soil lies fallow, the weeds grow rank,
And idle the poor man stands,
Whilst millions of hands want acres,
And millions of acres want hands.[5]

Enough good Labor men, ex-miners, ex-bushworkers, even town

labourers, had gone selecting to ensure sympathy for the selectors' interest, and a respectable Labor vote among small farmers reinforced loyalties. In the speech just mentioned, Hardacre was critical of the frequency of land legislation which he attributed to lack of a fixed policy, to the fact that influential interests "hurl the various Governments backwards and forwards to alter the law", and the fact that circumstances changed. To bring land law to "finality", he advocated three principles: use should be the only reason for granting tenure; security of tenure should be given only for improvements; land required for superior use should be available for that use without delay or costly compensation. Such principles would have the effect of hastening and intensifying pressures on the big pastoralists; anticipating the events of a decade later, Hardacre argued that alterations in tenures made by Land Acts were not analogous to other contracts, and therefore such alterations were not "repudiation". Leases were different because the supply of land was limited, and their duration was so long. But the Labor party did not go along with the small selector as far as freehold which, it was feared, would lock up the land against settlement and frustrate development. Instead it favoured perpetual leasehold. Perpetual lease selections had been introduced in 1908 as an alternative to agricultural farm selection, subject to similar conditions for occupation and improvements, but had had little impact on the land situation involving ten to twenty selections and ten thousand to twenty thousand acres per year.

Ryan's first secretary for public lands was John McEwan Hunter. One of the government's earliest, and most enduring, decisions was to proclaim a national park of forty-seven thousand acres at the Lamington Plateau, but legislation required the agreement of the Legislative Council. The first attempt at a Land Act Amendment Bill combined the cessation of freeholding and replacement by perpetual leasehold with provision that pastoral rents might be increased by more than 50 per cent on a review. The rents proposal was subsequently withdrawn, and becomes part of the story of the eventual abolition of the Legislative Council (see Chapter 4), but the establishment of perpetual leasehold got through the upper house after a free conference. It is difficult to estimate the consequences of the change. In 1956, the proportion of the state's area which had been or was being alienated was much what it had been in 1914, though by then almost all of the land involved had been alienated and only 0.6 per cent was still in process; the proportion had fallen slightly between 1914 and 1929, but was restored to 6.5 per cent by the brief period of freeholding under the Moore government and stayed at that figure for the next twenty-five years. Given depressed pastoral and agricultural conditions from about 1920 to 1945, it is questionable whether the steady alienation of 1900-14 would have continued, and it is certainly improbable that it would have accelerated. Once freeholding had been restored after Labor lost office in 1957, the proportion of the state's area alienated rose so that by 1974 it was 16.8 per cent (7.3 per cent alienated, 9.5 per cent in process), but these were other times. The anti-Labor opposition parties always remained committed to freeholding, and when they had the opportunity they restored it, but it was a matter of ideological predisposition rather than hard evidence that Labor policy slowed development.

The universal commitment to development through closer settlement provided an obvious solution to the problems of repatriated soldiers. The Federal Parliamentary War Committee identified land settlement as one means whereby returned servicemen could have a secure future; as the states controlled all Crown lands in Australia the matter was handed over to them. The policy had been agreed at a commonwealth-state conference in February 1916; the Discharged Soldiers' Settlement Act 1917 in Queensland was, Bernays affirms proudly, the first measure of its kind in the British Empire. The state government was empowered to acquire land by agreement or compulsion or to set aside Crown land for soldier settlement. Perpetual leases would be granted on favourable terms as to rent and survey fees, though subject to stringent residence requirements. Advances would be provided by the Government Savings Bank. The first plans were grandiose: in January 1917, Hunter spoke of 1222 settlers at Beerburrum, 250 at Pikedale — and 6700 in the Callide Valley and 9,000 in the Upper Burnett. Numbers were quickly scaled down to 2,800 to be settled by January 1919; in the event only 956 had been settled by June 1919, although the number then rose steadily to a maximum of 2577 in 1921 after which it declined. Ryan sought British ex-servicemen as well, with very little success as despite extensive advertising in Britain only thirty-nine came of the 1600 expected. The disruption of European agriculture had left prices high after the cessation of hostilities; fruit and maize particularly benefited, and soldier settlers were encouraged to grow them. (A further encouragement to maize-growing at Atherton-Tolga was that it justified the ejection of Chinese farmers whose lands were compulsorily acquired for the purpose. The 1907 Labor-in-Politics Convention had carried a resolution to prohibit non-whites from holding leasehold or freehold, and so several goals could be realized simultaneously. The unfortunate solider settlers who replaced the Chinese were handicapped in marketing their crop until the north coast railway was completed in 1924.)

The weaknesses of the soldier settlement scheme were many — and much the same in each state. The Queensland government had a selection programme of sorts, administered first by local Land Settlement Committees and after 1919 by a sub-committee of the Soldier Settlement Branch of the Lands Department, but inadequately staffed and acting on minimal evidence. There was a training programme, based on the group settlements, but the training supervisors and assistants were of dubious quality, and the selection in some cases of returned soldiers who were current settlers themselves was particularly unsatisfactory. Gatton Agricultural College ran a short course, but only forty-four men passed through it. Even when the settlers proved effective farmers, they might be poor managers, with no idea of budgeting or how to run a farm as a business. The settlement scheme was based on commercial principles: settlers were put on land purchased or compulsorily resumed and paid rent of 1½ per cent of capital value, that is the price that the government had paid. They had also to pay interest on advances, and eventually repay the whole sum advanced and a survey fee for the subdivision of the property. Consequently they needed a high rate of turnover to meet commitments, and to pay their production costs. Saddled with a 100 per cent mortgage on high land values, when the generally accepted limit for a successful settler was two-thirds, the returned soldiers were at risk. Drought and pests, poor soils in some areas, inadequate areas in some, and the inevitable decline in agricultural prices multiplied their difficulties.

Interest deferments were granted by the Lands Acts Amendment Act 1922 which merely transferred unpaid interest to capital. Valuation adjustments were made in 1923 which knocked £77 off an average debt of £634. Some resettlements to new areas were made, with a writing off of old debts and the grant of new loans, but the drift of soldier settlers from the land continued. By 1929 the scheme was at an end, and thereafter ex-servicemen received no special treatment although the Revaluation Board continued to write down their debts. Overall the government had lost £1.85 million, about £300 for each settler assisted or £550 for each who remained on the land. Viewed as repatriation welfare, or even as a means of encouraging land settlement, such losses were not too bad, but it had been expected that there would be no loss at all.[6]

After World War II, governments were much more cautious. The Rural Reconstruction Commission, which had reviewed the extensive problems of rural industry in Australia, warned against expansion of agricultural production without adequate consideration of markets, and its second report (1944) made elaborate proposals to make any new programme for soldier settlement more successful. Emphasis was place on rehabilitation of men with previous rural experience. In Queensland, by December 1949 the Lands Department had acquired and distributed over 157,000 acres and the Agricultural Bank had approved loans totalling £4 million, while more than 3280 ex-servicemen had been rehabilitated in grazing, mixed farming, sugar and tobacco. Experience dictated more realistic areas, so that, for example, the sixty-three grazing blocks opened exclusively for ex-servicemen averaged 30,000 acres each. Whilst the new programme did little to promote closer settlement, the ex-servicemen were spared the hardships of the earlier soldier settlers.[7]

Labor's first two secretaries of public lands, Hunter and Coyne, left politics to become, respectively, agent-general and a member of the Land Court. The third, William McCormack, was responsible for most innovations of Labor's 1915-29 term. The Closer Settlement Acts Amendment Act 1923 introduced another new tenure, the settlement farm lease midway between a grazing selection and an agricultural farm. The Upper Burnett and Callide Land Settlement Act 1923 created an ambitious scheme comprising 2.4 million acres, about half of which was Crown land and the rest resumed for the purpose, and gave the government power to provide water supplies. The Land Acts Amendment Act 1924 gave power to control settlement in the scheme by requiring that certain areas be cultivated, and to indicate what crops should be grown. It also increased the secretary's powers to prevent dummying. The Land Acts Amendment Act 1927 sought to promote closer settlement of pastoral lands by allowing a grazing selector to apply for a new lease up to seven years before expiry of his existing lease, thereby establishing whether the holding would be subject to sub-division or not; the residence requirement was also eased to personal residence for seven years, followed by occupation only, and in the case of a transferred lease only five years personal residence was required. The holder of an inadequate grazing area was enabled to enlarge his holding to a living area from vacant Crown land or other lands which had become available; in 1950 the royal commission on pastoral lands settlement complained that "additional areas was still one of the most onerous and vexatious features of land administration" because of abuses the 1927 act introduced.[8] Probably the greatest achievement of McCormack's term at Public Lands was the victory over prickly pear. A royal commission on the pest led to the Prickly-Pear Land Act 1923 under which a permanent board was appointed. By 1925, infestation was at its height with sixty million acres affected, twenty-two million acres densely infested, and the cactus spreading at the rate of a million acres a year. Cactoblastis was introduced in 1925, and within ten years in the twenty-two million acres of dense infestation the pest was virtually eradicated and its spread had been stopped.

Although changes to basic land legislation were infrequent and minor during the 1915-29 period, settlement continued steadily. It was most conspicuous in the sugar industry, the backbone of state agriculture. The acreage under cultivation for cane had risen slowly from 50,000 acres in 1890 to 110,000 in 1900, 140,000 in 1910 and 160,000 in 1920. Encouraged by the Theodore government in particular, it shot up to almost 300,000 acres in 1930, after which it levelled off to rise to 350,000 in 1940 and 380,000 in 1950. Then a new expansion under the Hanlon government took the acreage up again until by 1953 it was approaching 470,000, three times the figure when Labor first came to office. Nevertheless, the total acreages were small in comparison with Queensland's vast area, and the proportion of land holdings actually under cultivation very high in the sugar industry. Acreage held, acreage cultivated, cane crushed, sugar produced, constituted a chain which was tightly controlled by the industry authorities, and access to land was only one consideration among many for the cane-grower.

The 1930s were largely barren of land legislation, apart from the introduction of a new and minor tenure, forest grazing leases, in 1934, and in 1937, the creation of the office of President of the Land Court. (The first appointee was W.L. Payne, then chairman of the Land Administration Board, and a central figure in land policy in Queensland for many years). In 1951, the assessment period of Crown rentals of perpetual leaseholds was reduced from fifteen to seven years, and in 1952 there was some tinkering with grazing leases ostensibly to encourage closer settlement. The opposition charged that it was camouflage for the abandonment of closer settlement as a result of the AWU's success at the 1950 Toowoomba Labor-in-Politics Convention. The platform was amended to require the government to refrain from sub-dividing grazing leases when it was satisfied that more people would derive a livelihood from work on the land than if it were subdivided, and provided the lessee provided adequate accommodation and amenities for his employees. More likely the AWU's intention was merely to induce pastoralists to be better employers by reducing the risk of sub-division to which they were subject, though the dispute also carried overtones for the Movement's policy of encouraging closer settlement which later disrupted the Victorian Branch of the ALP.

By far the most unusual development of Labor's second term of office was the short-lived Peak Downs scheme. After early caution about the post-war economy, primary production's future appeared promising and high prices for rural products, especially wool, encouraged the Hanlon government to promote closer settlement once more. The Labour government in London was anxious to augment the British food supply, and on a visit in 1947 Colin Clark interested the Ministry of Food in large-scale production in Queensland. Expansion of peanut growing was quickly ruled out because of the scarcity of cleared land and the shortage of machinery to clear more, and the two governments settled on the growing of sorghum on extensive acreages at Peak Downs west of Rockhampton; the sorghum would be fed to pigs in Queensland and Britain. A statutory corporation, the Queensland-British Food Corporation, was created, and the co-ordinator general empowered under the State Development and Public Works Organization Acts 1938-40 to acquire land. The area chosen was rundown grazing country, in transition from sheep to cattle raising, but the black soils were thought to have some of the agricultural potential of the Darling Downs further south. Some 700,000 acres were assembled, 75 per cent freehold acquired from large properties; production targets were set on a grand scale rising to 250,000 acres under cultivation, the proposition being that each 100,000 acres would produce 55,000 tons of sorghum which, with supplements, would feed 200,000 pigs. The corporation was capitalized at £2 million, one-quarter coming from the Queensland government and the balance from the British Overseas Food Corporation which was also engaged in an even grander, and more ill-fated, project to grow peanuts in East Africa.

Sorghum was a new crop for Queensland. The dwarf variety which alone was capable of mechanized production had been introduced only in 1932 and first grown commercially in 1938 although by 1946-47 some 116,000 acres were being grown in the state. Peak Downs failed badly. The QBF Corporation failed to meet the acreage under crop targets; the overall yield per acre was in the best season two-thirds of target and in the worst less than one-quarter although in some areas production targets were met and exceeded; losses mounted so that the corporation's capital had to be increased by 25 per cent. In four seasons, a total of only 54,800 tons of sorghum was produced. The East African debacle and return of a Conservative government in Britain, together with an easing of world food supplies, ended British interest in the project; Hanlon's death removed its strongest local supporter. In February 1953, it was decided to wind up the scheme, the Queensland government buying out the British share for the purpose. After the disposal of all assets, the land being offered in leasehold as sixty-three agricultural and seventeen grazing blocks, there was a net loss of £390,000, but the Queensland government now had an annual income of £17,000 from the new leaseholds. The opposition had bitterly opposed the scheme, arguing that it foreshadowed the advent of collective farming and, more plausibly, that the increased production sought could have been met by private enterprise. Although its enemies in Britain and Australia condemned the idea as socialist doctrine run wild, its immediate parentage was pragmatic — the British government's concern for food supplies, and the Queensland government's desire to be helpful to Britain and to secure some developmment for a backward area. As an experiment in state enterprise, it took its place in Queensland political mythology with the state cattle stations of Ryan's day, but it could also be counted as one more piece of evidence of the intractability of the inland Queensland environment to closer settlement.[9]

Over forty years, Labor governments did little to alter Griffith's land system of 1884. Despite their "ruralist" bias, it would appear that they did less to encourage settlement than other Australian state governments, if readiness to advance money to settlers is a good measure. At the end of 1933 (when the figures first appear in the *Commonwealth Yearbooks*) total advances then made for Queensland were only £10 million, compared with Victoria's £60 million, New South Wales' £43 million, Western Australia's £30 million, and South Australia's £20 million. Only Tasmania with £1.35 million had paid out less. Queensland governments also appeared to have been tougher bankers: sums outstanding and the number of persons owing them reflect a similar pattern — Queensland £3.8 million owed by 14,457 persons compared with Victoria's £20.9 million and 20,921 persons for example. Some basis for comparison is provided by the rural population of each state at the 1933 census: Queensland 445,000, New South Wales 795,000, Victoria 629,000, South Australia 215,000, Western Australia 183,000 and Tasmania 110,000. By the end of 1956 Queensland's total advances had risen to £34.4 million, barely ahead of South Australia's £33 million and well behind New South Wales with £157.7 million and Victoria with £127 million; however, by then the proportion of debt outstanding was much the same for each state at about one-third of the total advanced.[10] No doubt the exclusion of the Country party from office helped keep the Queensland figures down, but perhaps manipulation of the leasehold system in favour of settlers made more of a contribution to their survival in Queensland than in New South Wales and Victoria where a much higher proportion of land had been alienated and cash had to be paid out. In 1957, Queensland was still predominantly a pastoral state, with half the beef cattle and one sixth of the sheep in Australia, but, apart from sugar and tropical fruit, contributing a disproportionately small share to national agricultural production. That mix may help explain the relatively low cost of settlement policy. Labor's electoral success in rural areas (except where dairying predominated) up to 1957 suggests that there was little active dissatisfaction with what the party did, or failed to do.

NOTES

1. Report of the Royal Commission on Pastoral Lands Settlement, *QPP* 2 (1951-52) :180.
2. T.A. Coghlan, *Labour and Industry in Australia* IV (Melbourne: Macmillan, 1969, reprint) :1987-91.

3. See J.C.R. Camm, "Land Settlement and the Developing of Farming under the Agricultural Lands Purchase Act of 1894 and Closer Settlements Acts 1906-1917", *Queensland Heritage* 1, no. 9 (1968) :25-31.
4. For a detailed account of land administration about the turn of the century, see T. Weedon, *Queensland Past and Present* (Brisbane: Queensland Government Printer, 1898), pp. 372-98; and P.W. Shannon, "The Land Laws" in *Queensland Official Year Book 1901* (Brisbane: Queensland Government Printer, n.d.), pp. 126-45.
5. *QPD* CVI (4 October 1910) :1226.
6. The preceding paragraphs drew extensively on E. Milton, "Soldier Settlement in Queensland after World War I" (B.A. thesis, University of Queensland, 1968).
7. W.J. Jackson, "The Government and Economic Growth in Queensland, 1946-1951", (B.A. thesis, University of Queensland, 1968), pp. 43-44. 43-44.
8. *QPP* 2 (1951-52) :187.
9. For a detailed study, see P. Rogers, "The Peak Downs Scheme" (B.A. thesis, University of Queensland, 1960).
10. *Commonwealth Yearbook No. 27* (Canberra: Commonwealth Government Printer, 1934) and *No. 44* (1958).

11 Labour Relations — Law

E.I. Sykes

During its period of rule the Labor government in Queensland passed substantial legislation designed to ensure industrial safety, viz., the Factories and Shops Acts, the Inspection of Machinery Acts, and the Inspection of Scaffolding Acts. Such legislation however, followed a pattern common to the United Kingdom and other Australian states and the main lines of some of it ante-date the coming into power of Labor. The most outstanding contributions in the industrial field of the Labor government were in relation to industrial conciliation and arbitration, strikes, trade unions and workers' compensation.

In earlier days, Queensland looked like following the model of Victoria in relying on wages boards, i.e., bodies consisting of employer and employee representatives endowed with direct powers of fixation of wages. When Labor came to power in 1915, the legislation on the statute book comprised the Denham government's Industrial Peace Act of 1912. This act continued the wages board concept though the bodies were termed industrial boards, but it also set up as a second element an industrial court comprising a judge. It was the main contribution of the Labor era to make the second element the predominant one and in fact to produce the most centralist of the Australian state industrial systems — a result rather surprising in view of the geographical situation. The industrial board, as a piece of possible machinery, was not actually phased out completely until Forgan Smith's review of industrial legislation in 1932, but the use of such bodies had long become exceptional and concentration was on the "curial" type of body, though the actual name was subject to a considerable process of change.

The first piece of industrial legislation by the Labor government was the Industrial Arbitration Act of 1916. This replaced the existing Industrial Court by a Court of Industrial Arbitration consisting of not more than three judges, though three judges were never appointed. The president was to be a judge of the Supreme Court and lengthy legal proceedings followed the appointment of the Crown solicitor, T.W. McCawley, to the Supreme Court and the presidency of the Industrial Court. The previous industrial boards set up under the Industrial Peace Act were abolished though the act gave power to create boards of the same type. By an amendment of 1925 the place of the Court of Industrial Arbitration was taken by the Board of Trade and Arbitration comprising a Supreme Court judge as president and two other lay members. So far as personnel was concerned, this set the pattern until the act of 1961 by which time Labor had lost power.

In 1929, an act passed during a brief period of non-Labor rule changed the terminology by abolishing the Board of Trade and Arbitration and replacing it by an "Industrial Court", but constituted in much the same manner as under the 1925 act. With the return of Labor to government in 1932, an Industrial Conciliation and Arbitration Act was passed which remained the basic statute for the rest of the era of Labor rule. This provided again for a court of three members (changed in 1948 to "not more than five"), one of whom had to be a Supreme Court judge. The judge was to act as president. The act did not forbid the appointment of other judicial members but in point of fact the members other than the president were neither judges nor judicially qualified.

The 1932 act gave the court a very wide jurisdiction in point of subject matter, defining "industrial matters" in very wide language and giving the court all the powers and jurisdiction of the Supreme Court — a provision which had some interesting possibilities. The activities of the court comprised the making of awards in relation to specific callings and the promulgation of general rules as to matters common to all industries. This latter power was of course denied constitutionally to the Commonwealth Court.

Crown Solicitor, T.W. McCawley, formerly a student of the English Fabian movement, believed that the law should be harnessed as a tool of reform, not conservatism. (Photograph by courtesy of Queensland Newspapers Ltd.)

However, the act kept considerable control by the government over the direction of the activities of the court. Thus the court's awards had to conform to certain minimum standards of favourableness to employees, e.g., as to annual leave and overtime. The act also empowered the court to make general rulings as to the basic wage and the standard hours, but these again were subject to certain standards laid down by the Labor government. Whilst the court determined the basic wage, the concept was one defined by the legislature. This again was true in respect of the notion of a maximum working week. The maximum hours for which an employee could be worked were set out in the act itself. Thus first the forty-eight-hour week (1916), then the forty-four-hour week (1924), and finally the forty-hour week (1947) were introduced by the legislature itself and in response to pressure from the constituent Labor organizations. However, the court had power to order conditions more favourable to the worker. Long service leave and sick leave on the other hand were different. These were not only introduced by the parliament but the conditions were also spelt out by the parliament.

The making of specific awards and the giving of general rulings comprised the arbitral and legislative functions of the court. However, the court had a considerable jurisdiction in respect to enforcement of awards and also in dealing with offences under the act. The arbitral-judicial dichotomy had never compelled the setting up in the state sphere of separate tribunals. Moreover, it was only at the end of the period of which we are speaking that such a necessity was fastened on to the federal system. However, the Queensland Industrial Court was given power to remit proceedings for penalties whether for breach of award or in respect of breach of the Act to industrial magistrates and many types of proceeding were in fact so remitted.

Industrial magistrates, who were also local stipendary magistrates, were first provided for by the act of 1916. They represented whatever centrifugal tendencies existed in the system. However, whilst they exercised functions of conciliation they did not arbitrate or make awards. Their functions were and are limited to dealing with claims for recovery of wages and with claims for penalties in respect of breach of award or breach of the act.

Although the industrial arbitration legislation made and still makes certain strikes illegal and gave certain powers to the court in respect thereof, certain other legislation dealt with civil claims for damage for strikes and other manifestations of industrial pressures.

Certainly the Labor party as a legislator did not betray any particular sympathy for strikes. The industrial arbitration statute indeed only made a strike illegal if it occurred without a majority in favour of it at a union secret ballot and such a provision had a democratic ring. However, it was fairly obvious that in certain callings the holding of a pre-strike ballot by the union was a virtual impossibility. Moreover, the act did not say that a strike preceded by a pro-strike ballot was legal and in fact in 1949 there was a dramatic Industrial Court decision in relation to a tramways strike. Here the court ruled that a ballot favouring a strike did not prevent the court from ordering the strikers to resume work and imposing penalties on those who refused to comply with such order. The Labor government of the day took no legislative steps to remove the effect of that decision and presumably approved of it.

The 1932 act gave the court wide powers of issuing injunctions to restrain breaches of the act or of an award and mandatory orders to compel compliance. Only a non-ballot strike would be a breach of the act but it was widely assumed in the era which we are discussing that any strike — ballot or non-ballot — was a breach of the award. This latter was subsequently shattered by a Supreme Court decision in the 1960s. Injunctions against strikes were just as frequent under the Labor governments of the 1932-57 period as under their non-Labor successors.

So far as civil actions for damages in tort for strike or associated activity under the headings of conspiracy and interference with contract were concerned, Queensland became the only Australian state to adopt the provisions of the English Trade Disputes Act 1906 — a distinction it retained until recently. The provisions were, so far as Queensland was concerned, enacted by the Trade Union Act of 1915. They were three in number. The first sought to render an act done by a combination in contemplation or furtherance of an industrial dispute not actionable unless the act, if done without such combination, would be actionable; the second proclaimed that an act done in contemplation or furtherance of an industrial dispute was not actionable on the ground only that it induced breach of a contract of employment or that it was an interference with the trade, business or employment of some other person or with the right of some other person to dispose of his capital or labour as he wills; the third one simply removed the power to sue a trade union in tort at all. It is to be remarked that the first arm of the second provision referred only to inducing breach of a contract or employment and the second arm seemed to have no impact at all. It would be inappropriate to go into the mass of English decisions on these provisions; so far as the writer is aware there were no Queensland decisions.

The Labor government by the Trade Union Act 1915 had provided for the English-type registration of trade unions which was optional in character and mainly related to the holding of property. More important was the adoption by the various Industrial Arbitration Acts of a system of registration of industrial unions. Such registration was necessary to enable the union to participate in the process of court arbitration under the industrial arbitration system as representative of the employees whom it covered by its rules and to be entitled to the benefit and be bound by the obligations of awards. A registered union became, for the purposes of the Conciliation and Arbitration Act, a corporate entity. Cancellation of registration could be effected on certain stated grounds. On the whole, the basic pattern was that to be found in the federal act and the acts of such other states as adopted the court system rather than the wages board one.

A distinctive Queensland feature, however, was the system of so-called "preference to unionists". Section 8(2) of the new Industrial Conciliation and Arbitration Act, passed by the Forgan Smith government in 1932, allowed the granting of preference "either generally or to any particular union or organization", either where it was mutually agreed by the parties concerned or considered advisable by the court. Under this umbrella, the typical provision in Queensland awards provided for something which went considerably beyond preference and was popularly called "compulsory unionism", but was probably more correctly referred to as "union shop". Not only did the award provide for absolute preference to be given to the member of the named union, but it also provided that the non-union employee be not continued in employment unless he joined or applied to join the relevant union within fourteen days of his being first employed. This general pattern had been upheld by the Court of Arbitration in 1917 decisions even before section 8(2) found its way into the act and continued to be a characteristic of Queensland awards. However, after the demise of the Labor government in 1957, the "union shop" clause was, following High Court precedents dealing with the federal act, held to be beyond the powers given by the act.

At the time of the advent of the Labor government in 1915, there had been prior Workers Compensation Acts of 1905 and 1909, but they were of limited application and did not, for instance, cover industrial diseases. Nor did they cover injuries occurring during the course of the worker's journey to and from work. The Workers Compensation Act 1916 filled in these gaps. Still more important was the fact that it swept away the old requirement that the injury had to arise out of and in the course of employment. What was covered comprised injuries by accident whether occurring at the place of employment or on the journey to or from such place or, being in the course of the employment or while under the employer's instructions, away from the place of employment. It will be noticed that the concept of "course of employment" took a secondary place and that it was possible for the worker's injury to be covered by compensation even though not incurred in the course of employment. The older concept of arising "out of" employment, which connoted a causal relationship between the work and the injury, disappeared altogether.

It was, however, in the institutional framework that the new Queensland legislation departed most from the traditional pattern. The usual pattern was that, assuming that the accident or injury was compensatable, the worker or if deceased, his dependants, would be entitled to certain designated sums of money, but the liability was that of the employer and proceedings were taken against the employer; later a system of compulsory insurance against the liability was introduced.

However, under the Queensland legislation introduced by the Ryan government, there was no direct recourse by the worker against the employer at all. In the first place, there was created a State Accident Insurance Fund out of which all payments in respect of compensation were to be made. A State Accident Insurance Office (later the State Government Insurance) was set up to be managed and controlled by an officer called the insurance commissioner. If the worker's entitlement to compensation was disputed then it was against the insurance commissioner that proceedings lay. Later under non-Labor governments the office of insurance commissioner was abolished and the legal entity became simply the State Government Insurance Office.

Every employer who employed workers was obliged to apply to the insurance commissioner for a policy for the full amount of the liability to pay compensation under the act and to thereafter maintain the policy in force and pay the prescribed premium. Nowhere under the act was there a liability on the part of the employer to pay compensation to the employee. The key section 9, which spelt out the entitlement of the worker, merely conferred a claim to "compensation in accordance with this Act" out of the State Accident Insurance Fund. In fact, the liability of the employer to pay compensation arose only if he had failed to take out a policy and the claim of the worker had been paid by the insurance commissioner in which case the employer became liable to the insurance commissioner. Hence, as was judicially pointed out by the Queensland Supreme Court, the concept of "insurance" was rather a strange one as there was no principal liability on the part of the "insured" except to the "insurer" in certain contingencies!

The State Government Insurance Office came to have a monopoly of the business of workers' compensation insurance. The first act of 1916 by Section 7 allowed the governor-in-council to permit a private company to carry on a business of accident insurance. As, however, the primary obligation of the employer to insure with the SGIO was unaffected by any insurance with a private company, this part of the act proved to be unworkable and it was not without reason that Chief Justice Cooper, in a 1916 case in the Supreme Court of Queensland, referred to it as a "legislative curiosity". In 1921, the legislature removed the anomaly by repealing Section 7 and provided that accident policies should be issued only by the insurance commissioner and not by any other person, company or firm.

This scheme of direct recourse to a government fund carrying a state monopoly of accident insurance under the act has remained an enduring part of the Queensland scheme and was not disturbed by succeeding non-Labor governments which took control after 1957; in fact they extended it to cover the liability of the employer for industrial accidents at common law.

The actual procedure in the case of disputed claims was peculiar to Queensland as it made use of the industrial arbitration system. In the other Australian states the procedure in general was either to refer matters to the normal civil courts of the state or to set up special boards or commissions. However, under the Queensland Act of 1916, applications in the first instance were to be allowed or rejected by the insurance commissioner, but any person who objected to the ruling of the insurance commissioner might require the matter to be heard and determined by an industrial magistrate. From the decision of the magistrate, an appeal on a question of law lay to the president of the Industrial Court. Up to 1941, however, it was a peculiarity of the Queensland system that on such appeal not only was there no right of legal representation, but the parties themselves could not appear and the point of law was to be decided without argument. This rather bizarre provision resulted in the president on quite a number of occasions trying to imagine what points would have been put to him had argument been allowed. However, the government was amenable to suggestion and in 1941 the system was changed to permit a full appeal both on questions of law and questions of fact.

It can be said that the Queensland system was at point of introduction in 1916, both as regards liberality of provisions and scope of financial benefits available, considerably in advance of that available in the other states at the time. This was helped by the liberal and paternalistic attitude of the SGIO. In more recent years, however, Queensland has rather suffered by comparison with New South Wales where the legislature has proved extraordinarily responsive to the pressures for reform.

There were other specific areas where Labor governments legislated to protect workers. The Workers Accommodation Acts were designed to require employers within the limits set out to provide accommodation for workers and the Workers Homes Acts designed to provide homes for workers, either by way of easy terms for purchase or by way of lease in perpetuity. The Wages Act 1918, in addition to providing for a summary method of recovery of wages, also provided for a method of attachment of wages due to a workman by a contractor or sub-contractor over moneys due by the ultimate employer or head contractor as the case might be. A more comprehensive scheme, based on a New Zealand model and designed to give a lien over land or charge over moneys in favour, not only of workmen but sub-contractors, was embodied in the Contractors and Liens Acts. This legislation was initiated in 1906, but considerably refurbished by the Labor government in 1921. The legislative drafting, however, was so bad as to evoke hostile judicial comment and the whole scheme — perhaps deservedly — was consigned to oblivion by a subsequent government in the post 1957 period.

12 Labour Relations — Issues

D.J. Murphy

When the first general council of the Australian Labour Federation met in Brisbane in August 1890 to draw up the platform for the Labor party that was about to be born, the delegates promised that: "In one year, a People's Parliament will give Queensland workers more than can be wrung from capitalistic parliaments in a generation". Their political goals were set out in an eight point document whose first clause read: "The Nationalisation of all sources of wealth and all means of producing and exchanging wealth". The political platform was sent out to the affiliated organizations which rejected it by a large majority. In May 1891, a more sober minded general council met again and drew up a completely new platform which dropped all references to nationalization. This new platform reflected the practical reforms sought by the miners, shearers, labourers, other workers and farmers who made up the new Labor party.[1]

For the following twenty-five years the Labor party developed as a political organization committed to legislating for wide practical reforms sought by workers and farmers. When it won office in 1915, Labor quickly set about fulfilling the hopes of its founders of the early 1890s.

Three men were to be responsible for providing Queensland with the farthest reaching reforms of benefit to the working man that any Australian government was to attempt until World War II. These men were E.G. Theodore, the treasurer and minister for public works, W.R. Crampton, the newly appointed director of labour, and T.W. McCawley, then Crown solicitor. Theodore and Crampton had both been union officials, Crampton with the Australasian Meat Industry Employees Union, while McCawley

E.G. Theodore earned the nickname of "Red Ted" as a result of implementing a series of acts which became the basis of Labor's industrial programme. (Photograph by courtesy of the John Oxley Library.)

had been a student of the English Fabian movement and believed that the law should be harnessed as a tool of reform, not conservatism. All were concerned to use the power of the state to provide institutions that would permanently benefit and protect the working man and his family. They began publication of the *Queensland Industrial Gazette* so that awards, regulations and reports would be made clear to union leaders and employers.

Between 1915 and 1923, Theodore passed a series of acts which, with subsequent amendments, became the basis of Labor's industrial programme until it lost office in 1957. It was these acts plus several similar acts relating to advances for primary producers that earned him the nickname of "Red Ted" from his political opponents.[2] Unquestionably, the most important of these were the Industrial Arbitration Act and the Workers Compensation Act of 1916. The Industrial Arbitration Act made the eight-hour working day the law in Queensland. Now an employee could not be made to work more than eight hours a day or more than six consecutive days in any seven-day period. In practice, the new court was able to rule on overtime and could award holidays. Queensland thus had a statutory forty-eight hour week from 1916. In a 1924 amendment to the Industrial Arbitration Act, the goal of a forty-four hour week was achieved, again by legislative action, and before workers in other states or under awards of the Commonwealth Arbitration Court had obtained this. Employees could not be dismissed from their jobs because of union membership, as had occurred during the 1912 tramway strike and a union could now sue its members for fines, levies or outstanding dues.

Prior to the 1916 act, state government employees were prohibited from forming industrial unions and had their salaries, wages and working conditions determined by legislative and administrative actions of the government. At the first cabinet meeting after being sworn in, in June 1915, Ryan's government granted pay increases to policemen, teachers and public servants, that had been held back in July 1914 by the previous Liberal government. It also granted a shilling a day increase to railway construction workers. More importantly, under the Industrial

Arbitration Act, it provided for government employees to form trade unions and put their case for improvements in wages and conditions to the new Court of Industrial Arbitration. In an amendment to the act in 1923 the Police Union was allowed to affiliate with other trade union organizations.

McCawley had followed closely the working of the Commonwealth Arbitration Court and was something of a disciple of its president Henry Higgins. He played a considerable role in the drafting of the 1916 act, and on the strong recommendation of Theodore, he was appointed as the first president of the Court of Industrial Arbitration on 12 January 1917. In the act a minimum wage was broadly defined and the court, once it had established that wage, could not award a lower wage. McCawley and Theodore defined the minimum wage as being:

> sufficient to maintain a well conducted employee of average health, strength and competence, and his wife and a family of three children, in a fair and average standard of comfort having regard to the conditions of living prevailing among such employees in the calling in respect of which such minimum wage was fixed.

Equal pay for males and females was provided under the act, but the implementation of this was left to the court. An adult female minimum wage was defined as: "not less than sufficient to support her in a fair and average standard of comfort having regard to the nature of her duties and the conditions of living prevailing amongst female employees in the calling in which such minimum wage was fixed."[3]

Apart from its initial adjustment of the wages of government employees in 1915 and a reduction in the salaries of higher public servants, judges and politicians following the general reduction of the basic wage by the court in 1921, the Labor government left the fixing of wages to the court itself. There was to be one further notable exception to this rule in 1925 which is discussed later in the chapter. The court did not actually set a minimum wage until February 1921. For its first four years, it was concerned with establishing wage rates in a number of important industries, with attempting to settle several major disputes, particularly in the railway and meat industries, and in laying down a system of preference to members of particular unions in various awards. When McCawley and the second judge of the court, A.W. Macnaughton, came to the question of a Queensland basic wage, they were able to draw on the experiences of the commonwealth and New South Wales courts and on the reports of the Basic Wage Commission of A.B. Piddington.

In laying down a Queensland basic wage in 1921, McCawley and Macnaughton applied a combination of cost of living and capacity of industry to pay in providing the standard basic wages of four pounds five shillings a week for southern and central Queensland and four pounds fifteen shillings for north Queensland. The basic wage was then twelve shillings and sixpence a week more than the commonwealth basic wage for Brisbane. When the cost of living in Queensland dropped by almost 12 per cent during 1921, the court reduced the standard basic wage to four pounds a week. To reduce its own costs at a time of increasing unemployment and reducing state revenue, the government successfully approached the court for a reduction of government employees' wages by five shillings a week. The ensuing battle between the affiliated unions and the government at QCE meetings, at the 1923 Labor-in-Politics Convention and during the 1925 strike for a restoration of the basic wage cut is discussed in Chapters 1, 18 and 19. After three years of internal party argument and debate, the government passed a special Basic Wages Act in September 1925 which restored the standard basic wage to four pounds five shillings a week, with an additional five shillings and sixpence a week for the Mackay region and ten shillings for Townsville and northern centres.

While the 1923 Labor-in-Politics Convention had narrowly rejected a motion to instruct the government to restore the five shillings to the state basic wage, the same convention wrote the forty-four-hour week into the Labor platform. When this plank in the platform was not quickly implemented, considerable heat was raised in the party and Theodore agreed to amend the Industrial Arbitration Act to provide for a forty-four-hour week only when a majority of the PLP forced this on the cabinet.

McCawley and Theodore possessed very rational logical minds and by 1924 they were concerned to have more precise means of determining fair wages, hours of work and other matters covered in the Industrial Arbitration Act. In December 1924, McCawley established an Economic Commission on the Queensland basic wage to report on the productivity of the state and the adjustment of wages according to that productivity. The commission consisting of J.T. Sutcliffe (chairman) from the Commonwealth Statisticians Office, R.C. Mills, dean of the Faculty of Economics at the University of Sydney and J.B. Brigden, professor of economics at the University of Tasmania, reported on 21 February 1925.[4] The report does not seem to have had the influence sought by McCawley, although his successors continued to use a combination of cost of living and average productivity statistics in setting basic wage rates. Theodore retired from the office of premier in February 1925 and McCawley's own death occurred in April that year. Crampton had long since resigned as director of labour and become manager of the *Daily Standard*.

In October 1925, the Act was again amended to change the Industrial Court to the Board of Trade and Arbitration. This new board was to fulfil the dual roles of a court of conciliation and arbitration and a standing committee on social and economic conditions. Perhaps of greater moment was that only one of its members, the president, was required to have legal training and to be a judge of the Supreme Court. William Webb, who had succeeded McCawley as Crown solicitor, became the first president of the Board of Trade and Arbitration in 1925. The other two positions were filled by laymen. In 1925, these were W.N. Gillies who had recently retired as premier, and W.J. Dunstan, the former secretary of the AWU. A pattern was established in 1925 that was to be retained until 1952. The judge chosen to be the president was one known by the government to be reasonably disposed towards the worker (though not a member of the Labor party) while one of the two lay commissioners was the AWU secretary who resigned his union office to take up the position. The other lay commissioner was to have a non-union background.

Both the Industrial Court and the Board of Trade and Arbitration used conciliation conferences extensively. On occasions several conferences were held at the same time, often before a stoppage of work had actually occurred. Arbitration was introduced to settle those issues on which the parties could not agree. Not suffering from the constitutional limitations which restricted the scope of the Commonwealth Arbitration Court, the Queensland court could and did make "common rule" awards which were binding on all employers in an industry irrespective of whether they had been parties to the hearing before the court. Awards could extend for a maximum period of three years. Outside Brisbane, and particularly in north Queensland, industrial magistrates who were also stipendary magistrates, acted with success as conciliation commissioner. Industrial boards, which had been established under the Wages Board Act of 1908 and continued under the Industrial Peace Act of 1912, were retained under the 1916 act, but were rarely used after 1916.

Queensland did not become an industrial utopia after 1916 and, in fact, McCawley and his successors were compelled to deal with several long and bitter disputes where members of unions refused to obey the court's instructions to return to work. Under the Industrial Arbitration Act, strikes and lock-outs were prohibited, but a strike could be called if a ballot was taken among the workers concerned and a majority voted in favour of strike action. As Professor Sykes has pointed out in Chapter 11, a successful ballot could be and was overruled by the court itself. McCawley used the threat and withdrawal of preference clauses as his principal means of having the more militant unions abide by the decisions of the court. In the main, unions and unionists in Queensland abided by the decision of the Industrial Court which, over the thirty-nine years of Labor government, provided them with superior awards to those of the Commonwealth Arbitration Court and many of the awards of other state tribunals. In 1954, 73 per cent of wage and salary earners in Queensland remained under state awards, the second highest proportion in Australia. Only 6.6 per cent of Queensland wage and salary earners were not covered by awards in that year, by far the lowest figure in Australia.[5]

During the Labor period of government working days lost in Queensland through industrial disputes were comparatively small. Apart from the years 1917, 1919, 1925, 1927, 1946, 1948 and 1956 when there were major strikes in the labour intensive railway and meatworks industries, man days lost through industrial disputes in Queensland accounted for only 7.5 per cent of man days lost throughout Australia. Queensland workers were about 19 per cent of Australian wage and salary earners. (See figure 1). The railways accounted for the peaks in 1917, 1925 and 1948, railways and meatworks in 1919 and 1946, railways and sugar works in 1927 and the pastoral industry together with rail, road transport and storage industries in 1956. While these disputes provided the years of exceptionally high numbers of working days lost, there was continuing industrial trouble in the mining and stevedoring industries for the whole period (see figure 2). In this respect, Queensland was no different from the rest of Australia, or indeed from the rest of the world, where bad labour relations and bad and insecure working conditions produced a pattern of continuing industrial conflict. On the other hand, while the railways provided peak years of man days lost through strikes, it was not an industry with a continuing pattern of strikes. Between the end of the 1927 strike and 1945, there were fourteen years in which the railways registered no strikes at all. The railways show up in the accompanying graph (figure 2) as accounting for the second highest percentage of man days lost, but 75 per cent of man days lost in the railways, between 1919 and 1957, were during the 1948 strike. (See Chapter 19).

The Industrial Arbitration Act was underpinned by the Profiteering Prevention Acts of 1920 and 1948 which regulated the prices of essential items in a worker's budget, by the Workers Homes Act, the Fair Rents Act and Landlord and Tenants Act, the Workers Accommodation Act, acts regulating safety in industry, the Wages Act, the Trade Union Act and a series of Health Acts. After the passing of the Industrial Arbitration Act, the Factories and Shops Act, provided originally in 1896, was overshadowed as an instrument of reform and a protector of male and female employees. Theodore amended the Factories and Shops

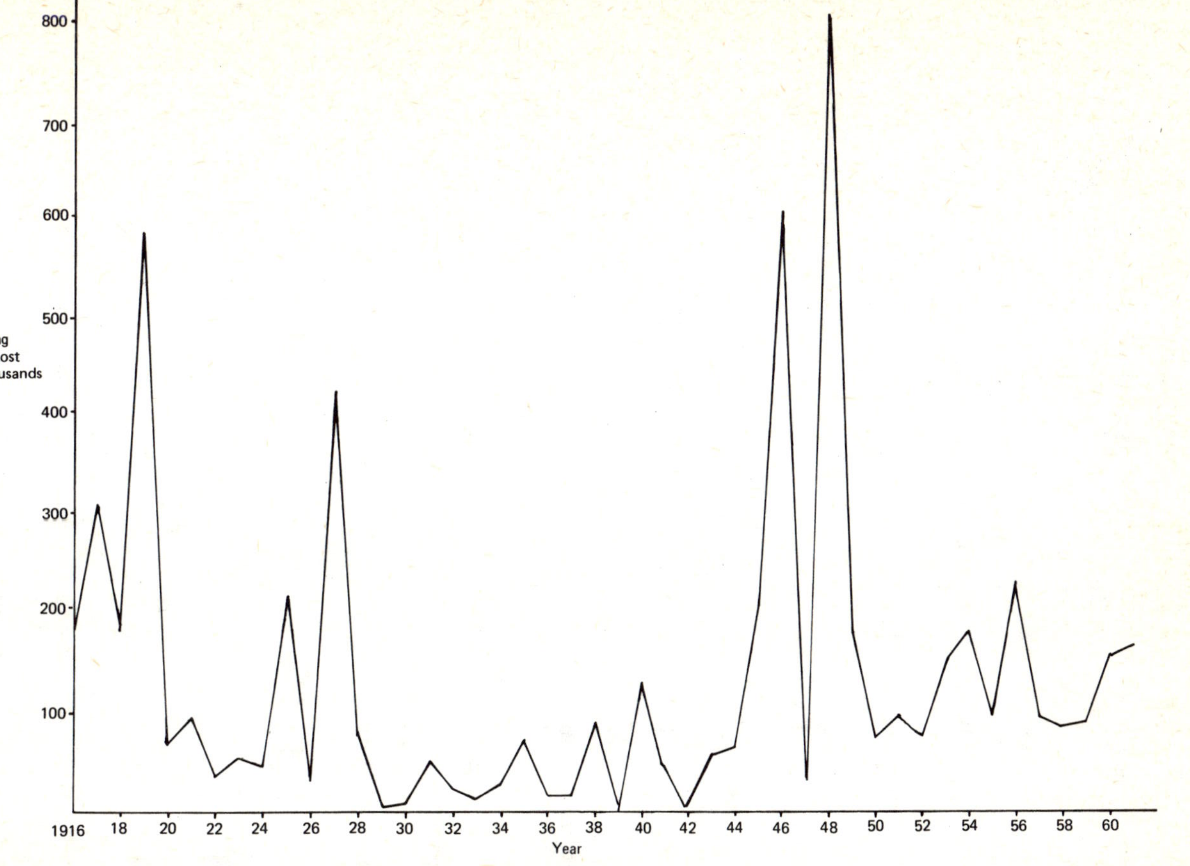

Figure 1. Working days lost in industrial disputes in Queensland, 1916-61.

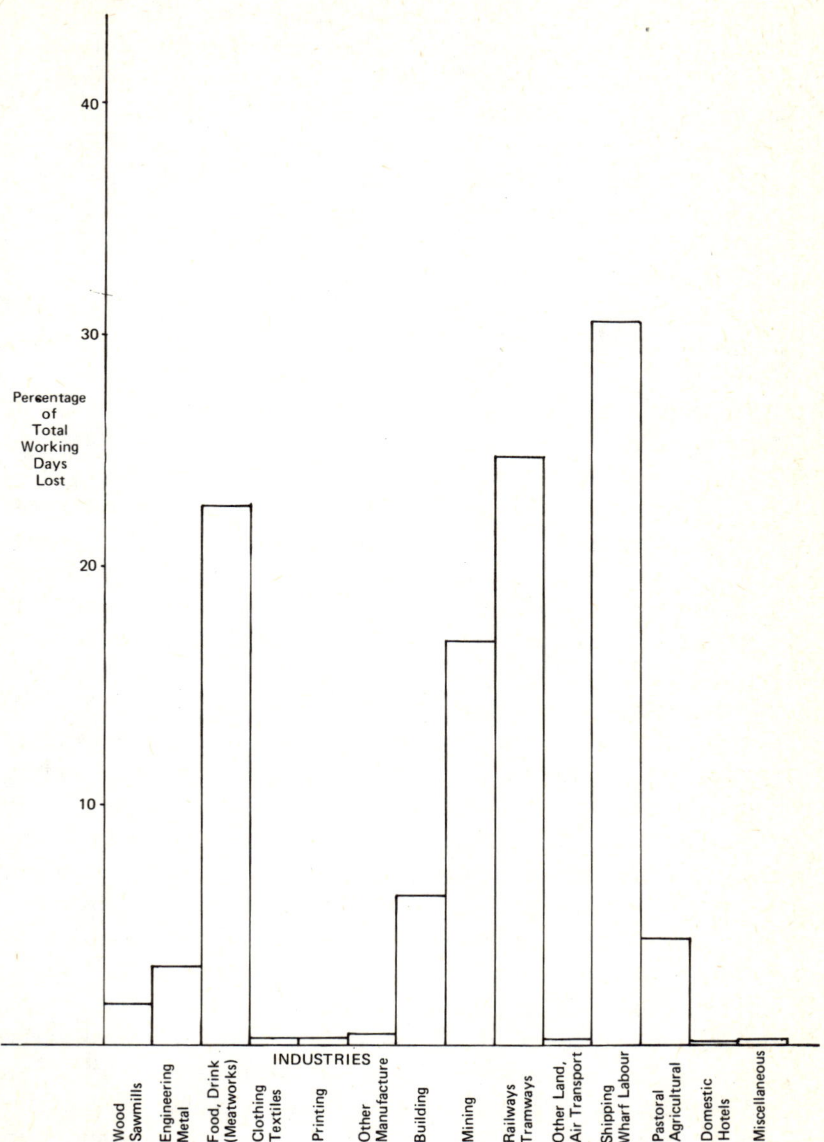

Figure 2. Proportion of working days lost in industrial disputes, Queensland, 1919-57.

Act in 1916 to provide for the entry of inspectors to all shops and factories, but under the Industrial Arbitration Act, industrial inspectors were created who were also classed as inspectors under the Factories and Shops Acts. When a provision of the Factories and Shops Act conflicted with an award of the Industrial Arbitration Act, the latter act prevailed. This inspectorate, which was principally concerned with policing awards, expanded quickly to cover the whole state. There were ten separate districts in the state each with its own labour agent and inspector. In addition there were travelling inspectors whose job involved not merely enforcing the Industrial Arbitration Act awards and the Factories and Shops Act regulation, but also the Workers Accommodation Act. There were over three hundred separate state awards.

Industrial inspectors were authorized to enter any premise or property where labour was being employed. More importantly, from a union viewpoint, union officials were given the right to enter premises to interview employees and to take legal proceedings, through the court, for breaches of awards. They could and did take these proceedings independently of the Department of Public Works and later the Department of Labour and used this right to recover substantial wages owing to their members. In practice, both employers and unions drew on the knowledge and experience of the industrial inspectors regarding interpretation of awards concerned the payment of wages and this caused numbers awards regarded the payment of wages and this caused numbers of complaints in the 1930s when jobs were scarce and some employees accepted employment on below award wages. Penalties for breaches of awards were increased by amendments to the Act in 1935 and 1937.[6] Industrial inspectors prosecuted employers each year for breaches of awards and for non-payment of correct wages. By the 1950s, £30,000 a year in back wages was being obtained for workers by industrial inspectors.

Public images of nations tend to change with their leaders. Much the same applies with the six Australian states. While Ryan and Theodore were the premiers, Queensland had a public image of radicalism; some of Theodore's political opponents would even have used the term "Bolshie". In addition to the legislation mentioned, Theodore proposed a system of child endowment related to a worker's income, but economic conditions of the 1920s held this back, and the restoration of the basic wage to four pounds five shillings absorbed the government funds proposed to finance the scheme. In 1915, he had established state operated labour exchanges and caused private, profit-making exchanges to be licensed and regulated by the state. His other, more ambitious programme for unemployment relief was an Unemployed Workers Bill which he introduced in 1919. It provided for an Unemployment Council on which the government, employers and employees were to be represented; relief work on government and local authorities' projects; provision of extra employment by private employers; unemployment insurance; employment farms for the chronically unemployed and technical instruction for a worker who had lost his job through his lack of technical knowledge. Opposition to the bill from the conservative side of Queensland politics was fierce. The *Brisbane Courier*, the leading anti-Labor newspaper in the state, insisted on referring to the bill as the "Loafers Paradise Bill", while E.B. Swayne, one of the leading members of the newly formed Country party, argued, in the Legislative Assembly, that "legislation such as this is going to sap our moral fibre instead of making us a virile race". In 1919, the Unemployed Workers Bill was defeated in the Legislative Council, but after the abolition of the upper house (see Chapter 4) William Forgan Smith, then minister for public works, had the bill passed into law in 1922 as the Unemployed Workers Insurance Act. It was to remain the only such act passed by a state government until the commonwealth took over the responsibility for employment in World War II.

The Unemployed Workers Insurance Act came into operation in March 1923. It provided a compulsory scheme of unemployment insurance for all workers, male and female, over eighteen years and covered by state awards (except for some under certain agricultural awards). The employer, the employee and the government, initially, each contributed three pence per week which was paid into an Unemployed Workers Insurance Fund. A worker had to have been employed for six months before being eligible for unemployment insurance which covered him for thirteen weeks in any one year. For workers employed for less than twenty-six weeks, unemployment insurance was paid on the basis of one week's benefit for each two weeks of employment. Weekly benefits were not large. For single or widowed male or female workers, there was a payment of fifteen to seventeen shillings a week; a married worker with a wife received twenty-four to twenty-nine shillings and sixpence a week with a four to five shillings a week allowance for each child up to a maximum of four children. The scheme was really designed to cope with seasonal or short-term unemployment, not that of a depression or long recession. However, such were the economic problems of Queensland after 1925, that the contribution had to be raised to four pence per week in 1927 and sixpence in 1928 to cope with the number of unemployed workers claiming insurance benefits. In 1929, 59,160 workers applied for unemployment insurance.[7]

In the list of priorities that workers and unions had for a Labor government, the first was providing jobs at fair and reasonable wages and in safe conditions. The second priority was the protection of the worker and his family in case of accidents or sickness. The Queensland Labor governments did not introduce legislation for sickness benefits; these had to wait for the Commonwealth government of John Curtin. However, the Workers Compensation Act of 1916, with subsequent amendments, remained something of a model for other states. It was based on the experiences of Ryan, the barrister, conducting cases for the AWU and other unions under the previous act, and on the experiences of Theodore, the union leader. It was drafted by McCawley who searched for examples in the other Australian states and elsewhere, that could be adapted. It too had a stormy passage through the Parliament and, in fact, it was allowed to pass only through the over zealous bungling of some insurance company directors in the Legislative Council. Workers compensation in Queensland promised to be a very lucrative insurance, but the Ryan government had planned it as a state monopoly.[8]

The Workers Compensation Act made it compulsory for employers to ensure their employees, with the newly created State

Insurance Office, against accidents occurring at work or going to and from work. An employer could not deduct his workers compensation insurance payments from an employee's wage. The employee was no longer required to take legal proceedings against his employer for compensation and the compensation payments began from the date of the accident. A schedule of payments was included in the act, which provided lump sum payments for death, incapacity or the loss of limbs. Initially, the rate of compensation was fixed at 50 per cent of the basic wage for a single worker. This was raised to 66⅔ per cent in 1926. For a married worker with children, the compensation payment was increased in 1926 to a sum about equal to the basic wage.

Two other pieces of legislation, the Apprenticeship Act of 1924 with its 1927 amendment, and the Electrical Workers Act of 1923, amended in 1927, completed the major thrust of Labor legislation in the 1920s.[9]

By 1929, Labor had been in office for fourteen years. With increasing economic problems in the second half of the 1920s, the government had not attempted any new labour legislation. It had been a constant criticism of the Labor government's industrial legislation by the Country and National parties that the reforms introduced had been beyond the capacity of the state's industries to bear. Between 1929 and 1932, the Moore government revoked the forty-four-hour week and rural arbitration awards, and removed the power of the court to grant preference in employment to unionists. Government employees were removed from the jurisdiction of the Industrial Court and later also shearers and miners.

In January 1932, the fourteenth Labor-in-Politics Convention was held in Brisbane. The convention delegates divided into two major groups: those who were anxious to have a Labor government returned to office at the coming election and those who wanted to commit the Labor party to a radical platform. Each side won some debates. The convention voted for a restoration of the forty-four-hour week, but rejected a call for a forty-hour week; it rejected a proposal for a Labor government to legislate for a return to the standard basic wage of four pounds five shillings a week (the Queensland basic wage had by then been reduced to three pounds fourteen shillings a week) in favour of the basic wage being set by the Arbitration Court; it overrode objections by Forgan Smith, the parliamentary leader, to the introduction of a child endowment scheme and wrote into the platform a plank covering widows' pensions. A lengthy debate took place on the legislative and administrative restoration of awards and other rights removed by the Moore government. Forgan Smith and Clarrie Fallon, the rising star in the AWU, opposed this. They argued that a Labor government would inherit a deficit of £5 million and wanted a policy which would involve the Arbitration Court restoring awards, state and local government works being carried out under award conditions and the restoration of all rights to state employees. It was a classic example of that unresolved debate about the central problem of how far Labor governments should go in legislating directly in the labour area and how much they should leave this to the Arbitration Court. Jim Larcombe, Syd Bryan, Frank Waters and Harry Harvey argued that a Labor government should be prepared to legislate directly, while Forgan Smith, his deputy leader, Percy Pease, and Fallon were more cautious. The convention voted by thirty to twenty-eight to accept the Larcombe argument. There was no opposition to providing absolute preference to unionists when the Industrial Arbitration Act was reintroduced.[10]

With the election of the Forgan Smith government in 1932, the basic industrial legislation of Theodore was returned with a re-enactment of almost all of the Industrial Arbitration Act and its amendments.[11] The court was to reintroduce the forty-four-hour week, but in certain occupations such as domestic servants, some agriculural workers and seamen on coastal and river vessels, it could waive the forty-four-hour week. The basic wage continued to be set on a combination of cost of living and the productivity of average industries.

In the area of industrial legislation, the Forgan Smith governments were not to be as adventurous as those of Ryan and Theodore. Their overriding priorities were in the development of land and agricultural programmes and the restoration of employment. Hanging over the Forgan Smith governments was the spectre of the Moore government and what it had done in three years to destroy the previous fourteen years of Labor's industrial reform. To Forgan Smith and Fallon, who became secretary of the AWU in 1933 when Riordan went to the Industrial Court, it was more important to remain in office and use the re-established arbitration system and the Industrial Arbitration Act, than to embark on radical new programmes.

While the government did not proceed with the child endowment or widows' pensions schemes as laid down by the convention, it did re-establish the right of the court to grant preference in employment to unionists. The proportion of wage and salary earners in Queensland who belonged to unions had been high throughout the 1920s, usually over 55 per cent. This had fallen to 45 per cent in 1932, but grew during the 1930s, 1940s and early 1950s, reaching 81 per cent in 1948. (See Appendix D from pages 549-50, for a national comparison.) After 1933, the Industrial Court wrote absolute preference clauses into state awards. Queensland did not have compulsory unionism, but only workers with designated union tickets were given preference in employment. Those without union tickets were given a certain time in which to join a union set out in the award. Non-unionists could be employed only if it could be shown that there was no union member seeking the job.

In 1935, the International Labour Conference adopted the forty-hour week convention, which sparked off a union campaign throughout Australia for the introduction of the forty-hour week. Queensland unions argued that the state Labor government had already led the way by legislating first and directly for the forty-four-hour week and that a shorter working week would help spread the available employment. The debate was taken up at the 1938 Labor-in-Politics Convention when a resolution for the forty-hour week was moved by A.D. Murgatroyd, a Townsville railwayman and friend of Tom Aikens, and Syd Bryan, president of the Trades and Labor Council from 1929 to 1937, and soon to become vice-president of the QCE. Still the spectre of Labor's defeat in 1929 and the regressive actions of the Moore government hung over the "old hands" at the convention. In his final presidential address to a convention, Billy Demaine warned of trying to proceed too quickly:

> Prior to 1929 some of us — industrialists mostly — became impatient . . . the discontent resulted in a sad harvest and at the 1929 election Labor suffered a reverse, and the legislative social gains of many hard-fought years went by the board . . .
> The Statute Book is rich in the legislation which two Parliaments [1932-35, 1935-38] have built up, but still some of our people are dissatisfied, and while divine discontent is a good thing, we must recognize that there are limits and frame our policy accordingly.
> While there is still room for improvement, the workers of this community have gained very materially and today they have not only the shortest working week, but they have the highest basic wage and the lowest cost of living in the Commonwealth . . .
> It is questionable whether the activity to achieve this desirable objective [forty-hour week] should not be on an Australian wide basis and the question attacked as one which concerns all States and not one State in particular. To attempt to introduce in one State a reform of this nature, while other States remain on no fixed legal basis at all, may have dangerous repercussions to the prosperity of Queensland and re-act to the disadvantage of the Labor Movement in this State.

Forgan Smith opposed the forty-hour week being introduced legislatively in Queensland at that stage on the grounds of cost. This, he said, the state would accept if it were introduced federally so that "every State would be on the same footing". He also warned that a unilateral introduction of the forty-hour week in Queensland would force one hundred thousand Queensland workers into less favourable federal awards which still had a forty-four-hour week, or as he put it "into the jaws of the Commonwealth Arbitration Court". There, they would "lose the advantages of policing awards . . . have no power and authority to secure the proper administration of those awards . . . and deprive all bush workers of Queensland of the advantages of the Workers Accommodation Act". In a division, Forgan Smith's amendment, affirming the desirability of a forty-hour week and seeking the collaboration of other governments to secure a forty-hour week throughout Australia, was carried by fifty-seven votes to thirty-seven.[12]

Some of the advances to which Demaine had referred in his presidential address were in the areas of employment, wages and hours of work. In 1938, Queensland had the lowest level of unemployment of any of the states, the highest average weekly wage, the lowest average number of hours worked per employee each week, and the lowest index figure for the cost of living. It also had the highest rate of taxation of any of the states and the lowest budget deficit per head of population. The Bureau of Economics and Statistics that Moore had established in 1930 to provide independent economic advice to the government was transformed by Forgan Smith into a Bureau of Industry. J.B. Brigden, whom Moore had brought to Queensland to be the director of the bureau, remained in that position until 1938 when he was replaced by Colin Clark. Forgan Smith used the bureau to investigate major developmental projects that required large capital and provided long term employment for a considerable number of men. It was after investigation by the bureau that loans were raised to finance the building of the Story Bridge and the Somerset Dam. The Unemployment Relief Tax, introduced by Moore in 1930, was continued by Forgan Smith. It remained a source of contention in the Labor party because of its low base of sixpence in the pound for incomes over £104 a year and at one shilling in the pound was heaviest on those on incomes over £499 a year. Forgan Smith raised the base to £208 in 1938 and changed it to the State Development Tax. There remained problems with relief workers who were paid award rates but received only a couple of days work a week. The government refused to abandon relief work as a means of providing temporary jobs for the unemployed, but by 1938 relief works were progressively being converted into fulltime jobs. (See Chapter 20). During the 1930s, workers compensation payments for death and incapacity had been increased along with accident payments. Eligibility for workers compensation had been widened to include diseases contracted by workers in mines, the sugar industry, abattoirs and in the ambulance service. On the other side, although Forgan Smith had repealed Moore's Railway Strike and Public Safety Preservation Act which contained an all embracing State of Emergency clause, he re-inserted the same clause in the 1938 State Transport Act. This emergency power was to be used in 1946 against meatworkers, in 1948 against railway workers and in 1956 against electrical workers and shearers.

Throughout the war, modest changes were made in workers compensation, but the emphasis on unemployment relief and welfare swung over to the commonwealth government which gained constitutional powers in this area after the 1946 referendum. It was to be after World War II that there was a resurgence of industrial legislation.

In 1945, the Industrial Arbitration Act was amended to provide that overtime payments were to be at the worker's rate of pay, not at the minimum wage prescribed in the award; an employer was prohibited from offering to pay an employee less than the award rate in return for a job. The act was again amended in 1946 to provide two ten minute "smokos" or rest pauses in the first and second half of a working day or shift. One week's sick leave on full pay was to be provided in all awards. Annual leave had previously depended on the Industrial Court, but after 1946 all workers under state awards were to receive two weeks' paid annual leave a year with three weeks for shift workers. The 1946 act further regulated the conduct of union ballots. Unions were required to provide quarterly lists of financial members to the Industrial Court which could order a fresh pre-strike ballot if it thought that the ballot had not been properly conducted.

The amendment to the act in 1947 providing for a forty-hour week was a fulfilment of an undertaking that the premier, E.M. Hanlon, had given to the Labor-in-Politics Convention in February that year. The Queensland government supported the federal Labor government and the unions in the successful forty-hour case in the Commonwealth Arbitration Court that year. When that court unanimously agreed to the forty-hour week in September that year, it meant that Queensland workers under both state and federal awards enjoyed a forty-hour week from January

1948.[13] Under the same amending act, a worker dismissed from his job was to receive the cash equivalent of his annual leave.

Amendments to the Industrial Arbitration Act continued right up to 1956. Long service leave was introduced in 1952 and was later extended to seasonal workers. There were further improvements to long service and sick leave after 1952 when V.C. Gair was premier. The court was extended from two to four laymen in 1948 when Harry Harvey, secretary of the Miscellaneous Workers Union and president of the Trades and Labor Council, was appointed to one of the additional positions. When Riordan retired from the court in 1952, he was not replaced by a commissioner with a union background and at the fall of the Labor government in 1957, Harvey was the only member of the court with a union background. By then there was a constant stream of union complaints about delays in obtaining judgments from the court, court members having other duties and the unsatisfactory quality of some of the members. The 1953 and 1956 Labor-in-Politics Convention debates on the arbitration system were filled with complaints about the Industrial Court. Gerry Goding, a senior AWU official, remarked at the 1953 convention:

> The whole arbitration system in Queensland wants a general overhaul. That is the opinion of many workers in Queensland. The treatment that the Australian Workers Union has had is scandalous. Although the Government makes provision for a smoko and sick pay in the Act, we in the field section of the sugar industry have been consistently refused smoko or sick pay. That is the treatment the Court has handed to us. In other cases we have waited eight months for a decision after the case has been heard. If the position is not altered in some way, by either legislation or some other method, there is no doubt that the workers will refuse to accept the principle of arbitration any further.[14]

In response to union complaints about members of the court being involved in other work, when Mr Justice Brown was appointed president of the court in 1955, he remained a judge of the Supreme Court, but was to devote more time to the presidency.

Perhaps the most contentious piece of labour legislation introduced was the Industrial Law Amendment Act of 1948 which arose out of the lengthy railway strike. The act gave police extensive powers against strikers and union pickets. It was aimed principally at members of the Communist party who, the government argued, were the instigators and perpetrators of the strike. The act was repealed by Hanlon when the strike concluded. (See Chapter 19).

In 1949, the Workers Compensation Act was amended to increase the weekly payments to 75 per cent of the worker's average weekly earnings. Payments for an injured worker's wife and dependent children were also raised along with lump sum payments for death or incapacity. When Labor lost office in 1957, although the state basic wage was lower in Queensland than in the other states and the "C" series index showed a slightly lower cost of living, weekly workers' compensation payments were among the highest in Australia.

For the first fourteen years of Labor rule, average wages in Queensland were above the national level and about equal to or above the average wage levels of the other states. While wages fell in 1930, they were restored by the Industrial Court throughout the 1930s and by the end of the decade were either the highest or second highest in Australia. They declined relatively in the post-war period to become the second lowest in Australia. By comparison with the commonwealth basic wage for Brisbane, however, the Queensland basic wage remained higher. This higher basic wage and the greater simplicity of the state arbitration system were the principal reasons for most unions remaining under Queensland state awards. A second factor of importance relating to wages in Queensland between 1916 and 1956 was the significance of the lower cost of living which was underpinned by a wide ranging price control scheme. While average nominal wages in Queensland declined relative to those of other states after the war, real wages, adjusted for prices, remained the highest in Australia.

Throughout the years of Labor government in Queensland, unions had placed considerable faith in what could be achieved by political as against industrial action. Although unions were highly regulated in their internal government, throughout the thirty-nine years of Labor government, their faith in what a distinctively labour-oriented party could achieve had produced its rewards. Only in New South Wales and in Western Australia were comparable industrial reforms achieved in this period. The unions and the Labor party had both sought permanent, practical legislation that would benefit the working man and his family. However, one of the key institutions established by the Labor government to provide this political reform was proving less than efficient by 1956. That was the arbitration system. In his presidential address to the 1956 Labor-in-Politics Convention, Harry Boland, the AWU secretary and QCE president, put his finger on the major problems facing the unions:

> I suggest we can have the best legislative enactments in legislation, but it is the administration of these enactments which the people desire. If they are not administered to the welfare of those who are employed in industry we will surely have dissension. At one time the arbitration system in Queensland was looked upon as the greatest in its time in the Southern Hemisphere, and probably the greatest in the world, but we find on examination of those who are administering the Arbitration Act and those who are in the Arbitration Court that unions will be told, after a delay of 18 or 19 months, and sometimes two years, their applications will be rejected, and the advocates of the applicant unions will be told, 'You did not put sufficient information before the Court'.
>
> We must have sympathetic administration by those who are employed in high positions.[15]

This "sympathetic administration" had involved a close personal relationship between the leaders of the parliamentary party and the leading trade union officials. The success of this relationship depended largely on the trust and respect that each group had for the other and a readiness on the part of Labor ministers to meet and hear deputations from the unions, even if they could not grant the unions' requests. This trust, respect and willingness to confer sympathetically with unions declined from the early 1950s and it was this decline that was basic to the split in the Labor party in 1957 and its loss of office.

NOTES

1. For the political goals of unions in Queensland, see D.J. Murphy, ed., *Labor in Politics: The State Labor Parties in Australia, 1880-1920* (St Lucia: University of Queensland Press, 1975); chap. 2; and J.D. Armstrong, "Closer Unity in the Queensland Trade Union Movement, 1900-1922" (M.A. thesis, University of Queensland, 1975).
2. On Theodore's role in Queensland politics see D.J. Murphy and R.B. Joyce, eds., *Queensland Political Portraits 1859-1952* (St Lucia: University of Queensland Press, 1978), chap. 11.
3. *Industrial Arbitration Act of 1916.* Two short histories of this act are contained in B.H. Matthews "A History of Industrial Law in Queensland with a Summary of the Provisions of the Various Statutes", *Historical Society of Queensland Journal* 4, no. 2 (December 1949), R.F. Delaney "The Development and Progress of Industrial Arbitration in Queensland", *New South Wales Industrial Gazette* 109, no. 3 (June 1953).
4. *Report of the Economic Commission on the Queensland Basic Wage* (Brisbane: Government Printer, 1925).
5. Percentage of employees affected by state and federal award in 1954, (males and females combined)

State	Under federal awards	Under state awards	Not covered by awards
NSW	41.7	48.2	10.1
Vic	56.3	32.3	11.4
Qld	20.2	73.2	6.6
SA	51.4	35.4	13.2
WA	13.9	75.9	10.2
Tas	48.2	36.8	15.0
Aust*	42.5	47.0	10.5

Source: *Labour Report* 58, 1973

* Excludes Northern Territory and ACT, members of the defence forces, employees in agriculture, and certain other very small groups of employees.

6. For a summary of the working of the Factories and Shops Act, the Industrial Arbitration Act and the Workers Accommodation Act, see "Labour Inspection in Queensland", *International Labour Review* XXXIX, no. 2 (February 1939).
7. Annual Reports of the Unemployed Workers Insurance Acts were discussed in short articles in the *International Labour Review* XIII (January 1926), XVII (March 1928) and XIX (February 1929). A longer article "Unemployment Insurance and Unemployment Relief in Queensland in 1932" outlined the first few years operation of the act and is contained in the *Monthly Labor Review* 35, no. 4 (October 1932).

8. For an outline of the introduction of the Workers Compensation Act, see D.J. Murphy, *T.J. Ryan: A Political Biography* (St Lucia: University of Queensland Press, 1975), chaps. 4-6.
9. A useful summary of the Labor government's legislative and administrative actions prior to 1929 is contained in *Administrative Actions of the Labour Government in Queensland: during the period 1915 to 1925* (Brisbane: Government Printer, 1926); and *Legislative Record of the Labour Government of Queensland From the Session of 1915 to the Session of 1928* (Brisbane: Government Printer, n.d.).
10. *Official Record of the Fourteenth Queensland Labor-in-Politics Convention* (Brisbane, 1933)
11. William Webb, who had succeeded McCawley as Crown Solicitor in 1917, was appointed president of the Industrial Court, on McCawley's death in April 1925. (MacNaughton was president for a month until May 1925). Webb became successively president of the Board of Trade and Arbitration, president of the Industrial Court constituted by the Moore government, and president of the Labor instituted Industrial Court until 1946. When Gillies died in 1928, he was replaced by T.A. Ferry who remained on the bench until 1947. Under Forgan Smith, Ferry was also to fill the offices of chairman of the Licensing Commission, Commissioner of Prices, a member of the Coal Board, and an electoral redistribution commissioner in 1935. W.J. Dunstan died in 1930 and was not immediately replaced. J.B. Brigden served for a short period in 1932 as a commissioner. In February 1933, W.J. Riordan resigned as secretary of the AWU to become the second lay member of the Industrial Court. For the details of subsequent members of the Industrial Court, see Clem Lack, *Three Decades of Queensland Political History* (Brisbane: Government Printer, 1960), pp. 723-30.
12. *Official Record of the Sixteenth Queensland Labor-in-Politics Convention* (Brisbane, 1939).
13. For the case in the Commonwealth Arbitration Court, see O. de R. Foenander, "The 40 Hour Case and the Change in Standard Hours in Australian Industry", *International Labour Review* LVIII, no. 6 (December 1948).
14. *Official Record of the Twenty-First Labor-in-Politics Convention* (Brisbane, 1955), p. 121.
15. *Official Record of the Twenty-Second Labor-in-Politics Convention* (Brisbane, 1956), p. 67.

13 Manufacturing

Kenneth Wiltshire

Although it is true that during its long term of office in Queensland Labor gave little positive encouragement to manufacturing, it is possible, nonetheless, to identify periods with subtly distinct differences of outlook in this respect. The criteria for distinguishing these periods are political for they do not correspond to any indentifiable economic cycles in Queensland's history. The direct causal links and timing between government policy and responding changes in economic activity are tenuous in any situation and were particularly so in Queensland. Thus, if the question is to what extent did government policies, or the lack of them, affect the development of the manufacturing sector, the answer can only be: indirectly and vaguely. So attention will be directed primarily at Labor's manufacturing policies, and not at the pattern of the state's economic development and industrialization.

On this basis, the discernible periods of policy evolution are:

1. 1915-29 when the only positive attempt to promote industrialization came by way of state enterprises, i.e., the government itself engaging in manufacturing;
2. 1932-45, characterized first by Labor's reaction to innovations made by the Moore government to give government assistance to private industrialists, and then by the concept of large scale public works expenditure to prevent unemployment from which factories would benefit indirectly;
3. 1945-57, which reflected the impact of the World War II upon the manufacturing sector, and a greater awareness of the stimulus which secondary industries could impart to the state's economy as a whole, but more importantly to the goal of decentralization.

In 1915, Labor inherited an economy in which manufacturing played a very minor role in comparison with the rural industries of the state, and also in comparison with the importance of manufacturing in other states of Australia. Accurate data are not available, but it seems likely that the proportion of the Queensland labour force engaged in manufacturing in 1915 would not have exceeded 14 per cent, while secondary industries at this time would have accounted for about 20 per cent of the net value of all recorded production in the state. Queensland's share of Australian factory activity would have been about 14 per cent, corresponding to its share of 13.5 per cent of the national population. Factories were geared mostly to the processing of primary products to such an extent that these enterprises (butter factories, abattoirs, sugar mills, sawmills, etc.) were often popularly regarded as primary industries and their affairs were administered by government departments which also handled agricultural and pastoral industries. Queensland factories on average were smaller units than those in southern states. Federation had not helped, because the erection of external tariffs and the abolition of internal tariffs favoured growth of manufacturing in the more densely populated states. Having achieved economies of scale in these locations, New South Wales and Victorian firms were quick to discover the concept of marginal pricing and, assisted by tapered rail freights, they presented stiff competition for actual or potential rivals in Queensland. The state's widely scattered population presented a fragmented market for any firm which wished to establish a plant in Brisbane.

In the early days of federation there had been little interest in Queensland in industrial development, either from governments or from private enterprise. Although a considerable body of legislation on industrial affairs had been passed prior to 1915, much of which had a direct bearing on factory operations, there had been no attempt by Queensland governments to introduce a positive emphasis regarding the expansion of manufacturing. Queenslanders perceived their state as a primary producing one and were proud of their supposed superiority in rural activities. There was little in the Labor party's platform prior to 1915 to indicate any change in outlook should Labor gain office. Ryan's election speech in 1915 contained only two items with any sort of bearing upon manufacturing: further reforms to existing legislation on industrial relations, and the establishment of a number of state enterprises, some of which would be manufacturing ventures. The latter included a sugar refinery (to aid sugar growers), manufacture of cheaper farm implements (to benefit farmers), and abattoirs (to ensure clean and wholesome meat).[1]

Between 1915 and 1929 Labor's sole attention to manufacturing came through the attempted state enterprises. No encouragement was given to the private sector, and in fact the government was usually at loggerheads with industrialists because of its reforms in industrial affairs such as wages and conditions of employment, and the rate of company tax said to be the highest in Australia and a discouragement to prospective investors. The story of the state enterprises is told in Chapter 6, but it is worth noting here that the prime objective in establishing them was not to stimulate manufacturing but rather to save the community from exploitation by private capitalists, to counteract monopolies, and to supply goods and manufactures at a reduced cost.[2] Nevertheless, some of the proposals, had they been successful, would have accelerated industrialization of the state through their linkage effects, e.g., a state iron and steel works could have spawned a whole array of metal-processing and fabrication industries.

During the 1920s, economic development had proceeded apace in Australia, but Queensland, like the other outlying states, did not enjoy this rising prosperity to the same extent. The federal arbitration system, with its tendency to equalize wages and working conditions, made it difficult for manufacturers in the poorer states to compete with established firms in New South Wales and Victoria. After World War I, the commonwealth government had adopted a deliberate policy of industrialization, but as this meant import replacement, which invariably implied consumer goods where Queensland could not compete with southern firms because of their economies of scale, there was little benefit for Queensland. At the end of the 1920s, for example, there was only one cement factory in the state, and Queensland's share of textile production was only 7 per cent.[3] There seems to be little doubt that Queensland's manufacturing growth during this period was the lowest of all the states.[4] At this time some 15 per cent of the Queensland labour force was engaged in manufacturing, though secondary industries now contributed about 30 per cent of the state's value of production.

As might well have been expected, the appearance of the Moore Country-National government in 1929 produced a change of viewpoint. Apart from efforts to rid Queensland of the state enterprises and to repeal much industrial legislation, the best tangible indication of a change in government attitudes was the Industries Assistance Act, 1929. This was the first sign of state government encouragement to *private* secondary industry in Queensland, apart from earlier measures to help co-operatives and other operators of plants which processed primary products. The act was designed to foster the development of secondary industries by financial advances or guarantees, but the advent of the Depression ensured that its immediate effects were negligible.

Introducing the legislation, Moore had claimed that the high taxes imposed by the Labor government had chased business away from the state, and the new incentives would offset this handicap to some extent. Forgan Smith first objected that the measure mixed state enterprise with private enterprise and was therefore unworkable, and would reduce the amount of money available for development.[5] However, a fortnight later, he changed his tack and proposed that the bill be sent to a select committee "for the purpose of taking evidence and reporting to the house upon the most efficient means of encouraging existing secondary industries and establishing further secondary industries as a means of increasing opportunities for employment."[6] Whatever the motives for the change — fear of antagonizing local manufacturers, wish to avoid appearing apathetic to the unemployment problem, a tactical device to make the Moore government appear not to be genuinely concerned about the plight of manufacturing when it rejected the proposal — it does represent a turning point in Labor thinking about manufacturing, so that Labor policy would now accommodate some acceptance of the principle of government assistance for private industrialists.

However, Queensland had suffered least from the Depression because of the small size and nature of its manufacturing sector. Its factories were still geared mainly to the processing of primary products whose prices remained high on world markets, the servicing of the local market with building materials, and some production of consumer goods. The state's more favourable experience during the Depression caused members of all political parties to pay tribute to the resilience of the state's rural sector, and by the time Labor returned to office in 1932 this thinking pervaded their policies. The new-found interest in helping private manufacturers was to all intents and purposes forgotten. Nevertheless, although secondary industry was clearly relegated to a subsidiary place, it was not entirely forgotten. At the end of 1932, Labor introduced the Bureau of Industry Act. The act created a bureau of fifteen members to conduct economic inquiries and investigate development proposals, replacing the Bureau of Economics. However, it should not be thought that the new bureau would be preoccupied with secondary industries: the promotion of employment was its main goal and for this purpose the government considered that public works and rural industries would offer greater potential.[7] In 1933 there were amendments to the Industries Assistance Act and the Bureau of Industry Act. For the first, the qualification "secondary" was deleted so that government assistance could be given to "industry" as a whole, a change intended to bring the construction of roads and bridges within the ambit of the act. So, for example, a guarantee of £100,000 was given for the Hornibrook Highway, so that the company concerned could complete the project. For the second, the bureau was made a construction authority with power to borrow money and issue debentures under government guarantee, enabling it to assume oversight of the Story Bridge, another measure designed to combat the Depression. The consequence was that the bureau became more of a works planning authority than an aid post for industry.

These moves set the tone of Labor policy throughout the

1930s: manufacturers might be encouraged but solely in the interest of reducing unemployment. By the outbreak of World War II, Queensland's relative position in the manufacturing sector compared with the national total had not changed to any appreciable extent. A relatively unheralded, but extremely significant, event occurred in 1938 when Colin Clark, formerly lecturer in statistics at Cambridge, became state statistician and director of the Bureau of Industry.

In 1945, Clark was appointed for a further seven years as director of the Bureau of Industry, under-secretary for labour and industry, and financial adviser to the state treasury. Through the pages of the bureau's publication, *Economic News*, and in various submissions to the state government, Clark argued incessantly in favour of rural industries and paid little heed to the manufacturing sector. It has been claimed that ruralism, an anti-city bias, and a defence-oriented economic policy, the three key elements in Labor governments' thinking in this period, were expressed in the strongest terms by Colin Clark.[8] His ideal was rapid closer settlement of the state with towns of around fifteen hundred in population growing to serve new farming areas, each town being autonomous and run on a co-operative basis. There was little scope for manufacturing in such a vision.

Clark did leave behind one important contribution after his resignation because of disagreement with government policy in the mid-1950s. He had classified the state's secondary industries into three broad categories:

1. Processing industries, which were an essential associate of primary production and because of the bulk or perishability of the raw materials they treated had to be located close to the source of those materials, e.g., sugar mills, butter factories, meatworks, and sawmills;
2. Sheltered industries, which because of the bulk or perishability of finished product had to be located within reasonable distance of the market, e.g., bakeries, motor-repairing, ice-cream making, newspapers;
3. Competitive industries, which comprised the rest and were in open competition with similar industries in other locations.

This classification scheme was used extensively in Queensland's official statistics, and apart from neatly providing a picture of the nature of manufacturing in the state, also conveniently distinguished those industries which were easiest for the government to promote because of natural advantages, e.g., the first two types. Moreover, since it was those industries which also happened to be of the greatest benefit to the rural sector and provincial areas, there was no questioning the merit of encouraging them, while the third type, the competitive industries, was hard to attract and would thus absorb public funds which could otherwise be allotted to primary industries.[9]

During World War II, Queensland's industrial structure was fully taxed and its deficiencies became very apparent. While a number of industries geared to wartime needs were established in Brisbane under commonwealth government supervision, the state lacked the industrial base for munitions manufacture, and the siting of defence industries in the north of Australia was thought to be unwise. The census of 1947 revealed that manufacturing now claimed about 21 per cent of the state labour force, a significant increase over the inter-war period, and this was complemented by an increasing share for factory production which represented nearly 35 per cent of all production in the state. However, because of the greater industrial growth of the southern states during the war, Queensland's position relative to the rest of Australia had declined. Its share of national factory production fell well below its share of national population, 8.5 per cent compared with 14.6 per cent.

At the 1944 election, Labor was prodded a little when J.B. Chandler, leader of the Queensland People's party, promised a ministry for secondary industries, and G.F.R. Nicklin, leader of the opposition, proposed a Council for Industrial Research and Development. In 1945, after winning the election, the Hanlon government appointed a public body known as the Queensland Secondary Industries Committee to survey existing secondary industries in the state and consider proposals for the expansion and development of existing and new industry. This could have been partly a response to the opposition's 1944 promises, but was more probably intended to maintain the stimulus which manufacturing had imparted to the state's economy during the war, and to ensure that Queensland could secure a handout if commonwealth assistance was given to the development of manufacturing. Queensland had been represented on the Commonwealth Secondary Industries Commission by S.F. Cochran, the state liaison officer who was also chairman of the State Electricity Commission and had the oversight of secondary industry matters as a part-time job. Cochran was chairman of the Secondary Industries Committee which included the co-ordinator general of public works (J.R. Kemp), the director of the bureau of industry (Colin Clark) and the director of employment (A.C. Sorenson). There were no representatives of capital or labour, but numerous submissions from both were received on a confidential basis.

The committee's report was the most comprehensive official attempt to consider the role and prospects of manufacturing in Queensland. The committee delved into theories behind industrialization, and the practical problems which confronted manufacturers in Queensland, and concluded that the state had a long way to go. The report went so far as to say that the machinery set up under the Industries Assistance Act and the Bureau of Industry Act had been inadequate, and so had been the "practical aids" such as the public works programmes of the 1930s. Something more was required, and the committee suggested a permanent government authority to aid the development of a "secondary industrial economy in Queensland".[10] This was done by the establishment of a Secondary Industries Division within the Bureau of Industry, and transfer of the administration of the bureau to a minister who would be responsible for the promotion and decentralization of secondary industries.

The necessary legislation came in the Labour and Industry Act 1946. An Industries Assistance Board was created to handle and investigate applications for government assistance to industries, and private enterprise would be represented on the board by two members. Financial advances might be made or guaranteed to help industries. The Secondary Industries Division came into existence in April 1947 with the appointment of the former manager of the State Stores, P.J. Ross, as director of secondary industries and chairman of the Industries Assistance Board; Clark was made a member of the board.

Such speedy action on the report by the Hanlon government and the fact that the committee's recommendations were followed so closely in administrative details might have suggested a change of heart on the part of the Labor party, but in the light of the parliamentary debates of this period such an interpretation is unlikely. The politicians' appreciation of the role of manufacturing was still obviously limited to one idea, that secondary industries would provide the means of absorbing a rural workforce made redundant by mechanization and other changes in the rural sector. In the minds of many others, the only justification for industrialization was decentalization, and they saw no reason why the two should be incompatible.

The efforts of the Secondary Industries Division and the Industries Assistance Board represent the only efforts in the post-war years to develop manufacturing. Two of the major fields of activity for the division in its formative years were the provision of land and factory space, and the granting of financial assistance. The former munitions factory at Rocklea was acquired from the commonwealth, and other surplus wartime buildings in the Brisbane suburbs and in the country were acquired for industrial purposes. In 1948, plans were announced for a new type of development by the conversion of Crown land at Hamilton into industrial blocks available for lease to approved industries with provision for conversion to perpetual leasehold if substantial capital improvements were carried out.

However, the staff of the division remained exceptionally small, and the loans from the Industries Assistance Board were relatively few and meager, being distributed mainly to manufacturers or fabricators of products linked with the building industry. The largest contribution was made to Mount Isa Mines, a primary producer. Policy had been stated clearly in 1950 that it was not the government's intention to usurp the functions of banks or other financial institutions in catering for the financial requirements of industrialists, and an elaboration in 1956 explained that it was not then the board's policy to make advances although it was being done in exceptional cases. At the same time banks and other financial institutions were refusing to accept government guarantees, or were imposing outrageous conditions on the acceptance of a guarantee. The general impression can only be that the government, with or without advice from the board, was not prepared to venture far in gaining industries for the state. Most of the money went outside Brisbane, a large proportion of it to non-manufacturers, and virtually none to "competitive industries" of which Queensland had the greatest need. In the 1950s the state government was wont to complain that the national government was discriminating against Queensland as far as developmental expenditure was concerned. Although to some extent the complaint was legitimate, it became an over-used scapegoat to be employed whenever accusations were made that Queensland was not doing enough to stimulate manufacturing.

The absence of any coherent, positive policy in relation to manufacturing during Labor's long term in office is sufficiently significant to warrant some form of explanation. But how does one explain a vacuum? Unquestionably, economic factors were important: the state's relatively small and scattered population presented too fragmented a market; large southern firms indulged in marginal pricing of goods sent to outlying states aided by tapered freight rates and uniform pricing policies in capital cities. Although the state was well endowed with mineral resources, these did not form the basis for any related manufacturing activity. In the period after World War II, Queensland did not receive anything like its proportionate share of immigrants, though it is also likely that union opposition in Queensland to competitive labour may have prevented any positive action to attract immigrants. Indeed, opposition by the dominant Australian Workers Union to the encouragement of rival blue-collar unions has been held to be a major factor militating against Queensland Labor governments fostering manufacturing,[11] though there is little tangible evidence to suggest that this was a determining factor. Commonwealth monetary and fiscal policy often did not help the situation. Such policies were framed in Melbourne or Canberra, and reflected conditions prevailing in the south-east of the continent, so that more than once deflationary measures caught the Queensland economy on the wrong foot. Political factors should not be overlooked. The ideology of the Labor party in Queensland was not conducive to welcoming private investment as witnessed by the fears of national businessmen about the state's high and discriminatory taxation. Public capital might have provided a substitute, but there were always portions of the public sector, railways and irrigation, which quickly gobbled up any idle public funds. Labor in Queensland was not an urban party. It had been nurtured from roots in outlying areas of the state and since industrialization invariably meant urbanization and drift of labour from rural areas, there was little to be gained electorally in encouraging manufacturing, whereas there was much to lose. Finally, the official, expert advice available to Labor throughout this period from the government bureaucracy served only to entrench these priorities.

However, it cannot be overstressed that a major reason for a lack of drive towards manufacturing was the general contentment of Queenslanders with the *status quo*. There were simply no votes to be gained from encouraging large scale development which would have upset traditional ways and indicated favourable treatment for one part of the state over another. The longer Labor's term in office, the more entrenched this outlook became, and the harder to rearrange priorities favouring rural pursuits which the electorate understood and welcomed. Very few Labor politicians of this period appreciated the role of manufacturing in stimulating economic development; few had any personal experience of working in manufacturing. Given their past successes, and the apathy of Queensland voters, there was little incentive for them to change.

NOTES

1. See T.J. Ryan's policy speech in D.J. Murphy, R.B. Joyce and Colin A. Hughes, eds., *Prelude to Power: The Rise of the Labour Party in Queensland 1885-1915* (Brisbane: Jacaranda Press, 1970), Document 19, pp. 292-99.
2. *Worker*, 1 April 1915.
3. C. Forster, *Industrial Development in Australia 1920-1930* (Canberra: Australian National University Press, 1964), p. 88.
4. For a rather elaborate statistical attempt to verify this contention, see G.E. Hart, "A Study of Australian Manufacturing Employment 1911-1961" (B.Econ. thesis, University of Queensland, 1964).
5. *QPD* CLIV (31 October 1929) :1339.
6. Ibid. (12 November 1929) :1560.
7. For example, the three sub-committees of the bureau were Rural Development, Roads Mining and General Works, Administration Finance and Industrial. Manufacturing did not rank highly.
8. W.J. Jackson, "The Government and Economic Growth in Queensland 1946-1951" (B.A. thesis, University of Queensland, 1968), p. 49. Colin Clark's views on ruralism are fairly clearly set out in his evidence to the 1950 Royal Commission on Pastoral Lands Settlement.
9. K.W. Wiltshire, *Portuguese Navy: The Establishment of the Queensland Department of Industrial Development* (Brisbane: Queensland Group of the Royal Institute of Public Administration, 1973).
10. *Report on the Development of Secondary Industries in Queensland* (Brisbane: Queensland Government Printer, 1946), p. 14.
11. M. Gough et al., *Queensland Industrial Enigma* (Melbourne: Melbourne University Press, 1964), p. 19.

14 Mining

K.H. Kennedy

The turn of the century was marked by a revival in Queensland mining. Gold was the mainstay of the state economy with three fields producing over 100,000 fine ounces year after year — Charters Towers (1885-1911), Mt Morgan (1888-1917) and Gympie (1902-6). Between 1892 and 1906, the state's gold yield surpassed half a million fine ounces annually. Similarly, the base metal industry was experiencing good times as "the nineties were going out in wars and rumours of wars".[1] Instant townships sprang up on the Chillagoe and Cloncurry fields which emerged as major producers of copper. Thousands of miners and their families populated the isolated regions of the northwest and Cape York Peninsula, working either as independent prospectors or wages-men. Bolton has suggested that the "most glorious evening" in the north's mining capital, Charters Towers, was Mafeking night, "From the balcony of Collins's Hotel a popular tenor, supported by two jockeys led the Mossman Street crowd in a series of patriotic songs, while church and fire bells pealed, Cornish and Welsh miners sang glees, and the thousands in the streets blocked all traffic, cheering, roaring choruses, and occasionally clearing a space for fights."[2] No doubt the scene suggested the prosperity and stability which the mining industry appeared to have attained; and the large majority of people would have dismissed or scoffed at any prediction that the golden age was rapidly coming to its end.

When the Ryan government came to office in 1915, the mining industry was in a state of decline. The revival of the late nineteenth century had succumbed to adversity: the gold yield was one-third of the 1900 output; silver returns were only one-fifth of 1908 production figures; the value of tin concentrates had decreased to one-third of the 1907 values; lead output had diminished nine-fold in just seven years; copper production was falling, and the tonnage of coal mined was lower than in preceding years.[3] The outbreak of the war in Europe had a significant impact on mining. A labour shortage was created by men rushing to enlist for military service; the world metal market had collapsed and was not full recovered; overseas contracts were dislocated — Mt Morgan and Mt Elliott companies in particular were affected by the loss of sales to Germany.

The causes of the decline could not be attributed exclusively to the outbreak of war. British investment in Queensland had all but ceased after sustaining considerable losses, which according to Blainey, was "less because so many mines were worthless than because Britain paid too much for both the rich mines and the poor."[4] Typical was the Chillagoe Company, heavily backed by British capital, which had ceased operations in 1913 with accumulated losses of £2,000,000 in less than fifteen years. From 1912 to 1914, severe drought in north Queensland had forced the suspension of mining operations on many fields. Further, Australian mine managers had failed to adopt new ore extraction methods, especially the flotation process; they continued to work with aging and inefficient machinery; but most important, they had been reluctant to earmark sufficient capital to test ore reserves and to undertake development work. When the rich surface lodes were exhausted, profits and dividends dwindled as mining companies endeavoured to cope with increased production costs and low grade ore bodies.

The only gratifying feature of the industry was the spiralling copper and lead prices from wartime demand for munitions: copper prices escalated from a high of £66 a ton in 1914 to £153 a ton in 1916. Similarly, lead prices doubled in the same period. The under-secretary for mines commented in his annual reports for 1915 and 1916 that the "improved return has been secured in the face of peculiarly adverse circumstances, which more than counterbalanced those arising on the outbreak of the war",[5] and which were "brought about by the improved value ruling for industrial metals — or rather it should be said for the metals required for the manufacture of munitions for war."[6] At Mt Morgan and on the Cloncurry field, mining companies welcomed the metal prices bonanza which permitted them to mine and process low grade deposits at a profit. But the revival was short-lived: by 1920, copper prices had fallen to a low of £70 per ton and continued to slide. The Cloncurry field shut down, and Mt Morgan was confronted with serious financial difficulties which threatened closure of the mines and smelters. In far north Queensland, the Chillagoe Company had been unable to raise sufficient capital to recommence working its copper and lead deposits to capitalize on the high metal prices. Instead, the Ryan government entered into what was to prove the most disastrous experiment in state capitalism in Australian history.

In his policy speech in 1915, Ryan emphasized the importance of the mining industry which had employed "nearly 20,000 men" and had yielded £4,000,000 in output annually. He claimed the Denham government had done "practically nothing to foster or encourage mining or prevent the decline of the industry", "beyond giving infrequent grants in aid of deep-sinking and small loans for the purchase of mining machinery". Labor promised state batteries at which "miners will get their ores treated at substantially reduced rates"; refining and treatment works; state coal mines; an iron and steel works; and a vigorous oil exploration programme. In addition, miners could anticipate regulations for improved ventilation in the mines; more stringent safety measures; and the "appointment of workmen's inspectors of mines."[7] Many of these promises were to be honoured, but the financial burden on the state was enormous.

The State Experiment

The several mining enterprises established by the Ryan and Theodore governments were designed to halt the population exodus from depressed areas by creating more job opportunities, and to provide state facilities for individual prospectors and small concerns which, despite the odds, retained confidence in the industry's future. The majority of the enterprises were located in north Queensland, and, by no coincidence, in Labor strongholds. With members in caucus from Cook, Chillagoe, Charters Towers, Queenton, Flinders and Mt Morgan, it was understandable that attention should be given to mining.[8] State batteries were established at Bamford (near Irvinebank) in 1915, at Kidston (on the Einasleigh field) in 1921, and at Charters Towers in 1923. Assay offices were opened at Cloncurry in 1916 and Mareeba in 1917 at which miners were able to obtain advances on their ore parcels. Diamond drilling equipment and pumping plants were purchased for the Mines Department to conduct state-wide geological surveys, especially for coal and oil. In January 1918, a state arsenic mine was opened at Jibbinbar, south of Stanthorpe, to supply low cost grey arsenic for prickly-pear destruction, but it was abandoned within a few years with an operating loss of over £50,000.[9] The three major state undertakings were the Chillagoe smelters, the Irvinebank treatment works, and the state coal mines.

The closure of the Chillagoe Company's operations had deprived nearly five thousand men of employment; thus by acquiring the company's assets the government not only would be able to redress the serious unemployment position but also would redeem its election pledge. Spearheading the state takeover was E.G. Theodore, member for the region and Ryan's treasurer, whose faith in the region was limitless. Ryan also considered other merits: escalating wartime copper prices augured well for its profitability, while any additional production would contribute to the war effort. Legislation to acquire the enterprise was introduced in December 1915. After three years of constant wrangling with a hostile upper chamber, during which time the proposition was investigated by two select committees of inquiry, the bill finally received assent in the month the war ended. The purchase price, which included the railways from Mareeba to Mungana and from Almaden to Charleston, the smelters, plant and machinery and the Einasleigh mine, was in excess of £700,000.[10] The delay proved costly: no sooner had the enterprise commenced operations than copper prices plummeted. Despite the legislative restrictions which the council had inserted prohibiting state mining at Chillagoe, Theodore, on becoming premier, endeavoured to make the enterprise a viable proposition. Amending legislation in 1920 enabled the state to purchase successively the Mungana group of mines, Consols, Muldiva, Redcap and the Wilson mine to ensure adequate ore supplies. Within a short time, it was evident that Labor's commitment to state enterprise at Chillagoe had become a matter of ideology transcending reason. This helps to explain the mines minister's persistence with keeping the smelters open, despite low metal price, high production costs, lack of suitable high grade ores, and huge accumulated losses. Nevertheless, in February 1927, after it had been disclosed that over-valuation of assets and financial chicanery on the part of the general manager had boosted the losses in excess of £1 million, McCormack ordered the closure of the Chillagoe venture.[11]

The Irvinebank treatment works were acquired from the Irvinebank Mining Company in October 1919 to sustain tin mining on the western tablelands. After closing in 1922 for lack of ore supplies, the works were re-opened and leased to a private company in 1925. In only three years as a state enterprise, it had cost the Treasury nearly £68,000.[12] Similarly the state coal mines were far from successful. The Warra mine, west of Dalby, was acquired in December 1915 to supply steaming coal for the railways. Operations in the unstable mine were suspended in 1919 after a heavy influx of water, and the mine eventually closed after capital expenditure and a trading loss of nearly £40,000 was written off.[13] A second coal mine at Baralaba to supply Mt Morgan was commenced as a state venture in April 1919, but like Warra, was abandoned in 1928 with accumulated losses of nearly £60,000 which were also written off.[14] Two other mines, Styx No. 1 and Styx No. 2 proved to be financial disasters. Situated on Ogmore in central Queensland, they were opened to supply both the railways and the navy, but after excessive fire damp was detected they were abandoned in 1925 at a loss to the state of some £70,000.[15] Equally burdensome to the treasury was Mt

Mulligan, a coal mine acquired from the Chillagoe Company in July 1923 to reduce fuel costs at the state smelters. Large sums were required to restore the mine after the 1921 disaster when an explosion of coal dust and fire damp had wrecked the pits, killing seventy-nine men. No sooner had operations recommenced than the state smelters were closed, and in 1929, the mine was leased on tribute to the workers. In its six years of operations Mt Mulligan had accrued losses to the state totalling £146,000.[16]

Two other mines were initially profitable in the short term. The Styx No. 3 mine, known as the Hartley State Colliery, was opened in 1924 and soon showed small profits.[17] The Bowen colliery at Collinsville, the largest of the coal ventures, earned nearly £40,000 profits in the 1920's after a rail link to Bowen was completed in 1922. Unlike the other coal mines, the Bowen colliery had the advantage of working a high grade seam exposed after only a small expenditure on development. Railway and shipping contracts aided constant operations; and the output per shift was one of the highest in the state.[18]

State enterprise, especially in mining, was far from being the success that its advocates had prophesied in 1915. In 1926, the McCormack government announced that it intended to cut its losses on state enterprise "which do not give a reasonable prospect of success, and will shut down on, or dispose of, any enterprise which continues to be worked at a loss."[19] It was a bold move, but a necessary one as the state could ill-afford the financial and political liability of huge accumulated losses. Even Labor members to whom state mining was ideologically sacrosanct and electorally advantageous, could no longer resist the financial arguments. State mining was just one factor in Labor's defeat in 1929, but an important one which almost certainly cost the government the electorates of Chillagoe and Cook. The closures of the smelters and state mines at Chillagoe, the Mareeba assay office, the arsenic mine, the Warra, Baralaba and Styx coal mines; the leasings of the Bamford and Charters Towers batteries, the Irvinebank treatment works, Mt Mulligan Colliery, and the drilling equipment to tributors or private companies; and the history of accumulated losses did not show the Labor government in a favourable light.

Indeed, it mirrored the depressed condition of the industry: the value of output was the lowest since the post-war depression of 1921; copper production was a sixth of the 1920 output; only forty-two tons of lead were produced in the state; silver, gold and tin yields had decreased considerably; and only coal production to meet increased domestic demands retained any semblance of stability.[20] The number of persons engaged in mining had fallen from 9631 in 1915 to 5069 in 1929.[21] The deserted townships in north and north-western Queensland littered with rusting machinery and overgrown mullock heaps testified to earlier boom years, but now reflected the world-wide depression in mining.

Not that the Labor administrations from 1915 to 1929 failed to halt the decline in mining for want of effort: state enterprise aside, successive governments resorted to a variety of means to sustain the industry. In 1921, after copper prices had collapsed, Mt Morgan experienced losses amounting to £2300 per week. The company proposed general wage-cuts of 20 per cent which the workers rejected outright. As Blainey relates: "No slag was poured while the company and the government and the men argued on who should make those sacrifices without which the mine was doomed."[22] The government finally concluded arrangements with the employees, who agreed to accept a reduction in wages to be offset by a government subsidy of £1100 per week in the form of rebates on rail freights which was paid to them. But the struggle to keep nearly fifteen hundred men in work was lost when the mine caught fire in 1925, and the board of directors wound up the old company two years later.[23]

One decision of the McCormack government to assist mining which reaped dividends for the state nearly three decades later was the construction of the Duchess to Mount Isa rail link. This link was the key to the development of the silver-lead deposits on which Mount Isa Mines Limited and its general manager, William Corbould, pinned their hopes of raising sufficient overseas capital to develop the field. For two years the government had been pressed for assistance and although a royal commission reported in favour of the proposal,[24] the deciding factor was probably the vested interests of Theodore, McCormack and the mines minister, Alfred Jones, which ultimately decided the issue. Four years later, it was revealed that they had acquired considerable parcels of shares in Mount Isa Mines Limited and Mount Isa Proprietary Silver-Lead Limited. It is an odd but undeniable fact that this mining enterprise, which was eventually to prove of enormous benefit to the state, would probably not have been undertaken but for a corrupt and cynical bargain by members of a Labor cabinet.[25]

Writing of the mining depression of the 1920s, Blainey has made a general observation critical of the role of governments:

> The mining industry, compared to other industries, has been highly taxed in good times but has got comparatively little aid from governments when that aid is essential. The state steps in, not when a new field is born and urgently wants railways and schools and telegraph and water, but when the field has faded beyond even the power of governments to resurrect it. Perhaps that is because mining regions usually have more political pull when they are old and declining than when they are new and vital to the country,[26]

His contention does not completely account for the decline in the mining industry in Queensland. Certainly the state enterprises at Chillagoe and Irvinebank were examples of a government endeavouring to resurrect a dying field for political considerations, but the state in this instance had a vested interest in the areas as provision had been made for the government to take over the private railways in the original legislation. By its activities at Mt Morgan, Charters Towers, Cloncurry, Kidston and Croydon,[27] the state endeavoured to provide facilities to encourage mining until world metal prices had improved; and by an amendment in 1915 to the Mining Machinery Advances Act giving the minister discretion to determine the contributions of applicants for state assistance, the government more than doubled subsidies for mining plant to promote investment in the absence of speculative capital.[28] At Mount Isa, the rail link and the leasing at low rates of the state drilling equipment, demonstrated an initiative on the part of the government to open new job opportunities. The symptoms of the industry's ailment were to be more adequately diagnosed by the royal commission on mining in 1930.

Depression to Post-War Recovery

One of the last actions of the McCormack government was the setting up of a royal commission to ascertain the mining industry's future. Its report isolated the many problems confronting the industry and the "fundamental causes responsible for the decline." Summarized under four headings, the causes were found to be:

(i) Deterioration in ore values at depth as existing deposits become worked;
(ii) Difficulty of finding new deposits of suitable location, size and grade;
(iii) Increased cost of production due chiefly to increased costs of mining stores, explosives, fuel and transport, and to altered labour conditions, respecting hours, wages, and output;
(iv) Instability in the metal market and in the case of some metals its continued adverse condition.[29]

It recognized that "the first and fourth causes are beyond any control in Queensland"; but, at the same time, listed no fewer than sixty-six recommendations through which the government could assist the industry. These embraced amendments to the Mining Act and its regulations; revised labour conditions; new provisions governing mining plant, machinery and transportation; altered taxation schedules to provide incentives for private companies; and a greater emphasis on Mines Department activities in geological and mining surveys. This report dominated state mining policy for the next fifteen years.

The Moore government tackled the problem of locating new ore bodies by amending the Mining Act to provide for enlarged areas for mineral leases and miners' homestead leases, with less restricted tenure and lower rental; to sanction gold mining leases outside the limits of a proclaimed mineral field; to facilitate easier transfer and amalgamation of leases; and to permit authorities to prospect to be granted at the minister's discretion. These amendments coupled with the special concessions under the Mining Trust Limited Agreement Ratification Act and the Palmer Development Company Limited Agreement Ratification Act were designed to encourage overseas interests to invest in mining in the state.[31] Large scale foreign investment was a feature of the pre-1913 mineral boom and has been fundamental to the expansion of mining activities since World War II; but in the early 1930s, only Mount Isa Mines Limited recorded any success in attracting investment capital, and this was partly attributable to the fillip of a guarantee from the Moore government, of £500,000 on a debenture issue.[32]

In addition, the Moore government attempted to reduce the cost of mining overheads to offset the effect of low world metal prices. These costs had escalated significantly since 1915, and in no small way had come about because of labour legislation introduced by the Ryan government. Between 1915 and 1918 a series of acts had been passed designed to improve the lot of the miners and other employees in the industry. The Workers' Compensation Act (1916) provided for payments to mine workers injured in accidents or afflicted by industrial diseases, most notably phthisis, from a State Accident Insurance Fund to which all employers were required to contribute in proportion to their payrolls. The Wages Act (1918) contained a section dealing with the security of miners' wages, under which wages became the first charge against an employer or contractor, or the first call on mortgages. The Industrial Conciliation and Arbitration Act (1916) governed hours, wages and conditions of employment in the industry, although the awards were usually based on agreements between the employers and the industrial union representing the workers. The provisions of the Mines Regulation Act, and later the Coal Mining Act (1925), emphasised safety measures in the mines for the protection of workers. Collectively, these acts, welcomed by miners and basic to Labor philosophy, added substantially to the cost of mining operations. The Moore government, particularly the mines minister, E.A. Atherton, who represented the mining constituency of Chillagoe, fully appreciated the political and industrial implications for both employers and employees of amending labour legislation under which wages had doubled in the mining industry since 1915. Rather than reduce miners' wages and conditions, the Mining Act was amended to facilitate less stringent labour requirements: the number of men to be employed on gold mining leases was reduced from one man to every four acres, with a minimum of three men, to one man to every ten acres; on all mineral leases, it was no longer necessary to man areas used for stacking tailings; and capital expenditure was to be regarded as the equivalent of employing the prescribed number of men.[33] On the other hand, the state government had no control over tariffs which had drastically increased the cost of mining plant and stores, and while the commonwealth government sympathized with mining companies and owners, it was reluctant to allow imports to under-cut Australian-made mining equipment.

The Moore government's record in mining was by no means as harmful to recovery as Labor politicians suggested. The value of production figures reflected no credit on the government, as the under-secretary for mines noted:

> The year 1932 saw record low levels in the prices of both lead and silver, while the other base metals struggled in a slough of depression. It is futile to prophesy what the coming year holds in store, because the disastrously low prices realised during 1932 were reached in spite of the fact that world production receded by roughly 50 per cent. International revival in the industry must take place before base metal mining can hope to thrive.[34]

Aside from the rail concessions to Mount Isa Mines Ltd., and subsidies to small companies, the Moore government reopened the Chillagoe smelters to provide employment on the depressed northern mineral fields, despite cynical claims that Atherton was merely attempting to retain his seat in Parliament. Gold mining was encouraged with commonwealth government assistance; and prospects for an upsurge in mining were heightened by the investment incentives conferred by the Mining Act Amendment Act.

Unfortunately, politicians appeared preoccupied with mining scandals which did not enhance confidence in the industry. These scandals revolved around E.G. Theodore, the federal treasurer and strongman in the Scullin government, and William McCormack, the former Labor premier. Rumours had persisted in the late 1920s that Theodore and McCormack had been involved in shady dealings in mining shares in Mount Isa and the state mines at Mungana. In October 1929, it was revealed that Theodore held 5480 £1 shares in two Mount Isa companies, while McCormack similarly held 5925 £1 shares.[35] In the same month, it was disclosed that McCormack held 5000 £1 shares in Mungana Mines Limited, the company from which the state had purchased the mines.[36] Theodore's name was connected with Mungana by inference, as it was known that he held shares in Argentum and Fluorspar mines in the same region which had also had dealings with the state smelters.[37] Prompted by motives of political advantage, a royal commission was set up to investigate Mungana. Its report declared that Theodore, McCormack and others "were guilty of fraud and dishonesty in procuring the state to purchase the Mungana mines for £40,000", and that the money was shared between them.[38] These findings ruined the careers of Theodore and McCormack, and rocked the Scullin government. Although they were found "not guilty" of conspiracy to defraud in subsequent civil proceedings, the bitterness instilled in political life at both state and federal level rubbed off on the Moore government,[39] and in no small way discredited the Chillagoe region, and to a lesser extent, Mount Isa Mines Limited, although the company involved in corruption in the 1920s was an altogether different concern from the present one.

The Forgan Smith government did not undertake any major revisions of mining legislation enacted by its predecessors: it was satisfied to adhere to the guidelines laid down by the royal commission. In fact, mining tended to assume a much less prominent position in Labor programmes in the 1930s, for while the value of output increased nearly four-fold in the decade, it represented only about six per cent of the value of primary production. The change in emphasis in state mining policies involved the government co-operating with private mining companies, rather than directly intervening in the industry by a series of state undertakings. The period was marked by the gradual recovery and expansion of the gold, copper, silver-lead and coal industries.

By 1930, gold prices had commenced an upward movement as a consequence of the Great Depression, intensified by the depreciation of both the Australian and British pounds. Added incentive was provided by the commonwealth government's Gold Bounty Act (1930) which paid a bounty of one pound per fine ounce on gold output in excess of the average production for the years 1928-30.[40] In turn, investment capital flowed into renewed gold mining activities. In Queensland, the Mt Coolon field south-west of Bowen, discovered in 1915, was the first to benefit from the upsurge in gold mining. Taken over by Gold Mines of Australia Limited in 1930, the area yielded over 150,000 fine ounces in the ten years before it was abandoned in 1939 when the proved reserves were exhausted.[41] The second field to achieve prominence was Cracow. Traces of gold had been found in the area as early as 1875, but in 1931 after Charles Lambert and William Reynolds located the Surprise Reefs, a Melbourne syndicate floated the Golden Plateau No Liability Company to acquire the reefs which yielded over £800,000 in dividends by 1939.[42] Cracow continued as the state's major gold producer until its closure in 1976. Of the old mines, Mt Morgan was the most successful. In 1929, Adam Boyd had floated Mt Morgan Limited to acquire the old company's assets with the intention of working the mine by open cut methods. Three years later, Boyd's efforts were greatly assisted by a £15,000 loan to enable gold mining to recommence, made available through the Mines Department by the Loan Council.[43] The loan was repaid in six months, and by 1934 Mt Morgan was once again a profitable undertaking, attracting investment necessary to erect a new treatment mill and to mechanize the open cut mine.[44] Even Charters Towers relived its golden past for a short time. The Venus battery treated an increasing number of parcels of ore, and to cope with demands, the Mines Department allocated extra funds in 1934 to repair and upgrade the plant.[45]

The state government provided additional incentives for the gold mining industry by ear-marking £130,500 for assistance to miners over the three-year period 1933-36.[46] The renewed activity in gold mining was reflected in the changes in output values and employment in the three years from 1929: the value of production increased from £27,494 to £69,928, while the number of men engaged in the industry increased from 326 to 3893.[47] The revival peaked in 1938 when 151,432 fine ounces were yielded, but by 1942 a decline in output had recommended,[48] attributable on the one hand to many miners enlisting in the armed services, and on the other hand to the relocation of men in the base metal industry as part of the war effort. The old gold mining towns soon reverted to the tranquility of the previous decade.

Mt Isa became the focus of the base metal industry after the treatment plant was fired in 1931. In contrast to the scattered "instant" townships of earlier years, Mt Isa was a planned development in which large sums had been expended on workers' accommodation and civic facilities before a ton of ore was treated. When the American general manager, Julius Kruttschnitt, assumed control, he had to cope with debts of near £3.5 million, and to complicate matters, had to contend with an alarming incidence of plumbism. Between 1931 and 1933, no fewer than 288 case were reported, resulting from the dust given off by the treatment of lead sulphide ores.[49] The state government reacted by issuing special regulations under the Mines Regulation Act which compelled Mount Isa Mines Limited to install expensive machinery and to conduct regular medical checks on workers to reduce lead poisoning. By 1937, when the company had shown its first profit, and when the Industrial Court had accepted the principle of a lead bonus, plumbism had been successfully countered with only six reported cases for the year.[50]

Blainey has contended that by the outbreak of World War II, the company's most notable achievement had been "merely to survive".[51] Certainly the first decade had been difficult: strikes in 1933, problems with treating low grade ores, the financial burden of erecting a plant for zinciferous ores, and the accumulated debts justified the under-secretary for mines' comment in 1938 that the company "has courageously persisted in its large scale operations despite all the difficulties associated with unfavourable market fluctuations".[52] But the company's perseverance and the support of American Smelting and Refining, which had provided substantial investment capital, paid dividends. Re-armament and later the war in the Pacific created a new demand for strategic minerals. Extensive copper deposits were discovered after the commonwealth government appealed for increased copper production in 1942. When the transition from wartime was nearly finalized, Mount Isa Mines Limited paid its first dividend and at the same time initiated a development programme designed to make the mine one of the world's principal and most profitable base metal ventures.[53]

Mt Morgan also benefited from the increase in wartime copper prices, as its average annual output of ore over five thousand tons compared very favourably with returns from gold production. Similarly, Queensland tin mines remained profitable due partly to high metal prices, and partly to developments before the war. In 1933, the Forgan Smith government had resumed the Irvinebank treatment works from private tributors, and had undertaken a modernization programme. Within a few years, when world tin prices stood at £200 per ton, Tableland Tin No Liability had commenced large scale dredging operations in the Mt Garnet district.[54] By 1947, the value of tin output was nearly £400,000, more than ten times the 1931 value.

The revival of the base metal industry was attributable mainly to the initiative of Mount Isa Mines Limited. The extent of state assistance was almost negligible.[55] Paradoxically, the coal industry experienced considerable state intervention. By 1933, the Forgan Smith government had resolved to restructure the coal industry to halt indiscriminate and unplanned colliery developments and to regulate production and marketing. Queensland's coal output was geared for local consumption; it was not dependent on world demand or world prices, and offered practically the only stable avenue of employment in mining in the inter-war years. Its past left much to be desired. The Ryan government had attempted to stabilize coal prices and standardize working conditions by example with the state mines competing with private collieries. In 1925, special legislation had been enacted to supplement the state experiment: the Coal Mining Act consolidated laws relating to coal mining and stipulated a code dealing with licences and leases, drainage, ventilation and safety measures. Without impinging on the features of the 1925 legislation and an amendment in 1928 ensuring security of tenure for colliers, the Coal Production Regulation Act (1933) contributed significantly to the stabilization and subsequent revival of the industry in which output had decreased by nearly 40 per cent between 1929 and 1931.[56] The act provided for a central coal board and five district boards to administer production and marketing. The arrangement gave "satisfaction to colliery proprietors and the coal mining industry generally", "stabilized coal production and increased employment", and more important, caused output to double over the following fifteen years without a significant increase in the number of small collieries.[57] For the coal miners, state intervention had improved their conditions considerably. Accidents were less frequent due to strict application of the Mines Regulation Act; improved ventilation standards reduced the threat of fire damp; and the Coal and Oil Shale Mine Workers (Pensions) Act (1941) inaugurated a contributory pension scheme for coal workers and their dependents. Considered a major achievement in social welfare, the pensions, provided on retirement at sixty or sixty-five depending on occupation or upon previous incapacity, were paid from a trust fund administered by a tribunal to which employers, the government and employees contributed.[58]

The upsurge in production which could be achieved by greater state control of the coal industry was apparent during the war years. In August 1941, the National Security (Coal Control) Regulations, promulgated by the commonwealth government, established a Coal Commission which in turn delegated powers to a Queensland Coal Committee to ensure increased output to meet wartime requirements. Despite a decrease in the number of skilled miners due to enlistment, production was maintained at an annual rate in excess of one and a half million tons.[59] The experience of wartime regulation and the post-war demands greatly influenced the Hanlon government's decision to adopt even greater state controls on the industry. Three measures were noteworthy in the major restructuring of the coal industry in the late 1940s. Firstly, an English firm of mining consultants, Powell-Duffryn Technical Services Limited, was commissioned to compile a comprehensive survey of the industry and to recommend guidelines for its expansion.[60] Secondly, the Coal Mining Acts Amendment Act (1947) ensured improved safety, health and ventilation in the mines, and better amenities for workers. While this measure aimed at overcoming many of the grounds for industrial unrest, the opposition under Francis Nicklin, no doubt pressured by private colliery owners resentful at the increase in overheads, protested against the changes, claiming that the state had gone too far in regimenting the industry. Even a further amendment to reduce royalty rates as a palliative to the colliery owners did little to appease hostility to the changes.[61] Thirdly, the 1933 act which had set up district coal boards was repealed, and the Coal Industry (Control) Act (1949) was passed. The legislation incorporated the Queensland Coal Board, staffed it with technical experts, and endowed it with wide-ranging functions and powers to regulate all aspects of development, production, marketing and miners' welfare. Though not as sophisticated as the Joint Coal Board instituted by NSW-Commonwealth complementary legislation for the rehabilitation and development of the NSW coal industry, the Queensland Coal Board had a major impact on the industry in the 1950s, contributing significantly to its growth, although in recent years with opencut developments governed by special legislation its role has become less influential.

A project which was abandoned for want of capital, but which foreshadowed the export coal developments of the 1960s, was Blair Athol. The Electric Supply Corporation (Overseas) Limited Agreement Act (1947) had empowered Hanlon to negotiate with a British firm to open up Blair Athol on a large scale at an estimated cost of £18 million. Initially approved by the opposition, the Blair Athol franchise later became a divisive political issue. In March 1949, Hanlon announced that the British firm had concluded an arrangement with Power and Traction Company Limited to assign its rights and obligations under the act to a new company to be known as Central Queensland Coal Development Co. Pty. Ltd. in return for substantial equity which Power and Traction Company Limited would be able to acquire on the completion of a satisfactory technical investigation and on an undertaking to provide the finance to develop the deposits.[62] During a volatile debate, it was claimed that the franchise was being hawked to foreign interests, and finally in September 1949, Hanlon admitted that the project had fallen through for lack of capital for rail and port facilities.[63] Ironically, twelve years after the project was abandoned, the non-Labor parties had reversed their attitudes to concessions and overseas capital in the coal industry, and had generously accommodated Theiss-Peabody-Mitsui and Utah International Incorporated to develop export coal deposits in central Queensland.

The Labor administration continued with coal mining operations at Mulligan, Ogmore and Collinsville throughout its long period in office, even though the enterprise sustained heavy trading losses in the 1950s. Mt Mulligan was resumed from tributors in 1947, but ten years later in November 1957, by one of the first actions of the Nicklin administration, was closed after accumulating losses of £700,000 since its inception.[64] The Hartley colliery at Ogmore probably should have been abandoned in 1934 when an explosion of fire damp wrecked the mine. It seemed that the cost of re-opening the mine in consideration of the employment factor had been justified by the small trading profits in the late 1930s, but after the war, large losses were incurred amounting to over £400,000. Ogmore was eventually handed over to Theiss-Peabody-Mitsui in April 1964.[65] The Collinsville colliery had been one of the few profitable state enterprises in its early years. In 1933, coke works were located at Bowen drawing coal from Collinsville to supply Mount Isa and the Chillagoe smelters, and for a brief period for export to Noumea.[66] After the war, the Collinsville colliery absorbed considerable public capital when a mechanization programme was undertaken in 1949; similarly, the upgrading of the Bowen coke works was costly. The enterprise faced an uncertain future following a royal commission in 1954 to investigate the asphixiation of seven miners at Collinsville and the impact of mechanization on the mine. Its report favoured continued mining under new regulations, but the reprieve was short-lived.[67] In April 1961, after a spell of industrial unrest, the Nicklin government called tenders for the sale of the mine and the coke works which had accumulated losses of over £900,000 and £150,000 respectively, thus effectively concluding the Labor experiment in state coal mining.[68]

After 1932, successive Labor governments assisted the mining sector in a number of ways, all of which indirectly contributed to the revival of the industry. Firstly, in line with the recommendation of the royal commission, the geological survey of the states' resources was stepped up. The Mining Survey Act (1935) committed the state government to participate with the commonwealth and Western Australian governments in a combined aerial and land geological and geophysical survey of north Australia.[69] At the same time, Geological Survey decentralized its operations, opening offices in Rockhampton and Charters Towers, and stationing geologists at Cloncurry and Ipswich. Secondly, compressors, drilling plants, portable batteries and pumping and hoisting units were purchased and leased at low rental to companies or groups of miners to encourage exploration and small developments.[70] In addition, the state continued to maintain batteries at Kidston and Charters Towers and to provide an assay service at Cloncurry. Thirdly, the Mines Department committed increased sums for financial assistance to prospectors; it offered repayable subsidies for the development of mining properties; it made grants for the provision of roads, bridges and water supplies in mining areas; and it advanced to small operators loans for the installation of mining machinery. One of its major activities was the search for oil to which the state was heavily committed.

Since the discovery of natural gas in 1900 on Hospital Hill at Roma, the search for oil had been a major pre-occupation of successive administrations. The Ryan government's Petroleum Act (1915) attempted to confine oil search exclusively to government activity: the rights of the Crown were declared, and the state was authorized to conduct a drilling programme.[71] By 1920, after considerable public expenditure, an amendment to the act permitted individuals to obtain prospecting licences over areas up to two thousand acres, or leases over sixty acres. Three years later, the government endeavoured to encourage private capital to the Roma area, and, by amendments in 1927, 1929 and 1939, progressively enlarged the areas over which a prospecting permit could be granted. Private companies responded almost immediately: the Roma Oil Corporation and Roma Blocks Oil Company were particularly active in the late 1920s. An absorption plant at Roma processed twenty-seven thousand cubic feet of gas, recovering only five thousand gallons of petrol before closing in 1931. Drilling results were promising, but the small quantities of crude obtained were too small to be of commercial importance. As the search expanded from localized to regional explorations the government was required to amend legislation to prevent operations by merely speculative concerns with insufficient capital backing. It reserved a small area around Roma, and insisted on a minimum annual expenditure in proclaimed areas. By 1936, the commonwealth government was providing financial incentives for private oil companies, but it was clear that there was not only insufficient capital to finance oil exploration but also a lack of geological expertise to supervise any programme. One the outbreak of war, the Shell Company took advantage of liberal prospecting rights and acquired an area of 136,000 square miles on which it intended to carry out investigations through a subsidiary company, Shell (Queensland) Development Pty. Ltd. Shell's programme was interrupted by the war, but on resumption of geological surveys and drilling in 1946, hundreds of thousands of pounds were invested and a large number of wells were sunk. By the late 1950s overseas capital was flowing into Queensland's oil search, but it was not until nearly five years after the Labor government was defeated that a commercial oilfield was tapped at Moonie, over sixty miles south-east of Roma.[72]

A New Era

The post-war mining boom in base metals was reflected in the rapid expansion of Mount Isa Mines Limited in the 1950s. The substantial increase in the price for lead in the immediate post-war years influenced the company to revert to the mining and treatment of silver-lead ores; but the copper lodes were not forgotten. In 1948, construction commenced on a new copper smelter which took nearly five years to complete, during which time large sums were invested in exploration and assessment of reserves. Despite a drop in copper prices from £350 per ton to £285 per ton in 1953, production began in earnest. By 1956, the under-secretary for mines was able to report that copper "has assumed the role of the state's greatest revenue producer as far as the mining industry is concerned, and it would appear that it will continue to hold this position for many years to come."[73] Indeed, Mount Isa Mines Limited now accounted for 60 per cent of the state's value of output, employing more than half the miners in Queensland, and paying out over £11 million in wages and salaries. The Labor government was conscious of the company's contribution to the state, and readily supported its submission for funds to reconstruct the railway to Townsville in early 1956. The finance was not forthcoming, as the commonwealth government turned down the state's request for £10 million. It was only after three years of wrangling that the funds were made available: and the rebuilding of the Townsville to Mount Isa rail link was not completed until 1965.[74] Just as Mount Isa had contributed significantly to the industry's gradual recovery in the 1930s, it reflected the growth and prosperity of base metal mining in the late 1950s.

The recession in mining in Queensland in the inter-war years had been greatly influenced by the condition of the world metal market and world demands for base metals. The post-war era witnessed demands for new metals, particularly mineral sands, uranium and bauxite. Technological developments in the 1940s created markets for rutile, zircon and ilmenite, which occurred in natural beach and dune concentrations in south-east Queensland.

In 1941, Mineral Deposits Syndicate commenced mining a seam of mineral sands near Beenleigh, and was soon joined by Rutile Sands Proprietary and Southport Minerals. Within five years, nearly £400,000 worth of black sands had been extracted, the bulk of which was exported as mixed mineral concentrate until a commonwealth government ban in 1946 compelled the separation of the minerals into high grade rutile and zircon concentrates.[75] Two years later, the Hanlon government exerted limited controls on mineral sands developments by amending the Mining Acts to provide for the granting of dredging leases in lieu of dredging claims together with sludge abatement clauses dealing with the pollution of water courses. This act not only applied to mineral sands, but also to other minerals, notably tin; it was reinforced by a further amendment in 1951. By 1957, mineral sands was a £2 million a year industry, and in only a decade had yielded concentrates valued in excess of £7 million.[76] It was not until the 1960s that tourism and conservation interests checked the rapid expansion of beach sand mining.

In 1954, after the commonwealth government had foregone its monopoly on uranium, the north-western areas of the state experienced an upsurge in prospecting activities. Small parties of prospectors competed with large companies, including Mount Isa Mines Limited, Gold Mines of Australia Limited, and Australasian Oil Exploration Limited to locate radio-active ore bodies. When samples confirmed the presence of pitchblend, speculative frenzy gripped the stock exchanges in capital cities. On 17 July 1954, a party of eight discovered uranium deposits at Mary Kathleen; and within a month the leases had been acquired by Australasian Oil Exploration Limited for more than £250,000.[77] This deposit was developed by Mary Kathleen Uranium Limited, a company in which Rio Tinto Limited obtained major equity; and only months before the Labor split of April 1957, it was announced that an £8.5 million treatment plant was to be constructed. A mining code was prepared by the Australian Atomic Energy Commission; and a modern township had been constructed by the company by 1959 when the treatment plant commenced operations. Nearly four thousand tons of uranium oxide valued at £40 million were produced between 1959 and 1963, by which time overeas stockpiles had been built up sufficiently to cause the closure of Mary Kathleen.[78]

One of the most important developments in the state's history was the discovery of bauxite outcrops on Cape York Peninsula in mid-1955, by a party of geologists during a reconnaissance of possible oil bearing structures. The find coincided with a decision by the commonwealth and Tasmanian governments to construct a smelter at Bell Bay, Tasmania, to process imported bauxite to meet increasing demands for aluminium. Since 1950, the Commonwealth Bureau of Mineral Resources and the State Geological Survey had been conducting investigations for bauxite deposits on Tambourine Mountain and in the South Burnett district, but with little success.[79] The disclosure of the Weipa deposits which Blainey later described as "the largest area of payable mineralization ever found in Australia"[80] was shortly followed by the registration of the Commonwealth Aluminium Corporation Pty. Ltd. in December 1956, the company having obtained authorities to prospect over the area. The Weipa Agreement was concluded by the Nicklin government only twelve months later, and the first shipments of bauxite were commenced in 1963.[81] In only twenty years, Weipa has yielded bauxite valued in excess of $300 million; though the terms and concession of the 1957 agreement and the subsequent favourable treatment extended to Comalco Limited by the state government has been justifiably criticized in recent years.[82]

By 1956, the Queensland mining industry had not only regained a position of economic importance for the state but was on the brink of an expansion phase which over the next two decades would transform it into the state's major export earner.[83] The value of production in 1956 was in excess of £37 million; in 1976, mining was worth nearly $1500 million. The industry's rapid recovery from the recession of the inter-war years was attributable as much to the adoption of improved mechanical equipment and extraction and processing techniques as to the increase in metal prices from heavy overseas demands for minerals.[84] Technological advances accelerated the search and

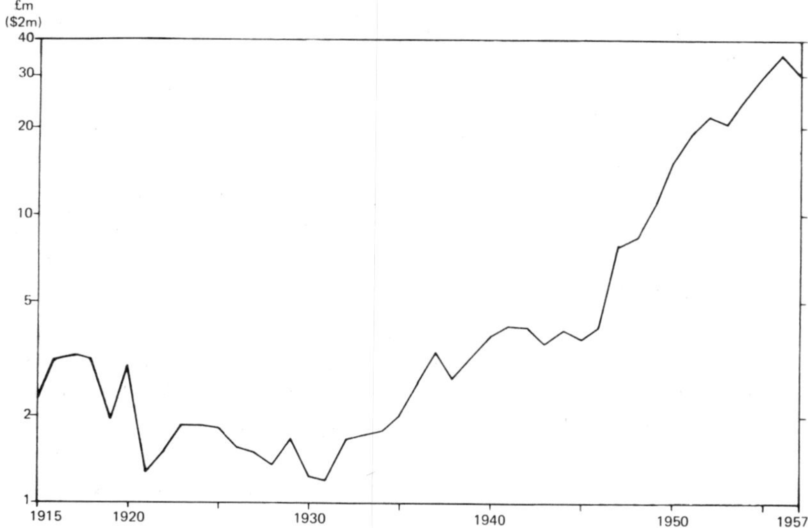

Figure 1. Value of minerals raised.

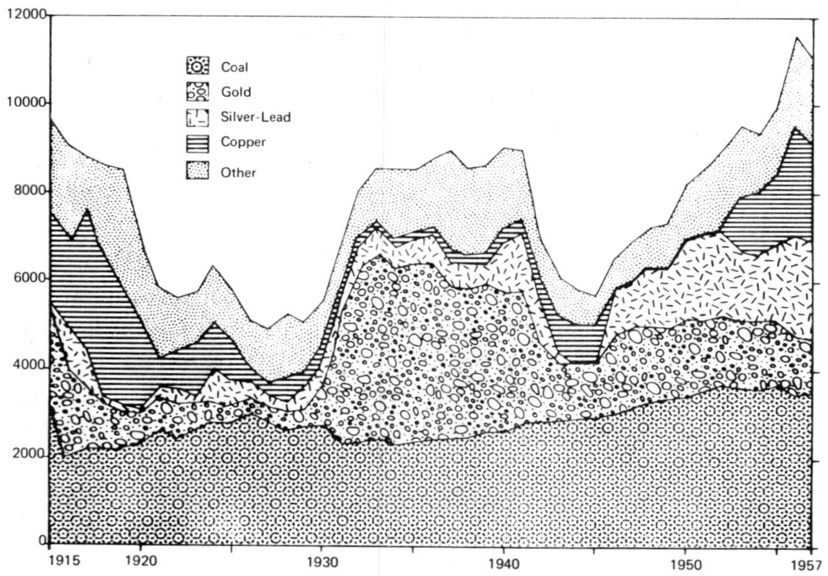

Figure 2. Employment in the mining industry.

development of deposits, financed not by speculative capital raised from investors on the London and Australian exchanges, but by established overseas mining companies with financial reserves sufficient to cope with the high infrastructure costs of working extensive low grade deposits in isolated areas. These companies assumed responsibility for communications and workers' accommodation, costs which forty years ago would have been met by government public works programmes at intervals in a mining field's development. In only four decades, mining was converted from a labour intensive industry to a capital intensive one. Further, fluctuations in employment no longer reflected movements in world metal prices and overseas demands. Long term contracts introduced stability in employment in the industry.

For its part, the Labor governments, which in earlier years had shown a commitment to mining not found in most other industries, had gradually modified the state's role from direct participation in mining and smelting to indirect encouragement of the industry. The policies of state capitalism introduced by the Ryan and Theodore governments were rejected after the experience of huge losses of public revenue. The recommendations of the royal commission of 1930 which had emphasised the importance of private capital investment and the need to locate sizable ore deposits justified the change of direction. After its electoral success in 1932, the Labor government concentrated on encouraging overseas investment, and assumed a role in which it sought to regulate developments by legislative sanctions, evidenced by amendments to laws relating to the search and mining of ore bodies; to mining on alienated lands; to the imposition of safety and health standards; to labour conditions; and to controls on oil exploration and coal mining activities.[85] The industry was fundamental to decentralization objectives, more so as the Labor governments relied heavily on the non-metropolitan areas for political support, especially in the north and northwest, which was reflected in Hanlon's redistribution in 1949. After the split in 1957, the Labor party adopted new attitudes to the mining industry, emphasizing Australian ownership and increased royalty return from highly profitable large-scale developments; but even these aspects have been encouraged by the National-Liberal coalition. In retrospect, apart from the dozen years of Labor commitment to state enterprise, mining policies have not divided the parties fundamentally. The Moore government's policy was foreshadowed by McCormack and continued by Forgan Smith's reversal of Ryan's mining policies; while those of the present administration and its non-Labor predecessors were clearly foreshadowed by the innovations of Hanlon and Gair in the 1940s and 1950s. Queensland Labor today, though critical of some instances of government policy, has no radical alternative and its coming to power would not result in any dramatic change in direction.

NOTES

1. G. Bolton, *A Thousand Miles Away* (Canberra: Australian National University Press, 1972), p. 278.
2. Ibid., p. 269.
3. *Annual Report of Under Secretary for Mines, 1915*, Table D, p. 30.
4. G. Blainey, *The Rush That Never Ended* (Melbourne: Melbourne University Press, 1963), p. 250. Blainey claimed that the impact of British money also carried its advantages: "It stimulated so much prospecting and the sinking of shafts that many concealed deposits were found decades before they might otherwise have been found. It re-opened old mines that would have otherwise been shunned. It equipped many mines so efficiently that they could work poorer ore and make higher profits. Although British companies worked scores of gold and copper mines that should probably not have been touched, such mines increased the output if not the profits of Australian mining."
5. *Annual Report of the Under Secretary for Mines, 1915*, p. 1.
6. Ibid., *1916*, p. 1.
7. T.J. Ryan's Election Speech at Barcaldine, 1915 in *Prelude to Power: The Rise of the Labour Party in Queensland, 1885-1915*, eds., D.J. Murphy, R.B. Joyce and C.A. Hughes (Brisbane: Jacaranda Press), p. 296.
8. The mining fields had produced a number of venerated Labor leaders: Anderson Dawson, Andrew Fisher and W.H. Browne. In Ryan's administration, E.G. Theodore, William McCormack, Alfred Jones and William Hamilton had worked as miners in their earlier years.

9. "Report of the Auditor-General upon the Accounts of the State Enterprises 1922-23", *QPP* II (1923), pp. 1162-64.
10. For full details, see: Chillagoe Railways and Mines Ltd. [Reports, forms of agreement, memoranda and correspondence related to the Chillagoe Railways and Mines Ltd. 1898-1920.] *QSA*, JUS/54/57.
11. "Special Report of the Auditor General on State Smelters, Ore Reduction and Treatment Works and Mines", Chillagoe, *QPP* I (1927) :1399-433.
12. *Annual Report of the Auditor General, 1922-23, QPP* I (1923), pp. 205-6.
13. Ibid., *1918-19, QPP* I (1919-20) :866.
14. Ibid., *1927-28, QPP* I (1928) :111.
15. Ibid., *1925-26, QPP* I (1926) :179-80.
16. Ibid., *1928-29, QPP* I (1929) :156-59. See also: Report of the Royal Commission upon the Mount Mulligan Colliery Disaster, etc. *QPP* II (1922) :709-944.
17. *Annual Report of the Auditor General, 1928-29*, QPP I (1929) :159-60.
18. Ibid., pp. 151-56.
19. *QPD* CXLVII, p. 326.
20. *Annual Report of Under Secretary for Mines, 1929*, Table C, p. 23.
21. See Appendix: "Employment in the Mining Industry".
22. Blainey, *The Rush That Never Ended*, p. 284. The situation at Mt Morgan was adequately analyzed by James Stopford in Parliament on 18 August 1921. *QPD* CXXXVII, pp. 144-50. See also: *Annual Report of Under Secretary for Mines, 1922*, p. 1.
23. B.G. Paterson, "The Story of Mount Morgan Mine", *Queensland Government Mining Journal*, 51, no. 584 (June 1950) :378-81.
24. "Report of Royal Comission on Public Works on the advisableness of completing Section D of the Great Western Railway, and upon a proposal to build a railway to the Mt Isa Mineral Field", *QPD* III (1925) :595-699.
25. In debate on the Mining Trust Limited Agreement Ratification Bill, it was alleged that Labor ministers had accepted parcels of shares to expedite the Duchess to Mount Isa railway.McCormack, Theodore and Jones were accused of "utilizing public funds and prostituting the high offices which they held in the State". *QPD* CLIII, pp. 712-17. Randolph Bedford, who had proffered the shares claimed: "The value of shares I gave away to friends in mere good will, would be today about £11,000; and I don't expect mean little suburban 'pikers' to understand either mateship, gratitude or generosity." p. 717.
26. Blainey, *The Rush That Never Ended*, p. 288.
27. The Ryan and Theodore governments had financed drilling programmes on the Palmer and Etheridge field, but with little success. In 1926, the Mines Department financed the erection of a small battery at Stanhills, near Croydon, under the Mining Machinery Advances Act.

28. *Annual Report of Under Secretary for Mines, 1915*, p. 24. Returns under the act were published annually in Queensland Parliamentary Papers.
29. "Report of the Royal Commission Appointed to Inquire into the Mining Industry of Queensland", *QPP* I (1930): 1309.
30. For a synopsis of the amendments, see: "Mining Acts Amendment Bill", *Queensland Government Mining Journal* 31, no. 367 (December 1930): 515-17.
31. For details on the Mining Trust, see G. Blainey, *Mines in the Spinifex* (Sydney: Angus & Robertson, 1960), pp. 135-38. The Mining Trust secured from the government sole prospecting rights over 100,000 acres on the Lawn Hills field near Burketown. *QPD* CLIII, pp. 568-75. The Palmer Development Company Limited was given rights over 573 acres on the Palmer River, and the government agreed to subsidize drilling and development to the extent of £2 per foot. *QPD* CLVII, pp. 2426-28.
32. *QPD* CLVI, pp. 62-63.
33. Ibid CLVII, pp. 2424-26; 2555-58.
34. *Annual Report of Under Secretary for Mines, 1932*, p. 1.
35. *QPD* CLIII, pp. 847-48; 933.
36. *Brisbane Courier*, 10 October 1929.
37. List of Shareholders, Argentum Mining Company, No. 180/23, *Queensland Companies Office*, Brisbane; List of Shareholders, Fluorspar Mining Company, No. 181/23, *Queensland Companies Office*, Brisbane.
38. "Report of the Royal Commission to Inquire into and Report upon Certain Matters Relating to the Mungana, Chillagoe Mines, etc.", *QPP* I (1930) :1372.
39. For full details of the Mungana scandal, see: K. Kennedy, *The Mungana Affair* (St Lucia: University of Queensland Press, 1977).
40. The bounty was short-lived. Payments were reduced in 1931, and suspended following economic cut-backs in 1932. *Commonwealth Year Book* (1935), p. 664.
41. C.B. Simmons, "Gold Discoveries in Queensland", *Queensland Government Mining Journal* 51, no. 584 (June 1950) :406.
42. Ibid.; Blainey, *The Rush That Never Ended*, pp. 311-12.
43. *Queensland Government Mining Journal* 33, no. 386 (July 1932) :189-90.
44. For details on developments at Mt Morgan in the 1930s, see: Paterson, "The Story of Mount Morgan Mine", pp. 381-88.
45. *Annual Report of Under Secretary for Mines, 1934*, p. 2.
46. *Queensland Year Book* (1937), p. 124.
47. See Appendix: "Employment in the Mining Industry".
48. The gold output of 1938 was valued at £643,344; but an increased in price from £4.5.0 per fine ounce to £10.13.9 per fine ounce conferred higher values during the war despite decreased in output. *Annual Report of Under Secretary for Mines, 1938*, p. 1; *1941*, pp. 1-2.

49. *Annual Report of Under Secretary for Mines, 1931*, p. 3; *1932*, p. 3; *1933*, p. 3.
50. Ibid., *1937*, p. 3.
51. Blainey, *The Rush That Never Ended*, p. 331.
52. *Annual Report of Under Secretary for Mines, 1938*, p. 1.
53. Mt Isa ceased lead production in 1943 to concentrate on copper. In 1946, it reverted to treating silver-lead ores, and commenced erecting a copper smelter. For full details, see: Blainey, *Mines in the Spinifex*, pp. 182-200.
54. J.M. Newman and B.G. Paterson, "Fifty Years of Queensland Mining", *Queensland Government Mining Journal* 51, no. 584 (June 1950): 365-66; *Annual Report of Under Secretary for Mines, 1938*, p. 1; *1940*, p. 1.
55. The major benefit had been freight concessions on the state railways; while on the other hand, high taxes offset the concessions.
56. *Annual Report of Under Secretary for Mines, 1933*, p. 1.
57. *Annual Report of Under Secretary for Mines, 1935*, p. 1. The number of collieries working in 1933 was eighty-seven; in 1947 there were eighty-five in production.
58. This act was complemented by the Coal Mining Industry Long Service Leave Act (1951) which instituted a trust fund, and provided for the payment therefrom to employers in the industry of amounts paid by them to employees in respect of long service leave accrued by employees under certain awards.
59. *Annual Report of Under Secretary for Mines, 1942*, p. 1; *1947*, p. 92.
60. Ibid., *1948*, p. 90; for terms of reference, see: *QPD* CXCI, pp. 1638-40.
61. For details, see: *QPD* CXCI, pp. 1706-14.
62. *QPD* CXCV, pp. 2091-92. For details on the field, see: "History of Blair Athol", *Queensland Government Mining Journal* 68, no. 553 (1947) :347-50.
63. *QPD* CXCVI, pp. 422-24.
64. *Annual Report of the Auditor General*, 1958
65. Ibid., *1963-64, QPP* 1964-65 session, pp. 151-52.
66. *Annual Report of Under Secretary for Mines, 1933*, pp. 1-2; *1938*, p. 2.
67. "Report of the Royal Commission appointed to inquire into certain matters relating to the State Coal Mine, Collinsville", *QPP* II (1956).
68. *Annual Report of the Auditor General, 1968.*
The coke works were retained as a state enterprise.
69. *Annual Report of Under Secretary for Mines, 1934*, p. 1; *1938*, pp. 1-2. The survey was conducted over six years at a cost to the state of £37,500.
70. In 1947, V.C. Gair, minister for mines, announced that Broken Hill South Ltd had been given prospecting rights over 2,900 square miles in the Chillagoe region in an attempt to have the mines re-opened. *Queensland Government Mining Journal* 68, no. 546 (1947) :115.
71. *Annual Report of Under Secretary for Mines, 1915*, p. 24.

72. For details on oil exploration, see: A. Wade, "Fifty Years Searching for Oil in Queensland", *Queensland Government Mining Journal* 52, no. 584 (1950): 456-68.
73. *Annual Report of Under Secretary for Mines, 1956*, p. 5.
74. For full details of the project, see: *Annual Report of the Auditor General, 1961-62, QPP* 1962 session, pp. 110-12.
75. See O.J. Carlson, "The Beach Sands Minerals Industry of South East Queensland", *Queensland Government Mining Journal* L1, no. 586 (1950) :493-98.
76. *Annual Report of Under Secretary for Mines, 1957*, p. 6.
77. Ibid., *1955*, pp. 82-83.
78. Ibid., *1963*, p. 16.
79. Ibid., *1950*, p. 7.
80. Blainey, *The Rush That Never Ended*, p. 340.
81. For details of the agreement, *QPD* 219, pp. 1408-18.
82. Comalco became the centre of political controversy in 1970 when it was disclosed that six cabinet ministers had been offered and had accepted parcels of preferential shares. *QPD* 256, pp. 5-44. The state expenditure on the Gladstone Power Station to supply power at a cheap rate to the proposed smelters at Gladstone has often been criticized in Parliament, more so because Comalco refuses to confirm whether or not it will proceed with the plant.
83. For details of the expansion of the industry, see: I.W. Morley and A.W. Norrie, "The Mining Industry of Queensland", *Queensland Government Mining Journal* LXIII, no. 729, 1962.
84. For details on the fluctuations in metal prices in the inter-war period and late 1940s, see: B.I. Thomas, "Metal Price Variations Over the Past 50 Years", *Queensland Government Mining Journal* L1, no. 584, pp. 569-71.
85. For details on mineral holdings available for prospecting and exploration, see: "The Mining Laws of Queensland", in *Queensland Mining Guide* (Brisbane: Government Printer, 1958), pp. 118-71; and "Mines Department Activities", *Queensland Government Mining Journal Year Book* (Brisbane, 1967), pp. 43-47.

15 Health and Social Welfare

P.K. Jordan

Indifference seemed to characterize Queensland state health and welfare policies in the early decades of the twentieth century. This indifference was related to the notion that only paupers, who thrived in slum conditions, were recipients of aid. Institutional squalor was therefore considered fitting and satisfactory for such nuisances who interfered with a society, preoccupied with its own growth and development. To declare that the government cared for them, would not be as exact as to say that it minimized their inconvenience.[1] Why did such situations and attitudes apply in Queensland, when in Britain, Europe and America, there were movements underway to shift the emphasis in social welfare from punitive regulations and undeserved charity to consideration of individual needs and "kind" service? Queensland could not, with any persuasiveness, plead ignorance of overseas trends through its unavoidable isolation. Its learned and cultural societies maintained avid contact with British ideas through lectures and literature, and the government was usually informed of any overseas legislation in the health and welfare sphere.

With the advent of a Labor government in 1915, there were changes directed towards the provision of new and extended material handouts, and to institutions concerned with relatively inexpensive welfare. By 1957, Labor boasted of its health and welfare achievements, particularly those associated with the late premier, E.M. Hanlon. In his policy speech of 1950 Hanlon had indicated his party's concern with all aspects of human needs and not only their material requirements.

> We believe that we have a society in which there will be no exploitation of human bodies or souls, a society in which cheating

> and lying can have no place and preventible disease and hunger eliminated . . . We visualise a society in which the citizens will have health, happiness and security. The family will be the unit of that society, the morale will be lifted by the conscious drive of the common good.[2]

Measured over the forty years of Labor government, Hanlon's vision emerged as a piece of rhetoric, amid tentative action and at times, piecemeal planning. Although Theodore, from 1915, had budgeted for increased welfare services and Hanlon, as minister for health and home affairs and then as premier, had been outstanding in the welfare area, the idealism of the Labor party was not fully translated into comprehensive humanitarian policies and actions during its years in power.

A feature, to which the Labor party has looked with a great source of satisfaction in the health and welfare fields, was the reorganization of hospital services, especially the free hospital

As minister for health and home affairs and later as premier, E.M. (Ned) Hanlon, was outstanding in the welfare area. (Photograph by courtesy of the John Oxley Library.)

scheme, which it was able to implement fully by 1945. The secretary for health and home affairs, T.A. Foley, stated during the debate on the 1945 Hospital Benefits Agreement Bill:

> Those changes have been brought about mainly by Federal and State Labor Policy and nothing else. They have been embodied in the platform and policy both of the Federal Labor Party and the State Labor Party over a period of years, purely as the result of the desires of the individual members of the party translated into concrete proposals at its triennial conventions, which agreed from time to time that it should be the duty of its representatives in Parliament, when circumstances permitted, to give these free hospital service and free treatment to the people in the case of sickness.[3]

However, it had taken the Labor party some thirty years to implement a programme of free hospital care despite the clear desire of the party generally to achieve this much earlier. Had it not been for the special qualities of the Curtin and Chifley commonwealth governments, it is doubtful that this reform could have been achieved and sustained. By the end of the Labor period, there were also serious questions being raised about the quality of hospital services and the need for centralized control.[4]

The Brisbane Hospital (now the Royal Brisbane Hospital) was in a grave financial situation when Labor took office in 1915. This provided an opportunity for the party's platform of nationalization to be implemented if it could have the necessary legislation passed. However such legislation was not introduced because, as John Huxham, the home secretary, told the 1918 Labor-in-Politics Convention, there was insufficient finance for hospital nationalization and he had to appeal for public help for much needed finance. Another factor which retarded the scheme for immediate nationalization of hospitals was the intransigence of the Legislative Council regarding welfare legislation. A bill, introduced in 1917, to cope with the urgent financial problem at the Brisbane Hospital was rejected by the non-Labor members of the upper house because they claimed it failed to provide a satisfactory scheme for the whole of Queensland. However, the government was compelled to assume control of the Brisbane Hospital under a proclamation made in 1917.

Finance remained the central problem for health and welfare services for the next forty years. Some monies for hospitals were provided through the Golden Casket lottery which had been originated in 1916 by the Entertainments Committee of the Queensland Patriotic Fund, in aid of the Repatriation Fund of the Queensland War Council (see Chapter 6). In 1920, the government decided to continue the scheme with the proceeds being allocated to public hospitals.[5] However, country and provincial city hospitals were also finding it very difficult to cope with their costs through contributions.

In 1923, the home secretary, J. Stopford, introduced a Hospitals Bill to establish new administrative controls and financial assistance to local hospitals. Local contributors to the hospital, the local authority of the area and the government now shared the administration of the hospital boards. However, Stopford was doubtful about solving hospital problems by this one act. He said that it would take some ten years before public hospitals would be able to provide adequate treatment for the poorest man in the community. More significantly, Stopford indicated an important change in Labor thinking when he stated that hospitals could function much better under proper local control than under centralized control, and he was against any nationalization scheme. Such a view was opposed officially by Labor party policy. The act was amended in 1928 to provide additional government support and relieve more of the financial burden on the local authority.

Whilst the Labor government was not prepared to implement a nationalization scheme, neither was it willing to bow to pressure from the medical profession which saw the family medical practitioner service as being more important than hospital-based medical care. The Labor administration further refused to grant the medical profession the influential role it had hoped for in hospital administration; instead the government positively supported lay control of medical officers. Such an attitude adopted by the ALP to the medical profession appeared to stem from a general attitude of anti-intellectualism within the party, and a fear that if the medical officers obtained prominent positions on hospital boards they would eventually control the provision of services. There was also a class concern that the working man should not be made to feel inferior because of his treatment in free hospitals by a professional middle class bureaucracy. When hospital boards were established in accordance with the 1923 Hospital Act, it was determined that no medical officer could sit on a board, and their exclusion from hospital administration greatly annoyed their profession. Professor Douglas Gordon has since commented that such an attitude being adopted by a party which advocated socialism was unusual.

> Social planners tend to espouse rather than alienate highly trained experts. It was probably a product of essentially local conditions, an organized profession which willy-nilly had become closely concerned with a hospital administration and quite knowledgeable therein and a numerically strong Labor Party which derived its power particularly from an unskilled rural work force, well-imbued with anti-intellectualism and a simple doctrinaire socialism. Bureaucratic as well as political urges contributed to the progress of events.[6]

Because of the Labor party's suspicion of private medical practitioners and the British Medical Association (BMA), any changes recommended by the medical profession were delayed unnecessarily. Two such changes which eventuated during the 1930s were the introduction of intermediate wards into public hospitals, and the abolition of the honorary medical system in hospitals. These changes occurred during the period of greatest development in the health and welfare services between 1932 and the conclusion of World War II. The work commenced and completed during that period, both in the metropolitan area and the country districts of the state, was the coping stone on which the development of the Queensland hospital system was based. Two significant figures who influenced such developments were Hanlon, home secretary 1932-35 and secretary for health and home affairs 1935-44, and Sir Raphael Cilento, director-general of health and medical services.

Cilento, who already had a distinguished career in public health, was appointed to co-ordinate the health and medical services, to survey the overall services, and to come up with definite proposals for a system of free public hospitals providing comprehensive medical treatment. Hanlon was aware of deficiencies in his department and in the state's health services, and he appointed Cilento to provide the professional expertise necessary to reorganize the department. In 1934, Hanlon told the Parliament:

> It is realised that the public health service in Queensland has been considerably starved and has neither the equipment nor the staff to do really preventive work. I do not value any public health service that is not preventive, for without minimising the importance of the curative side of medicine one can stress the importance of an organisation that will prevent epidemics and outbreaks of disease.[7]

Cilento's role was also to act as a liason between the government and the BMA. Hanlon's contribution to the state's health services was to be his most notable achievement in twenty-five years in politics. Late in the session in 1936, he introduced an amended Hospitals Act which repealed all the previous acts and placed all aspects of public health care under the one piece of legislation. In essence the act vested absolute power in the Department of Health and Home Affairs with regard to finance, administration and appointments at the Brisbane and South Coast Hospital Boards, which, through the General, Childrens and Womens Hospitals, dominated that state's health care. In 1939, the government passed the Medical Act which required registration of all medical practitioners and para-medicals. It provided a sound basis for recruitment of staff to public hospitals and was many years ahead of comparable legislation in other states.[8]

In 1944, the state government assumed full financial responsibility for all public hospitals and in the same year, the Queensland Health Education Council and the Queensland Radium Institute were established. Because of Queensland's size and dispersal of population, it was necessary to expand the Radium Institute to other centres and to provide free rail travel for patients. Hanlon had a particular concern for women and their children. During the

1930s he established firmly a government role in pre-and post-natal facilities. Initially these were established in Brisbane but their expansion to the rural areas was delayed by the war. In 1938, Hanlon opened the Women's Hospital in Brisbane, where his statue stands today.

The Labor-in-Politics Convention reports during the 1930s reveal a lack of concern with health matters, and certainly no concrete proposals for future legislation. Jobs and wage rates dominated the convention debates. Consequently Hanlon looked to the public service rather than to the Labor party to provide him with definite proposals for health and welfare reforms. However, there were many factors which prevented or delayed such public servants from carrying out their programmes, including the lack of finance which was available for health care only when there was a budgetary surplus and the problem of coping with pressure from Labor parliamentarians seeking vote-winning facilities in their own electorates. The acceptance of such pressure as being legitimate meant that overall planning of services was extremely haphazard. Jack Duggan, a minister from 1947 onwards stated stated that he sought to have one major building project such as a school, court house or hospital, for Toowoomba every year.[9] Another example was the placement of an institution for retarded boys at Dalby in the late 1930s to build up flagging electoral support in that area. Finally, the public service was influenced by the extent to which individual ministers and premiers allowed their departmental programmes to be decided by senior officials rather than by the ministers themselves.

Hanlon was one minister who was able to exert full ministerial control over the public service. Jack Duggan told the author that while Hanlon could "fall to flattery", he was less susceptible to bureaucratic control than previous or successive ministers, while Sir Raphael Cilento also saw Hanlon as a strong minister who stood up to his departmental staff. He used the public service to implement programmes he saw as being necessary. During the debate on the Hospitals Act Amendment Bill of 1943, L.J. Barnes, the Independent member for Cairns remarked "I congratulate the minister [Hanlon] as an individual — his efforts as a unit is a faithful carrying out of his job — but I do not offer those congratulations to the government collectively."[10]

Given this reputation it was not unnatural that Hanlon should have been credited with the establishing of the free hospital system in Queensland. The legend was not fully based on fact, since it was not until September 1945, by which time Hanlon was treasurer and T.A. Foley, minister for health and home affairs, that the commonwealth Labor government provided the financial grants that enabled the Queensland government to provide free public ward care. A significant element which enabled Queensland to establish speedily free hospitalization was the restructuring of the hospital service which had been carried on since the passing of the Hospitals Acts in 1923 and 1936. Under this legislation the state was divided into hospital regions and those into hospital districts. Each region had a base hospital which was responsible for the co-ordination of the hospitals in its region. Each hospital in the region was administered by a Hospital Board. The Labor government maintained a tight control over these boards, through its appointment of board members and its administrative and financial controls.

The general acceptance of Labor's free hospital proposals was exemplified by the support of the leader of the Queensland Peoples party in the late 1940s of the acts whereby the government accepted full financial responsibility for public hospitals. Conservative governments, since 1957, have continued to uphold the principles of free hospitalization establised by Labor.

The thrust for reforms in the hospital system came from the state and federal Labor politicians in the 1940s and it is arguable whether the Labor party organization, as such, had much influence in restructuring of the hospital system. It did advocate nationalization of the system and the eventual restructuring could be seen partly as a move in that direction. There was no attempt or intention to interfere with private or religious hospitals which received considerable government subsidies for building and maintenance. The party's contribution was limited to passing resolutions at three-yearly conventions. It established no machinery to enforce these resolutions and developed no concrete schemes for their implementation.

While the Labor administration may be favorably remembered for its achievements in general hospitals, its work in the field of "mental illness" suggested a lack of interest and an inability to understand the problem. There was also a reluctance to allocate extensive finance for new facilities. It was not until the 1950s that such finance was available. Shortly after his election as premier, Ryan received a letter from Sydney which claimed: "The conditions at Goodna Asylum are attracting attention outside Queensland . . . . If the articles have been a substratum of truth, your Government is not directly responsible. At the same time, the fact that your party was in opposition does not relieve it from all onus in the matter."[11]

Ryan took the opportunity for his new government to show some positive action, by appointing a royal commision to look into the management of the hospital for the insane and the treatment given to the patients. The findings of the royal commission confirmed the unfavourable reports. Overcrowding in rat-infested, condemned buildings was verified. The hospital was understaffed, and the patients were handled brutally. However, the commission found the external appearance of the hospital satisfactory, noting that it had one of the best cricket ovals in Australia. This was due to the fact that patient labour was used to maintain the oval, such activity being described as "outdoor therapy", though patients were seldom allowed to use the oval for sport or recreation themselves.

Raymond Evans in his study of Queensland charitable institutions noted that the findings of the commission were denied because recognition of the situation would have caused major reassessments of government policy at a time when there were other pressures for government action. There was no public outcry regarding the conditions under which citizens were treated for mental illnesses and the Labor party organization, as well as Labor and Conservative politicians, ignored the situation apart from isolated comments which were indicative of the attitudes of the time.[12]Little progress was made in the 1920s and it was not until the 1930s that the influence of Cilento's and Hanlon's changes in the Department of Health and Home Affairs were felt. In 1938,

£250,000 had been spent on the insane. Such small expenditure was seen as a blot on the civilization of Queensland, and it was suggested by H.M. Russell, the UAP member for Hamilton, that something was wrong with the social system.[13] However, Cilento's view was there were practically no funds for improving the care of the mentally sick, and that one had to creep and crawl to gain such finance. He said that in the 1930s credit was still given to the administrator who could save money, rather than improve the service.[14]

In 1938, possibly as a result of pressure from the BMA, it appeared that new initiatives in psychiatric services were to be taken. Dr. Stafford, director of mental hygiene, was sent overseas to attend a world conference on mental health and to study the 1930 British mental health legislation. The 1938 Queensland Mental Hygiene Bill was practically a copy of the 1930 British act and aimed at curing the patient rather than confining him to an institution. To copy overseas legislation was inevitable because of the lack of interest in mental illness. After Parliament had passed the 1938 act, the *Courier-Mail* headed its report of the debate "Teeth Blamed for Mental Disorders"[15] although this reference by a back-bencher was unrelated to the act. Only in the conclusion of the article was some reference made to the 115 clauses passed.

Political pressure operated even in the placement of special hospitals. The opening of the Charters Towers Mental Hospital in 1954 resulted from long standing pressure from Labor party branch members. As far back as 1928, the Charters Towers and Queenton Combined Branch had sought a northern institution for the insane at Charters Towers. Their justification was that as the mining industry in Charters Towers had collapsed, the city needed some help to enable those out of work to obtain employment.[16] The branch continued to lobby for the mental hospital, and even though Dr. Stafford stated, in 1944, that Townsville was geographically the right place for the hospital, the decision to place it at Charters Towers was still taken. The local ALP branch viewed the institution and its patients in terms of future employment opportunities and accepted uncritically that untrained staff could cope with mentally ill people. For political reasons the Labor government acceded to their requests. New approaches concerned with the personal welfare of the mentally ill in Queensland emanated from the directors of Psychiatric Services. But because of the widespread indifference they were not given scope to develop their ideas; mental health facilities remained archaic and disjointed.

Queensland, the most decentralized state in Australia, in 1919 had the questionable distinction of having the largest lazaret, and one of the largest benevolent asylums in Australia. These institutions were located in the far south-east corner of the state on isolated islands in Moreton Bay. Eventually in 1947, the elderly people at the Benevolent Asylum at Dunwich were transferred to former RAAF buildings at Sandgate, while the inebriates were transferred to a small farm at Marburg. The Sandgate home was regarded as temporary, for the long huts were assessed as being unsuitable. When Labor lost office in 1957, the temporary buildings had grown ten years older but had not been replaced. They remained for a further ten years after the change of government in 1957. "Eventide" homes for the aged were established at Charters Towers and Rockhampton and local authorities received a 50 per cent subsidy for the construction of pensioners' cottages. The leper colony at Peel Island stayed until 1959.

There seemed little interest displayed by Labor, Country party or National-UAP politicians and cabinet ministers in the plight of those who were placed in charitable institutions. In January 1920, after unsuccessfully begging a visit from a home secretary since 1910, patients on Peel Island wrote: "Much of the treatment meted out to us makes us doubt that we or our parents ever helped to shape the destiny of this great state, or that we were ever respectable members of the community."[17] Patients at Peel Island received: "less than half the prescribed dosage of Roger's Treatment, and Dr. Moore explained, that the full quota would require direct supervision of a resident medical officer and that was not considered necessary."[18] When eventually the government closed the Dunwich Benevolent Asylum, it did so without taking definite steps to assess the needs of those people at

Dunwich or to provide institutions suitable for caring for the incapacitated elderly and the alcoholics.

Lack of finance, and the unwillingness to set aside sufficient finance for health and welfare, contributed to the low level of child and family services in the 1920s. To cite one example: in response to a resolution by the Labor-in-Politics Convention in 1920 for better protection of infant life and the establishment of a State Mothers and Infant Home, McCormack, then home secretary, stated that it would cost half a million pounds to look after those who could not help themselves, although "the Government would probably have some money for social work next year, especially if the season was good".[19] However pressure from Labor-in-Politics Conventions, and McCormack's own concerns, were instrumental in having the Motherhood and Child Welfare Scheme launched in 1922. The scheme was aimed at providing better ante-natal and post-natal care of the mother and child and it was especially directed towards those in outlying regions.

In 1925 the Labor party brought forward progressive legislation in the form of the Child Endowment Bill which envisaged that money would be raised by a levy on all employers thus providing an allowance to be paid to mothers for maintenance of their children. In spite of strong pressure from the party organization, the Child Endowment Bill was never enacted, again due to a lack of finance (see Chapter 12). At the 1926 Labor-in-Politics Convention McCormack claimed:

> It was not possible to outline a scheme at a conference such as that, it was all a matter for investigation as to the amount of surplus wealth available between the cost of producing the wealth and the full amount to see whether there was an amount available out of which they could pay Childhood Endowment.[20]

In his thesis on state child care in Queensland between 1864 and 1965, George Schofield expressed doubts about the Labor administration's attitudes to services for "State children" who were the wards of the state.

> Apart from the elevation of the assistance rate in 1917 to the

> same rate as for foster mothers, it appears to have largely ignored the pleas of Directors to increase staff and facilities for care. Although the Forgan-Smith Ministry was responsible for a programme of State-aided renovations to the denominational institutions in the 1930s, their contributions to child care in Queensland remain undeniably small.[21]

During the 1920s the State Children's Act was twice amended to provide assitance to "State Children" going on to secondary education and to protect all children against exploitation in employment. No child under twelve could be employed in street trading and special permission was required to employ children over twelve. Under the 1922 Maternity Act, baby clinics were established and special wards in hospitals could be devoted to the treatment of women's diseases. Adoption laws were tightened also to protect the adopted child and to prevent "baby farming". The 1935 Adoption of Children Act took away the embarrassing legalisms of adoption procedure and gave Queensland perhaps the most straightforward adoption laws of any of the states. However, matters did improve during Hanlon's term as minister and premier when ante-natal facilties were placed on a firm basis, maternal and child welfare clinics established and the creche and kindergarten services extended.

Certain health and welfare services provided by Labor governments point to their concern for Queenslanders living in outback regions. For example, maternal and child welfare nurses travelled to isolated townships regularly and, with the return to normal conditions between 1947 and 1950, twenty-one new maternal and child welfare centres were established in country districts. The government also subsidized a number of existing charities. Voluntary groups, such as the Sub-normal Children's Welfare Association, the Spastic Organization, the Creche and Kindergarten Organization and the Blind Welfare League, obtained assistance provided they could prove to the government that their services were of need and value to the community. Subsidies to denominational bodies to build hospitals and provide welfare services were extended in the 1950s. After 1949, religious organizations building hospitals received a 50 per cent subsidy on capital costs and a bed-day subsidy of seven shillings and sixpence for public ward patients.

There was a reluctance by Labor governments, and no apparent pressure from within the party, to train and use skilled welfare workers within its programme. This attitude has been partly attributed to the identification of welfare workers with hospital almoners. A major role of almoners was to assess a patient's ability to pay hospital fees, and this function caused them to earn the disfavour of the Labor party which sought free hospitalization for all. Moves to provide a course in social welfare at the University of Queensland began in the 1940s. The senate of the University submitted to the government a proposal to institute such a course, but it was rejected on the basis of cost. The Queensland Council of Social Welfare, and the Queensland Branch of the Australian Association of Social Workers together with interested medical officers continued to apply pressure to the Labor government to accept trained social workers, but the fact that a course in social work commenced at the University of Queensland in 1956 was not as a result of any new initiatives from the Labor party.

Dr. H.W. Noble, Liberal minister for health, commented in 1961:

> I might say that when I took over the portfolio of Health and Home Affairs they would not have social workers in the department. Over the years of Labor's brainwashing and administration social workers were regarded as meddlesome busy-bodies. The only social worker they had was a dear old lady without any special skill, and it took me quite a time to alter Departmental thinking about them.[22]

The Labor party in office committed itself more to securing social reforms on a community-wide basis, e.g., the Workers' Compensation Act of 1915-16, the establishment of the Public Curator's office as a "poor man's solicitor", the State Government Insurance Office, legislation for unemployment insurance, the abortive Child Endowment Bill of 1925 and the welfare and hospital reforms of the 1930s. Labor's emphasis after World War I, as T.H. Kewley points out, shifted from pre-war social experimentation, to a concentration on material development.[23] Thus during its term in office in Queensland it tended to provide an environment favourable to the establishing of humane welfare legislation. However, in the health field, except for the legislation relating to general hospitals, there was little evidence of planning and research until 1945 when the Queensland Institute of Medical Research was established. It began work in 1947 and was the only medical institute wholly funded by a government for research work alone.

The strongly rural-based working class Labor party under the influence of the conservative Australian Workers Union reacted against the apparent intellectualism and wealth of professional workers, especially medical officers. Until late in the government's long term of office, such hostility inhibited research and restricted the development of new initiatives. The services provided under Labor governments arose mainly from initiatives within the public service, but there, emphasis on promotion through seniority contributed to a scarcity of new ideas. Schofield has noted that new initiatives in State Child Care Services came when directors were appointed from outside the department.

The Hanlon era saw the re-organization of the Health and Home Affairs Department, the encouragement of new mental hygiene and child care proposals and the implementation of the free hospital scheme. The Labor party organization provided some general guidelines within which its political wing should work, e.g., nationalization, equal opportunities for all citizens, but it left the task of shaping these concepts into action to ministers and their departments.

In the 1940s, the initiative in health and welfare passed from the state to the commonwealth government. This became evident during the war when the Menzies government introduced child endowment in 1941 and the Curtin government provided widows' pensions, unemployment benefits and a large commonwealth involvement in welfare housing. With the passing of the 1946 amendment to the commonwealth constitution, the central government was given specific power to legislate for maternity allowances, widows' pensions, child endowment, unemployment, pharmaceutical, sickness and hospital benefits, medical and dental

abor premier, Vince Gair, unveiling the E.M. Hanlon Memorial Statue at the Brisbane Women's
ospital, 6 February 1955.

services, benefits to students and family allowances. The commonwealth government had the financial resources, the lack of which had deprived the Queensland Labor governments of the opportunity to legislate for extensive welfare services. Chifley's National Health Act was the starting point of a national health and hospital scheme and the provision of Section 96 grants enabled Queensland to build a special chest hospital at Chermside as a part of the national campaign against tuberculosis. In 1956, a new major public hospital, the Princess Alexandra Hospital, was opened in South Brisbane. It seemed to breathe new life in the Queensland hospital system and reflected the first movement away from the highly centralized system of control envisaged by Hanlon in 1936.[24] It was, moreover, the first sign of new capital works on an unprecedented scale, but also a symbol of the extent to which major decisions on health and welfare, in the future would be taken outside Queensland.

NOTES

1. R.L. Evans, "Charitable Institutions of the Queensland Government to 1919" (M.A. thesis, University of Queensland, 1970), p. 293.
2. Larcombe papers, S.9, John Oxley Library.
3. *QPD* CLXXXV (17 October 1945) :904.
4. C.A.C. Leggett, "The Organization and Development of the Queensland Hospitals in the Twentieth Century" (M.A. thesis, University of Queensland, 1977), chap. 3.
5. J.E.R. Pearson, "Growth and Development of Social Services in Queensland" (B.A. thesis, University of Queensland, 1953), p. 87.
6. D. Gordon, "An Arranged Marriage: The Story of an Unusual Teaching Hospital", *Medical Journal of Australia*, (8 April 1967), p. 695.
7. *QPD* CLXVI (21 November 1934), :1583.
8. P.A. Cloake, "The Government of William Forgan Smith" (M.A. Qualifying thesis, University of Queensland, 1978).
9. J.F. Duggan interview, 19 August 1972.
10. *QPD* CLXXXI (7 September 1943) :297.
11. Cited by Evans, "Charitable Institutions", p. 105.
12. Ibid., p. 110.
13. *QPD* CLXXIII (19 October 1938) :1066.
14. P.K. Jordan, "Mental Health Service of the Queensland Government,

1920-1962" (B. Soc. Work thesis, University of Queensland, 1973), p. 98.
15. *Courier-Mail*, 5 November 1938.
16. Jordan, "Mental Health Service", p. 139.
17. Correspondence relating to Lazarets, COL/323, 2 January 1920, QSA.
18. Ibid., 18 September 1923.
19. *Official Record of the Labor-in-Politics Convention* (Brisbane, 1920), p. 39.
20. *Official Record of the Labor-in-Politics Convention* (Brisbane, 1926), p. 60.
21. G. Schofield, "An Overview of the Methods of State Child Care in Queensland 1864-1965" (B. Soc. Work thesis, University of Queensland, 1971), p. 192.
22. *QPD* 231 (16 November 1961) :158.
23. T.H. Kewley, *Social Security in Australia* (Sydney: Sydney University Press, 1965), p. 169.
24. Leggett, "The Organization and Development of the Queensland Hospitals", chap. 5.

16 Aborigines

"The Duty We Owe . . ."[1]

Raymond Evans

But the native is passing, and who cares? Those, who are capable, help least of all . . . . It would be interesting to know with what anathemas future generations will pour contempt upon our neglected opportunities . . . .

R. Hamlyn-Harris. 1917[2]

. . we are doing all that is expected of us as a governing race.

Hon. E.M. Hanlon,
Labor Home Secretary. 1934.[3]

Why do you deliberately keep us backward? Is it merely to give yourselves the pleasure of feeling superior?

Aborigines Progressive
Association Manifesto. 1938.[4]

When Cecil Jesson, the Labor member for Kennedy, confidently informed Parliament in September 1939 that "one thing of which Queensland can be proud is the fact that this Government have always looked after the interests of what I might term our black brothers", he was merely rephrasing a sentiment which had, by this time, become a well-worn political cliche. Such a self-congratulary tone is, no doubt at certain times, a conventional enough indulgence of most governments and would probably merit no more than a passing mention, were it not for the surprising fact that the parliamentary opposition invariably showed itself to be in full accord with such complacent views. Thus, in October 1928 honorable members would witness the unfamiliar spectacle of the leader of the opposition, A.E. Moore, actually initiating a protest debate against "unfair" criticism of the home secretary's and chief protector's handling of Aboriginal Affairs by the executive of the Police Union. Similarly, in March 1946, it was the assertion of the opposition leader, G.F.R. Nicklin, that "Queensland has done a good job in looking after her aboriginal people" which paved the way for the argument of the secretary of health and home affairs, T.A. Foley, that, although "It was true that before Labor attained office the aboriginals were neglected and little or no attention was paid to preserving the race or to raising their standards", since 1915 "definite progress" had been made.[5]

Such unusual displays of unanimity between normally antagonistic political parties reveal, to begin with, the very low priority which all politicians attached to the Aboriginal question. It was rarely an issue upon which political capital could be made or much electoral enthusiasm aroused. Thus, behind the chorus of uncritical support for the familiar refrain that "splendid work is being done" lay a predominant mood of political indifference and neglect. Years would often pass without the Queensland government once initiating debate or the opposition raising queries upon any item of native welfare. Most discussions which did occur arose only as the annual estimate for the "relief of Aboriginals" was being moved — but even here the fluctuating vote was often accepted in silence. The Labor party, after its election to power in 1915, did not hold a serious debate upon Aborigines until 1918, and did not again return to the problem until September 1921. When, in 1928, the Aborigines Protection and Restriction of the Sale of Opium Act was amended for the first time since 1901 — "to increase the penalties for persons having opium in their possession" — the alteration was made without discussion or demur.[6] When this legislation was again reshaped during 1934 in much greater detail, and a substantial dialogue did at last occur, an opposition spokesman observed at one critical point: "The vacant benches on the Government side of the House indicate the amount of interest taken by Government members in this Bill. There is only one member sitting behind the Minister."

Whenever parliamentary members did speak at any length about Aborigines, their words revealed a general, fairly fixed image of the native, to which they all seemed confidently to subscribe. In short, possible party differences were constantly overriden by common racist assumptions. As late as 1946, it was happily claimed during debate that Aborigines indulged in "head-hunting" and tended to be "cannibalistic because they were barbarians and pagan people" — erroneous conceptions which had persisted since the earliest frontier contacts. The Labor member for Carpentaria, Alfred Smith, illustrated the "primitive instincts" of Aborigines with the story of how: "every year when the moon is at a certain stage every native, even the younger natives in the school, irrespective of the job he is doing, drops everything and walks for miles on what they call a walkabout. It will be hard to kill that instinct."[7] Because of such ingrained "backwardness" and ascribed intellectual "inferiority",[8] it was concluded that a "blackfellow is not worth a white man." E.P. Decker, of the Queensland People's party (Sandgate), after allowing for the fact that "the black men are very useful to the squatter and pastoralist", nevertheless, concluded that he could not: ". . . place the blackfellow on a level with the white man. I do not think the aboriginal will ever have the mentality to reach the same standard as we whites have attained." Labor member, George Devries (Gregory) fully agreed, with the modest comment that "I do not admit for a minute that the nigger is as good as I am . . . ."[9]

The Aborigine's attributed inferiority — or "his inferiority complex", as members modishly classified it — had earlier been explained by the secretary for health and home affairs, Ned Hanlon, in terms of outdated evolutionary theory: "The aboriginal, in his natural state, is about 1,000,000 years behind the white race. He is still in the food-gathering stage of human development, instead of the food producing stage . . . ." It was therefore the duty of all partliamentarians, agreed the leader of the opposition, E.B. Maher, to help him in his upward climb "as he fought to catch up and bridge the great gap between his stage in human evolution and the stage that the white race had reached." The most common prediction among his fellow politicians, however, was that "human evolution" would most likely "catch up" with the Aborigine first.

The widespread belief that the Aborigines were "a dying race so far as Queensland was concerned"[10] was re-echoed in the Assembly as an article of faith, and was retained there with a stubborn, almost desperate persistence. It is significant here to note that, as early as 1922, J.W. Bleakley, the chief protector of Aborigines had concluded:

> A perusal of the statistics for the last two years . . . discloses an interesting fact — that, contrary to the common belief, the natives are not dying out fast . . . . It is not inevitable that they should die out. The evidence does not support such a conclusion sufficiently to justify treating their case with indifference . . . .[11]

Yet, even in March, 1946, it was still being maintained that "if a census was taken now we should find that those numbers [of 15,700 in 1921] had dropped considerably." Decker of Sandgate added authoritatively: "We have evidence that over the years there has been a gradual decline and that eventually the race will disappear. The best we can do is to preserve the race as long as possible and we do this on our settlements."

It was therefore by this strong commitment to a "final solution", at a time in history when the playing out of "final solutions" upon "settlements" was so much at a discount, that Queensland politicians provided some telling insights into their psychological and emotional reactions to the Aboriginal presence. Plainly, the argument served as a kind of functional illusion which shielded those who subscribed to it from some perplexing truths about the indigenous population. In the first place, such a continued insistence upon a "doomed race" theory allowed ministers to overlook the necessarily complex task of formulating an adaptable long-term native affairs policy. If they were only patient, it was temptingly suggested, the problem would go away. Nothing more clearly reveals their bankruptcy of ideas, and their unthinking reflection of popular distortions about Aborigines as a people than this. Even more importantly, however, this sombre theory supplied a convenient alternative to facing what certainly was, to them, the racially unpleasant prospect of a permanent and growing black minority in white Australia. As Godfrey Morgan (Country party, Murilla) had frankly stated in October 1925, without encountering disapproval from any government member:

> Some persons say that we should perpetuate the race. I am not one of those who think it would be advisable to do so. The time is rapidly drawing nigh when the race will become extinct . . . the blacks, like the native birds and animals will . . . eventually disappear . . . . Speaking broadly I do not know that it would be beneficial to the blacks themselves at present or in the future if we assisted them to multiply.

In the years immediately following World War I, the Labor government adopted for a time the pose of a party seeking a new approach to Aboriginal affairs. In both 1920 and 1921, the chief protector of Aborigines had indicated "the urgent need for a definite and generous policy . . . a definite scheme for providing for the thousands of aboriginals in this State who are still wandering unprotected . . ."; [12] while, at the same time, the home secretary, William McCormack, candidly admitted: "He did not know that there had been any definite policy in Queensland that properly dealt with the treatment of aboriginals. Governments came and went, and, of course, the aboriginal was a decaying race, and was not given much consideration." [13]

During 1919, an independent group from the University of Queensland, calling itself the Social Worker's League had presented a scheme for purported Aboriginal "betterment" to the government which had reached the draft bill stage before it was abandoned, for the official reason that "funds were not available." [14] Consequently, it would not be until September 1939 that the secretary for health and home affairs, Hanlon, could announce that "a concrete policy" had at last been evolved. In the intervening decades, Labor would pursue an approach to the problem which differed only in degree to that of preceding non-Labor regimes.

This approach, officially protectionist and — in practice — highly authoritarian, exclusionist and separatist, had developed under earlier Aboriginal protectors, Archibald Meston, Walter E. Roth and Richard B. Howard, all of whom had emphasized the pressing necessity for comprehensive administrative control over every facet of Aboriginal life. J.W. Bleakley, who had worked under Howard and succeeded him as chief protector in February

1914, essentially perpetuated this existing order, but placed a much greater emphasis upon the tactic of racial segregation. Previously, those Aborigines removed to government reserves or governmentally-subsidized missions had been mainly those who were either unable or unwilling to accommodate themselves to European economic enterprises as a cheap labour source, controlled via the police force by a system of agreements and permits similar to the one applied to colonial indentured labour, particularly that of Melanesians on Queensland sugar plantations. From 1919, however, Bleakley began to call for "complete segregation" of Aborigines from whites, a suggestion which, despite its financial infeasibility was echoed by the home secretary in 1921.[15] Between 1915 and this latter year, the protector's annual reports enumerated 2183 individual removals of natives onto various Queensland settlements.

This new insistence upon segregation was encouraged, initially, by Labor's traditional concern for protecting white workers against "unfair" economic competition from other ethnic groups. Although in October 1914, a Labor opposition member, Harry Coyne, had assured the Assembly that no union desired "to take a nigger down", events would subsequently reveal a high level of rank and file sensitivity towards blacks being "used to do a white man's work" and "to squeeze out the white man on the score of expense."[16] Early in 1916, in Bleakley's words: ". . . instructions were issued to Protectors and Settlement Officials that, in districts where suitable white labour was available, aboriginals were not to be engaged at rates which would allow them to unduly compete with such white workers.[17] In November of that year, the *Cairns Post* noted that due to Aborigines being utilized as strike-breakers during a sugar industry dispute, police had notified farmers that "aboriginal labourers duly signed on and paid the required rates must not for the present be employed."[18] Subsequently, the application of higher wage rates under the McCawley award to Aborigines as well as to whites resulted in the former's virtual exclusion from this industry, the remuneration being "more than growers were prepared to pay" for native labour.[19] Lack of trade union support for black workers was here sufficient to convert a putative benefit into a positive liability. Indeed, in 1921, a Country party opposition member charged that:

> He knew there had been a movement by different unions in Queensland to prevent the blacks from obtaining employment in work they had been engaged in for many years. Certain hon. members opposite had been doing their best to prevent them from getting employment, evidently preferring that they should remain idle, which was not a good thing for a black man anymore than for a white man[20]

No refutation of these claims was forthcoming from the government benches. By 1924, the chief protector was commenting that greater vigilance was needed against Aborigines "engaged as houseboys on sugar farms being illegally employed at 'chop-chop', which is work covered by the Sugar Workers' Award."[21]

Thus, from the year of this award's inception in 1917 until 1927, there was a gradual though inexorable decline in the number of Aborigines employed under annual agreement — from 4365 to 2205, a fall of almost fifty per cent. Though numbers rose to 3068 in 1929, there was a particularly dramatic plunge again with the Depression — only 1640 agreements being issued as late as 1935. These figures accurately mirrored Bleakley's growing conviction that the "policy of absorbing them in the labour market has, after over twenty years' trial, proved itself a failure." The Aboriginal labourer, he had already concluded, was "looked upon by many with hostility" and treated as "a pariah . . . a social outcast". Employers too often held "too cheap an estimate of the value of aboriginal labour", he maintained: ". . . and their treatment of him — so far as accommodation, food, and other working conditions are concerned — would, in some places, convey the impression that he is regarded more as a part of the stock or working plant than as a human being." Then there were, additionally, "many moral dangers" resulting from what Bleakley would consider *too* human an intimacy with native employees, especially female domestics:

> . . . first that the girls will in time fall a prey to unscrupulous men and increase the already predominating number of half-castes,

> and again that they will develop a taste for town life and conditions that will unfit them for their only legitimate future — marriage with men of their own race.[22]

These considerations reveal a common pattern in any exercise of the government's segregation policy towards Aborigines: firstly, a racially exclusionist pressure is coupled with a protectionist concern, and, secondly, that concern takes on a racist dimension of its own which renders at least questionable any humanitarian intention it purports to have.[23] If Bleakley's integrity is to remain unimpeached, it seems clear that he was genuinely concerned about "degeneration . . . destitution and degradation", and believed that reserves and missions, as morally-policed, subsistent sanctuaries, away from "outside contamination", could overcome these abuses.[24] Yet he was at least equally disturbed about another kind of "contamination" which tended to make his humanitarian stance something of an equivocal one. Like the majority of his white Australian contemporaries, he was intent upon safeguarding "the purity of our own blood" from "the half-caste evil". As he stated in 1919, the European population must have already been "contaminated to an extent sufficient to warrant serious reflection".[25]

The presence of "half-castes" in ever-increasing numbers stood as living proof of the alarming discrepancy between a vaunted ideal of racial purity and the natural behaviour of mixed human populations. Their acknowledged existence mocked the cherished hope that impregnable racial barriers could be indefinitely maintained. As the perplexed chief protector revealed, as he tried to explain his opposition to "half-castes": "what they inherit of the superior intelligence and tastes of the whites is nullified by the retarding instincts of the blacks. In other words they seldom make either a steady white or a contented black." The "half-caste" was "rarely able to hold his own in the business or labour world and is nearly always socially ostracised", Bleakley observed, but, even more crucially, "the *blood* is always an obstacle." Thus, as early as 1923, the chief protector was ready to admit, "The most vexing problem the administration is faced with is that of the half-caste."[26] Politicians on both sides of Parliament took longer to realize this, but eventually they too were ready to agree. In October 1932, Labor's new home secretary, Hanlon, reiterated, "The half-caste problem . . . is the outstanding problem of the Aboriginal Department", while one opposition member spoke gloomily of the production of "a mongrel race in this State" and a second confided: "it makes one apprehensive lest ultimately we shall be called upon to deal with a quadroon problem. Any action the Home Secretary can take to retard the increase in the number of half-castes will meet with the approbation of all concerned."

One finds, therefore, the chief protector placed in the rather contradictory position of, upon the one hand, applauding the fact that "the people are not dying out but . . . are apparently holding their own", whilst, on the other, worrying over "an undue inflation" in the number of "cross breeds of all shades."[27] By the same token, whereas in 1917 Bleakley had placed a major stress upon "social progress" for Aborigines, by 1933 he had shifted his emphasis sufficiently to be warning against forcing them into "an unnatural hothouse condition of civilization."[28] At the centre of this quandry lay the potent taboo against inter-racial sexual relations: the Aborigines should increase, but not physically encroach; from a safe distance, they should watch and copy, but never approach and touch. "To combat the half-caste evil", Bleakley wrote in 1923, "it is essential that the gulf between the white and black races should be widened as far as possible." In 1928, he added, "The policy is to check as far as possible the breeding of half-castes by firmly discouraging miscegenation."[29]

Using powers granted by the 1901 Amendment Act to control Aboriginal legal marriages, Bleakley embarked upon a scheme "of restricting, as far as is reasonable the . . . mating [of half-caste and Aboriginal women] with others [sic] than of their own race." Whereas in 1915 thirty of these marriages had been permitted, by 1921 the chief protector had reduced this number to two. When in 1925, six such unions were allowed, Bleakley explained this higher total as: " . . . 3 Asiatic half-castes to men of Malay extraction, and 3 who were nearly white to men of European descent." In 1930, when he agreed to only one "quadroon" marrying a Europan, he pointed hopefully to that year's statistical increase of twenty in the number of "half-castes" as "encouraging evidence that the department's efforts to check miscegenation are proving effective."[30] By 1934, no "mixed marriages" whatever were allowed.

Over the same period, he was gradually decreasing the number of "half-castes" granted exemption from the Aboriginal Act. In order to qualify for this, applicants had to convince their local police protector[31] that their lives were solid examples of thrift and sobriety, that their parents — one of whom needed to be a European — had been legally married and that they lived "in a civilized manner", mixed usually with Europeans and were not "habitually associated with Aborigines". Even then, an application could still be refused for arbitrary reasons like: "I cannot see what benefit [s]he would derive by becoming exempt";[32] or, perhaps if granted, it could be later revoked for some detected moral or "racial" lapse. The sub-Department of Aboriginal Affairs showed itself to be inordinately cautious and suspicious about releasing part-Aborigines from its control, with Bleakley often discerning "The wiles of the unscrupulous" behind the applications — either those of "designing employers or . . . natives of the flash type, quite unfit to be given their freedom."[33] In 1918, he had granted twenty-nine of the thirty-four applications (87 per cent), but in 1929, he allowed only thirty-three out of seventy-eight (40 per cent) to pass, commenting, ". . . it is questionable whether more than 10 per cent of those granted the privilege honestly live up to it." Four years later, only eight out of forty-two applicants (20 per cent) were so "freed".

The increasing alarm over racial and sexual "contamination" reached a peak in 1934, a factor reflected in both administrative concern and legislative action taken during that year. In August, a memo from the under-secretary of the home secretary's department to the Governor of Queensland remarked: "Inferior races will have to go, and in my opinion Governments sooner or later will have seriously to consider the question of sterilization of the half-caste." The governor, however, disconcertingly replied, ". . . I cannot believe that any Government would be *brave* enough to legislate in that direction."[34] When the Forgan Smith Labor government did introduce new Aboriginal legislation in November, it failed, as the governor had predicted, to display this kind of "courage". Yet what this act did achieve was effective management over the lives of most part-Aborigines who had previously remained beyond the state's bureaucratic control. As home secretary Hanlon explained, "It is aimed particularly at taking control of all Asiatic and island people who are crossed with aborigines." The act further prescribed a range of penalties against inter-racial sexual contact which covered both white male/black female and black male/white female liaisons. Hanlon stated categorically: "No-one can argue that it is desirable that any white person should cohabit with or have carnal knowledge of any female aborigine or half-caste . . . . These are undesirable things and the department is endeavouring to repress [them] as much as possible . . . ."[35] Several clauses therefore provided for the fining or imprisonment of any white male involved in cohabiting or consorting "for immoral purposes" with "any female aboriginal or half-caste." Such females or even "any male aboriginal or . . . half-caste" who became involved in these arrangements — in the latter instance for "procuring" — could be additionally fined.[36] The intention was, the home secretary explained:

> . . . to put down the practice of whites who have lost all sense of decency and of public morals, associating with aboriginal women. It is important to remember that in looking over our aboriginal institutions, the increase in population is intensely half-caste, . . . the increase in the birth-rate of half-castes is alarming to the authorities, and we are taking steps to punish any white man who consorts with aborigines for immoral purposes.

The suggestion of Aboriginal male/white female sexual contact was even more discomforting, and it is here important to note that Assembly members found it practically impossible to conceive of this happening outside the bounds of rape. Such concern led to the introduction of "one very important clause" which the home secretary gingerly introduced as "one that I do not like myself, but there is no other way of dealing with the situation."[37] Clause 21 allowed for the minister to direct that "any aboriginal or half-caste", deemed "uncontrollable", should be: "kept in some institution . . . either for such time as he shall think fit or until he shall direct that such aboriginal or half-caste shall be released. . . . the term 'Institution' shall also mean and include any prison within the meaning of *The Prisons Act of 1890*." The offending native, who could thereby be imprisoned *indefinitely* in a state gaol, was defined as "uncontrollable" firstly, if he had been "convicted of an offence included in the offences mentioned in Chapters XXII and XXXII of *'The Criminal Code'*."[38] It was these chapters, the minister reminded the House, which covered "offences against women, assaults on females and abductions". An opposition member (James Kenny, Cook) added: "In these two chapters . . . we have altogther twenty-five different crimes. They include, in addition to rape and similar major crimes, an attempt to procure abortion . . . supplying drugs to procure abortion; indecent acts; obscene publications and exhibitions." Kenny therefore wanted to confine the "uncontrollable" offence to that of rape against white women alone, but the home secretary interposed: ". . . none of the offences prescribed under these two sections of the Criminal Code could be treated as light offences . . . an aborigine guilty of repeated offenses coming within the category mentioned in these chapters should certainly be put where he could not continue them."[39] Most significantly, Hanlon confided, that where such offences occurred *between* Aborigines no assault was really involved as "the complainants are *practically consenting* parties", but, to the contrary, "when white women are involved *consent more or less willing is not a factor*" meaning, in short, that this category of "miscegnation" was officially seen as fully synonymous with rape, whatever the circumstances.

Country-National members raised only a feeble protest to this forbidding clause, and the most critical comment came instead from the Independent member for Fassifern, I.M. Weinholt, who observed: "It really strikes at the whole principle of the writ of habeas corpus, and takes one back to the days of the Bastille when a person could be permanently incarcerated on a lettre de cachet signed by the King." Yet even he was quick to reassure the govenment that he did "not discuss the matter in any hostile way, but merely as a matter of debate." The opposition was actually far more worried about the particular case which, the home secretary alleged, had led to his inclusion of this item in the bill. An Aborigine in Stewart's Creek Gaol, Townsville, was due for discharge after having been "convicted of three offenses for rape on white women". Yet the minister, being unwilling to release again this "menance to society", was now calling for "power to imprison [him] . . . beyond the period which he had been sentenced by the court." An available "solution" of sending this man into legal detention upon Palm Island Reserve was quickly rejected because of the presence of: "white women there — the wife of the superintendent and her daughters and also female employees. The only thing we could do was to send him to one of the adjoining islands and provide a couple of native policement to camp there with him." Because this was "a lonely form of imprisonment" (not to mention a most expensive one), the explanation concluded, as it came full circle: "the offender would be better off in Stewart's Creek."

Rather than condemning this gross executive invasion into the judicial sphere, opposition members were more perturbed about why "he could get a discharge after three offences of that nature." James Kenny stipulated:

> If the law of the bush were permitted to operate in such a case there would be no need to bring down this clause because he would not commit that offence a fourth time.
> The Home Secretary: You are not advocating that should be permitted?
> Mr. Kenny: I am not. If I thought that sterilisation would meet the case I would advocate it and put it to the vote . . .

Weinholt was likewise upset that:

> It would certainly create the greatest astonishment in other places of the world, as for example, in the southern part of the United States and in South Africa if it was thought that a native could be three times convicted of such a crime . . . . It seems . . . that the basic trouble was in the sentence of the court.

This logically allowed the home secretary to plead, "Does it not show that it is obvious we should have some means of dealing with these people?" and to emphasize the extent of this present "danger" by informing the Assembly that, "There are other aborigines at present undergoing sentences for similar offences . . ." What was needed, he maintained, was a special "aboriginal gaol or reformatory" where "any aborigine found guilty of an offence upon a white woman" could be perpetually incarcerated. The "supposed harshness" of this solution was simply "an attempt to deal with a very difficult situation"; and, in any case, he soothingly averred: "ordinary imprisonment is no great punishment for an aborigine beyond the deprivation of his liberty, because he is better housed, fed and clothed when in prison than when he is free".[40] As well as revealing once more the deeply racist rationale which lay at the centre of official attitudes towards the Aborigine, this key discussion serves to introduce the way in which the segregationalist emphasis of state policy tended to maintain and perpetuate itself by its own kind of internal logic. The impulse to segregate highlights more the *removal* of a problem from its relevant cultural context than a positive attempt to solve that problem by the detection and elimination of its various cultural "causes". Indeed, such a response represents a tacit admission that the problem in its original social milieu is, for the present at least, a seemingly insoluble one. The early removal onto separate settlements of Aborigines who were seen as creating and/or experiencing serious problems within an imposed "white" social system, set a precedent for handling, in a similar fashion, other related problems (usually of a moral, sexual, "racial" or medical nature) which eventually arose *within* these newly-formed dependent communities themselves. There is not sufficient space here to trace the various appurtenances of this trend in the development of lockups, gaols, closed dormitories, isolated barracks and lockwards internally upon reserve and mission settlements. Yet the chain reaction which a segregationalist policy sets in motion, can be demonstrated effectively enough by firstly examining the rationale behind the formation and development of the Palm Island institution.

Once missions, to accommodate nomadic Aborigines in areas sparsely settled by Europeans, and reserves, to contain detribalized native remnants removed — usually forcibly — from fringe camps at the periphery of European towns and stations, had been set in motion, their ultimate survival as viable "closed" institutions came to depend upon further rationalizations of the segregative process. In May 1916, the chief protector reported to the home secretary upon the urgent need for "another settlement" in north Queensland, occasioned by the fact that none of the missions were "willing to receive troublesome characters" and because the southern reserves, Barambah and Taroom, similarly, could not cope with "discharged criminals and bad characters". A year later he repeated the call for a "Northern penitentiary" at Great Palm Island, and added that "the demand for such an establishment for southern and central natives is equally insistent".[41]

After a cyclone destroyed the Hull River settlement, near Tully in March 1918, this "pressing demand" became an "absolute necessity", and the Palm Island Reserve was commenced forthwith. Since its inception in 1915, Hull River itself had had a turbulent history of rigorously enforced segregation, trouble with opium-addicted and absconding Aborigines, "raids and prosecutions" as well as police intervention in "controlling these deportees."[42] An island reserve, twenty miles out to sea, would, in Bleakley's own words, provide "the security from escape required with such characters",[43] and "problem cases" from all over Queensland would henceforth be "drafted" there. Significantly enough, and despite its high death-rate, Palm Island fast became the largest Aboriginal reserve in the state, with 737 inmates in 1925 and 1129 by 1934. Year by year, more Aborigines would be "deported" to this island than to any other settlement — usually, more than to all other settlements combined. For instance, in 1921, 140 Aborigines were sent to Palm Island compared with seventy-one to Taroom, twenty to Barambah, thirty to Yarrabah Anglican Mission, thirty-five to Cape Bedford Lutheran Mission, eight to Mona Mona (Seventh Day Adventist) Mission, one to Purga, near Ipswich and one — a leper — to

Darnley Island.[44] Discipline naturally received a high priority upon Palm Island. In 1918, a concerted campaign against gambling was launched and, by 1919, a lockup was in operation for "combating unruliness, gambling and other breaches of regulations."[45] During the late twenties, stories of the flogging of Aboriginal women by the superintendent began to appear in the press[46] and, when in February 1930, this man "ran amuck" in the settlement, firing many of the building as well as the government launch, seriously wounding European white staff members and killing his own children, only to be fatally shot in turn by a native inmate, the resulting furore led to an even greater intensification of disciplinary procedures.[47] An understandably reticent chief protector mentioned in his report, at the end of this fateful year, the "distubed state" of the inmates, but was quick to add that they had "settled calmly again under discipline". By 1933, he was recording:

> At Palm Island the native police squad was reorganized and strengthened and strict training given, which resulted in marked improvement in discipline all round. A new and effective lock-up was built and also a barracks for the police . . . . Moral offences were most frequent owing to the preponderance of males. Twenty-five natives absconded, but seventeen were recaptured and dealt with.

Yet despite these restraints, Bleakley could still comment, ". . . at Palm Island effective control cannot be exercised under existing staff conditions."[48] As shown above, the Aboriginal Department was by now unwilling to send native "sex-offenders" to this reserve, because of white females attached to its staff. In addition, the 1934 Amendment Act allowed for the definition of "uncontrollable" Aborigines — who might thus be fully imprisoned at the chief protector's command — to include those who were considered "a menace to the peace, order and proper control and management of an institution." Hence Palm Island, itself a repository for "many refractory characters" whom other institutions would not tolerate, was provided in turn with its own disciplinary outlet — a further intensification of the segregative process.[49]

Parallel to this development ran a new scheme, undertaken by the chief protector, for the further segregation of "half-castes", both from other Aborigines and from Europeans. During 1933, Bleakley had rejected a suggestion from interstate that the "half-caste problem" should be solved by a process of sexual absorption — "the marriage of half-caste women to European men" — for, as he reported, in agreement with "certain prominent scientists": "it was highly unlikely that many whites would be willing to marry crossbreeds, no matter what the inducement, and those few [who would] would probably be of a low type. Futhermore . . . the evils of hereditary transmission would always be a menance to the happiness of such unions." On missions and reserves, more-over, the number of "cross-breeds" was increasing constantly at the expense of "full bloods", helped along always by what Bleakley saw as the "over-sexed" nature of "coloured" inmates. What he proposed for part-Aborigines, therefore, was "segregation from both races" upon separate "self-contained communities under benevolent supervision" — both the Salvation Army mission at Purga, outside Ipswich and the Roman Catholic mission at Hammond Island, Torres Straits, being advocated for this purpose.[50] As C.D. Rowley comments, with somewhat characteristic understatement: "It is worth a note that stated Queensland policy should have been so explicit in assuming an indefinite apartheid arrangement for the 'inferior' half-castes."[51]

After the first Aboriginal Welfare Conference of State and Commonwealth Authorities, held in Canberra during April 1937, to adopt a uniform national policy, however, the chief protector's escalating segregation system received a significant check. This conference, by agreeing theoretically upon an eventual "absorption", of all part-Aborigines into the general "white" community, represented potentially a virtual rejection of the "separate and unequal" hierarchy of native settlements, advocated by Queensland officials. The first indication of its impact came with the remarkable rise in the number of exemptions granted in 1937: forty-five on the mainlaind and 157 on Thursday Island.[52] Following this, a new Aboriginal Preservation and Protection Act in October 1939 exempted all "half bloods" not in habitual association with "aboriginals", and even held out the prospect that "civilized full bloods" in "exceptional cases" might also be granted "freedom". Instead of becoming closed institutions, as originally envisaged, Purga and Hammond Island were now to be designated as "clearing stations."[53]

Yet, overall, Queensland's accommodation to this new concept of "absorbtion" would involve more of a half-hearted resignation to change than any major about-face in policy-making. Under the new act of 1939, any mixed marriage still required the permission of the chief protector, and "illicit intercourse" between the races remained a punishable offense. In 1937, there were 2659 Aborigines on state reserves, and 3090 more within the missions. Such inmate numbers dropped marginally during the war years, due more to both a high death rate on reserves and, as J.P.M. Long intimates, to "the increase in employment available outside and the restriction of settlement development" than to any significant alteration in the philosophy behind departmental policy.[54] From the late 1940s, settlement totals would again continue to grow, augmented still by "removals", but now swollen most noticeably by natural increase, which at last became apparent in the post-World War II era. There were, also 6858 natives in recognized "bush camps" in 1937, segregated and supervised by local police acting as "protectors" under the act. In 1939, there were twenty-five such areas designated as "country-camps", operating particularly as local cheap labour reservoirs. The new act allowed for both the choice of each camp site by the said "protector" and a stiff penalty for "any *person* . . . found in or within five chains of any such camp."[55]

Concurrently, the expressed attitudes of most state parliamentarians had not markedly altered. In 1939, W. Dart of the United Australia party, mixing "humour" with caution, informed other members:

> It may not be wise to give the half-caste the same privileges as those enjoyed by the white man. One of the speakers told us that the blackfellow — and I think he meant the black gin too — was very lovable . . . [but] we do not want any further mixing of the population. We want to keep the white race white . . . . The half-

> caste is a danger to the population. He has already had a leg in (laughter) and we want to see that the position does not get any worse . . . . I hope that too much liberty is not given to the half-caste who wishes to live among the white people. We do not desire to see any more half-blood people born into this world.

The Labor representative for Cook, Harold Collins, during the same debate, then went so far as the suggest that "a big part of Cape York Peninsula" be set aside, so that "the whole of the Aboriginal population of the state could be put into that area gradually."[56] Later, in March 1946, when the Labor member for Carpentaria, Alfred Smith had the temerity to predict: "It may not be in this generation or the next but the time is coming when the Aboriginals will be able to take their place alongside the white races of the Commonwealth . . . ." Hostile Opposition members muttered, "what are left of them . . ." and "Never!"

Despite a further verbal endorsement of "assimilation" in 1951, the official position upon Queensland Aborigines remained essentially the same in 1957, when Labor lost power, and even beyond that date. As Colin Tatz rather conclusively demonstrated in 1961: "The administrative practices of the Department of Native Affairs are difficult to reconcile with the assimilation policy aims expressed and accepted by the Queensland government, aims, which, from their wording, embrace the concept of civil liberty or the Rule of Law." Indeed, as C.D. Rowley has more recently commented: "By the end of the 1930s the effort at protective and restrictive control had reached a climax which was reflected in the Aboriginal legislation. Much of it was to remain for over two decades. In Queensland, a good deal of it was repeated in 1965."[57] Clearly, a nominal policy shift from separation to "assimilation" had largely failed to overcome the tenacity of long-established bureaucratic precedures and the fixity of mental attitudes about Aborigines, whenever practical decision had to be made. Such a situation has led Frank Stevens to surmise:

> . . . what is remarkable . . . is that the resistance to change has taken place in a community which, in keeping with world standards, is both highly educated and liberal . . . . More importantly, recalcitrance on the part of legislators has taken place

> in the face of the general pattern of enlightenment on the question of race relations throughout the world, and, indeed, even clear expressions of opposition from the electorate."[58]

Lacking both the challenge and the contrast of any clearly formulated state opposition approach towards Aborigines, the Queensland government, which happened to be an almost continuously Labor one from 1915 to 1957, operated almost unhindered, an increasingly anachronistic "protectionist" policy towards Aborigines, based squarely upon racist premises. Given this situation, one is hard pressed to see how the story for Queensland natives would have read much differently if a non-Labor coalition had dominated the treasury benches in this period instead. Under the banner of "protection", and ostensibly for "their own good", Aborigines were subjected by a white executive and administration to enforced population transfers, confinement to particular areas under relatively arbitrary and quite authoritarian regimes, excessive moral scrutiny, interference in intimate human relationships, supervised breeding, imposed placement and calculatedly inferior educational training for their children,[59] control over their labour conditions, wages and personal property and even suppression of their "injurious" or menacing "customs" or practices".[60] As Stevens acknowledges above, there had been a minority trend of largely extra-parliamentary protests against this almost total denial of basic human, civil and property rights, but officials and politicians utilized a substantial armoury of rationalizations to counter virtually all of these.

When white residents wrote to the home secretary's department complaining of the enforced removal of "the children of the aboriginals from their parents", and of the "crying and wailing of the blacks" in the camps as a result; or of the taking of Aboriginal men, "chained together like murderers whilst theirs relatives and friends . . . howled and shrieked with agony", the chief protector would simply explain that an "outcry" was being made "mostly by persons to whom they had been useful as cheap labour".[61] During a debate in November 1934, after an opposition member had called attention to "the taking of an aboriginal away from his kith and kin — leaving his wife and children behind", home secretary Hanlon merely responded, "They often want to leave them behind" and the matter was quickly dropped. The fact that "the natives fear going to settlements" was explained in March 1946 by another Labor man, Smith, as a terror of "witchery" — "The same boodgery that they had in their primitive days, that the witchcock would still come about." Again, native discontent upon these same settlements, evidenced by occasional strikes, incidents of insubordination and abscondings was seen as occuring either because "a few recalcitrants are sure to be found" anywhere or because: ". . . the Australian native, being a descendent of nomadic tribes, is more or less hard to handle, particularly when an attempt is made to confine him on a settlement where he must conform to rigid disciplinary conditions." Similarly, Aboriginal abscondings were attributed to "a survival of the native instinct of wanderlust".[62]

Different and more plausible explanations could no doubt be readily suggested and authenticated were the necessary information about the experience of actually having to live under these "protective" laws presently available.[63] Yet, during the entire era of Labor rule in Queensland, no independent Aboriginal voices were ever officially allowed to surface and make themselves heard. Not a single statement from an Aborigine was ever reiterated in Parliament or reproduced in printed government reports while Labor remained in power. So one is left, for the present, interpreting data with a heavily weighted European bias — and largely, wondering what the total picture was really like. Yet, even in this data, there certainly seems to be sufficient indication that, when a comprehensive history of Aboriginal life under Queensland Labor governments is at last written — calling, as it must, upon both black and white sources and memories — its conclusions will diverge rather sharply from the old Labor cry that "the Government are doing the right thing by the Aboriginals."[64]

NOTES

1. Significantly, both the home secretary in 1897 (Tozer) and the home secretary in 1934 (Hanlon) employed this kind of expression to introduce "protective" legislation for Aborigines. See *QPD* LXXVIII (15 November 1897) :1538 and CLXVI (22 November 1934) :1687. I would like, at the outset, to express by gratitude to Kay Saunders for the large amount of help she gave me in researching for this article.
2. R. Hamlyn-Harris, "Some Anthropological Considerations of Queensland and the History of its Ethnography", *Proceedings of the Royal Society of Queensland* XXIX, no. 1 (1917) :11.
3. *QPD* CLXVI (27 November 1934) :1736.
4. Manifesto of the Aborigines Progressive Association, *Argus*, 13 January 1938, quoted in C.D. Rowley, *Outcasts in White Australia* (Ringwood: Penguin Books Australia, 1972), p. 79; see also J. Horner, *Vote Ferguson for Aboriginal Freedom* (Brookvale: Australia and New Zealand Book Co., 1974).
5. *QPD* CLXXVII (19 March 1946) :2026, 2028.
6. *Public Acts of the Parliament of Queensland* (19 Geo V): *An Act to Amend "The Aboriginals Protection and Restriction of the Sale of Opium Act, 1897" in Certain Particulars* [assented to 14th November 1928]; *QPD* CLI (5 September 1928) :496.
7. *QPD* CLXVI (27 November 1934) :1735; CLXXVII (19 March 1946) :2030, 2035.
8. *Brisbane Courier*, 23 March 1927.
9. *QPD* CLXXVII (19 March 1946) :2037, 2040.
10. Ibid. CLXXII (20 October 1938) :1115 and CLXXIV (19 September 1939) :453, 457; CXXVII (28 September 1921) :976.
11. *Annual Report of the Chief Protector of Aborgines for 1922, QPP* I (1923) :1071.
12. Ibid., *1920 and 1921, QPP* II (1921) :561; *1922*, QPP II (1922) :475.
13. *QPD* CXXXVII (28 September 1921) :977.
14. *Annual Report of the Chief Protector of Aborigines for 1919, QPP* I (1919) :1.
15. Ibid., p. 5; and *1920*, p. 561.; *QPD* CXXXVII (28 September 1921) :975.
16. See E.M. Land (Cunnamulla) to home secretary, 15 January, 9 and 6 March 1919; T. Loose, deputy chief protector to under home secretary, 6 March 1919. COL A1136 in letter no. 671 of 1919.
17. J.W. Bleakley, *Annual Report 1919, QPP* I (1919) :1.
18. *Cairns Post*, 7 November 1916.
19. *Annual Report of the Chief Protector of Aborigines for 1921, QPP* II (1922) :471.
20. *QPD* CXXXVII (28 September 1921) :976. *Daily Mail*, 16 February 1920.

21. *Annual Report of the Chief Protector of Aborigines for 1924, QPP* I (1925) :1089.
22. Ibid., *1919*, p. 5; *1918*, pp. 2, 6; *1919*, p. 4; *1916*, p. 7; see also *QPD* CXXX (13 September 1918) :2314.
23. *QPD* CLXVI (27 November 1934) :1733; CLXXVII (19 March 1946) :2038.
24. See *Annual Report of the Chief Protector of Aborigines for 1918*, p. 6; *1919*, p. 5; and *1920*, p. 561.
25. Ibid., *1919*, p. 5 and *1923, QPP* I (1924) :989.
26. Ibid., *1928, QPP* I (1929) :1215; ibid., *1923* and *1924*, p. 989; *1925, QPP* I, p. 1091. My own emphasis.
27. Ibid., *1929, QPP* I (1930) :947; *1935*: "Aboriginal Department — Information Contained in Report . . .", *QPP* I (1936) :1032.
28. Ibid., *1917*, p. 9; "Aboriginal Department — Information Contained in Report for . . . 1933", *QPP* I (1924) :894.
29. Ibid., *1923*, p. 989; *1928*, p. 1215.
30. J.W. Bleakley, *Annual Report 1918*, p. 4; "for 1915", p. 9; *1921*, p. 474; *1925, QPP* I (1926) :1019; *1930, QPP* I (1931) :891.
31. *QPD* CLXX (6 November 1936) :1435.
32. See, for instance, the refusal of exemption to Freddy Fox and Miss E. Hutchinson. P.J. Murphy (Rockhampton) to F.M. Forde, 7 January 1919. QSA COL A 1135 in-letter no. 572 of 1919.
33. *Annual Reports of the Protector of Aborigines for 1924*, p. 1091; *1928*, p. 938.
34. Under-secretary, Home Secretary's Department (W.J. Gall) memo to Sir Leslie Wilson, 7 August 1934 and reply, 13 August 1934. QSA Special Bundle on Aborigines: Gall Collection. My own emphasis.
35. *QPD* CLXVI (22 November 1934) :1687; 27 November 1934, p. 1730.
36. *Public Acts of the Parliament of Queensland* (25 Geo. V): *An Act to Amend the Aborigines Protection and Restriction of the Sale of Opium Acts in Certain Particulars.* Clauses 9-11.
37. *QPD* CLXVI (20 November 1934) :1555-56.
38. *Public Acts* (25 Geo. V), Clause 21.
39. *QPD* CLXVI (22 and 27 November 1934) :1690; 1733-34.
40. Ibid., p. 1734. My own emphasis; 20 November 1934, p. 1556, 22 November 1934, p. 1690; 27 November 1934, p. 1734; 20 November 1934, p. 1557 and 27 November 1934, pp. 1734-35, respectively.
41. Chief Protector J.W. Bleakley to under home secretary, 6 May 1916 and 28 May 1917. QSA Special Bundle on Aborigines: Gall Collection.
42. *Annual Reports of the Chief Protector of aborigines for 1915*, pp. 13-14 and *1916*, p. 6. See also D. Jones, *Cardwell Shire Story* (Brisbane: Jacaranda Press, 1961), p. 305.

43. Chief Protector J.W. Bleakley to under home secretary, 28 May 1917, QSA Special Bundle on Aborigines: Gall Colection.
44. *Annual Report of the Chief Protector of Aborigines for 1921*, p. 473.
45. Ibid., *1918*, p. 7 and *1919*, p. 5.
46. See, for instance, *Smith's Weekly*, 27 April 1929 and 15 February 1930: *Townsville Evening Star*, 5 February 1930. Note also a counter-view: "Aborigines' Paradise" by F.C.B., *Sydney Morning Herald*, 29 June 1929, mentioned in C.D. Rowley, *The Remote Aborigines* (Ringwood: Penguin Books Australia, 1972), p. 91.
47. See, for instance, *Brisbane Courier*, 5 February 1930; *Truth*, 16 February 1930, 2 March 1930, 9 March 1930; *Daily Standard*, 3 March 1930, 7 April 1930; *Townsville Evening Star*, 4 March 1920, 14 August 1930. The *Brisbane Courier* (5 February 1930) reported: "The Aboriginal settlement superintendent [R.H. Curry] shot Dr and Mrs Maitland Pattison, blew up and burnt his son and daughter, and burnt two of the settlement residences, an office, the aboriginal school, the main store and the launch ESME . . . [H]e was [later] shot by some natives who were posted under cover . . ." R.H. Curry, a returned soldier, had been in charge of Palm Island since its commencement. Significantly, a further development was the arrest of part-Aboriginal inmate Peter Prior on the charge of having murdered Curry. On 11 February 1930, Curry's father asked the *Telegraph* to "probe why blackfellows were made to shoot my son. That aspect of the situation is scandalous, and it will have a most serious effect on the morale of blacks in other settlements." Subsequently, to quote Bleakley's terse report for 1920 (*QPP* I [1931] 895): "As a result of a Magisterial Inquiry, charges of 'murder' against Peter Prior and of 'procuring to kill' against Dr Pattison and Mr Thos. Hoffman [Assistant Superintendent] were laid by the Justice Department. The Crown afterwards withdrew the charge against Dr Pattison and at the later trial, the charges against Thos. Hoffman and Peter Prior were dismissed." At this trial, it was reported that "His Honor", at one crucial point, remarked " . . . is the prosecution proceeding because he was shot by a black man and not a white man?" *Townsville Evening Star*, 18 August 1930.
48. *Annual Report of the Chief Protector of Aborigines for 1930*, p. 895; "Aboriginal Department — Information Contained in Report for . . . 1933", *QPP* I (1934) :890-91.
49. *Public Acts* (25 Geo. V), Clause 21 (b); "Aboriginal Department — Information Contained in Report for . . . 1934", *QPP* I (1935) :992.
50. "Aboriginal Department — Information Contained in Report for . . . 1933", pp. 884-85; "for . . . 1934", p. 982.
51. Rowley, *Outcasts in White Australia*, p. 28.
52. "Aboriginal Department — Information Contained in Report for . . . 1937", *QPP* II (1938) :1097, 1106.

53. Ibid., "for . . . 1939", *QPP* (1940) :1077-78; *Public Acts of the Parliament of Queensland* (3 Geo V): *An Act to Consolidate and Amend the Law Relating to the Preservation and Protection of Aboriginals, and for Other Purposes*. passim.
54. J.P.M. Long, *Aboriginal Settlements: A Survey of Institutional Communities in Eastern Australia* (Canberra: Australian National University Press, 1970), pp. 103-4; 111. 117.
55. "Aboriginal Department — Information Contained in Report for . . . 1937", p. 1104; *Public Acts* (3 Geo VI), Sections 29-30. My own emphasis. Rowley, *The Remote Aborigines*, p. 228.
56. *QPD* CLXXIV (19 September 1939) :458, 461-62.
57. C.M. Tatz, "Queensland Aborigines: Natural Justice and the Rule of Law", *Australian Quarterly* XXXV, no. 3, p. 49; Rowley, *Outcasts in White Australia*, p. 43.
58. F.S. Stevens, "Parliamentary Attitudes to Aboriginal Affairs" in *Racism: The Australian Experience*, ed. F.S. Stevens (Artarmon: Australia and New Zealand Book Co., 1972), p. 121; in the same volume, see A. & R. Doobov, "Queensland: Australia's Deep South", pp. 159-70; see also G. Nettheim, *Outlawed: Queensland's Aborigines and Islanders and the Rule of Law* (Artarmon: Australia and New Zealand Book Co., 1973).
59. On Aboriginal education, see *QPD* CLXXVII (19 March 1946): 2025, 2027; *QPD* CLXII (27 October 1932): 1208; and *QPD* CLXVIII (12 November 1935): 1119; *QPD* CLXXVII (19 March 1946): 2028-29.
60. *Public Acts* (3 Geo VI), Section 23.
61. W.C. Knoullton (Bloomfield) to home secretary, 12 November 1915, QSA COL A 1036 in-letter no. 997 of 1916. G. Bardon (Tumoulin) to N. Gillies, 23 June 1915; Herberton Local Protector to Chief Protector, 9 August 1915, QSA COL A 1013 in-letter no. 6961 of 1915; J.W. Bleakley, "Annual Report 1916", p. 6.
62. "Aboriginal Department — Information Contained in Report for . . . 1937", p. 1098; "for . . . 1936", *QPP* II (1937) :1204; *QPD* CLXX (6 November 1936) :1434.
63. Thankfully, this information is now beginning to appear. See, for instance, Len Watson, "1945: Enter the Black Radical", *National Times Magazine* (1 April 1974), pp. 4-13 and Bill Rosser, "Palm Island: First the Bad News", *Australian* (26 October 1974), p. 36.
64. *QPD* CLXX (6 November 1936) :1431.

17 Education

J.R. Lawry

The provision of education was never a major political concern between 1915 and 1957. The operation of the public education system was relatively uneventful, and Labor politicians placed little importance on education as a political issue. The portfolio of the secretary for public instruction in the first Ryan government ranked second last, the position it held when the Gair government was defeated in 1957. The education programme, which was followed almost without variation until 1957, had been commenced or forecast by state education authorities by 1915; it owed little to distinctively Labor policies, reflecting more the general pattern of developments in public education systems in the English-speaking countries. A distinction must be drawn between the on-going activities of professional educators, including the advisers to Labor governments, and the policies of the Labor party. Politicians could regulate the momentum of the education system in varying degrees through control of finance and power over public servants. Even so, Labor's thinking on education remained limited, while radical policies and major innovations were ignored. The system was allowed to respond slowly to developments in the wider educational sphere, but within the ability and willingness of the people to pay.

Before Labor came to power in 1915, the under-secretary of the department of public instruction, J.D. Story, compiled an illustrated brochure to inform the public "what the Education Department is doing to educate their children, and how the money voted for education is being spent."[1] The account is important in understanding Labor's attitudes to education. Story pointed to the educational ladder from kindergarten to the university, and claimed rapid progress in a number of special areas such as the provision of medical and dental services and of itinerant teachers and part-time schools for isolated families. Secondary education had been extended with the establishment of state high schools and secondary departments at smaller centres, the award of scholarships to candidates who passed the qualifying examination, and means-tested living allowances. So, Story claimed, "secondary education in Queensland is free to those who prove their fitness . . . and that . . . it is just as possible for the son of the wharf labourer, the sugar-worker, or the shearer to enjoy a full course of secondary education as for the son of the shipowner, the sugar-planter, or the station-owner."[2] The Education Department had improved buildings, established libraries, and issued readers and copy-books. Free places at technical colleges had been introduced in 1910, and tuition by correspondence in 1911. The University of Queensland, founded in 1909, had commenced teaching in 1911. The staffing of schools was improving, following the establishment of the teachers' training college in 1914. The primary course had been upgraded with a new syllabus in 1915, kindergarten methods were being adopted in all infant schools, and physical training was encouraged as part of the commonwealth defence scheme. By 1915, education was compulsory to the age of fourteen, and there were plans to extend activities, particularly in vocational education.

Labor's education policy for the 1915 election was more modest than Story's departmental plan, but both represented the general framework within which Labor was to operate. Ryan promised an investigation of the department, and the provision of more money if "required to complete its efficiency",[3] and was critical of the department's organization and its standing in comparison with those in southern states. After Labor assumed office, school papers, copy books and other requisites were provided free by the department, one of the few developments which followed an election promise. Labor claimed for its first term of office significant developments in education: improved lighting, ventilation, classroom arrangements, and recognition of the general principles of hygiene; schemes for the extension of agricultural education — which had figured in Ryan's policy; increased medical and dental services; extension of technical education, preparatory trade schools, high schools and scholarships, and the Workers' Educational Association[4] But these achievements reflected Story's plans rather than Labor's policy, as a study of discussion at Labor-in-Politics Conventions confirms. By 1926, L.D. Edwards, chief inspector of schools, claimed that the developments proposed by Story in 1915 had been implemented, and new activities had begun: teachers' remuneration and professional training had improved; primary correspondence tuition had been inaugurated in 1922; travelling domestic science and manual training schools visited railway centres in the north and north-west, and a motor travelling dental clinic covered western districts; rural schools had been opened in many centres, and the Gatton Agricultural College brought under the department in 1923; opportunity classes for retarded pupils had been established in 1923; physical instructors were appointed in 1926. Edwards observed that the primary education of children in Queensland "may now be regarded as systematic and complete", but queried whether secondary education "will be altered to coincide with the system adopted, in principle at least, by most of the other British colonies".[5]

Labor cautiously supported secondary education, but what was achieved was limited by adherence to the scholarship system. Labor was not prepared to support open access to secondary education at any stage, although in its early years the provision of more government scholarships did much to increase the number of secondary school students. In 1915, 883 scholarships had been awarded, of which 73 per cent were held at grammar schools; in 1916, the number was increased to 1360, and by 1926 it had grown to 3429, of which only 42 per cent were held at grammar schools. Labor's interest in secondary education was primarily practical and utilitarian, coupled with a wish to widen access and to protect the demoninational schools. The major thrust of this interest was displayed in the "emphasis on technical training and apprenticeship, commercial and industrial courses for boys and domestic science courses for girls, agricultural and rural courses for country children."[6] Whilst Labor supported provision of free technical eduation "to workmen desiring to improve their skill and to pupils selected in demonstrated evidence of fitness",[7] few members ever showed awareness of education as a means of social change to obtain political goals. The party's original intention to provide access to secondary education for able students became involved with the vested interests of the grammar and approved schools, the churches, many parents and students, and as a consequence the extension of secondary education to all adolescents was inhibited. With the exception of the development of three state high schools from the Central Technical College and the take-over of the Maryborough Grammar School, no new state high schools were established in Queensland between 1924 and 1934. Not until World War II was some attention given to the future control and development of the total education system.

In the 1941 election campaign, Forgan Smith promised improved education, especially "in training pupils attending our schools for suitable avenues of employment", but also proposed a conference on education at which interested parties might indicate "ways in which the educational facilities of the State can be improved, extended, or widened."[8] Following the conference in May, Forgan Smith introduced the National Education Co-ordination and The University of Queensland Acts Amendments Act, designed to "co-ordinate all forms of education from kindergarten to university . . . and to secure to the people of Queensland the best possible education for the money that the State is able to provide for it."[9] The act created a Board of Post-Primary Studies and Examinations and dealt with a number of reorganizations in university affairs. E.R. Wyeth attributes authorship of the legislation to J.D. Story, now vice-chancellor of the University of Queensland,[10] and certainly the act appears to have stemmed not from Labor party policy, but from Forgan Smith and his advisers, including Story, in response to growth in the university and to some dissatisfaction with public examinations.

Any assessment of Labor's control of education finds that "it has been difficult to discern evidence of any policy working itself out."[11] Most developments, whether in curriculum, organization, teacher training, or special services, may be attributed to general developments in education rather than to party policy which was less related to political ideals and aspirations than to any assessment of what was feasible given existing resources. Before Labor came to power in 1915 very little of its "policy towards education was concerned with ideology", and once in office Labor was concerned largely with practical matters and "a lack of recognition of the importance of education was to remain a feature of Labor party policy for sixty years."[12] When the 1920 Labor-in-Politics Convention debated a proposal to hold a royal commission into the state education system, those "who appreciated that education could be the most powerful tool in the party's armoury . . . were outnumbered by those who saw Labor politics in narrower, less radical, and more mundane terms."[13] It is tempting to conclude that Queensland Labor, like the British Labour party, "derived its ambitions, not from political principles, nor from broad visions of a different society, but from the social and ecnomic opportunities of which its members already had experience."[14] Several state politicians with limited formal education can be quoted to support this conclusion. H.A. Bruce, secretary for public instruction 1947-50, believed "we all believe that the best education is obtained after leaving school",[15] while G. Devries, secretary 1950-56, stated that "A man in the university with scholastic attainments has never been able to apply commonsense and commonsense was what is needed in the Australian Workers Union."[16] Nevertheless, despite the apparent discounting of the value of education by Labor politicians, part of their political rhetoric was a claim that "education reform was a special feature of Labor Government policy and work."[17] Statements about education policy made at Labor-in-Politics Conventions and during election campaigns help to explain why so little importance was attributed to education as a social and political issue, and why such policy as there was came to be implemented so slowly.

In 1913, Labor policy had included the extension of free education, compulsory education up to the age of fourteen, secular education in state schools, secular and free university education for all qualifying by examination, and the reform of technical education. The 1915 election policy merely extended these points. At the 1918 election it was proposed to open up educational opportunity "so that the sons and daughters of the poorest in the community can go from State school to university absolutely free of all cost to their parents."[18] The 1920 Labor-in-Politics Convention proposed raising the compulsory age to sixteen, providing free technical tuition, and regulating the subjects required for university education. Although W.H. Demaine's presidential address to the 1923 Convention criticized the direction of education, its competitiveness and lack of co-operativeness, and urged a radical reform of the system by a government commission, one of the few party statements which reflected a radical policy, the convention merely refined the education programme without much discussion. At the 1925 Convention, the president proposed free technical and university education, but convention voted to restrict free books and school requisites to "children of invalid pensioners and sufferers from phthisis only who attended primary school".[19] A motion that the government introduce "the teaching of Socialism, Civics, and economics" was not supported. Members "did not want propaganda carried on among children, but to have them trained in subjects in which they could think for themselves", or believed "a child should be taught along lines that would fit the child to take his or her place as a citizen of the State in any walk of life and enable them to live life as it ought to be lived." The motion was amended to read: "That this Convention affirms the principle of education that encourages the desire for investigation of all social and other human questions."[20] The 1928 Convention gave limited support to the concept of free education by agreeing that books at cost price be provided only "for children whose parents did not earn the basic wage",[21] while a suggestion that the number of children who might be taught by pupil teachers and student teachers should be reduced to twenty-five was defeated because of the additional cost. McCormack stressed vocational training in the closing stages of education before entry into the industrial world, and convention agreed that "industrial history and elementary economics be taught in all State schools."[22]

At the 1929 election campaign, McCormack returned to the need for sound pre-vocational and vocational education, and proposed a reorganization of education between the ages of twelve and fifteen, based on a course that would be "not only broad and liberal, but practical rather than academic", with intermediate and industrial high schools. Both the 1932 Convention and Forgan Smith's policy speech in the 1932 campaign promised restoration of educational advantages withdrawn by the Moore government, and pursuit of Labor's commitment to "equal educational opportunities", but improvements were slow in the period of recovery from the Depression. Two new schemes were introduced: the farm scholarship scheme which provided one year on approved farms and were arranged by the Juvenile Employment Bureau established in 1935 to assist juveniles to find employment, and the farm training scheme for boys administered by the Department of Labor and Industry. The 1932 Convention had sought strict adherence to the platform rule requiring the teaching of industrial history and elementary economics in all state schools — despite some opposition to "doctrinaries at Convention attempting by resolution to inflict upon the children their idea of education".[23] F.A. Cooper addressing the 1938 Australian Workers Union conference was able to remind delegates that on the Friday before Labor Day 1937, lessons to Grades 5, 6 and 7 "were on the struggle and triumph of the Labor Movement in Australia."[24] But by 1938 many Australian history courses incorporated civics and Australian history, so that Labor's achievements in Queensland were by no means radical. The Labor-in-Politics Convention in Feburary 1938, paid unusual attention to education. The platform was amended to require "State Education, secular and free, from Kindergarten to University" and that "night classes in all University subjects be available to working students in all centres of population", but resolutions to provide free books and requisites at state primary schools, with or without a means test, and to make all secondary schools part of a free state system with no public examinations were lost, while a resolution for "regular propaganda for peace and against war" in state schools and the portrayal of war in its proper perspective in textbooks was moved and subsequently withdrawn. However, in Forgan Smith's policy speech the following month, education was diluted to a statement of past achievements and a promise of more university scholarships. The 1941 Convention virtually ignored education while the policy speech returned to an emphasis on vocational training.

From the early 1940s education policy discussion moved out of the Labor-in-Politics Conventions into the politicians' hands, particularly at election time, and to interested groups such as the Teachers Union. In the immediate post-war years the Department of Education faced staff shortages, increased school population, and inadequate accommodation. "Always the problems were met by makeshift arrangements, by using any available accommodation, by employing untrained and partially trained teachers. Each problem was solved by expediency."[25] The Technical Correspondence School was established in 1945, a Research and Guidance Branch was created within the department in 1949, and the decentralization of administration commenced with the appointment of four regional directors in 1949, the last two following 1947 election promises which had included provision of university colleges at Rockhampton and Townsville. Responding to local pressures, particularly from the north and west, and to the promises of the opposition to introduce some decentralized control as proposed by the Committee on Regional Boundaries in 1943, Labor began decentralization of the department. At a conference called in April 1948 to discuss decentralization, premier E.M. Hanlon revealed the essentially pragmatic approach adopted: "It is not a popular thing in politics to look forward too far . . . . There has not been much long-range planning. Everyone wants to do the little jobs that can be done quickly. Concentrate on the little jobs that will placate public opinion for the time being until the next hurdle is reached and that is the next election. On that basis one never does anything big."[26] The Education Department was "a suitable guinea-pig for the experiment" of decentralization, but regionalization was meant to avert growing criticism from potential separatists, and linked to the decentralization of education was a public works and housing programme for outback areas on which Labor relied heavily for electoral support.

Increasing public criticism of Labor's efforts, and a growing awareness of education as a political issue mark the subsequent years. The Queensland Teachers Union was hostile to Labor's plans to meet the teacher shortage by reintroducing the Junior Examination entry to teacher training as an emergency measure, and opposed continuation of the scholarship system on educational grounds. Labor politicians had difficulties in coping with the educational ideas presented to them, and the departmental administrators, who advocated substantial revisions of primary education and the provision of secondary education for all adolescents, were frustrated in their efforts. By 1956, education, once claimed to be a prime concern and a field of major achievement, had become an electoral liability. The Teachers Union regarded the fact that the estimates of the department were debated in Parliament for the first time in six years as evidence of the minister's negative policy towards the teacher shortage; the opposition politicians realized the public concern over education. J.C.A. Pizzey, a former pupil teacher who became minister for education in 1957, asserted that "the real foundations of our present education were well and truly established before Labor came into power", and then listed what Labor had achieved since 1915. "We find no fault with what they have done but we do complain that it is little enough in comparison with what they have not done." Labor did not raise the leaving age, did not provide sufficient teachers, limited secondary education mainly to scholarship holders, did not build a decent teachers' training college, did not consolidate small schools, and did not bring parents "into the educational system sufficiently".[27] Education questions figured prominently in the 1953 election, but following a substantial victory Labor ignored much of the criticism as politically motivated. Modest increases in expenditure represented Labor's approach during the remaining years of office. In 1952, the first suburban high school since 1924 was established, and between 1953 and 1957, some fifteen new state high schools and twenty new secondary tops were established. In the period 1950-7 the number of state teachers increased from 5739 to 7637, state school enrolments grew from 164,803 and 214,626 and other school enrolments from 43,239 to 63,510, and government expenditure on education rose from £4.6 million to £11.9 million, but the rapid development passed almost without political comment.

Following the expulsion of V.C. Gair from the party, J.E. Duggan presented Labor's policy for the 1957 election. He claimed that Labor had "always looked on education as the vehicle fashioned by an intelligent society to give equal opportunities to all in the acquisition of knowledge." Labor would rename the Department of Public Instruction the Department of Education, with the minister being an experienced and dynamic person. More finance and federal support for capital expenditure were proposed, and the scholarship system would be reviewed without depriving private schools of government benefits. The policy promised the training of technicians, development of a balanced secondary programme, improved engineering education, financial assistance for students, more science teachers and improved science supplies, more teaching scholarships, grants to kindergartens and pre-schools, expansion of the Kindergarten Training College, provision of a new teachers' college near the university, residential teachers' colleges, an undergraduate university college at Townsville, investigation of secondary education modifications by state and private school teachers, reduction in primary class size, and improved teaching conditions and recruitment.[28] In other circumstances this policy might have won votes. Just as power slipped away from Labor, a modestly enlightened policy was produced. Whether it would have been implemented is another matter.

NOTES

1. *State Education in Queensland — A Retrospect and a Forecast* (Brisbane: Queensland Government Printer, 1915), p. 6.
2. Ibid., p. 35.
3. *Worker*, 29 March 1915.

4. Ibid., 21 February 1918.
5. *Report of the Secretary for Public Instruction, 1926*, p. 43.
6. R.D. Goodman, *Secondary Education in Queensland*, (Canberra: Australian National University Press, 1968), p. 230.
7. *Official Record of the Eighth Labor-in-Politics Convention* (Brisbane, 1916), p. 25.
8. *Worker*, 11 March 1941; see also 4 February 1941.
9. *QPD* CLXXVII (21 October 1941) :800.
10. E.R. Wyeth, *Education in Queensland*, (Melbourne: Australian Council for Educational Research, 1955), p. 197.
11. Ibid., p. 206.
12. M.G. Sullivan, "Education and the Labour Movement in Queensland, 1890-1910" (M.A. thesis, University of Queensland, 1971), p. 66.
13. D.J. Murphy, ed. *Labor in Politics* (St Lucia: University of Queensland Press, 1975), p. 213.
14. R. Barker, *Education and Politics 1900-1951: A Study of the Labour Party* (Oxford: Oxford University Press, 1972), p. 136.
15. *QPD* CXCIII (23 September 1948) :496.
16. *Courier-Mail*, 21 April 1949.
17. J. Larcombe, *Notes on the Political History of the Labor Movement* (Brisbane: Worker Newspaper, 1934), p. 53.
18. *Worker*, 28 March 1918.
19. *Official Record of the Twelfth Labor-in-Politics Convention* (Brisbane, 1926), p. 64.
20. Ibid., p. 6.
21. *Official Record of the Thirteenth Labor-in-Politics Convention* (Brisbane, 1928), pp. 54-55.
22. Ibid., p. 56.
23. *Official Record of the Fourteenth Labor-in-Politics Convention* (Brisbane, 1932), p. 60.
24. *Worker*, 1 February 1938.
25. Goodman, *Secondary Education in Queensland*, p. 324.
26. "Report of Conference on Decentralization of the Department of Education (Brisbane, 15 April 1948).
27. *QPD* 201 (28 August 1951) :1034, 1035.
28. *Worker*, 8 July 1957.

SECTION C

POLITICS

18 The Anti-Communist Pledge Crisis

K.H. Kennedy

In 1925-26, the labor movement in Queensland was so seriously divided over internal issues that the Labor government in office was threatened: there was a strong possibility of a significant defection of traditional Labor supporters at the 1926 state elections. Only in 1957, when the Gair government fell, and to a lesser extent in 1916-17, during the conscription crisis, has the labor movement in Queensland experienced more widespread disunity.

The issues were many and overlapped; but three stood out as important. Firstly, there had been a sustained ideological conflict between the cabinet and its supporters, including the powerful Australian Workers Union (AWU), and a number of Trades Hall unions over the policies and administrative decisions of the Labor government. Following the London loan failure of 1920, the government was forced to adopt stringent financial measures, unpopular with many public service unions, culminating in a basic wage reduction and postponement of a universal forty-four-hour week. Militant unions complained that the politicians had abandoned Labor principles, and by way of job disputes and strikes, agitated for immediate "workers' control" of all state undertakings. For its part, the government was unable to reconcile its objectives of sound economic management and electoral popularity.[1]

Secondly, there was the claim by the Parliamentary Labor Party (PLP) that it had the right to interpret the party platform as it saw fit, and the authority to decide when its planks should be implemented. As Morrison has pointed out, this raised the question of the powers of the Queensland Central Executive

(QCE), and also of the authority of the policy-making Labor-in-Politics Convention.[2] The politicians rejected any suggestion that they were merely delegates of the labor movement, submitting that they were responsible to the electorate in general.

While the first two issues reflect the tensions always present when a Labor government is in power, the third issue, involving industrial union rivalry, did not, as similar struggles were occurring in other states under non-Labor governments. There had been a continuing confrontation between craft unions, supported by the AWU, and the militant industrial unions over industrial tactics, organization and objectives. The militants were advocating the merger of existing unions into One Big Union (OBU) with sufficient weight and cohesion to impose its will not only on employers, but also on politicians and industrial courts. However, such a scheme cut across the AWU's aims of amalgamating small unions into a confederation of semi-independent industry groups, still retaining their craft characteristics. In addition, the AWU's constitution and rules firmly committed the union to the traditional processes of parliamentary reform and arbitration, thus conflicting with the social reconstruction aims of the OBU. In Queensland the OBU campaign was spearheaded by the officials of the large Australian Railways Union (ARU); and the AWU, sensing its very existence threatened, readily sided with Labor politicians in opposition to the scheme. As Turner observed:

> It was, however, the A.W.U. and the Labor Party which put the greatest obstacles in the way of the One Big Union — the A.W.U. because its officials would be submerged and their positions of power in the labour movement destroyed, and the politicians because they feared the consequences of revolutionary trade unionism for their electoral prospects.[3]

With the more pragmatic AWU officials at loggerheads with the doctrinaire socialists of the ARU and other unions, it was not unexpected when their quarrel impinged on the Labor party machine. It was against this background of conflict that the anti-communist pledge emerged.

For some time, state branches, particularly the New South

Wales branch had been concerned with communists being freely admitted to the Labor party, not only for electoral reasons, but also for reasons of party unity. By 1924, both the New South Wales state executive and the state conference had affirmed their opposition to the practice. Consequently, at the Federal Conference later that year, it was not unexpected when the issue was raised and debated at length.[4] By thirty votes to six, conference resolved that the Communist party could not affiliate with the ALP and that individual communists were ineligible for membership of the party. In accordance with party rules it was left to the respective state branches to adopt the resolution and implement its instructions.[5]

No action was taken by the Queensland branch until the following year, when at the February meeting of the QCE, on a motion by E.G. Theodore and William McCormack, the public lands minister, a pledge was drawn up and circularized to all branches within the state with the instruction that all ALP members sign by 31 July 1925.[6] At first sight, the pledge seemed simply an administrative procedure, implementing the Federal Conference decision of the previous year: subsequent events leave no room for doubt that the ruling group in the QCE, and Theodore and McCormack in particular, had seized upon the pledge as a means of isolating and subjugating their opponents within the labor movement.

The lines of the opposing groups in the forthcoming confrontation were drawn in July 1925, when McCormack moved in the QCE for rejection of Fred Paterson's endorsement for the seat for Port Curtis.[7] Paterson, a salaried officer with the ARU, was a former member of the Communist party, who had resigned to rejoin the ALP but remained a strong communist sympathizer, and perhaps more pertinently, a strong critic of the Labor government in the columns of the *Advocate*. McCormack's motion was carried by eighteen votes to five, with G. Rymer, E. Foley and J. Hayes (ARU delegates), P. Carney of the Australian Meat Industry Employees Union (AMIEU) and C. Dawson of the Waterside Workers Federation (WWF) recording their dissent.[8] The reaction of these delegates, particularly the ARU members, probably suggested to McCormack and his supporters the next step, even though the enforcement of the pledge in New South Wales had aroused bitter resentment and controversy.

From returns lodged with the state organizer, J.S. Collings, in August 1925, it was evident that less than a third of the branches throughout the state had responded to the February directive: only eight-two of the 300 branches circularized had complied with the pledge; three had refused; six had returned "indefinite replies"; while 209 branches had ignored the correspondence.[9] Lewis McDonald, the state secretary of the ALP, immediately requested all branches to sign the pledge by 12 September. Even then, the branches were less than co-operative, whereupon McDonald indicated that 7 November was the deadline, after which the QCE would consider action against recalcitrant branches.[10]

At the monthly meeting of the QCE, on 27 November 1925, R.J. Carroll, a strong supporter of McCormack who had been elected premier less than a month beforehand, disputed ARU state secretary Moroney's membership on a QCE committee of inquiry into plebiscite discrepancies, on the grounds that he had not signed the anti-communist pledge. Clearly, the challenge to Moroney had been pre-arranged, as McCormack immediately moved that all QCE delegates sign the pledge before the meeting proceeded any further. An amendment seeking to refer the question to the forthcoming Labor-in-Politics Convention was overwhelmingly defeated by twenty votes to three. Rymer and Moroney protested at length, but were ordered to comply with the motion or to leave the meeting, which they subsequently did.[11] The third ARU delegate, Hayes, signed the pledge at the meeting, claiming later that he "did not feel disposed to disenfranchise 11,000 railwaymen on the QCE";[12] but this action was interpreted in a different light by ARU state council delegates, and underlay his dismissal as southern district secretary some five months later.

Rymer, the ARU state president, who saw his removal from the QCE as a carefully engineered move by McCormack and his supporters to bring the ARU to heel and discredit its leaders, publicly declared that he was not a communist; but more important, complained that the QCE had overstepped its authority.[13] His reaction was almost certainly designed on one hand to protect some ARU officials who were communists, and on the other hand, to deny the QCE the right to apply any criteria of its own to delegates representing industrial unions.[14] Further, had Rymer and Moroney yielded to the QCE's directive, they would have found themselves at odds with other ARU delegates at state council level. Accordingly, Moroney wholeheartedly supported Rymer's statement, fully aware of the QCE threat to withdraw his endorsement for the Brisbane plebiscite preceding the 1926 state elections.

Their stand attracted considerable attention: not only the state council of the ARU but also every district committee of that union endorsed their action. A series of letters, dated 23 December 1925, revealed the ARU officers' strategy in the now serious rift. Moroney gave notice of appeal to the president of the Labor-in-Politics Convention over the removal of Rymer and himself as QCE delegates, on the grounds that the federal conference resolution was not valid in Queensland until it had been endorsed by convention and written into the party rules of membership, and further, that the QCE had no authority under the rules to demand such a pledge by signed.[15] A second letter gave joint notice of appeal as ALP members on similar grounds, but added that there was insufficient justification under the rules to remove them from the QCE as representatives of an affiliated union. Copies of the letters were lodged with Lewis McDonald, who formally acknowledged receipt without comment.[16]

At the same time, a number of ALP branches in the metropolitan area, for differing reasons,[17] requested that the pledge be withdrawn, but the QCE stood its ground,[18] and ruled that any appeal should be referred to the convention scheduled for February 1926.[19] Thus, at the QCE level, McCormack and his supporters had isolated the ARU, and in doing so, had reaffirmed the AWU's paramouncy in the Labor party machine. An AWU official, Ernie Lane, who was one of the very few militants in the AWU hierarchy, later indignantly complained that the pledge "was not designed to eliminate Communists from the Party", but was "an effective weapon to . . . drive the militants out of the Labor Party", and render "the Q.C.E. a virtual monopoly of the politicians":[20] "Everyone knew the real purpose of the pledge was to 'purge' the Party of all who were troublesome to the politicians by insistently agitating that the Labor Party be one in something more than name."[21]

In the week preceding the Southport Labor-in-Politics Convention, it was clear that a major row was imminent: Rymer, Moroney, Foley and V. Hartley, as ARU delegates, had signed the pledge under protest, in an attempt to get around the QCE ruling of November 1925, without altering their stand.[22] It was not as though the ARU had gained substantial support in the interval: nearly one-sixth of the delegates were politicians, certain to support the QCE line; the largest bloc of union delegates was from the AWU, inveterate opponents of the ARU; while AWU members were numerous among electorate delegates. Clearly, McCormack and his supporters had the numbers, but could expect a volatile convention at which all the issues inherent in the anti-communist pledge would be publicly voiced.

No sooner had the convention opened than the pledge issue erupted when McCormack sought a ruling on the eligibility of delegates to vote in the election of a credentials committee, the first formal item on the agenda. Eager to silence the ARU delegates at the outset, McCormack claimed that their credentials were out of order, as "no candidate for Parliament would be endorsed if he signed the pledge under protest", and the same applied to convention delegates. Defending his union's position, Moroney argued that it was solely a matter for the credentials committee to determine, and that committee had still to be elected. The chairman of the convention, William Demaine, a strong supported of the premier, ruled that the ARU delegates were ineligible to vote: as president of the QCE, it would have been unlikely for Demaine to rule otherwise. His ruling was subsequently upheld on a vote of forty-six to twenty-three, and endorsed by the credentials committee as a matter of course.[23]

Aware that they had been out-manoeuvred by McCormack,

Australian Labor Party
— State of Queensland —
.MEMBER'S PLEDGE.

.... BRANCH

I hereby pledge myself to the Principles of the Australian Labor Party's State, Federal, and Local Government Platforms, and to any alterations thereto made by a duly constituted Labor Convention. I also pledge myself to do everything in my power to further the objects of the Party as set forth in its Constitution and General Rules.

I hereby declare that I am not a member of a Communist Organisation or Party, or of any political party having objects and methods in any way opposed to the Australian Labor Party.

Witnessed ....

Date 8. ....

pledge.

on instructions of the state Council

Geo. W. Rymer

Member's Signature

ARU delegates, Rymer, Moroney, Foley and Hartley, signed the pledge under protest, in an attempt to get around the QCE ruling.

the ARU delegates now argued that the matter had still to be placed before the convention, following the credentials committee's report. An amendment giving the option of signing the pledge unconditionally was narrowly lost by thirty-eight votes to forty-three, effectively terminating debate on the Credentials committee's report. Thereafter, Demaine ordered the ARU delegates, along with two electorate delegates — J. Kane (Toowoomba) and C. McLary (Aubigny), neither of whom had signed the pledge — to withdraw. However, several delegates from militant Trades Hall unions were concerned at the heavy-handed treatment of the ARU, and, on the following day, moved the suspension of standing orders to debate the issue.[24]

In debate, McCormack vigorously defended the exclusion of the ARU, claiming that the action was justified because of a sectional challenge to the authority of the convention and the QCE by persons "behind Rymer and his satellites".[25] The Labor premier was in full command: there was no strong defence of the ARU, although some union delegates considered that the ARU delegation should have been afforded an opportunity to re-assess their position. The big guns soon came out behind McCormack: Theodore, W. Forgan Smith, and David Gledson, but they were nowhere near as bitter in their denunciation of the ARU. The sixty-four to fourteen vote demonstrated the strength of the QCE-politician-AWU alliance, and thus effectively stifled militant opposition to the *status quo* for the remainder of the convention.

For the ARU, the outcome caused considerable concern: not only had the union's influence within the Labor party been restricted, but also their bid for leadership of the union movement had been seriously impaired, as representation on ALP bodies was fundamental to their success. Now for the first time since 1916 when trade unions had received direct representation at the convention and on the QCE, the ARU was without delegates.

McCormack might have been well satisfied with a victory which demonstrated so decisively the ascendency of his section of the party, but this was not to be the case. His actions were prompted by a desire not only to consolidate his authority as a strong and determined leader, but also to crush the ARU's influence completely. Immediately after his election to the parliamentary party leadership, McCormack had publicly declared his opposition to militant union pressures, and announced his intention to invoke the anti-communist pledge.[26] In addition, he was keen to settle old scores: as Theodore's strongest supporter, McCormack had not forgotten the November 1925 federal election result in Herbert, where the railway vote was instrumental in his friend's defeat.[27] There was also the memory of incisive criticism of the cabinet by the ARU, culminating in his predecessor's capitulation on the basic wage issue in September 1925. Yet if McCormack believed that the ARU's isolation from the Labor party would cause Rymer and Moroney to curb their militant activities, he was mistaken.

Following the convention, there was a major effort to re-establish the ARU's position: the union's state council instructed all delegates to sign the pledge unreservedly, and on 19 March 1926, advised the QCE that Rymer, Moroney and Foley had been elected as QCE delegates by the union, and now requested notice of the next meeting.[28] McDonald replied the next day, pointing out that the signed pledges had not been received. He also advised that the letter would be placed before the QCE.[29] Moroney subsequently admitted that the pledges had been "omitted in error", but questioned the necessity of a QCE decision on their re-admission, as the ARU was an affiliated union, and "everything is now in accordance with the rules".[30]

The ploy was clear: having isolated the ARU delegates at both convention and QCE levels, McCormack and his supporters were no longer prepared to compromise with the militants, as can be seen from the delay in correspondence on the re-admission of ARU delegates to the QCE. To further intimidate Rymer and Moroney, McDonald withheld the executive's decision on their re-admission until 14 June 1926, and then informed Moroney that the QCE objected to Rymer, Foley and himself as individuals, and under no circumstances would they be accepted as delegates, although other ARU members would be considered.[31] In a final effort, the ARU appealed for a reconsideration of such a decision,[32] but was informed that only a Labor-in-Politics Convention had the authority to re-admit to the QCE delegates who had refused to sign the pledge unconditionally.[33]

Faced with a situation in which the state president, state secretary and other officials of the union were "black-balled", the ARU had only two courses open to it: to bide its time without QCE representation until an appeal to the next convention could be heard, with no guarantee of success while McCormack held the reins, or to refuse to pay affiliation arrears and withdraw from the ALP, a move which McCormack, McDonald and W.J. Riordan, the AWU secretary, had no doubt anticipated. The option of sending alternative delegates to Rymer, Moroney and Foley had received short shrift, as like the AWU hierarchy, the ARU officials were also protective of their positions.

To Rymer and Moroney, an appeal to the convention seemed too much like back down to McCormack and the QCE, and probably would have been interpreted as such. Consequently, the ARU disaffiliated,[34] with a snowballing effect: the AMIEU and three other unions followed their lead, while ten smaller unions had their affiliation revoked for non-payment of dues.[35]

The split which resulted from the enforcement of the anti-communist pledge was not, as might first appear, an instance of division over ideological issues, even though the protagonists were ideologically in conflict. It was in, fact, an instance of cynical exploitation of an ideological issue for narrow sectional and personal advantage, particularly on the part of McCormack, McDonald and Riordan. As such it was completely successful in the short term: the politicians gained greater control over policy making; the AWU was assured of paramouncy in the industrial wing of the labor movement; and the Labor party, dominated by McCormack, was successful at the 1926 state elections.

However, in the long run, it showed itself as short-sighted. McCormack's rigidity and the ruthlessness with which he hit back at the ARU on the QCE was unwise: had he given way on their re-admission, he would have been able by weight of numbers to exert his authority, without bringing his government into open conflict with the militants, as occurred during the 1927 railway lockout.[36] The result of his forcing the militants from the Labor party was the creation of a group of unionists, no longer bound by ALP rules, intent on over-throwing the McCormack government,[37] an aim actually achieved in 1929, when the railway vote influenced the outcome in a number of seats.

NOTES

1. For full details, see: E.M. Higgins, "Queensland Labor: Trade Unionists versus Premiers", *Historical Studies: Australia and New Zealand* IX, no. 34 (May 1960) :140-55; A.A. Morrision, "Militant Labour in Queensland, 1912-17", *Journal of Royal Australia Historical Society* XXXVIII, no. 5 (1952) :209-26; B. Schedvin, "E.G. Theodore and the London Pastoral Lobby", *Politics* VI, no. 1 (May 1971) :26-41; K.H. Kennedy, "The Public Life of William McCormack, 1907-32" (Ph.D. thesis, James Cook University, 1973), pp. 150-268.
2. Morrison, "Militant Labour", p. 216.
3. I. Turner, *Industrial Labour and Politics* (Canberra: Australian National University Press, 1965), p. 188. For further details, see: V.G. Childe, *How Labour Governs* (2nd ed. (Melbourne: Melbourne University Press, 1964), pp. 195-210.
4. *Offical Proceedings of the Tenth Commonwealth Conference of the Australian Labor Party*, (held at Trades Hall, Melbourne, 1924), pp. 35-38, located at Labor House, Brisbane. Queensland's attitude was summed by the Labor premier, E.G. Theodore: "But I believe that the vast majority (of militant unionists) are not activated by heart motives, but by what they are being paid by disruptionists to see what disruption they can bring about in the Labor Party".
5. L.F. Crisp, *The Australian Federal Labor Party, 1901-1951* (London: Longmans, Green, 1955), p. 176. The rules were amended as follows:
   1. Neither the Communist Party nor a branch thereof may be or may become affiliated with the Australian Labor Party.
   2. No member of the Communist Party may by or may become a member of the Australian Labor Party.

   The Queensland delegation, comprising E.G. Theodore, MLA, L. McDonald, G. Lawson, W. Demaine, W.J. Riordan, and R. Sumner, strongly supported the decision.
6. "Manuscript Minutes of the Queensland Central Executive of the ALP (QCE minutes)", 25 February 1925, located at Labor House, Brisbane. The pledge read: "I hereby pledge myself to the principles of the Australian Labor Party's State, Federal and Local Government Platforms

and any alteration thereto made by a duly constituted Labor Convention. I do pledge myself to do everything in my power to further the objects of the Party as set forth in its Constitution and General Rules. I hereby declare that I am not a member of a Communist Organization or Party or any political party having objects and methods in any way opposed to the Australian Labor Party." See also Branch Circular, 11 March 1925, *Anti-Communist Pledge File 1925-6*, located at Labor House, Brisbane.

7. QCE minutes, (31 July 1925). From 1944-50, Paterson was the Member for Bowen, and the only communist ever elected to a Parliament in Australia.
8. Ibid., 31 July 1925. Hayes was acting as proxy for T. Moroney, the ARU state secretary.
9. Ibid., 25 September 1925; State Organizer's Notes, *Anti-Communist Pledge File 1925-6.*
10. Branch Circulars, 11 August 1925; 9 October 1925, *Anti-Communist Pledge File 1925-6.* The Organizers Notes showed 155 branches complying, five refusals, eight indefinite replies, and 128 branches failing to acknowledge the circular, at the end of September.
11. QCE minutes, 27 November 1925.
12. *Advocate*, December 1925.
13. *Brisbane Courier*, 28 November 1925. "[The] issue at stake is not the anti-communist pledge laid down by the QCE of the ALP, which I was called upon to sign as a member of that body, but the rights of the QCE to instruct me as a representative of an industrial union to do so. My refusal to sign is a challenge to their legal and moral rights to alter the ALP pledge without the express authority of a State Convention".
14. Several ALP branches had complained that affiliated unions contained Communist members and that nothing was being done about it. *Anti-Communist Pledge File, 1925-6.*
15. *Correspondence, Pledges etc. — re Expulsion of Messrs. Rymer and Moroney 1925-6*, located at Labor House, Brisbane.
16. Ibid.
17. *Brisbane Courier*, 9 January 1925. A meeting of representatives of ten ALP branches and a number of affiliated unions suggested the formation of a Minority Labor Party, but little came of the proposal. Ibid.,, 16 January 1926.
18. The pledge was, as might be expected, endorsed by the Pledges Disputes Committee in January 1925. *Correspondence, Pledges etc. — re Expulsion of Messrs. Rymer and Moroney, 1925-6.*
19. QCE minutes, 29 January 1926.
20. E. Lane, *Dawn to Dust* (Brisbane: Brooks, 1939), pp. 220, 308-9.
21. Ibid., p. 309, Lane described the pledge as the "trump card of the Australian Labor Party, QCE and AWU"
22. On instructions from the ARU State Council, the following remarks were

typed across each pledge: "The QCE has no authority under the rules of the ALP (State of Queensland) to demand this pledge. It is, therefore, signed under protest of and on instructions of the State Council of the ARU" *Official Proceedings of the Twelfth State Labor-in-Politics Convention*, held at Southport, February 1926, pp. 3-4, located at Labor House, Brisbane.

23. Ibid.
24. Ibid., p. 17.
25. Ibid. McCormack stated that the "attitude now taken up by Mr Rymer and Mr Moroney was purely tinkering with the question, as they had definitely supported every Communist who came before the QCE for endorsement. The underlying motive in connection with the refusal to sign the pledge was disruption of the Movement".
26. *Brisbane Courier*, 30 October 1925: "As long as I have any say, and while I am Leader of the Labour Party in Queensland, I intend to use my best endeavours to keep Communists out of the Labour Movement, and allow them to form their own party and fight their own battles".
27. Theodore was defeated by only 268 votes, notwithstanding 2,188 informals (4.68 per cent) and more than 5,000 electors abstaining from voting. Rymer had called for an informal vote or abstention in the November 1925 issue of the *Advocate*, as a protest against Theodore's past treatment of trade union demands.
28. *Correspondence, Pledges, etc. — re Expulsion of Messrs. Rymer and Moroney 1925-6.*
29. Ibid.
30. Ibid.
31. Ibid. Also, QCE minutes, 11 June 1926.
32. Ibid.
33. The QCE resolved "that any person, who has refused to sign the anti-Communist pledge unconditionally, or has been refused on a resolution of Convention the right of members of the ALP, must have the authority of the Convention before being again admitted to membership of the ALP" QCE minutes, 17 September 1926.
34. The ARU remained outside the Labor Party until 1957 when the QCE-politican-AWU alliance was shattered following Gair's expulsion.
35. *Official Proceedings of the Thirteenth State Labor-In-Politics Convention*, held at Townsville, May 1928, p. 13, located at Labor House, Brisbane.
36. Prior to the 1929 state elections, the Trades and Labour Council resolved by only forty-five votes to twenty to support Labor at the polls, clearly showing the extent of resentment and antagonisms which the militants harboured against McCormack.
37. In 1926, three Independent Labor candidates, including Fred Paterson in Port Curtis, contested government held seats: in 1929, there were five Left Wing Labor candidates contesting the election.

19 Ideological Conflict: The 1927 and 1948 Strikes

Margaret Bridson Cribb

The adoption by Labor governments in Queensland after 1920 of the basic working premise that political power was to be used "to ameliorate the worst evils of capitalism rather than to engage that system in the frontal attack that Ryan and Theodore had pursued from 1915",[1] was not well received by all sections of the labor movement. Socialists in the party were convinced that the actions of earlier Labor governments, such as the introduction of piece-meal co-operative ownership, had in no way weakened the power of capitalism in Queensland. They cited as evidence the success of "finance-capital" in withholding loan money and forcing amending legislation favourable to its interests upon the Theodore Labor government and in general bringing it to heel. Increasingly this discontent with the Parliamentary Labor Party (PLP) and its aims and methods came to be centred within the union movement and particularly among the Australian Railways Union (ARU) and its leaders George Rymer (president) and Tim Moroney (general secretary), and to be directed at both the government and its offspring, the new Arbitration Court.

Yet railwaymen and their leaders had been involved actively in labour politics in Queensland from the beginning and had individually, and through their unions, given vigorous and strong support to the infant Labor party and to the task of getting the working man into Parliament. The association between railway workers and the party had been strengthened when, following a recommendation of the ARU (then known as the Queensland Railways Employees Association) Annual Conference in 1914, several branches of the union affiliated with the Central Political Executive (CPE) of the ALP to be followed by the union as a whole in 1915. The increasingly close relationship between the ARU and political labor was part of a general pattern of growing participation by the unions which culminated in the formation of a Labor government in Queensland in 1915, and, after the 1916 Labor Convention, in the re-organization of the party administration so that henceforth affiliated unions, in proportion to their membership, would be directly represented at both the convention and on the CPE.[2] In March 1916, Tim Moroney became the ARU's delegate to the CPE and at the Labor-in-Politics Convention in January 1918, the union had direct representation for the first time.

With Labor in office, the right to share in the party's policy making accorded it through affiliation, and its own membership increasing, the ARU appeared well placed to play an influential role in both wings of the ALP. How does one account therefore, for the rapid deterioration in this seemingly close and harmonious relationship between Labor governments and the ARU, early evidence of which was the temporary resignation of Moroney from the QCE in protest against its acceptance of a delegate from the Returned Soldiers and Sailors Labor League;[3] a relationship, moreover, which was already strained by 1920 and which was to become increasingly acrimonious and difficult, as the 1920s progressed.

In the first instance the ideological beliefs of Rymer and Moroney were of considerable importance. These can best be described as socialist with strong syndicalist overtones. Much influenced by the Industrial Workers of the World (IWW) movement, and supporters of the concepts of industrial unionism, direct industrial action and workers' control of industry, the political philosophy of the ARU leadership was firmly rooted in a belief in and recognition of the class struggle. It was their view that the successful conclusion of this struggle in favour of the workers would be reached only if "old unionism" and craft unionism were to be replaced by the new form of industrial unionism, uniting all workers within each industry, regardless of occupation, skill or craft alignment.

Consequently the ARU leaders actively supported the

principle of One Big Union (OBU) as the basis on which would be built the socialization of industry and workers' control, and rejected the notion that even partial achievement of these goals necessitated political action. They believed that it was not necesary for trade unionism to have an organized political expression as all that was required for the achievement of workers' control of industry was the solidarity of the workers (as represented in the slogan "an injury to one is an injury to all"), their organization into industrial unions and their tactical use of direct industrial action. To some extent, part of their personal philosophy was a reflection of the fact that for the major part of their working lives the ARU leaders had been activists in a union which, from it original inception in 1886, had been established as an "all-grades" union, in a determined and conscious effort to organize all railway employees from top to bottom of the railway service into one industrial union.

Moroney also personally rejected the notion that any government at that time was capable, let alone desirous, of changing the capitalist system to one which gave control of its own destiny to the working class. This had to be tempered by the felt needs of the ARU membership for political association with the Labor party and in the case of arbitration, by the necessity to work the system for whatever could be got from it to benefit the union's members. Seeing the Arbitration Court as an instrument of the capitalist class, coercing the workers into accepting conditions against which otherwise they would fight, the ARU leadership took the attitude that there could be no agreement with the employers of labour which the workers had to consider sacred and inviolable.

Views of this kind ran counter to those held by the ALP hierarchy but were also unrepresentative of the thinking in the craft and sectional unions, into which, along with the ARU, the railway service was divided. The sectional unions in particular were staunch supporters of the arbitration system and of the "gradual reformism" policies of the government. This sectional breakdown of trade unionism which existed among railwaymen was also the cause of a good deal of inter-union rivalry, itself exacerbated by the provisons for *de facto* compulsory unionism and the "bracketing" of unions, which were incorporated in the Industrial Arbitration Act of 1916. With regard to the former, the ARU was in the unique position of offering to those men and women employed in the railways an alternative to the unions covering their own craft or calling and thus compulsory unionism placed it in a situation of competition with other unions for the right to represent railway workers forced by the act to join a union.

Sectionalism, compulsory unionism and bracketing were thus ever present factors capable of undermining the ARU's position of leadership within the railway service, a leadership always under threat because of ideological and tactical differences between itself and the majority of the smaller railway unions. These made no secret of their dislike for the philosophical and political idealism of Moroney and his colleagues and their own loyal adherence to the arbitration system led them to deplore the use of direct action except as a last resort and to be fearful of what they saw as the "spoiling" tactics of the ARU in industrial matters.

Within the wider context of the labor movement itself, the ARU's potential for playing an influential role in both the industrial and political wings of the ALP also was challenged from the beginning by a much stronger rival. As Murphy has noted,[4] E.G. Theodore, through amalgamation, had already forged by 1920, a powerful political instrument in the AWU, with a ready-made propaganda machine available to it in the *Worker* newspaper. Between then and 1930, under Theodore's premiership and continuing into that of W. McCormack, these early links were hammered into a permanent alliance between Queensland Labor governments and the largest union in the state.

The struggle between the AWU-government partnership and the ARU and other smaller militant groups within the party was not on the grounds of ideology alone, however, though there was little enough held in common between them in this area. The marked swing away from Labor in the 1920 state election and the powerful opposition mounted within the state to many of the government's earlier policies which had led, in turn, to a drying up of most of the traditional sources for borrowing overseas, convinced Theodore and his successors that there were tangible limits to what a Labor government could achieve in office and survive electorally. These limits were unacceptable to the ARU, who saw this commitment to gradual reformism as a betrayal of the labor movement; the slackening in momentum of the government after 1920 in putting forward radical legislation comparable to that of the first Labor government widened the rift between it and the socialists. It was a conflict, too, over who was going to control not only the ideology of the party but also the party machine and one which was further exacerbated by the strength of the personalities on each side: Theodore and McCormack on the one hand, Moroney and Rymer on the other.[5] While, by the end of the decade, the combination of the AWU and the government had won out and had isolated the ARU politically and industrially and forced it into the position of "a permanently protesting minority"[6] within the labor movement, little of this was clearly discernible between 1920 and 1925, as the ARU in that period appeared to be enjoying an astonishing success. Its membership climbed from 9094 in 1922 to reach the all time peak of 13,190 for the years 1925-26. Its prestige and influence were enhanced by the crucial role it played in a campaign on the political front to bring the PLP under a large measure of rank and file control.

As leader of a committee formed from twenty-nine unions — the Government Employees' Anti-Reduction Committee — to induce Theodore to rescind the five shilling reduction in the basic wage for both private sector and government employees handed down by the Arbitration Court in February and July 1922, the ARU was able to promote substantial opposition to both this action and other "economy" proposals put forward by the government to shore up its faltering financial position. Resentment within the movement mounted to such an extent that even the Labor press exhorted Theodore to seek sources of economy other than those of rifling the pockets of the workers, and it was only with the greatest difficulty that he held caucus and the QCE in line over his government's policy of across-the-board wage reductions.

The battle was really joined at the Labor-in-Politics Convention at Emu Park in the following year where the temper of much of the labor movement was evidenced in the repeated attempts by delegates to push through resolutions to control the PLP.

Having pressed the government very hard at Emu Park in 1923, the ARU capped this two years later with a clear-cut victory in the industrial arena. The 1925 strike of railway workers lasted for one week only and at its conclusion the government, as the employer, conceded all the claims made upon it. These included the restoration of the wage cut to state employees, and, most importantly, legislation to fix the basic wage at four pounds ten shillings. Thus was reaffirmed the principle, previously denied by the parliamentary leaders, that a Labor government *should legislate* general industrial reform.

The railway unions in this strike were able to paper over the cracks in their facade of solidarity and held together for the short time required to achieve victory. That they were able to do this was to some extent dependent on the fact that the strike was one over industrial demands, demands moreover that were longstanding, and had the full support of all workers, militant or not. The strike leaders were also fortunate in their timing. Theodore had resigned from state parliament in February 1925 in order to contest the seat of Herbert at the federal elections later in the year, and in their confrontation, the railway unions faced a much weaker personality in the new premier, W.N. Gillies. The conservative press, the business sector and the opposition were particularly outspoken in their criticism of Gillies' alleged capitulation to the unions, making the point that governments which could not control their own workers could not hope to attract overseas investment capital to the state. There is evidence to suggest that fear of such a retaliation by overseas financial interests was a factor in the government reshuffle which took place before the end of 1925. Gillies was elevated to the bench of a reconstituted Arbitration Court — the Board of Trade and Arbitration — and his place as premier filled by W. McCormack, a longstanding associate of E.G. Theodore in both the AWU and the ALP.

The conservative press, the business sector and the opposition were outspoken of their criticism of the new premier, William Gillies' alleged capitulation to the unions. (Photograph by courtesy of the John Oxley Library.)

Premier William McCormack operated on the premise that political enemies should be crushed and not allowed to live to fight another day. (Photograph by courtesy of the John Oxley Library.)

The winning of the 1925 strike with such comparative ease appeared to confirm the argument of the ARU leaders and the militants that a great deal could be achieved by the workers through solidarity in direct action, and that when necessary, Labor governments could be forced by united industrial strength to keep faith with the workers. On the other hand there were those who took a different view of the outcome of the strike. The conservative elements in the state were looking for a strong premier, one who would get tough with the militant minority in the unions and bring about stability, industrial peace and economic investment. At the same time, within the labor movement itself, particularly in the PLP and the QCE, there were those who wished to see the ARU's challenge to the supremacy of the parliamentary party put down firmly. Both groups found their man in McCormack.

McCormack represented those elements inside the ALP who had, by now, translated the basic need to present a solid and united front against Labor's enemies into a demand for uniformity and conformity by all elements of the movement;[7] moreover, a conformity with the expressed policies and beliefs of the parliamentary leadership, backed by the party machine, both an integral part of the AWU-government alliance, of which by background and natural inclination, McCormack had come to be the acknowledged leader. As expressed in one of his public speeches, McCormack believed that

> Labour cannot tolerate the men who believe in revolutionary methods. I have no fault to find in their political opinions any more than I have fault to find with the Nationalists — but I have told them not only lately, but for years, that their best place is outside the ranks of Labour. Let them adopt whatever policy they like but they have no right to destroy the discipline of Labour and compel Labour to take up false positions.[8]

The new premier operated on the premise that political enemies should be crushed and not allowed to live to fight another day. Having consolidated his position by winning handily the 1926 elections, McCormack moved immediately to deal with the ARU. He struck at the union's influence within the

ALP by engineering the expulsion of its leaders from both the QCE and the Labor-in-Politics Convention.

For once it seemed that the *Brisbane Courier* was the most discerning observer of the contemporary scene. It commented that "by excluding the extremist delegates, the Government, the Central Political Executive [sic] and the party managers of the A.W.U. have ensured a conference that will do its bidding . . . the suppression movement yesterday was actuated entirely in the interests of the politicians."[9]

So it proved to be. Robbed of its left wing leadership, round whom those of a more radical persuasion could rally, Convention was induced, though only with considerable difficulty and by the narrowest of voting margins, to alter and modify the party's "Objective". Convention resolved to redraft the "methods" to eliminate reference to the Supreme Economic Council and to nationalization of banking. Even this was far less than McCormack had asked for. His motion had been to the effect that all reference to "methods" should be eliminated from both the constitution and platform of the ALP. He contended that if they were to have "methods" at all they must be of a kind that he could go on to a platform and expound.

This highlighted quite starkly the basic ideological differences between the Labor leadership and the militants. The "methods" of achieving socialism were of vital importance to the latter's thinking and this statement by McCormack was, for them, the ultimate proof that the government had abandoned the ideal of socialism and was no longer concerned with either the aims or objectives of the ALP. It appeared to them that all McCormack and the cabinet required as "methods" was a list of innocuous proposals which they could defend on election platforms, safe in the knowledge that there was nothing contained therein which was likely to either offend or frighten Labor's traditional opponents.

Having used all its influence and power in labour circles to attempt to control a union which had defeated it industrially in 1925, the government appeared to have pulled it off. Many ARU members felt the desirability — indeed, the necessity — for some form of political organization and a certain amount of unrest arose within the union because the ARU was no longer part of the political labor movement. J. Hayes, the south-eastern divisional secretary, led a rebel movement from within and was dismissed from the union. From the outside, the ARU came under open attack from the AWU which launched a campaign to build a railway section within its own organization, confidently asserting that over five thousand members of the ARU would subsequently secede to it. The general exodus prophesied by the AWU did not eventuate. Moroney's assessment that fewer than four hundred members left his union seems closer to the truth.

Disgust with the Labor politicians and the disaffiliation of the ARU and the Australasian Meat Industry Employees Union (AMIEU) from the ALP caused tentative moves to be made towards forming a new Industrial Labour Party (ILP). A meeting was held at the Trades Hall, attended by representatives from twenty-five trade unions and metropolitan ALP branches at which the decision was taken to form an ILP to realize the aims and planks of the Labor platform. At the time nothing further came of this. Rymer and Moroney were both opposed to the formation of any new political organization within the labor movement. They were convinced that unless a better means of control over the elected political representatives of labour could be found, the workers could hope for little from any political organization.

1925 had appeared to bring the ARU to a pinnacle of success in achieving its policies. By the end of 1926 it had lost a great deal of ground and McCormack's star was in the ascendant. He had favoured and supported the AWU and the craft unions in their skirmishes with the ARU and driven the latter outside the political labor movement. The ARU was left with but one field of action — industry — and here McCormack returned to the attack in 1927.

The industrial disturbance which broke out in that year gave little indication, initially, of the deep-seated cleavage which by now existed within the labor movement. Trouble began with what seemed to be a comparatively minor issue, the question of preference in re-employment for sugar mill workers in north Queensland, and, more specifically, for those employed at the South Johnstone mill. It should have been possible to settle a dispute of this nature fairly quickly but this was not to be the case. Several ballots of the rank and file were taken by order of the Board of Trade and Arbitration, but on each occasion a motion supporting a return to work was overwhelmingly defeated. Reluctantly, the AWU executive, though sworn to arbitration, was forced to intervene and officially support direct action. As they explained it, the only way they could confine the conflict to the South Johnstone area was to make it an official strike.

The strikers' refusal to accept the Board of Trade's terms, in defiance of their union leaders, and their determined adherence to the principle of preference should have been followed by one of two things — the repudiation of the strike by the AWU executive, or their proper organization of the men to force the issue. In fact the AWU officials vacillated from day to day and in the absence of forceful leadership from above, members of the strike committee at South Johnstone took matters into their own hands. They appealed for assistance to the Innisfail Trades and Labor Council (TLC), which, in its turn, declared the mill "black". While the strike committee was anxious to enlist the support of railwaymen and waterside workers, the AWU at this stage specifically requested the railway unions to keep out.

A significant step, likely to provoke retaliatory union action was taken when the mill management decided to send a consignment of sugar south. The AWU executive appealed to the railway unions to handle the shipment, on the promise that they would not be asked to do so again. The normal outlet of Mourilyan Harbour was blocked by the waterside workers, who had already declared sugar from South Johnstone "black". Despite strong protests from the Townsville sub-branch of the ARU the railwaymen worked the sugar as far south as Bowen, where the adamant refusal of Rockhampton ARU men to take over the train forced a situation where Australian Federated Union of Locomotive Enginemen (AFULE) crews had to bring the sugar to Brisbane.

Up to this stage the whole strike scene in the north was notable for little other than confusion. Northern sub-branches of both the AWU and the ARU were at times taking action independently of their state executives in Brisbane, of each other, and of the South Johnstone strike committee. Co-ordination of strategy was lacking and no clear direction had come from the ARU state council to its northern membership. Clearly, the railwaymen were not looking for a showdown with the government. Little comment on or news of the strike was appearing in the metropolitan press. Nor was there much quickening of tempo even when on 21 August, the strike committee notified the ARU and the Waterside Workers' Federation (WWF) that in its eyes everything to and from South Johnstone, by rail or road, was "black". This opened the way for the Innisfail sub-branch of the ARU to issue a similar declaration. One by one, over the following week, the railwaymen at Innisfail refused to handle goods for the mill and were suspended from duty by the commissioner for railways along with those who refused to take over the suspended men's jobs. By 28 August there were approximately one hundred and forty railwaymen under suspension in the northern division.

Although tension had naturally become acute there was no indication that a crisis point had been reached until, without warning, McCormack dropped a bombshell on the labor movement on 29 August. Having just returned from an overseas loan-raising trip, he may have been unduly sensitive to finding an industrial dispute on his hands at that time. For whatever reason he clearly over-reacted and brushing aside Larcombe, the minister for railways, took over personal control of the Railways Department and issued an ultimatum to the ARU. All its members and all members of other unions who had defied the decisions of their executives and thrown in their lot with the ARU men were to be dismissed on Saturday 3 September; the commissioner would re-engage on the following Monday only those employees who signed a pledge to obey the rules of the Railway Department. Subsequently finding that under the arbitration law he could not single out one union in that way, and hoping, it was assumed, that by including within his pronouncement all the unions in the railway service he would weaken the solidarity of the workers, McCormack then dismissed all the railway employees. The entire railway service was shut down.

It is difficult to understand why the premier chose to take such extreme and arbitrary action against government employees at that time. Had he wished to defeat the ARU industrially he could have found any one of a dozen issues to suit his purpose, none of which would have struck, as McCormack's ultimatum did, at one of the fundamental principles of the labor movement — not to scab on one's fellow workers. It has been suggested[10] that by constant reference, in the pages of the ARU's journal the *Advocate*, to questionable aspects of both Theodore's and McCormack's involvement in the Mungana mining leases and the Chillagoe smelter affair, Rymer and Moroney had goaded McCormack into using a sledge hammer to crack a nut. With hindsight, McCormack has also been credited with political prescience of such an order as to foresee the coming Depression and to desire to have Labor out of office when the worst effects of it were felt in Queensland. More reasonably, it was a sheer case of overkill; that he underestimated the effect on the labor movement of his personal action in locking out all the railwaymen; at the same time he was supremely confident of his ability to control the situation.

Given the severity of the immediate reaction to the lock-out, particularly as expressed in the Labor press, it was surprising just how much McCormack was able to salvage and how quickly from the situation he had created. Cabinet was behind him throughout but it required all of his considerable talents to swing the PLP into support. A predicted revolt in caucus fizzled out with only four parliamentarians voting against him.[11] The QCE was also whipped into line with a threat of dissolution of Parliament, and by the time the Labor-in-Politics Convention met in Townsville in May 1928, the premier was firmly in command once again of the party machine and the political wing of the ALP.

The lock-out ended in defeat for the ARU whose members

were forced to return to work on the government's terms. The divisions between the ARU and the other numerous railway unions could not be contained on this occasion, a key role in the railwaymen's capitulation being played by Theo Kissick, president of the Queensland branch of the AFULE, who was ever anxious for a settlement and who treated with McCormack behind the backs of Rymer and Moroney. In the months that followed, the ARU leaders were made increasingly aware of the isolation of their union and that it was out of step with the majority of the labor movement. Union membership dropped dramatically to 8972 by the end of 1927 and to 7153 in 1928.

These factors were decisive in determining the attitude of the ARU to the Militant Minority Movement (also called the Left Wing of the Labour Movement) which was organized by militant industrialists prior to the 1929 state elections, with the aim of endorsing candidates to provide a focal point for those disillusioned Labor supporters who could not bring themselves to vote Tory. While joining the left wing committee himself, Moroney kept the ARU officially out of the movement, even though a number of ARU sub-branches requested their executive to support it and its candidates. Speaking to the ARU council which met to deal with these requests, Moroney, while admitting his hopes for a Labor defeat, made the point most forcefully that unless other unions could be persuaded to support the left wing movement, the ARU could not "go it alone". "It would not be of any advantage to the railwaymen or to the Left Wing candidates if, as a result of the support accorded them on this occasion, the ARU was put out of existence . . . we have been practically isolated because of the policy we have pursued".[12]

The five left wing candidates polled only 3194 votes together at the elections but the McCormack government was heavily defeated, losing sixteen seats. There was no abnormal increase in informal voting and some writers[13] have supported the belief, widespread within the labor movement at the time, that, unusual though it seemed, normally solid supporters voted anti-Labor in 1929, "not as a result of wrath against the A.L.P. but rather as retribution against McCormack."[14]

These may well be oversimplified assessments of the situation which give insufficient weight to many other background factors. What was important, however, was that the struggle in this decade which developed between the AWU-government alliance and the more radical elements in the labor movement set a pattern in Queensland for relations, both industrial and political, between a Labor government and the militant unions for many years to come; a pattern which was to be clearly seen twenty years later as underlying the great railway strike of 1948.

The industrial conflict in 1927 was also notable in being the first major dispute in Queensland in which communism was made an issue. The Communist party was still too small and weak in numbers and finance to be able to exert much influence in the actual industrial disputes of 1925 and 1927, though both Norman Jeffreys in his organizing tour of north Queensland in 1925 and H.J. Moxon later were able to engender a certain amount of support. During the South Johnstone strike, Communist party agitation and propaganda may have assisted in preventing a speedy and peaceful settlement, as their support strengthened the militants and provided them with leadership at a time when this was not forthcoming from the AWU. Claims by McCormack and the press that "fifty or sixty" communist organizers had crossed the border from the south after the strike began to assist in the dislocation of industry and the destruction of the labor movement would seem to be of doubtful authenticity as from what was known of the Communist party in 1927, party membership was small, there were few paid officials and lack of funds was a perpetual worry. Their involvement in the left wing movement, though numerically small, was more easily substantiated. It followed from the publication by the party in August, 1928, of what came to be called the *Queensland Resolution*. This embodied the Comintern's "new line" as it applied to the local situation and involved a turning away from support for the Labor government to one of challenging Labor party candidates at the ballot box. It was in conformity with these new tactics that the "Left Wing of the Labor Movement" was set up on communist initiative and local electoral committees were formed to assist left wing candidates.

By 1948, the communist story was a different one. The Depression and the later years of World War II brought a great change in the position of the party. While estimates vary, it has been authoritatively suggested that by 1945 the party may have been supported by nearly 40 per cent of Australian unionists.[15] In Queensland its strength was concentrated in a number of unions affiliated with the TLC and identified in the persons of such prominent union officials as Mick Healy, secretary of the TLC, Gerry Dawson, secretary of the Carpenters' Union, Ted Englart of the WWF, Alex. Macdonald, secretary of the Federated Ironworkers' Association (FIA) and Theo Kissick of the AFULE. Their influence upon the strategy and direction of the 1948 strike was crucial, as was the strike itself in terms of relationships within the political and industrial wings of the labor movement in the years that followed.

The immediate industrial claim which set off this dispute on 3 February 1948 was one made by the workshop and running shed tradesmen employed by the Railway Department, for a flow-on of the Mooney Award. Federal Conciliation Commissioner G.A. Mooney had awarded marginal increases to metal trade workers in 1947 and though railway unions in Queensland operated under state awards it was usual for these to be kept in line with those covering other state railway employees who were working under Commonwealth awards. An approach to the government in 1947 produced an offer unsatisfactory to the relevant unions and the Arbitration Court delayed a hearing of the railwaymen's claims.

Underlying the industrial demand were a variety of social, political and economic factors which were to be decisive in determining the strategy and duration of the strike and its ultimate outcome. One element was the federal government's persistence with many of its wartime control measures such as wage pegging, price controls and rationing which angered workers who understandably sought in the post-war period some of the things like better wages and working conditions denied them by the Depression and voluntarily foregone in the interests of winning the war.

It should be remembered also that from 1941 to 1945,

"Queensland's geographical position made it the battlefront state"[16] and that the brunt of the transport within Australia of the war requirements of the Australian and Allied armies was borne by the Queensland railway service. By 1948 the department was still operating with mainly obsolete and worn-out rolling stock, testimony to a lack of foresight and long range planning for post war needs by the department. The continuation in service of a number of locomotives, built for wartime use on the Garratt principle also placed an additional strain on their engine crews, as both the commissioner and the men who drove them attested to their danger in operation. A series of accidents and derailments in 1947, culminating in the Camp Mountain rail disaster in which sixteen persons, including the driver and firemen of the train, were killed, produced further stress and tension within the service and the conviction that men, in the course of their daily work, were being called upon to operate potential death traps.

On the political front, the growing ascendancy of the communists in the trade unions, which had given them by 1940 control of the Brisbane TLC had produced, in its turn, a countervailing force, the ALP Industrial Groups, backed by the Catholic Social Movement, which began the struggle to win back unions from communist control. The Labor-in-Politics Convention at Townsville in February 1947, agreed to the setting up of such groups in Queensland and in the following year the executive of the QCE established a three-man committee with its own separate funds to form, maintain and advance ALP Industrial Groups. Though only in its seminal stage at this time, the Communist-Grouper conflict ran like a hidden thread through the activities of the strike and early signs of it could be seen in the internal dissension in such unions as the Transport Workers and the AFULE. The AWU was committed to the anti-communist cause, two of its members, Walsh and Bukowski serving on the QCE's three-man Industrial Groups committee.

On the other side, the ARU's long and close association with men like Fred W. Paterson, Communist MLA for Bowen (1944-50), and militant industrialists on the TLC had been an issue between itself and the less radical railway unions, the government and the AWU at the time of the 1927 strike. The 1948 leadership of Mick O'Brien (president) and Frank Nolan (general secretary) maintained a similar personal political philosophy and commitment to industrial unionism and direct action as their predecessors. Though not themselves members of the Communist party, their beliefs were in closer harmony with the communists, especially on the principles of industrial unionism and the use of direct action than with those of any other faction in the trade union movement and directly antipathetic to those of the AWU leadership.

The events of the strike, briefly recorded hereafter,[17] were notable for the way in which each side orchestrated its strategy in response to the tactics of its opponent. Immediately the workshop employees struck, having taken ballots of their members which were overwhelmingly in favour of a strike action, the government lifted all restrictions on road transport, and applied for and was granted a stand-down order for its railway employees. Its purpose was to divide the railwaymen among themselves, a stratagem which had proved succesful in 1927. This was followed by a dramatic change in the composition of the Central Disputes Committee (CDC). The position of secretary, initially filled by E.J. Irwin, secretary of the small sectional Railways Salaried Officers' Union, was taken over by Alex Macdonald, communist secretary of the FIA, while the federal organization of the Amalgamated Engineering Union (AEU) sent one of its councillors, E.J. Rowe, to assist the CDC. Rowe was a communist and one of the experienced leaders of the Victorian AEU strikes of 1946-47. Between them, Macdonald and Rowe possessed a combination of tactical and oratorical skill which, backed by the organizational capacity of other militants on the CDC and of the Communist party outside it, gave a new and forceful direction to the strike and to the management of the campaign. The efficiency and expertise of the communists was observable in the well organized picketing and in the skilful and continuous use of pamphleteering and panels of speakers to keep in close communication with the workers and for general propaganda purposes. Even Premier E.M. Hanlon's unofficial but effective mass media blackout of the

CDC did not prevent it from informing the workers of what was going on. An attempt by members of the Transport Workers Union to get Arbitration Court intervention in the strike in the hope of promoting a "return-to-work" order was forestalled by the CDC long enough to enable Theo Kissick (AFULE) to persuade his own union to join the strikers. This was a significant decision as trains could not run, other than those authorized by the CDC for emergency food relief, while both the ARU and AFULE were on strike. Kissick, who had moved across the political spectrum since 1927 into membership in the CPA was unable to keep his members "out" for the duration of the strike but the AFULE's intervention at this stage was crucial.

The CDC then attempted, with only marginal success, to involve the tramway workshop employees of the Brisbane City Council in the dispute and mounted a massive picketing exercise at the Milton depot. The government's response was to proclaim a state of emergency under Section 22 of the Transport Act and an Order-in-Council prohibiting picketing and the counselling of strike action; arrests began on strike leaders and others for picketing. In its turn, the CDC was able to escalate the strike further, bringing out the WWF, the Seamen's Union and the miners.

The government retaliated swiftly and savagely, rushing through Parliament the Industrial Law Amendment Act which gave the police unusual powers of entry and arrest without a warrant and placed the onus of proof upon the defendants in cases of prosecution which arose under the act. Subsequently this legislation was used to support police action in physically attacking, on St Patrick's Day, a small groups of unionists who began a march from the Trades Hall in protest against the act. During the melee, amongst those injured was Fred Paterson, who was batoned down from behind while observing the incident from the footpath. Other marchers were arrested and gaoled. The following day, however, the police made no attempt to interfere in an illegal mass demonstration of thousands of people in King George Square.

Behind the scenes both government and strikers were

During the railway strike on St Patrick's Day, 1948, unionists march in protest against an Act giving police unusual powers of entry and arrest without a warrant. (Photograph by courtesy of the Trades and Labor Council.)

beginning to weaken and once it became clear to the CDC that the central Queensland railwaymen were determined to go back to work, a settlement was reached which went some of the way towards meeting the original demands. A general return to work followed on 6 April, almost nine weeks after the strike began.

There is no doubt that when the communists assumed direction of the CDC and the determination of strategy and tactics, the strike became a political one. The strikers themselves were aware of this but were prepared to accept communist leadership as more likely to gain for them a positive improvement in their industrial conditions. The evidence supports the view also that although there were differences of opinion between the communist trade union leaders and some CPA officials over "politicising" the strike, such action was in line with the tactics of the "left adventurist" elements in the party at that time; tactics which were developed out of a conviction that the world was facing a grave economic crisis, likely to end in the collapse of capitalism, and that by placing itself in the vanguard of the industrial upheavals of the immediate post-war period, the Communist party would be able to extend its working-class base at the expense of the ALP. At the same time the Communist party sought to raise the political consciousness of the workers so that each could play an effective part in the period of economic chaos which, they anticipated, lay ahead. On both counts they were unsuccessful as they misinterpreted not only the signs for the future, but also the militancy of the workers, which was born in the main, not out of ideological conviction, but out of their economic and industrial frustration. The Communist party failed to appreciate in 1948 how deeply rooted traditional working class support was for the ALP in spite of the repressive actions taken by some of its leaders. Consequently, although some material industrial gains were made, the strike was not a victory for the militants. The government had triumphed, in effect; the prolongation of the conflict beggared the workers financially and drained the coffers of unions like the ARU; the labor movement had been deeply and irrevocably divided within itself.

The part played by Hanlon in the strike is of great interest. His rigorous enforcement, as a Labor premier, of government authority over strikers by the use of such extreme legislation that libertarian opinion throughout Australia was outraged, was not in keeping with some parts of his own background, or with his earlier close ties with railwaymen. In a relatively short career in the railway service, Hanlon had been president of the Railway Strike Committe in the 1912 General Strike and prominent in the Queensland Railways Union, until he left the service. At the time of the lockout of the railwaymen in 1927 he had entered the debate in the Assembly in support of his former workmates. Press reports of the conflict which were invariably supportive of the government's actions alleged that he was outdoing McCormack in 1927 in suppressing disruptive and revolutionary elements within the trade union movement who were hostile to any government or to law and order. That the strike was fought out in the increasingly hysterical atmosphere of the cold war and that its opening coincided with the communist take-over in Czechoslovakia, cannot be discounted as factors influencing Hanlon and others in his government. In such an atmosphere political judgment can easily become oversimplified and political enemies magnified beyond their true proportion. Hanlon's most recent biographer[18] sees him as a sincere anti-communist concerned both to preserve the ALP from communist inroads and influence and to stop their forward march within the union movement. It has also been noted[19] that Hanlon was the first Labor premier of Queensland to have no personal ties with the AWU and that the Hanlon cabinet was the first for many years to have no more than half its members with discernible AWU associations. From this it has been argued that Hanlon's early release of the jailed strikers after the settlement of the strike and decision to repeal the "strike-breaking" legislation, over the opposition of party leaders, including the deputy premier, V.C. Gair, were indicative of the waning influence of the AWU in the last years of Hanlon's premiership. The situation on the government side at the time of the strike was clearly a more complex one than that implies; even now all the strands have not been teased out with complete reliability, but the dating of any observable decline in AWU influence within the ALP as the mid-1940s would seem to be premature.

Of the 1948 strike it can be said that in many ways it was a continuation of the 1927 situation, of the cleavage between the government-AWU alliance on the one hand, and the "industrialists" based on the TLC on the other, with the latter's militancy reinforced and extended by the communists for their own purposes. The long range effects of 1948 were much more far-reaching than those of 1927 however. The strike brought closer to the surface all the divisive elements at work by this time within the labor movement in Queensland, elements which were to erupt and split the ALP in 1957. It also produced some contradictory situations: the conformity and solidarity of all loyal party members became outwardly even more obligatory under the pressure of growing communist influence, but solidarity itself began to be eroded from inside the ALP as the Communist-Grouper struggle extended eventually into one for the control, for its own sake, of the party, its machine and the parliamentarians. At the same time, after 1948, began the eclipse of the influence of the "ideological" radicals in the trade union movement and the rise of the practical power-brokers, no longer located within the AWU but based in the Brisbane TLC. The influence of men like Frank Nolan and the communist officials began gradually to decline, as did the size of the ARU, while paradoxically that of the TLC of which their unions were members, began the upswing which, after 1957, was to enable it to supercede the AWU and take control of the party in Queensland.

NOTES

1. D.J. Murphy, ed., *Labor in Politics: The State Labor Parties in Australia, 1880-1920*, (St Lucia: University of Queensland Press, 1975), p. 214.
2. D.J. Murphy, R.B. Joyce and Colin A. Hughes, eds., *Prelude to Power: The Rise of the Labour Party in Queensland, 1885-1915*, (Brisbane: Jacaranda Press, 1970), pp. 89-107.
3. QCE minutes, 9 January 1920, held at Labor House, Brisbane.
4. Murphy, Joyce and Hughes, *Prelude to Power*, p. 105.

5. Murphy, *Labor in Politics*, pp. 213-15.
6. I. Turner, *Industrial Labour and Politics: The Labour Movement in Eastern Australia, 1900-1921*, (Canberra: Australian National University Press, 1965), p. 217.
7. Murphy, *Labor in Politics*, p. 210.
8. *Brisbane Courier*, 24 February 1927.
9. Ibid., 9 February 1926.
10. V. Daddow, *The Puffing Pioneers and Queensland Railway Builders*, (St Lucia: University of Queensland Press, 1975), p. 150.
11. By so doing, Collins, Hartley, Riordan and Weir earned a heroes' acclaim in the left-wing newspaper.
12. *Advocate*, 15 April 1929.
13. A.A. Morrison, " 'Militant' Labour in Queensland, 1912-27", *Proceedings of the Royal Historical Society, 1952-53*; E.M. Higgins, "Queensland Labor Governments, 1915-29" (M.A. thesis, University of Melbourne, 1954); and D. Volker, "The Australian Labor Party in Queensland, 1927-35" (B.A. thesis, University of Queensland, 1962).
14. Volker, "The Australian Labor Party in Queensland", p. 7.
15. Alastair Davidson, *The Communist Party of Australia: A Short History*, (Stanford: Hoover Institute Press, 1969), p. 126.
16. "Report of the Commissioner for Railways, 30 June 1945", *QPP* 1 (1945-46) :517.
17. For a detailed account of the 1948 Railway Strike see Margaret Cribb, "State in Emergency: The Queensland Railway Strike of 1948", in *Strikes: Studies in Twentieth Century Australian Social History*, eds. J. Iremonger, J. Merritt and G. Osborne, (Sydney: Angus & Robertson, 1973), pp. 225-48.
18. Kenneth W. Knight, "Edward Michael Hanlon: A City Bushman", in *Queensland Political Portraits, 1859-1952*, eds. D.J. Murphy and R.B. Joyce (St Lucia: University of Queensland Press, 1978), chap. 15.
19. R. Shearman, "The Politics of the 1948 Queensland Railway Strike" (B.A. thesis, University of Queensland, n.d.).

20 Labor and the Depression

B.J. Costar

The Great Depression placed the Australian labor movement under unprecedented political and economic pressures. In the states of New South Wales, Victoria and South Australia the Labor party experienced schisms from which it took many years to recover. The Queensland ALP also began the Depression badly in being defeated at the 1929 election after having ruled the state continuously since 1915. However, this defeat meant that the ALP had the good fortune to be out of office during the worst years of the economic crisis, and was thus spared the problems which destroyed the party in other states. Furthermore, the Country Progressive National (CPN) government of Premier A.E. Moore performed badly during its term of office. As the economic situation worsened, the CPN government became, in the eyes of the labor movement, increasingly more reactionary and class biassed. These developments had the effect of uniting almost all sections of the labor movement in the desire to see the return of a Labor administration at the 1932 election.

The years 1929-32 were generally ones of reconciliation and consolidation for the Queensland labor movement. The state of unity achieved over this period stood in stark contrast to the factionalism which plagued the party during the late 1920s. However, potentially divisive issues did confront the party during its years in opposition. The Australian Railways Union (ARU) remained outside the ALP and continued its battle with the Australian Workers Union (AWU). New problems in the form of Langism and the Premiers' Plan also threatened the stability of the party but were diffused before they could inflict serious damage.

Perhaps the most significant structural development within the ALP in Queensland during the Depression years was the consolidation of the hegemony of the AWU. From 1932 until the early 1950s the Labor party was effectively controlled by an alliance of the parliamentary leader and the secretary of the AWU. This alliance was confirmed and strengthened by the Depresssion.

The defeat of the government of William McCormack in 1929 was a consequence of Queensland's depressed economy. The 1920s in Australia are generally regarded as a period of economic boom. However, since the boom was centred on manufacturing industy,[1] and since Queensland was the most rural state in the Commonwealth, that state did not enjoy the full fruits of the buoyant twenties. Moreover the available economic indicators illustrate that by the financial year 1926/27 Queensland was in the depths of a severe recession. The value of wool exports (Queensland's major export) declined dramatically from £12.9 million in 1925/26 to £3.5 million in 1926/27.[2] A similar pattern emerges when the figures for factory production, overall production and the value of new buildings are examined. The slight recovery experienced by Queensland in 1928/29 was quickly swamped by the general economic downturn. The major cause of Queensland's premature depression was the decline of the pastoral industry which was precipitated by a severe drought. Drought conditions prevailed in wide areas of the north and west of the state throughout 1926, 1927, 1928 and part of 1929.[3] While the beef and woollen industries were most affected, abnormally low rainfall had deleterious effects in wheat and other agricultural areas. The drought broke early in 1929 but the woollen industry did not experience the anticipated recovery because of a marked fall in overseas prices.

Queensland's economy in the 1920s was heavily dependent on its primary sector. The strong linkage effects of the pastoral industry brought about a decline in economic activity not only in the country areas but also in the coastal ports, whose viability rested on the economic well-being of their hinterland. The value of new buildings approved in the Brisbane metropolitan area declined from £18 million in 1926 to £9.5 million in 1929. This fall off in economic activity in such key industries led to a steady increase in unemployment. While recorded unemployment in Queensland was lower than the national average for most of the 1920s, it reached 8.4 per cent of registered trade unionists in 1926 and increased from 6.4 per cent in the last quarter of 1928 to 7.6 per cent by May 1929. (The national increase for the same period was only 0.1 per cent; from 9.9 per cent to 10 per cent).[4] The significance of these increases was not lost on Queensland's trade unionists who regularly petitioned and criticized the government for failing to deal with the problem.[5] Arthur Moore and his party, realizing the government's vulnerability on the issue, made unemployment a major plank in their 1929 election campaign. As well as continually accusing the government of being responsible for the high level of unemployment, the CPN also promised that if it were elected to power it would immediately raise a £2 million loan to stimulate economic activity.[6]

While one may agree with David Butler's contention that the manner in which an "elector translates his economic circumstances into a voting intention is still largely a mystery",[7] it was true, at least until 1977, that Australian voters were quick to respond to variations in levels of employment. No Australian government which was forced to the polls during the years 1930 to 1934 survived the ordeal. Bearing in mind that Queensland commenced its depression before the other states, McCormack was as much a victim of the Depression as were Scullin, Hogan, Hill, Lang and Mitchell. Furthermore, the 1929 defeat was not an aberration. In the two other major elections Labor fought in Queensland in the late twenties, it achieved a poor result. The 1928 mayoralty election in Brisbane saw the Labor candidate poll only 38.60 per cent compared to the CPN's 61.40 percent, whereas in the Senate election in 1928, the Labor team could muster only 37.13 per cent to the Nationalists' 60.04 per cent.

However, contemporaries and scholars alike have hiterto explained Labor's 1929 defeat as the end-product of the division which existed within the labor movement in the late 1920s.[8]

Hal Eyre's cartoon of William McCormack "whitewashing socialism" at the 1929 election. (Photograph by courtesy of the John Oxley Library.)

They argue that McCormack and his cabinet had seriously alienated significant sections of the Queensland trade union movement and that these unionists, led by the ARU, retaliated by voting Labor out of office in 1929. There is no doubt that the labor movement was racked with internal divisions during the late 1920s. However, it cannot be assumed *ipso facto* that it was these divisions which occasioned McCormack's defeat. The entry of the left wing and communist candidates into the election did not cause the loss of any Labor seats because of vote splitting. However, the defeat of the Speaker, W. Bertram, in Maree together with the defeats of railway minister, Jim Larcombe, in Keppel and labour minister, D.A. Gledson, in Ipswich all occurred in centres of strong ARU influence, suggesting perhaps that the union rank and file did seek vengeance on the parliamentary party. However, an argument against the thesis that it was militant unionists who put out the government concerns the defeat of H.L. Hartley in the central coast seat of Fitzroy. Hartley was the doyen of the militants for it was he who had led the attack on Theodore's wage reduction policies at the 1923 Labor-in-Politics Convention. More recently it was Hartley who had been the most unrestrained in his denunciation of McCormack's handling of the 1927 South Johnstone strike, and was one of the four who had voted against him in caucus. Yet at the election Hartley was defeated in an eighteen per cent swing to the CPN. Furthermore, the militant unionists were located in specific areas and in specific electorates (notably Brisbane and provincial cities such as Rockhampton), yet the swing against Labor was remarkably uniform. (Only six seats went against the pro-CPN swing.) Such a uniformity of swing suggests that Labor's defeat was occasioned not by an aggregation of localized grievances, but was the result of the impact of a more general change of allegiance on the part of the electorate. This switch of allegiance can best be explained in terms of the economic condition of Queensland in the later 1920s.[9]

When the initial shock of the 1929 defeat had passed, the ALP was faced with the problem of whether or not McCormack was to remain as parliamentary leader. McCormack, who was in failing health, solved this problem by tendering his resignation as leader on 27 May 1929. In the subsequent ballot the deputy leader, William Forgan Smith, had an easy victory over David Weir.[10] McCormack then departed for the United Kingdom where, in a speech to a group of Labour MPs, he attacked the railway unions for bringing about the defeat of his government.[11] These comments were not favourably received by the Queensland trade union movement, and the TLC issued a call for McCormack's expulsion from the ALP.[12] However, McCormack's own actions again diffused the issue. On 21 February 1930, he resigned his seat of Cairns and in March resigned as a delegate to the QCE. It was fortunate for the unity of the ALP that McCormack chose to adopt this course of action, for a major dispute over his position in the party, coming so closely upon the 1929 defeat, would have opened up the divisions and animosities of the previous four years.

With McCormack no longer an issue, the new parliamentary leader was keen to respond to the suggestion of the TLC that their executive and that of the ALP meet together to settle any outstanding differences.[13] However, as a consequence of statements made about the PLP by trade union speakers at a public meeting convened to express opposition to the new government's Arbitration Bill, Forgan Smith attempted to suspend all discussions.[14] While he was not successful in this endeavour, any prospect of a "Unity Conference" was shelved indefinitely when the executive committee (the "inner executive") of the QCE announced that as a result of contacts with the executive of the TLC all contentious matters had been settled.[15] In retrospect the decision not to hold an open conference was a wise one, since the unifying influence of the Moore government had not as yet reached out to all sections of the labor movement.

As the Depression deepened, relations between the trade unions and the ALP became more and more harmonious. However, divisions did manifest themselves from time to time. Shortly after the 1929 election the AWU came into open conflict with the ALP member for Gregory, George Pollock. Pollock had been an AWU organizer prior to his entry into Parliament in 1915.

During late 1929 he wrote a series of articles outlining the parlous state of the woollen industry in Queensland. Since the electorate of Gregory was dominated by pastoral activities, Pollock was necessarily concerned with the problems of that industry. However, his suggestion that the cause of these difficulties was the high cost of production, provoked an angry response from the AWU, who, at the time Pollock went into print, were involved in an arbitration case surrounding the question of wages and hours in the woollen industry.[16] Pollock was subsequently summoned before the annual delegates meeting of the AWU and called upon to explain his actions.[17] The delegates were unimpressed with his arguments and voted unanimously to cancel his membership of the union. To incur the displeasure of the AWU could have severely hindered Pollock's future political career. However, the effluxion of time combined with more pressing political issues led to a reconciliation and Pollock was made Speaker on the election of the Forgan Smith government, a post he held until his death in 1939.

Similar success in resolving conflict within the party was evident in relations between the ALP and the Waterside Workers' Federation. Relations between the waterside workers and the McCormack-QCE group were characterized by hatred and bitterness. The sources of these problems were not removed by McCormack's departure from the political scene, and throughout the period of the Moore ministry, the WWF remained outside the ALP. However, non-affiliation created difficulties for the WWF since it was denied representation at ALP conferences and its members could not vote in party pre-selection ballots. This situation encouraged some within the union to lobby for re-affiliation and in January 1932 the union decided to seek admittance to the party provided that the QCE rescind the expulsion of the secretary, Andrew Brown.[18] The Queensland branch of the union had assisted the ALP during the 1931 federal election,[19] and as a result of the re-affiliation decision elected a committee of five to negotiate with the QCE the delicate matters of Brown's expulsion and the payment of accumulated affiliation fees.[20] Despite the support of the party's secretary, Lewis

McDonald, the QCE rejected the WWF's terms for reaffiliation. This rebuff hardened the attitude of those in the WWF who believed that the QCE was under the domination of a clique who did not wish to share power with unions such as themselves.[21] The election of the Labor government in 1932, however, encouraged the WWF again to seek formal links with the governing party and in March 1933 they were finally re-admitted.[22]

Neither the deepening of the Depression nor the activities of the Moore government could, however, affect a reconciliation between the ARU and the ALP. At the 1929 federal election the union softened its previous position and decided to issue a leaflet urging its members to vote for the Labor party.[23] This conversion to parliamentary politics proved to be short lived, and the ARU regarded the problems later encountered by the Scullin government as the result of the mistaken belief that political change could be enacted through parliamentary action alone.[24] With reference to the state ALP, the ARU adhered to its contention that the party remained under the domination of the group that had engineered its expulsion in 1926, viz., the AWU.[25] The ALP did make overtures to the ARU regarding reaffiliation of the union. This approach was part of the general strategy of the QCE to heal the breaches in the labor movement in preparation for the 1932 election. The ARU executive received the overture coldly, and when the matter came before the 1930 state conference of the union, a motion calling for reaffiliation was defeated fourteen votes to two after a very brief debate.[26] Major arguments put forward against the QCE were that the ARU had never voluntarily left the ALP — it had been expelled, and that the union was in no position to pay back affiliation fees.[27] Despite the hostility of the union's executive officers, there developed within the ARU a rank and file movement in favour of rejoining the Labor party. At the February 1931 ARU state council meeting, one delegate moved that the union re-affiliate, but was ruled out of order by the president. A subsequent motion to force the executive to place the question before the rank and file in a referendum lapsed for want of a seconder.[28] However, the Cairns sub-branch of the union ignored these motions and applied to the QCE for separate affiliation. This was refused and the union members were advised to take up party membership via their local branches.[29] As a consequence of these attitudes and decisions, the ARU was to remain outside the ALP until the events leading up to the 1957 split in the party.

While the refusal of the ARU to rejoin the party created some strain within the labor movement, the union had lost the ability to operate as a serious disruptive force in Labor politics. The antagonism between the ARU and its QCE opponents paled into insignificance when compared with the major schisms that were besetting the labor movement in other states. By mid-1931, the Scullin, Lang, Hogan and Hill Labor governments were raked with internecine warfare. Ostensibly the disputes concerned the relative merits of contending economic policies, but were characterized by power struggles and personality clashes of serious dimensions. The disputes reached a crescendo in mid-1931 when New South Wales Premier Jack Lang advanced his alternative to the Premiers' Plan. Space does not permit a detailed analysis of the politics of the "battle of plans", but it must be noted that Lang's plan was the product of his own political ambitions and hatreds, combined with the political situation within the New South Wales Labor government. As Jim Hutchinson has argued: "The Lang Plan was essentially proposed to maintain the support of the labor movement in order to preserve Lang's precarious basis for political primacy in NSW, and at the same time reduce the possibility of threat to his position as leader of the NSW Labor Party."[30] Thus Lang's plan was the product rather than the instigator of factionalism within the New South Wales ALP in the early thirties.

The influence of Langism soon spread beyond the boundaries of its home state. Many disenchanted and dissident Labor members saw in the person of its creator the possibility of salvation from the depths of economic chaos.[31] However, "Langism" meant more than an adherence to a particular economic programme; it represented an act of defiance of the federal executive of the ALP, and inevitably brought its supporters into open conflict with their respective state executives. Fortunately for the unity of the Labor party, Langism never became a serious, disruptive force in Queensland. The state parliamentary party disowned the Lang Plan, and after mid-1931, support for Langism was regarded as political heresy by the Labor party in Queensland. Despite the disapproval of the party's leaders and officials, a Lang Plan organization was formed in Brisbane by a number of Australian Labor party members. A series of branches had also passed motions expressing their support for the Lang Plan. The QCE sent a circular to all state branches informing them that any motions passed in favour of the Lang Plan were to be rescinded forthwith. The QCE threatened to dissolve any branch that did not comply with this directive.[32]

This attitude of the QCE and the QPLP was quite predictable. At a time when the organization was attempting to rebuild in preparation for the 1932 election it was in no mood to tolerate divisive and enervating factionalism. The AWU, now established as the chief reservoir of power in the ALP in Queensland, also determined that the party would adopt a hostile attitude to Lang and his proposals. When Lang first entered Labor politics in New South Wales in 1913, he found the party's executive dominated by the state's largest union, the AWU. After 1923, Lang sought the active support of unions affiliated with the New South Wales Labor Council in an attempt to break the hold of the AWU. The clashes between the Lang-Labor Council faction and the AWU faction rendered internal Labor politics in New South Wales in the early 1920s particularly torrid.[33] The final outcome was decided in Lang's favour, but the battles fought had embroiled both the ALP and AWU federal executives. Lang's political rivalry with Theodore also determined that the Queensland ALP would emerge as an opponent of his proposals. Since Theodore's entry into federal politics via the New South Wales seat of Dalley, Lang had viewed him as a major rival. Theodore, of course, was closely associated with the AWU, both in Queensland and New South Wales, and there is evidence to suggest that the New South Wales premier was eager to destroy Theodore politically and that his advocacy of the Lang Plan was but a part of that campaign.[34] Despite the strong stand taken by the Queensland ALP hierarchy against Langism, the QCE received reports in October 1931 indicating that at least four ALP branch members were actively involved in a pro-Lang organization.[35] As a consequence of further reports these members (V.D. Kearney, W. Mitchell, F. Pforr and J. O'Leary) were dismissed from the executive positions they held in their respective branches. Kearney was a quite prominent ALP member, being secretary of the Enoggera Electorate Executive Committee (EEC) and of the Lilley Federal Divisional Executive (FDE). The QCE was obviously concerned that a man who held such positions in the party, and who had stood as an ALP candidate in the 1926 state election, should so actively defy its rulings, and it instructed Kearney to hand over the books of both bodies to their respective presidents. However, Kearney was reluctant to do so, and the QCE was eventually forced to employ a solicitor in an attempt to recover the books. The QCE then took the step of again writing to all branches informing them that Kearney, Pforr, O'Leary, together with two others, had been expelled from the party because of their continued support of the Lang Plan. The QCE also took the opportunity to point out to the branches the party's official rejection of Langism.[36]

Nevertheless, quite a number of branches were unwilling to acquiesce in the QCE decision and after the Christmas recess eleven branches were given fourteen days to rescind motions they had passed supporting Kearney, and to declare their loyalty to the party.[37] After the expiration of the fourteen-day period, six of the above groups indicated that they were willing to adhere to the QCE's ruling. The failure of the remainder to reply led to their closure and the formation of new branches in their area.[38] In addition to Langite activities in Brisbane, the QCE found it necessary to take disciplinary actions against members in South Johnstone and Toowoomba. The "inner executive" of the QCE took the opportunity to express the opinion that such groups as the Lang planners were merely disruptionists attempting to effect Labor's defeat at the forthcoming election. The tone of the executive's statement reveals a determination that internal factionalism was not going to contribute to a Labor defeat in 1932.[39] However, the above events indicate a degree of support amongst the ALP rank and file for the Lang plan.

Langism also held a certain attraction for some sections of the Queensland trade union movement. In March 1931, a motion was proposed (but defeated) that the Brisbane Trades and Labor Council (TLC) send a telegram to the New South Wales branch of the ALP expressing its support for Eddie Ward, who was contesting the East Sydney by-election on the platform of the New South Wales branch, rather than that of the federal party.[40] The initial meeting to form a rank and file organization to support the economic policies of Jack Lang was held in the Brisbane Trades Hall. This meeting was the consequence of the enthusiasm engendered by Lang when he addressed a public meeting at the Brisbane stadium. After this initital meeting, further gatherings of the Lang group were held at the Trades Hall. On 23 May 1931, two New South Wales politicians, John Lamaro and Senator Arthur Rae, addressed a meeting on Lang's financial schemes. The Shop Assistants Union was particularly active in calling and organizing these meetings,[41] and the WWF invited John Beasley (the leader of the Lang faction in the Federal Parliament) to address their union.[42] Some members of the ARU also expressed support for Langism. Frank Nolan chaired at least one pro-Lang meeting,[43] and Mick O'Brien attempted unsuccessfully to censure the president of the TLC for his public support for Theodore's policies in preference to those of Lang.[44] However, the ARU, despite its hostility towards the ALP and the AWU, was never officially committed to Langism. Secretary Tim Moroney believed that the union would gain little by associating with a particular political party or faction. With these few exceptions, the Queensland trade unions remained loyal to the federal and state executives of the ALP and the 1931 Trade Union Congress passed a resolution deploring the divisive effect the Lang Plan was having on the Australian labor movement.[45]

The dispute over the Lang Plan flared up again at the 1932 Labor-in-Politics Convention, where Kearney appealed against his expulsion from the party. While the debate on a motion to re-admit Kearney was an extremely lengthy one, he received the support of only three branch delegates and two union officials. The unionists (Frank Waters of the APWU and Gordon Brown of the Shop Assistants) were rather lukewarm in their support and were careful not to appear as Langites.[46] Kearney's appeal was rejected by forty-four votes to twenty-two and his subsequent appeal to the federal executive was ruled inadmissable. By the time of the 1932 state election, Langism was a dead issue in Queensland and the two Lang candidates who stood both forfeited their deposits.

An important question is why Langism was unable to command popular, sustained support in Queensland during the Depression. In answering this question one must remember that the Lang Plan was primarily the result, rather than the cause, of the divisions which existed in various sections of the Australian Labor Party in the early thirties. Langism persisted in the states of New South Wales and South Australia only because there were serious divisions affecting the Labor parties there prior to Lang announcing his economic plan in mid-1931. The events surrounding the split between the federal Labor party and the New South Wales branch are too well known to need recounting here, but an examination of Lang Labor in South Australia is interesting because it illustrates why the Lang planners never gained a strong foothoold in Queensland. Don Hopgood has shown that there was a high level of factionalism present in the Labor party in South Australia prior to 1931.[47] The deflationary policies of the Hill Labor government had provoked the anger of the trade unions and large sections of Labor's rank and file. Thus, when Lang announced his plan at the 1931 Premiers' Conference, there existed dissident factions in South Australia who were eager to make use of it in their struggle for control of the Labor party. However, the situation in Queensland was quite different. By June 1931, the Queensland Labor Party was one of the most united in Australia. With no potential power base in the form of a strong group of party dissidents, Langism was destined to be very short-lived in Queensland Labor politics. As well as being denied the preconditions for survival, the Lang planners had other difficulties to face in Queensland. The fact that the parliamentary party was out of office ensured that it would not antagonize any section of the labor movement by legislative action. Also, Forgan Smith was sufficiently astute to express only guarded support for the Premiers' Plan, thereby depriving the Langites of the opportunity of accusing the parliamentary party of being "friends of the money power".

In states where Langism gained a foothold, it did so partly because the dissidents in the party made political capital out of Labor's support for the deflationary Premiers' Plan. For example, the Premiers' Plan caused a most serious split in the Labor party in Victoria, where the premier, E.J. Hogan, was expelled from the party for lending his support to it. When the Premiers' Plan was announced, the Brisbane TLC passed a very strongly worded motion condemning it, and called on the federal party to deal drastically with any ALP members who supported it.[48] Similarly, the QCE declared itself totally opposed to the contents of the plan.[49] Forgan Smith, however, found himself in a difficult position. His personal economic beliefs and a desire not to precipitate divisions in the party determined that he could not wholeheartedly support the plan. On the other hand, Smith knew that if he opposed the plan he could encounter difficulties with its federal and state government supporters should he become state premier. Shrewd compromise solved his dilemma. He announced that the parliamentary party was opposed to the deflationary provisions of the Premiers' Plan and would, if elected in 1932, review the plan and develop a more balanced policy to deal with the economic situation.[50] The party indicated that it still favoured a controlled inflationary policy and argued that while successful in effecting a reduction in the cost of government, the Premiers' Plan was lacking in the measures necessary to restore industry and commerce by reviving the purchasing power of the people.[51] By adopting this policy, Smith placated the party and the trade unions, whose main objection to the Premiers' Plan was that it provided for the reduction of wages and social service benefits, and at the same time ensured that Queensland's subsequent economic policies were not placed out of step with the rest of Australia.

While avoiding the schisms that befell the party elsewhere, the Queensland ALP underwent certain structural changes during the Depression years. The most significant of these was the consolidation of the power and influence of the AWU. As the state's largest union, the AWU had long been the major power base of the ALP. Its size, financial position and the distribution of its membership were all factors which maintained its influence within the party. As a result of the economic collapse, the AWU achieved a position of dominance in the ALP which was not broken until the 1950s. One effect of the Depression was a sharp decline in ALP membership. The Labor party, in 1925, possessed a membership of 9720 spread over 294 branches. By 1932 this had declined to 3144 members in 197 branches.[52] This low branch membership rendered the party more heavily dependent on the AWU infrastructure for organizational support. The AWU was organized on a regional basis (southeast, western, central and northern) and their organization, particularly outside the southeast, often doubled as the ALP organization. At election time AWU officials acted as ALP officials, the AWU car became the ALP car, and canvassers, booth workers and campaigners were drawn heavily from the ranks of the AWU.

This situation predated the Depression, but ALP dependence on the AWU was greatly increased in the early thirties. Power in the ALP was closely related to the number and size of the affiliated unions. The effect of the Depression on the Queensland trade unions assisted the AWU in its bid to achieve total hegemony within the ALP. The number of unions affiliated with the ALP declined from seventy-one in 1926 to fifty-nine in 1935. This ensured that it would be extremely difficult for an anti-AWU coalition to be formed within the party, particularly since the natural leader of such a coalition, the ARU, was outside the ALP. Furthermore, power in the ALP was determined by the size of affiliated unions. Most unions experienced a major loss of membership during the Depression and this reduced their representation at conventions and on the QCE. Because it represented many unskilled workers who were prone to unemployment and because the Moore government abolished the rural award, AWU membership declined by 54 per cent over the period 1927 to 1932, compared with an overall Queensland union membership decline of only 30 per cent.[53] However, between 1932 and 1935, AWU membership increased by 136 per cent compared with the overall union increase of only 42 per cent. This rapid AWU recovery can be partly explained by the Forgan Smith governments' unemployment relief scheme.

On its return to office in 1932, the Labor government retained, virtually intact, the unemployment relief scheme which it inherited from the Moore administration. However, the new government introduced legislation in September 1932 that amended the scheme in certain particulars. A graduated tax scale replaced the flat rate system that provided funds for the unemployment refief fund; the requirement that the unemployed must travel from place to place in order to qualify for rations was abolished; the government decided on a pilot land settlement scheme for unemployed men; and intermittent relief workers were paid basic wage rates. The government also restructured the Bureau of Economics and Statistics as the Bureau of Industry and through the new body encouraged the development of public works in an attempt to absorb the unemployed. This unemployment relief scheme persisted until 1938 when the relief tax was replaced with a development tax and all outstanding relief projects were converted to normal public works.

The government's 1932 decision to place relief workers under the ambit of industrial awards meant that a large number of these workers were required to join unions which were granted preference under the relevant award. Since most of the work was conducted on a rotational basis, a new gang of workers was required to take out union tickets every six or eight weeks. The AWU was the major beneficiary of this scheme since it was the AWU that covered the unskilled type of work carried out under the relief scheme. If the particular relief project was a lengthy one, the AWU was in a position to sell successive teams of relief workers multiple tickets for the one job, thereby boosting the book membership of the union.[54] Other unions which covered workers in the normal employment were unable to benefit in this way, and hence their membership grew much more slowly than the AWU's.

By 1935, AWU membership stood at 53,547 which accounted for 35 per cent of Queensland's unionists. Not only was the AWU the state's biggest union, but also there existed a huge gap between it and the second biggest union, the ARU, which in 1935 had only 6827 members or 13 per cent of the AWU's total. Prior to 1935, the Labor-in-Politics Convention was composed of one delegate for each state electorate plus delegates from unions, based on the formula that unions with a membership ranging from one thousand to three thousand were entitled to one delegate. Unions with a membership in excess of three thousand gained an additional delegate for each three thousand up to a maximum of ten. At the 1932 Convention only two unions were entitled to more than one delegate — the AMIEU earned two delegates and the AWU earned the full quota of ten delegates. The AWU delegates accounted for 40 per cent of the total union representation of tweny-four. When these ten delegates were added to those "branch" delegates who had close AWU connections, the union commanded a large block vote at convention, which in 1932 was made up of a total of seventy-three delegates.

At the 1932 Convention there occurred a major debate on a motion moved by Frank Waters of the APWU that the rules be amended to allow union representation on the following basis:

250 to 500 members = 1 delegate
501 to 750 members = 2 delegates
751 to 1000 members = 3 delegates
1001 to 2000 members = 4 delegates
With an extra delegate for each 1000 up to 16.[55]

Waters argued that the virtue of his formula was that it provided fairer representation for smaller unions. However, the AWU was strong on arithmetic and was aware that, despite the proposed increase in its delegates to sixteen, Waters' scheme involved a major diminution of its relative strength. If Waters' formula was applied to the 1932 Convention, the unions would have been entitled to over sixty delegates, only sixteen of which would have been from the AWU. In 1932, the AWU had 26,862 members which equalled 25 per cent of the total Queensland union membership. Under Waters' proposal the AWU would have been granted credit for fourteen thousand members while the other affiliated unions, most of whose membership ranged from fifteen hundred to three thousand five hundred, would have been entitled to four, five or six delegates each. When the delegates from each of these "small" unions were added together, the AWU would have only 26 per cent of the total union delegation. Since Waters did not advocate any alteration to the branch representation, which in 1932 equalled forty-eight delegates, the balance of power at convention would have been altered very definitely away from the AWU and in the direction of the other unions. While Waters gained strong support from the delegates from the Shop Assistants Union, the PIEUA, the AFULE and the Electrical Trades Union, he was vigorously opposed by the AWU faction. The AWU argued that Waters' motion was anti-democratic in that it disfranchised the larger unions and gave too much power to the representatives of what Clarrie Fallon called "the conglomeration of small unions operating with a purely craft outlook".[56] When the motion was put only sixteen of the seventy-three delegates voted in favour, which was a clear indication of where the numbers lay in 1932. However the maximum number of delegates permitted for one union was increased to twelve which had the effect of further entrenching the AWU in its position of dominance, because it was the only union capable of attaining the full quota of delegates.

The Queensland Central Executive of the ALP was charged with the administration of the party between conventions. The QCE comprised representatives elected from the parliamentarians, convention and the trade unions. A number of attempts were made at the 1932 convention to amend the rules governing the QCE but all were defeated. A study of the method of union representation on the QCE again reveals a pro-AWU bias. Affiliated unions were not entitled to a delegate unless they had at least two thousand members and in 1932 only sixteen Queensland unions (not all of which were affiliated to the ALP) fell into that category. Small unions of fewer than two thousand members were grouped to elect generally three delegates. To gain a second delegate a union required five thousand members which excluded all but three unions in 1932 (one of which was not affiliated to the ALP). However, unions with over twenty thousand members (of which there was only one — the AWU) received five delegates. The results of this formula were obvious when the past-convention QCE assembled on 26 August 1932. Of the nineteen members present eleven had close connections with the AWU. When the meeting chose the party's executive committee, no ballot was required for any of the eight positions decided and of those elected, only S.J. Bryan (the TLC president), and R.J. Carroll (AEU secretary) were not closely associated with the AWU, but represented Trades Hall unions.[57]

A similar pattern of AWU domination was found in the composition of the first Forgan Smith government. When the caucus completed its election for the nine-man ministry six of the successful candidates possessed a strong AWU background. This result reflected the influence the AWU had attained in the parliamentary party by its judicious use of the plebiscite system of candidate selection. The plebiscite method allowed not only ALP branch members but also members of affiliated trade unions to vote in pre-selection ballots. Since the total branch membership of the party in 1932 stood at only 3144 the potential influence of the unions was considerable. The AWU was placed at a great advantage compared with the other affiliated unions because its large membership was spread over wide areas of the state whereas the other unions had their members concentrated only in particular localities. Despite its recruitment of urban relief workers, the AWU was essentially a rural union, a fact which greatly aided its pre-selection strategy in a state where 68 per cent of the electorates in 1932 were situated outside the metropolitan area. In addition to these natural advantages, the AWU made great use of the "facsimile ballot" system. Prior to each ALP plebiscite a fascimile of the ballot paper was printed in the AWU paper, the *Worker* (a similar privilege was extended to the AMIEU). AWU members who were entitled to vote but could not reach a booth on polling day merely filled out the facsimile ballot, affixed one of the perforated voting slips which were attached to all AWU union tickets and posted the vote to the returning officer. The system of facsimile ballots was a constant source of tension within the ALP, and there were regular accusations of malpractice on the part of AWU officials who were alleged to have filled in ballots for members whom they knew would not vote in a particular plebiscite.[58] However, these complaints had negligible affect, since by 1932 the AWU/QCE coalition that was to dominate Labor politics until the early 1950s was formerly established. The coalition was maintained and nurtured by a complex system of patronage and trade-offs. In return for its organizational support and large financial donations,[59] the AWU received heavy representation on the QCE and in Labor ministries, favourable industrial awards and appointment of its officials to the industrial courts. (The AWU secretary, W.J. Riordan, was appointed to the re-established Industrial Court in December 1933). In the process the ALP became heavily dependent on the AWU.

In a frank editorial in the *Worker* in 1949, the AWU aptly summed up its relationship with the ALP over the previous twenty years:

> Whence, then, comes the power of the Labor Movement in Queensland? Where is the basic strength — the resiliency which has enabled Labor Governments to occupy the Treasury benches in this State ever since 1915 with the exception of three years from 1929 to 1932 . . . . The answer is the Australian Workers' Union . . . . The Australian Workers' Union provides the network of organisation, its secretaries and organisers, representatives and rank and file are everlastingly preaching the gospel of Labor in the places where votes count most . . . . With few exceptions every one of the huge membership in Queensland . . . is a disciple of Labor and where A.W.U. members do not participate directly in A.L.P. acitivities their unions supplies much of the funds to fight political campaigns.[60]

To suggest that this close relationship was due solely to the Depression would be a distortion. The AWU had played a leading role in Labor politics for many years prior to 1929. However, the events of the early 1930s confirmed and strengthened the AWU-ALP alliance in a way which rendered any opposition ineffectual. What further entrenched the AWU in its position of power was the blow that the Depression dealt the other unions. Had the ARU been capable of recovering from the defeats of the late 1920s and emerged as a leader of a viable anti-AWU union faction, the latter's dominance of the ALP may have been checked. Yet it was not until the late 1940s that the smaller unions had recovered sufficiently to commence a challenge to AWU hegemony.

Because the ALP was dominated by a union which was committed to moderate social and industrial reform through Parliament and the arbitration system, the Depression had little lasting impact on the party's belief system. The economic crisis did not lead to an upsurge of revolutionary thought or action within the ALP. Labor's newspaper, the *Daily Standard*, often engaged in flights of "rhetorical socialism". It believed, for example, that the capitalist system had been shaken to its foundations,[61] and that the Australian people were turning inexorably to socialist solutions.[63] Yet the paper displayed a contradictory attitude to the methods needed to establish a socialist system. At times it was prepared to condone open rebellion,[64] but on other occasions counselled against any attempts to stage a general strike to overthrow the capitalist system.[64] Such ideological confusion was common to many sections of the labor movement during the Depression and necessarily acted as a restraint on the development of avowedly socialist policies within the ALP.[65]

The 1932 Labor-in-Politics Convention witnessed a major debate on Labor's socialization objective. Some members of the ALP had obviously been impressed by the performance of the Socialization Units within the New South Wales ALP and moved the following motions at the convention:

> (1) That a definite review be made of the fundamental plank of the party, viz., Socialization of means of production, distribution and exchange. Either it is practicable to put same

into operation or, alternatively, it is to be an instruction to the political party to evolve plans for its full operation within two years of gaining office.

(2) That political candidates for election seek a mandate from the people for complete socialization by definitely advocating same from all public platforms at next election.

(3) That socialization of industry be placed on the ALP Fighting Platform and that a Socialization Committee by formed for educational purposes, and publication of literature, with power to circularise all ALP branches with same.[66]

These motions attracted some support from branch delegates but were vigorously opposed by the Forgan Smith/Fallon group. Forgan Smith argued that it was naive to think that there were a large number of dedicated socialists in Queensland, and that Labor would get little support if it campaigned solely on the socialization objective.[67] Smith suggested that the party should do more to educate the public in the tenets of socialism because "before we can achieve Socialism we must have a majority of the people already converted to Socialism, capable of thinking as Socialists and understanding Socialist theory."[68] The AWU secretary, Clarrie Fallon, felt that the Labor party was progressing steadily towards the attainment of the socialist objective and that to hasten the process would be to invite disastrous electoral consequences. David Riordan (the federal member for Kennedy) also reminded delegates that "the Labor party is not a revolutionary party; it is an evolutionary party".[69] In the face of such opposition the motions were soundly defeated and convention adopted an amendment moved by Forgan Smith that the principles contained in the objective be affirmed.

With the major repository of socialist militancy, the ARU, excluded from the ALP there was no organized alternative to the ideology of moderate social democracy adhered to by the dominant faction. Pragmatic considerations were strongly in evidence. As a last attempt to stave off electoral defeat the CPN attempted, in 1932, to associate Forgan Smith with the economic theories of Jack Lang. As a consequence Smith was determined that his party would not play into Moore's hands by adopting radical or "irresponsible" proposals on the eve of the election. When Smith was elected in 1932 he led a party whose ideological consensus favoured social and economic amelioration via the established consitutional methods. Queensland Labor's commitment to reformism was left virtually unchanged by the experience of the depression years.

The Depression had an appreciably different affect on the Labor party in Queensland when compared with the party in other states. After the conservative interregnum of 1929-32, the ALP continued in office in Queensland until the split in 1957. Obviously there are explanations for this long run of government which bear little relationship to the events of the Depression. However, the memory of the Moore government remained an important electoral advantage for the ALP long after Moore himself had sunk into oblivion. Similarly, the unity achieved by the party during its brief term of opposition stood it in good stead throughout the 1930s and 40s and was only broken by the traumatic events of the 1950s.

NOTES

1. M. Gough, et al., *Queensland: Industrial Enigma* (Melbourne: Melbourne University Press, 1964), p. 8.
2. *Queensland Year Book* 2, 1938.
3. See the governor's speech to Parliament, *QPD* 147 (28 July 1926): 5, CXLIX 24 August 1927, p. 2; and Department of Agricultural and Stock Reports, *QPP* II (1926) :401, 409; *QPP* II, (1927); *QPP* II (1928) :295 and *QPP* II (1929) :581; AWU Annual Delegates Meeting, *Western District Report* (Brisbane, January 1928), p. 17.
4. *Labour Report*, no. 20 (1929), p. 115.
5. Trades and Labor Council to home secretary, 15 November 1927; Notes of Deputation of Waterside Workers Federation to home secretary, 7 December 1927, item 47/1615 COL/300, QSA; and *Report AWU Annual Delegates Meeting* (Brisbane, January 1929), p. 26.
6. *Brisbane Courier*, 6 May 1929.
7. D. Butler, *The Canberra Model* (Melbourne: Cheshire, 1977), p. 89.
8. C.A. Bernays, *Our Seventh Political Decade* (Sydney: Angus & Robertson, 1931), p. 55; *Advocate*, 15 June 1929, p. 1; *Headlight*, 5 July 1929, p. 1; Interview with Frank Waters, 17 June 1975, transcript, p. 1; Interview

with Senator Bill Morrow, 21 August 1974, transcript, p. 1; Interview with Jack Read, 8 September 1975, transcript, p. 5; E.M. Higgins, "Queensland Labor: Trade Unionists versus Premiers", *HSANZ* 9: no. 34 (May 1960) :140; K.H. Kennedy, "The Public Life of William McCormack" (Ph.D. thesis, James Cook University, 1973), p. 384.

9. A more detailed analysis of the 1929 election is contained in the author's doctoral thesis: "Politics and Government in Queensland During the Great Depression 1925-1935".
10. Caucus minutes, 27 May 1929, p. 381.
11. *Worker*, 11 September 1929.
12. TLC minutes, 16 October 1929.
13. Ibid., 27 May 1929; QCE minutes, 2 December 1929.
14. QCE minutes, 13 December 1929.
15. Ibid., 13 May 1930.
16. *Worker*, 6 November 1929.
17. *Report AWU Annual Delegates Meeting* (Brisbane, January 1930), p. 24f.
18. WWF minutes, 6 January 1932, p. 95, E213/10, ANU Archives.
19. Ibid., December 1931, p. 79.
20. Ibid., 10 February 1932, p. 118.
21. Ibid., 2 March 1932, p. 141.
22. Ibid., 29 March 1933, p. 285.
23. ARU State Council minutes, 26 September 1929, p. 121.
24. *Advocate*, 16 March 1931.
25. Ibid., 15 February 1931; and 15 February 1932.
26. *Report ARU 12th Conference*, Brisbane, August 1930, p. 60.
27. *Advocate*, 15 February 1930.
28. ARU State Council minutes, February 1931, p. 72; and 6 November, 1931, p. 113.
29. QCE minutes, 13 April 1931.
30. J. Hutchinson, "The Lang Plan and Its Origin" (Unpublished paper, Lang Seminar, Macquarie University, Sydney, 1976), p. 13.
31. For a discussion of Lang's charismatic qualities see M. Dixon, *Greater than Lenin?: Lang and Labor 1916-1932*, Melbourne Political Monograph no. 2 (Melbourne: University of Melbourne, 1976), chaps. 1 and 2.
32. QCE minutes, 8 June 1931.
33. Dixon, *Greater than Lenin?*, p. 69f; and J. Hagan, "J.T. Lang and the Trade Unions" (Unpublished paper, Lang Seminar, Macquarie University, Sydney, 1976) pp. 1-3.
34. Hutchinson, "The Lang Plan", p. 8f.
35. QCE minutes, 7 October 1931.
36. Ibid., 16 October 1931.
37. Ibid., 4 February 1932.
38. Ibid., 22 February 1932.

39. McDonald to secretary of Cairns ALP, 28 October 1931, QCE minutes, Brisbane.
40. TLC minutes, 4 March 1931.
41. *Official Report of the Fourteenth Labor-in-Politics Convention*, 1932, p. 89.
42. WWF minutes, 2 September 1931, E213/10, ANU Archives.
43. F. Nolan, *You Pass This Way Only Once* (Brisbane: Colonial Press, 1974), p. 67.
44. TLC minutes, 10 June 1931.
45. *Official Report of the Eighth Queensland Trade Union Congress*, 1931, p. 12.
46. *Labor-in-Politics Convention*, 1932, pp. 95 and 99.
47. D. Hopgood, "Lang Labor in South Australia", in "The Great Depression in Australia", ed. R. Cooksey, *Labour History* 17 (1970) :161f.
48. TLC minutes, 10 June 1931.
49. QCE minutes, 12 June 1931.
50. *QPD* CLVIII (24 June 1931) :29; CLXIII (17 August 1933) :67.
51. Ibid. CLXI (16 August 1932) :4.
52. *Headlight*, 5 February 1932.
53. All union membership figures are taken from *The ABC of Queensland Statistics.*
54. Waters, Interview p. 4; Interview with Michael Healy, 13 May 1975, p. 10.
55. *Official Report of the Fourteenth Labor-in-Politics Convention*, 1932, p. 82.
56. Ibid., p. 84.
57. QCE minutes, 26 August 1932. The result of the ballot was:
President: W.H. Demaine, nominated by Messrs. W. Forgan Smith and G. Crooks — re-elected unopposed.
Vice President: W.J. Riordan, nominated by Messrs. J.C. Lamont and E. Rusling — re-elected unopposed.
Secretary: L. McDonald, nominated by W. Forgan Smith and R.J. Carroll — re-elected unopposed.
Executive Committee: Messrs R.J. Carroll, S.J. Bryan, W. Forgan Smith, M.P. Hynes, J.C. Lamont, were nominated and re-elected unopposed.
58. Healy, Interview, p. 19.
59. An accurate picture of ALP finances for the period under discusion is virtualy impossible to obtain. However the AWU's size determined that its contribution in capitation fees would be a large one. In addition, the AWU had the financial resources to make large donations to party election funds. For example, the AWU gave £2000 to the 1926 fund which amounted for 30 per cent of the total (*Daily Standard*, 15 April 1926). The union regularly made donations of £500 to municipal and federal campaigns. This was at a time when most other affiliated unions found it difficult to donate more than £25 to election funds (RTWU, Board of Control minutes, 23 July 1934, p. 124).

60. *Worker*, 24 January 1949.
61. *Daily Standard*, 1 January 1932.
62. Ibid., 9 September 1931.
63. Ibid., 3 May 1930.
64. Ibid., 14 September 1932.
65. Les Louis, *Trade Unions and the Depression: A Study of Victoria 1930-1937* (Canberra: Australian National University Press, 1968), pp. 30ff.
66. *Labor-in-Politics Convention*, 1932, p. 9f.
67. Ibid., p. 10.
68. *Daily Standard*, 12 January 1932.
69. Ibid.

21 The Protestant Labour Party

S.K. Fox

Catholics in Australia have always had an affinity for the Labor party, and the economic and social factors which supported the connection had been considerably strengthened by the ALP's split over conscription during World War I. The close and long standing Catholic-Labor alliance does much to explain the absence of a specifically Catholic party, but then neither have the Protestant parties formed on various occasions been conspicuously successful. Only three have managed to elect a candidate, the most recent in 1938, when G.A. Morris of the Protestant Labour Party won Kelvin Grove in the Queensland Legislative Assembly.

The demand for state aid for church schools has been the biggest single factor causing and perpetuating conflict between religious groups in the political sphere. The Education Act 1875 had abolished state aid and direct religious education in state schools, but the system of Catholic education survived and grew, supported by the provision of low-cost staff from religious orders and the readiness of Catholics to finance the system with fees and donations. During the Depression, the system came under increasing financial strains, and at the Australian Catholic Education Congress in 1936, the decision was taken to set up the Catholic Taxpayers' Association (CTA) to seek a remedy. In May 1937, the campaign was launched in Catholic churches throughout Australia; in Queensland the counter-attack came immediately from the Queensland Council of Churches and the United Protestant Association (UPA) formed the previous year. Within a few weeks the political parties were drawn into the debate. On 14 June, the acting premier, Percy Pease, declared that there could be no question of state aid to denominational schools from the Labor government. The next day, the leader of the opposition, E.B. Maher of the Country party, himself a Catholic, stated that although he had great sympathy for those parents who wished to have their children educated in demoninational schools, his opinion was that as approximately 70 per cent of the people of Queensland wished to retain the existing system of secular education and subsidies to demoninational schools would result in the deterioration and eventual disappearance of the state school system, the Country party could not support state aid.

Although the CTA, Archbishop James Duhig and the premier, Forgan Smith, issued statements to the effect that state aid would not become an issue in the state election due in the first half of 1938, the matter was already out of their hands. The archbishop tried to still the controversy by asking Catholics not to write to the press on the subject, and the matter did drop out of the newspapers for a time, only to be revived when the UPA called on Protestants to vote only for Protestants at the federal elections in October 1937. The event which really determined that sectarianism would be an issue, indeed the principal issue, of the state election was the formation on 8 December 1937 of the Protestant Labour Party.

The party's first statement brought together a number of Protestant grievances, including the belief that Catholics were coming to dominate the public service, the one source of job security in a state which had experienced massive unemployment and where many men were still on relief. The succession of four Catholic Labor premiers before Forgan Smith, and the fact that the current cabinet, although led by a Presbyterian, contained a majority of Catholics, had already convinced many Protestants that Queensland was being taken over by the church working through the Labor party. The Protestant Labour Party developed the theme of pointing to the fact that while Catholics comprised only 19.2 per cent of the population, in caucus there were twenty-seven Catholics and only sixteen Protestants, and complaining that the claim for state aid disregarded the wishes of Queensland and repeated Labor-in-Politics Convention decisions on the subject.[1]

Many of the Protestant Labour Party's first members were previously ALP supporters, but some of them had also been members of the the UPA which had not previously formulated a specific platform for political action. The UPA insisted from the beginning that it had no official links with the Protestant Labour Party, claiming that it supported all Protestant candidates regardless of party affiliations and under its consitution could not ally itself with any political party. Nevertheless, some of the Protestant Labour Party's candidates in 1938 claimed to be backed by the UPA, and the one successful candidate, G.A. Morris, maintained that the UPA had approached him and encouraged him to stand.[2] The list of Protestant candidates produced by the UPA were all Protestant Labour Party or United Australia Party (UAP), plus one Social Crediter. Although the Protestant Labour Party instructed its supporters not to exercise their contingent votes, for they could not support the ALP without violating the party's anti-Catholic principles nor the UAP without violating their Labor principles, the UPA's list reinforced the suspicion that Protestant Labour was both sectarian and anti-Labor.

The party's policies emerged gradually and a full formal platform was not issued until 18 August 1938, following the state election. However, a week after its formation, the executive committee set out the objects of the party in which it appeared that an effort had been made to please everyone except Catholics, and even in this regard its members claimed that they did not mind Catholic action organizations fighting for their own people provided they had only a "fair share" in the control of the country, that is 20 per cent. The first object listed was "The maintenance of Protestantism in Queensland, because it is recognized that once Queensland ceases to be Protestant she ceases to be the home of free men." Further down, items 11 and 12 forbade state aid and religious preference in state employment, but most of the objects were unexceptional commitments to industrial conditions and development which could have come from any party.

On 19 January 1938, the first public meeting was held in the Albert Hall, Brisbane, and a few more policies were added including making it an offence to cast doubt on the validity of a marriage conducted according to state law, i.e., a secular ceremony, and to repeal the recent amendment to the Local Authorities Act which had exempted church buildings from local rates. But, again recognizing its Labor antecendents, a number of policy items referred to relief work. Italian immigration was a subject of considerable interest in Queensland at the time; on 24 March 1938, the UPA forwarded a resolution to the prime minister, J.A. Lyons, opposing the influx of undesirable Italians into north Queensland, while the Protestant Labour Party sought a quota on the number permitted to enter the state and a requirement that all immigrants learn English within two years of arrival or be deported. (At the 1941 Labor-in-Politics Convention at Southport, Forgan Smith stated that he had been approached to amend the state's land laws to give Italians equal rights, but had refused because the ALP recognized the danger of gathering a population that lacked the background that the natives of the country and British subjects in general were likely to have.)

The five competing parties gave their policy speeches on 9-12 March; all were pre-occupied with the problems of relief work and getting the economy going again. The policies put forward by the UAP leader, H.M. Russell, most closely resembled the Protestant Labour Party's in that both were very generalized and piecemeal, but the latter managed to steal a march on the ALP by adopting the forty-hour week, a matter on which Forgan Smith had been rather cautious and suggested merely collaboration with the Commonwealth to introduce the shorter working week when it could be done without too much difficulty. In his policy speech delivered in the electorate of Ithaca, the Protestant Labour Party leader, G.S. Webb, attacked certain ALP actions which he claimed were opposed to the best interests of the people of Queensland: refusing to endorse UPA members in ALP plebiscites, exempting church property from rates (which he said had cost the Brisbane City Council alone some £140,000), allowing hotels to disregard trading hours, and encouraging racing. The issue of the *Protestant Clarion*, which reported Webb's speech, added its own accusations: 75 per cent of the public service and the police force were Catholics and

Catholics received 75 per cent of the benefit of relief spending.[3] Its editorial attacked Hanlon, Webb's opponent in the electorate, as the effective leader of the government and a pillar of the church.

Archbishop Duhig attempted to reply to these charges by declaring, and offering to repeat on oath, that he had never known of the existence of any undue influence on the government by the hierarchy or priesthood, and denied that he had ever given any direction to any group of Catholics or individual as to how they should vote.[4] At the Trades and Labour Council meeting on 20 April a letter from the Australian Builders Laborers Federation requested that the government be asked to investigate the allegations concerning favouritism in employment and promotions in government institutions and into the charges of influence on the government by the hierarchy, but the proposal was rejected on the recommendation of the executive.

Press reports of Protestant Labour Party campaign meetings describe them as well attended, but noisy. On occasions brawls and scuffles broke out, and Webb, whose attacks on the clergy were particularly outspoken, often had to be escorted by plain-clothes police. After two or more serious incidents, only approved persons were admitted to meetings, and at one stage the party considered the formation of a "Protestant Army". It had been expected that the election would be held in May, the usual month for state elections, but on 25 February, Fogan Smith announced that the polling day would be 2 April. It is likely that the decision was taken to reduce the Protestant Labour Party's opportunities to organize and spread its message, and its success in fielding twenty-three candidates, none of whom lost their deposits, within four months of the party's formation, suggests that a few more weeks might have made its intervention more damaging to the ALP's chances. The Labor party would have had to lose sixteen seats to go out of office; in the event it lost only three, one each to the Country party, the UAP, and the Protestant Labour Party.

The Protestant Labour Party contested fifteen seats in Brisbane; in two (Ithaca and Kelvin Grove) it polled more than one-third of the votes, in another two (Baroona and Nundah) more than a quarter, and in a further five (Buranda, Enoggera, Kurilpa, Merthyr and Wynnum) more than a fifth. Its performance in eight country seats, mainly provincial cities, was not quite so impressive: two (Gympie and Townsville) better than a quarter, one more (Cairns) better than a fifth. Two questions may be asked in an attempt to identify the party's voters: where did the votes come from, and under the non-compulsory contingent voting system then prevailing in the state where did their preferences go? An answer to the first is complicated by the strong showing made by Social Crediters at the previous state election, but a rough estimate is that the Protestant Labour vote came predominantly from the ALP rather than the opposition in ratios generally between 3:1 and 2:1, subject to a few exceptions. One was South Brisbane where the sitting member, V.C. Gair, lost 18 per cent of his 1935 vote and the opposition candidate only 2 per cent. As to the destination of Protestant Labour contingent votes, these were counted in only ten electorates, and in only two of those was there a clear-cut distribution between ALP and UAP: 9.0 per cent to the ALP in South Brisbane and 7.6 per cent in Merthyr. Elsewhere the Protestant Labour vote was masked by the distribution of Social Credit and other votes, but it would appear that a typical ALP share was 20 per cent of the Protestant Labour contingent votes. Thus it is indisputable that the Protestant Labour Party provided a vehicle for transferring normal Labor votes to the established anti-Labor parties, although the impact was mitigated by the non-compulsory expression of preferences so that only about one-half of Protestant Labour voters cast contingent second preferences. In the two most exciting contests where Protestant Labour had the best chance of winning the seat from the sitting ALP member, in Ithaca, Hanlon received only 7.5 per cent of UAP contingent votes but had a sufficient margin on first preferences to beat Webb, while in Kelvin Grove, Frank Waters, who received only 8.4 per cent of the UAP contingent vote, was overtaken and lost his seat to Morris. No doubt the experience of 1938 prepared the ground for the ALP decision to abandon contingent voting and retun to first-past-the-post which followed the loss of Cairns at a by-election in 1941.

After 2 April, public interest in the Protestant Labour Party was kept alive by a series of court cases and by the presence of Morris in the Legislative Assembly where he was the only member on the cross-benches. Two of the court cases were relatively trivial: an alleged assault on Morris' campaign director and a civil suit against Morris which acquired a political flavour when Morris claimed that it was politically motivated. The other two cases were more significant and involved state ministers. In Townsville, police proceeded against the Protestant Labour candidate under the Vagrants Act for distributing a circular containing insulting words — it alleged that the ALP secretary for labour and industry, M.P. Hynes, had scabbed in 1911. He was fined £20 and appealed unsuccessfully to the Supreme Court. More sensational still was Webb's election petition against Hanlon which alleged intimidation of voters, publication of false statements, issue of an unsigned pamphlet, removal of the ballot boxes to the Treasury on election night, and technical defects in counting. The tribunal judge found for Webb on the pamphlet and on isolated incidents of intimidation, but decided that he would not declare the election void because of illegal practices for that would have the effect of preventing Hanlon standing again for three years and he had acted under extreme provocation given by Webb and his supporters who attacked him on religious grounds. The Full Court found 2-1 that the Tribunal had been wrong in declaring Hanlon not duly elected, on the ground that an election could not be upset for an isolated breach of the law. Webb then took the case to the High Court where Hanlon's application to have the appeal set aside was granted, the point being that the matter was not one constitutionally for the High Court to intervene. The protracted litigation kept the Protestant Labour Party's affairs in the public eye for a year.

In the Legislative Assembly, Morris was a frequent and effective speaker, acting as a champion of the underdog especially when this gave an opportunity to attack the government for sectarian bias. As evidence of the favouritism shown to Catholics, he claimed that fifty-six of the eight-two teachers recruited by the Department of Public Instruction in 1937 were Catholics, as were twenty-six of the thirty-two police trainees then in barracks; motormen on the tramways were being notified that their rates were in arrears, yet Archbishop Duhig who, he claimed, owed £10,555 was not proceeded against. Notwithstanding his hostility to the Labor government, Morris insisted that he was still a supporter of the labor movement and believed in Labor legislation.

Conflict between the two strands, Protestant and Labor, was to cause the party's rapid decline. As early as October 1938 the *Protestant Clarion* warned that the election had shown the dangers in a divided Protestant vote, but the warning was not heeded. Sometime before August 1939, a split occurred in the Protestant Labour Party, the reasons for which are now obscure. One suggestion is that it was occasioned by a dispute over party finances, another that some members wished to drop the word "Labour" from the party's name to widen its appeal, a third that there were accusations that some of the party's candidates and officials were not Protestants. The first evidence of the split was a report that the new Protestant party was considering contesting the next Brisbane municipal election.

The Protestant Labour Party had already won two seats on the City Council at by-elections: Wynnum on 1 October 1938 and Baroona on 16 November. It also contested two of the four Legislative Assembly by-elections held on 27 May 1939, running second to the ALP in both. At the municipal elections on 27 April 1940, the party contested the mayoral election and two wards. The Protestant Labour candidate for Lord Mayor was Henry Bond, secretary of the Queensland Government Professsional Officers Association, who had been refused endorsement for the ALP plebiscite for Windsor in 1938 and subsequently stood as an Independent Labor candidate. The Protestant candidate was Webb who had moved over to the new party. Both lost their deposits in an election which was a landslide for J.B. Chandler of the Citizens' Municipal Organization. The Protestant Labour Party almost made one brief excursion into federal politics by contesting the Griffith by-election on 20 May 1939. Its candidate, Everett Graham who had become president after Webb's defection, polled well with 27.8 per cent of the primary vote, and over two-thirds of his preferences went to the UAP candidate who missed election by only eight votes. The close result was further confirmed for those who viewed the party as a close ally of anti-Labor forces.

The last election in which it figured was the 1941 state election. Its organization had run down badly, its financial resources had been exhausted by the series of electoral contests, while several leading members, including Morris and Graham, were in the armed forces. Morris offered again for Kelvin Grove but as an Independent; the UAP resolved that it would not oppose Morris as he was serving, and had two sons serving overseas, and had given an assurance that he would stand as an Independent. However, an Independent UAP candidate ran against him and polled eight votes more than Morris; the ALP candidate regained the seat with an absolute majority. Three endorsed candidates stood in provincial cities; in each case no candidates nominated from the opposition and thus it is difficult to say much about the remaining strength of the Protestant Labour appeal save that it does not seem to have increased the normal anti-Labor vote in those electorates by very much.

After the 1941 election, no mention was made of the Protestant Labour Party which simply faded away. One explanation would be that in wartime it was not considered good form to foster sectarian differences. Another might be that once the party had failed to achieve any solid power or influence, many of its supporters, including the more active, drifted back to the parties from which they had originally come. One aldermanic candidate recalled that the most faithful members had been women, but even the social side of the party ceased to function after the 1941 election. (It had been the first political party to provide meals for servicemen, and held dances for them at party headquarters.) It has always been difficult for minor parties to establish themselves in Australia, especially when they lacked the support of substantial interest groups, and the militant brand of

Protestantism advocated by the UPA and the two political parties, Protestant Labour and Protestant, would have been too strong to bring the Protestant churches into direct and open association with the political activities. Whatever the explanation, the life of the Protestant Labour Party was brief, less than four years. It had arrived on the Queensland scene with a bang, but passed from it without even a whimper.[5]

Appendix A
Labor's Policy towards Religious or Other Bodies

Having regard to Labor's well-known and long-established claim for the right of every individual to absolute freedom of conscience and action in relation to religious beliefs, the Queensland Branch of the Australian Labor Party hereby declares that no applicant for membership in the Party should be refused such membership, nor should any member of the Party be expelled from such membership, merely because of his or her membership in or association with any other body which is, or is understood to be, religious or denominational body, provided that such religious or denominational body is not party-political in character or activity, or subject to, or connected with any other body which is party-political in character or activity.

Ample provision is contained in the Constitution and General Rules of the Party for dealing with applicants for membership who, in the opinion of a majority of the members of a Branch, desire to join the Party for subversive reasons or purposes of disintegration. Such applicants should be refused membership in the Party.

Members of the Party who are believed by a majority of the members of their Branch to be using their membership detrimentally to the Party's welfare can likewise be dealt with under its Constitution and General Rules. They should be expelled from membership in the Party.

Any rejected applicant for membership in the Party and any member expelled from the Party has, within the Party's Constitution and General Rules, the right of appeal against such rejection or expulsion.

The Labor Movement stands for Freedom of Thought and Liberty of Organization. Labor is not subject to any religious dictation or denominational influence, and it will not dictate to nor will it dominate anyone in relation to religious beliefs.

The Labor Movement is non-sectarian and non-denominational. It welcomes to its ranks all those men and women who subscribe to its policy and programme in the interests of community welfare without any mental reservations.

By authority of Queensland Central Executive Australian Labor Party.

R.J. Carroll, Secretary.

*Leaflet held by Australian Labor Party, Labor House, Brisbane: Issued July 1938

Appendix B
Constitution of the Protestant Labour Party

(1) The name of the party is the Protestant Labour Party.

(2) Membership shall consist of bona fide Protestants of the age of 16 and over, who sign the party's pledge; but so that no person shall be deemed a member unless and until his application has been accepted by a branch of the State electoral district in which he resides, provided that if at the date of application there is no branch in that district, the approval of the Executive committee shall be substituted for the acceptance by the branch — the vigilance committee in each branch being the final arbiter as to admission to the branch.

(3) Administration — The party shall consist of (a) Branches; (b) Executive Committee; (c) Management Committee; (d) Protestant Labour Women's Auxiliary.

(a) Branches — Subject to approval of the Executive Committee in writing in any state electoral district in Queensland, any seven (7) persons who have signed the party pledge, may form a branch. Branches shall appoint their own officers and conduct their own domestic business subject to this constitution. Each branch shall have a vigilance committee.

(b) Executive Committee — Shall consist of not more than thirty members including 3 members of the P.L. Women's Auxiliary. The Executive Committee shall be appointed annually by conference. Vacancies that may occur in the Executive Committee shall be filled by the Executive Committee from time to time (i.e. appointment not election) — Quorum 9.

(c) Management Committee shall consist of not more than 9

members including President, Secretary and Treasurer: Shall be appointed from and by the Executive Committee — Quorum 5.

(d) P.L. Women's Auxiliary shall be subject to this Constitution and to the rules from time to time, authorized by the Executive Committee for the governing thereof: Shall be financial members of the P.L.P.

(4) Control of the Party: by the Executive Committee which shall exercise its control through the Management Committee, which shall report to the Executive Committee once each month.

(5) Vacation of Office: The office of a member of the Executive Committee shall ipso facto be vacated if a member of such committee absent himself from 3 consecutive committee meetings without tendering an apology which shall subsequently be accepted by the Executive Committee. Any member of the Management Committee ceasing to be a member of the Executive Committee shall automatically cease to be a member of the Management Committee.

(6) Candidates for any Federal, State or Municipal election shall be selected from members of the party of not less than 6 months standing, by the branches in the electorates concerned, provided that the nominations of candidates be in the hands of the responsible authority 3 months before any plebiscite, and that any necessary plebiscite be taken 3 months before the date of an election.

(7) Funds: The annual membership fee shall be 2/- per male member and 1/- per female member of which sums 1/3 rd shall be paid to the Executive Committee and 2/3 rd to the concerned branch. A general fund shall be established under the control of the Executive Committee. The signed pledge form duplicate receipt and 1/3 rd capitation fees to be forwarded together at the end of each month to the General Secretary of the Party.

(8) Publicity as to policy shall be under the absolute control of the Executive Committee.

(10) Badge: A triangular badge was adopted with a red centre containing the initials P.L.P., with gold borders containing the words "Liberty, Eternal Vigilance".

(11) Conferences of Delegates from branches, shall meet annually in the month of August, where and when to be decided by the Executive Committee.

(a) No councillor, alderman or member of Parliament shall be a delegate at convention. They may address the conference, at its request.
(b) Delegates to conference must vote according to instructions from their respective branches.
(c) The branches in each State electorate shall collectively be entitled to send to conference 3 delegates. Votes at conference may be given personally or by proxy, provided no person shall be appointed a proxy who is not a member of the party and that no person shall hold more than one proxy.
(d) The instrument appointing a proxy shall be deposited with the Secretary of the Party not less than 4 days prior to the date of the conference and in default of being so deposited will not become operative.
(e) The Conference shall have the power to decide the constitution of the party to revise the platform and to do all other things necessary to advance the interests of the Party.
(f) Suggestions for the agenda of Conference shall be forwarded by branches to the Secretary of the Party 4 months prior to the holding of conference and a copy of the agenda paper shall be submitted to the branches at least 2 months prior to the holding of conference. All suggestions by branches must be submitted by conference.

(12) No change shall be made in the constitution or name of the Party without the matter being submitted to all branches for discussion and approval.

NOTES

1. *Courier-Mail*, 9 December 1937.
2. Ibid., 2 April 1938.
3. *Protestant Clarion,* 17 March 1938.
4. *Courier-Mail,* 26 March 1938.
5. For a fuller account, see S.K. Young, "The Protestant Labour Party" (B.A. thesis, University of Queensland, 1971).

22 The Expulsion of George Cuthbert Taylor

M.G. Sullivan

Among the Labor party members in the Legislative Assembly during the late 1930s when the Protestant Labour Party was challenging the ALP from the Protestant right, was George Taylor who shortly afterwards was to present a different sort of problem from the secular left. George Cuthbert Taylor had been born in Warrnambool in 1886. His family was impoverished through his father's drinking, and after completing primary school in Hamilton he began to work at the age of eleven, eventually becoming a shearer. In 1908 he became organizer for the Australian Workers Union in Adelaide, but, typical of the itinerant worker of the period, he also had some experience as a miner, including five years at Broken Hill. On the outbreak of war he joined up, served at Gallipoli where he was wounded in the hand and subsequently discharged. Soon after he reached Queensland where in 1918 he joined the ALP and acquired a reputation as a soapbox orator who spoke on topics, usually involving political theory, economics and rationalism, in great detail and with utmost seriousness.

In 1919 he came to prominence in demonstrations against the commonwealth government's War Precautions Act and as a spokesman on behalf of the Russian community of Brisbane, then containing a significant pro-Bolshevik element. In March 1919 he was involved in the riotous processions and street meetings at which returned soldiers clashed with Russians and trade unionists, and was one of the fifteen "red flag" prisoners sentenced to six months for breach of the act "by exhibiting a red flag in contravention of a prohibition duly made by the Minister for Defence". His conviction was appealed to the Supreme Court where he was represented by the premier, T.J. Ryan. In a reserved judgment on 19 July 1919, the Supreme Court found for the commonwealth, but the same day all the prisoners were released under the general amnesty granted to mark the official declaration of peace. His appeal was the beginning of a close friendship with Ryan, which was instrumental in Taylor's securing a position in the public service as a clerk in the Tourist Bureau. The appointment provided the foundation for Taylor's subsequent political career as through the 1920s it provided him with the security to devote more time to politics.

The story of the Labor party in Queensland for the next decade is of a steady drift to the right. When Labor returned to office in 1932, the new premier, Forgan Smith, was popular with the party he had led back from the wilderness, and within the parliamentary party only Charlie Collins remained of the group prepared to criticize their party over such issues as the 1927 railway strike and Collins was already affected by the ill-health that preceded his death in 1936. Among the new MLAs were two potential radicals, George Taylor who had won Enoggera, and Frank Waters, assistant secretary of the Postal Workers' Union and a delegate to the Trades and Labour Council and the ACTU, who held the adjacent constituency of Kelvin Grove. Both might have joined any left wing faction that existed, but as new members they were too busy finding their parliamentary legs to start one.

Taylor's radical performance in 1919 made him the target of suggestions from the other side of the House that he was about to start leftist agitation within the ALP, but, apart from one pro-Lang reference in 1933, in his first Parliament, little that he said could have been criticized by the more conservative members of his party. However, in October 1936 he returned to the subject of Lang and declared himself in favour of repudiation.[1] The next day Forgan Smith replied to Taylor's remarks which had been given wide publicity. The premier made it clear that Taylor did not express the ALP's views, and amid regular "Hear, Hear" murmurs from the government side of the House declared that the Labor party had always honoured its obligations to all sections of the community and always would. That was not the end of the affair, for Taylor was summoned before the premier and made to withdraw his statement under threat of expulsion. On 14 October he made a personal explanation to the House in which he withrew and accepted the premier's statement. The incident is significant both as showing the start of Taylor's disenchantment with his own party, and as demonstrating the tremendous power that Forgan Smith now held in the ALP, for there is little doubt that he could have carried out his threat of expulsion if Taylor had not withdrawn. A more domestic demonstration of the premier's role in the party is provided by the arrangements in the parliamentary dining room: Forgan Smith sat the head of his table with his cabinet members arranged along the sides and the premier dished up!

After this first rebuff, Taylor did not criticize or depart from Labor policy, aiming his attacks instead at "the system". Over the years he acquired, at least outside the House, the label of being something of a "commie", a tag that he mostly ignored and sometimes denied. The tumultuous politics in the western suburbs revolving around the appearance of the Protestant Labour Party (see Chapter 21) largely passed Taylor by. In 1938 and 1941 he was unopposed for party selection for Enoggera, suggesting that even if he was suspected of leftwards leaning the feeling was not strong enough to bring a candidate against him in a pre-selection plebiscite. The ALP won the 1941 state election comfortably, but three months later Hitler's invasion of Russia placed new strains on party unity. Labor party members had supported the coalition federal government's action in declaring the Communist Party of Australia an unlawful body in June 1940. When the Soviet Union became a fighting ally of Britain, and thus of Australia, the ALP was placed in a dilemma which it solved by distinguishing between the alliance with Russia against Hitlerism and collaboration with the domestic Communist party which up to that point had opposed the war effort.

On 17 August 1941, the Australian Soviet Friendship League was proscribed by the central executive of the Victorian Branch of the ALP, and Clarrie Fallon, then president of the Queensland branch, was reported to have said that all such organizations were banned in Queensland and there was no intention of lifting the ban.[2] Taylor's attitude to the ban may be surmized from a speech in the Legislative Assembly ten days later when he said that the Tories would have to rely on communists to win the war. A subsequent speech praising the Russian war effort and suggesting that if communists were to be dealt with sternly then all Fifth Columnists should be so dealt with was challenged in caucus by Paul Hilton, but Forgan Smith mildly observed that a great deal of latitude was allowed in address-in-reply speeches although such speeches should be governed by "considerations of mateship and decency".

Lest there was any doubt about the ban of members of the ALP belonging to the Australian-Russian association in Queensland, on 5 September 1941 the Queensland Central Executive (QCE) ruled specifically that party members might not be members of or participate in the activities of the association. Taking its line from the declaration of the British Labour party and the Trade Union Congress in Great Britain, the resolution went on to compliment the people of the Soviet Union for their heroic struggle, but warned: "We strongly disapprove of the efforts being made by the members of or sympathisers of the former Communist Party of Australia to capitalise the Russian war situation on behalf of a movement which the A.L.P. has on many occasions stated to be opposed to the best interests of the working class."[3]

The office bearers of the Australian-Russian Medical Aid to Soviet Russia Association at the time included three ALP parliamentarians: Taylor as president, and G.H. Marriott and George Keyatta as vice-presidents. The association's executive declared that it could prove that no trace of communism or communist practice had ever appeared in its affairs, but the parliamentarians ignored press reports of the ban and waited formal notification. In the meantime a number of trade unions came out against the ban, the Enoggera Electorate Executive Committee (EEC) unanimously opposed the decision, and a meeting at Trades Hall decided to hold a public rally at the City Hall to allow the citizens of Brisbane to express their views on the association. On 18

September, the night before the City Hall meeting, Taylor made his first public statement to a meeting of one hundred people at the Ipswich Trades Hall. Referring to the QCE action as "stupid", Taylor claimed that the association "was nothing more than a humanitarian body, striving to bring medical aid to a country fighting nobly against the Germans."[4] On the nineteenth both Marriott and Taylor attended the meeting in the packed City Hall — Keyatta was in the army and did not attend — and criticized the QCE's decision.

A meeting of the ALP federal executive had been called for 20 September to discuss the matter, and Forgan Smith was absent from Brisbane in Sydney where he and Fallon were to be the Queensland delegates. The federal executive sought to find a formula to save such prominent party members as Maurice Blackburn, but ultimately on a unanimous vote upheld the ban already imposed by Victoria and Queensland. Speaking that week in Parliament, Taylor reaffirmed the theme that ran through so many of his speeches since he had entered the Assembly nine years earlier: "Upon an analysis of the war effort it will be found that capitalism as an institution is finished — it is doomed — and that in its place the people of Europe and then the rest of the world will adopt socialism and working class control . . . .[5] The same day the Trades and Labour Council voted thirty-nine to twenty-one to oppose the QCE's ban, but with federal support the QCE's position had been strengthened. On 23 September Taylor left for Canbera to attend an all Australia Conference on Aid to Russia, and during his absence caucus met to hear a report by Forgan Smith on the federal executive meeting after which it adopted the decision taken in Sydney. On 3 October public attention was distracted by the fall of the Fadden government and the appointment of John Curtin as prime minister, but the same day the Victorian branch expelled Blackburn.

A few party branches, including two in Marriott's electorate of Bulimba, declared themselves behind the QCE, and on 8 October a meeting of the full QCE unanimously adopted the decisions of the federal executive. After the meeting an unidentified member of the QCE stated: "They must choose between the Labor Party and the Australian-Russian Association. If they decide against the A.L.P. that is their concern."[6] Returning the onus to the rebels was a good tactic for it gave them an opportunity to retract even at this stage, although it was most unlikely that they would do so. Meanwhile the QCE sent a circular to party branches justifying their ban; the Enoggera EEC returned theirs with the comment that the QCE was misinformed about the bona fides of the association. On 22 October Fallon as president of the Queensland branch issued a statement that Taylor had "withdrawn" from the ALP. Taylor, on a tour of north Queensland on behalf of the association, denied that he had withdrawn or transgressed the party's platform or constitution.

An Aid to Russia Congress had been called for the last weekend of October. Forgan Smith declined an invitation to open it, but the congress was not banned by the QCE although two branches in the western suburbs were advised against issuing credentials to any of their members to be delegates to the congress. Early in the dispute, Keyatta, who had been in camp in Brisbane, made his peace with the QCE, and a statement by the ALP secretary, S.J. Bryan, that Marriott had complied with the QCE's decision — which he clearly had not — suggested that Taylor would be the sole target. Marriott's own branch voted by more than two to one not to issue credentials to the congress, but Marriott made it clear that he would continue to stand with Taylor. Caucus was scheduled to meet two days before the congress, and on the day of the caucus meeting Waters, who had failed to secure endorsement to the contest the plebiscite for Kelvin Grove in 1941, announced that a protest meeting would be held in the City Hall "by the Kelvin Grove executive and other A.L.P. bodies". The lines were now firmly drawn. Taylor was excluded from the caucus meeting on 29 October after a twenty-minute discussion in which he was defended by only Marriott whose position was not challenged. After the meeting Forgan Smith disclosed that caucus had passed a resolution approving the QCE's action in advising Taylor that by his actions he had forfeited his membership in the ALP, and the *Courier-Mail* carried an unusually detailed account of the caucus meeting which sounded suspiciously like an official report.[7]

Taylor's personal papers support his claim of widespread support, but it was largely from the unions. Seven branches of the ALP defied the QCE and sent delegates to the congress, the majority of the branches being in the western suburbs. The congress was attended by three thousand people at the first session which was opened and presided over by the president of the Trades and Labour Council, H.J. Harvey. The following Sunday, a meeting was held in the Enoggera electorate which set up an "A.L.P. Protest Committee" to seek reinstatement of Taylor; that committee decided to hold a protest meeting in the City Hall on 25 November. On 3 November the afternoon newspaper, the *Telegraph*, reported that Marriott had left the ALP, and on 5 November he withdrew from caucus claiming that his expulsion from the ALP had been the result of religious persecution. Despite a violent storm that broke over the city earlier in the evening, two thousand people attended the protest meeting on the twenty-fifth. The *Telegraph* reported fourteen branches and twenty-three unions represented, the *Courier-Mail* twelve branches and thirty unions and other oganizations; both agreed that four trades and labour councils were represented. Frank Waters told that rally that the movement would lead to the cleansing of the party, and on 30 November the protest committee decided to broaden its scope and proposed a variety of reforms for the ALP, some very general like "abolition of the Q.C.E. dictatorship", others quite specific like an annual conference to replace the triennial Labor-in-Politics Convention, and more emphasis on the socialist objective. The protest committee was overtaken by events — Pearl Harbour and the Japanese advance towards Australia. By early 1942 the protest committee had folded, and Waters had joined the army.

The QCE was not so easily distracted. On 12 January 1942 it appointed members to examine credentials and issue tickets in two offending branches, Enoggera Terrace-Ashgrove and Kelvin Grove-Newmarket, and from a later entry it appears that the Wilston-Grange Branch was also dealt with. The consequences of the dispute continued to appear in the minutes of the QCE over the next two years, as various attempts were made to secure reinstatement. One followed the Curtin government's raising of the ban on the Communist party, but as the president and secretary of the Queensland branch protested this action to Curtin and had their protest later endorsed by the QCE, this development did little for the rebels' cause. During Taylor's tour of north Queensland on behalf of the association, a comparable body had been set up in Townsville (see Chapter 23) but the strong action taken in Townsville may well have been influenced by the view that anything less could lead to the reinstatement of Taylor and Marriott. They continued to sit on the government side of the House and were broadly sympathetic with their former colleagues in what they said in debates. However, they were ostracized by many members of the ALP who did not even offer the normal courtesies when they met in the corridors of Parliament House. Before the 1944 state election they tried again for reinstatement in company with a group of about twenty-five supported by the Queensland Labour Reinstatement Committee, a body created to replace the defunct ALP Protest Committee. The application for reinstatement was badly organized, and did not come before the QCE until the day on which nominations closed. The QCE referred the matter to the branches; in Enoggera there was only one branch functioning and it recommended his reinstatement and a plebiscite to choose between Taylor and the endorsed candidate, J.S. Fraser, with party supporters being subsequently advised to vote for whichever man won the plebiscite as both men were now on the ballot paper. No mention of action on the recommendation can be found in the QCE minutes. Taylor stood as "Enoggera Labour Party" and although he outpolled Fraser 3:2 the seat was lost to K.J. Morris of the Queensland People's Party, successors to the UAP. In Bulimba, a safer Labor seat, Marriott survived.

In the last analysis, Taylor's well known radicalism went against him. His falling out with the ALP as it became in Queensland in the 1930s was inevitable. Taylor went into Parliament firm in his belief that he was merely representing the working class and unresponsive to the view that the ALP had to please other classes if it was to stay in power. Taylor could see only ill in the capitalist sytem, but for many of his Labor colleagues it had been kind. Some, with little education and a lifetime of hard physical labour behind them, were in secure positions that were reasonably well paid; others could be said to have made modest fortunes from their parliamentary service. Still others had found in Parliament a task that completely engrossed them and through it they felt tht they were improving the lot of the rank and file unionist. Taylor could not wait, and when an issue appeared which seemed to show his party going not merely too slowly but actually in the wrong direction, their parting was certain.[8]

NOTES

1. *QPD* CLXIX (1 October 1936): 709.
2. *Worker,* 5 August 1941.
3. *Courier-Mail,* 6 September 1941.
4. Ibid., 19 September 1941.
5. *QPD* CLXXVII (18 September 1941): 378.
6. *Courier-Mail,* 9 October 1941.
7. Ibid., 30 October 1941.
8. For a fuller account, see M.G. Sullivan, "Dissent in the Labor Party 1938 to 1944" (B.A. thesis, University of Queensland, 1968).

23 The Expulsion of Tom Aikens

Ian Moles

On the eve of the 1977 Queensland state elections the "father" of the legislature, the man who had held a seat longer than any other incumbent, the man who may well hold the record for longevity as an Independent in any parliament acknowledging the paternity of Westminster, was Thomas Aikens, since 1944 leader and sole parliamentary representative of the North Queensland Labour Party (NQLP).[1] The NQLP, originally the Hermit Park branch of the ALP until its "expulsion" in 1942 by the ALP's Queensland Central Executive (QCE), dominated the municipal politics of Townsville, by then Queensland's largest provincial city, from 1939 to 1949. For three of those years (1943-46) the NQLP ruled Townsville in coalition with the Communist party — the first of only two occasions in Australian electoral history when the Communist party gained not merely elected representation but also active participation in government.

Historically, the isolation of north Queensland communities from both one another and the main centres of population in the south had produced what its historian has described as "fierce local loyalties", "go-it-along patriotism" and "direct-action radicalism".[2] Aikens' election to Parliament in 1944 was a manifestion of all three phenomena; so, too, were two other features of the same election — a spectacular drop in public support for the Labor government that had ruled Queensland continuously, with a single brief interruption, since 1915, and the electoral success of two other radicals (one of them the only communist ever to enter an Australian legislature) in north Queensland seats which were traditional Labor strongholds. The 1944 election was the more remarkable to the extent that in the entire period 1915-41 Labor had at no stage held less than three-quarters of the state seats between Mackay and Cairns, and for three successive elections (1935, 1938, 1941) won all nine of the electorates in the northern region.

"Go-it-alone patriotism" was aroused whenever north Queenslanders felt that Queensland governments were neglecting the north. Mass defections from the Labor party were one way in which they registered their disapproval, but the 1944 election was merely the culmination of a long series of disputes going back to the 1860s. All the grievances could be epitomized in the catch-cry that "Queen Street governments were indifferent to the north and even contemptuous of it." Labor governments were sensitive to northern criticism and tried to combat it. Indeed, in addition to being a party that deliberately set out to attract all classes and all interests throughout the state, Labor was also the only consistent "northern" party. By spending loan moneys freely in northern and far northern Queensland on public developmental works such as roads, bridges, harbours, sewerage, forestry, schools and other buildings, the party set out to "kill with one stone both the Separtation Movement and the Country-National party."[3] The north also received a generous allocation of cabinet portfolios, not to mention premierships (Theodore, Gillies, McCormack and Forgan Smith all represented north Queensland constituencies); it had influential voices within the councils of the ALP; its major industry, sugar, was well protected. But to many in the north such solicitude was often seen as inadequate or insincere, or both — as indeed it seemed in itself a tacit admission on the part of governments that the north really had been neglected.

"Direct-action radicalism" was an amalgam of two regional peculiarities. On the one hand, isolation and localism bred self-reliance, independence of spirit, the sort of "irreverent" radicalism, according to Bolton, "that chose a man irrespective of his label and enjoyed cocking a snook at respectable party politicians."[4] On the other hand, the very nature of most employment in the north, which was seasonal, irregular and itinerant or semi-itinerant in the mines and the bush or on sugar farms, wharves and railways, itself bred a "conditioned recklessness" and "undisciplined vehemence" that merely reinforced the primary influences of history and geography.[5]

Both essential elements of the north Queensland tradition fused in the upbringing and education of Thomas Aikens who was born in Hughenden on 28 April 1900. As a schoolboy in Charters Towers, Tom was brought up in an aggressively anti-capitalistic environment, a product both of the miners' collectivist vigour in remedying their grievances and of the exceptional quality of their leadership which life on the gold fields seemed invariably to engender and attract.[6] Later, as a roustabout in the shearing shed of Oxton Downs station outside Julia Creek, he also absorbed the rebellious spirit of the "nomads" and "ramblers" — the shearers and itinerant bush workers of north Queensland whose militancy was a byword in the labor movement.[7] Finally, in Cloncurry, he joined the Queensland railways and completed an exacting political apprenticeship as acting secretary, vice-president and president of the Australian Railways Union (ARU), delegate to the northern district committee of the ARU, secretary of the Cloncurry branch of the ALP, councillor and deputy chairman of the Cloncurry Shire Council.

The years during which Aikens held elected office in Cloncurry were also characterized by a progressive disillusionment among workers with the Labor government that ruled in Brisbane. When the ALP eventually fell from power in 1929, after fourteen years continuously in office, this was because large numbers of its hitherto loyal supporters deserted it.[8] The root cause of the problem was twofold. On the one hand, some sections of the labor movement deplored the snail's pace at which socialization appeared to be proceeding; on the other hand, a much larger core of workers discovered to its chagrin that the Labor government was not the model employer that they had expected it to be but a downright unsympathetic one. Nowhere in Queensland were these feelings more pronounced than in the north and in the ranks of railway workers. As early as 1919, railwaymen had begun to denounce their employer for bureaucratic "injustice, pin-pricking and tyranny."[9] Of the men who long led the ARU, Cribb remarks that they were "left-wing oriented", though not communist, "vigorous" in their beliefs, "frequently sounding like communists" and constantly proselytizing an ideological position which was "one of socialism with strong Marxist overtones."[10] Increasingly the government responded by stigmatizing them as "revolutionaries" and "communists".

Transferred to Townsville during the interregnum of the Moore government, Aikens became a foundation member of the Hermit Park branch of the ALP whose members, almost to a man, belonged to the ARU. He also found that the political climate of Townsville was even more militant, if that were possible, than the one in which he had earlier received his political initiation. Many of the ramblers and nomads from the west eventually ended up in Townsville; the place had also acquired a reputation for industrial anarchy that most residents traced back to "Bloody Sunday" in 1919 — the riotous culmination of a meatworkers' strike in which police fired on workers and a number of people were injured. After 1922, Townsville's radical reputation was further enhanced by her status as organizational centre of the communist movement in north Queensland. Throughout the 1930s the Communist party enjoyed a period of "remarkable growth" which was without parallel anywhere else in Australia, culminating in 1944 when F.W. Paterson, barrister, Townsville alderman, former Rhodes Scholar, became the first and so far the only Communist member of an Australian parliament.[11]

An accomplished bush orator, Aikens played the role of acknowledged left-wing spokesman with relish and panache. In 1936 he was elected to an aldermanic seat on the Townsville City Council; on his second try in 1939 he became deputy mayor after polling more votes than any other Labor candidate. Most lunchtimes, the Labor municipal caucus met conspiratorially behind the locomotive foreman's office and, huddled over their battered black tucker boxes, thrashed out the policies which were to shape Townsville's destiny over the next decade. What eventually emerged was a determination not only to proceed with the public acquisition of the city's main utilities, but also to initiate municipal competition in a great many lesser fields traditionally reserved to private enterprise; in short, to inaugurate a bold, thoroughgoing and, in many respects, novel programme of municipal socialization. During and immediately after World War II, a City Council controlled by a coalition of Hermit Park "ALP" and Communist aldermen (which in 1943 went to the polls as the "Greater Townsville Labour party") effected the public ownership of a remarkable range of utilities and services — a ladies' rest room (incorporating a free baby-stroller service for mothers shopping in the city), a wood depot, a fruit and vegetable mart, a legal aid department, a municipal ice works and a child care centre; by 1949, plans were well in hand for the development of "workers' housing", a people's bakery and the "municipalization" of all bus services — when the Hermit Park group finally fell from power.

From the very outset, however, there was a snag. Tom Dougherty, later federal secretary of the Australian Workers Union (AWU) and then its northern district secretary, a man whose stature and pertinacity made him at least the equal of Aikens, challenged the left-wing champion for leadership of the labor movement in Townsville. As the principal local mouthpiece and representative of Labor right-wing orthodoxy, which was gradualist, multi-class and moderate, the two rivals were bound to clash — each so very much alike in the strength of his ambition and ideological conviction, but each facing the other from opposite ends of their party's ideological spectrum. Towards the end of 1940, Dougherty was able to engineer Aikens' expulsion from the ALP on the grounds of the latter's occasional but always sensational "benders".

Aikens never again became a member of the ALP, though he did soon resume membership of the Hermit Park branch. The explanation for that apparent anomaly lay in the fact that the branch itself was presently "expelled" from the ALP. By an astonishing quirk of fate, Tom Aikens regained his political platform; then, with supreme political aplomb and in defiance of every known canon of political survival, he made the renegade Hermit Park branch into the dominant political force in Townsville, slaying the Goliath of the ALP and reversing the electoral behaviour of a generation.

In January 1942, four leading members of the Hermit Park ALP, all aldermen, were advised by the QCE that they had voluntarily "left the Party" because of their connections with a Townsville Aid to Russia committee which, along with other "communist subsidiary organizations", the ALP had recently placed under interdict. In fact, the Townsville membership of the anathematized committee was politically heterogeneous, respectable and unexceptionable; accordingly, in a gesture of loyal solidarity, all other members of the Hermit Park branch chose to join their comrades in exile and, moreover, to "fight the tyranny of the QCE" by fielding a "strong team of candidates" in the 1943 municipal election. Since it was impossible to conceive of any "strong" team which did not include the popular deputy mayor, Tom Aikens, the branch invited its prodigal son to return to the fold after more than two years of party obloquy. In the subsequent election, Aikens topped the poll, seven of the ten successful aldermen were Hermit Park rebels, and not a single ALP alderman was returned.

Of course, it was not merely local outrage at QCE "despotism" which resulted in such a dramatic reversal of fortunes. Townsville was also at war, and probably no other community in Australia during World War II was thrown back quite so rudely on its own resources in the face of such formidable odds. At least that was the judgment not only of Townsvilleans themselves but also of a host of surprised and concerned outsiders. All testified to the demoralization of a citizenry beleaguered by Japanese air raids, the threat of imminent invasion, widespread evacuation, protracted military occupation by forces heavily outnumbering the civilian population, persistent shortages of essential goods, a sense of isolation from the mainstream of Australian life and of actual abandonment by remote and insensitive governments — of which the QCE's ostracism of the Hermit Park branch seemed merely a palpable and particularly crass example. As late as mid-1944, north Queenslanders still nurtured "an abiding sense" that southern governments in Brisbane and Canberra were ignorant of their total wartime experiences and indifferent to them. The chief spokesman of that mood was Tom Aikens and in 1944

Don't Be Misled! For Maximum Aid Support Labor's War and Defence Effort

Front cover of pamphlet on aid to Russia, 1942. (Permission: Australian Workers Union; Photograph by courtesy of the Mitchell Library.)

Townsvilleans elected him to Parliament in Brisbane to evoke it, to shame and bludgeon government with it.

There were several reasons why Aikens was subsequently re-elected to Parliament over and over again. "As far as orators go, there were only two men in Australia, that was Menzies and Aikens, and Aikens had it on Menzies because he put humour in his speeches"; as a campaigner he was a politician's politician, continually refining the techniques of his art.[12] But pre-eminently it was becaused he proved a "local" member *par excellence*. As a representative, he was always visible, accessible and helpful; his policy — "A Square Go for the North" — was consistently attuned to the deepest of his constitutents' emotional and historical predilections. Among political *cognoscenti* the notice he attracted often seemed ambivalent, even censorious, but it was never muted. To one, he was "a unique phenomenon in the desert of Queensland politics"; to another, he was "the last representative in the Australian parliaments of a style of inspired, conscientious, vulgar, 'irresponsible', legislative behaviour that Southerners are apt to assume disappeared with *The Wild Men of Sydney* sixty years ago."

NOTES

1. In 1974 the word "Labour" was dropped from the party's name. This did not signify that the party was abandoning its traditional sympathy for the "little man" nor that some other subtle ideological re-orientation had occurred. It was just that the party leader's prognosis of Labor's infirmity, at a time when elections loomed, was perhaps more confident than it had ever been.
2. See G.C. Bolton, *A Thousand Miles Away: A History of North Queensland to 1920* (Canberra: Australian National University Press, 1970), pp. 163, 320, 336.
3. See T.P. Fry, "State Elections — Queensland", *Australian Quarterly* (June 1935,), p. 90.
4. Bolton, *A Thousand Miles Away*, p. 337.
5. Cf. T. Cutler, "Sunday, Bloody Sunday: The Townsville Meatworkers' Strike of 1918-1919", in *Strikes: Studies in Twentieth Century Australian*

Social History, eds. J. Iremonger, J. Merritt, G. Osborne (Sydney: Angus & Robertson, 1973), pp. 81-102, esp. pp. 82, 85.

6. See J. Stoodley, "Labour and Gold-Mining", in *Prelude to Power: The Rise of the Labor Party in Queensland 1885-1915*, eds. D.J. Murphy, R.B. Joyce, C.A. Hughes (Brisbane: Jacaranda Press, 1970), esp. pp. 164-67.
7. See Cutler, "Sunday, Bloody Sunday", pp. 83-84.
8. See D. Vockler, "The Australian Labor Party in Queensland, 1927-35" (B.A. thesis, University of Queensland, 1962), p. 14.
9. *The Militant,* 1 June 1919.
10. See M.B. Cribb, "Some Manifestations of Ideological Conflict within the Labor Movement in Queensland (1924 to 1929)" (B.A. honours thesis, University of Queensland, 1964), pp. 29, 39. See also M.B. Cribb, "State in Emergency: The Queensland Railway Strike of 1948", in *Strikes: Studies in Twentieth Century Australian Social History*, eds. J. Iremonger, J. Merritt and G. Osborne (Sydney: Angus & Robertson, 1973), pp. 228, 236.
11. See A.E. Jones, "Electoral Support for the Communist Party in North Queensland: A Study of F.W. Paterson's Victory in Bowen, 1944 (B.A. thesis, University of Queensland, 1972), pp. 57, 91.
12. See author's study of the 1963 state election campaign in Townsville South, in *Images and Issues: The Queensland State Elections of 1963 and 1966*. C.A. Hughes (Canberra: Australian National University Press, 1969), pp. 304-18.

24 The Affiliation of Unions: A Study of Four Unions, 1947-57

Joy Guyatt

The Labor party derives its name from having trade unions directly affiliated with it, thought it is not, and never has been, a purely trade union party. A question to be answered is whether this connection has been of benefit to the unions and to the political party. The evidence suggests that it has been of benefit to both.

During the period of the Labor government, unionism in Queensland reached its highest level ever in Australia in 1948, with 81 per cent of male and female wage and salary earners being members of unions. Preference clauses for unions, a favourable arbitration system and the access of unions to Labor cabinet ministers provided an environment in which unionism prospered. It was not until the last years of the Labor government that this relationship soured.

Unions affiliated with the Labor party were entitled to send delegates and items of business to the Queensland Central Executive (QCE) and to the Labor-in-Politics Conventions, and to vote in plebiscites for the selection of candidates for governmental and party offices. Theoretically if a union could have a policy item passed by a convention, then the Labor government was bound to legislate on that policy. Those unions affiliated with the Trades and Labour Council saw this affiliation as a means of achieving their goals through industrial action. A great number of unions affiliated with both. Affiliations were withdrawn and renewed from time to time, reflecting the circumstances of unions and their political attitudes. Relationships between union and union, between individual unions and the QCE, between individual unions and the Parliamentary Labor Party (PLP), and between the Trades and Labour Council and individual unions, the QCE and PLP were complex and changing, yet this wide range of relationships must be considered for any meaningful insight into interactions between "the trade unions" and the Labor governments that held office between 1915 and 1957.

As a practical compromise, four important unions have been selected as a sample from the great diversity — in terms of size, comprehensiveness, etc. — and the story concentrated on Labor's last decade in office, 1947-57.[1]

The first, and most obvious choice, is the Australian Workers Union (AWU). This union dominated the QCE and successive Labor-in-Politics Conventions; it provided money and facilities to fight elections and many candidates from amongst its members; it was the trade union which came closest to achieving the ideal of One Big Union through the extent of its cover of rural workers. The second union chosen, the Australian Railways Union (ARU) is an industrial union, seeking to cover all workers in the railways, and was the only one in the sample not affiliated to the Australian Labor Party, (ALP). Its affiliation lapsed after a dispute in 1926 and was not renewed until 1957. The other two unions in the sample are the Queensland State Service Union (QSSU) and the Boilermakers Society of Australia (BSA) which provide examples of two different kinds of unions. The QSSU is a union of white-collar employees of the state government, and the BSA a craft union. Both were active in channelling demands, in the form of agenda items, through Labor-in-Poltics Conventions.

The AWU had affiliated with the TLC when it had been reformed in 1922, subsequently withdrew, then affiliated again in 1929 only to withdraw in 1939 on the ground that the union was inadequately represented by only six delegates on a body it regarded as dominated by communists. It re-affiliated for a short and crucial time in 1956 during the pastoral strike which created considerable tension between the Gair government and the AWU. In contrast to some of the militant unions of the TLC, the AWU was not only conservative in politics but also moderate in industrial action, generally preferring arbitration to strike action.

Part of the political influence of the AWU was due to the considerable contributions in money and services it made to the ALP. AWU organizers gave invaluable help during election campaigns by providing transport, and AWU offices served as bases for organization in country areas. Discussing at the 1947 Labor-in-Poltics Convention a proposal for the appointment of an organizer to the QCE, E.J. Walsh, then minister for transport, reminded the convention:

> If the balance sheets were dissected it would be seen that the A.W.U. made substantial contributions apart from capitation fees towards assisting the campaign of the Labor Party not only in the State but also in the Federal arena. I go futher and refer to the help given by this organization throughout the State, particularly in the west and in the north, where members of Parliament and political candidates find it difficult to get transport over long distances.[2]

The dominance of the AWU in ALP affairs gave it certain advantages in maintaining that position: the procedure whereby AWU members could cast absentee votes in ALP plebiscites was said to be manipulated by union officials; the AWU members and officials held party posts throughout the state and provided a substantial proportion of the PLP; while other parliamentarians who had not worked in industries covered by the AWU still found it expedient to take out AWU tickets.

As an affiliated union, the AWU sent few agenda items to the Labor-in-Politics Conventions, for it had other means of channelling its demands to Labor governments. Its members were well represented amongst activists in ALP branches, and matters of interest to AWU members were frequently sent forward by the branches. There was one item from the central district of the AWU on the Labor-in-Politics Convention agenda in 1947, none in 1950 and 1953, and seven in 1956 when other avenues of approach were becoming ineffective and the union's relationship with the PLP had deteriorated. In contrast to the relative lack of interest in sending items to Labor-in-Politics Conventions, every year some hundreds of items were submitted to the delegate meeting of the Queensland branch of the AWU.

Because the AWU covered employees with the least bargaining

power, viz. the unskilled and semi-skilled workers, it relied heavily on the awards of the Industrial Court and on the power of industrial inspectors to enforce awards. At the 1941 Labor-in-Politics Convention, Fallon said that the AWU had been able to collect fifteen thousand pounds in back wages owed to its members through the laws instituted by Labor governments. This, to him, well repaid the affiliation fees paid by the AWU to the ALP. The AWU was further advantaged by the appointments to the Industrial Court. Two former AWU secretaries — W.J. Dunstan and W.J. Riordan had been made commissioners. It was expected that, when Riordan retired in the early 1950s, he would be replaced by an AWU man. In two other areas, sick leave and long service leave, the government legislated directly after having been approached by a group of unions which included the AWU.

When a Labor government was the employer, the AWU often found a direct approach to the minister more effective than the submission of claims to the Arbitration Court. In 1952, Edgar Williams, as AWU spokesman, met the minister for mines, W. Power, in the office of his under-secretary, to make representations for a pay increase for workers at the state-owned coke works at Bowen and was promised an extra pound a week. At a subsequent conference, the public service commissioner reduced the amount to ten shillings which the AWU refused to accept. The minister than reaffirmed his previous offer of one pound, and the Arbitration Court legalized it by bringing down an award as arranged between the minister and the AWU.[3] This happy co-operation was not to continue indefinitely. When in 1948 the QCE had set up the ALP Industrial Group executive committee to combat the influence of communists in the unions, R.J. Bukowski, then southern district secretary of the AWU and a member of the QCE executive committee, was one of the three members. Later, however, AWU officials began to feel their union and party positions were being threatened by Industrial Group candidates, and in the *Worker* of 28 February 1955, Bukowski charged that the "Movement" aimed to oust top AWU officials.

Tension then shifted from the political to the industrial sphere. In November 1955, on the application of the United Graziers' Association, the Industrial Court in Queensland reduced the minimum wage for shearers by 10 per cent as from 1 January 1956. In February 1956, Commonwealth Conciliation Commissioner Donovan imposed a 5 per cent reduction in wages for shearers elsewhere in Australia. The men decided not to offer for work, and their decision was supported by the union and by the Trades and Labour Council. The disputes committee of the TLC collaborated with the AWU, and black-banned wool from a number of sheds, the names of which were supplied to the AWU. On 4 July 1956 the Industrial Court, on the application of the UGA, deleted the preference clause from the State Shearing Industry Award. The AWU overcame its objections and re-affiliated with the TLC. Twenty-six unions refused to handle non-union labour products. The September wool sales were cancalled, and the premier, V.C. Gair, approached the acting prime minister and leader of the Country party, A.W. Fadden, for help in shipping *all* wool, both black and white, an action tantamount to inviting the use of the military as strike-breakers.

Relations between the premier and the unions were strained almost to breaking point. In a broadcast from the Labor radio station, 4KQ, Bukowski, now president of the Queensland branch of the AWU, warned that ". . . as a Labor Premier, Mr. Gair should understand that once a man steps across the line against the people within the Labor Movement, it is very, very hard to step back again".[4] In July the strike was settled in the southern states by an increase in wages, but a conference between the UGA and the Queensland unions, convened by Gair at the end of September, failed. On 4 October, despite union protests, the premier introduced emergency legislation and ordered storemen and packers and AWU members engaged under the Wool Classers' Award back to work with penalties of up to one hundred pounds for failure to obey. Wool brokers were also ordered to reinstate the men in employment in an effort to prevent the introduction of free labour into the wool stores. In the *Worker* of 8 October 1956, Bukowski characterized Gair's emergency legislation as "one of the greatest examples of non-Labor action that this State has seen since the tragic days of 1912". On 9 October, the public service commissioner was directed under the emergency legislation to seek a review of the shearing award on an interim basis; the AWU accepted the interim award and the TLC withdrew its black ban.[5]

The strike was over, but during it there had been bitter public exchanges between the premier and AWU officials. The AWU began to feel that its interests were being neglected, and at the 1956 Delegate Meeting, Bukowski moved for a meeting between the union executive and senior ministers to discuss matters relating to the union and the Industrial Court with a view to avoiding strike action.[6] When the executive met the premier in July, it was the first meeting that Gair had had with the AWU state executive in his five years as premier.[7]

As a sign of its extreme disaffection, in 1956 the AWU declined to make its usual general contribution to election funds and failed to invite Gair to address its delegate meeting. It explained that money was not subscribed directly to the party because Gair had collected £12,000 from sources unknown to the Labor party, and the premier was not invited because, as he had not attended the Hobart Federal Conference, his presence would not have been welcomed by the delegates. When Gair was finally challenged on the three weeks' annual leave issue, three AWU men, Boland, Bukowski and Schmella were respectively president, vice-president and secretary of the QCE. Five of the six delegates from the AWU to the QCE voted for the expulsion.

In sharp contrast with the AWU's long and close association with successive Labor governments was the ARU's long history of stress and strain. State Railway Department employees were covered by three kinds of union — craft unions, section unions, and one industrial union, the ARU. The division of the industry among a number of unions weakened their bargaining power *vis-a-vis* the one employer, the Queensland government, and the ARU was active in both the state committee of the Combined Railway Unions and the All Services Union which were formed to overcome it. The ARU's approach to industrial disputes was generally militant and it was openly critical of the actions of successive railway commissioners. Clashes with the Labor government entailed more or less prolonged strike action by the ARU between 1945 and 1957.

In March 1945, the ARU decided to strike for annual leave, penalty rates for nightwork, adequate housing, the right of appeal against dismissal, and increases in wages. The result of a strike ballot conducted by the All Services Union was conveyed to the premier, and following a conference most of the demands were granted; only penalty rates for nightwork were not secured. In 1946, the ARU supported a strike by the Australasian Meat Industry Employees Union members at the Murrarie bacon factory, and as a result railwaymen were fined for refusing to handle "black" goods. However, their intention to remain on strike in support was dropped following a restraining order from the Industrial Court. Then an old grievance flared up again. Prior to 1926, employees had been allowed five minutes in which to wash their hands before lunch and ten minutes for the same purpose at the end of the day. The ten minutes was reduced to five, and then both periods were withdrawn in 1929 after the report of the Harris-Cameron Commission on Workshops, but employees continued to take the time off and were challenged for it by departmental officers. In May 1944, union officials met the minister for transport who was prepared to restore "wash-hand" time to employees in sections where it was thought necessary; the ARU insisted that there should be no discrimination, cabinet agreed to three and six minutes, the employees continued to take five and ten, and the privilege was again withdrawn. Negotiations dragged on for twelve months in 1945-46, and eventually in April 1946, the Industrial Court's suggestion of three and five minutes was accepted.

Conflict continued and in November 1947, the ARU ordered a twenty-four hour stoppage over the railway commissioner's power to impose fines. The stoppage was in defiance of a restraining order by the court, and the ARU's president and secretary were fined for contempt of court and for having contravened an order. In 1948, the ARU as an affiliate of the All

Services Union was involved in a nine weeks' strike to obtain an additional marginal increase already paid under the Mooney Award to railway workers in other states and penalty rates for weekend work. (Chapter 19). The bitterness engendered by the repressive actions of the Labor government during this strike remained with railwaymen for many years.

The ARU retained its role as a militant, left-wing union which emphasized industrial strength against reliance on political action. Its 1954 Conference adopted the secretary's report which declared: "Trade union policy must never be made subservient to political expediency, as is the policy of ALP groups."

The editorial policy of the *Advocate*, the Union's fortnightly newspaper, was to advise its readers to "keep the Tories out", rather than to advise positively the return of a Labor government: "Parliamentary Labor in office is not responsive to elementary working-class demands and is compelled definitely to align itself with employers against the working class as in the railwaymen's and miners' strikes. So we should rejoice at the defeat of the Tories rather than the election of Labor men."[8] Although the ARU was affiliated to the TLC, except for the period 1931-33, so deep was the animosity towards the AWU and the ALP that motions to re-affiliate with the ALP were defeated at every state conference from 1948 to 1957. Only after the expulsion of Gair did the ARU show a change of heart when the state executive passed a resolution calling on members to support the QCE and, in the event of an election, support the return of official Labor candidates.[9]

The ARU was openly critical of Labor governments on the administration of the liquor laws, the Industrial Conciliation and Arbitration Acts, especially its provisions for the holding of court-controlled secret ballots, the Queensland Traffic Act 1949, and the Printers and Newspapers Act 1953. The union negotiated day-to-day administrative issues with the commissioner of railways. Representations on railway matters were made by letter and deputation to both the commissioner and the minister for transport. Requests for action on more general matters were sent to the TLC. The state executive conferred with other unions with a view to co-operative action for common ends and, when all else failed, the railwaymen were ready to stop work for mass meetings to discuss grievances, to assist other unions by refusing to handle goods declared "black" in disputes in which the ARU was not directly involved, and, if necessary, to come out on strike.

Some demands on the government, such as those for improved housing and accommodation for workers forced to live away from home, continued in varying forms for many years. Rising standards of living for the community as a whole made past gains seem less than adequate, and new amenities such as refrigerators, electric lights and fresh fruit and vegetables in remote centres were sought. Some requests were obviously reasonable and granted as a result of union representations to the minister, but other objectives were followed for some years, not achieved and ultimately discarded, such as the provision of canteens at depots and shops with one hundred and more employees.

From time to time the ARU pressed for worker participation in management decisions: in 1945, it agreed to a ministerial suggestion for a Railway Re-organization Board to discuss re-organization, and in 1947, when there was a dispute over working overtime in the workshop, the proposal was made for a committee with union participation to discuss modernizing the workshops. In 1948, the idea was rejected by the minister who said that opportunities for the unions to make suggestions was as far as cabinet would go. The union continued to press the suggestion, but consultative committees were never appointed. The union's campaign against the commissioner's power to impose fines and for stricter rules of evidence in disciplinary proceedings failed to win improvements, neither did its requests to make the railway commissioner subject to the statutory controls and inspection imposed on private employers. Yet although some of their demands were not met, or only partially fulfilled, ARU members acknowledged that substantial gains were made under Labor governments and that "bad" Labor governments were preferable to non-Labor governments.

The defeat of Labor in 1957 caused concern among members about their future under a Tory government. The ARU leaders were aware that political pressure could succeed and used all the channels open to them, including appeals to the general public, to improve the lots of their members. They made effective use of strike action, knowing when to compromise and send the men back to work. They consistently opposed the ALP Industrial Groups and were prepared to work with communists on industrial matters.

Like the ARU, the BSA was a militant union, forthright in its relationships with the state government which employed a number of its members. However, membership of the BSA depended on trade qualifications acceptable to the society, and its constitution carefully protected standards of workmanship as well as the employment opportunities of members. The society's objects also included a guild welfare component to assist members "in case of unemployment, dispute or injury by accident while working at the trade" and for payment of benefits on the death of a member and to members who were victimized or oppressed. The BSA concerned itself with the wages and working conditions of its members in general and with the wrongs of individual members, though from time to time it expressed opinions on wider issues such as the need for kindergartens, price control and freedom of speech.

Its methods of negotiation included correspondence between the district committee of the society and relevant ministers, especially the minister for transport, and constituent branches were urged to write to their local members of Parliament on issues raised at society meetings. Ministers were asked to intervene with private employers when direct demands by the society were unsuccessful. The district committee co-operated with other unions: strikes, stoppages and refusals to work overtime were part of the negotiating structure though direct action in a particular dispute was not always supported. Items relating to the society's interests were sent to Labor-in-Politics Conventions and to Trade Union Congresses. The BSA took its political affiliations seriously, and items on convention agendas were discussed at length by the district committee so that delegates were properly informed of the society's views. From time to time the government was pressed, through QCE delegates and circulars to individual politicians, to implement convention decisions, and in the final confrontation between the QCE and the PLP on the issue of the implementation of the party policy of three weeks' annual leave for all workers, John Egerton, full-time secretary of the BSA since 1950, was one of the strongest proponents of the doctrine that Labor parliamentarians were servants of the party bound to carry out decisions made by Labor-in-Politics Conventions.

The BSA had an unbroken affiliation with the TLC since 1885 and with the ALP from 1945. While not particularly anti-communist, it rejected attempts by communists to influence its affairs, and equally rejected the ALP Industrial Groups' approaches in 1948 and 1952. In general, the BSA obtained little satisfaction from its approaches to the QCE or from the passage through convention of the items it submitted. Although *pro-rata* long service leave, improved compensation payments, increases in the basic wage, the daytime training of apprentices and the extended application of the provisions of the Shops and Factories Acts were introduced they were due as much to rising standards in the community and continued pressure from particular trade unions as to direct responses by Labor governments to convention resolutions.

Concerned to safeguard the employment of its members, the BSA criticized the government for letting contracts to outside firms and asked that it intervene to have outside work done under state awards which were more favourable than federal awards at that time. In 1955, the society resolved to circularize every politician in Queensland, and the QCE as well, to protest against the letting, to a foreign company, of contracts for a bridge over the Brisbane River at Indooroopilly. It instructed branches to hold protest meetings on the job and asked the TLC to take the matter up. The exercise was unsuccessful as the government refused to reconsider the contracts. Protests by the BSA also failed to prevent the sale, by the state government, of its mines at Blair Athol to private enterprise. The society expressed interest in the design of railway workshops, and in 1948 it asked the minister for transport to allow its representatives to study the plans of new workshops and to suggest improvements. In due course, the minister sent the plans and promised to consider all suggestions, but the amount of consultation on these matters depended, on the responsible minister — in this case Jack Duggan — and not on formal consultative procedures.

The fourth union considered here, the QSSU, illustrates yet another set of relationships within the ALP. This union covered clerical workers in government employment; it was politically and industrially moderate, and for the most part pragmatically concerned with the relations of its members with their employer. The QSSU's executive negotiated to further their interests by letters and deputations to the Public Service Commission, to the premier who was the minister responsible for public service matters, and to other ministers, and as an affiliated union, by the submission of motions to the QCE and to Labor-in-Politics Conventions. It submitted twenty items to convention in 1947 and again in 1950, thirty-four in 1953 and twenty-five in 1956, more than any other union on each occasion.

As much of the day-to-day business of the union was conducted with the public service commissioner, a good deal of the union's dissatisfaction at any failure of negotiations was directed towards the commissioner. The premier seems to have used the commissioner to deflect some union pressure away from himself. The statutory responsibilities of the commissioner gave him a large measure of independence, although as a senior public servant he was directly responsible to the premier and therefore likely to be influenced by what he thought to be the premier's attitude and by the effect of decisions which he might make on government policy and finance.

The QSSU executive communicated directly with the premier and other ministers by letters and deputations, and undoubtedly by personal contact as they moved in ALP circles. It also tried unsuccessfully to use the QCE as a vehicle to press its demands on the government as the employer of its members. A number of issues can be followed through the pages of the QSSU's journal, *State Service*. Some were important because they continued to exercise the executive, such as demands for improved superannuation benefits, and others because they appeared and reappeared as convention items, such as the request for a three-member Public Service Commission and access to appeal boards for all Crown employees. Some demands were eased by the effluxion of time, such as the date from which extended leave might be taken again after the restrictions on leave imposed during World War II, or by government action to grant requests, as when legislation was enacted in 1946 to implement a decision made at the 1944 Convention that public servants be not called upon to resign from the service to contest elections. Some demands, especially for improvements in workers' compensation, were pursued more vigorously through Labor-in-Politics Conventions than through other channels available to the union. Here the union joined with other unions and succeeded in having the compensation payments raised.

Superannuation was a continuing issue because the expectations of QSSU members were related to rising standards in the community in general and to the Commonwealth Public Service in particular. Improvements were made under the Labor governments. The QSSU was less successful in its negotiations for access to appeal boards for some of its members and in demands that decisions of appeal boards be final. The rejection of the appeal board's decisions by the governor-in-council was seen by the union as an attempt by the government "to estrange and antagonise the Public Service",[10] and a threat was made to withdraw affiliation with the ALP "if Convention did not discipline the Cabinet Ministers".[11] No discipline was applied and no withdrawal by the union occurred. The union also pressed unsuccessfully for the establishment of a three-member Public Service Commission, one of whom was to be elected by the service. In January 1947, the premier declared himself opposed to the idea on the grounds that it would be difficult "to determine the person responsible for delay or shortcomings generally if authority were divided between three Commissioners". As the Commonwealth, Victorian and New Zealand governments had established boards with employee representation, the president of the QSSU concluded "that organisations unaffiliated and opposed to the Labor movement receive more favourable consideration from Labor Governments than affiliated unions do".[12] The QSSU did not subscribe to strike action in spite of the government's failure to satisfy some of its important demands. Relationships between the QSSU and the government were complicated by the political aspects of the situation in that the premier seemed unable to isolate his role as employer from that of leader of the government, and this confusion extended to the union executive.

Referring to the government's unwillingness to meet representatives of the union to conciliate matters in dispute, the president said:

> This unrealistic approach to the relationship of employer and employee is the cause of most of the Union's dissatisfaction with the present Government . . . . The Australian Labor Party was established because employers exploited their employees, and it ill becomes the present Labor Government to play traitor to the ideals of the progenitors of the Movement.[13]

In spite of this dissatisfaction, the QSSU maintained its affiliation with the ALP (except for the years 1929-32 when the Moore government was in office) and with the TLC (except for the years 1946-47 and 1953) over the period 1924 to 1958. Although the TLC was a potential means of bringing pressure to bear upon a Labor government to meet union demands, the affiliation of the QSSU, at least after 1947, was continued primarily as part of its campaign against left-wing leadership of the unions, a campaign in which it endorsed the work of the Industrial Groups and approved the successes of anti-communists in the TLC and the provincial councils of the TLC.

Affiliation with the ALP was undertaken as a result of the political convictions of the executive and council of the QSSU. Although the union allied itself with "right-wing" unions and maintained its affiliation with the party for wider political purposes than the satisfaction of the demands of its members, it nevertheless, from time to time, carried important claims previously refused by the premier to the QCE and Labor-in-Politics Conventions in the hope of bringing about a satisfactory outcome through endorsement by the policy-making bodies of the party. It submitted items to convention asking it to *instruct* the PLP and setting a time within which convention's decisions were to be implemented by the PLP.[14] However, in 1956, when the issue was the obligation of the government to implement official policy, the QSSU delegate to the QCE believed that the QCE had no right to direct the government.[15] The three weeks' leave issue was not an immediate matter for public servants who already enjoyed three weeks' leave, and while approving in principle its extension to all workers, the QSSU disapproved of "any direction by any body outside Parliament whatsoever as to when this legislation should be introduced"[16] and voted with the politicians against the Trades Hall unions and their allies.

This brief discussion of the relationships of four unions with a succession of Labor governments shows that while many union demands were satisfied, some were not. Labor governments, as employers, were criticized for not complying with the minimum requirements for safety, health and accommodation laid down in their own industrial legislation, and unions expected to be able to confer with Labor ministers on industrial and political matters. There were five major issues in which almost all unions were interested: control of prices, the forty-hour week, long service leave, the provisions of the Industrial Conciliation and Arbitration Act, and workers compensation. In these areas substantial gains were made under Labor governments.

From about 1953, when relations between cabinet and the trade union movement began to deteriorate, unions found themselves in a much more difficult position. The AWU, which for years had believed its interest to be almost identical with the government's, thought it was being neglected. Many unions affiliated with the TLC had a similar feeling, and in December 1953 the TLC resolved that a circular be prepared "explaining the full facts concerning the refusal [by certain ministers] to meet deputations on compensation and other matters."[17] Ministerial replies were rejected as unsatisfactory by a meeting in June 1955, and demands for meetings pressed again without success. At the 1953 Labor-in-Politics Convention, five items of interest to unions had been carried against ministerial opposition, and there was evidence in several debates of failing faith in the government. The 1956 Convention showed clearly the degree of disunity within the party, and this disunity polarized around the issue of three weeks' leave. Failure to legislate for three weeks' annual leave not only weakened the support of the unions for the parliamentary wing of the ALP, but endangered the relationship between union officials and their members. It was an issue which affected almost all the unions, and unions which were ideologically divided on issues related to anti-communism closed ranks against politicians in upholding the right of convention to instruct the parliamentary wing.

It is open to debate whether improvements in wages and working conditions achieved under Labor governments during this period might not have been achieved under non-Labor governments by industrial action, through arbitration and in response to rising expectations and community standards. (Indeed, three weeks' annual leave for all workers was granted soon after the Gair government had been defeated.) Yet an examination of the total 1915-1957 period certainly indicated that Queensland workers and unions had benefited by having distinctively labour oriented governments in office in these years. However, by 1957 the memory of the harsh anti-union legislation of the Moore government was losing its strength and this allowed union leaders to argue that they would be no worse off under a non-Labor government.

It is true that the unions had originally formed their own political party because this was the most effective way to achieve the industrial and social reforms their members required. However, it may also be argued that some unions remained affiliated with the ALP, not only because of industrial rewards gained or expected, but because of the political convictions of their influential members and the trappings of power that were shared by union officials who were members of the QCE. This was to be an important factor in maintaining the affiliation of many unions in the years after Labor lost office.

Don Rawson argues that affiliation with the ALP provides

important satisfactions for the more active minorities of union members, including union officials:

> To draw attention to them now is not to suggest that partisanship is maintained solely or even largely for the material benefit of union elites. On the contrary, the most important satisfactions which it gives are probably those which are felt by the lowest level of unpaid officials and the active minority of rank and file members, who see the success of the Labor Party as steps towards a better society, for which they are prepared to contribute much time and trouble. On the other hand, it is also relevant that union partisanship has been the means of taking many union officials to parliament and to other positions in which they enjoy power and influence.[18]

This latter satisfaction is most obviously illustrated by the activities and political successes of members of the AWU, but both the QSSU and the BSA displayed the importance of political convictions in maintaining affiliation and pursuing goals wider than the narrow interests of their own members. In contradistinction, the ARU, because it was ideologically to the left of the majority at the time in the ALP, was not affiliated during this period, although it was nevertheless highly aware of political issues.

NOTES

1. For more detailed discussion see J. Guyatt, "Trade unions and the Australian Labor Party in Queensland 1947-57" (M.A. thesis, University of Queensland, 1971).
2. *Official Record of the Nineteenth Labor-in-Politics Convention*, Brisbane, 1947, pp. 22ff.
3. Interview with C.E.W. Williams at Dunstan House, Brisbane, 17 June 1970.
4. *Worker,* 10 September 1955.
5. For a more detailed account of the pastoral dispute of 1956 see J. Guyatt, "The Labor Government and the Queensland Shearers' Strike of 1956", *Labour History,* no. 33 (November 1977).

6. *Worker,* 20 February 1956.
7. *Courier-Mail,* 11 July 1956.
8. *Advocate,* 15 September 1949.
9. Ibid., 15 May 1957.
10. *State Service,* August 1949, p. 1.
11. Ibid., December 1949, p. 2.
12. Ibid., January 1947, p. 14.
13. Ibid., January 1953, p. 2.
14. Agenda for Labor-in-Politics Convention 1950, items 69 and 158; 1953, items 275 and 290.
15. *State Service,* February 1956, p. 5.
16. Ibid., December 1956, p. 15.
17. Trades and Labor Council minutes, 2 December 1953 (held at Trades Hall, Brisbane).
18. D.W. Rawson, "The paradox of partisan trade unionism" (Unpublished paper delivered at ANZAAS Congress, Perth, 1973), p. 30.

25 The 1957 Split: "A Drop in the Ocean in Political History"

D.J. Murphy

The Queensland labor movement, at the end of World War II, had three forces competing for support amongst its members. By far the largest, and in many respects the least well organized and co-ordinated were the traditional ALP forces in the trade unions and party branches. The two other forces, the Communist party and the Catholic Social Studies Movement (called the "Organization" in church circles, but better known later as the "Movement"), owed their inspiration and ideologies to non-Australian sources; they were smaller than the ALP, tightly disciplined and organized and lacking the pragmatism of the ALP. Both had penetrated the trade unions, but only the "Movement" had infiltrated the ALP and wielded some influence there.

Just as World War I had thrown up an increased militancy within many unions, an increase in the belief in a Marxist revolution and a rejection among small groups of the Labor party's slow, constitutional approach to reform, so World War II repeated the pattern. The comradeship of the service units during the war, the courage of the Russian soldiers and people in holding off the best Nazi forces,the vigorous support of the Communist party for the prosecution of the war and the hard work of communists within and for the unions, contributed to the size and strength of the Australian Communist party in 1945. For the only period in its history, the Communist party had had its own Australian identity and was not merely an overseas arm of the Communist party of the Soviet Union.[1] Yet so long as the ALP held the loyalty of most active trade unionists, the Communist party could never become the Australian workers' party.

With the end of the war, the communists had resumed their

fight against the Labor party. They derided the ALP and its substantial industrial reforms as being mere palliatives which tempered and destroyed, what the communists argued, was the workers' natural desire for revolution. However, the communists overestimated their strength, mis-read the aspirations of the Australian workers and alienated their own union members. By the mid-1950s they had effectively destroyed their influence in the unions.

At the 1947 Labor-in-Politics Convention, the QCE was authorized to establish Industrial Groups in unions in Queensland as they had been established in New South Wales and Victoria. In July 1948, Joe Bukowski, then southern district secretary of the AWU, Tom Rasey, formerly an official of the Transport Workers Union and now an alderman in the Brisbane City Council and Ted Walsh, deputy premier prior to the 1947 election, were appointed as the ALP Industrial Group executive committee by the QCE. Their role was to defeat communists in union elections.

At this convention there were several significant debates on industrial questions. Comments by two delegates deserve noting because of their relevance in 1956 and 1957.[2] Ted Walsh was a determined anti-communist, in the Fallon tradition, and one who had developed a mild obsession about communists being involved in the agitation for changes in industrial laws. This made him ultra-sensitive to any suggestion that the convention might instruct, as distinct from recommend to, the government on how it should legislate. A motion by Artie Cole, secretary of the Queensland Railway Maintenance Union, "that Convention recommends ... that ... they [PLP] consult railway unions ...." immediately brought Walsh to his feet. "I oppose the motion", he said, "because I do not think that any section of the community can instruct the Government as to the nature of the legislation that should be introduced". When Harry Harvey, president of the TLC, secretary of the Miscellaneous Workers Union and a member of the "inner executive" put the motion in broader terms and emphasized the "Convention recommends" wording, Walsh accepted it without any fuss.

Labor governments had been supported by workers and

Ted Walsh was a determined anti-communist and developed an obsession about communists being involved in the agitation for industrial law changes. (Photograph by courtesy of Queensland Newspapers Ltd.)

farmers because they had legislated directly on their behalf. However, there was a problem in defining the line between what a Labor government might do directly for employees and what should be left for their unions to argue before the Arbitration Court. In February 1947, Jack Duggan was still a back-bencher but would replace Walsh in the transport portfolio after the election. He was uneasy about the government's legislating directly in questions of the basic wage and hours of work. He supported Hanlon's proposal for a forty-hour week as convention had recommended (see Chapter 1), but took a longer view backwards and forwards of the problems posed by such direct legislation.

> I emphasise the fact that the ALP and the Government are committed to a policy of arbitration. We have been advised to resist demands for alteration of working conditions from time to time

> because the Government were committed to a policy of arbitration. Where is there to be a line of demarcation on these things? If we agree in this case to introduce a 40 hour week, it is possible that at some future time the Industrial Movement will ask us to increase the basic wage by £1 a week. If we adopt the policy of other Labor Governments we will tell them to go to the Court.

Unfortunately in 1957 that was not to be a possible solution to the three weeks' leave issue.

The ALP in Queensland had contained a large proportion of Catholics since 1916 and Labor cabinets up to 1952 contained four or so Catholics in cabinets of eleven ministers. Both the Catholic church and the Labor party had kept each other at a safe distance. The archbishop of Brisbane, James Duhig, was a conservative Edwardian man of property who had supported conscription in World War I and was not in sympathy with many of Labor's goals and aspirations. When the Catholic Social Studies Movement disbanded itself in July 1956 to regroup as a new lay organization freed from the direct authority of the bishops, Duhig immediately affiliated the Brisbane archdiocese with the new organization which shortly was to become the National Civic Council. Bishops H.E. Ryan (Townsville), A.G. Tynan (Rockhampton) and W. Brennan (Toowoomba) likewise affiliated their dioceses.[3] For its part, the ALP, whether under Catholic premiers like Ryan and Theodore or Protestant premiers like Forgan Smith and Cooper, determined to keep church and state apart and was conscious of the electoral consequences of being publicly allied with any one church.

Within the ALP, the emergence of communists as a force in the unions, produced two counter reactions. One was from traditional ALP trade unionists, such as George Whiteside, of the Federated Engine Drivers and Firemen's Association (FEDFA), who organized their own anti-communist groups within their unions to defeat communists at union elections. The other reaction came from the Catholic Social Studies Movement, started in Melbourne in 1942, which, while carefully and secretly remaining in the background, joined with other anti-communists to form ALP industrial groups to contest union elections against the communists. Membership of an industrial group was not synonymous with membership or even knowledge of the "Movement". Most "Groupers" had no knowledge of the secret "Movement" cells within their group. Some who did were not conscious of the contradiction in their own simple goals of defeating communists in the trade unions and the longer term goals of "the Movement". The majority of "Groupers" were genuine anti-communists and loyal ALP supporters who wanted to see a continuation of the practical reforms that had characterized Queensland Labor governments since 1915.

At the time of the formation of the industrial groups in Queensland few people knew of the existence of the Catholic Social Studies Movement.[4] Nor was it appreciated that this branch of Catholic action, officially under the authority of the Catholic hierarchy, had as its most powerful official, a Melbourne lawyer, B.A. Santamaria. His aggressive Catholicism was that of the sixteenth century Counter Reformation, not that of the defensive Irish church that had sought and achieved acceptability in a predominantly Protestant Australia. Santamaria wanted to "roll back the tides" of communismm, freemasonry, industrial urban capitalism, liberalism, Protestantism and agnosticism, an ambition worthy of his crusading zeal. In a *Catholic Worker* article on "The Movement" in July 1959, Santamaria was quoted as having said, in 1952, that the movement should not only try to depose communists from union positions but also "Individuals who refuse to fight organised atheism or who, in fact, objectively side with it or its supporters, [and] individuals who oppose the broad social policies laid down, for instance, in the Social Encyclical".[5]

A reading of Santamaria's written works suggests that his long term ambition for Australia was a type of corporate theocratic state, of 20 to 30 million people, organized into self-supporting agricultural communities. The "Movement" was not merely an anti-communist organization, but a positive force with a goal of using the Labor party and Labor governments to carry out the migration, agricultural and other programmes which the

"Movement" sought to implement. Santamaria's central thesis about the role and goals of the Communist party in infiltrating the trade unions fits well with the role and goals that he had for the Catholic Social Studies Movement. Not all of his closest followers understood or appreciated the intellectual basis of the "Movement". There were two full-time officers of the "Movement" in Queensland, A. Poulgrain and W. Thornton.[6] The latter became a QCE delegate representing the Clerks Union in 1950.

According to Archbishop Mannix: "The 'Movement' began in Melbourne in 1943 [it began in 1942] as a lay organisation whose members undertook loyally to follow the policies and programme laid down by the Executive. In 1945, it received the backing of the Bishops as a national Organisation with a commission to fight Communism wherever it showed itself".[7] It was a highly disciplined organization. Bishop F.P. O'Collins of Ballarat put this more strongly to the other bishops in January 1956: "The decisions of the National Executive of the 'Movement' were binding on its members in all dioceses which belonged to the 'Movement'. Although delegates from dioceses had the right to take part in the making of decisions, no member of the 'Movement' could go his own way after a decision had been made and still remain a member".[8]

In a report on the 1957 ACTU Congress, submitted to the archbishop of Perth, Santamaria described the success of the "Movement" prior to 1949: "The National Executive of this Movement, representing every State and region in Australia, was able to survey the whole of the Communist plan, and to take disciplined and co-ordinated counteraction in every trade union and political labor branch in every part of Australia."[9] Santamaria noted the ill-effects that the revelation, in 1954, of the "Movement's" existence and role had had on setting Catholic against Catholic in the trade unions. "While this sad spectacle of division reigns in Catholic ranks, the Communists are completely united", he said. "They are backed by Freemasonry, which is ruthlessly using the opportunity afforded by Catholic division, to purge every Catholic influence from Public life".

He may have been boasting too grandly of the penetration of

his organization into the Australian labor movement, but, by 1950, there was a growing uneasiness among some trade union officials that there was some other organization behind the industrial groups. It was felt that the groups were not just straight out organizations of anti-communist trade unionists committed to restoring ALP officials to communist controlled unions. Remarks by Fallon during the 1948 rail strike about a new political organization emerging in the labor movement and his taking leave from the AWU secretaryship for "private political research" are hints that Fallon too was concerned about this new political force. Suspicions were heightened at the 1949 federal elections, when Labor in Queensland found that the Liberal and Country parties were receiving assistance from people linked with the industrial groups. In the early 1950s, leaflets and how to vote "tickets" which recommended voting against well-known ALP union members and even ALP union officials, began appearing at union elections. Increasing suspicions about the people behind the groups was the observation that while most ALP branches and branches of unions were perennially "broke", the groups always seemed to have sufficient funds.[10]

At the 1950 Labor-in-Politics Convention, which commended strongly the work of the industrial groups, it was clear that the groups held the power within the Queensland labor movement. There were conflicts, in 1950 and 1951, between the TLC and the ALP affiliated unions about who should organize the Labour Day march and whether communists should be allowed to march as a separate body. However, with Mick Brosnan, a state parliamentarian, president of the Electrical Trades Union and Walsh's replacement on the Industrial Group Committee, Bukowski and Cole as the president, secretary and treasurer, respectively, of the Labour Day Celebrations Committee, the industrial groups controlled this also. Of more significance was the composition of the QCE's inner executive. Gone was the balance that Forgan Smith and Fallon had maintained among the PLP, AWU and Trades Hall unions (see Chapter 1). Harry Boland, state secretary of the AWU after Fallon's death in 1950, was the president, but C.R. Muhldorff, a

"Grouper", from the State Service Union was now vice-president. The premier and Walsh (re-elected to Parliament in 1950) were from the PLP, Bukowski was there as the other AWU official, but instead of there being two Trades Hall union officials, there were Rasey, now a member of the state parliament, and Cole, secretary of a small railway union not affiliated with the TLC. The groups and the "Movement" knew what was happening at the core of the ALP, but the ALP did not know what was happening at the core of the groups.

The Labor party in Queensland, and in the rest of Australia, was divided in its attitude to the referendum on the dissolution of the Communist party in September 1951. Opposition to communism was entwined with a desire to keep the party together and to regain office in the federal parliament. The Queensland ALP took two seemingly different courses on the referendum. Its two federal executive delegates, Syd Bryan, the QCE secretary, and Cole, voted to direct the ALP majority in the Senate to pass the Dissolution Bill, over the objections of Chifley and Evatt. However, the QCE supported the official "No" campaign. Boland and Bukowski threatened disciplinary action against those in the ALP and affiliated unions who were conducting an undercover "Yes" campaign.[11] There was a heavy "Yes" vote in Queensland and at the federal executive in 1952, Walsh and Bryan argued for lifting the ban placed on the "Movement's" paper, *News Weekly*, for its role in supporting the referendum. It was a measure of the strength that the "Movement" and groups held in the ALP.

Until 1953, the industrial groups continued to hold power easily within the Labor party in Queensland. They received an overwhelming vote of confidence from the delegates at the 1953 Labor-in-Politics Convention. However, the debate on the report by Bukowski, Rasey and Brosnan outlining the groups' success in union elections indicated that, among those who had supported the groups' campaign against the communists, there were many who were dismayed at what was happening. Many ALP union officials, who had fought the communists in the later 1940s, now found themselves being opposed for union positions through "how to vote tickets" drawn up outside the union. The explanation given for these ALP union officials being opposed or removed from office suggested a certain naivety among the "Groupers", and a lack of understanding about human beings' reactions. Bernie Parker, president of the Electrical Trades Union Industrial Group and a member of the "Movement" cell at Wavell Heights, a north Brisbane suburb, explained how his group worked:

> Prior to the meeting for the election of officers the *bona fide* of all candidates nominated for office are carefully examined so that Communists and fellow travellers may be weeded out. We have had some complaints that in the process some good Labor supporters have failed to get endorsed .... The Labor men who are not endorsed are notified and the position is further explained to them when the group pamphlet is sent out.[12]

The "Movement" was to be "a means to an end" according to Cardinal Gilroy. However, as information about the "Movement's" part in the industrial groups started to filter through to those trade union leaders who were paying particular attention to the groups' methods of action, there was a questioning about the "ends" of the groups. What were their ultimate ends? Jack Devereux of the Amalgamated Engineering Union had supported the industrial groups, but by 1953 he was questioning their future role inside the unions. He told the convention:

> I believe that the time has arrived when attention will have to be given to Industrial Groups and their activities. They were formed, and in a number of instances they accomplished the work for which they were formed — the defeat of Communists in the unions. Having done so the question of their further activities arises .... If we are prepared to get down to a stage of giving some consideration to where the Groups might move, having removed the Communists from the organisation, something might be achieved.[13]

There remained that strong traditional Labor opposition to communism and, despite the doubts expressed at the convention, 105 delegates, including Devereux, voted to adopt the report of

Bukowski, Rasey and Brosnan supporting the continuation of the work of the industrial groups. Only seven delegates walked to the other side of the hall when the division was called.

Unlike earlier Labor premiers, Vince Gair, premier after Hanlon's death in 1952, was a stranger at the Trades Hall and rejected an invitation to open the AWU Conference in 1953. The decline in the close association between the AWU and the cabinet was reflected, not only in complaints from the AWU itself, but in its campaign donations. The AWU had provided £3000 for the 1950 state election campaign, £1000 in 1953 (which it insisted be received by Gair personally), but stood over the question of a donation in 1956 until its January 1957 meeting when it gave £500. So much had the PLP drifted away from its close ties with the AWU that, in April 1955, five cabinet ministers, including Walsh and George Devries, a former AWU district secretary and Queensland vice-president, were informed that they would not be issued with AWU union tickets in future.

Confidence in the QCE was not inspired in Trades Hall affiliated unions in October 1953 when the new "inner executive" was elected. Boland and Muhldorff were unopposed, while Gair, Walsh, Cole and Brosnan were elected to the executive positions. Duggan, though elected deputy-premier in 1952, was kept off the QCE "ticket" by Gair and did not become a member of the QCE and of the "inner executive" until 1956. Two moderate, anti-communist union officials, Bert Milliner from the Printers Union and George Whiteside of the FEDFA were defeated in the ballot for the "inner executive" positions. *News Weekly* gleefully described them as having been "sponsored by an industrial clique from the Trades Hall".[14]

The growing divisions in the Labor party and its affiliated unions were not solely due to the presence of the "Movement" and the industrial groups. Unions felt that the government was not as responsive or as sympathetic to their industrial needs as a Labor government should have been. Deputations from affiliated unions waited on the QCE secretary to ask him to use his influence to persuade ministers to meet and confer with union delegations. A major source of union complaints, for both "left" and "right" unions was the performance and composition of the Industrial Court. It was overloaded with work; there was dissatisfaction with Mr Justice T.M. Barry, the president from 1952 to 1955; unions had long waits for decisions and the government seemed oblivious to union requests to activate the court. When W.J. Riordan retired from the Industrial Court in 1952, it was expected that Boland or Bukowski or at least another unionist would replace him. However, no new appointment was made until January 1956 when, instead of a unionist, the ailing public service commissioner, J. McCracken, was promoted sideways on to the bench. He died in September that year.

On the other hand, there were significant industrial reforms by the Gair governments. The most important of these was the provision of long service leave for all employees in Queensland in 1952. This was indeed a major reform which had come about, not through any convention recommendation, but after a deputation from the AWU and the Shop Assistants Union. The government also granted three weeks' leave to public servants. There were further amendments made to the Industrial Conciliation and Arbitration Act, the Workers Compensation Act and increases in sick leave and long service leave. For its part, the government defended its industrial record by arguing that it was providing stable employment through investing in developmental projects and higher real wages through its control of prices. The *Labour Reports* of the period confirm this latter argument. While average male wages in money terms in Queensland were well below the national average, real wages, adjusted for prices, remained the highest in Australia.[15]

Unions, however, were not entirely convinced by these arguments and between 1953 and 1957, industrial grievances and religion became enmeshed in the battle between "Groupers" and "anti-Groupers". This fight dragged Queensland into the controversy over Evatt's revelation of the existence of the "Movement", and the ALP split in the southern states. An indication of the division in the Queensland ALP came in November 1954 when Gair and the new QCE secretary, Jack Schmella, both Catholics, voted against each other at the federal executive meeting which decided that the Victorian branch of the ALP had to be reconstituted and the "Movement's" grip over the party broken there. In the reaction to the decision on Victoria, the "Movement" seemed to intensify its forces in Queensland to combat the growing anti-grouper feeling there. Catholic unionists and ALP members found themselves in a fearsome ideological battle which few understood. Communism seemed to be only a side issue. They heard priests using their Sunday sermons to urge Catholics to vote for the Gair Labor party in Queensland in 1953 and 1956, but to vote against the Evatt and Calwell Labor party in the 1954 and 1955 federal elections. Catholic unionists particularly were aware of the intense pressure on themselves and their families, within Catholic parishes, not to oppose the "Movement" in the unions or in the ALP. A Catholic fitter in the Amalgamated Engineering Union who had been recruited by the industrial groups after the war, and who became a brother in a Catholic teaching order after the split, put the issue to the author in these terms. "By 1956 a lot of us had become disillusioned. There was a feeling about that the industrial groups had lost their goal of fighting the Coms and were engaged in an ideological battle outside normal Australian politics. Nobody had heard of Santamaria."

There were other issues that divided the labor movement. The Printers and Newspaper Act of 1953, in its provisions for compulsory annual registration of printing presses (and even roneoing machines) and for the legal seizure of such machines was seen as an illiberal piece of legislation designed to intimidate "left wing" union leaders. The Legion of Ex-Servicemen and Women to which many trade unionists belonged and of which Frank Waters, an arch opponent of Gair and the industrial groups, had been the president, felt that it was being harassed by the police. Gair became the focal point of this "Grouper" and "anti-Grouper" battle and of the unions' campaign for a better deal, industrially, from the government. Added to this were those, opposing Gair, who were motivated by more than negative sentiments. Their campaign went back into the 1930s. They sought to break the oligarchic power of the inner executive, and to remove the AWU hold over the whole Labor party organization. They hoped to prevent any one man whether he was the QCE president or parliamentary leader from ever holding absolute power in the party and to open the Labor party out again to some fresh social democratic air. "Gair Must Go" became the combined slogan.

Gair himself was an intelligent, traditional, pragmatic ALP premier, steeped in the Labor party, known to be stubborn, but much in the same mould as other Labor premiers throughout Australia. He often appeared devious to his colleagues, but he was a capable administrator and was willing to legislate directly for changes that would benefit working men and their families. However, he was deeply involved in the politics surrounding the industrial groups. Although he rejected the AWU's offer of union membership, in 1950 he joined the Federated Clerks Union, a stronghold of the industrial groups, and three years

Premier Vince Gair seemed to have invited the martyrdom by his own supporters, which led to the second great split in the history of the Labor party in Queensland. (Photograph by courtesy of the John Oxley Library.)

later he took on as his private secretary, Brian Mullins. Mullins is now the Queensland president of the National Civic Council, but in 1953, he was a member of the "Movement" cell or team at Wavell Heights. Gair seems to have kept himself personally unconnected with the "Movement", though this has been recently disputed.[16] In any case, however, the presence of Mullins as his private secretary meant that the "Movement" had penetrated right to the heart of the Labor government. In January 1975, Gair told the author that he did not meet Santamaria until well after the split. Nevertheless, Gair was too shrewd and too experienced a politician not to have known what the "Movement" was doing. His story of the almost haphazard appointment of Mullins as his private secretary, as told to the author, and also recorded in Frank Mines, *Gair* (Canberra, 1975) has an implausible ring. If Gair was being totally frank about the appointment of Mullins, this suggests that the "Movement" deliberately planted one of its senior members right in the premier's office.

Because of the direct assistance thrown behind him by the Catholic hierarchy in 1953 and 1956 (partly through the greater opportunities he represented for state aid to Catholic schools) Gair was to prove one of the most popular vote getters among all Queensland premiers ranking with Ryan and Forgan Smith.[17] It might have been better for him as premier and for the ALP, if his majorities in 1953 and 1956 had been smaller. They certainly contributed to his willingness to fight his ALP opponents to the death, rather than to seek a normal political compromise.

One could read the 168-page verbatim report of the 1953 Convention and almost miss a motion, passed without opposition or debate: "that it be the aim of the Labor Movement to obtain for the workers three week's annual holidays in southern areas and four weeks in the northern and western areas". This became the great issue in 1956 and 1957 which destroyed the political coalition that Ryan, Theodore and McCormack had built, which Forgan Smith and Fallon had perfected and which Cooper and Hanlon had maintained.

In 1953, the dominant AWU-PLP coalition, with some other unions, still held together. Both supported the industrial groups.

However, following the public revelation of the "Movement's" involvement behind the groups, and the reversal of attitudes to the groups by Tom Dougherty, the AWU federal secretary, the AWU in Queensland, through Bukowski, dramatically withdrew its support from the groups in January 1955.[18] Boland, Bukowski and the AWU retained their firm anti-communism, but a new, uneasy coalition was being formed inside the ALP. This consisted of Schmella, the AWU officials, state parliamentarians such as "Johnno" Mann and Felix Dittmer who were in dispute with Gair and Walsh in the caucus, and a group of Trades Hall affiliated unions. The key figure in this last group was Jack Egerton, secretary of the Boilermakers Society, whose chief tutor was Frank Waters, by now one of the most experienced men in the labor movement with an increasing knowledge of and great dislike for the "Movement".

Jack Egerton was a key figure in a group of Trades Hall affiliated unions. It was said of him: "Egerton was magnificent. The only weapon he knew how to use was the blunt end of an axe and he used it." (Photograph by courtesy of Queensland Newspapers Ltd.)

Egerton was then inexperienced in Labor politics. Prior to 1956, he was not a member of the QCE, and had attended only one Labor-in-Politics Convention as a delegate. That was in 1950. He was personally a very courageous and ambitious man, but also a brilliant, though ruthless, organizer who paid close attention to every detail of his campaign. Letters and reports written by Egerton and his closer allies (and seen by the author) reveal Egerton's thoroughness as a political organizer. There was also the other side to his character. In 1957, he lacked political acumen. The late Bert Milliner described the Egerton of the early 1950s to the author in these terms: "Egerton was magnificent. The only weapon he knew how to use was the blunt end of an axe and he used it". Building the Trades Hall affiliated unions as his power base, Egerton worked tirelessly and with effect for twelve months before the 1956 Convention delegates were elected. He, Schmella, Bukowski, a few state politicians and the AWU district secretaries swung an overwhelmingly Grouper majority in 1953, into a comfortable anti-Grouper majority in 1956. The establishment of this unstable coalition was assisted by Gair and Walsh whose handling of two deputations of moderate and "right-wing" union officials on the three weeks' leave decision of the 1953 Convention turned possible allies among the unions into opponents.

The Federal Conference at Hobart in 1955 confirmed the dismissal of the "old" Victorian executive which had been a power centre of the industrial groups. The boycotting of the conference by Gair, Walsh, Cole, Tom Bolger of the State Service Union and Clarrie Bushell of the Bricklayers Society produced contradictory reactions in Queensland. The PLP passed a vote of confidence in Gair, but endorsed the decisions passed by the remaining delegates at the conference. Similarly, the QCE voted to support Gair, but also endorsed the platform of the Hobart conference at which Boland had remained. Both reactions were evidence of the broader desire to maintain unity within the Labor party in Queensland and to keep the split in the southern states outside Queensland. If reflected the desire to hold on to government in Queensland, which still overrode personal and ideological conflicts.

At another time in the party's history and with different men holding power, the three weeks' leave issue would not have been the cause of a split. However, such were the personal animosities, between Gair and Walsh on one side and Schmella, Boland, Bukowski and Egerton on the other, that any major issue on which there was disagreement could have been made the grounds for an all out power struggle. This personal struggle, though it had Catholics, Protestants and agnostics on both sides, was to become heavily laced with sectarian suspicion and bitterness. One contemporary described it as a fight between the "Grippers and the Groupers" (i.e., Freemasons and Catholics), with the "Grubs" sitting on the sidelines. For a Catholic, like the ALP organizer, Jim Keeffe, who was at the centre of the anti-grouper organization, it was a very difficult period. His two older children (aged twelve and eight) were later abducted by an elderly female pillar

Jim Keeffe, QCE organizer at the time of the "split".

of the Catholic church who harangued them for an hour about their "evil" father who was so closely involved with the ALP and therefore with communism!

As it turned out, in 1956 and 1957 three weeks' leave was the best possible issue about which to unite a coalition against Gair. It became a genuine industrial grievance which cut temporarily across "Grouper" and "anti-Grouper" divisions in the unions and in the ALP.

After the 1953 Convention, it became evident that certain communists at the Trades Hall were planning to embarrass the ALP and to outmanoeuvre the ALP union officials by seeking to gain the extra week's leave through industrial action. In view of the convention decision, and to spike the communists' campaign, a group of unions sent a delegation led by George Whiteside and Jack Devereux to the cabinet to seek an amendment to the Industrial Conciliation and Arbitration Act to provide for three weeks' leave, instead of two, for employees working under state awards. The delegation met Gair, Walsh now treasurer, and Arthur Jones, the minister for labour and industry. They explained their purpose and left with the clear impression that the government would outflank the communists by legislating for the three weeks' annual leave. This was what they reported to their unions.[19] At about the same time, the QCE was also considering the industrial items passed at the convention and on 15 July 1955 appointed a sub-committee of Bukowski, Devereux, Bolger, Bill Barry from the Clerks Union, Archie Dawson of the ETU and Wally Major of the Shop Assistants Union to meet the premier on long service, sick and annual leave. Gair indicated to this committee that Arthur Jones was preparing amendments to the act on sick leave and long service leave and that "it was not a bad idea to have something in their policy speech about three weeks' leave". That is, three weeks' annual leave would not be introduced during the 1953-56 Parliament, but unions could expect to receive it after the election.[20]

This was reported to the QCE on 23 September when the changes in long service leave and sick leave were endorsed and when it was recommended to the cabinet that the act be further amended to provide for three weeks' annual leave. No answer to this recommendation was received by either the QCE or by the delegation that Bukowski had led. However in the Brisbane *Telegraph* of 25 October it was reported that the government would not be providing for the extra week's leave. The PLP had endorsed the view of Gair and Walsh that the state's economic situation would not allow for the additional cost that the extra leave would entail. Gair told the QCE that as the three weeks' leave was only a recommendation to the government and not an instruction, it did not bind the government to any time-table. Now by a vote of thirty-eight to ten, the QCE instructed the PLP to introduce the three weeks' leave.

It was now November and the state elections were due sometime between March and June of the following year. Hanging over the members of the PLP was the spectre of Victoria where Labor had lost office in June 1955 following the bitter divisions in the party there. This fear of losing their seats and perhaps even the government was heightened by a threat from Gair to resign. Reversing the precedent of the PLP support for the forty-four-hour week issue in 1924, (see Chapter 1) the PLP, by twenty-eight votes to twenty, decided to stand by Gair and the cabinet against the QCE. For the affiliated unions, the problem of how to achieve the additional leave was thrown back into the Labor party itself. Gair had advised the shop assistants to go to the Industrial Court which in turn told this union that it had no power under the act to grant more than two weeks' leave unless this was by agreement between employers and employees. In December, the QCE asked the PLP to reconsider its decision, but in January, the PLP, fearing what the newspapers would say during the election campaign about their receiving a direction on the leave issue, reaffirmed their earlier decision by thirty votes to nineteen. There was nothing more that the QCE could do other than to refer the whole question to the party's supreme policy making body, the Labor-in-Politics Convention which was to meet at Mackay in March. The QCE decision to do this was without opposition.

Labor conventions have been occasions of great political drama when divisions have been overcome by careful agreements or widened out into party splits. The 1956 Convention could have been either, however since most of the leading figures came armed to do battle, it was more likely that the latter description would apply. Only Duggan and Devereux seemed determined to avoid open conflict at all costs and to hold the Labor party together by tact, commonsense and normal political compromise.

There were 134 delegates at this convention, seventy-five representing branches in each of the state electorates and fifty-nine representing affiliated unions. This understated the union strength since many union officials were there as branch delegates. To take two AWU examples: Gerry Goding, the central district secretary represented the Isis electorate and Edgar Williams, the northern district secretary, represented Townsville. There were twenty-four members of state parliament including two representing unions; two senators and one member of the House of Representatives. Schmella represented the Barambah electorate and therefore had a vote.

Harry Boland was elected chairman without opposition. He was unwell and was to die four months after the convention. There were ballots for all other positions and there would have been a ballot even for the scrutineers to check the votes if it had not been agreed to have two scrutineers from each side. The first ballot, for returning officer, was won by Bukowski by eighty votes to fifty-two. This indicated the strength of the anti-Gair and pro-Gair sides. The ballot for vice-chairman was won by "Johnno" Mann now Speaker in the Legislative Assembly. Subsequent ballots for credentials committee, appeals committee, agenda committee and one later to resolve an appeal were all won by the anti-Gair forces and followed the same voting pattern with only a few votes difference.

The changes from the 1953 Convention were further apparent on Tuesday morning when Muhldorff moved for the establishment "of an efficient organised fighting force in trade unions to combat communism". Official ALP endorsement of the industrial groups had been withdrawn at the 1955 Federal Conference. The groups could still operate legally in the unions, but could not use the title "ALP" and could not be officially sanctioned by the party. Muhldorff's motion almost lapsed for want of a seconder. An amendment by Egerton reaffirming the ALP's continued opposition to communism, in similar terms to that adopted by the federal conference, was easily carried.

On the third day, Boland delivered his presidential address. It was not an inspiring speech that would unite the convention, but a prosaic call for a more sympathetic administration of the state's industrial laws. A motion calling for party unity, which followed Boland's address, produced the opposite effect and signified the depth of the division at the convention. Bukowski leapt in to criticize the lack of support for the federal Labor party in Queensland at the 1955 election and to complain of Catholic priests instructing their congregations not to vote for Labor candidates then. Walsh retaliated by criticizing branches in Brisbane who had not supported Mick Lyons in the 1955 Lord Mayoral elections on the grounds that he was a "Grouper".

Shortly before lunch on the Wednesday, Devereux moved the central motion of the convention:[21] "That the Conciliation and Arbitration Act be amended as under: Section 10A Sub-section 2(i): Delete 'three weeks' and insert 'four weeks'. Section 10A Sub-section 2(ii): Delete 'two weeks' and insert 'three weeks'." His speech traced the history of the three weeks' leave debate and touched only briefly on the power of the QCE to interpret convention decisions. Devereux's motion laid down no specific timetable for the government, nor did it make any reference to the convention's directing the government. These matters were already covered in the general party rules, but Devereux was anxious to conciliate, not to fight. General rule 16 then stated: "The State Parliamentary Labor Party to introduce during the next term of Parliament succeeding Convention, all legislation covering decisions of Convention", a rule often broken by previous Labor governments. A further rule stated: "All endorsed Australian Labor Party Members and Candidates shall be bound by the decisions of the latest convention and the latest platform . . . ." Devereux's motion was seconded by Barry of the Clerks Union.

Now, however, the debate moved away from conciliation

when Vince Hefferan, secretary of the Shop Assistants Union, moved to amend Devereux's motion by adding the words "and the Arbitration Act be amended this year, 1956, and to take effect from 1st January 1957". It was symptomatic of the general feeling of frustration with the Gair government by the unions, on this issue, that the secretary of the Shop Assistants Union should advocate a clear convention instruction to the government. The Shop Assistants Union had been characterized by its avoidance of direct industrial action and its commitment to conciliation and to the arbitration system. The seconder, Leo Connolly, was a strong supporter of the industrial groups and also came from a decidedly non-militant union, the Railway Traffic Employees Union. He wanted a definite time limit on the implementation of Devereux's motion.

Gair himself now rose to speak. He opposed Hefferan's amendment, but supported Devereux's motion. "I say that the resolution moved by Mr Devereux is quite in order", he told the convention ". . . the Government will implement this legislation as soon as possible". He delivered a short homily on responsible government, which was to become his stock speech after 1957, but which, somehow, did not fit Vince Gair the politician in 1956. It now reads like an artificial argument prepared before the convention to get around a party rule which he had not opposed in twenty-four years in Parliament. If the convention directed the government as to when it should introduce three weeks' leave, he said, "you members of this Convention would be a party to the unconstitutional decision and to an unconstitutional act". Gair did not oppose the government's legislating directly for the extra leave; his opposition was to being directed by the QCE or the convention to do this within a certain time.

There was a case for caution in 1956 in granting an extra week's annual leave to all employees. The Forestry Department was preparing to sack seven hundred employees and the Railway Department was also looking at possible staff retrenchments. Although Walsh had budgeted for a small surplus in 1955-56 and would budget for a small surplus again in 1956-57, he was using cash reserves of £12 million, acquired during the war, to bridge the gap between income and expenditure. These reserves were all used by 1956-57 and Tom Hiley, the financial spokesman for the opposition, argued that Queensland should now have been applying to the Commonwealth Grants Commission for additional financial assistance. On the other hand, Queensland had done somewhat better from Commonwealth tax reimbursements in 1956, receiving an additional £2.5 million and Walsh conceded to the convention that the extra cost of the three weeks' leave could have been borne by the government. However, he and Gair argued that the future financial position was unclear and that it would be better to keep men employed with two weeks' leave a year than to have men put off through the extra cost of three weeks' leave. If union leaders were not impressed by this argument, it was because they had already received two clear indications that the government would introduce the legislation and because they had heard employers and governments cry "wolf" so often before when similar reforms were being sought, particularly at the time of the forty-four-hour and the forty-hour week legislation.

Egerton followed Gair and supported Hefferan's amendment in a speech that allowed for no compromises. "I think there is much logic in what the Premier said", he told the delegates, "but the time for logic had passed". He wanted the convention to give a direction to the government because without that specific direction, the QCE's authority on this issue would be considerably lessened. Again, he told the convention, "The time for logic has passed". Gerry Goding, one of the senior AWU officials at the convention, followed Egerton and foreshadowed a further amendment: "And the Premier include this in his policy speech with the assurance that this resolution will be implemented during the first session of the new Parliament." He told the convention that his amendment, in no way, was to be construed as a direction to the government. George Pont, the far northern district secretary of the AWU, followed and supported Devereux.

Duggan now entered the debate and, in a masterly speech in support of Devereux, tried to bridge the chasm between the two conflicting sides, or as he said himself, he was "trying to retrieve the situation". Duggan understood better than his cabinet colleagues the frustrations felt by the unions over the handling of the leave issue by Gair and Walsh. He also appreciated the bitterness of many unions regarding other matters that were dividing the labor movement. In cabinet, Duggan had not supported the extra week's leave because of the costs involved and the loss of jobs already predicted by government departments. As in 1947, he was not thrilled about the direct use of government power to increase annual leave. However, he appreciated that there was now a different atmosphere in the ALP from that of 1947. "I am not too arrogant to accept a direction", he told the convention. He conceded that a Labor-in-Politics Convention had the technical authority to direct the Parliamentary Labor Party, but he understood better than most delegates the determination of Gair and Walsh not to yield to such a direction. He was concerned that the convention would force Gair and Walsh into a corner, from where they would fight. He urged the delegates to "consider the political repercussions which could result and be a great danger to the Labor Government in this State".

Eight other delegates followed Duggan, including Bart Lourigan, the delegate from Sherwood, and supported either Devereux or Hefferan. Then Walsh spoke. If any speech should have urged caution on the delegates, it was that of Walsh:

> I would say that the motion as moved by Mr Devereux and as debated by him indicated that he was prepared to trust the Government if the Labor Government is returned. I say very definitely and advisedly that the wrong decision on this question tonight could result in one of the most sensational political developments in this State.

Egerton laughed. But Walsh was not in a humorous mood. "I am prepared to ignore a direction from this body, or any other body," he said. What of the rules regarding the implementation of convention decisions that Edgar Williams had raised earlier? In tones reminiscent of his 1947 address, Walsh answered:

> Surely you have the intelligence to know that while we are bound by those particular rules here that we are not expected to apply

> them in a way that the Government is going to be surrendered to this or any other body. I would be surprised if you advocated along these lines, because it is getting near the Communist technique.

"Johnno" Mann appealed for support for Devereux's motion, while Devereux himself, in summing up, rejected any notion of directing the government and said: "I am prepared to trust the Government on its being returned".

The convention now prepared to vote. Hefferan's amendment was defeated on the voices. Goding moved his foreshadowed amendment which was, in substance, not different form that of Hefferan. When this amendment was seconded, Boland gave a ruling from the chair whose effect was little noticed at the time, but which was critical to the whole debate. He immediately closed the debate and would allow no discussion on Goding's amendment for which a division was called without names being recorded. The convention divided seventy-five votes for and fifty-eight against. It then became the motion and was carried. As the convention adjourned at 10 o'clock, Gair announced that he was summoning a cabinet meeting that night to consider the government's position.

Few convention delegates gained much sleep that night as the cabinet, the various factions and groups of party members met to review the serious situation which now faced the party two months before an election. An attempt by Gair and Walsh to have the whole cabinet resign so as to force a rescinding of Goding's amendment, was dropped when five of the eleven ministers refused to agree to any resignation. On the following day however, the Gair forces recognized that they were outnumbered at the convention, by offering no opposition to the ticket of Boland, Bukowski, Duggan, Egerton, Whiteside and Dittmer for the federal conference whose delegates were being elected by the convention for the first time since 1918. When Gair, Boland and Schmella were nominated for the two federal executive positions, also being filled by the convention for the first time since 1918, Gair withdrew his nomination. Yet, if any delegates thought that Gair had conceded defeat on the three weeks' leave issue, they were quite mistaken. Towards the close of the fourth day, after the convention had heard an address by Evatt and a "hearty vote of thanks" to Evatt by Gair, the premier rose in his place to report on the previous night's meeting. Throughout the controversy, even when there were divisions within the cabinet, the traditional solidarity of cabinet was maintained. "Cabinet considered the matter very carefully", he told the convention, "and unanimously decided that, having regard to all factors and circumstances, it did not accept the direction contained in the resolution". A convention committee, headed by Bukowski, and consisting of Pont, Devereux, Col Maxwell, Hec Chalmers, Whiteside and Egerton was immediately formed to meet with Gair and Duggan. No agreement could be reached on a proposal to be put to the convention, but Gair privately gave the committee an under-taking to include three weeks' leave in his policy speech provided that he did not have to mention it specifically, but could camouflage it in phrases about general social and industrial welfare. As the convention closed, a vote of confidence was passed in Gair and in the Labor government.

Ranks were closed for the election with Gair addressing a meeting at the Trades Hall (his first ever), but remaining pretty sceptical about the support he would receive there. Nevertheless, based on what Gair had said to the Bukowski committee at the convention, there was a confidence that some reference to the three weeks' leave would be incorporated in his policy speech. There was no such reference when the speech was delivered. While the AWU, for the first time, held back its campaign donation, Gair provided £12,000, "in a brown paper bag", which was almost the total cost of the campaign. When Bukowski's committee met Gair on 30 May, after the election, he was again reported to the unions as having given an undertaking that the legislation would be brought in. On 1 June, the full QCE, including Gair, endorsed unanimously the inner executive's recommendation: "That in regard to the question of three weeks' annual leave, the QCE has every confidence that the Parliamentary Labor Party will carry out the policy of the Labor Party". S. Wright, the AFULE delegate on the QCE and a supporter of Gair, reported back to his divisional council meeting on 12 July 1956, that "it does appear that the legislation will be brought down in the first session of parliament".[22] But, once more, there was no mention of the legislation when the governor opened the new Parliament in August.

In July 1956, Boland died and Bukowski became state secretary of the AWU and president of the QCE. He and Gair had attended the same Christian Brothers College in Rockhampton and there developed a dislike for each other that was to grow over the years.[23] It was certainly not a partnership comparable with that of Fallon and Forgan Smith or even Fallon and Hanlon. Bukowski had none of the political balance and commonsense that had characterized Fallon's years as QCE president. His behaviour between 1956 and 1958 suggests instability and a certain paranoia developing in his personality.

As president of the QCE, Joe Bukowski's partnership with Vince Gair was not a happy one. He later voted for the expulsion of the premier. (Photograph by courtesy of Queensland Newspapers Ltd.)

One more event of 1956 was to exacerbate this personal relationship and strengthen the "Gair Must Go" campaign. In November 1955, the Industrial Court reduced the shearing rate per 100 sheep by 10 per cent. The AWU had asked for an increase of 10 per cent. The dispute grew into a major pastoral strike that lasted throughout 1956. Its effects on the labor movement were momentous. The AWU re-affiliated with the TLC after a break of seventeen years; the TLC affiliated unions gave physical support to the shearers and declared "black" all wool shorn at non-union rates; Gair supported the graziers in their attempt to ship their wool out and declared a state of emergency.[24] Late in 1955 also, the Industrial Court awarded five shillings a week to Electrical Trades Union (ETU) members seeking a rise of two pounds five shillings a week. At the same time parliamentary salaries (then tied to the public service award) rose by eight pounds thirteen shillings a week. An eighty-one day strike followed, involving other unions as well as the ETU and Gair imposed another state of emergency.[25]

The dominant issue for the new QCE that met after the convention and the election was the three weeks' leave. There was a contrast between the premier's assurances to delegations that it would be introduced and his apparent unwillingness to bring forward the necessary legislation. When there was no mention of the legislation in the governor's speech, the QCE directed its attention to the members of the PLP. In September, Schmella wrote to all state Labor parliamentarians asking if they were prepared to abide by the rules of the ALP and support the introduction of the three weeks' leave. Gair's supporters in the PLP remained firm and, by a vote of twenty-eight to nineteen, reaffirmed the premier's contention that the time was not ripe. In October, the QCE considered the politicians' replies and heard again from Gair that, while there should be three weeks' annual leave, the state's finances would not yet permit this. An impasse had now been reached as, in November, the Legislative Assembly adjourned until the following March.

While the QCE and the cabinet had been wrestling with the leave dispute, other matters had come before the parliament which would not normally have concerned the QCE, but which were now taken up as a part of the anti-Gair campaign. The University Act Amendment Bill, the Motor Spirit Distribution Bill and the royal commission into allegations of corruption into certain Crown leaseholds, all came to involve the QCE in conflict with the cabinet. The last of these brought about the expulsion of Tom Foley, the former minister for lands, from the ALP and reduced Gair's PLP support by one. At about the same time, the suspension by the QCE of H.R. Gardiner, the member for Rockhampton, took one further caucus vote from the premier. Len Eastment, the member for Ithaca, died in July 1956. He belonged firmly in the Hanlon camp in Labor politics and thus had an aversion for Gair. Nevertheless, he supported Gair's stand in the caucus, on the three weeks' leave issue, and his replacement by Pat Hanlon, who supported the QCE, in the by-election in December 1956, increased the size of Gair's opposition within the PLP.

As an experienced Labor politician, Gair should have been wary of forcing his challenge to the constituted authorities in the ALP. He had already lost at the convention and, through the same thorough anti-Gair organizing among the Trades Hall unions by Egerton and others, Gair no longer held majority power on the QCE as had his predecessors. He could have reasserted his own authority and divided the uneasy and temporary coalition against him by accepting the convention decision and providing the additional week's leave. It was this that held the anti-Gair coalition together. He chose not to and he and his allies plunged in to a battle that they had already begun to lose.

In the new year, matters began moving quickly to a head as Gair threw down a challenge in his New Year message, by rejecting any three weeks' leave legislation in 1957. After the first QCE meeting, Schmella again informed PLP members of their obligation to obey the decisions of the convention. It looked as though a confrontation between the two centres of power, the QCE and the PLP, was inevitable. Once more, Duggan sought to avoid this by bringing the warring parties together to reach a compromise that would avoid a split. With some considerable difficulty he successfully proposed that the inner executive, which now consisted of Gair, Bukowski, Egerton, Whiteside, Dittmer, Jim Donald plus Schmella, should meet a PLP committee of Gair, Walsh, Duggan, Jack Dufficy, the PLP representative on the QCE and A.J. Skinner, a supporter of Gair, to try to resolve the issue. Members of the Bukowski committee from the convention were added to this meeting. Others, outside the QCE and the PLP, were warning of a split in the party if one or both sides did not look beyond the immediate conflict to the good of the Labor party and the government. However, such warnings went unheeded. About the corridors of the Trades Hall there was considerable discussion about the possible effects of a move to expel Gair. There was no Labor party "old hand" about the Trades Hall to caution against such an expulsion though Claude Jones, then president of the Communist party, was cautioning against any such expulsion. He urged that Gair be not re-endorsed at the following election. When Egerton was urged to consider the consequences of expelling Gair and to adopt a cautious approach to such a step, he replied: "So what. We haven't got a Labor government now. They are only masqueraders and the Tories couldn't be any worse."

Twenty years later, it is difficult to recapture the intensity of the feelings of those involved in the QCE, PLP, unions and ALP branches. Rumours and speculation of Gair's expulsion; deals between Gair and the Democratic Labor Party; accusations that Walsh was really egging Gair on in order to have him expelled so that he (Walsh) could become premier; speculation that the federal executive would not allow Gair to be expelled for fear that this would cause a loss of the Queensland government; these and more passed about, often as political facts. The federal executive, at its meeting in Brisbane in March 1957 had no formal discussion of the Queensland problems.

Frank Nolan was the secretary of the ARU which was still not affiliated with the ALP. He was a militant trade unionist and totally opposed to the "Movement" and to the industrial groups. However, being outside the "Gair Must Go" circle at the Trades Hall, he was able to view the impending disaster for the ALP from a more critical perspective than those deeply immersed in the conflict. He spoke to Bukowski of the serious split that would follow any expulsion of Gair. He warned Walsh about the precarious position that Gair now occupied in the party, but Walsh dismissed his warning as being wrongly based. Walsh claimed he had "inside knowledge" about the strength of the anti-Gair forces. In his memoirs, Nolan wrote:

> A serious split in the Party was now almost certain and head-counting started . . . . I was convinced that there were people holding high official positions in the Australian Labor Party who hated Vince Gair so much that they were prepared to do irreparable damage to the Labor Movement to wreak vengeance on him.

Gair's opponents were convinced that they "had the numbers" to expel him. Beyond that point Egerton's and Bukowski's logic seems to have prevailed. On the other hand, Gair's supporters were sceptical about who really "had the numbers". A member of the office staff at the QCE was "leaking" information to Gair on the situation there. In any case, Gair's supporters believed that Schmella, Bukowski and Egerton would not go beyond the brink and actually expel the premier. There was some taunting also that "they did not have the guts to expel Gair". The federal leader, Evatt, was not so sure about the intentions of Schmella, Bukowski and Egerton and on two occasions came to Brisbane to argue against any motion to expel Gair and to argue for federal intervention if Gair was expelled.

By March 1957, both Gair and his leading opponents seemed determined to have war and nothing else. Nolan recalled: "I had a couple of hours discussion with him [Jack Schmella] on the situation. However, he was adamant that they had the numbers and Gair would go." Schmella told his private secretary, Kath Gallogly, that Gair's expulsion would be "a drop in the ocean in political history". From his forty years experience in trade union politics, Nolan concluded: "Those with the numbers never stop to think of what might be the long range effect from the use of these numbers."[26]

The inner executive, the PLP committee and Bukowski's convention committee met on 5 April. If war is defined as the breakdown of diplomacy, then war began in the Queensland ALP on this date. The meeting broke up without reaching agreement and both sides returned to mobilizing their forces. On 18 April, the QCE passed a vote of no confidence in Gair by thirty-five votes to twenty-seven and summoned him to a special QCE meeting on 24 April to show cause why he should not be expelled. On the day before this QCE meeting, Gair called a special caucus meeting, which, by twenty-six votes to twenty-one, passed a vote of confidence in him. (See Appendix: no. 2.) Gair's opposition to the extra leave remained his rejection of any direction by the QCE or convention on the timing of the legislation. For the March quarter of 1957, the basic wage for Queensland remained unchanged although average weekly wages in the state dropped during 1957. Manufacturing industries increased their profits substantially during 1956-57, while primary producers, especially the wool growers, had a very good year.

Lobbying of QCE members was intense right up to the meeting since many of those who opposed Gair on the leave issue drew back from actually expelling from the party a man who was the premier of the state. Edgar Williams, for example, moved in the early part of the QCE meeting "that the only matter before the meeting be the matter of three weeks' annual leave." After some debate Bukowski ruled this out of order and again the delicate question of expelling a premier from the party and the possible consequences of this became the issues facing the sixty-five delegates. It was partly on this sentiment that the Gair forces were counting, though they underestimated the personal animosity that Gair had engendered over the betrayal that many union officials felt on the three weeks' leave issue. After the QCE meeting, H.L. Edmonds the divisional manager of the AFULE (i.e., the state secretary) reported to his union that: "he had been approached prior to the meeting to support the Premier and he told the contact man that he could tell the Premier that if he would give a definite date when he would apply the three weeks' leave he would get his vote and a number of other QCE delegates as well."[27]

Gair faced a long list of charges (see Appendix: no.3.) some pretty thin, but the most serious was that he had failed to abide by the decision of the Labor-in-Politics Convention at Mackay. He spoke at length in his own defence, not retreating from his position, but emphasizing the support of cabinet and the caucus for his refusal to abide by the convention decision. Even now, he could have retrieved the situation by giving some indication as to when he would bring down the legislation which, he argued, he supported. He was asked: "At this late hour will the Premier give a definite undertaking to bring down a Bill granting 3 weeks' leave as soon as Parliament meets in August?" But in contrast to the answer that Hanlon had given to a similar question, on the forty-hour week, in 1947, Gair replied: "No, I'll not do that as the position might be worse than it is now."[28] After a five-hour debate, the delegates prepared to vote. Gair left the room.

A legal opinion had been sought from the ALP solicitors E.E. Quinlan and A.J. Miller, regarding Gair's right to vote on a motion for his own expulsion. The opinion had been that he could not be a judge in his own case, which was upheld by thirty-four votes to thirty.

One last effort was made by two union secretaries, Bert Milliner and Archie Dawson, to avoid the catastrophe that now hung over the party. They sought to amend the expulsion motion by having one more meeting between the QCE and the PLP to try to reach some agreement. (See Appendix: nos. 1 and 5.) This was rejected by thirty-five votes to thirty and Gair was expelled with the same voting figures. Several of those who had been in delegations to Gair over the three weeks' leave issue and who had been involved in the vain attempts to have Gair abide by his undertaking on the matter, voted against his expulsion. (See Appendix: nos. 4 and 6.)

Why such an experienced politician as Gair, who had grown up in the Labor party, should have allowed himself to be boxed into such a corner, particularly after the Mackay convention and the QCE meetings which followed, remains the mystery of the split. He seemed to have invited the martyrdom that his supporters were to confer upon him. Perhaps the answer lay with Gair's own personality. Between January and October 1973, the DLP senators and the DLP federal executive went through similar problems regarding Gair's resignation as parliamentary leader, as the ALP in Queensland had faced over the three weeks' leave issue before 1957. Gair equivocated; on several occasions he said he would resign by a certain date, but didn't.[29] It seems, again, that he had to be delivered an ultimatum which he accepted in 1973, unlike that of 1957. The three weeks' leave issue was not one that was worth taking to the brink and causing the destruction of a government. On the other hand, Gair believed that the federal executive would intervene to overrule any QCE decision to expel him and this seems to have been one of the reasons for his remaining uncompromising right to the end.[30] There were good political reasons for thinking that the federal executive would regard the expulsion of a Labor premier as affecting the good of the Labor party as a whole. This was certainly the attitude of the federal president, Joe Chamberlain who, though a rigid anti-Grouper, sought to have the federal executive intervene to prevent the Queensland ALP being wrecked as had been the Victorian party.[31] However, both the composition of the federal executive and Gair's own standing then in the ALP were against such an intervention. The former federal secretary, Pat Kennelly, though no longer a delegate, still wielded considerable influence and was a vigorous opponent of Gair. Of the twelve-man federal executive, Bukowski and Schmella, the Queensland delegates had voted for his expulsion; the two Victorians represented the new "anti-Grouper" executive and the two South Australian delegates were strongly "anti-Grouper" with no particular regard for Gair. Both Schmella and Bukowski argued strongly against any federal intervention, and on 26 April, the federal executive decided not to intervene.

The "Gair Must Go" campaign had succeeded, but now, the party which Ryan had held together in the conscription split of 1916 and which Forgan Smith had kept intact through the Depression, was torn apart. Gair held the loyalty of nine of his ten cabinet ministers and fifteen other members of the PLP. These twenty-four, plus Gair, formed the Queensland Labor Party (QLP). Duggan resigned from the cabinet to lead the ALP. Gair held a conference with Frank Nicklin, the Country party leader, who was then prepared to support Gair as a minority premier. He was talked out of this by Artie Fadden and no QLP-Country party alliance was formed. The Legislative Assembly refused to pass supply, an election was called and Labor lost office after twenty-five years. For the extra-parliamentary leaders in the QCE and in the unions, their principal task in 1957 and 1958 was to try to hold the party branches together. Here Keeffe, Egerton, Duggan and a number of Catholic and non-Catholic union officials played a major and, in retrospect, successful role.

The Labor split had not been inevitable. At several stages it could have been avoided. Unfortunately those most deeply involved on both sides were never able to stand back and view the consequences of their decisions. Ideological differences had played their part, but while most of those who had voted to support Gair could be termed "right-wing", his opponents were far from being "left-wingers". In the final analysis of the causes of the split, ideology was a smaller influence than clashes of personality even though these were often cast in ideological terms.[32] In the end obstinacy, pride, the exercise of power and personal ego, over-ran commonsense, tact and political nous. The baby went out with the bath water.

This was the second great split in the history of the Labor party in Queensland. After the first split — over Premier William Kidston — a group of talented Labor parliamentarians, led by Ryan and Theodore, had put the split behind them and set the party's sights on winning office and bringing in significant reforms. The same did not occur after 1957. Labor was handicapped by an unfavourable redistribution of electoral boundaries brought in by the new Country-Liberal government, but it was handicapped even more by its own concentration on internal politics and an internal power struggle. Stalking phantom enemies within became more important than confronting the real political enemy without. Labor had to wait for new political leaders who would regain the trust of the trade unions and who would build a coalition of urban and rural and provincial city support needed to return the party to office. More importantly, it had to regain its sense of purpose as a party of reform and regain some quality in its parliamentary representation. Returning the party to such a position would depend not only on the competence of the parliamentary leaders, but also on the political sense, the desire for reform and the administrative competence of those union leaders who controlled the party machine.

Appendix

1. Motion of No Confidence in Gair, passed by the QCE, 18 April 1957.

"This Meeting of the full Queensland executive is of the opinion that the Leader of the State Parliamentary Labor Party no longer has the confidence of the Labor Movement in Queensland in view of the fact that he has deliberately flouted the decisions of the Labor-in-Politics Convention, which is the highest authority in the Queensland branch of the ALP. Because of his continued and openly expressed defiance of the Convention and the Queensland Central Executive, which is the ruling body in the Labor Party between Conventions, it is obvious that the Leader of the State Parliamentary Labor Party will not accept the rules and constitution of the party whose representatives in Parliament he is appointed to lead.

"Further, the Leader of the State Parliamentary Labor Party has deliberately broken the pledge which he and all other members of the party are required to sign, and which pledges them to uphold the policy and platform of the party.

"Further, this Executive is of the opinion that the Leader of the State Parliamentary Labor Party has acted in such a way as to bring discredit on the party, and confusion and embarrassment within the ranks of the party itself. It also calls on him to appear before a special meeting of the Central Executive to show cause why he should not be expelled from the party".

2. Document signed by cabinet ministers, 23 April 1957.

Resolution of Cabinet: The Premier, having reported today on the meeting of the Queensland Central Executive of the Labor Party held on 18 April, and otherwise on the dispute between the Executive and the Government, Cabinet declares:

1. That it has complete confidence in the Premier and recognises the distinction with which he has led the party, and his outstanding work as head of the Executive Government.

2. That at no time, or on any matter, has the Premier done other than execute the decisions arrived at by Cabinet in accordance with the principle of Cabinet responsibility.

3. That therefore Cabinet regards as a matter of the utmost gravity the attempt being made to impose on the Premier responsibility for decisions to which we individually and jointly subscribe, and to which we adhere. And, we, the undersigned members of Cabinet wish it known that any punitive action by way of expulsion, suspension, or otherwise, taken against the Premier will therefore be regarded as having been taken against each Minister individually.

Duggan signed the document, but included with his signature "with the exception of the final paragraph, I agree".

3. The charges brought against Gair at the QCE meeting, 24 April 1957.

1. Defiance of the decision of the Labor-in-Politics Convention at Mackay, and on numerous occasions since — in Press statements, at meetings of the Parliamentary Labor Party Caucus, and at meetings of the Queensland Central Executive.

2. Refusal to accept decisions of the QCE interpreting Convention decisions.

3. Breach of the Pledge signed by all Members of the Party requiring them to uphold the policy and platform of the Party.

4. Discredit brought on the Party by such procedures as:
   - (a) Redcliffe Commission — designed to discredit one individual.
   - (b) Lands Commission — designed to discredit an Affiliated Union but only brought discredit on the Party and the Minister.
   - (c) Club legislation initiated because of representations made by one individual (invasion of rights of privacy, and the principle that a person is entitled to choose his own company).
   - (d) University Bill initiated at the instigation of one individual and against all accepted authorities connected with the Uni-

versity of Queensland and all other Universities in British countries.

(e) Petrol Bill which contains some provisions of Fascist or Communist character, such as onus of proof on the accused and concentration of power in one man.

(f) Consistent false leadership by encouraging members of the Parliamentary Labor Party to refuse to accept decisions of the Labor-in-Politics Convention and the Queensland Central Executive.

(g) Soliciting and obtaining financial support from non-Labor sources and sources definitely un-sympathetic to Labor and the rank and file interests of the Labor Party, without accounting to any individuals or any body such as the QCE.

5. Repudiating a personal Pledge given to a number of delegates at Convention and inferring that the report given by these delegates was untrue.

6. Organising and arranging the issue of a statement by Cabinet which is a direct challenge to the Queensland Central Executive and undoubtedly political blackmail of the most vicious type, by stating, in effect, that if the Leader could not run the party his way (without reference to the rank and file or its representatives) he would abandon the party and form or join another party opposed to Labor.

Note: Important Rules covering this matter are Rule 32 (r) which obliges the QCE to guard the interests of the Party generally, and Rule 32 (a) empowering the Executive to suspend or expel any member violating its Rules and Platform, and Rule 32 (v) empowering the QCE to interpret its own Rules and decisions of Convention, and to expel any member who refuses to abide by its interpretation or decision.

4. The motion to expel Gair, 24 April 1957.

This Executive, after hearing Mr. Gair state his case in showing cause why he should not be expelled from the Australian Labor Party, decides that he has not refuted the charge that he has defied Convention decision on the matter of three weeks' leave, and that he has not shown that he has not repudiated his personal pledge in the matter of three weeks' leave, given to a number of delegates. This Executive is satisfied that there was a pledge given to the Convention delegates and that Mr. Gair has since repudiated that pledge.

This Executive declares that the Premier's reply as to why he has not carried out Labor-in-Politics Convention decision in connection with three weeks' leave is entirely unsatisfactory. His continued refusal to accept ALP rules and platform render him unfit to be a member of the Labor Party.

This Executive emphasises that it regrets very much the necessity which forces it to adopt this decision. Every possible means has been examined with a view to obviating the regrettable deterioration in the relationship between the State Parliamentary Labor Party and the Executive Body. Nevertheless the Executive has an undeniable obligation to see that the rights and the wishes of the industrial unions and the rank and file of the Labor Party must be preserved and protected and that the Convention decisions must be observed. The Mackay Convention, after prolonged discussion and after extended negotiations following on the discussions at the Rockhampton Convention, arrived at a definite decision that legislation for three weeks' leave should be implemented. Mr. Gair must accept responsibility for his leading role in this organised defiance of the recognised authority in the Party, with particular reference to the three weeks' leave question, and this Executive must accept its obligation also, as distasteful and regrettable as it undoubtedly is. We therefore decide that the membership of Mr. Gair be terminated forthwith; that is, that he be expelled from the party and that the Parliamentary Labor Party be advised accordingly, and that the Executive Committee request the Parliamentary Labor Party to meet them to hear views and reasons of the QCE for arriving at this decision on Monday next at 2.30 pm.

5. Amendment moved by Bert Milliner and Archie Dawson to the above motion:

This meeting of the QCE recognises that the interests of the Party are paramount in all discussions and it is out duty to present a united front to the enemies of the Party. On this occasion we realise that the Cabinet and the Parliamentary Labor Party have adopted a policy in their respective spheres which could plunge the Party into two forces and could cause embarrassment because of a false sense of loyalty to differing ideals of the objects of the Australian Labor Party. However, we believe that a further attempt to reconcile the views of individual members of the Party should be made, and in this spirit we offer to further discuss with the Cabinet, the Secretary of the Parliamentary Labor Party, and the Parliamentary Labor Party delegate to the QCE, features of the dispute, and report back to a meeting of the Queensland Central Executive on Friday afternoon at 2 pm.

6. Voting in the QCE division to expel Gair, 24 April 1957.

FOR		AGAINST	
Name	**Organization**	**Name**	**Organization**
Adsett E.	Federated Storemen and Packers Union	Allman J.	Federated Clerks Union
Ashmore E. (proxy for E.J. Barr)	Amalgamated Postal Workers Union	Bennett F.	Queensland State Service Union
Beale R.M.	Building Workers Industrial Union	Bolger T.	Queensland State Service Union
Bright E.	Boilermakers Society	Buchanan C.	Australasian Meat Industry Employees Union
Bukowski R.J.	Australian Workers Union	Burke M.L. (proxy for H.G. Peebles)	Federated Iron-workers Association
Campbell P. (proxy for L. Burnett)	Operative Painters and Decorators Union	Bryan E.	Theatrical Employees Union
Darby T.	Amalgamated Engineering Union	Cannon F.W.	Liquor Trades Union
Devereaux J.	Amalgamated Engineering Union	Cole A.	Queensland Railway Maintenance Union
Dickson W.	Convention delegate	Connolly L.F.	Queensland Railway Traffic Employees Union
Dittmer F.C.S. (MLA)	Convention delegate	Currie F.	Queensland Shop Assistants Union

Donald J. (MLA)	Queensland Colliery Employees Union	Dawson A.	Electrical Trades Union
Egerton J.	Convention delegate	Dufficy, J. (MLA)	State PLP delegate
Farthing D.	Australian Workers Union	Duggan J. (MLA)	Convention delegate
Edmonds H.	Australian Federated Union of Locomotive Enginemen	Doyle T.J. (proxy for R.C. Janson)	Transport Workers Union
Grundy R.J. (proxy for F.W. Hulme)	Plumbers and Gasfitters Union	Edmonds W.F. (MHR)	Federal PLP
Howman F.	Australian Workers Union	Fraser R.	Amalgamated Foodstuffs Union
Laing W.	Federated Engine Drivers and Firemen's Association	Goding G.	Australian Workers Union
MacColl A.C.	Federated Miscellaneous Workers Union	Hefferan V.	Queensland Shop Assistants Union
McCarter W.J.	Australian Workers Union	Hough B.V.	Transport Workers Union
McCormack W.	Small Unions (Tramways)	Kelso C.J.	Federated Clerks Union
McWatters J.	Federated Miscellaneous Workers Union	Major W.	Queensland Shop Assistants Union
Merrell C.	Amalgamated Engineering Union	Marshall A.L.	Federated Storemen and Packers Union

Milliner B.R.	Printing Industry Employees Union	McPherson S.	Australasian Meat Industry Employees Union
Newton F.	Building Workers Industrial Union	Ryan J.J.	Vehicle Builders Union
Robinson C.L.	Amalgamated Postal Workers Union	Scanlan M.	Amalgamated Foodstuffs Union
Rogers W.C.	Federated Furnishing Trades Union	Taylor K.E. (proxy for W.J. Barry)	Federated Clerks Union
Schmella J.	Convention delegate	Thornton W.T.	Federated Clerks Union
Shaw E.	Australian Workers Union	Tyrell W.H.	Australian Builders Labourers Federation
Smith B.	Small Unions	Wilkinson E.	Waterside Workers Federation
Spence W.K.	Convention delegate	Williams C.E.W.	Convention delegate
Summers A.	Australasian Meat Industry Employees Union		
Walpole B. (proxy for S. Baker)	Building Workers Industrial Union		
Walton W.	Federated Engine Drivers and Firemen's Association		
Whitby F.W. (proxy for E. Stokoe)	Small Unions		
Whiteside G.	Convention delegate		

NOTES

1. See Alister Davidson, *The Communist Party of Australia, A Short History* (Stanford: Hoover Institute Press, 1969).
2. *Official Record of the Nineteenth Labor-in-Politics Convention,* Brisbane, 1947, pp. 59-60 (Walsh). p. 14. (Duggan).
3. Letter from B.A. Santamaria to Archbishop R. Prendiville, Perth, 4 September 1956, copy held by author.
4. There is an increasing amount of material written on the "Movement" and the Industrial Groups. See B.A. Santamaria, *"The Movement" 1941-60 An Outline* (Melbourne: Hawthorne Press, 1960); B.A. Santamaria, *The Price of Freedom* (Melbourne: Hawthorne Press, 1964); Tom Truman, *Catholic Action and Politics* (rev. ed. London: Merlin Press, 1960); Henry Mayer, *Catholics and The Free Society* (Melbourne: Cheshire, 1961); Paul Ormonde, *The Movement* (Melbourne: Nelsons 1972); Robert Murray, *The Split, Australian Labor in the Fifties* (Melbourne: Cheshire, 1970); Niall Brennan, *The Politics of Catholics* (Melbourne: Hill of Content, 1972); Frank McManus, *The Tumult and the Shouting* (Adelaide: Rigby, 1977); "The Movement — its origins, aliases, decline", *Catholic Worker* 281 (July 1959); D.W. Rawson "The ALP Industrial Groups" in *Australian Labour Relations Readings,* eds. J.E. Isaac and G.W. Ford (Melbourne: Sun, 1971); Ian Campbell, "An aspect of ALP Industrial Group development", *Australian Quarterly* 33 (1 March 1961); Ian Campbell, "ALP Industrial Group — A Reassessment", *AJPH 8,* no. 1 (1962); F.G. Clarke, "Labour and the Catholic Social Studies Movement", *Labour History* 20 (May 1971); John Warhurst, "United States' Government Assistance to the Catholic Social Studies Movement, 1953-54", *Labour History* 30 (May 1971); H. Arndt and B.A. Santamaria, "The Catholic Social Studies Movement", *AJPH* 2, no. 2 (1957); R. Murray, "*News Weekly*'s March", *Dissent* 6, (1966); B.A. Santamaria, "Review of *The Split* ", *Australian Quarterly* 43, no. 2 (1971). In writing this section I have been able to see copies of correspondence which passed between Joe Bukowski, John Maynes and Jack Kane and to read the minutes of the ALP Groups Interstate Liaison Committee. These were lent to me by Frank Waters.
5. "The Movement — its origins, aliases, decline", *Catholic Worker* (July 1957), p. 9.
6. Letter to Prendiville, signed by three national officers of the "Movement", the manager of *News Weekly,* Santamaria, and the full time officials in Perth, Hobart, Melbourne and Brisbane, 18 July 1956, copy held by author.
7. Letter from Archbishop D. Mannix to Cardinal N. Gilroy, 27 August 1956, copy held by author. The "Movement" began in 1942, not 1943 as stated by Mannix.

8. Contained in letter referred to in note 6.
9. Correspondence from Santamaria to Prendiville, "Report on National Congress of the Australasian Council of Trade Unions, 23rd-27th September 1957", 8 November 1957. Copy held by author.
10. A great deal of material for this aspect of this chapter was obtained from retired union officials and ALP members. See note 20.
11. See Leicester Webb, *Communism and Democracy in Australia, A Survey of the 1951 Referendum* (Melbourne: Cheshire, 1954), for an outline of this referendum. For the Queensland part in the referendum see James Beatson, "Communism and Public Opinion in Queensland 1949-1951: An Explanation of Queensland's Vote in the 1951 Anti-Communist Referendum" (B.A. thesis, Queensland, 1974).
12. *Official Record of the Twenty-first Labor-in-Politics Convention*, Brisbane, 1955, p. 67. For reactions inside Parker's own union, see Archie Dawson, *Points and Politics, A History of the Electrical Trades Union of Queensland* (Brisbane: Colonial Press, 1977), chaps. 14-16.
13. Ibid., p. 72.
14. *News Weekly,* 4 November 1953.
15. *Labour Reports,* Nos 42-44, 1953-55/56.
16. John Warhurst, The "Communist Bogey". Communism as an issue in Australian Federal Elections, 1949 to 1964. (Ph.D. thesis, Flinders University, 1977).
17. In 1918, under Ryan, Labor obtained 53.68 per cent of the valid vote; in 1935, under Forgan Smith, Labor obtained 53.43 per cent of the valid vote and in 1953 and 1956, under Gair, Labor obtained 53.21 and 51.22 per cent of the valid vote, respectively. Colin A. Hughes and B.D. Graham, *A Handbook of Australian Government and Politics* (Canberra: Australian National University Press, 1968).
18. For a contemporary assessment of the effect of this change see Don Whitington, "Will the Movement Smash the ALP?", *Australian Monthly,* (15 February 1955) and in the debates, articles and "Capital Letters" in the Sydney journal *Voice* during 1954 and 1955.
19. Devereux's account, substantiated by both Gair and Walsh, at the 1956 Labor-in-Politics Convention.
20. The information for this part of the chapter was obtained from interviews with Archie Dawson, Bert Milliner, Frank Waters, Vince Gair, Jack Duggan, Manfred Cross, Wally Major, Joy Guyatt, Kath Gallogly, Fred Whitby, Jim Keeffe and other surviving participants who did not wish to be identified; from a very full newspaper clipping file that the late Alan Morrison deposited in the Fryer Library; *Labor-in-Politics Convention* reports; Queensland Parliamentary Debates; trade union records in the ANU archives and Frank Waters' private collection of documents and reports of the 1950s. For other participants' views, see Wayne Swan

"Factionalism — the Case of Queensland Labor 1959-1966" (BA thesis, University of Queensland, 1975); QCE records and the minutes of the PLP for this period are both closed to access.

21. *Hansard* reporters were employed to record a verbatim report of the convention. For this debate see *Official Record of the Twenty-second Labor-in-Politics Convention,* Brisbane, 1956, pp. 75-105, 107, 133-34.
22. AFULE, Divisional Council minutes, 12 July 1956, E212/31, ANU Archives.
23. Interview with Gair, January 1975. The extent of the personal and mutual dislike was confirmed in interviews with contemporaries.
24. For a full discussion of the 1956 pastoral strike see Ann McMurchy "The 1956 Shearers' Strike" (B.A. thesis, University of Queensland, 1977).
25. On this strike of electrical workers, see Archie Dawson, *Points and Politics, A History of the Electrical Trades Union of Queensland,* ed. Denis Murphy, (Brisbane: Colonial Press, 1978), chap. 21.
26. Frank Nolan, *You Pass This Way Only Once, Reflections of Trade Union Leader,* ed. Denis Murphy, (Brisbane: Colonial Press, 1974), pp. 128-36.
27. AFULE, Divisional Council minutes, 8 May 1957, E212/32, ANU Archives.
28. Ibid.
29. See McManus, *The Tumult and the Shouting*, pp. 114-15. McManus was careful not to try to force Gair to resign; others in the DLP were not so generous.
30. In January 1975, Gair was emphatic that the refusal of the federal executive to over-rule the QCE decision to expel him had been crucial to the whole split.
31. Interview with Miss Kath Gallogly.
32. On the other hand, Swan, in his thesis on the post-split period, places a greater emphasis on ideological factors.

Appendix A:

Labor Vote, 1915-57

	1915 %	1918 %	1920 %
BRISBANE (17)			
Inner Urban			
Brisbane	60.8	60.6	54.0
Buranda	56.2	60.8	55.9
Fortitude Valley	68.2	65.5	64.2
Ithaca	63.7	55.5	52.3
Kurilpa	54.1	49.3	44.0
Maree	60.2	53.1	51.2
Merthyr	57.3	52.7	48.4
Paddington	68.4	60.9	61.6
South Brisbane	59.4	55.0	51.6
Toowong	40.4	32.3	28.1
Windsor	53.0	49.5	45.4
Suburban			
Bulimba	51.6	47.5	44.3
Enoggera	56.4	50.8	47.6
Logan	43.9	53.1	39.9
Nundah	48.3	42.4	37.5
Oxley	51.2	47.8	41.1
Toombul	43.2	39.5	35.2
SOUTH-EAST (9)			
Albert	-	37.9	30.5
Bremer	61.5	66.0	61.5
Fassifern	23.0	46.7	32.9
Ipswich	53.4	56.5	56.4
Lockyer	16.9	52.5	46.7

	1915 %	1918 %	1920 %
WIDE BAY (8)			
Bundaberg	69.0	66.5	57.4
Burnett	43.9	41.4	33.8
Burrum	46.6	51.6	42.3
Cooroora	39.4	35.5	-
Gympie	52.7	56.7	54.8
Maryborough	55.7	61.8	58.1
Musgrave	53.5	54.6	41.9
Wide Bay	48.4	52.7	47.2
CENTRAL (6)			
Fitzroy	51.1	54.0	54.0
Keppel	67.4	57.8	54.3
Mt. Morgan	66.2	65.6	65.3
Normanby	56.5	59.6	56.6
Port Curtis	50.7	52.9	47.5
Rockhampton	66.1	68.3	65.6
SOUTH-WEST (4)			
Balonne	*	60.9	59.2
Maranoa	69.0	59.1	50.7
Murilla	45.8	45.8	42.3
Warrego	*	74.3	68.7
CENTRAL-WEST (4)			
Barcoo	77.4	73.8	70.4
Gregory	*	70.5	58.9
Leichhardt	*	68.7	60.2

Rosewood	23.4	64.8	51.6
Stanley	39.6	46.5	37.3
DARLING DOWNS (9)			
Aubigny	28.2	48.3	37.8
Carnarvon	49.0	47.8	45.8
Cunningham	-	36.3	-
Dalby	42.5	43.1	37.5
Drayton	34.1	47.3	40.2
East Toowoomba	44.8	48.6	38.2
Pittsworth	30.7	46.1	-
Toowoomba	46.7	54.1	46.2
Warwick	26.2	46.0	45.0

Burke	48.2	58.9	66.6
Charters Towers	58.3	56.7	54.7
Chillagoe	79.7	72.8	77.8
Cook	53.9	60.6	55.9
Flinders	*	75.7	64.5
Kennedy	67.8	61.1	48.0
Queenton	70.2	63.5	65.0
NORTHERN (8)			
Bowen	57.5	59.4	57.6
Cairns	70.4	61.4	54.7
Eacham	66.5	54.8	55.3
Herbert	64.6	63.4	54.6
Mackay	54.4	56.0	53.2
Mirani	43.8	46.4	44.3
Mundingburra	70.2	70.1	60.0
Townsville	52.2	54.6	45.0

- No Labor candidate
* Labor win uncontested

LABOR VOTE 1923-1929

	1923 %	1926 %	1929 %
BRISBANE (20)			
Inner urban			
Brisbane	59.8	59.8	47.1
Buranda	56.6	60.3	51.3
Fortitude Valley	61.8	62.8	53.7
Ithaca	54.3	58.8	51.8
Kelvin Grove	55.6	54.3	45.6
Kurilpa	44.7	44.7	47.0
Maree	52.9	50.5	43.0
Merthyr	52.4	51.5	43.0
Paddington	64.3	73.1	71.6
South Brisbane	53.1	50.8	45.0
Toombul	-	-	26.5
Toowong	30.3	32.0	26.3
Windsor	42.4	41.7	36.5
Suburban			
Bulimba	53.8	55.6	48.2
Enoggera	41.3	38.7	33.2
Logan	47.4	46.4	35.2
Nundah	38.6	40.8	32.9
Oxley	35.5	39.6	30.1

	1923 %	1926 %	1929 %
WIDE BAY (7)			
Bundaberg	59.0	59.4	51.1
Burnett	39.8	37.8	40.0
Burrum	49.4	45.0	39.8
Cooroora	-	-	-
Gympie	56.1	57.0	46.1
Maryborough	59.8	59.3	52.0
Wide Bay	-	26.3	-
CENTRAL (6)			
Fitzroy	52.4	58.4	40.2
Keppel	60.7	58.2	41.6
Mt. Morgan	71.3	66.3	52.3
Normanby	46.9	43.3	37.4
Port Curtis	52.7	45.6	44.3
Rockhampton	61.4	67.7	38.3
SOUTH-WEST (4)			
Balonne	62.6	56.9	63.9
Maranoa	57.5	54.8	52.4
Murilla	44.7	42.0	42.9
Warrego	70.2	*	57.7

Sandgate	-	40.2	32.5
Wynnum	40.3	38.4	31.7
SOUTH-EAST (9)			
Albert	-	30.1	27.0
Bremer	55.6	66.2	51.2
Fassifern	-	-	-
Ipswich	54.7	56.2	43.1
Lockyer	41.1	26.9	-
Murrumba	26.4	28.2	-
Nanango	39.7	34.6	-
Rosewood	54.1	57.6	43.4
Stanley	-	37.0	-
DARLING DOWNS (7)			
Aubigny	40.9	30.5	-
Carnarvon	46.7	46.0	39.3
Cunningham	36.1	30.9	-
Dalby	37.7	31.1	31.2
East Toowoomba	38.4	38.2	29.8
Toowoomba	52.7	56.7	48.6
Warwick	46.2	45.4	44.0

CENTRAL-WEST (4)			
Barcoo	*	*	*
Gregory	66.8	*	*
Leichhardt	58.7	61.4	54.5
Mitchell	65.2	*	58.4
NORTH-WEST (7)			
Burke	61.1	*	65.8
Charters Towers	61.7	62.2	54.0
Chillagoe	64.3	67.5	47.1
Cook	51.7	62.0	47.2
Flinders	62.9	65.9	66.2
Queenton	51.3	55.9	51.1
NORTHERN (8)			
Bowen	63.0	57.6	51.6
Cairns	58.8	66.4	56.6
Eacham	59.4	51.5	41.1
Herbert	66.5	57.3	57.1
Kennedy	51.3	50.2	54.3
Mackay	57.9	64.6	57.9
Mirani	49.0	47.8	41.5
Mundingburra	64.5	74.0	81.5
Townsville	52.0	64.2	54.5

- No Labor candidate
* Labor win uncontested

LABOR VOTE 1932

	1932 %
BRISBANE (19)	
Inner urban	
Brisbane	59.9
Bulimba	62.7
Buranda	66.0
Fortitude Valley	69.2
Hamilton	40.0
Ithaca	59.6
Kelvin Grove	56.6
Kurilpa	56.5
Maree	54.5
Merthyr	51.6
South Brisbane	52.2
Toowong	34.2
Windsor	37.7
Suburban	
Enoggera	52.2
Logan	47.6
Nundah	51.1
Oxley	43.1
Sandgate	45.1
Wynnum	42.9

	1932 %
WIDE BAY (6)	
Bundaberg	59.3
Cooroora	31.6
Gympie	48.4
Isis	37.3
Maryborough	58.7
Wide Bay	37.6
CENTRAL (5)	
Fitzroy	46.2
Keppel	48.4
Normanby	59.9
Port Curtis	51.2
Rockhampton	60.7
WEST (8)	
Barcoo	*
Carpentaria	*
Charters Towers	63.6
Cook	49.6
Gregory	*
Maranoa	62.2

SOUTH-EAST (8)	
Albert	36.6
Bremer	*
Fassifern	-
Ipswich	59.3
Murrumba	33.0
Nanango	33.0
Stanley	32.0
West Moreton	32.8
DARLING DOWNS (7)	
Aubigny	33.2
Carnarvon	44.1
Cunningham	33.2
Dalby	46.2
East Toowoomba	41.2
Toowoomba	52.4
Warwick	45.5
Murilla	41.4
Warrego	55.3
NORTHERN (9)	
Bowen	57.1
Cairns	65.3
Herbert	66.5
Kennedy	49.4
Mackay	61.4
Mirani	43.8
Mundingburra	66.9
The Tableland	52.0
Townsville	73.0

- No Labor candidate
* Labor win uncontested

LABOR VOTE 1935-1947

	1935 %	1938 %	1941 %	1944 %	1947 %
BRSIBANE (20)					
Inner urban					
Baroona	69.2	49.6	59.9	55.3	55.5
Brisbane	64.4	66.0	57.4	58.4	50.9
Bulimba	66.8	59.8	70.1	24.5	27.7
Buranda	64.1	50.9	56.9	50.7	52.9
Fortitude Valley	72.3	56.4	56.5	60.5	59.8
Hamilton	34.2	31.3	-	24.8	26.3
Ithaca	*	49.8	56.9	54.0	57.5
Kelvin Grove	69.7	42.5	50.7	53.1	50.5
Kurilpa	63.9	46.7	48.4	53.5	51.6
Maree	69.8	53.3	49.8	46.7	49.4
Merthyr	66.5	49.3	58.4	54.7	55.4
South Brisbane	67.6	49.8	56.6	56.3	53.1
Toowong	39.1	26.0	36.2	-	29.8
Windsor	57.5	46.2	44.6	40.8	41.95
Suburban					
Enoggera	69.0	54.7	50.5	22.0	42.5

	1935 %	1938 %	1941 %	1944 %	1947 %
WIDE BAY (6)					
Bundaberg	52.4	44.1	48.9	33.4	33.0
Cooroora	-	25.4	-	37.5	22.7
Gympie	56.7	43.0	52.4	47.8	41.6
Isis	44.9	35.2	40.8	35.5	31.6
Maryborough	90.4	61.2	59.1	*	55.9
Wide Bay	-	20.1	43.2	42.9	21.1
CENTRAL (4)					
Fitzroy	63.3	55.0	*	51.4	54.7
Keppel	33.1	-	38.4	40.1	41.1
Port Curtis	55.0	57.1	64.3	59.3	41.4
Rockhampton	72.4	60.9	72.9	65.5	50.4
WEST (7)					
Barcoo	*	*	79.6	*	66.7
Carpentaria	*	55.8	51.8	57.5	70.2
Charters Towers	64.5	*	63.2	67.5	63.2
Gregory	*	64.9	54.2	*	59.6

Logan	61.0	49.6	55.0	47.3	39.3
Nundah	66.5	48.4	53.3	51.6	50.8
Oxley	46.6	39.7	38.5	42.8	40.4
Sandgate	55.0	45.4	38.7	40.5	41.7
Wynnum	50.5	36.5	40.5	36.6	52.7
SOUTH-EAST (8)					
Albert	-	28.6	37.6	31.9	31.4
Bremer	87.5	83.4	83.5	*	69.3
Fassifern	37.9	32.6	35.3	29.6	28.4
Ipswich	*	66.0	66.8	*	61.9
Murrumba	-	17.7	29.1	-	-
Nanango	-	28.4	40.8	36.2	22.8
Stanley	36.0	37.8	40.3	35.8	-
West Moreton	-	-	34.6	25.4	18.9
DARLING DOWNS (7)					
Aubigny	-	24.0	36.7	31.8	28.4
Carnarvon	52.8	56.2	*	56.5	52.7
Cunningham	-	-	32.7	32.8	27.7
Dalby	48.1	50.3	56.0	51.5	40.9
East Toowoomba	54.3	45.4	45.8	41.2	48.2
Toowoomba	58.8	52.5	67.7	*	59.8
Warwick	45.8	52.8	55.0	54.4	48.3
Maranoa	70.5	60.0	59.2	56.2	59.9
Normanby	68.0	53.8	58.2	54.6	48.3
Warrego	*	69.7	*	69.6	49.3
NORTHERN (10)					
Bowen	52.6	39.2	52.7	38.6	30.5
Cairns	69.3	56.3	55.4	34.3	40.0
Cook	53.7	59.0	57.0	54.5	55.7
Herbert	63.7	52.9	56.2	57.0	48.0
Kennedy	63.9	63.8	57.7	50.7	44.8
Mackay	71.6	80.6	67.5	58.0	60.8
Mirani	48.9	48.8	58.9	47.5	41.9
Mundingburra	67.4	50.3	56.3	28.5	22.9
The Tableland	66.4	57.8	58.5	47.0	49.6
Townsville	76.9	50.0	*	62.9	67.8

- No Labor candidate
* Labor win uncontested

LABOR VOTE 1950-1957

	1950 %	1953 %	1956 %	1957 %	QLP
BRISBANE (24)					
Inner urban					
Baroona	61.7	*	64.8	26.5	(40.6)
Brisbane	58.8	75.2	60.0	38.4	(32.3)
Bulimba	35.7	64.0	56.6	37.0	(28.8)
Buranda	53.0	63.4	55.5	34.4	(22.8)
Clayfield	25.4	-	-	-	(-)
Coorparoo	37.0	42.5	38.0	29.4	(-)
Fortitude Valley	57.6	72.1	57.2	32.0	(30.1)
Ithaca	60.7	65.0	61.6	43.9	(18.3)
Kelvin Grove	56.2	61.9	54.3	37.7	(20.7)
Kurilpa	57.4	62.7	57.2	28.7	(32.4)
Merthyr	56.0	63.8	59.8	27.4	(35.6)
Norman	48.8	59.2	56.1	41.1	(18.7)
South Brisbane	56.5	64.6	58.6	24.2	(44.1)
Toowong	33.0	37.2	-	-	(-)
Windsor	50.1	60.2	56.3	22.4	(38.6)
Yeronga	41.2	48.8	40.5	23.8	(21.6)
Suburban					
Chermside	39.9	48.4	41.5	25.6	(20.2)

	1950 %	1953 %	1956 %	1957 %	QLP
WIDE BAY (7)					
Barambah	24.8	-	-	-	(29.6)
Bundaberg	44.6	65.6	*	22.6	(53.8)
Cooroora	27.4	29.9	31.8	24.1	(-)
Isis	38.1	41.3	37.7	-	(32.0)
Marodian	30.2	32.4	-	24.7	(-)
Maryborough	65.4	56.0	66.2	53.1	(14.6)
Nash	50.1	56.1	56.0	23.1	(35.4)
CENTRAL (5)					
Callide	34.2	36.1	34.9	-	(-)
Fitzroy	61.9	69.5	62.6	43.1	(25.9)
Keppel	56.1	55.4	58.5	30.9	(26.1)
Port Curtis	57.8	67.7	64.5	49.4	(14.7)
Rockhampton	51.3	61.8	50.0	24.6	(36.3)
WEST (10)					
Balonne	53.9	61.2	56.7	37.9	(19.0)
Barcoo	68.5	*	67.6	40.8	(29.9)
Belyando	58.9	*	58.7	24.3	(38.5)
Carpentaria	62.8	62.7	60.1	31.2	(38.6)

[illegible]	[illegible]	[illegible]	[illegible]	[illegible]	(21.3)
Mt. Coot-tha	39.9	42.7	37.6	21.8	(19.8)
Mt. Gravatt	52.3	63.5	59.6	39.3	(20.4)
Nundah	52.3	61.9	55.5	29.4	(31.3)
Sandgate	46.0	55.9	56.6	35.5	(27.3)
Sherwood	41.6	48.4	45.2	32.0	(18.6)
Wynnum	61.0	69.5	65.4	52.3	(12.2)
SOUTH-EAST (9)					
Bremer	65.8	*	72.7	59.7	(14.1)
Darlington	-	30.7	32.1	20.3	(-)
Fassifern	23.8	-	-	-	(26.9)
Ipswich	64.0	94.6	61.2	45.6	(20.9)
Landsborough	-	-	26.9	-	(-)
Lockyer	25.2	32.9	-	-	(-)
Murrumba	34.9	42.2	38.0	19.5	(18.7)
Somerset	42.2	50.9	55.9	23.0	(36.0)
Southport	28.8	39.8	34.0	26.1	(-)
DARLING DOWNS (7)					
Aubigny	20.6	-	27.4	-	(-)
Carnarvon	50.8	61.4	58.2	13.7	(46.2)
Condamine	37.9	50.5	54.9	7.7	(48.4)
Cunningham	-	39.0	35.9	-	(-)
North Toowoomba	54.4	61.8	59.0	44.3	(17.4)
Toowoomba	55.7	66.1	63.0	38.7	(16.9)
Warwick	31.6	35.2	36.4	-	(34.7)

Charters Towers	59.2	*	67.5	25.3	(43.8)
Flinders	47.5	*	58.1	34.4	(25.8)
Gregory	64.1	*	65.2	30.5	(21.9)
Mackenzie	51.3	55.0	49.5	24.9	(20.1)
Roma	46.7	51.6	50.1	15.3	(36.0)
Warrego	65.0	*	67.7	44.7	(25.8)
NORTHERN (13)					
Burdekin	44.0	42.0	33.3	28.4	(19.6)
Cairns	59.0	59.6	58.9	38.4	(32.2)
Cook	49.2	53.1	63.6	17.7	(44.2)
Haughton	46.9	59.2	70.4	27.6	(48.1)
Hinchinbrook	55.9	59.3	52.1	35.2	(17.2)
Mackay	55.0	64.5	58.0	42.0	(19.2)
Mirani	37.0	42.1	40.7	22.5	(20.8)
Mourilyan	43.5	67.3	59.5	42.2	(22.6)
Mulgrave	44.0	51.1	51.9	23.8	(31.0)
Mundingburra	23.9	27.7	22.1	19.2	(-)
Tablelands	53.6	66.3	66.4	25.9	(36.6)
Townsville	51.6	58.4	46.9	40.1	(25.0)
Whitsunday	36.5	44.8	40.6	29.1	(15.6)

- No Labor candidate
* Labor win uncontested

Appendix B:
Membership of the Queensland Central Committee, 1916-60

Records of membership of the QCE during the 1920s and 1930s have not been well preserved. It is therefore not possible to provide accurate membership for the period 1920-1935.

1916-18 W.H. Demaine President, R. Sumner vice-president, L. McDonald secretary

Convention delegates: W.H. Demaine, T.J. Ryan MLA, L. McDonald, R. Sumner, T. Wilson MLA, J. Larcombe MLA, C. Collins MLA, W. Gillies MLA, J.S. Collings, J.G. Hall, W.F. Smith MLA

State PLP: M.J. Kirwan MLA

Federal PLP: J. Page MHR

Union Delegates: *Australian Workers Union*: W.J. Dunstan replaced by M. Kelly, E.H. Lane, J.A. Moir replaced by W. Williams; *Australasian Meat Industry Employees Union*: E.G. Jones replaced by C. Boulton; *Waterside Workers Federation*: M. McCabe; *Queensland Railways Union*: T. Moroney; *Small Unions*: G. Lawson, D. Gledson MLA

1918-20 W.H. Demaine MLC President, R. Sumner MLC vice-president, L. McDonald MLC secretary

Convention delegates: C. Collins MLA, T.J. Ryan MLA, W.H. Demaine MLC, L. McDonald MLC, J.A. Fihelly MLA, W. McCormack MLA, R. Sumner MLC, T. Moroney resigned January 1920 replaced by E.J. Hanson, R.J. Carroll MLC, J.G. Hall resigned March 1920, J.S. Collings MLC

State PLP: E.G. Theodore MLA

Federal PLP: J. Page MHR

Union delegates: *Australian Workers Union*: E.H. Lane, W.J. Riordan replaced by W.J. Dunstan, J. Stopford MLA replaced by F.W. Martyn; *Australasian Meat Industry Employees Union*: C.A. Boulton; *Amalgamated Society of Engineers*: P. Watson; *Queensland Railways Union*: J. Heeney replaced by I.W. Williams, V.W. Speering; *Waterside Workers Federation*: D.K. Heggie; *Small Unions*: G. Lawson MLC, D. Gledson MLA

1920-23 W.H. Demaine MLC President, W.J. Dunstan vice-president to 28 January 1921, W.J. Riordan vice-president, L. McDonald MLC secretary

Convention delegates: W. Demaine MLC, R. Sumner MLC, L. McDonald MLC, J.S. Collings MLC, C. Collins MLA, J. Mullan MLA, D. Gledson MLA, B. McLean, W. McCormack MLA, H. Bruce, T. Wilson MLA

State PLP: E.G. Theodore MLA

Federal PLP: J. Page MHR (died 3 June 1921), replaced by F.M. Forde MHR.

Union delegates: *Australian Workers Union*: E.H. Lane, F.W. Martyn, W.J. Dunstan replaced by W.J. Riordan 28 January 1921; *Australasian Meat Industry Employees Union*: C.A. Boulton replaced by E. Jones; *Australian Coal and Shale Employees Federation*: C. Kilpatrick; *Amalgamated Engineering Union*: P. Watson replaced by R.J. Carroll; *Queensland Railways Union (Australian Railways Union)* A.E. Welsby expelled, D.T. Beatson withdrawn, G. Rymer, D. Weir MLA; *Waterside Workers Federation*: D.K. Heggie; *Small Unions*: G. Lawson MLC, J.P. Teefey

1923-26 W.H. Demaine President, W.J. Riordan vice-president, L. McDonald secretary

Convention Delegates: L. McDonald, R. Sumner, W.H. Demaine, W. McCormack MLA, B. McLean, W.J. Dunstan, W.F. Smith MLA, D. Gledson MLA, W. Liddle, T. Wilson MLA, J. Mullan MLA

State PLP: E.G. Theodore MLA replaced by W.N. Gilles MLA, replaced by M.P. Hynes MLA

Federal PLP: F.M. Forde MHR

Union delegates: *Australian Workers Union*: W.J. Riordan, G.W. Martens replaced by R. Funnell, J.C. Lamont replaced by P. Cahill, S. Brassington, R. McMullen; *Australian Railways Union*: J. Hayes, V. Hartley, T. Moroney; *Australasian Meat Industry Employees Union*: P. Carney; *Amalgamated Society of Carpenters and Joiners*: F. Brazier replaced by L. English; *Amalgamated Engineering Union*: R.J. Carroll; *Queensland State Service Union*: H. Dever replaced by P.K. Copley; *Carters and Drivers Union*: G. Lawson; *Small Unions*: G. Lawson replaced by F. Harris, C. Burke replaced by G. Marriott, J.C Valentine, S.J. Bryan

1926-28 W.H. Demaine President, W.J. Riordan vice-president, L. McDonald secretary

Convention delegates: J.S. Collings, L. McDonald, W.H. Demaine, W. McCormack MLA, W.F. Smith MLA, D. Gledson MLA, G. Lawson, G. Pollock MLA, B. McLean, J. Mullan MLA, T. Wilson MLA

State PLP: M.P. Hynes MLA

Federal PLP: F.M. Forde MHR

Union delegates: *Australian Workers Union*: J. Lough replaced by O. Lewis, W.J. Riordan, G. Martens, G. Crooks, J.C. Lamont; *Australasian Meat Industry Employees Union*: P. Carney; *Amalgamated Society of Carpenters and Joiners*: E. Ellis resigned August 1928; *Amalgamated Engineering Union*: R.J. Carroll; *Amalgamated Road Transport Workers Union*: G. Lawson; *Australian Federated Union of Locomotive Enginemen*: J. Valentine; *Amalgamated Foodstuffs Union*: J. Bourke replaced by J. McDonnell; *Queensland Shop Assistants Union*: L. Day, E. Rusling replaced by G. Brown; *Federated Clerks Unon*: W.C. Blakemore; *Storemen and Packers Union*: J.A. Turner; *Queensland State Service Union*: P.K. Copley replaced by J.F. Ruddy; *Small Unions*: R.H. Watson, T. Fallon, A.J.H. Pickford replaced H. Milton, S.J. Bryan, W. Richardson

1928-32 W.H. Demaine President, W.J. Riordan vice-president, L. McDonald secretary

Convention delegates: W.J. Riordan, L. McDonald, W.H. Demaine, W.F. Smith MLA, W. McCormack MLA, D. Gledson MLA, J. Collings, J. Mullan MLA, G. Pollock MLA, D. Riordan MLA, S.J. Bryan

State PLP: M.P. Hynes MLA

Federal PLP: F.M. Forde MHR

Union delegates: *Australian Workers Union*: G. Crooks; J.C. Lamont, C. Fallon, W. Hay replaced by G. Devries, J. Perrett replaced by J. Carpendale; *Australasian Meat Industry Employees Union*: P. Carney; *Amalgamated Road Transport Workers Union*: G. Lawson; *Amalgamated Engineering Union*: R.J. Carroll; *Australian Federated Union of Locomotive Enginemen*: J. Valentine; *Amalgamated Foodstuffs Union*: J. Bourke replaced by D. Brown; *Queensland Colliery Employees Union*: C. Kilpatrick; *Queensland Shop Assistants Union*: G. Brown, E. Rusling; *Federated Clerks Union*: W. Blakemore replaced by A.W. Gee; *Federated Miscellaneous*

Workers Union: A. Crockatt, H.J. Harvey; *Federated Storemen and Packers Union*: J.A. Turner replaced by J. Reid, replaced by J.A. Turner; *Queensland State Service Union*: J.F. Ruddy replaced by W.J. Copley, resigned January 1930 (union disaffiliated); *Small Unions*: R.J. Mulvey, G.H. Marriott, T. Fallon, G. Fry

1932-35 W.H. Demaine President, W.J. Riordan vice-president to 15 March 1933 replaced by C.G. Fallon, L. McDonald secretary

Convention delegates: S.J. Brassington, J. Dash MLA, W.H. Demaine, L. McDonald, J. Mullan MLA, G. Pollock MLA, D. Riordan MLA, W.J. Riordan replaced by T. Wilson MLA died 6 June 1934, replaced by T. Foley, W.F. Smith MLA, S.J. Bryan, P. Carney

State PLP: M.P. Hynes MLA

Federal PLP: J. Collings Senator from November 1932

Union delegates: *Australian Workers Union*: G. Crooks, J.C. Lamont, C.G. Fallon, G.H. Devries, J. Carpendale; *Australasian Meat Industry Employees Union*: P. Kennedy; *Australian Federated Union of Locomotive Enginemen*: J. Valentine; *Amalgamated Engineering Union*: R.J. Carroll; *Amalgamated Road Transport Union*: K.A. Sanders; *Federated Miscellaneous Workers Union*: H.J. Harvey; *Federated Storemen and Packers Union*: J. Reid; *Queensland Colliery Employees Union*: C. Kilpatrick replaced by A.E. Phillips 14 June 1935; *Queensland Shop Assistants Union*: E. Rusling; *Small Unions*: T. Lourigan from 11 May 1933, W. Richardson, J. Cranitch

1935-38 W.H. Demaine President, C.G. Fallon vice-president, L. McDonald secretary, died 18 September 1936, replaced by R.J. Carroll

Convention delegates: W.F. Smith MLA, C.G. Fallon, E.M. Hanlon MLA, W.H. Demaine, J.C. Lamont, S.J. Bryan, H.A. Bruce MLA, J. Mullan MLA, J. Dash MLA, T. Foley MLA, R. Leggatt

State PLP: M.P. Hynes MLA

Federal PLP: J.S. Collings Senator

Union delegates: *Australian Workers Union*: J. Lough, O. Lewis, G. Crooks, J. Perrett, C.E. Fallon; *Australasian Meat Industry Employees Union*: A.J. Neumann; *Amalgamated Engineering Union*: R.J. Carroll; *Amalgamated Society of Carpenters and Joiners*: A. Andrews; *Amalgamated Foodstuffs Union*: J. Bourke; *Amalgamated Road Transport Workers Union*: A.C. Milton; *Federated Clerks*

Union: K.A. Sanders, T. Lourigan; *Federated Engine Drivers and Firemen's Association*: E. Shaw; *Federated Miscellaneous Workers Union*: W.C. Gollan; *Federated Storemen and Packers Union*: J. Reid; *Queensland Colliery Employees Union*: A.E. Phillips; *Queensland Shop Assistants Union*: E. Rusling, V.T. Hefferan; *Queensland State Service Union*: C.R. Muhldorff; *Small Unions*: W. Cotter, H.J. Harvey, J. Cranitch, B.F. McCabe, R. Battye

1938-41 C.G. Fallon President, S.J. Bryan vice-president, R.J. Carroll secretary, died 7 February 1940, replaced by S.J. Bryan

Convention delegates: W.F. Smith MLA, C.G. Fallon, E.M. Hanlon MLA, J.C. Lamont, S.J. Bryan, H.A. Bruce MLA, J. Mullan MLA, J. Dash MLA, T.A. Foley MLA, F.A. Cooper MLA, G. Pollock MLA died April 1939, replaced by A.C. Milton

State PLP: M.P. Hynes MLA died March 1939, replaced by J. O'Keefe MLA

Federal PLP: J.S. Collings Senator

Union delegates: *Australian Workers Union*: J. Lough replaced by J. Perrett, O. Lewis, G. Crooks replaced by A. Elliott, W.B. Hay, C.E. Fallon; *Amalgamated Engineering Union*: R.J. Carroll, died February 1940, replaced by R. Leggat; *Amalgamated Meat Industry Employees Union*: A. McHardy died April 1939 replaced by R. Dixon; *Amalgamated Clothing Trade Union*: W.H. Sparks; *Amalgamated Foodstuffs Union: J. Bourke; Amalgamated Society of Carpenters and Joiners*: H.H. Long; *Federated Clerks Union*: K.A. Sanders, T. Lourigan replaced by W.J. Barrett; *Federated Engine Drivers and Firemen's Association*: E. Shaw; *Federated Miscellaneous Workers Union*: W.C. Gollan; *Federated Storemen and Packers Union*: J. Reid; *Queensland Colliery Employees Union*: A.E. Phillips; *Queensland Shop Assistants Union*: E. Rusling, V. Hefferan; *Queensland State Service Union*: C.R. Muhldorff; *Transport Workers Union*: A.C. Milton became Convention delegate, replaced by B.V. Hough; *Small Unions*: W. Cotter, H.J. Harvey, W. Richardson, A. Cole.

1941-44 C.G. Fallon President, A.E. Phillips vice-president, retired 11 June 1943, S.J. Bryan secretary

Convention delegates: W. Smith MLA, S.J. Bryan, C.G. Fallon, H.A. Bruce, E.M. Hanlon MLA, F.A. Cooper MLA, T.A. Foley MLA, A.C. Milton, H.J. Harvey, W.B. Hay resigned 26 February 1943, replaced by J. Larcombe MLA, J. Reid

State PLP: J. O'Keefe MLA died February 1942, replaced by E.J. Walsh MLA

Federal PLP: J.S. Collings Senator, B. Courtice Senator alternative delegate

Union delegates: *Australian Workers Union*: J.W. Perrett replaced by T. Dougherty, O. Lewis replaced by G. Devries MLA, R.A. Elliott replaced by H. O'Shea MLA, C.E. Fallon replaced by R.J. Bukowski, J. Doyle replaced by J. Lough, *Amalgamated Engineering Union*: R. Leggat; *Australian Federated Union of Locomotive Enginemen*: J.C. Valentine from May 1942; *Federated Clerks Union*: K.A. Saunders, W.J. Barrett, T. Lourigan; *Federated Engine Drivers and Firemen's Association*: E. Shaw withdrew 1942; *Federated Miscellaneous Workers Union*: W.C. Gollan; *Federated Storemen and Packers Union*: A.L. Marshall replaced by W. Dorricot; *Queensland Colliery Employees Union*: A.E. Phillips replaced by J. Donald; *Queensland Shop Assistants Union*: E. Rusling, V. Hefferan; *Queensland State Service Union*: C.R. Muhldorff; *Transport Workers Union*: B.V. Hough; *Small Unions*: P.A. Davis, W. Cotter died March 1942, A. Cole, T. Fallon

1944-47 C.G. Fallon President, A.C. Milton vice-president, S.J. Bryan secretary

Convention delegates: F.A. Cooper MLA resigned 23 May 1946 replaced by W. Power MLA: S.J. Bryan, C.G. Fallon, E.M. Hanlon MLA, H.J. Harvey, H.A. Bruce MLA, V.C. Gair MLA, A. Jones MLA, A.C. Milton, T. Rasey, C.R. Muhldorff

State PLP: E.J. Walsh MLA

Federal PLP: J.S. Collings Senator, B. Courtice Senator, alternative delegate

Union delegates: *Australian Workers Union*: C.E. Fallon, J. Lough, H. O'Shea MLA, G. Devries MLA replaced by W.F. Edmonds MHR, R.J. Bukowski; *Amalgamated Engineering Union*: R. Leggat; *Australian Federated Union of Locomotive Enginemen*: H.S. Burton replaced by D.W. Trewin; *Federated Clerks Unigon*: W.H. Wood, W.J. Barrett replaced by T. Lourigan, G. Knight replaced by S.H. Martin; *Federated Engine Drivers and Firemen's Association*: G. Whiteside; *Federated Miscellaneous Workers Union*: W. Gollan; *Federated Storemen and Packers Union*: W. Dorricot; *Queensland Colliery Employees Union*: J. Donald MLA; *Queensland Shop Assistants Union*: E. Rusling replaced by T.M. Taylor, V. Hefferan; *Queensland State Service Union*: M.F. Moriarty replaced by T. Bolger; *Transport Workers Union*: B.V. Hough; *Small Unions*: A. Cole, T. Fallon, P.A. Davis, E.T. Henry

1947-50 C.G. Fallon president, died 11 January 1950, A.C. Milton vice-president, died 6 February 1948, H.J. Harvey vice-president, resigned 26 October 1949, C.R. Muhldorff vice-president, S.J. Bryan secretary

Convention delegates: C.G. Fallon, A.C. Milton, died replaced by W.J. Copley, H.J. Harvey, C.R. Muhldorff, E.M. Hanlon MLA, E.J. Walsh, V.C. Gair MLA, A. Jones MLA. A. Cole, T. Rasey, W. Power MLA

State PLP: T.A. Foley MLA

Federal PLP: J.S. Collings Senator, B. Courtice Senator, alternative delegate

Union delegates: *Australian Workers Union*: C.E. Fallon, J. Schmella, H. O'Shea MLA, R.J. Bukowski, G. Devries MLA; *Australian Federated Union of Locomotive Enginemen*: D.W. Trewin replaced by S. Wright; *Australian Theatrical Amusement Employees Union*: S.J. Bryan; *Australasian Meat Industry Employees Union*: A.J. Neumann; *Amalgamated Engineering Union*: R. Leggat; *Amalgamated Foodstuffs Union*: J. Cowan; *Electrical Trades Union*: A.H. Dawson; *Federated Clerks Union*: T.E. O'Driscoll replaced by K.W.S. Murray, W. Wood replaced by H. Dean, T. Lourigan replaced by T.H. Callinan; *Federated Engine Drivers and Firemen's Association*: G. Whiteside; *Federated Miscellaneous Workers Union*: W.C. Gollan died 9 November 1947 replaced by R.S. Greig; *Federated Storemen and Packers Union*: J. Lindsay replaced by A.L. Marshall; *Queensland Colliery Employees Union*: J. Donald MLA; *Queensland Railway Traffic Employees Union*: P.A. Davis; *Queensland Shop Assistants Union*: T.M. Taylor, V.T. Hefferan; *Queensland State Service Union*: T. Bolger; *Transport Workers Union*: B.V. Hough, *Small Unions:* B.R. Milliner, E.T. Ashmore, J.V. Quinn, W. McCormack

1950-53 H. Boland President, C.R. Muhldorff vice-president, S.J. Bryan secretary retired 31 July 1952, replaced by J. Schmella

Convention delegates: E.M. Hanlon MLA died 15 January 1952, replaced by W.J. Copley, E.J. Walsh MLA, A. Cole, T. Rasey MLA, V.C. Gair MLA, A. Jones MLA, W. Power MLA, E. Williams, M.T. Brosnan MLA, G. Whiteside, C.R. Muhldorff.

State PLP: T.A. Foley MLA

Federal PLP: B. Courtice Senator replaced by W.F. Edmonds MHR
Union delegates: *Australian Workers Union*: H. Boland, J. Schmella, R.J. Bukowski, G.H. Devries MLA, C.E. Fallon replaced by N. Williamson; *Australian Federated Union of Locomotive Enginemen*: S. Wright; *Australian Theatrical and Amusement Employees Union*: S.J. Bryan; *Australasian Meat Industry Employees Union*: A.J. Neumann, S.J. MacPherson; *Amalgamated Engineering Union*: R. Leggat died 11 May 1951, replaced by C. Merrell; *Amalgamated Foodstuffs Union*: J. Cowan; *Amalgamated Postal Workers Union*: E.T. Ashmore; *Electrical Trades Union*: A.H. Dawson; *Federated Clerks Union*: K.W.S. Murray, H. Dean replaced by W.T. Thornton, T. Lourigan replaced by J.P. Madden, replaced by W.J. Barry, S.H. Martin; *Federated Engine Drivers and Firemen's Association*: P.C. Johnson; *Federated Ironworkers Association*: H.J. Chant (affiliated 30 June 1952); *Federated Miscellaneous Workers Union*: R.S. Greig absent nine months 1952, A. Macpherson proxy; *Federated Storemen and Packers Union*: A.L. Marshall, P.A. Fulloon; *Printing Industry Employees Union*: B.R. Milliner; *Queensland Colliery Employees Union*: J. Donald MLA; *Queensland Railway Maintenance Employees Union*: J.V. Quinn; *Queensland Railway Traffic Employees Union*: P.A Davis; *Queensland Shop Assistants Union*: T.M. Taylor, V.T. Hefferan; *Queensland State Service Union*: T. Bolger; *Transport Workers Union*: B.V. Hough; *Vehicle Builders Employees Federation*: J.J. Ryan; *Small Unions*: N.L. Buchan, E.A. Stokoe, W.H. Tyrrell

1953-56 H. Boland President, C.R. Muhldorff vice-president, J. Schmella secretary (not a delegate to the QCE)
Convention delegates: V.C. Gair MLA, A. Cole, E.J. Walsh MLA, W. Power MLA, C.R. Muhldorff, J. Devereaux, A. Jones MLA, H. Boland, V.T. Hefferan, M.T. Brosnan, J. Cowan
State PLP: T.A. Foley MLA
Federal PLP: W.F. Edmonds MHR
Union delegates: *Australian Workers Union*: W.J. McCarter, G.H. Devries MLA replaced by J.V. Bliss 12 December 1955, G. Goding, N. Williamson, R.J. Bukowski; *Australian Builders Labourers Federation*: W.H. Tyrrell; *Australian Federated Union of Locomotive Enginemen*: S. Wright; *Australian Theatrical and Amusement Employees Union*: S.J. Bryan Mrs E. Bryan proxy for almost all meetings; *Australasian Meat Industry Employees Union*: A.J. Neumann died 14 October 1955, replaced by R.F.G.

Neumann, A. Summers proxy for A.J. Neumann March-October 1955, S.J. MacPherson; *Amalgamated Engineering Union*: C. Merrell, T. Darby additional delegate from 25 May 1955; *Amalgamated Foodstuffs Union*: W.T. Gibson resigned 25 July 1955, replaced by R. Fraser, J. Pleace additional delegate from 13 September 1954; *Amalgamated Postal Workers Union,* E.T. Ashmore replaced by W.K. Spence 30 September 1955; *Building Workers Industrial Union* (affiliated 11 November 1955): W. Davidson, F. Smith, F. Newton; *Electrical Trades Union*: A.H. Dawson; *Federated Clerks Union*: J.V. Bliss replaced by C.J. Kelso, J. Allman, W.T. Thornton, W.J. Barry replaced by T.J. Heike; *Federated Engine Drivers and Firemen's Association*: G. Whiteside; *Federated Furnishing Trades Society* (affiliated 20 July 1954): W.C. Rogers; *Federated Miscellaneous Workers Union*: W.J. Costello retired, replaced by W. Ward, W.T. Lake additional delegate 15 December 1954, replaced by A. Sullivan 28 September 1955; *Federated Storemen and Packers Union*: A.L. Marshall, P. Fulloon retired, replaced by E.E. Adsett 1 July 1953; *Printing Industry Employees Union*: B.R. Milliner; *Queensland Colliery Employees Union*: J. Donald MLA; *Queensland Railway Maintenance Employees Union*: J.V. Quinn; *Queensland Railway Traffic Employees Union*: P.A. Davis retired replaced by L.F. Connolly 23 September 1955; *Queensland Shop Assistants Union*: W.F. Major, T.M. Taylor, A. Stockwell additional delegate 8 December 1954; *Queensland State Service Union*: T. Bolger, F. Bennett additional delegate 1 March 1955, J.A. McGuire proxy for Bolger while ill; *Returned Sailors, Soldiers and Airmens Labor League*: J.B. Quinlan; *Transport Workers Union*: B.V. Hough, R.C. Jansen additional delegate 22 March 1955; *Vehicle Builders Employees Federation*: J.J. Ryan; *Small Unions*: E.A. Stokoe, E.J.G. Irwin, C.J. Bushell

1956-60 H. Boland President, died 25 July 1956, R.J. Bukowski President suspended 19 December 1958, G. Whiteside President; R.J. Bukowski vice-president; G. Whitside vice-president, J. Duggan vice-president, J. Schmella secretary

Convention delegates: V.C. Gair MLA expelled 24 April 1957 replaced by F.W. Whitby 31 October 1957, H. Boland died, replaced by F. Howman, J.E. Duggan MLA, F.C.S. Dittmer MLA, J. Schmella, J. Devereaux, W. Dickson, W.K. Spence, G. Whiteside, E. Williams, J. Egerton

State PLP: T.A. Foley MLA replaced by J.J. Dufficy MLA, 25 May 1956

Federal PLP: W.F. Edmonds MHR replaced by A. Benn Senator 23 March 1959

Union delegates: Australian Workers Union (disaffiliated 23 February 1959) W.J. McCarter, G. Goding, E. Shaw, N. Williamson replaced by E. Tiley 27 July 1959; *Amalgamated Foodstuffs* Merrell died 15 May 1958, replaced by B. Lourigan, T. Darby replaced by E. Tiley 27 July 1959; *Amalgamated Foodstuffs Union*: R. Fraser, J. Pleace replaced by M. Scanlan 14 February 1957; *Amalgamated Postal Workers Union*: C.L. Robinson, E. Barr replaced by E.T. Ashmore; *Australian Builders Labourers Federation*: W.H. Tyrell, J.J. Taylor; *Australian Federated Union of Locomotive Enginemen*: S. Wright replaced by H.L. Edmonds died 15 September 1958, F.E. Doyle; *Australian Railways Union* (affiliated 16 May 1957); W.R. Bousen, R.J. Patterson, F.G. Nolan; *Australian Theatrical and Amusement Employees Union*: Mrs E. Bryan; *Australasian Meat Industry Employees Union*: R.F.G. Neumann, S. McPherson, C. Buchanan, A. Summers, H.E. Edmonds appointed delegate 11 September 1957, A. McArthur appointed delegate 11 September 1957; *Boilermakers Society:* E. Bright; *Building Workers Industrial Union*: F. Smith replaced by S. Baker 14 February 1957, replaced by C. Cusack 22 August, replaced by R. Anderson 28 September 1959, F. Newton, W. Davidson replaced by R.M. Beale 14 February 1957, replaced by T. Chard 22 November 1957; *Electrical Trades Union*: A.H. Dawson, R.J. Green additional delegate 23 February 1959; *Federated Clerks Union* (disaffiliated 30 June 1957): C.J. Kelso, W.T. Thornton, T.J. Heike, J. Allman, W.J. Barry from 28 February 1957; *Federated Engine Drivers and Firemen's Association*: W. Laing, W. Walton; *Federated Ironworkers Association* (disaffiliated 16 August 1957): H.G. Peebles; *Federated Liquor Trades Union*: F.W. Cannon; *Federated Furnishing Trades Union*: W.C. Rogers; *Federated Miscellaneous Workers Union*: A.C. MacColl, J. McWatters elected 28 March 1957, F. Bromley elected 28 August 1958, W. Ward elected 25 May 1959; *Federated Storemen and Packers Union*: E.E. Adsett, A.L. Marshall replaced by H. Starker; *Operative Painters and Decorators Union*: L. Burnett replaced by T. Conway; *Plumbers and Gasfitters Employees Union*: F.W. Hulme replaced W.J. Gardiner 1 May 1958 replaced by J.S. Stewart 22 May 1958;

Printing Industry Employees Union: B.R. Milliner; *Queensland Colliery Employees Union*: J. Donald MLA; *Queensland Railway Maintenance Union*: A. Cole; *Queensland Railway Traffic Employees Union* (disaffiliated 31 December 1957): L.F. Connolly; *Queensland Shop Assistants Union*: T.M. Taylor died 12 October 1956 replaced by F. Currie, W.F. Major, A. Stockwell replaced by V. Hefferan 28 June 1956; *Queensland State Service Union* (disaffiliated 5 June 1957): T. Bolger, F. Bennett; *Returned Soldiers Labor League* (disaffiliated 1956): J.B. Quinlan; *Transport Workers Union*: B.V. Hough replaced by T.J. Doyle 27 May 1959, R.C. Jansen replaced by S.H. Milton 27 May 1959; *Vehicle Builders Employees Federation*: J.J. Ryan replaced by J.S. Park 27 July 1959, replaced by L. Townsend; *Waterside Workers Federation*: A. Arnell replaced by E. Wilkinson 22 August 1956, replaced by P. Healy 22 August 1957; *Small Unions*: E.A. Stokoe, E.J. Irwin replaced by B. Smith 14 September 1956, C.J. Bushell replaced by W. McCormack 14 September 1956.

Appendix C:
Membership of the Executive Committee ("Inner Executive"), 1918-60

1918-20	W.H. Demaine (President), W.J. Riordan, L. McDonald (Secretary)
1920-23	W.H. Demaine (President), W.J. Dunstan (Vice-President), replaced by W.J. Riordan, R.J. Carroll, L. McDonald (Secretary)
1923-26	W.H. Demaine (President), W.J. Riordan (Vice-President), R. Sumner, G. Lawson, R.J. Carroll, L. McDonald (Secretary)
1926-28	W.H. Demaine (President), W.J. Riordan (Vice-President), R.J. Carroll, D. Gledson MLA, M.P. Hynes MLA, J.C. Lamont, W.F. Smith MLA, L. McDonald (Secretary)
1928-32	W.H. Demaine (President), W.J. Riordan (Vice-President), R.J. Carroll, W.F. Smith MLA, J.C. Lamont, M.P. Hynes MLA, D. Gledson MLA (resigned 13 September 1929), S.J. Bryan (from 13 September 1929), L. McDonald (Secretary)
1932-35	W.H. Demaine (President), W.J. Riordan (Vice-President, resigned 15 March 1933), R.J. Carroll, S.J. Bryan, W.F. Smith MLA, M.P. Hynes MLA, J.C. Lamont, L. McDonald (Secretary)
1935-38	W.H. Demaine (President), C.G. Fallon (Vice-President), W.F. Smith MLA, M.P. Hynes MLA, S.J. Bryan, J.C. Lamont, R.J. Carroll (Organiser 28 November 1935, Secretary from 12 February 1937), L. McDonald (Secretary, died 18 September 1936)
1938-41	C.G. Fallon (President, 2 December 1938), S.J. Bryan (Vice-President, acting Secretary from February 1940), W.F. Smith MLA, J Reid, M.P. Hynes MLA (died March 1939), J.C. Lamont (resigned 8 August 1941), B. Hay (replaced Lamont), F.A. Cooper MLA (from 14 November 1939), A.E. Phillips (from 14 December 1938), R.J. Carroll (Secretary, died 7 February 1940)
1941-44	C.G. Fallon (President), A.E. Phillips (Vice-President, retired 11 June 1943), W.F. Smith MLA, F.A. Cooper MLA, A.C. Milton, J. Reid, W.B. Hay (resigned 22 March 1943), R.J. Bukowski (from 22 March 1943), S.J. Bryan (Secretary)
1944-47	C.G. Fallon (President), A.C. Milton (Vice-President), E.M. Hanlon MLA, F.A. Cooper MLA (resigned 23 May 1946), E.J. Walsh MLA (from 23 May 1946), R.J. Bukowski, H.J. Harvey, C.R. Muhldorff, S.J. Bryan (Secretary)
1947-50	C.G. Fallon (President, died 11 January 1950), A.C. Milton (Vice-President, died 6 February 1948), E.M. Hanlon MLA, E.J. Walsh MLA, H.J. Harvey (Vice-President 17 March 1948 to 26 October 1949, resigned), C.R. Muhldorff (Vice-

	President from 23 December 1949), T. Rasey (from 17 March 1948), A. Cole (from 23 December 1949), S.J. Bryan (Secretary)
1950-53	H. Boland (President), C.R. Muhldorff (Vice-President), E.M. Hanlon MLA (died 15 January 1952), V.C. Gair MLA (from 6 February 1952), E.J. Walsh MLA, R.J. Bukowski, T.Rasey MLA, A. Cole MLA, S.J. Bryan (Secretary, retired 31 July 1952), J. Schmella (Secretary, from 1 August 1952)
1953-56	H. Boland (President), C.R. Muhldorff (Vice-President), V.C. Gair MLA, E.J. Walsh MLA, A. Cole, R.J. Bukowski, T. Brosnan MLA, J. Schmella (Secretary)
1956-60	H. Boland (President, died 25 July1956), R.J. Bukowski (Vice-President, President, suspended 19 December 1958), G. Whiteside (Vice-President July 1956-February 1959, President from February 1959), J.E. Duggan (Vice-President from February 1959), V.C. Gair (expelled 24 April 1957), F.C.S. Dittmer, J. Egerton, J. Donald MLA, L. Wood MLA (died 29 March 1958), A.H. Dawson (from 23 February 1959)

Queensland Trade Union Membership, 1915-60

Year ending December	No. of Unions	Union Membership Thousands	Proportion of Queensland wage and salary earners as union members: Percentage			Total Australian unionists as a proportion of wage and salary earners	ALP Affiliated Unions		
			Male	Female	Total		No. of Unions	Membership	% of Qld. Unionists
1915	89	58.3	na	na	na	na	39	35,667	61.2
1916	93	66.8							
1917	96	75.4					52	51,158	67.8
1918	102	87.7							
1919	106	97.4					58	69,529	71.4
1920	115	103.8							
1921	118	103.8							
1922	118	100.9					61	69,817	69.2
1923	119	109.2							
1924	117	112.2	59.8	31.2					
1925	107	127.7	65.0	38.6			71	95,386	74.7
1926	109	143.0	71.3	37.8					
1927	104	150.7	72.1	46.0			62	97,776	64.8
1928	102	154.8	71.3	52.2					
1929	106	154.6	70.9	48.2					
1930	107	141.9	63.7	44.0		52.7			
1931	107	123.1	54.3	37.4		47.0	na	na	na
1932	107	110.1	47.6	34.9		45.0			
1933	107	121.3	53.8	42.3	51.8	44.4			
1934	106	129.4	53.4	50.1	52.9	43.4	59	74,858	57.8
1935	109	148.1	60.4	57.1	59.8	44.7			
1936	111	159.0	64.4	55.0	62.6	44.1			
1937	110	162.2	64.8	54.1	62.8	45.7	59	92,810	57.2
1938	111	169.6	66.1	53.0	63.6	46.6			

Year ending December	No. of Unions	Union Membership Thousands	Proportion of Queensland wage and salary earners as union members Percentage			Total Australian Unionists as a proportion of wage and salary earners	ALP Affiliated Unions		
			Male	Female	Total		No. of Unions	Membership	% of Qld. Unionists
1939	114	180.7	70.6	51.3	66.8	47.6			
1940	115	189.7	71.6	59.1	69.2	47.9	59	129,559	68.3
1941	115	192.0	66.1	70.2	66.8	49.3			
1942	113	190.6	na	na	na	52.2			
1943	113	194.2	60.0	66.4	61.3	53.6	37	106,884	55.0
1944	112	192.1	67.1	60.9	65.7	54.2			
1945	110	192.1	62.5	66.6	63.3	54.2			
1946	110	199.7	69.4	67.9	69.1	59.5	47	104,068	52.1
1947	110	218.1	78.8	71.5	77.2	62.9			
1948	112	234.5	84.5	69.6	81.1	64.9			
1949	125	259.3	71.9	55.2	67.7	57.0	53	149,742	57.7
1950	128	262.6	70.1	55.2	66.4	58			
1951	128	277.0	75	59	71	60			
1952	129	274.9	76	60	72	60	58	177,262	64.2
1953	129	285.7	78	62	74	60			
1954	129	305.3	79	70	77	62			
1955	130	305.5	77	65	74	59	63	211,112	69.1
1956	135	314.8	78	70	76	59			
1957	133	310.8	77	66	74	59			
1958	131	313.7	77	64	73	58			
1959	129	322.2	78	66	75	58	51	138,334	42.9
1960	133	327.4	78	66	75	58			

Sources: A.M. Johnston, Bureau of Census and Statistics, Brisbane,
Reports of the Labor-in-Politics Conventions

Appendix E:
Endorsed Labor Candidates, 1915-57

[Surnames of candidates who ever won an election are shown in capitals, and the dates of elections won in heavy type.

* indicates a candidate who stood prior to 1915; particulars will be in *Prelude to Power*, Appendix 1.

‡ indicates a candidate who stood for the Q.L.P. in 1957.]

ADAIR, Herbert Arthur	*publican*	Cook **1953, 1956**,‡
ADAMSON, John	*clergyman*	*Rockhampton **1915**
Alexander, William Charles	*public servant*	Aubigny 1956
Alke, Michael Philip	*bootmaker*	*Toowoomba 1915; Drayton 1918
Archibald, John	*farmer*	Cunningham 1932
ARMFIELD, Thomas Gummersall	*coachmaker*	Musgrave 1915, **1918**, 1920; East Toowoomba, 1923
Armstrong, Thomas Henry	*timber-getter*	Nanango 1915
Arnell, Geoffrey Ernest	*health inspector*	Cooroora 1950, 1953, 1956
Baker, Adolphus Allan Stanley	*railway worker, storekeeper, business manager*	Carnarvon 1926, 1929; Dalby 1932; Aubigny 1941
BARBER, George Philip	*seaman*	*Bundaberg **1915, 1918, 1920, 1923, 1926, 1929**
Barron, John	*auctioneer*	Isis 1953
Bartlett, Victor Leonard	*tram conductor*	Hamilton 1947
Barry, John Micharel	*solicitor*	Bowen 1947
Bauers, Paul Charles	*railway employee*	Warwick 1915
BAXTER, William Edward	*engine driver, railway clerk*	Norman **1953, 1956, 1957**
Baxter, William John	*clerk, miner, journalist, farmer, canefield worker, railway construction*	Burnett 1926
Beatson, Donald Thomas	*public servant*	Warwick 1920
BEDFORD, Randolph George	*journalist*	Carnarvon 1918; Warrego **1923**(by), **1926, 1929, 1932,**

		1935, **1937**(by), **1938**, **1941**
Belford, William James	*schoolteacher*	Southport 1956, 1957
BERTRAM, William	*union secretary, grocer, storemen*	*Maree **1915**, **1918**, **1920**, **1923**, **1926**, 1929
Binstead John	*farmer*	Mirani 1915
BOW, Richard Rowland	*shearer, union secretary*	Mitchell **1928**(by), 1929
BOWMAN, David	*bootmaker, newsagent*	*Fortitude Valley **1915**
Boyden, George Henry	*teacher*	Carnarvon 1915
Bradfield, Robert Joseph	*clerk*	Cunningham 1953
Brady, William John	*butter factory manager*	Aubigny 1920
BRASSINGTON, Samuel John	*A.W.U. official*	Balonne **1927**(by), 1929; Murilla 1932; Fortitude Valley **1933**(by), **1935**, **1938**, **1941**, **1944**, **1947**, **1950**
Bray, John Walter	*truck driver, salesman*	Albert 1938, 1941
BRENNAN, Frank Tenison	*barrister*	Toowoomba **1918**, **1920**, **1923**
Brennan, John Francis	*hotel keeper*	Mundingburra 1956
Bromley, Charles Henry	*accountant*	Lockyer 1915
BROSNAN, Michael Timothy	*linesman, union organiser*	Fortitude Valley **1950**(by), **1953**, **1956**,‡
Brown, John	*butter factory worker*	Wide Bay 1932
BROWN, John Innes	*alderman*	Logan **1935**, **1938**, **1941**, **1944**
Brown, Leslie	*barrister*	Maree 1947
BROWN, Richard Kidston	*insurance inspector, blacksmith*	Logan 1920, 1926; Buranda **1947**, **1950**, **1953**, **1956**, 1957
Brown, Thomas E	*labourer, candle maker, fruit grower*	Carnarvon 1923
Brown, Vivian George	*schoolteacher*	Bundaberg 1947
BRUCE, Henry Adam	*bushworker, miner, AWU organiser*	Kennedy, **1923**, **1926**, **1929**; The Tableland **1932**, **1935**, **1938**, **1941**, **1944**, **1947**
Buchan, Norman Lewis	*alderman*	Baroona 1957
BULCOCK, Frank William	*journalist, AWU organiser*	Barcoo, **1919**(by), **1920**, **1923**, **1926**,

		1929, 1932, 1935, 1938, 1941
Burns, George	*AWU organiser*	Whitsunday 1956
BURROWS, James	*farmer, hospital secretary*	Port Curtis 1947, 1950, 1953, 1956, 1957
Burton, Walter Pigott	*storekeeper, farmer*	Nanango 1918
BUTLER, Robert John Cuthbert	*secretary, journalist*	Toombul 1915; Lockyer 1918, 1920
BYRNE, Peter	*cangrowers' secretary*	Mourilyan 1950, 1953, 1956, 1957
Campbell, George Thomas	*farmer*	Warwick 1923
Campbell, Sydney Henry	*caterer*	Marodian 1953
Campbell, Thomas Norman	*city council employee*	Merthyr 1957
Carroll, Daniel Noel	*farmer, solicitor*	Nanango 1944, 1947
CARTER, George	*bushworker, bookseller*	*Port Curtis 1915, 1918, 1920, 1923, 1926, 1929
Casey, John Patrick	*carrier*	Whitsunday 1950
Chataway, James Cosmo Mant	*grocer*	Mirani 1957
Chataway, Seymour Darcy Eagle	*railway worker*	Cook 1957
Christiansen, Donald	*schoolteacher*	Barambah 1950
CLARK, James	*miner, AWU secretary, hospital board secretary*	Fitzroy, 1935, 1938, 1941, 1944, 1947, 1950, 1953, 1956, 1957
Clayton, William Francis	*timber worker*	Keppel 1932
Collings, Joseph Silver	*grocer, boot-factory manager, party organiser*	*Murilla 1915
COLLINS, Charles	*labourer, miner, organiser*	*Bowen 1915, 1918, 1920, 1923, 1926, 1929, 1932, 1935
COLLINS, Harold Henry	*farmer*	Cook 1935, 1938, 1941, 1944, 1947; Tablelands 1950, 1953, 1956,‡
Collins, Robert Bernard	*wheatgrower, cattle breeder*	Murilla 1923

Connolly, James	*Crown lands ranger, farmer*	Dalby 1915, 1920
CONROY, Charles William	*tobacconist*	Maranoa **1920, 1923, 1926, 1929, 1932, 1935, 1938, 1941**
Cook, Sidney	*theatrical manager*	Nundah 1918; Windsor 1923
COOPER, Frank Arthur	*clerk, journalist, union official*	Bremer **1915, 1918, 1920, 1923, 1926, 1929, 1932, 1935, 1938, 1941, 1944**
Cooper, George	*carpenter*	Enoggera 1929
COOPER, Vivian Joseph Northcote	*coach painter, signwriter*	Keppel **1952**(by), **1953, 1956**,‡
COOPER, William	*blacksmith*	Rosewood **1915, 1918, 1920, 1923, 1926, 1929**
COPLEY, Patrick Kerry	*barrister*	Kurilpa 1929; Maryborough 1929(by); Kurilpa **1932, 1935, 1938, 1941, 1944, 1947**
COPLEY, William John	*public servant*	Bulimba **1932, 1935**
Costin, Benjamin Green	*insurance inspector*	Aubigny 1932
COYNE, John Henry	*bushworker, union organiser*	*Warrego **1915, 1918, 1920, 1923**
Cranitch, Joseph	*postal employee*	Logan 1932
Crilly, Andrew Anthony	*linesman*	Lockyer 1950
Crooke, Percy Clement	*carpenter*	Logan 1915
Crosby, Vincent Joseph	*farmer*	Landsborough 1956
Crowley, David Patrick	*foreman*	Cairns 1942(by), 1944
CROWLEY, Thomas Martin	*commission agent*	Cairns **1947, 1950, 1953**
Curtis, Clive Goff	*insurance superintendent*	Dalby 1929
Dalton, John James	*hospital attendant*	West Moreton 1944
Darby, Thomas	*turner*	Nundah 1929
Darveniza, Vladislav	*commission agent, auctioneer*	Mt Coot-tha 1953, 1956
DASH, John	*union organizer*	Mundingburra **1920, 1923, 1926, 1929, 1932, 1935, 1938, 1941**

Davis, Aaron William	*grazier*	Wide Bay 1926
Davies, David Swiss	*licensed victualler*	*Burke, 1915; Warwick 1918
DAVIES, Horace Jason	*schoolteacher*	Nanango 1938; Maryborough **1953**(by), **1956, 1957**
Davies, Robert Henry	*hospital employee*	Charters Towers 1957
DAVIS, Edward William	*AWU secretary*	Barcoo **1943**(by), **1944, 1947, 1950, 1953, 1956, 1957**
Day, Leslie Harry	*secretary*	Toowong 1929
Dean, Harold	*public servant, alderman*	Sandgate 1957
Delaney, William George	*barrister*	Stanley 1920
DEMAINE, William Halliwell	*printer, newspaper proprietor*	Maryborough **1937**(by)
Dent, Roy Maurice	*fitter, tramway workshop employee*	Yeronga 1957
Desmond, James Joseph	*solicitor*	Aubigny 1918
DEVRIES, George Henry	*AWU organiser*	Gregory **1941, 1944, 1947, 1950, 1953, 1956**
DIPLOCK, Leslie Frank	*school inspector*	Condamine **1953, 1956**,‡
DITTMER, Felix Cyril Sigismund	*doctor*	Oxley 1943(by), 1944; Mt Gravatt **1950, 1953, 1956**, 1957
Dixon, John James	*accountant*	Hamilton 1944
Dobinson, William	*carpenter*	Kurilpa 1923
DOHRING, Alfred	*forestry worker*	Roma **1953, 1956**,‡
DONALD, James	*(colliery employees) union secretary, winding-engine driver*	Bremer **1946**(b), **1947, 1950, 1953, 1956, 1957**
Donges, Jacob	*farmer*	Drayton 1915
DONNELLY, John Burton	*dentist*	Wynnum 1932, 1933(by), **1935**, 1938
Doyle, Edward James	*contractor*	Cunningham 1926
Doyle, Thomas Joseph	*carrier, alderman*	Yeronga 1950, 1953; South Brisbane 1957
Drew, Frank Harold	*railway clerk*	Warwick 1956
DUFFICY, John Joseph	*shearer, AWU organiser*	Warrego **1951**(by), **1953, 1956, 1957**
DUGGAN, John Edmund	*grocer*	Toowoomba **1935**(by), **1938, 1941, 1944,**

		1947, 1950, 1953, 1956, 1957; Gregory 1957 (postponed)
DUNSTAN, Thomas	*printer, newspaper proprietor*	Gympie 1915, 1918, 1920, 1923, 1926, 1929; Nash 1950
Durkin, John Michael	*shearer*	Murilla 1918
Eastaughffe, Francis Eric	*railway driver, dairyman*	Isis 1944, 1950
EASTMENT, Leonard	*motor mechanic, hospital employee*	Ithaca 1952(by), 1953, 1956
Easton, Robert Matthew	*auctioneer*	Toowong 1923
Egerton, John Alfred Ray	*boiler maker, union secretary*	Fortitude Valley 1957
Eggington, William Russell	*electrical fitter*	Condamine 1957
Elson-Green, William	*barrister*	Bundaberg 1957
ENGLISH, Charles Bernard	*sawmiller*	Mulgrave 1950, 1953, 1956,‡
Falk, Edward Alexander	*public servant*	Norman 1950
FARRELL, David	*engine driver*	Maryborough 1938, 1941, 1944, 1947, 1950, 1953
FARRELL, George Pritchard	*teacher*	Rockhampton 1923(by), 1923, 1926, 1929
FERRICKS, Miles Aloysius	*teacher, miner, sugar farmer, mailroom worker, journalist*	South Brisbane 1920, 1923, 1926, 1929
FIHELLY, John Arthur	*clerk, journalist*	*Paddington 1915, 1918, 1920
FOLEY, Thomas	*building trades labourer*	*Mundingburra 1915, 1918
FOLEY, Thomas Andrew	*miner, timber supplier*	Leichhardt 1919(by), 1920, 1923, 1926, 1929; Normanby 1932, 1935, 1938, 1941, 1944, 1947; Belyando 1950, 1953, 1956,‡
FORDE, Francis Michael	*teacher, electrical engineer*	Rockhampton 1917(by), 1918, 1920; Flinders 1955 (by), 1956, 1957

Forde, William John Aloysius	*labourer*	Murrumba 1920
Francis, Harold Lesina	*school teacher*	Dalby 1926
Fraser, James Neville	*ambulance bearer*	Rockhampton 1957
Fraser, Thomas Scott	*railway engine driver*	Enoggera 1944
FREE, Edgar Noah	*dentist*	South Brisbane **1915, 1918**
Friis, William	*stationmaster*	Murrumba 1926
FUNNELL, Robert	*AWU organiser fruiterer*	Brisbane **1932, 1935**
GAIR, Vincent Clair	*clerk*	South Brisbane **1932, 1935, 1938, 1941, 1944, 1947, 1950, 1953, 1956,‡**
Gardner, Alexander	*union organiser*	Mirani 1932
GARDNER, Harold Raymong	*garage proprietor*	Rockhampton **1956,‡**
GARDNER, Robert James	*foreman painter, public servant*	Bulimba **1944, 1947, 1950, 1951**(by), **1953, 1956,‡**
Gardner, William	*railway guard*	Cook 1932
GILDAY, John Theophilos	*butcher, union secretary*	*Ithaca **1915, 1918, 1920, 1923**
Gillies, Frank D.	*farmer*	Stanley 1938
Gillies, James	*engine-driver*	Stanley 1926
GILLIES, William Neal	*cane farmer*	*Eacham **1915, 1918, 1920, 1923**
GLEDSON, David Alexander	*miner, union secretary*	*Ipswich **1915, 1918, 1920, 1923, 1926, 1929, 1932, 1935, 1938, 1941, 1944, 1947**
Gleeson, Daniel Thomas James	*mechanic*	Mundingburra 1953
Gould, Charles Herbert	*shearer, farmer*	Aubigny 1923
Gow, Douglas George Thompson	*orchardist*	Carnarvon 1957
GRAHAM, Frederick Dickson	*railway employee*	Mackay **1943**(by), **1944, 1947, 1950, 1953, 1956, 1957**
Gralton, John Austin	*meatworker*	Burdekin 1957
GUNN, William Morrison		Wynnum **1944, 1947, 1950, 1953, 1956, 1957**

HADLEY, James William	*public servant, labourer*	Kedron 1950; Nundah **1956, 1957**
HAMILTON, William	*shearer, miner*	*Gregory **1915**
Hanley, Timothy Edward	*contractor*	Burrum 1929
HANLON, Edward Michael	*grocer, railway employee*	Ithaca **1926, 1929, 1932, 1935, 1938, 1941, 1944, 1947, 1950**
HANLON, Patrick Joseph	*accountant*	Ithaca **1956**(by), **1957**
Hannay, David Patrick Vincent	*farmer*	Cunningham 1923
HANSON, Edward Joseph	*plumber, union secretary*	Buranda **1924**(by), **1926, 1929, 1932, 1935, 1939, 1941, 1944**
HARDACRE, Herbert Freemont	*butcher, union official*	*Leichhardt **1915, 1918**
HARTLEY, Harold Leslie	*engineer*	*Fitzroy **1915, 1918, 1920, 1923, 1926,** 1929
HARTLEY, William	*textile worker, labourer, insurance agent*	Kurilpa **1915**, 1918
Harth, William	*coalmine worker*	Aubigny 1944
Hay, William Hold	*locomotive driver*	Roma 1957
HAYES, John Vincent	*shop assistant*	Nundah **1932, 1935, 1938, 1941, 1944**
Hayes, Patrick	*cane farmer*	Kennedy 1932
Hayes, William Michael	*farmer*	Pittsworth 1915
HEALY, John Joseph O'Connor	*sheet-metal worker, railway clerk*	Warwick 1932, **1935, 1938, 1941, 1944, 1947**
Heffernan, William Vincent	*machinist*	*Fassifern 1915; Stanley 1918
Herbert, Henry Wilson	*research officer*	Oxley 1941
Herbert, John Armstrong	*surveyor*	East Toowoombas 1926
Hill, Edgar Charles	*station master*	Southport 1950, 1953
Hill, Francis Alexander	*baker*	Burnett 1920
Hilton, John Geralbert Michael	*station master*	Cunningham 1941, 1944, 1947; Lockyer 1953
HILTON, Paul Jerome Remigius	*clerk*	Carnarvon **1932, 1935, 1938, 1941, 1944, 1947, 1950, 1956,**‡

HISLOP, Roland William	*foreman cabinet maker, furniture manufacturer*	Sandgate **1935, 1938, 1941**
Hogan, James	*engine driver*	Stanley 1941
Holden, Richard Lawrence	*painter and decorator*	Albert 1920
Holman, John	*tailor*	Fassifern 1938
Hooper, George Edward	*forestry overseer*	Nash 1957
Hopkins, Lister	*jeweller*	Drayton 1920
HOUSTON, John William	*technical teacher, electrician*	Bulimba **1957**
Howman, Frederick Ernest	*construction worker*	West Moreton 1941
Hoy, William James	*railway employee*	Windsor 1944
HUNTER, John McEwan	*storekeeper*	*Maranoa **1915, 1918**
Hurley, Bryan Dominic	*public servant*	Mt Coot-tha 1950
HUXHAM, John	*merchant*	*Buranda **1915, 1918, 1920, 1923**
HYNES, Maurice Patrick	*labourer, organiser*	Mirani 1918, 1920; Townsville **1923, 1926, 1929, 1932, 1935, 1938**
Inch, Alexander James	*winding-engine driver*	Carpentaria 1957
INGRAM, Walter Charles	*secretary*	Keppel 1941, 1944, **1947, 1950**
Ivey, William Denis	*AWU organiser*	Isis 1941
JAMES, Alfred Arthur	*journalist*	Logan **1918**
James, George James	*saddler, miner, insurance inspector*	Warwick 1926
James, William George	*contractor*	Mackenzie 1957
JESSON, Cecil George	*commission agent*	Kennedy **1935, 1938, 1941, 1944, 1947**; Hinchinbrook **1950, 1953, 1956, 1957**
JONES, Alfred James	*driver, storekeeper, miner*	*Maryborough **1915**; Carnarvon 1920; Paddington **1922**(by), **1923, 1926, 1929**; Hamilton 1932
JONES, Arthur	*AWU organiser, public servant*	Burke **1929**(by); Charters Towers **1939**(by), **1941, 1944, 1947, 1950, 1953, 1956**,‡

Jones, Hamilton Cuffe	*labourer, gas worker, waterside worker*	Kurilpa 1926
Jones, John	*ganger*	Aubigny 1915
JONES, Thomas Llewellyn	*merchant*	Oxley **1915**, 1918; Logan 1923
KANE, James David	*railway telegraphist, journalist, insurance agent*	East Toowoomba 1934(by), **1935**, 1938, 1941; Roma 1950
Kane, Myles Joseph	*solicitor*	Kurilpa 1957
Kavanagh, John Patrick	*teacher*	Sandgate 1929
Keane, Terence John	*railway clerk*	Warwick 1950
Kearney, Victor Dennis	*salesman*	Nundah 1926
KEHOE, Gregory Brian	*clerk*	Nash **1953**, **1956**,‡
Kemshead, Kenneth MacLean	*bank officer*	Windsor 1957
KEOGH, James Patrick	*storeman, labourer*	Merthyr **1932**, **1935**, **1938**
KEYATTA, George	*shopkeeper*	Townsville **1939**(by), **1941**, **1944**, **1947**, **1950**, **1953**, **1956**, **1957**
KING, William Thomas	*barrister*	Maree **1932**, **1935**, **1938**, 1941
KIRWAN, Michael Joseph	*bootmaker, railway porter*	*Brisbane **1915**, **1918**, **1920**, **1923**, **1926**, **1929**
Kluck, Albert C.	*farmer*	Lockyer 1923
Knoll, Charles William	*building contractor, carpenter*	Darlington 1953, 1956, 1957
Krause, Bertram Charles	*farmer*	Murrumba 1957
Krebs, Lorenz Albert	*schoolteacher*	West Moreton 1932
Lake, William Henry	*shop assistant, storekeeper, manager*	Albert 1926
LAND, Edward Martin	*storekeeper, bushworker, selector*	*Balonne **1915**, **1918**, **1920**, **1923**, **1926**
Laracy, William John	*truck driver*	Wynnum 1941
LARCOMBE, James	*butcher, carter*	*Keppel **1915**, **1918**, **1920**, **1923**, **1926**, 1929; Rockhampton **1932**, **1935**, **1938**, **1941**, **1944**, **1947**, **1950**, **1953**
Laurison, John	*canegrower*	Burrum 1926

Lawson, William John	*carpenter*	Albert 1918
Laws, Thomas John	*schoolteacher*	Toowong 1941
Lee, Arthur	*contractor*	Stanley 1944
Leggat, Richard	*pattern marker, union official*	Logan 1929
LENNON, William	*auctioneer, merchant, bank clerk*	*Herbert 1915, 1918
Lilley, Arthur Shipley	*barrister*	*Toowong 1915
LLEWELYN, Evan John	*ambulance superintendant*	Toowoomba 1925(by), 1926, 1929, 1932, 1935
LLOYD, Eric Gayford	*public servant*	Murrumba 1950; Kedron 1951(by), 1953, 1956, 1957
LLOYD, William Field	*teacher, college principal*	*Enoggera 1915, 1918, 1920; Kelvin Grove 1923, 1926, 1929
Londsdale, Thomas John	*union secretary*	East Toowoomba 1915
Lough, James	*AWU organiser*	Toombul 1929
Lourigan, Bartholemew Roger	*fitter, instrument maker*	Sherwood 1956
Lyle, Robert Miller	*engineer, miner*	Normanby 1923, 1926
Lyons, Michael Gerard	*solicitor*	Condamine 1950; Buranda ‡
Lythgo, Thomas Michael	*storeman*	Fassifern 1950
McAnally, Hugh	*farmer*	Dalby 1923
Mcarthur, James Begg	*railway employee*	Oxley 1929, 1932; Chermside 1950
McAuliffe, Ronald Edward	*railway clerk*	Sandgate 1947
McCabe, James Joseph	*tailor*	Nundah 1923
McCafferty, John Francis	*bus proprietor*	Cunningham 1956
McCATHIE, Colin George	*accountant*	Houghton 1950, 1953, 1956,‡
McCorkell, Lavis Arthur William	*teacher*	Murilla 1926
McCORMACK, William	*miner, AWU secretary*	*Cairns 1915, 1918, 1920, 1923, 1926, 1929
McCosker, William	*compositor*	Toowong 1918, 1920
McDonald, Alexander	*civil engineer*	Toombul 1918
MacDougall, James Henry Arthur	*minister of religion*	East Toowoomba 1918; Maranoa 1919(by)
MacGinley, John Joseph	*barrister*	Murilla 1920

McKenzie, Donald	*public servant*	Windsor 1926
McKeon, Austin	*farmer*	Dalby 1918
McLACHLAN, Peter Alfred	*compositor*	*Merthyr **1915, 1918, 1920, 1923, 1926, 1929**
McLaughlin, John James	*whipmaker, cattle breeder, fruitgrower*	Wynnum 1923, 1926
MacLennan, Hugh	*engineer*	Whitsunday 1953
McLEAN, Bernard	*railway employee*	Bundaberg **1935, 1938, 1941, 1944**
McMahon, Patrick Michael	*farmer*	Warwick 1929
McMahon, William	*agent*	Burnett 1923
McMINN, Hugh Cameron	*storeman, secretary*	*Bulimba **1915**, 1918
McNulty, John Joseph	*commission agent*	Maree 1944
McPHAIL, Herbert George	*shop assistant, optician*	Windsor **1915, 1918,** 1920; Sandgate 1932
McRae, Kenneth Scott	*photo engraver*	Chermside 1953
Mack, Albert George	*carrier*	Burnett 1915
Maher, Gerald Jeremiah	*public servant*	Coorparoo 1953, 1956
Maher, Thomas Andrew	*engine driver*	Fitzroy 1932
Mahony, James Martin		Pittsworth 1918
Mahony, James William	*technical teacher, boiler maker, union secretary*	Mundingburra 1950, 1957
Manchester, Ernest James	*civil engineer*	Windsor 1932
MANN, John Henry	*builders labourer*	Brisbane **1936**(by), **1938, 1941, 1944, 1947, 1950, 1953, 1956, 1957**
Mansfield, Robert Charles Edward	*grocer*	Sherwood 1950, 1953
Marginson, Evan	*hospital board secretary*	Somerset 1957
MARRIOTT, George Henry	*engine driver*	Bulimba 1920, **1938, 1941**
MARSDEN, Ivor	*clerk*	Ipswich **1949**(by), **1950, 1953, 1956, 1957**
Martin, Robert William	*farmer*	Burnett 1929
Mattingley, John Thomas	*railway engine driver*	East Toowoomba 1920
MAY, John	*farmer, station worker, organiser, produce salesman*	*Flinders **1915**
Moir, John Alfred	*lithographer*	Cunningham 1918; Aubigny 1926; Hamilton

		1935
Moorcroft, David Turner	*butcher*	Murrumba 1923, 1932
Moore, Frederick John	*carpenter, fruitgrower*	Wynnum 1929
Moore, Patrick	*grazier*	Callide 1950, 1953
MOORE, William Matthew	*insurance inspector*	Merthyr **1940**(by), **1941, 1944, 1947, 1950, 1953, 1956**, ‡
MOORES, Thomas	*alderman, plumber*	Kurilpa **1949**(by), **1950, 1953, 1956**,‡
Moran, Edward Lancester	*licensed victualler*	Albert 1929
Mulherin, John Martin	*sugar grower*	Mirani 1926, 1929
MULLAN, John	*postal clerk, organiser*	Flinders **1918, 1920, 1923, 1926, 1929**; Carpentaria **1932, 1935, 1938**
Munro, Robert Roy	*managing storekeeper*	Murilla 1929
Murray, John Cade	*tobacco farmer*	Isis 1932
Myers, Charles Albert	*hairdresser*	Murrumba 1956
Nelson, Peter Henry George	*clerk*	Fassifern 1941
Nowotny, Henry Richard	*teacher*	Windsor 1929
O'Brien, Daniel Augustus	*inspector of shops (1917)*	Cooroora 1915
O'Brien, John Joseph	*public servant*	Warwick 1953
O'KEEFE, John	*miner, publican*	Chillagoe **1926**, 1929; Cairns **1930**(by), **1932, 1935, 1938, 1941**
O'Neill, Matthew Thomas	*cane farmer*	Mirani 1950
O'SHEA, Harry	*union secretary*	Warrego **1943**(by), **1944, 1947, 1950**
O'Shea, John	*law student, public servant*	Toowong 1938
O'SULLIVAN, James	*fitter, blacksmith, union official*	*Kennedy **1915, 1918, 1920**
Ouston, Bernard William	*pipe inspector*	Coorparoo 1957
Owens, Vivian John	*AWU organiser, teacher*	Haughton 1957
Parker, George Frederick	*AWU organiser*	Mundingburra 1947
Parker, Montague Vincent	*licensed victualler*	Burrum 1923
Pascoe, Albert Edward	*fruit farmer*	Keppel 1935, 1936(by)
Patterson, Hurtle Austin	*painter*	Enoggera 1926
PAYNE, John	*shearer, blacksmith, union official*	*Mitchell **1915, 1918, 1920, 1923, 1926**
PEASE, Percy	*accountant, merchant*	Herbert **1920**(by), **1920, 1923, 1926, 1929, 1932, 1935, 1938**

Perrett, John Wort	*AWU organiser, public servant*	Somerset 1950
PETERSON, James Christian	*builder*	Normanby **1915, 1918, 1920**
Pinder, William Alfred	*clerk*	Hamilton 1938
POLLOCK, George	*union organiser, labourer*	Gregory **1915**(by), **1918, 1920, 1923, 1926, 1929, 1932, 1935, 1938**
POWER, William	*tramway employee, alderman*	Baroona **1935, 1938, 1941, 1944, 1947, 1950, 1953, 1956**,‡
Pringle, John	*engineer*	Kurilpa 1920
Quinlan, John Barron	*clerk*	Fassifern 1920
RASEY, Thomas William	*transport worker, union organiser, alderman*	Windsor **1950, 1953, 1956**,‡
Raven, Desmond Edwin	*carriage painter*	Mt Coot-tha 1957
Reid, John Francis	*journalist*	Oxley 1920
Reid, Roy Spence	*clerk*	Cooroora 1932
Reordan, Thomas Lawrence	*licensed victualler*	Nanango 1932
Richards, Roy Barton	*farmer*	Fassifern 1944
Ridings, William Shakespeare	*butcher*	Oxley 1923
RIORDAN, David	*railway worker*	Burke **1918, 1920, 1923, 1926, 1929**
RIORDAN, Ernest Joseph	*waterside employee, political organiser*	Bowen **1936**(by), **1938, 1941, 1944**; Flinders **1950**
Ritchie, Thomas	*Agricultural Council organiser*	Normanby 1929
Robbins, George Arthur Howard	*herbalist*	Nundah 1920
Roberts, Edmund George	*commission agent*	Clayfield 1950
ROBERTS, Frank Edward	*solicitor, barrister*	Hamilton 1943(by); Nundah **1947, 1950, 1953**
ROBINSON, Herbert Framont	*railway guard*	Sandgate 1950, **1953, 1956**,‡
Rosser, John Hall	*beekeeper*	Albert 1944, 1947
Round, Samuel	*farmer*	Isis 1947
Russell, Ernest William	*carpenter*	Burdekin 1950
RYAN, Cornelius James	*miner, publican*	Eacham **1926**, 1929

RYAN, Daniel	*public servant*	Townsville **1915, 1918, 1920**
RYAN, Henry Joseph	*miner, union official*	*Cook **1915, 1918, 1920, 1923, 1926, 1929**
Ryan, James		Fassifern 1935
Ryan, Jack Hay	*railway employee*	West Moreton 1947
RYAN, Thomas Joseph	*barrister*	*Barcoo **1915, 1918**
Ryder, Dudley Francis	*station master*	Isis 1935; Chermside 1956; Nundah 1957
Salter, Hylton Barry	*schoolteacher*	Isis 1956
Sampson, Arthur	*farmer*	Murrumba 1915, 1918
Sampson, Leslie Harold	*policeman*	Chermside 1957
Scanlan, Mark Deveney	*carpenter*	Enoggera 1947
Scanlan, Roger Terence	*schoolteacher*	Mirani 1953, 1956
Scholl, Ferdinand Charles	*clerk*	Logan 1947
Schull, Christopher	*farmer*	Aubigny 1950
Searle, William George	*union secretary*	Oxley 1926
Sherlock, John	*farmer*	Somerset 1915
Sherrington, Douglas John	*city council employee*	Sherwood 1957
SKINNER, Alexander James	*fitter*	Somerset **1953, 1956,‡**
Skinner, Henry William	*painter*	Burdekin 1956
SLESSAR, Aubrey Robert	*garage proprietor, mechanic*	Dalby **1938, 1941, 1944**
SMITH, Alfred James	*picture show proprietor*	Carpentaria **1941, 1944, 1947, 1950, 1953, 1956,‡**
Smith, Ralph Arnot	*engine driver*	Cooroora 1957
SMITH, William Forgan	*painter*	Mackay **1915, 1918, 1920, 1923, 1926, 1929, 1932, 1935, 1938, 1941**
Spencer, Robert Alexander	*assistant station master*	Cooroora 1944, 1947
Spratt, Hector Charles	*farmer*	Cooroora 1918
Staples, Ralph Loye	*coal miner*	Whitsunday 1957
Staunton, Francis Edgar	*farmer*	Stanley 1932, 1935
Stock, William Edmund	*secretary*	Toowong 1926
Stockwell, George Alfred	*AWU organiser*	Wide Bay 1947
STOPFORD, James	*organiser, mine engine driver*	*Mount Morgan **1915, 1918, 1920, 1923, 1926, 1929;**

		Maryborough 1932, 1935
Strohfeld, James Joseph	*solicitor*	East Toowoomba 1932; Aubigny 1938
Stutz, Norman Edward	*truck driver*	Yeronga 1956
Sumner, Richard	*manufacturer (fruit canner)*	*Nundah 1915
Sweeney, Joseph Anthony	*farmer*	Fassifern 1918; Lockyer 1926
TAYLOR, George Cuthbert	*motor mechanic*	Enoggera 1932, 1935, 1938, 1941
TAYLOR, John Russell	*organiser*	Maronoa 1944, 1947; Balonne 1950, 1953, 1956, 1957
Telfer, Benjamin	*locomotive driver*	Wide Bay 1938
THACKERAY, Mervyn Herbert	*engine driver*	Keppel 1957
THEODORE, Edward Granville	*miner, union organiser*	*Chillagoe 1915, 1918, 1920, 1923
THEODORE, Stephen	*cane farmer*	Herbert 1940(by), 1941, 1944, 1947
Thieme, Wilhelm Frederich Ernst	*public servant, journalist*	Oxley 1935, 1938
THOMPSON, Andrew	*farmer*	*Wide Bay 1915, 1918, 1920; Cooroora 1938
Thompson, Vincent Gavvin	*AWU official*	Gregory 1929(by)
Thorpe, James F.	*railway clerk*	East Toowoomba 1944
Thorpe, Thomas George	*public servant, farmer*	Wide Bay 1941, 1944; Fassifern 1947
Tomlins, Lionel E.D.	*solicitor*	Mundingburra 1944
Tomlinson, John Arthur	*hotel-keeper*	Aubigny 1947
Tracey, Cecil John	*baker*	Nanango 1941
Trembath, Leslie Robert	*cane farmer*	Mulgrave 1957
Tullipan, Sidney Ernest	*AWU organiser*	Tablelands 1957
Tully, James John Parnell	*hotel proprietor*	Cook 1950
Turnbull, Reginald	*labourer*	East Toowoomba 1929
Turner, Edward Henry	*clerk*	Toowong 1932, 1935
Turner, Henrietta Ethel	*domestic duties*	Mirani 1923
TURNER, John Alber	*storeman and packer, union organiser*	Kelvin Grove 1941, 1944, 1947, 1950, 1953, 1956, 1957
Valentine, John Crozier	*railwayman, union secretary*	Enoggera 1923

Venables, Frank Albert	*coach painter*	Toowong 1947, 1950, 1953
Wall, William Garnet	*farmer*	Burdekin 1953
Wallace, Robert Albert Renforth		Nanango 1920
WALLACE, George Walter Gordon	*meat worker, butcher*	Cairns **1956, 1957**
WALSH, Edward John	*party organiser, farmer*	Mirani **1935**, **1938**, **1941**, **1944**, 1947; Bundaberg **1950**, **1953**, **1956**,‡
Warmington, Joseph Frederick	*farmer*	Burnett 1918
WATERS, Francis John	*postal employee, union secretary*	Kelvin Grove **1932**, 1935, 1938
Watkins, John Taylor	*commercial traveller*	Toombul 1920
Watson, George Alexander Hilary	*bus operator, publican*	Murrumba 1938, 1941
Webster, Robert Joseph	*farmer*	Nanango 1923, 1926
WEIR, David	*railway officer*	Maryborough **1917**(by), **1918**, **1920**, **1923**, **1926**, **1929**
Weir, James	*miner, farmer*	Sandgate 1926
Weir, William Alexander	*farmer*	Marodian 1957
Weitemeyer, Eric Thorvald	*clerk, accountant*	Sandgate 1944; Windsor 1947; Coorparoo 1950
WELLINGTON, William John	*miner, secretary*	Charters Towers **1915**, **1918**, **1920**, **1923**, **1926**, **1929**, **1932**, **1935**, **1938**
WHITFORD, Albert Edward Victor	*tailor*	Burrum 1915, **1918**, 1920
WHYTE, Patrick James	*railway employee*	Mackenzie 1950, 1953, 1956
Widdup, Ernest	*agricultural instructor*	Isis 1938
Wilkes, George Daniel	*locomotive driver*	Dalby 1935, 1947
WILLIAMS, Herbert	*clerk*	Windsor **1935**, **1938**, **1941**
Williams, John Francis	*hotel-keeper, AWU organiser*	Belyando 1957
WILLIAMS, Thomas Lewis	*journalist*	Port Curtis **1932**, **1935**, **1938**, **1941**, **1944**; Marodian 1950

Willis, Eric Joseph	*farmer*	Callide 1956
Wilson, Henry James	*dentist*	Albert 1932
WILSON, Thomas	*pastoral worker, miner*	Fortitude Valley 1916(by), 1918, 1920, 1923, 1926, 1929, 1932
WINSTANLEY, Vernon	*miner, brick and tile manufacturer*	*Queenton 1915, 1918, 1920, 1923, 1926, 1929
WOOD, Leslie Arnold	*schoolteacher*	East Toowoomba 1946(by), 1947; North Toowoomba 1950, 1953, 1956, 1957
Wood, William Henry	*hospital employee*	Oxley 1947
WRIGHT, Albert Henry	*blacksmith*	Bulimba 1923, 1926, 1929

Name Index

Subject Index